# Not by Love Alone

# Not by Love Alone
## The Violin in Japan, 1850–2010

Margaret Mehl

The Sound Book Press
Copenhagen
2014

Published 2014 by
The Sound Book Press
Copenhagen, Denmark

ISBN 978-87-997283-0-5 (hardback)
ISBN 978-87-997283-1-2 (paperback)
ISBN 978-87-997283-2-9 (epub)
ISBN 978-87-997283-3-6 (mobipocket)

Typeset by Taylormade Book Production

In memory of
Mizuki
whose violin fell silent far too soon.

# Contents

# Illustrations and Credits

Cover: Postcard of geisha posing with violin, c. 1905, courtesy of "Okinawa Soba" with thanks for providing a print quality copy of the picture found at http://www.flickr.com/photos/24443965@N08/2402722304/in/photostream/

# Acknowledgements

Many people helped me with the research and the completion of this book and I dare not attempt to list them all for fear of forgetting several of them. Research in Japan was at various stages supported by the Danish Universities' Rectors' Conference (now Danish Universities), the Japan Society for the Promotion of Science and the Department of Cross-Cultural and Regional Studies at the University of Copenhagen. An Edward T. Cone Membership in Music Studies at the School of Historical Studies of the Institute for Advanced Study at Princeton in the spring term of 2009 enabled me to concentrate on research and writing for this book as well as to present my work and discuss it with faculty and fellow members of the Institute and with colleagues at the University of Princeton. My heartfelt thanks go to them all and in particular to the Edward T. Cone Foundation and to the Institute for Advanced Study for providing me with this wonderful opportunity. My thanks also go to the staff of the Rosenthal Archives of the Chicago Symphony Orchestra and their help in using their materials relating to August Junker.

In Japan, Waseda University proved itself a most hospitable institution for foreign scholars several times. The staff at the university's libraries were most helpful. So were the staff at other institutions I visited regularly, including the library at Tokyo University of the Arts and the Archives of Modern Japanese Music (Nihon Kindai Ongakukan), now, sadly, closed down, although their valuable collection has been moved to Meiji Gakuin University. During a two-week research trip to Berlin in 2010, the staff at German libraries and archives were equally helpful. My thanks also go to the individuals and institutions who provided pictures and gave permission to use them.

Among the many individuals without whose support, encouragement and patience over many years this book could not have been written, my special thanks for intellectual stimulation, practical advice and moral support go to Furukawa Eriko and Furukawa Takahisa, Okayama Yoshiko and Okayama Kiyoshi, Gaye Rowley, Suzuki Akiko and Suzuki Jun, David Schoenbaum and Tsukahara Yasuko.

Heartfelt thanks also to Tessa Carroll for copy-editing and Jill Campbell for proof-reading, both with an attention to detail that must have been hard to sustain given the manuscript's length. Many thanks also to Marie-Pierre Evans who did a far better job indexing the book than I would have done.

Finally, I thank an anonymous reader for a major scholarly publisher who strongly recommended publication of my manuscript. As a result, when the publisher presented me with a draft contract that reserved the right not to publish, "should market conditions make the publication of the work unprofitable," I felt encouraged to take matters into my own hands. The valuable feedback from this and another (not quite so enthusiastic, but still encouraging) reader helped me revise the manuscript and rethink some of my choices. It also led me to conclude that my book may well be a writer's answer to "crossover" violinists, a work that defies easy categorization as either "academic" or "popular." I hope it will nevertheless appeal to the diverse readership it is intended for.

# Notes on Usage

The romanization of Japanese words, with a few exceptions, follows the modified Hepburn style. In the transliteration of "violin" I have tried to be faithful to the phonetic rendering of the source; this accounts for irregularities like "baiorin", "vaiorin" and "vwaiorin."

Japanese names are given with the surname first in the main text, according to Japanese usage. In the interest of consistency, this applies even to names known to English speakers in the English order, such as Seiji Ozawa and Mitsuko Uchida. In the notes and bibliography they are given in the same order as Western names. Since the notes contain full citations, I have opted for a select biography of English language works on music in Japan. A full bibliography will be posted on my website, www.notbylovealone.com

To avoid confusion, the present-day Tokyo University of the Arts is called Geidai (the abbreviation commonly used in Japan) throughout for the period from 1949, even though its official name changed a few times.

# Prologue and Introduction

## 1. A Resounding Success Story

When I first heard Hattori Yoshiko play in the early 1970s, I never wondered where she had learnt it all; it did not occur to me to ask how someone born and raised in a country far from the heartland of classical music as I knew it had come to master that music so perfectly. "Frau Okayama," as people called her, was performing with the amateur orchestra my parents played in. Both she and her husband Okayama Kiyoshi were well-established members of the musical scene in Bonn. As a teenager I took their proficiency and their position for granted.

The Okayamas came to Bonn in 1971, when Okayama Kiyoshi was appointed concertmaster of the Beethoven Orchestra in Bonn. Both had graduated from Tokyo University of the Arts in 1968 and come to study in Hamburg with a scholarship from the German Academic Exchange Service the same year. They had won competitions individually and as a duo (Ysaÿe Medal in Brussels, 1971), and continued to perform together as a duo or as a string quartet with members of the Beethoven Orchestra. Hattori Yoshiko had to take a career break when their two children were born. Perhaps this was why during that first performance I heard, there were moments when nerves caused her to falter. But the moments were few and soon disappeared, and to me she became an example of what a woman, even with small children, can achieve if she puts her mind to it.

Even when I became her pupil in 1978, I did not at first give much thought to the fact that she was Japanese. The Okayamas' appeal to audiences in Bonn and elsewhere may well have been enhanced because, as Japanese, they looked mildly exotic as well as beautiful when they performed as a couple; but mainly their audience recognized them as outstanding musicians, and I cannot remember anyone around me expressing surprise at the fact. Moreover, by the example of her playing,

1

she taught me to appreciate and love Bach's Preludium from the Unaccompanied Partita in E major, which under my most recent previous teacher (trained in the former Eastern Bloc) I had come to regard as a tedious étude. Whenever I hear the old stereotype about "Asians" not being able to play European composers with due expression, I cannot but remember that it was my Japanese, not my German, teacher who revealed to me the beauty of Bach's solo violin works.

By the time Frau Okayama became my fifth violin teacher, it was clear that I would not pursue a career in music. In 1981 I enrolled at the University of Bonn to study for a double major in history and Japanese studies. History was my first choice, while Japanese was an afterthought. I continued to take lessons until 1983, when the Okayamas returned to Japan; he to take up an appointment as concertmaster of the Yomiuri Nippon Symphony Orchestra in Tokyo, and she to become head of the strings department at Aichi University of the Arts in Nagoya, commuting from Tokyo by bullet train and staying over three days a week. The children attended Tamagawa Gakuen in Tokyo, a school known for its liberal climate and holistic approach to education. Both the Okayamas continued to perform as soloists with orchestras and as chamber musicians. During my first stay in Japan in 1984–85, I visited the family, and we kept in touch between subsequent visits. While in Japan, I often received invitations to their concerts.

Meanwhile, I had specialized in the history of Meiji Japan (1868–1912), the period when Japan successfully modelled itself on Western nations and not only escaped colonization, but itself became a colonial power. A brief notion of writing my M.A. thesis about German musicians in Japan came to nothing, and I wrote about German–Japanese military relations instead – the two are not unconnected, as I soon found out. Then, in 1988, while researching for my doctoral thesis, I met Irene Suchy, an Austrian doctoral candidate working on German and Austrian musicians in Japan between 1868 and 1945.[1] Only then did I begin to realize just how remarkable was the way the Japanese made Western classical music their own in only a few decades. We were witnessing the height of the "bubble" economy, which among other ways found its expression in several newly opened concert halls and ever more foreign artists touring Japan. In fact, among them was another previous violin teacher of mine, Heinz Schopp, a violist in Bonn's Beethoven Orchestra and a regular member of the Bayreuth Festival Orchestra. In 1989 the latter performed in Tokyo to celebrate the opening of Bunkamura, a multi-storey complex of shops, theatres, and a concert hall, billed as "the first and largest multimedia, cross-cultural complex of its kind in Japan."[2]

Traditional Japanese music, meanwhile, seemed as exotic to most Japanese as to any Westerner. Through Irene Suchy I met the Kawamuras, roughly the same generation as the Okayamas and likewise leaders in their profession: Kawamura Taizan is a *shakuhachi* (end-blown flute) player and Kawamura Toshimi, a *koto* (plucked zither) player. In their efforts to bring indigenous music to a wider audience, they organized the Mutsunowo concert series (named after Japan's oldest plucked instrument). It is a mark of what the Kawamuras were up against that they roped in both Irene Suchy, a professionally trained cellist, and this amateur violinist to boost the popular appeal of their concerts. "Internationalization" was the buzzword of those years and it was not unusual to present an event as "international" by engaging (white) foreigners. The programme of the Mutsunowo summer concert in 1989 included *Haru no Umi* (Sea in Springtime) a well-known piece composed in 1929 by Miyagi Michio, originally written for *koto* and *shakuhachi,* but performed on this occasion on the *koto* and the violin, as indeed it had been as early as 1932 by the composer himself and the French violinist Renée Chemet. The concert ended with the theme song of a then popular computer game named "Dragon Quest," accompanied by an ensemble of Japanese and Western instruments.

The Kawamuras came to Cologne in 1990, during a tour of Europe supported by the Association for International Exchange of Japanese Music (est. 1988) and the Japan Foundation. When performers of traditional music travel abroad, they often do so to perform at events sponsored by official bodies in order to represent "traditional" Japanese culture. In general, however, traditional Japanese music is a closed world even in Japan. Artists may win national prizes, but there is no international *shakuhachi* or *koto* competition, although the *shakuhachi,* is the one Japanese instrument (apart from the *taiko* drums) that has a significant international following.

The almost complete separation of Western classical music and traditional Japanese music in post-1945 Japan (at least until relatively recently) is an intriguing phenomenon, given the Japanese reputation for "Japanizing" foreign influences. The violin in particular would seem to lend itself to Japanization: when Japan opened its doors in the mid-nineteenth century, the violin was still the most widely used (Western) musical instrument in the world, both across social classes and across continents, replacing indigenous bowed instruments wherever it went.[3] Arnold Steinhardt, first violinist of the now disbanded Guarneri String Quartet, has even described the history of the violin as "downright Darwinism."[4] In Japan, however, the violin did not replace existing instruments completely; nor did it become integrated into existing musical styles. Instead, it came to play a major role in the performance of Japan's modern traditions.

The Japanese government systematically introduced Western music in the mid-nineteenth century as part of its deliberate programme of modernization in accordance with Western models. By means of military bands and singing in schools, Western music was harnessed for the purpose of strengthening the nation. It fulfilled new functions for which traditional music seemed unsuitable. The possible exception was *gagaku*, the music of the court, which did in fact retain a limited role in modern ceremonies. *Gagaku* musicians began to study Western music in addition to *gagaku* and many of them played an important role in the dissemination of Western music. Traditional music in general was largely neglected by the government, but remained popular among the people for a long time.

Once music education became firmly established in the nation's schools from the 1880s onward, in the hands of music teachers the violin found its way into the remotest parts of the country. Japanese craftsmen, seeing a business opportunity, began making violins. The most successful one was Suzuki Masakichi, the father of Shin'ichi, who is known in the West for the "Suzuki Method." Like no other, the name "Suzuki," one of the most common surnames, has come to represent violins for the masses in Japan. By the 1890s, Suzuki violins were available almost nationwide at relatively cheap prices. Affordable, portable and versatile, the violin became one of the most popular Western instruments. After the Second World War, from the 1960s, when Japanese violinists had begun to win international competitions and the Suzuki Method took America by storm, the Western world marvelled at this success without knowing how to explain it. The roots of this success lie in the nineteenth century when Japan embarked on its successful course of Westernization.

Politics and economics go a long way towards explaining the triumph of Western classical music in Japan. Nevertheless, although the government could force its people to study and perform the foreign music, it could not force them to like it, and a liking for unfamiliar music does not usually come easily. Even in our time, the ethnomusicologist Bruno Nettl has observed that American and Western European university professors (whom we can assume to be open to foreign cultures at least on an intellectual level) tend to be particularly ethnocentric about food and music: "They read *The Tale of Genji* but don't want to hear *gagaku.*"[5] Professors and other Western observers in nineteenth-century Japan did not even try or pretend to like Japanese music, convinced as they were that their own music was superior. Basil Hall Chamberlain, who lived in Japan for nearly 40 years from 1873 to 1911 and whose knowledge of language and culture was probably unsurpassed by any of his foreign contemporaries, wrote under "music" in his famous *Things Japanese*: "Music, if that beautiful word must be allowed to fall so low as to denote the strummings and squealings of Orientals, is supposed to have existed in Japan ever since mythological times."[6] He claimed, probably rightly, that most Western observers felt the same. At least Chamberlain was fair enough to point out that "Dislikes are apt to be mutual" and remarked that "Of all the elements of Europeanization, European music is the one for which the Japanese have been the slowest to evince any taste."[7]

All the more remarkable then, that the Japanese learnt not only to play to and listen to Western music, but to like it. This book aims to trace the process and to show how this transformation came about. It is not so much about music itself, as about the people who embraced Western music and the violin and the historical circumstances they were moved by. Ultimately the story of how the Japanese made the violin and Western music their own is about much more than music: it is part of the story of Japan's entry into an emerging modern, globalized world. The most salient feature of globalization is the speed of communication and the resulting contemporaneity. No one has expressed this more vividly than the Viennese-born writer Stefan Zweig (1881–1942), describing the experience of his generation. "When bombs smashed houses in Shanghai, we knew it in our rooms in Europe before the wounded had been borne from their houses."[8] By the time Zweig wrote this, his experience of contemporaneity was chiefly negative; he felt he had no means of escaping the horrors of the Second World War. But for many Japanese around the turn of the century, contemporaneity represented opportunity; they believed in the progress of civilization and wanted to be part of the latest developments in all areas of life, including music.

In order to understand the changes we must look at a variety of complex processes by which tastes, including musical predilections, are exported but also imported and acquired independently of official political agendas, whether international or national.[9] And we must finally accept and appreciate that "Western" classical music played in Japan sounds much the same as it does in the West, but that it is nevertheless just as much "Japanese" as it is "Western"; so completely have the Japanese made it their own, even while keeping it on a pedestal and holding on to the belief that it is only at home in its European heartlands. They have come to be major players in the world of Western classical music: literally, through Japanese musicians populating conservatoires and concert stages worldwide, but also as composers, consumers and even as teachers. The Suzuki Method represents one of the most important innovations in string pedagogy in the twentieth century. Yamaha is a household name for musical instruments. Western classical music is only "Western" in the sense that it originated in the West, in Europe, but it has long ceased to belong to Europeans.

Books about the violin in the West tend to deal with the "great men" (and, occasionally, women), virtuosos and famous makers. I have emphatically not set out to describe the "great men" (or even the "great women"), although, inevitably, I have included well-known names. It was not "great masters" that made Japan one of the great players in the field of Western classical music and especially violin music today. It was the combined effort of numerous men and women, Japanese and foreign, whose names are largely forgotten even in Japan by all but a few specialists. Violin virtuosos emerge in environments where many are teaching and learning the violin, and it is this environment I have set out to describe. I have selected violinists I see as illustrating something of the story of the violin in Japan particularly well; many were teachers of particular importance in spreading the art of violin playing. I have even given space to that underrepresented and little understood species, the amateur, because I believe that the best musicians are produced in a culture where music is widely pursued for the love of it. I have privileged those who have written books or had books written about them. This has practical reasons and reflects my preferences as a historian; but it also reflects one of the ways the Japanese learnt about Western music, especially before recordings became widely available. To this day, many Japanese music enthusiasts love to expand and deepen their knowledge through books and magazines. One reason may well be that they still feel that they in some way need to "catch up" with Western musicians.

So are we over-optimistic or incorrigibly Euro-centric if we speak of a success story? Some Japanese today would no doubt say, yes. They would cite the marginalization of indigenous traditional music or the continuing "Western music complex"; others might even claim that the Japanese, despite what looks like overwhelming evidence to the contrary, do not really like Western classical music.[10] Measured by the goals of the people responsible for its introduction in the nineteenth century, however, the appropriation of Western music *was* a success. Even the more elusive goal of creating a music of their own by synthesizing the music of East and West has to some extent been reached, although not in the way they envisaged. The most successful synthesis arguably took place in popular genres they would have condemned as vulgar.

Meanwhile we live in a different age from the Japanese who first took up the violin in the 1870s and 1880s. No matter where we are in the world we have many more ways of learning about music from other cultures than reading books. Even at the end of the nineteenth century sound technology was beginning to revolutionize the performance, the study and the enjoyment of music. Image technology had similarly profound effects. More recently, the internet has revolutionized the dissemination of musical performances both old and new. My own gradual discovery of the possibilities it offers has been one of the reasons my book has taken longer to complete than I hoped.

Then, just as I thought I was finally close to finishing, Japan was hit by the triple disaster of 11 March 2011. Almost immediately it became clear that the catastrophe had repercussions in the world of music. Within days it gave rise to a wave of charity concerts worldwide that may well have set a new record. Many of them were organized by Japanese musicians living abroad, others by Western musicians who had fond memories of performing and teaching in Japan. The Sendai Philharmonic Orchestra had to cancel its regular concerts, but its members gave charity concerts and performances in emergency shelters throughout their home region and beyond. Kino Masayuki, solo concertmaster of the Japan Philharmonic Orchestra based in Tokyo, gave special performances in support of the badly damaged Sanriku railway line in July 2011, in Ōfunato and Rikuzentakata, as well as in Morioka station. In London, Hakase Tarō, violinist of many genres, busked in St Pancras Station, played among glass cases with designer goods in Mitsukoshi department store and among fruit baskets in the famous Fortnum & Mason store, and gave a more formal concert in Cadogan Hall, all within a week of the disaster. The Berlin Philharmonic Orchestra, who in Kashimoto Daishin appointed its second Japanese concertmaster in 2009, formally addressed their friends in Japan in a video message given by chief conductor Sir Simon Rattle and violinist Sebastian Heesch; Heesch even spoke in Japanese. The orchestra and smaller ensembles of its members subsequently gave several concerts in support of Japan. In Denmark, Yasui Yūko, a violinist in the Copenhagen Phil staged seven of the at least twelve concerts in Copenhagen between 26 March 2011 and 11 March 2012.

Ivry Gitlis, a 90-year-old veteran violin virtuoso who has been visiting Japan regularly for the last 30 years, ventured to the hard-hit town of Ishinomaki as early as June 2011 to play for people living in emergency shelters and school children. Early in 2012 it was announced that on 11 March, Ivry Gitlis would be the first to play the violin made by Nakazawa Muneyuki, partly of tsunami driftwood, in a relay to mark the anniversary. Starting with the inaugural concert in Rikuzentakata, Iwate Prefecture, the violin would travel around the world to a total of 1,000 violinists. Gitlis duly performed, and a month later overseas performers from the United States, Canada, Australia, Britain and Germany had applied to take part in the relay, playing on a newly completed second driftwood violin.[11]

Already in June 2011, another violin, a Stradivarius no less, the "Lady Blunt," had been sold by the Nippon Music Foundation to raise funds for recovery and fetched a record price of nearly $16 million. The Foundation's collection of valuable instruments is another testimony to Japan's importance in the violin world.

It is hard to imagine a more visible (not to mention audible) manifestation of Japan's role as a major player on the world musical stage than the musical aftermath of the 2011 disaster. And, as often as not, the violin took the lead.

## 2. The Violin's Forgotten Japanese Cousin and the Musical Worlds of Japan

*The young man sitting on the raised tatami floor behind the counter repairing a* shamisen *looked up in surprise at the foreign woman standing in his tiny shop. The surprise was mutual. The advertisement in the Yellow Pages described his shop in the busy Ikebukuro area of Tokyo as a "main store" and listed a large selection of Japanese traditional musical instruments. So I had expected something like Yamaha's main store in the fashionable Ginza district, with its many floors packed with everything to do with music: musical instruments and accessories, sheet music and CDs, books, a recital space, a music school – everything to do with Western music, that is. Japanese musical instruments are conspicuously absent, although the CD section does include a small selection of traditional Japanese music. Where then, did one go to buy the instruments for traditional music?*

*Having nearly walked past the small entrance of this "main store," I now surveyed what was on offer. To my right, just by the door I saw a wall full of* shakuhachi *(end-blown bamboo flutes). Straight ahead was a glass case with* koto *(plucked zithers). In between the two, another glass case contained what I took to be* shamisen *(three-stringed plucked lutes) in different sizes. Only two looked ready to be played, their little wooden square sound boxes covered with white skins. When I hesitantly asked for a* kokyū, *the young man came and pulled out one of the instruments I had taken to be* shamisen *– the smallest one, skin-less, string-less and not a bow in sight. He promised he would have it ready in a week.*

The *kokyū,* Japan's very own bowed lute, is rarely seen or heard, and even shops specializing in traditional instruments are more likely to stock the Chinese two-stringed fiddle *erhu,* which, confusingly, is also known as *kokyū* (as well as *niko*) . To avoid misunderstandings it is best to speak of the "*Nihon* (Japan) *kokyū.*" Many Japanese, particularly those playing

Western music, have no idea that a Japanese bowed lute even exists: "Japan has no history of bowed instruments," claims the violinist Tanaka Chikashi in his book about violin playing, *The Five Pillars*.[12] The violin has almost completely ousted its Japanese cousin and the *kokyū* is seldom heard today.

1: Miyagi Michio playing the *kokyū* (bowed lute).

No one knows for sure where the *kokyū* came from. It differs significantly from the Chinese *erhu* and its closest relatives. These have a small cylindrical or polygonal body and pegs on one side or at the back of the instrument and are played with the bow passing between the strings. The *kokyū* on the other hand, has a larger body, shaped like that of a *shamisen*. The pegs of the three or four strings are on both sides. The strings pass over a high, arched bridge. The bow is free of the instrument and is played over the top of the strings, another significant difference to the *erhu*. The *kokyū* stands on a long spike while its body usually rests on the player's lap. The player turns the whole instrument to change strings, while the bow remains at the same right angle to the instrument; in this the bowing technique resembles that for the Iranian *kamancheh*.[13] The strings are usually tuned in fourths; in the four-stringed version the two upper strings are in unison. The hairs of the bow are quite loose and the player tightens them by grasping them with the ring finger and the little finger of the right hand, while holding the bow like a chopstick.

In fact, the *kokyū* may well be distantly related to the violin, whose origins are likewise disputed and whose ancestors (or at least bowed predecessors) include the rebec, adopted from Moorish culture, and the viol family.[14] The earliest Japanese descriptions of the *kokyū* and its origins link it to the Ryūkyū Islands or to the "Southern Barbarians," meaning the Portuguese and Spanish Westerners, who reached Japan in the sixteenth century. Curiously, the two most important sources on the origins of the *kokyū*, attributing it to the Ryūkyūans and the Westerners respectively, mention its use in chasing away snakes. One of them claims that the inhabitants of the Ryūkyū Islands used the *kokyū* (which in its Okinawan version has a round soundbox covered with snakeskin and is played with a taut bow, or even – today – with a violin bow[15]) to imitate the cry of a beast called, "raheika," which feeds on the feared poisonous adder. The name of this remarkable creature is neither Ryūkyūan nor Japanese, but resembles the modern Japanese work for rebec; *rabeika,* which appears in a seventeenth-century collection of haiku.[16]

In the mid-sixteenth century the Jesuit missionaries arrived on Japan's main island, Honshu. They brought with them their music as well as their faith, and they taught their Japanese acolytes to sing and play hymns. The terminology surrounding musical instruments is maddeningly unclear, but Jesuit sources – Japanese sources are virtually non-existent – mention a variety of bowed instruments, most notably the *viola da arco* (first mentioned in 1561) and the *viola da braccio* (1580).[17] The missionaries used viols widely in religious services and taught Western musical instruments to a few Japanese students. As small churches multiplied, the viol was most commonly used as a substitute for the organ. One missionary recorded that after the organ and the clavier, the Japanese liked the viol best.[18]

Between 1582 and 1590 a delegation of Jesuit missionaries and four Japanese converts travelled to Europe, where they were received by the pope and visited several musical centres, where they both listened to performances and played themselves. They even spent a couple of days in Cremona, and a Japanese luthier based there today has speculated that they may have seen, heard and possibly acquired a violin from the Amati family, on which they may have performed at an audience with Toyotomi Hideyoshi, the supreme military ruler of Japan, after their return.[19] A nice idea, linking as it does the history of the violin in Japan to the very cradle of the violin's history in Europe, where pre-1800, Italian-built violins from Cremona remain the gold standard to this day.[20] The link is not inconceivable, but the evidence is inconclusive. According to Jesuits' reports of the audience, the instruments the young Japanese played on included the *rabequinha*, a generic term for bowed treble, arm-held and fretless instruments of the *braccio* family. By the time the Japanese toured Southern Europe, instruments of the violin family were being played alongside viols, and so the instrument in question may have been a violin. If so, the description of the performance for Toyotomi Hideyoshi would be the first record of a violin being played by a Japanese in Japan. Another report, in 1593, mentions *violas de arco* (a viol consort) and a *viola* (*viole d'arco* and *viola semplice* in an Italian translation of the report) being played at mass. By this time, however, Toyotomi Hideyoshi had begun expelling the missionaries. In the following years, the persecutions of the Christians and the culture they had brought with them increased, culminating in their complete expulsion in 1613. Virtually all traces of missionary activity, including musical instruments, were destroyed. The last explicit mention of bowed instruments is the report of a performance for Hideyoshi's son Hideyori in 1607, which mentions a *viola* and a *rabeca* being played for him.

Some researchers have surmised that the introduction of Western music in the sixteenth century paved the way for the adoption of Western music in the nineteenth century, but this is speculation and perhaps another indication of the desire to enhance the legitimacy of Western music in Japan by giving it as long a history as possible. The triumph of Western music in modern Japan can be plausibly explained without referring to earlier history. In the sixteenth century Japan's rulers had powerful reasons to keep the Westerners and their culture out of Japan; in the mid-nineteenth century they had equally powerful reasons to let them in and learn from them. The only people who played Western music in Japan in the following 250 years of Tokugawa rule were the Dutch merchants who languished at their trading post on the artificial island of Deshima in Nagasaki Bay waiting for the next Dutch ship to take them home. Japanese illustrations show scenes of music-making with viols and other instruments, but whether the painter or other Japanese personally witnessed these scenes is uncertain.[21]

Even if viols and possibly violins disappeared by the seventeenth century, they may well have inspired Japanese musicians to start playing a *shamisen*-like instrument with a bow. It seems plausible that the *kokyū* was developed in the late sixteenth century from the *shamisen,* which itself came to Japan from the Ryūkyū islands, and the Okinawan *kokyū* (*kūchō,* whose ancestors most likely include the rebec); probably with inspiration from the viol. By the early eighteenth century the *kokyū* had become a popular folk instrument. The most typical players around 1800 appear to have been wandering minstrels performing music to accompany Buddhist morality tales. But the *kokyū* was also played by actors and by courtesans at drinking parties and to accompany dancing. In addition, it commonly featured in the three-piece chamber ensembles known as *sankyoku*, together with the *koto* and the *shamisen*, until the mid-nineteenth century, when it was replaced by the *shakuhachi*.[22] From then on it gradually sank into oblivion, although Miyagi Michio (1894–1956), one of the foremost representatives of "new Japanese music," played the *kokyū* and even developed a new type with a larger resonance box. Today it is played by some specialists of classical ensemble repertoire, namely the *jiuta,* a sung genre with instrumental interludes. Occasionally the *kokyū* can be heard as part of the accompaniment in the *bunraku* puppet theatre as well as in the folk music of certain regions (including parts of Aichi, Mie, Nagano, Niigata and Toyama Prefectures[23]).

The *kokyū*'s obscurity is an extreme case of traditional music's niche existence in general.[24] For over a hundred years, from the 1880s until the end of the twentieth century, music lessons in schools taught only Western classical music. The leaders of the imperial government which replaced the rule of the Tokugawa shoguns in 1868 decided from the start that Western music served its educational purposes better than what their own country had to offer. For a while some sort of synthesis was envisaged, but it came to nothing.

What, then, was the music like that the Meiji government deemed so inadequate? For one thing, "music" did not exist at all. More precisely, music as an abstract concept had no psychological reality for most Japanese; the word *ongaku* for "music" only gained currency when it came to be used as a Japanese translation for the Western word, and people still tend to associate it with Western music. Rather, the Japanese had and have preserved to this day what ethnomusicologists like to call "musics," several different types and styles of music played in different settings and by different kinds of people. Many genres originated on the Asian mainland, but were assimilated so thoroughly that they had long ceased to be perceived as foreign. We could also speak of musical worlds, essentially self-contained, although there could be connections between them, a phenomenon by no means unique to Japan.[25] Each of these musics had its own name and its own social setting. Among the most elevated was *gagaku*, the orchestral music of the imperial court and certain shrines. It came to Japan from the continent between the seventh and the ninth centuries, and while it has changed over the centuries it can still claim to be one of the world's oldest continuous orchestral traditions.[26]

By the late Tokugawa period (1602–1868), Japan had a great variety of musical genres, including *shōmyō* (Buddhist chant), *kagura* (music performed at Shintō shrines), the accompanying music of the *nō, kabuki* and *bunraku* theatres as well as various styles of recitation and song to the accompaniment of the *biwa, shamisen* and *koto* as well as a few purely instrumental genres. Several styles were associated with the pleasure quarters. Folk songs (*min'yō*) and other folk performing arts (*minzoku geinō*) with music were enjoyed by the common people. The Ainu in the north of Japan and the Okinawans in the south each had their own musical traditions. The *tonkori* (a kind of zither with vertically stretched strings) of the Ainu may well be the only stringed instrument that does not appear to have origins outside the Japanese archipelago.[27]

In other words, when Westerners encroached on Japan's shores for the second time in the mid-nineteenth century, Japan had a rich and varied musical culture which included many different forms, both old and new. Its different musical genres were highly context-bound, played by different social groups in different settings, although social and economic changes and the increasing commercialization of culture had begun to blur the boundaries between different musical worlds.[28] There was no universal system of notation. Transmission was almost exclusively by ear, from teacher to pupil, and often organized in the so-called *iemoto*-system of fictive family ties, with a hereditary master as the "head of house" (*iemoto*) ensuring the continuation of the lineage. Much music was performed in small, intimate settings. Except, possibly, at the larger festivals, there were no large-scale public performances comparable to the symphony concert or the military parade. In short, Japanese music and musical culture lacked several qualities deemed indispensable for fulfilling the functions expected of music in a modern nation state: the potential for large-scale displays of power uniting many people in musical performance, a system of transmission suitable for teaching large groups at once in schools, and a theoretical framework and vocabulary to enable intellectual discussions about the nature of music (in the abstract) and its uses. Western music came to Japan with all these elements already in place, ready-made for the Japanese to adopt full-scale together with so many elements of Western civilization.

Most of this book, starting with the next chapter, will be about the introduction of Western music centring on the violin. Japanese music, however, continued to be played, and like everything else it was profoundly affected by the changes that swept Japan after 1868. *Gagaku,* closely associated with the imperial court, was the one music that did have a place in the government's reforms and was changed fundamentally by the typical government measures of the time: centralization, standardization, regulation. The different orchestras and their traditions were brought together in Tokyo, the musicians were ordered to copy and edit their repertoire according to general principles and their status was newly defined. Several of them began to study Western music in addition to *gagaku*. Their salaries decreased, causing some to leave and make a living elsewhere.[29]

Other types of music were affected by the national and local governments' policies to various degrees. Music associated with Shintō and Buddhism was affected by the government's policies relating to religion. Some Buddhist reformers even looked to Protestant hymns in their efforts to reform religious music. Many of the instrumental genres were affected by the abolition of specially protected guilds, including the guilds of blind *biwa, koto, kokyū* and *shamisen* players and the Zen-Buddhist *komusō* guild of *shakuhachi* players. The *shakuhachi* became widely popular as a solo or chamber music instrument. New schools emerged and the repertoires were standardized. The enterprising *shakuhachi* player and teacher Nakao Tozan (1876–1956) introduced a new school with its own teacher licensing system.

Popular music in the nineteenth century also included a style that originated in China and became known as *minshingaku* (Ming and Qing dynasty music).[30] Fashionable among men of letters since Tokugawa times, it reached the height of its popularity in the period from the 1860s. The instruments of *minshingaku* included several types of Chinese fiddles, but the most popular instrument was the *gekkin*, a plucked lute with a round, flattish body (like the full moon from which it takes its name) and frets. From the 1880s a veritable craze for the *gekkin* swept Japan; easier to learn than the fretless *shamisen*, it became popular among geisha in Kyoto and in ordinary families. But during the Sino-Japanese war of 1894–95, *minshingaku* lost its popularity and never really recovered, although it was taught as a separate genre in Osaka until 1940.[31] It may well be that people's familiarity with the Chinese fiddles paved the way for the popularity of the violin.

By the early twentieth century, Japan's musical life was more vibrant and varied than ever. Not only had Western music gained a firm foothold with some quite decent performances (although the general level was still low) and private teachers as well as public education contributing to its spread; many genres of traditional music, including the folk performing arts, were thriving as well. In the early years, some traditional genres suffered from official efforts to reform Japanese arts so that they could measure up to Western arts (deemed superior by the reformers) and enable Japan to prove to the West that its culture was as civilized and noble as their own.[32] *Kabuki*, for example, the theatre of the people, was cleansed of its perceived vulgar elements and new, supposedly more edifying plays were staged, at least for a while.

Japanese popular music for *shamisen* and *koto* was treated in a similar way, mainly by sanitizing the lyrics of the songs. But such official attempts at reform were soon given up, and subsequent efforts centred on Western music. Only the *koto* continued to be taught at the Tokyo Academy of Music and heard at its concerts, partly because of its use as a substitute for the prohibitively expensive piano. The *koto* was also taught at schools for the blind.[33] Perhaps official neglect was an advantage for traditional music, allowing its musicians to develop their art without government interference. Enterprising performers of Japan's traditional music as well as *minshingaku* (which after all was more similar to Japanese than to Western music) renewed their chosen genre in different ways. They played at public concerts – a type of event unknown before the introduction of Western musical culture – and, later, on the radio. They taught more pupils. They composed new pieces, fairly close to traditional idiom at first, but then increasingly influenced by Western music.[34] They published old and new pieces in some revised form of traditional notation or in Western staff notation. This enabled people to study new pieces by themselves rather than pay a teacher for each piece they wanted to learn.

Musical experiments included attempts to combine and to "harmonize" Japanese and Western music. The violin – cheap, portable, available and widely studied – seemed especially suited to this enterprise. It is even perfectly possible (in theory) to play the violin not only using Japanese scales and tuning, but also conforming to expectations of sound quality. Indeed, for a while in the early twentieth century, it looked as if the violin might become integrated into Japan's traditional music. Enterprising musicians published Japanese *koto* and *shamisen* tunes for the violin in Western notation, sometimes complete with advice on playing together with Japanese instruments. High school and university students took up the violin. Respectable families let their daughters learn the violin instead of the *shamisen*.[35] Even geisha abandoned their *shamisen* for violins, although in some cases only to pose for picture postcards. Self-taught minstrels, the *enkashi,* wandered the streets accompanying their own songs on the violin.

Increasingly, however, the trend moved towards separating indigenous and Western music. Before 1945 there were still many efforts to "renew" Japanese music with the help of inspiration from the West, and styles we might call hybrid (often merely dismissed by critics as kitsch) flourished. But after the Second World War, a second wave of profound change under Western influence swept Japan, and Western music increasingly dominated people's preferences. So thoroughly did it conquer Japan that Bach is more familiar to most Japanese today than *gagaku,* Mozart is more popular than *shamisen* or *koto* music, and Beethoven sounds less exotic than the drums and flutes of the *nō* theatre. Even music perceived as "traditional" has as often as not been written recently by composers trained in Western music. Indeed, Western music *is* traditional music for today's Japanese. Songs like "The Last Rose of Summer" have been – favourites for well over a hundred years. Beethoven's Ninth Symphony probably sees more performances per year in Japan than in Beethoven's homeland. Western classical and traditional Japanese music constituted and to a large extent still constitute separate worlds whose representatives rarely meet. Eta Harich-Schneider (1894–1986), a pioneer of the harpsichord in the twentieth century and scholar of Japanese music, observed in *A History of Japanese Music* (1973): "Not a single one of my students of European music knows the name of the old Japanese instruments in my collection."[36]

Still, while Western classical music still dominates the schools[37] and popular music of various descriptions has the largest audience, Japanese traditional music continues to be played, often in niches and unnoticed by the general public. The imperial court still has its *gagaku* orchestra. *Nō* and *kabuki* are still performed in special theatres and attract fans. Other traditional genres are most often practised by amateurs, paying their teachers for the privilege to play and perform. New "traditional music" has evolved, including *taiko* drumming groups, Tsugaru *shamisen* (Tsugaru-jamisen) and Okinawan pop. Tōgi Hideki, a *gagaku*-musician turned feel-good performer has given the *hichiriki* (a double reed) of the *gagaku* orchestra new prominence, and even the *kokyū* has found a champion in Azechi Keiji, amplified and combined with synthesizer on CDs like *Songs from the Heart: Oasis*.[38]

Perhaps the most remarkable result of the introduction of Western music into Japan is the fact that to most Japanese today their own indigenous music sounds as exotic as it does to non-Japanese, indicating that within the space of a few decades Japanese musical sensibilities have changed beyond recognition.[39] "Japanese music," like "Japanese culture" in general, has been placed on a pedestal as something to be preserved in its "pure" form, but it is not the music most Japanese regularly listen to.[40] Back in 1583 the missionary Valignano wrote, "Our vocal and instrumental music wounds their ears and they delight in their own music which truly tortures our hearing."[41] He may have been exaggerating, but both then and 300 years later many Japanese must have found Western music uncomfortable to listen to, since it sounded very different from their own. If anything the gap widened, for what we know today as art music had barely begun to emerge in Valignano's time, and what is perceived as most distinctive about traditional Japanese music only fully developed in the Tokugawa period. Eta Harich-Schneider surely has a point when she observes that Japan adopted Western art music at a point in history when its contrast with indigenous music was at its strongest and that the nineteenth-century Western idea of "absolute music" had no equivalent in Japan (where music was played as part of a ceremony, or a theatre play or to accompany words in the many recital styles).[42] Japanese music is based on different scales and modes and has very little of the kind of vertical harmony that characterizes Western art music, even in *gagaku,* where there is some polyphony. Another obvious difference lies in what is considered a beautiful sound; unlike the Western *belcanto* tradition with its ideal of pure notes, the unstable pitch of a twanging string or the sound of blowing mixed with the note of a *shakuhachi* are an essential ingredient of the music; the skilled musician creates variety by subtly changing timbres. Moreover, in contrast to the passionate expression of the Classical and particularly Romantic music of Europe, most Japanese music lacked strong emotional expression; sober refinement or decorum characterized the performance of the most highly regarded music.[43]

In the twentieth century, sound recording brought music from around the world to people's ears, and musicians, whether of the Western classical tradition or of other traditions, have experimented and sought to extend the possibilities of the genres they worked in. As a result, we have all become accustomed to and enjoy a wider range of musical sounds and styles. By the end of the century, distinctions such as "classical music" and "popular music" or "European" and "Eastern" were losing their meaning.[44] But in the mid-nineteenth century the two musical traditions seemed virtually irreconcilable to anyone but die-hard proponents of harmonization of Western and Japanese Music. Western visitors to Japan who heard Japanese indigenous music in the nineteenth and early twentieth centuries tended to be contemptuous of it. Those who taught music, professionals even more than amateurs, were convinced of the superiority of their own music. Few of them took the trouble to learn about Japanese traditional music, even if their busy schedules permitted it. Many of their students accepted their teachers' privileging of Western classical music, because they associated the music with other achievements of Western civilization. But that does not by itself explain the profound changes in aesthetic sentiment over the following decades. If we want to explain the overwhelming dominance of Western classical music today, we must look beyond Western imperialism and political power.

# Part 1: Confrontation with the West: The Modernization of Japan and the Role of Music from the Mid-nineteenth Century to the End of the First World War

On 14 October 1872 the Meiji emperor, wearing traditional clothes (which he would soon exchange for a Western military uniform on public occasions) arrived in a horse-drawn carriage at Shimbashi station in Tokyo for the official opening of Japan's first railway line. Outside the station building a bugle corps from the army played the French military march *Aux Champs*, while inside, a *gagaku* orchestra played *Manzairaku* (Dance of Longevity). The emperor made a speech before boarding a special railway carriage. The invited dignitaries manned the other eight carriages. The navy band played, canons saluted, fireworks exploded, the whistles blew and the train steamed and roared off on its way south. Thus the modern era of "civilization and enlightenment" announced itself with noisy concert never heard before in Japan.[1]

The day, still known as "railway day," represented an important landmark on Japan's journey towards modern times: modern times which came to be symbolized by the Meiji emperor, the railway, the military – and by music. Western music was not adopted and systematically advanced by the Meiji government because of any intrinsic musical value. It came to Japan as part of a package. In the 1850s and 1860s, following Commodore Perry's arrival in Japan in 1853, the government of the Tokugawa shoguns was forced to conclude treaties with North America and several European countries. This forceful end to over 200 years of relative seclusion combined with an internal crisis to bring down the Tokugawa shoguns. In 1868, a group of samurai and nobles from the imperial court staged a palace coup and proclaimed a new era, Meiji, and direct imperial rule. The new government devoted all its efforts to defending Japan against further Western encroachment by strengthening the country and turning it into an economic and military power. A rapid succession of reforms transformed Japan into a modern nation that could compete with the Western powers on their own terms. They created a central government, a conscript army, a tax system, a public education system, the foundations of an industrial economy and, in 1889, a parliamentary constitution. The "unequal treaties" with the foreign powers were revised, and Japan began to realize imperial ambitions of its own, winning wars against China in 1895 and Russia in 1905. By the time the emperor died in 1912, Japan had fulfilled its ambition of rivalling the Western powers; it joined the First World War on the side of the Allies and participated in the Versailles peace conference.

Music had an important role to play in the enterprise of modernizing on Western terms.[2] Perry had demonstrated the power of Western music when he had his military band play to enhance his display of military power. No wonder military music was the first kind the Japanese emulated; even before the Meiji government took control, the shoguns and the regional lords organized drum and fife bands. Until the Meiji government centralized the administration and created a conscript army, the domains still maintained their own armies, including military bands. The domain of Wakayama employed a German, Carl Köppen, to train its troops in Prussian military tactics from December 1869 to May 1871. In his memoirs Köppen mentions a band playing marches he himself composed (or, more likely perhaps, played from memory of his time as a soldier in Bückeburg), and a photograph is preserved in the archives of Köppen's home town of Bückeburg which shows the band, complete with drum, brass and woodwinds.[3] In 1869, the domain of Satsuma sent about 30 men to Yokohama, where British troops were stationed, to be trained by the bandmaster John William Fenton.[4] When the national army and navy were established in 1871, members of Fenton's band, also known as the "Satsuma Band," were recruited into the new national military bands and Fenton was employed by the Ministry for Military Affairs for 18 months from November 1871. Fenton continued as musical instructor of the navy band until 1877. The band played on ceremonial occasions such as the opening of the first railway line, the emperor's visits within Japan and receptions for foreign dignitaries. From April 1872, the army and the navy were under the jurisdiction of two separate ministries. The army, including its band, continued to employ French instructors; in 1871, Gustave Charles Dagron (1845–88?), a musician in the French army, was appointed to direct the band and stayed (with a brief interruption in 1878) until 1883. He was succeeded by Charles Leroux (1851–1926), a musical director in the French army, who came to Japan as a member of the third French military mission and taught from 1884 to 1889. From 1879 onwards, military music training received a boost with the appointment of Franz Eckert (1852–1916) as the musical director of the navy band. Trained at Breslau and Dresden and employed as musical director by the German navy, Eckert probably contributed more than any other foreign musician to the development of Western music in the early years. During his 20 years in Japan he taught not only the musicians of the navy (from 1879 to 1889 and 1895 to 1899), but also of the army (from 1890 to 1894) and the musicians of the imperial court, where he held official appointments from 1887 to 1899, having first taught some of the *gagaku* musicians privately. Between 1883 and 1886 he also taught for the Music Investigation Committee (Ongaku Torishirabe Gakari) established in 1879. Besides teaching he harmonized and arranged numerous pieces of music, most famously the national anthem "Kimi ga yo." His funeral march, *Kanashimi no kiwami* was first performed at the funeral of the dowager of Emperor Kōmei in 1897 and was also played at the funeral of Emperor Shōwa in 1989. Eckert left Japan in 1899. He briefly returned to Germany before moving to Korea in 1901, where he played a similarly pioneering role in the introduction of Western music there.[5]

Not only the military provided music on ceremonial occasions. The Meiji government reorganized the *gagaku* musicians in the imperial household's *gagaku* department.[6] In 1870, musicians were ordered to submit information about the music and the training, including pieces and methods of playing that had always been transmitted secretly from teacher to disciple. This system of secret transmission was now abolished; in 1873 the government permitted the study of *gagaku* to anyone who wished, provided they applied for permission. *Gagaku* musicians, just like the samurai, were no longer privileged by virtue of their birth, and they had to share the function of performing music at important ceremonies with the new army and navy bands. The officials in the Department of Court Ceremonies, which included the *gagaku* department, obviously read the signs of the times. In July 1874, having persuaded the Navy Ministry to agree to their proposal, they sent a request to the Council of State for their musicians to receive instruction in Western music. The first problem that had to be addressed was providing the *gagaku* musicians with instruments. They would also need tuition. Eventually an agreement with the navy ministry was reached; the ministry would help them to acquire instruments as cheaply as possible and have them taught by the ministry's teachers. By 1875, about half of the court musicians, 35 men, were receiving instruction, and the following year Fenton was employed by both the navy and the Department of Court Ceremonies, while two court musicians were appointed conductors.

The German pianist Eta Harich-Schneider, who taught court musicians just after the Second World War, heard stories from them about how their predecessors had struggled to learn the foreign music. Reading music proved particularly difficult, and in the end most of them ended up learning it by ear, listening to Fenton singing the entries for them and ignoring the sheet music on their stands, which as often as not was placed upside down.[7] The court musicians gave their first performance of Western music on 3 November 1876, at the celebrations for the emperor's birthday. The concert was deemed a success and plans for a string orchestra were made. The musicians continued to study with the Japanese musicians in the navy after Fenton's departure. Some began to receive instruction from Eckert, even before his formal appointment in 1887. A rehearsal schedule published in English by the *gagaku* department in December 1878 (the rehearsals were open to the public) stated that Western music was rehearsed on Wednesdays and Saturdays, the other days being devoted to "Kagura or music belonging to the oldest Japanese song" and "Gaku or several kind [sic] of classical music."[8]

Opportunities for performing Western music increased. Realizing the need for more in-depth study of Western music, the *gagaku* musicians began to widen the scope of their activities. In 1879, four of them applied for permission to learn the piano from Clara Matsuno (1853–1941), who taught at the kindergarten department of the government-run Tokyo Normal School for Women (Tōkyō Joshi Shihan Gakkō Fuzoku Yōchien). Born in Berlin as Clara Zitelmann, she had married an employee of the Japanese Ministry of the Interior, whom she met when he was studying in Berlin. Trained as a kindergarten teacher, she was also an accomplished pianist and later taught music at the Girls' Peers School (Joshi Gakushūin). The piano lessons do not seem to have continued for long, but they testify to the *gagaku* musicians' determination to master Western music.

To further the study and performance of Western music, the court music department established the Society for Western Music in November 1879, renamed the Society for Music in 1882. The court musicians played on an increasing variety of occasions and did much to bring Western music to an audience beyond the confinements of the imperial court. At the same time the department worked equally hard to preserve their traditional music.[9] The heads of the traditional *gagaku* families received government stipends to ensure that they continued to practise and teach their art. Thus *gagaku* was not completely displaced by Western music and continues to play a limited but significant role to this day.

Even more than the military and the imperial court, the education system brought Western music to the people of Japan. The government leaders knew that Western educators and governments promoted music education, particularly singing, in order to foster national cohesion and cultivate physical and mental health as well as civilized moral conduct. This chimed in with Confucian notions of the moral power of music. Putting the ideas into practice, however, took time. The Education Law promulgated in 1872 provided for a universal, compulsory education system with public schools at all levels and a Western curriculum which – on paper – included music: singing at elementary level and instrumental music at secondary level, but in both cases with the addition, "omitted for the time being." The implementation of the Education Law took several years. Music education in particular lagged behind, since schools lacked qualified teachers, instruments and textbooks. But that music was mentioned at all shows that government officials recognized its important educational role in the West. In preparation for the law several Japanese officials had inspected Western education systems and they knew what they wanted for their country.

Several years after the promulgation of the Education Law in 1872, the Ministry of Education began to implement music education in earnest.[10] Three men in particular were responsible for this: Tanaka Fumimaro

(1845–1909), who had studied European education systems as a member of the Iwakura Embassy, the Meiji government's first major diplomatic mission, Megata Tanetarō (1853–1926), who had graduated from Harvard in 1874, and Isawa Shūji (1851–1917), who studied at Bridgewater Normal School in Massachusetts and Harvard University between 1875 and 1878. In April 1878, Megata, who was then in America as a supervisor of the Japanese students, and Isawa submitted a report to Tanaka, then Vice-Minister of Education, about the introduction of Western music in Japanese schools. They praised the physical, emotional, social and moral benefits of teaching children to sing and stated that, since no suitable musical style existed in Japan, Western music should be adapted to suit the Japanese. An additional document signed by Megata detailed the practical implementation.[11] He proposed setting up a "singing course" in the Tokyo Normal School and Tokyo Normal School for Women and employing Luther Whiting Mason as a teacher and Isawa Shūji as his assistant.

Luther Whiting Mason (1828–96), born in rural Maine, had received a general education and trained as a teacher; most of his musical training was informal, including private instrumental and singing lessons and experience as a conductor of church choirs.[12] He had studied at the Boston Academy of Music and at the New York Normal Musical Institute in summer 1853; most American music teachers in his time acquired their musical training at summer courses. From 1853 to 1855 Mason worked as a teacher for public schools in Louisville, Kentucky, where he started to develop his method of teaching singing by rote. He continued his work as a teacher for public schools in Cincinnati from 1855 to 1864. His experience of teaching German immigrant children in America was to serve him well in Japan. He established a reputation for himself, which resulted in an invitation to teach music for the Boston public schools. Mason continued to edit and publish textbooks, including his *National Music Course* with accompanying charts. Mason's methods were eclectic. The songs he included were mostly German folk songs, and many of his exercises came from Christian Heinrich Hohmann's *Praktischer Lehrgang für den Gesang-Unterricht in Volksschulen,* translated into English as *Practical Course of Instruction in Singing* (1856–58), which he had used in Cincinnati. Mason travelled to Europe in 1872 and 1874 to observe musical education and collect song books.

During his time in Boston, Mason firmly established his reputation as a music educator; his *National Music Course* was the most influential series of music textbook in America in the 1870s and early 1880s and earned him honours at the world exhibitions in Vienna (1873) and Paris (1878) as well as the Philadelphia Centennial Exposition in 1876. Mason hoped to develop an international music course, and in the 1890s headed an editorial committee that published a German work, *Neue Gesangsschule,* based on his methods. It is not surprising that Mason's work attracted the attention of Japanese studying education and teacher training in America. Megata consulted him about music education. Isawa had private lessons from him while studying at Bridgewater. Apparently music was his worst subject; he had even been advised to drop it by the school's principal, A.G. Boyden, who otherwise spoke highly of Isawa, describing him as "well-trained in the schools of Japan."[13]

Isawa returned to Japan in 1878 after having continued from Bridgewater to study physics at Harvard. He became head of Tokyo Normal School in May 1878. In spring 1879 he got a high-ranking official in the Ministry of Education to express his – Isawa's – ideas in a "Plan for the Establishment of a Music Instruction Centre" (dated 8 March). In June 1879 Mason was formally appointed "Instructor of Musics in the School of Musics" for a period of two years, although no institution of that name existed. In October Isawa became head of the Music Investigation Committee, which functioned both as a research and experimental committee and a teacher training institute; its tasks were to investigate music at home and abroad in order to develop suitable educational materials and to implement musical education, starting with singing, at the kindergarten and primary school affiliated to the Tokyo Normal School and the Tokyo Normal School for Women.

Mason arrived in Japan in March 1880.[14] In preparation for his work in Japan he had bought musical instruments and tools to tune and repair them and collected pentatonic folk songs from Scotland, Ireland and Wales. His work with Japanese students in America had led him to believe that these were most suited to Japanese ears. His responsibilities in Tokyo were not so different from those in Boston: teaching children, training teachers, organizing and directing performances, and creating educational materials. He taught at the Tokyo Normal School, the Tokyo Normal School for Women and the affiliated schools and kindergarten, at the Peers' School and the Music Institute of the Music Investigation Committee. The Music Institute's first 22 students, including several court musicians and 13 women, were accepted in October 1880 to study singing, piano, organ, violin and theory of music, as well as Japanese instrumental music. The students were a mixed group aged 12 to 50. Only three of them completed the entire course and graduated in 1885. The court musicians, with their previous experience in Western music, were soon promoted to assistant teachers, and Mason found able helpers in them.

Isawa had outlined his ideas for the work of the Music Investigation Committee in October 1879, when he spoke of combining Eastern and Western music to create a national music. The most immediate task, however, was the selection of songs deemed suitable to be taught in schools. Aesthetic considerations hardly troubled Isawa, whose only musical qualifications consisted in having beaten the drum in a drum and fife band in 1866 and commissioned a Japanese version of "Lightly Row" as director of the Aichi Prefecture Normal School in 1874. He was far more concerned with the moral content of the songs' lyrics than with their musical qualities. In order to compile a series of graded music textbooks, Isawa chaired a committee including Mason, an interpreter, three poets, five court musicians and two general scholars.[15] The committee began publishing song books in 1881. Most of the melodies come from Western sources, while the lyrics, not necessarily translations, were composed by Japanese. Many of the songs are still popular in Japan today.

In July 1882, Mason left Japan for Europe to learn more about music education there, particularly for the blind. He expected to return to Japan, but his contract (he had been granted a one-year extension of his original contract), was cancelled that November. The reasons for this are not wholly clear, but by the 1880s, the Japanese government was keen to reduce the number of foreign teachers. Besides, disagreements between Mason and Isawa might have influenced the decision. Mason, who regarded Japanese music as having "a wrong scale" and was convinced of the necessity of converting his pupils to "civilized music,"[16] presumably had little time for Isawa's vision of a "national music" which amalgamated Japanese and Western music, and Isawa may well have felt that the Japanese could now continue implementing Western vocal music in the education system without Mason. In 1883 students from teacher training schools in several prefectures were enrolled for a short course at the Music Investigation Committee's Music Institute, and in 1884, 22 students selected by their home prefectures were formally registered as students. In this way the government hoped to disseminate singing in schools as rapidly as possible.

Instrumental music was another matter though. Only a few Japanese mastered a Western musical instrument well enough to teach it. Several *gagaku* musicians taught on the music course, mainly singing, musical theory and Japanese musical instruments; but one of them, Ōno Hisayori also taught the violin.[17] In March 1882, Nagai Shigeko (or Shige), one of six girls who in 1871 travelled to America with the Iwakura Embassy, began teaching the piano at the Music Institute. She had studied at Vassar College and graduated with a Certificate of Music the previous year.

In March 1883 Franz Eckert (1852–1916) was appointed to teach at the Music Investigation Committee's training institute in addition to his commitments with the navy. When his contract expired in March 1886, he was succeeded by the Dutchman Guillaume Sauvlet (1843–1902), who taught until March 1888. Sauvlet has often been described as an amateur, but although he does not appear to have been conservatoire-trained, he made his living as a performer, conductor and teacher.[18] He first came to Japan in 1885 as a conductor and pianist for the English Mascotte Opera Company. From April 1886 Sauvlet taught part-time at the training institute. A subsequent contract for 1887 details the subjects as singing, piano, organ, strings, wind, harmony, composition and counterpoint. Sauvlet's contract was renewed once more in 1888, but by then negotiations were underway to appoint Rudolf Dittrich (1861–1919) as artistic director. Dittrich's appointment and the upgrading of the Music Investigation Committee to the Tokyo Academy of Music (Tōkyō Ongaku Gakkō) marked the first steps towards an institution that provided musical training to the highest level.[19] Unlike his predecessors, Dittrich was an outstanding professional who had trained at one of Europe's leading conservatoires. During his time at the Tokyo Academy of Music, from 1888 to 1894, he not only taught, but performed in 50 concerts, including solo performances and chamber music with pupils, colleagues and foreign amateurs and conducting choral concerts. His professional excellence as a musician is illustrated by the fact that he enjoyed a distinguished career after his return to Europe, something hardly any of the Western music teachers who succeeded him achieved. In 1901 he became court organist and in 1906 professor at the Vienna Conservatoire.

A few months after Dittrich's arrival, the school was reorganized into a preparatory department and a core department; the latter included a two-year teacher training course and a three-year specialist course. That same year, 1889, Kōda Nobu (1870–1946), one of only three students at the first graduation in 1885, became the first music student to be sent abroad by the Meiji government. She returned to teach in 1895, having studied violin and piano in Boston and Vienna. Gradually, foreign teachers and the school's graduates, often after studying abroad, raised the standards at the Tokyo Academy of Music.

In this way – led by programmatic and utilitarian rather than aesthetic considerations, based on questionable theoretical reasoning and on prejudice against Japan's popular musical tradition, and with makeshift arrangements and minimal training – began the official import of Western music into Japan. Measured against the government's aims, it was successful. By the mid-Meiji period, Western music was well-established in government institutions, namely the army, the navy, the imperial court and the public education system.[20] Each of these institutions had a group of active specialists who were recruited and trained through formal channels. Equally importantly, occasions for the performance of Western music had been created as part of the process of reform: imperial tours, diplomatic events such as welcoming foreign representatives and state visitors, court ceremonies, and various new ceremonies in schools and business. This systematic importation by the government, together with the establishment of formal systems of transmission and the creation of occasions which required its performance is one of the main reasons why Western music was able to take such a strong hold in Japan within a short time. On the other hand it took time for these developments to reach beyond the capital and the larger cities; the dissemination throughout the country's schools had only begun, and most people still had few opportunities to hear Western music.

Although in the early years of Meiji, government measures played the most important role in the introduction of Western music, they could not have worked on their own. The Western music teachers invited by the government were not the only foreigners who taught music in Japan. Christian missionaries, whether Russian orthodox, catholic or protestant, taught music in the private schools they established well before the Meiji government introduced music education in the public schools.[21] Mission schools played a particularly significant role in education for girls, to which the Meiji government gave low priority in the early years. While most of them were in Tokyo, Yokohama and Kobe, others offered a Western education in towns far from the capital, where the public schools were slow to develop. The private Morioka School for Girls in the northern prefecture of Iwate, for example, opened in 1892 by French catholic sisters, had what may well have been the only piano in town, imported from France. Some pupils were taught the piano and the violin. Schools like the Aoyama Academy for Girls in Tokyo, established in 1889 had music departments, where girls were taught musical instruments as well as singing. At another school in Hakodate in northern Japan, the (Methodist) Caroline Wright Seminary, established in 1882, all girls learnt to sing and some to play the organ; the seminary had a preparatory school in Hirosaki, where many of the seminary students came from.[22] Even when music was not an independent subject in the curriculum, pupils were taught to sing hymns. At the first of these schools, the private academy of James Hepburn in Yokohama and the Ferris Seminary established as part of Hepburn's school in 1870, music was formally introduced into the curriculum only in 1887. But hymns were taught from its establishment.[23] The influence of protestant hymns was particularly significant, because many of them were translated and published in song collections from 1874 onwards. Some, like "Joy to the World," became regular hits, as popular as any non-Christian song.[24]

Christian missionaries and teachers also associated informally with the Japanese around them, offering opportunities for music-making at social gatherings. An example is the family of Clara Whitney, who came to Japan in 1875. Clara mentions several musical events in her diary, including a tea party at the Matsudaira residence in 1878, where she witnessed a performance which included several types of Chinese bowed instruments and where she herself played the reed organ. In January 1879 the Whitneys gave a musical entertainment at their own home, where the invited court musicians played *gagaku*, Clara played and sang, and all together attempted to perform a piece composed by one of the court musicians.[25] We can imagine similar occasions of informal social and musical exchanges between foreigners and the Japanese around them. The lively cultural activities of the foreign community in Yokohama were largely conducted for the foreigners themselves; visiting artists and resident amateurs performed for them and music teachers taught mainly foreigners. When Sauvlet extended his services as private teacher to the Japanese it was worth a special mention in an article in the *Japan Weekly Mail* (5 December 1885).[26] Even before Sauvlet, Christian Wagner (1819–91) arrived in Yokohama in 1872. In 1862 he had settled in Hong Kong as a music teacher, like Sauvlet. In an advertisement in 1875 he offered lessons "on wind or stringed instruments" as well as piano tuning and instrument repairs.[27] He also composed and performed, chiefly on the flute, but also on the violin and the concertina, giving at least thirteen concerts during his time in Yokohama. Wagner even founded the first amateur orchestra in Yokohama. So prominent was he that in October 1876 the *Japan Punch* jokingly referred to his concert on 29 September as a "Wagner Festival," alluding to the first performance of Richard Wagner's complete *Ring der Nibelungen* at Bayreuth from 13 to 17 August that year.[28] In 1876 Christian Wagner founded an amateur group. Largely thanks to his efforts, a symphony orchestra was established in Yokohama as early as 1892.[29]

Since Wagner and Sauvlet earned their living with music, we can call them professionals, even if some writers describe them as amateurs. But amateurs did play an important role in making Western music heard in Japan. At a time where the record player, the radio and the cinema were still unknown, people who wanted to hear music had to make their own. Amateurs performed publicly at concerts arranged by Sauvlet and others, but the programmes usually only describe them as "amateur lady" or "amateur gentleman," so we cannot know who they were. Amateurs may have been particularly important outside the Tokyo-Yokohama region; after all, the supply of expert musicians far from the capital was limited. One example is the German merchant Hans Ramsegger (1867–1933), who conducted, performed, composed and taught in and around Kobe.[30] Many foreigners, however, were most active in the foreign community, so we cannot know for sure how much they contributed to making Western music known among the Japanese.

Military musicians who left the army and navy as a result of reorganizations in the late 1880s contributed to the dissemination of Western music among the wider population by teaching or establishing their own bands.[31] By this time, the number of functions which called for Western music, including balls, had risen substantially, making it impossible for the existing bands from the military and the court to meet the demand, in particular because they needed permission to play at non-official events. In 1883 the Rokumeikan (Deer Cry Pavilion) was opened, an impressive building designed by the Englishman Josiah Conder in an eclectic style mixing neo-Renaissance and Indo-Islamic features. Its purpose was to provide a space where Japanese political leaders and their wives could mingle with foreign dignitaries and demonstrate that Japan was well on the way to "civilisation and enlightenment." Social events included concerts of Western music and, most famously, grand balls, for which military bands provided the music.[32]

Several associations promoted Western music by staging concerts. In 1887 high-ranking aristocrats, government officials and leading industrialists, together with members of the Imperial University and the Tokyo Academy of Music founded the Great Japan Music Society (Dai Nihon Ongakukai).[33] Its president was Marquis Nabeshima Naohiro (1846–1921); Isawa Shūji acted as vice-president. Their aim was to disseminate Western music by sponsoring regular concerts. The foreign music teachers, including Eckert and Sauvlet, were roped in as a matter of course and took part in the concerts organized by the society. Sixteen concerts were held between the society's establishment and 1894; the society disbanded in 1897 in the wake of the Sino–Japanese War. It was replaced in 1898 by the Meiji Music Society (Meiji Ongakukai), which had similar aims and organized 54 concerts in Tokyo and in the Kansai area between 1898 and 1910. The Tokyo Municipal Music Society (Tōkyō Shichū Ongakukai) was founded in 1886 by a former navy band member as a joint stock company with financial support from the leading businessman Shibusawa Eiichi (1840–1931). The new band recruited 20 young men, bought musical instruments and hired an Italian director. As the first commercial ensemble for Western music, the band played at private functions and public ceremonies; it even managed to secure a regular engagement at the weekly ball at Yokohama Grand Hotel. The band did much to introduce Western light music to the public. Soon, however, it received competition from another band formed by retired military musicians, the Music Society of the East (Tōyō Ongakukai). The bands attempted to merge, but the difference in abilities was too great. In 1892, 15 members and their director left and established their own band in Kobe, where they played regularly at the Oriental Hotel as well as at private functions. Meanwhile, the reduced Tokyo Municipal Music Society continued to be active in the capital region.[34]

Professional opportunities for musicians gradually increased. As early as 1888, Akita Zenzō established an agency in Tokyo which provided advertising and other services for businesses. He employed musicians to play at functions or promotional events. The major department stores even established and employed their own youth bands. Led by former members of the navy, the bands recruited and trained young people who had to commit themselves for a fixed number of years. The Mitsukoshi store recruited 12 youths between the ages of 11 and 15 in 1909. They were not expected to have previous experience with instruments or written music. Rehearsing after school, they gave their first performance after two months. Membership lasted four years, after which several members turned professional. The Osaka Mitsukoshi Band followed in 1914. In 1911 the Itō clothing store in Nagoya, which in 1925 became the Matsuzakaya department store, advertised for musicians for its band and recruited 20. In 1914 it performed together with the Mitsukoshi band in Ueno Park; at this time string players were added. Several of them later became professionals.[35] The Mitsukoshi Band ceased performing in May 1925, but new youth bands formed in the 1920s; the Izumo Band and the Takashimaya band in Osaka in 1923 and 1924 respectively, and the Toshima-en band in Tokyo in 1927.

While the Tokyo Academy of Music remained the most important institution of professional music education well into the twentieth century, private music schools also appeared. Many of the early ones in Tokyo acted as preparatory schools for the Academy, but also provided basic music training for music lovers and primary school teachers. Some were run by teachers of the Academy of Music.[36] More schools were founded in the early twentieth century; most of them offered elementary music education. The first private colleges offering professional training were the Japan Music School (Nihon Ongaku Gakkō), founded in 1903 by Yamada Gen'ichirō, and the Music College of the East (Tōyō Ongaku Gakkō), founded in 1907 by Suzuki Yonejirō, both early graduates of the

Tokyo Academy of Music.[37] Yamada concentrated his efforts on teacher training, including kindergarten teachers, while Suzuki's connections with the business world made it possible to provide his graduates with employment. By the early twentieth century, music societies began to flourish at many universities and colleges, and Western music came to be seen as an important element of Western education. Tokyo Imperial University had a lively music society whose members often took part in concerts at the Tokyo Academy of Music. The predecessors of the private Keiō and Waseda Universities also had active music societies. In Kyoto, members of the intelligentsia at Kyoto Imperial University and the private Dōshisha University contributed to the spread of Western music in the area.[38]

Magazines did much to spread knowledge of music, not only in the cities, but throughout the country.[39] Even before the first magazine devoted to music, *Ongaku zasshi* (The Musical Magazine), began publication in September 1890, articles about music had appeared in scholarly and literary journals. The editor and publisher of *Ongaku zasshi* had studied at the Tokyo Academy of Music, as had the editors of *Ongaku no tomo* (Friend of Music), founded in November 1901 and succeeded by *Ongaku* (Music) in April 1905. *Ongaku shinpō* (Music News), with the German subtitle *Die Musik*, began publication in February 1904 and was edited by a student of the Academy. In 1908 it merged with *Ongaku* to create *Ongakukai* (Music World), which was published until 1923 and attained the largest readership of all the music magazines. The Academy's alumni association began publishing a magazine also named *Ongaku*, perhaps the most scholarly of the magazines, in 1910. Thus, Tokyo Academy of Music graduates played an important role in disseminating knowledge and stimulating interest in Western music, including the violin, which was the subject of several articles and "how-to" series. Music stores also published magazines. From 1907 to 1916 the musical instruments division of the Jūjiya store in Kyoto published *Ongaku sekai* (The World of Music; Latin subtitle *Mundus Musicae)*. The first issue contained an article entitled "A Talk on the Violin." Yamano Gakki, a company based in Tokyo, published *Gekkan Gakufu* (Monthly Scores) from 1912 to 1941. As the title suggests, the magazine included music scores, as did some of the other magazines.

Gradually the number of people listening to and playing Western music in some form increased and spread from the upper classes to other sections of the population. By the early twentieth century most school children received at least minimal instruction in Western-style singing and learnt to sing Western melodies. Bands parading in the streets or performing in public parks were a common feature in the cities and school performances of music took place throughout the country. Educated Japanese with money and time to spare learnt to play the violin or the reed organ, or made their children learn. Book stores throughout the country included musical instruments, sheet music and other equipment among their wares. One of the first was Jūjiya on the Ginza in Tokyo, which opened in 1874 and sold musical instruments and scores from 1880 and gramophone records from 1906.

Adopting something that seems useful is one thing; really taking a liking to it and making it part of one's life is quite another. Although hundreds of people attended the concerts given at the Tokyo Academy of Music, Basil Hall Chamberlain observed "It is to be presumed that most do so out of curiosity, and some bring infants who accompany the performance with their squalls."[40] The members of Japan's elite who attended these and other concerts did not necessarily like what they heard. But they recognized it as an integral part of the civilization they were striving to appropriate. Intellectuals who venerated Western culture did their best to appreciate the music that formed part of it. Many of them read about Beethoven and Wagner and admired them long before their music could be heard in anything like its original form in Japan. Even to the less educated people, the music they heard performed at school concerts or by military bands came to be associated with modern times. Nevertheless, until well into the twentieth century the majority of the Japanese people turned to the country's own music for pleasure and enjoyed the genres that had flourished since before the Meiji Restoration.[41] For many well-to-do families, the *koto* (13-stringed plucked zither) was still the instrument of choice for their daughters. Indeed, in the early years of the Music Investigation Committee, the *koto* was regarded as a useful substitute for the prohibitively expensive piano, and in 1888 the Tokyo Academy published a collection of *koto* music in Western notation. It included, for the first time the song *Sakura, Sakura*, the melody of which is cited in Puccini's opera *Madame Butterfly* and which even found its way into school song books in the West. The *koto* was the only Japanese instrument taught at the Academy and played at its concerts. Public concerts, an innovation of the Meiji period, often featured both traditional and Western music, and the standard of performance was often much higher in traditional music. Concerts, especially outside Tokyo, often included a variety of Japanese musical genres, played on different instruments, Japanese and Western. In fact popular tastes in general tended to be eclectic.[42] But while traditional music also came to be written down in Western notation and performed with Western instruments, the reverse seldom happened.

Soon new kinds of music emerged which combined characteristics of Western and Japanese music. Songs, in particular, could be sung and enjoyed by almost everyone, and many new ones were based entirely or partly on Western musical idiom. The Meiji wars against China in 1894–95 and Russia in 1904–05 created a surge in patriotic feelings, which found their expression in military songs with rousing rhythms. As more and more Japanese people passed through the modern schools and learnt Western-style songs, musical tastes evolved and new popular songs appealed to changing musical sensibilities. In 1914, the actress Matsui Sumako, who had gained fame in Ibsen's *Doll's House,* had a hit with "Kachusha's Song," composed for the performance of Tolstoy's *Resurrection*; it sold 10,000 gramophone records in 1915 alone.[43]

As the railways expanded to reach most parts of the country, they drew the nation together, making travel faster and easier and bringing the latest fashions from Tokyo and Yokohama to distant parts of the country in a matter of days. Symbolizing modern times, the railway was celebrated in the popular "railway songs" describing landmarks along the main lines. To promote the song for the Tōkaidō line from Tokyo to Kobe, published in 1900, the Osaka music dealer Miki Sakichi even hired a large band and an entire railway carriage and sent the musicians to perform around the country.[44] Travelling entertainers, including musicians playing for concerts, circuses and film shows, could make themselves heard all over the country. A few of them even ventured abroad, not to study, but to perform, most famously Miura Tamaki, of *Madame Butterfly* fame. A graduate of the Tokyo Academy of Music, she sang in operas at the newly opened Imperial Theatre; during the First World War she performed in the title role of Puccini's opera in London, Boston and Chicago.

The First World War also provided opportunities for two Japanese pioneers in the manufacture of musical instruments: Suzuki Masakichi and Yamaha Torakusu. Both regarded 1887 as the beginning of their business; by the early 1890s Suzuki was selling violins and Yamaha was selling reed organs throughout Japan, exploiting the new market created by music education in schools. In 1900 Yamaha's company, Nihon Gakki, made the first piano with a Japanese soundboard. Just before the First World War the company began to produce harmonicas, until then the almost exclusive domain of German manufacturers such as Hohner. When Germany went to war in 1914, Yamaha and Suzuki took over German markets in Europe and America.

In Asia, meanwhile, Japan had begun to assert itself as a colonial power, acquiring Taiwan in 1895 at the end of the Sino–Japanese war and annexing Korea in 1910. After 1895, Chinese students flocked to Japan to learn from the victor; many trained as teachers and the expertise they brought back to China with them included Western music.[45] Following the annexation of Korea in 1910, the colonial government introduced singing into the school curriculum and Korean schoolchildren learnt songs from Japanese schoolteachers. In 1925 a music department was established at the Ewha (or Iwha) College for Women (now Ewha Womans University) in Seoul. Japanese merchants sold instruments. The violin, portable and relatively cheap, fascinated the Koreans no less than the Japanese. Wandering peddlers played simple tunes on it to attract potential customers; the Korean-born Japanese luthier Chin Shōgen (1929–2012) remembers hearing and seeing a violin for the first time in the hands of a wandering medicine vendor visiting his home village.[46] The introduction of Western music in Taiwan and Korea (as in Japan) owes much to Western missionaries, but also to the Japanese colonizers.[47] When these countries regained their independence after the Second World War they continued to assimilate Western art music, for much the same reasons as the Japanese, and today Koreans and Chinese from Taiwan or mainland China vie with the Japanese on the international music scene.

In short, by the early twentieth century, Japan had begun to assert itself beyond its national borders as a musical power.

## 1. Early Evidence of the Violin in Japan

In the city of Ōita on the island of Kyushu, by the Prefectural Government Office, stands a group of bronze statues entitled "Statue in

Memory of the First Appearance of Western Music," on the site where on Christmas Eve in 1557 Christian missionaries gave a performance. The group consists of a priest playing a fiddle of uncertain description, while three Japanese boys are singing. In this way a relative of the violin symbolizes the introduction of Western music in Japan. We cannot know for sure whether the performers in 1557 actually played bowed instruments on the occasion.[48] Nor can we know who the first Japanese to play a modern violin was. There are unsubstantiated reports of Nagasaki geisha playing the violin in the Tokugawa period,[49] during which time members of the Dutch trade station on Deshima may have played the instrument.

2: "Statue in Memory of the First Appearance of Western Music," Ōita.

We are on firmer ground in 1853, when Commodore Perry forced Japan to take up negotiations and to open its doors to trade with the West. Among the things he brought with him to impress the Japanese were musicians, first and foremost a military band. He returned to Japan in 1854, and on 27 March gave a banquet followed by an "Ethiopian Concert" on the steamship Powhatan. Members of Perry's crew, made up with blacked faces, danced, sang and played instruments including two violins. Such shows by "Negro Minstrels" were popular in Britain and the United States in the nineteenth century, and the groups commonly included a violinist or two. The printed programme on the Powhatan records an unspecified violin solo – probably folk rather than classical music – by Charles McLewee, who also acted as the show's musical director. Until further records emerge we can regard him as the first named foreign performer on the violin in Japan. Apparently the Japanese officials enjoyed the show, which was repeated in Hakodate, Shimoda and Naha on the Ryūkyū Islands.[50]

The opening of the country in the 1850s brought more Westerners to Japan, and they brought their music with them. Almost certainly they included fiddlers; the violin was one of the most important instruments in both Western classical and folk music. An example is the Dutch naval officer Willem J.C. Ridder Huyssen van Kattendijke, who came to Japan in 1857. He not only taught drum lessons, which were very popular, but also played the violin for Shimazu Nariakira, the lord of Satsuma, at a party.[51] Presumably quite a few foreigners played the violin, but evidence is patchy. Japan, however, had barely emerged from its isolation, when the first travelling professionals appeared on its shores. They played mainly for the foreign community, and were often joined by local amateurs. Musical activities by amateurs began wherever a significant number of foreigners settled in foreign port towns, mainly Yokohama and Hyōgo (Kobe) and to a lesser extent Niigata, Hakodate and Nagasaki, the ports open to them by the treaties forced upon Japan. From the 1860s, Yokohama began to develop a lively amateur scene, which from 1870 centred on the Gaiety Theatre, and, from 1885, the new Public Hall.

The first violin virtuoso to visit Japan was the Italian-born Agostino Robbio (known as "Signor Robbio") in 1863. He appears to have been a successful violinist in his time who called himself a pupil of Paganini's and gave concerts in London, New York and Shanghai.[52] Robbio played at four concerts, together with local amateurs, and his programme included works by Paganini. Another early visiting violinist was the American Jenny Claus, who performed in Tokyo and Yokohama in 1875. According to the *Japan Weekly Mail*, she played Beethoven's "Kreutzer" Sonata, Vieuxtemps' *Faust* Fantasy, Brahms' Hungarian Dances arranged by Joseph Joachim (1831–1907) and various encores.[53] Not much seems to be known about her, but she previously toured Australia, where a condescending critic for the *Brisbane Courier* observed that her playing represented the French school, and that she was "certainly not a great violinist," but that her "pleasing" performance of the musically less demanding solo pieces was suitable to "satisfy a mixed audience, such as she will meet in a travelling career."[54] The third foreign violinist to visit Japan was J.C.H. Iburg from the Netherlands in 1880, who performed works by Schumann, Bellini, Spohr, Haydn, de Bériot, Beethoven and others and stayed in Yokohama for two months, during which he taught violin, piano and singing.[55]

A few stayed considerably longer. In 1872 Christian Wagner (1819?– 91) arrived from Hong Kong as mentioned earlier and established himself as a music teacher and performer. He expected to make a living from music, but amateurs are reported to have taught music too. These include Gottfried Wagener (1831–92), who came to Japan in 1868 and from 1870 taught science and technical subjects at various government schools; he is best known for his contribution to the development of Japanese industrial crafts. He was also a great music lover and an amateur violinist, and apparently taught music in Tokyo for a time.[56]

How much impact did performances by foreign artists for the expatriate community have on the Japanese? Not much perhaps, but they must have brought home to the Japanese the importance of music for the foreigners. A few Japanese took private lessons. The family of the composer Taki Rentarō (1879–1903) whose father was a minor government official, lived in Yokohama from 1882 to 1886, and during this time Rentarō's sisters received violin and accordion as well as *koto* lessons.[57] They may have been taught by Christian Wagner. Taki himself reportedly astounded his classmates in Takeda with his ability on the violin in the early 1890s.[58]

Once the Music Investigation Committee's training institute (renamed the Tokyo Academy of Music in 1887) opened, it began to hold regular concerts attended by members of the Japanese elite as well as foreigners. The Frenchman Paul Maurel, on the other hand, performed in Tokyo as well as in Yokohama; the programme of his concert at the Music Investigation Committee on 8 June 1885 included Vieuxtemps' *Fantasy and Caprice*, Beethoven's Romance in F, *Fantasie concert sur "Faust"* (Op 47) and another fantasy on Verdi's *Il Trovatore* (?) by Jean Delphin Alard (1815–88), de Bériot's Grand Concert, and Haydn's *Souvenir de Don* (arranged by Hubert Léonard). The programme also included two Japanese pieces for *sankyoku* ensemble, performed by members of the Institute.[59]

The greatest violinist among the early visiting performers was Ede Reményi (1828–98), who arrived in Japan in summer 1886 and is the first foreign virtuoso known to have officially performed for the emperor. Reményi, one of the most colourful among the travelling violinists of the nineteenth century, was born to Jewish parents in Miskolc, Hungary, as Eduard Hoffmann. He later changed his name and cultivated the image of a Hungarian gypsy violinist, but far from learning to play the violin in the Puszta, he attended the conservatoire at Vienna and studied with Joseph Böhm (1795–1876), making his debut in Budapest in 1846. In the revolution of 1848–49, he made a name for himself in the Hungarian uprising, becoming a kind of "musical aide-de-camp" to General Arthur Görgey, rousing revolutionary fervour by playing the Czardas or the Racokzy March. When the revolution failed, he had to flee and travelled to America, where he gave his first performance in New York in 1850. Returning to Europe he performed in Hamburg and met Johannes Brahms, who became his accompanist, and introduced Reményi to Joseph Joachim. But after meeting Franz Liszt in Weimar, Reményi and Brahms parted ways. Reményi later accused Brahms of plagiarizing folk songs heard from Reményi as well as Reményi's own melodies for his Hungarian Dances. From 1854 to 1860 Reményi toured Europe. Queen Victoria appointed him court violinist. An amnesty allowed him to return to Hungary in 1860, but he soon resumed travelling and performed in Europe, Egypt, America, Australia, New Zealand, India and East Asia. He collapsed and died during a concert in San Francisco in 1898.[60]

In Japan, Reményi performed in Kobe and Yokohama with the pianist Isidore Luckstone (1861–1941) and a singer. On 10 August 1886 he played at the Rokumeikan in Tokyo, to a full house of over 300 people, most of them foreigners.[61] Remenyi's performance in Kobe occasioned the first reference to the violin in a Japanese-language newspaper in the Kansai area, although his instrument was not mentioned.[62] His performance for Emperor Meiji took place on 10 August 1886, and he was accompanied on the piano by Guillaume Sauvlet, a versatile musician who had made his home in Japan a year earlier.

Another early visiting violinist was the young Constantine Domcheff (1879–1948) in 1894 (he returned in 1899). The Belgian Ovide Musin (1854–1930) performed at the Public Hall in Yokohama on 15 and 16 January 1896. Musin had studied in Liège and Paris with Hubert

Léonard. He repeatedly toured Europe and, from 1884, America; from Japan he continued to Shangai and Southeast Asia. After Reményi he was the first major violinist to tour Japan in ten years; like Reményi he performed at the imperial palace.[63] A few more touring violinists played in Japan before the First World War. Max Schlüter (1878–1945) a Dane who had studied with Joachim, performed at the Public Hall in Yokohama in September 1901 and apparently stayed long enough to give lessons to the amateur violinist H. Poole in Yokohama. He settled in his native Copenhagen in 1909, where his pupils included Jacob Gade, the composer of the famous *Tango Jalousie*. Another violinist who performed in 1901 was J. Marquardt.[64] Anna Schäfer, a native of Frankfurt, played at the Public Hall in March 1907 with local musicians; she performed Tartini's Sonata in G minor, Wieniawski's Scherzo Tarantelle and Bruch's Concerto in G minor, and the *Japan Weekly Mail* praised her highly.[65] In 1909 the Polish-born Leopold Premislaw, who had studied with Joseph Joachim in Berlin, came for the first time; he returned in 1924. Mishel Piastro (1891–1970), a pupil of Leopold Auer in St. Petersburg, came in 1912 and again in 1918. Dora von Möllendorff (1886–1971), a German violinist, performed at the Gaiety Theatre in December 1913.[66] Premislaw and Piastro were among the first of several East European violinists to visit Japan between the world wars.

If the foreign musicians mainly played for and taught foreign residents, it was Christian missionaries who taught music to young Japanese at their schools. Much has been written about the hymns they taught Japanese school children, and the organs they introduced, but some taught the violin. An early example comes from the Russian Orthodox Church. The Russian Orthodox missionaries attached great importance to church singing. In 1873, Iakov Tichai arrived in Hakodate to teach singing for the missions; he soon moved to Tokyo. Not much is known about him, but he appears to have studied music professionally, and he used the violin to teach. In Tokyo, besides training in four-part singing, seminary students at the Russian Orthodox Cathedral could study the piano or the violin on request.[67]

Some public schools made efforts to introduce music education of sorts soon after the promulgation of the Education Law in 1872. The Tokyo Normal School for Women included music training in its programme as early as 1874. In 1877 training for kindergarten teachers was added to the programme.[68] The first teacher to teach music playing the violin at a public school outside Tokyo may well have been Nose Sakae in Nagano. A graduate of the American Pacific University, he was appointed head of Nagano Prefectural Normal College in July 1892.[69] He had brought a violin with him, the first to be heard in Nagano Prefecture, and began to train teachers. Because violins were not generally available – Nose's own violin reportedly cost 70 or 80 yen, a staggering sum at the time – aspiring music teachers attempted to adapt *shamisen*, "and here and there you could hear sounds like that of a cat being strangled," according to one contemporary.[70] In January 1886, Nose organized a music teacher training course to train teachers sent by the district governors. That year the district of Chiisagata became the first in Japan to ask Isawa Shūji to send an expert from the Music Investigation Committee to train music teachers locally.[71]

A few musicians at the imperial court studied the violin before they enrolled at the Music Investigation Committee's training institute. Their teacher was Franz Eckert. After Mason's arrival members of the Imperial *gagaku* department asked to be taught by Mason, who was impressed that representatives of traditional music were so willing to study Western music. He had two of them learn the violin, and the other two the viola and the cello. The violin students, Ōno Hisayori and Shiba Sukenatsu, taught the violin after Mason's departure.[72]

Overall, evidence of Japanese learning the violin before the opening of the Music Investigation Committee's Music Institute and the dispatch of trained teachers to the regions is scanty. Only a few Japanese would have had a chance to hear and play a violin, mainly those who had the opportunity to mix with foreigners or attended mission schools. Once the Music Investigation Committee systematically began to train students with the help of foreign teachers the violin became more widely heard.

## 2. Foreign Teachers

With the establishment of the Music Investigation Committee the violin's progress becomes easier to trace. Although it would be wrong to ignore local developments independent of government efforts, it was through the Music Investigation Committee, elevated to become the Tokyo Academy of Music in 1887, that music education was introduced in schools throughout the country. The violin played a central role in this process. Luther Mason, the first foreign teacher appointed to the Institute, used the violin to teach singing in schools; it enabled him to turn any classroom into a music room as well as to move around the room while teaching. Mason had learnt the violin as part of his general music training, but was not a performer on the instrument and could only devote limited time to teaching it. Almost from the start those Japanese students who had previously begun to study the violin became his assistant teachers. Mason's farewell concert, at which he himself conducted, consisted mainly of singing and a few piano solos and only a single instrumental ensemble item at the end, when the assistant teachers and some of the students played three songs.[73]

Among Mason's violin pupils were Kōda Nobu and Takamine (née Nakamura) Sen, the daughter of a wealthy banker. Nakamura was among the 22 students who were recruited in 1880 and studied the violin, *koto* and piano. As early as 1881 she was promoted to teach English and *koto*. She became Mason's interpreter and he gave her his piano when he left Japan.[74] Sen left without graduating when she married Takamine Hideo (1854–1910), the principal of Tokyo Normal School. The American zoologist Edward Morse recorded a visit to the Takamine home in June 1882, where Sen performed on the *koto* and the violin. She impressed him, "for she played with great strength and accuracy 'Auld Lang Syne', 'Home Sweet Home,' and 'Glorious Apollo,' after having received instruction on the violin for only forty-seven days."[75] Kōda Nobu, who received lessons from Mason as a ten-year old, subsequently became the first violinist to be trained to professional level and taught at the Tokyo Academy of Music for many years (see following chapter).

Franz Eckert, Mason's temporary replacement at the Music Investigation Committee, taught there from February 1883 to March 1886.[76] His contract stipulated that he was to teach the subjects of instrumental music and harmony for two hours each on two afternoons a week. It was the "Rokumeikan era," when the political leaders held grand balls and concerts at the newly-built hall in the hope of softening foreign diplomats for the purpose of revising the unequal treaties. The events called for music, and Eckert was a sought-after man. A Japanese scholar has reconstructed Eckert's (hypothetical) schedule for the first week in November 1885, when the yearly grand ball in the emperor's honour demanded his service conducting the navy band. Every morning,

Monday to Saturday, from 8:00 a.m. to 2:00 p.m. he would instruct the navy band. On Monday afternoons, from 4:30 to 7:30 he instructed members of the *gagaku* ensemble. On Tuesday and Thursday afternoons he would teach at the Music Investigation Committee from 4:30 to 6:30. On Tuesday, 3 November, he would then have had to rush to the Rokumeikan in time for the evening's festivities. On Wednesdays and Saturdays he had the afternoon off, but no doubt he spent much of them arranging and composing music or giving private lessons.[77]

Given his busy schedule, Eckert too could only devote a limited time to teaching musical instruments to students at the Institute, which makes his achievements all the more remarkable. Unlike Mason, Eckert worked to develop instrumental music. At the first end-of-term concert Eckert conducted the ensemble he had inherited in an arrangement of a piece from Richard Wagner's *Tannhäuser*. Other excerpts from operas and dance music followed. The first graduation concert on 20 July 1885 included two pieces played by four court musicians on the violin, viola, cello and flute and directed by Eckert, an arrangement from Gounod's *Faust* and an unspecified Haydn string quartet. This may have been the first performance of a string quartet, but we cannot be sure whether they actually played it as a string quartet. Only one violinist, Ōno Hisayori, is named, so whether the other violin part was played by Oku Yoshihisa on the flute or whether the description of Eckert as "leader" in *katakana* phonetic script indicates that he played with the group on the violin is anybody's guess. Another mixed ensemble played Beethoven.[78] As was typical for the concerts in those days, this one also included choral singing, piano solos and Japanese music for *koto*, *shamisen* and *kokyū*.

Even before his appointment at the Institute, Eckert had taught some of the court musicians the violin.[79] The first time the court musicians played Western music for the emperor (on 9 July 1881) their ensemble included four violinists, four violists, one cellist and two bassists. But we do not know for certain whether Eckert actually played the violin himself. He is said to have studied the oboe at music college. In view of his career it seems likely that he studied a wind instrument at professional level, but he may still have learnt to play the violin, perhaps as a boy, before changing to a wind instrument. All we can say for certain is that he did not stand out as a performer on the violin. According to one of his students he did not demonstrate in lessons either.[80] Nevertheless, judging from his achievements, he must have been a competent teacher.

But however good, two afternoons a week at the Institute of tuition by Eckert were just not enough to fulfil the ambitions Isawa had for it. When Eckert's contract expired, Isawa asked for an Italian instrumentalist to be hired full-time. Nothing came of this, however, and another part-time teacher was hired, Guillaume Sauvlet.[81] Unlike the other early foreign teachers, Sauvlet performed music for a living – one of the many travelling musicians who took advantage of the new overseas markets created by increasing ease of travel and Western expansion and colonization. Expatriates tended to hold on to the culture they came from, perhaps even more so than they would have done had they stayed at home. And many of them were wealthy and willing to pay to hear visiting artists. While the most famous and successful virtuosos like Reményi played to large audiences and soon moved on, others stayed in one place for months or even years, teaching, conducting amateur choirs and ensembles, and becoming part of the local music scene.

Sauvlet, the son of a travelling musician, had been educated at the Dutch high school in Java. In 1884 or earlier he had settled in Hong Kong, where on 11 November he introduced himself in a concert, playing mainly the piano, but also the violin. With Hong Kong as his family base, Sauvlet travelled to Shanghai to perform. In June 1885 he joined the English Mascotte company, who had arrived in Hong Kong from Singapore, and accompanied them to Shanghai, Kobe and Yokohama. When they left Japan, Sauvlet stayed on and gave performances of his own. Later that year, he returned to Japan with the Melville Opera Company, with whom he also performed in Shanghai. In November 1885 he settled in Yokohama with his wife and son, where he taught music and gave concerts together with local amateurs and as a conductor of the choral society. Reviews in the English language press show that he soon made a name for himself, particularly as a conductor and pianist. It was a good time for a musician to arrive in Japan. The "Rokumeikan era" was in full swing, and the Japanese elite cultivated Western music to demonstrate their high level of civilization and invited foreigners from Yokohama to perform for them. Already Tokyo was taking its first steps towards becoming part of the world market for classical music.

A versatile musician, Sauvlet conducted, performed on the piano both as a soloist and an accompanist, played the violin and composed. Although he also performed on the violin, he appears to have regarded the piano as his main instrument, and in his debut concert as a soloist in Yokohama on 22 September 1885 he played only piano works, while a "popular" (unnamed) local amateur played a violin solo. Once Sauvlet had established himself as a teacher, he had his pupils perform as well. Sauvlet reportedly taught Japanese private pupils as well as foreign ones. Even more significantly, he formed a link in musical life between Yokohama and Tokyo, just as the demand for classical music in Tokyo rose. Under his leadership amateur instrumentalists and singers took part in concerts held at the Rokumeikan.

Sauvlet's many talents ought to have made him an ideal candidate for the Music Investigation Committee. So why was his appointment in 1886 only part-time, when the Institute so urgently needed a full time teacher? Perhaps he valued his freedom and was not interested. More likely, Isawa and his like-minded fellow members of the Japan Music Society had set their sights higher. They wanted Japan to train musicians at the highest level at an institution that could rival the best conservatoires in Europe, and they may well have looked down on a mere travelling musician. In October 1887 the Music Investigation Committee was upgraded and became the Tokyo Academy of Music. Earlier that year Sauvlet received a new contract; his hours were increased to three times five hours a week. He was to teach singing, piano, organ, strings, wind instruments, harmony and composition.[82] The contract ran for one year only and was not immediately renewed when it expired. Sauvlet did eventually receive another contract to teach until January 1889, but it is not clear whether he continued to teach after the arrival of his successor Rudolph Dittrich in November 1888. Nevertheless, despite being employed as a stopgap measure, Sauvlet too did much to further instrumental music in Japan. During his term, at the graduation concert on 19 February 1887, an ensemble of graduates gave what is generally believed to be the first performance of a Beethoven symphony in Japan, although this probably consisted of only one or two movements arranged for a small group, presumably by Sauvlet himself.[83] Sauvlet also conducted the ensemble in his own compositions and played the piano in several concerts. In a concert at the Institute on 9 July 1888 he played a violin solo, and a reporter for the journal *Kyōiku jiron* (Current Views on Education) praised him for his outstanding technique and musicality, concluding that with a teacher like that, music in Japan could soon be expected to thrive.[84]

Sauvlet gave a final concert in Yokohama on 30 May 1889. In September the *Japan Gazette* announced that he was auctioning his effects before moving on to Hawaii and San Francisco. Whether because of difficulties making a living, or because of being deemed second class compared to Dittrich, Sauvlet had decided to try his fortune in another part of the world. He obviously lost no time in resuming his career, for on 16 November 1889 he gave a concert in Honolulu together with local musicians. A year later he was in San Francisco. The *Japan Daily Herald Mail Summary* reported that Sauvlet had composed an opera. According to the San *Francisco Chronicle* it had a Hawaiian theme and was dedicated to King David Kalakaua of Hawai'i (1836–91), to whom Sauvlet had already dedicated his *Kalakaua March*.[85] No performance of the opera is recorded, perhaps because the king died in 1891; however, a note of a forthcoming concert by Sauvlet and local artists in the *San Francisco Chronicle* in February 1894 announced that "Several numbers from Mr. Sauvlet's Hawaiian opera will be given, (...)."[86] A year later Sauvlet was involved in a court case when he sued H.W. Schmidt, who had asked him to set to music his lyrics for a Hawaiian national anthem and then refused payment for the composition.[87] An entry in a San Francisco directory of 1896 lists Sauvlet as a music teacher, living at the same address as William Sauvlet Jr.[88] He was still in San Francisco in 1898 when Reményi died there during a concert. The two musicians had known each other since their performance for the Meiji emperor in 1886, and the report of Reményi's death names Sauvlet, "a well-known pianist," as one of the musicians with whom Reményi had planned to perform.[89] Sauvlet may himself have died that year or moved away; his whereabouts after 1898 are unknown.

Meanwhile the newly upgraded Tokyo Academy of Music had finally hired the kind of high-class musician Isawa envisaged, after a lengthy search through Japan's diplomatic representatives in Italy, Germany and Austria. One of the difficulties was that Isawa wanted a candidate who could teach in English. Eventually, the choice fell on Rudolf Dittrich (1861–1919), recommended to the ambassador in Vienna (Toda Uchitaka) by Joseph Hellmesberger senior (1828–93), the director of the Vienna Conservatoire. Japanese authors make much of the fact that

Dittrich was an artist rather than a mere pedagogue like Mason, and of how the choice reflected Isawa's high ambitions for Western music in Japan.[90] Dittrich's credentials were indeed impressive. Born in Biala in what was then the Austrian section of Poland, he received his early training from his father Anton Julius Dittrich (1825–1914), a music teacher. According to the curriculum vitae he submitted to the Tokyo Academy of Music, he studied piano from the age of five, violin from age seven, organ from age nine, and music theory from the age of ten. At the age of 15 he moved to Breslau, where he graduated from high school. In 1878 he enrolled at the Vienna Conservatoire (Konservatorium der Gesellschaft der Musikfreunde), where he studied violin with Josef Hellmesberger junior (1855–1907), organ, harmony, counterpoint and composition with Anton Bruckner (1824–96) and Franz Krenn (1816–97), and piano with Wilhelm Schenner (1839–1913). He excelled as a student, receiving top grades in all his subjects and even winning several prizes; in 1880 he came second in a violin competition with a performance of Spohr's Concerto in D minor, and in 1882 he won first prizes on the organ and the violin playing a fugue by Bach (G minor) and the Chaconne from Bach's unaccompanied Violin Sonata in D minor. Dittrich also participated in an orchestra and played chamber music with his fellow students. He enjoyed particularly close relationships with Bruckner and members of the Hellmesberger family; his violin teacher's younger brother Ferdinand (1863–1940), a cellist, was a fellow student. In 1882 he graduated, receiving a silver medal from the Gesellschaft für Musikfreunde with his violin diploma.

After graduation, Dittrich continued to perform on the organ and the violin. He played the organ for Baron Nathaniel Mayer Anselm Frh. von Rothschild (1836–1905) and for services in a synagogue, possibly the large one in Schmalzhofgasse (destroyed by the Nazis in 1938), as well as in various churches and at choral concerts conducted by Hans Richter (1843–1916). He played the violin (or sometimes the viola) with the Hellmesberger Quartet when they performed works for larger ensembles. His invitation to Japan resulted from his relationship with the Hellmesbergers; Hellmesberger senior, who had recommended him to the Japanese ambassador, advised him to take the job. His other mentor, Bruckner, was not impressed. When Dittrich came to say goodbye, he could hardly contain his agitation: "What, where are you going? To Japan

– to Japan? Farewell!" [91] Bruckner may well have wondered why on earth Dittrich was leaving a promising career behind. Competition in Vienna, however, was stiff and the immediate future promised no vacant position. The Japanese government offered a generous salary, and thanks to Dittrich's insistence and possibly Hellmesberger's backing, he received the title "artistic director," a title which, however, did not imply corresponding powers of decision.

Dittrich arrived in Yokohama on 4 November 1888, together with his wife Perine (née Lammer), whom he had married in 1886. His contract ran from 1 November 1888 to 1 September 1891 and stipulated that he would teach up to five hours per day in violin, harmony, composition and singing. Many of his students became pioneers of Western music. Kōda Nobu, one of the first to study the violin with Dittrich, described him as an excellent, if strict, teacher. Other students commented on his strictness too.[92] One student even gathered a group of fellow students and planned a strike. Dittrich, he felt, was too harsh and treated them with contempt because of their inability to meet his unrealistically high standards. No doubt Dittrich was often impatient with his pupils, most of whom had little knowledge of Western music before enrolling at the Academy. His particular brand of sarcasm, delivered in a foreign language, could give rise to misunderstandings; one student, on being pulled by his ears and told to wash them, took this literally, much to the amusement of his fellow students. He often reduced female students to tears. Nevertheless, by the standards of his day, whether European or Japanese, he does not appear to have been excessively strict, and many also remembered him for his kindness. One can imagine his strictness being tempered with Viennese charm.

Dittrich also set new standards by his performances, playing some of the most virtuoso pieces of the violin repertoire, such as concertos by Vieuxtemps and Spohr. Particular favourites were Spohr's Concerto No. 9 and Beethoven's Romance in G.[93] His first public performance took place in March 1889, when he played a violin solo. In a concert in May he accompanied his wife, who sang, on the violin. A year later, on 12 May 1890 the Academy's own concert hall the Sōgakudō, was dedicated. It was Japan's first purpose-built concert auditorium, providing a venue for the Academy's regular public concerts. During his six years in Japan – his contract was extended by another three years in 1891 – he performed in over 50 concerts; as a soloist, in ensembles with students, colleagues, and foreign amateurs, as a conductor of the Academy's choir, and with touring virtuosos, such as the flautist Adolf Terschlak (1832–1901), who had studied in Vienna, in 1890; Dittrich joined him and his pianist Luisa Schuller for several concerts, including one at the Rokumeikan on 11 March.[94] Besides playing two violin solos, Dittrich may well have helped Terschlak acquire scores for the two Japanese songs (*Sakura* and *Hanakurabe*) he performed. Terschlak also visited Dittrich at the Tokyo Academy of Music and observed his classes. In an article in the *Japan Weekly Mail*, which appeared in Japanese in *Ongaku zasshi*, Terschlak pronounced himself impressed with the level of musical achievement in Japan and praised Dittrich's work highly.[95]

Like Eckert and Sauvlet, Dittrich composed and arranged music, partly in response to his employers' expectations. His arrangements include one of Strauss's Pizzicato Polka for *koto* ensemble; he did not have enough competent violinists to perform the piece in its original version. He also arranged several Japanese pieces for piano or violin and piano, and composed works based on Japanese melodies. On 15 November 1891 he himself performed *Rakubai* (Falling Plum Blossoms), arranged for *koto, violin* and piano. Several of his scores were published by Breitkopf & Härtel in Leipzig, and Puccini may well have used them when he composed *Madame Butterfly*.[96] Dittrich also composed anthems for official occasions like the proclamation of the Meiji Constitution on 11 February 1889. In a lecture about Japanese music given in 1895 and published in 1897, he explained and justified his efforts to harmonize Japanese tunes and adapt them to fit Western stylistic conventions.[97] Dittrich's lecture is a typical example of the condescending attitude towards Japanese music shared by most of his Western contemporaries; nevertheless it shows that he at least made an effort to study it.

For his violin lessons at the Tokyo Academy of Music Dittrich compiled his own collection of 69 exercises, some of them based on the tutor by Rode, Kreutzer and Bailliot. It was later revised with his permission by his former students Andō (née Kōda) Kō and Shimazaki Akatarō and published in 1924.[98]

Dittrich left Japan on 1 August 1894, his departure coinciding with the start of the Sino–Japanese War. He received high honours from the Japanese government and was celebrated in an official farewell concert at the Academy on 1 April 1894, where he played several violin solos. He gave his last public performance at the Academy's graduation concert in July, when he conducted the choir. Dittrich helped lay the foundations of Western music not just as something to be taught in schools but as an art to be cultivated and brought to the highest level. Whether (as has been suggested[99]) he is also responsible for the image of classical music as something terribly serious, to be practised with endurance rather than enjoyment, is open to question. Music in Meiji Japan was a serious business long before Dittrich arrived, and in the early years many practitioners and listeners probably did not expect to enjoy it. The well-born women who represented the majority of the early violin students at the Academy had their own reasons to emphasize the seriousness of their pursuit; under no circumstances did they want to be likened to the geisha in the pleasure quarters.

Just before his departure, Dittrich deposited at the consulate of the Austro-Hungarian Empire in Yokohama a pledge to pay a yearly sum for the education of his illegitimate son by a Japanese mistress, Mori Otto, (confusingly named the same as the son of the famous writer Mori Ōgai), which he duly paid until Otto reached maturity. Mori Otto followed in his father's footsteps and became a violinist. He developed a special interest in the training of small children.

Dittrich's own career after his return to Vienna proved that he was indeed an outstanding musician; very few of the foreign musicians who taught in Japan did as well as Dittrich in their home country. He played second violin in two concerts by the Hellmesberger Quartet in December 1894, but his subsequent career as a performer and teacher centred on the organ rather than the violin – unlike his time in Japan. He played the organ for the imperial court, and in 1901 was officially appointed court organist. From 1906 he taught organ at the Conservatoire, where he was appointed professor in 1909. Besides performing, he was also active as chairman of the Austrian Imperial Association of Music Pedagogy, as an organ expert and a conductor of several choirs. He continued to compose shorter works, based on the Japanese melodies he had collected. His *Tekona March*, premiered at a musical garden party, found such great acclaim that the band repeated it.[100] He enjoyed success of another kind when he received permission to dedicate his paraphrase of the *Kaiserlied* to the Austrian emperor in summer 1915. In 1916 he suffered a stroke during a concert and never recovered his health. He died in 1919, survived by his second wife and two sons.

With Dittrich's departure, the Tokyo Academy of Music had to do without an outstanding foreign teacher for several years. The Sino–Japanese War drained government finances. In the rising tide of nationalism, war songs became hugely popular and helped familiarize the general population of Japan with Western musical idioms, but promoting art music at a high level took a back seat. Indeed, the continued existence of the Tokyo Academy of Music was debated in parliament and in the media as early as 1891, and in June 1893, it lost its independence and became a department of the Higher Normal School. From September it was headed by Kanō Jigorō, better known as the founder of the Kōdōkan style of judo. It did not become independent again until April 1899. During this period Dittrich had no foreign successor.

At the same time as Tokyo Academy of Music regained its independence, August Junker (1868–1944) was appointed professor of music; not much seems to be known about the circumstances and accounts of who recommended him vary.[101] Like Sauvlet but unlike Mason, Eckert and Dittrich, Junker was not invited to Japan, but came on his own initiative and made a name for himself in the musical world in Yokohama before attracting the attention of the authorities in Tokyo. Born on 28 January 1868 in Stolberg near Aachen in Germany,[102] Junker received his first violin lessons from his father, an engineer. In 1881 he enrolled at the conservatoire in Cologne, where he studied with Gustav Holländer and Ferdinand Hiller.[103] As a student he played chamber music with Johannes Brahms. In 1887 he graduated with flying colours, and was rewarded with the opportunity to study with Joseph Joachim in Berlin for three years. He gave some performances in Germany and played in the violin section of the Berlin Philharmonic Orchestra for a period, but apparently left before he could become a regular member.[104] At any rate, he decided to try his luck in America. Whether he went to Chicago directly or after a stint in Boston is unclear, but from early 1892 his name appears in the records of the Chicago Symphony Orchestra, where he led the viola section until 1897. He joined at a good time; in the run-up to the World Exhibition in 1893, the orchestra was expanding and Junker helped to find more German players. He also performed on the violin as a soloist and as a member of the Bendix String Quartet (several performances of which are mentioned in the *Chicago Tribune* in 1893) and taught violin at the Columbian College of Music.

Why Junker, who now called himself Yunker and became naturalized in 1897,[105] decided to leave Chicago, we cannot know. His grandson Iwakura Tomokazu believes that his interest in Japan was aroused by Ernest Fenollosa (1853–1908), whom he had met in Boston, where Fenollosa worked as curator of oriental art in the Museum of Fine Arts. Fenollosa, who had been professor at Tokyo University from 1878 to 1886 and lecturer at the newly established Tokyo Academy of Fine Arts from 1889 to 1890, may have told him that Japan could offer exciting opportunities for a well-trained German musician. Accounts of what Junker did between quitting his post in Chicago and arriving in Yokohama vary, but on 18 February 1898 he performed with local amateurs at a meeting of the Yokohama Literary Society. The *Japan Times* described his violin playing as "in many respects the most distinctive feature" of the evening and concluded, "Mr. Junker will undoubtedly be an appreciated acquisition in musical circles."[106] On 10 March he performed solo and chamber music works at the Public Hall in Yokohama, "Kindly assisted by Yokohama Ladies and Gentlemen."[107] Several of these were the same amateurs who had played in the February concert. Junker's fame spread quickly. On 19 March, he performed in a concert in the Academy's concert hall in Tokyo. This time the programme included a sonata with a fellow professional, Raphael von Koeber (1848–1923), at the piano. Koeber, who in addition to his training as a pianist held a doctorate in philosophy, had come to Tokyo as a professor at the Imperial University in 1893, a post he continued to hold until 1914. The Academy had appointed him to teach piano and history of music in 1898. Junker began his performance with de Bériot's Concerto No. 9 and "took the house by storm and roused at this early point the enthusiasm of the audience. The performance stamped him at once as a violinist of rare gifts and mastery of his instrument."[108] The concert also included a *nō-kyōgen* performance and singing by the choir of the Academy of Music. We can be sure that those members of the Academy who decided its future followed Junker's performance closely. If Junker turned out to be a suitable candidate, it would save them the trouble of a search abroad and the expense of bringing someone to Japan.

Meanwhile Junker continued to make himself an indispensable part of musical life in Yokohama, assembling the members of several amateur groups to form a choir and an orchestra. When it performed its "Second Grand Concert" it had sixteen violinists, two violists, three cellists and two bassists, as well as a pianist and wind and percussion players.[109] Junker also formed a string quartet with three amateurs, H. Poole, F Schmid and R. Schmid. Their first performance took place on 21 December 1898; besides solo items the programme included Mendelssohn's Quartet in D major, Haydn's variations from the "Emperor" Quartet, Tchaikovsky's Andante Cantabile (presumably from his Quartet No.1 in D) and Mendelssohn's Canzonetta (presumably from Op. 12 in E flat). The following January saw "The Second Grand Concert by Herr Junker's Choral and Orchestral Society" in Yokohama Public Hall with a selection of short works and movements.[110]

Junker must have passed muster with the representatives of the Tokyo Academy of Music; in 1899 he was appointed professor with effect from 1 April at a salary of 400 yen per month and a teaching load of four hours per day on average. Junker's contract at the Academy was renewed six times. When his appointment ceased on 28 December 1912, he had taught at the Academy for longer than any previous foreign music teacher. Soon after his appointment, on 21 April 1899, Junker performed a sonata by Rubinstein with von Koeber for the visiting empress. Junker, like most of the foreign teachers, taught a wide range of subjects; not only all the stringed instruments, but also voice, harmony and composition. He himself recalled his early years at the Academy: "For I had to teach solo and choral singing, as well as all the string instruments including the double bass. And behold; after only two years we had quite a nice Japanese string orchestra that gradually became worth hearing."[111] Indeed, Junker is remembered chiefly as "father of the Japanese symphony orchestra."[112] Under his baton the orchestra began to play more and more original works, rather than arrangements, and complete works began to take the place of single movements, although, unfortunately, the programmes do not always make clear whether a work was performed in its entirety or not. Among the works he premiered in Japan were several movements from Bizet's *Carmen* Suites (in 1900), the Shepherd's Symphony from Bach's *Christmas Oratorio* (1907) and the overture to Carl Maria von Weber's *Freischütz* (1912). Movements from symphonies included the first movement of Mendelssohn's "Scottish" Symphony (1900) and of Beethoven's "Eroica" Symphony (1909). The first symphony to be performed in its entirety may have been Niels Gade's Symphony in B flat Major; the programme lists all four movements. This was at the last concert he conducted at the Academy, on 1 December 1912, and it was highly praised.[113]

Junker's achievements are all the more remarkable considering that the general level of instrumental mastery was low. Most of his students had not begun to learn musical instruments before they entered the Academy of Music in their late teens or early twenties. One student, Okano Teiichi, reported that he played the violin at first, until he was told to study the cello with Junker. Later, Junker corrected his bow hold; Okano surmised that Junker had learnt how to hold a cello bow correctly from a cellist in the foreign amateur orchestra he conducted in Yokohama.[114] The Academy did not train wind players, but thanks to Eckert, Junker could draw on a supply of trained military musicians to assemble a full orchestra. Even so, some instruments were still missing, and Junker himself played and taught the horn, which he had learnt during his military service. When the navy decided to train string players, they appointed Junker to help build up a string section. Evidently Junker considered his efforts worthwhile: "After seven years I succeeded in founding the first complete orchestra in Japan, the orchestra of the Imperial Music Academy in Ueno. And after seven years of hard work we even played the prelude to *Lohengrin* and the first movement of the *Eroica*. And now the Japanese audience began to take an interest, and German music became the mainstream music in Japan."[115] Even Basil Hall Chamberlain, fastidious in matters musical, was full of praise for Junker, "who, in the brief space of five or six years, has done marvels, evolving a pleasing chorus of some eighty singers out of a chaos of disagreeable nasal voices, producing too a respectable orchestra, of forty executants and two hundred and fifty pupils who possess a considerable amount of theoretical knowledge."[116]

Junker's pioneering role also extended to chamber music. Besides his continued activities in Yokohama, where he played string quartets with three amateurs, Otto Fehling, H. Poole and Davis,[117] he regularly performed with his foreign colleagues at the Academy. He often played sonatas with Koeber at the piano. Soon Junker gained more foreign

3: August Junker (standing on the podium) and the Kōda sisters with the orchestra (left; front desk) and choir of the Tokyo Academy of Music around 1900; the other foreigners are the pianist Raphael von Koeber (right) and Noël Péri, who taught organ, harmony and composition.

colleagues as the Academy began to appoint specialized teachers for piano, voice and violincello. With the appointment of Heinrich Werkmeister (1883–1936) in December 1907, the Academy and Junker gained an outstanding cellist, and in Hermann Heydrich (1855–?, tenure 1902–09), they gained another professional pianist, who was also able to play second violin in a string quartet. On 15 December 1907 Junker, Heydrich and Werkmeister performed Beethoven's String Quartet Op. 18.4 with Kōda Nobu playing the viola, as well as Robert Schumann's Piano Quintet with Koeber at the piano.[118] This may well have been the first professional performance of an entire string quartet.[119] In subsequent quartet performances the second violin part was often taken by Kōda Nobu's younger sister Kō.

Not all were happy with Junker's tenure at the Academy, however. In September 1908 the *Tokyo Asahi shinbun* (Tokyo Asahi Newspaper) published a series of articles attacking the Tokyo Academy of Music.[120] The newspaper described Junker as a person of poor character and an indifferent artist and accused him of gross favouritism, especially towards Kōda Nobu. Two years later, an article in the newspaper *Kokumin shinbun* (the People's Newspaper) was similarly negative.[121] The circumstances of Junker's appointment after his arrival in Japan rather than by invitation from abroad were held against him, as was his position of relative power as a conductor. His skills as a violinist were compared negatively with those of Wilhelm (Guglielmo) Dubravcic (1869–1925), who in 1901 was appointed by the imperial court as director of the *gagaku* orchestra and to teach the violin.[122] Born in Fiume in Italy, Dubravcic had studied at the conservatoire in Vienna between 1881 and 1885; he remained in his appointment until the year of his death. The criticism of Junker as a second-rate musician may well say more about the growing confidence of some Japanese in their country's musical achievement than about Junker himself. As more and more Japanese gained proficiency in or at least knowledge of Western music, often through study abroad, they were able to make comparisons, although we might question their ability to make qualified judgements. On the other hand, Junker, who had received high praise for his performances in America and among the foreign community in Japan, and his Western colleagues may well have found it difficult to develop further as musicians in an environment where the general level was still relatively low and outstanding foreign artists did not yet visit regularly, as they would only a few years later.

Junker left Japan in January 1913 with high honours from the government. With him went his Japanese wife Nobu (née Kamada) and his two daughters Vera and Marion. The family settled in his home town of Stolberg. Junker taught at a private conservatoire in Aachen and conducted the amateur orchestra of the Aachen Orchestral Society. The concertmaster was Georg Talbot, from a local industrialist family, and Junker performed at social events for industrialists of Aachen, Düren and Stolberg. In 1934 the Junker family returned to Tokyo. Junker had joined the Nazi party even before Hitler came to power, but the Nazis treated his Japanese wife as a liability and refused his daughter Vera permission to marry a Japanese, Iwakura Tomokazu's father.[123]

In the 20 years of his absence, Japan had come a long way; it now boasted professional orchestras and private music schools, and artistic standards had reached the level of some of the minor European countries. Junker's grateful students, many by now in leading positions, received him cordially. Besides teaching at the private Musashino Academia Musicae, Junker performed, sometimes accompanied by his daughter Marion on the piano. He also conducted some of the new professional orchestras. In 1936, when Wilhelm Kempff visited Japan, Junker conducted the New Symphony Orchestra in some of his concerts, and Kempff publicly praised Junker for his work in Japan. The Japanese too, continued to hold him in high esteem. In 1943, the Japanese–German Cultural Society and the alumni association of the Tokyo Academy of Music planned a big concert in his honour at the Academy's Sōgakudō concert hall for 23 October; Junker himself and his former student Yamada Kōsaku were to conduct. That morning, however, Junker collapsed and the event had to be cancelled. He died on 5 January 1944.

The Tokyo Academy of Music continued to employ German violinists after Junker's departure. In January 1913 the violinist Gustav Kron (1874–?) succeeded Junker and taught at the Academy until March 1925. A native of Braunschweig, he studied at the conservatoire in Dresden. From 1896 to 1898 he was a soloist and Kapellmeister in Hamburg. According to his curriculum vitae at the Tokyo Academy of Music, he toured Europe as a soloist with the Berlin Philharmonic Orchestra under Nikisch in 1900 and under Strauss in 1904.[124] In the year of his arrival in Tokyo, on 7 December, he became the first to perform a movement from the Beethoven Violin Concerto with a full orchestra.[125] Heinrich Werkmeister, who taught the cello at the Academy, conducted. Apart from teaching the violin, Kron is especially known for having premiered several of Beethoven's symphonic works, including the Fifth Symphony in 1918 and the Ninth in 1924.[126]

By the time of Kron's tenure, however, the Tokyo Academy of Music and the German musicians it employed were losing their overwhelming dominance. Japanese musicians, many of them Academy graduates, had begun to found new institutions, and upheavals on the Eurasian continent sent many more European musicians travelling East.

## 3. Pioneering Sisters: Kōda Nobu and Andō Kō

The achievements of the foreign teachers were remarkable; yet they were only possible because they had dedicated and talented students, among them many women. This need not surprise us. Music may have been on the government's agenda for a strong nation that could compete with the Western powers, but singing or playing an instrument did not count as a suitable occupation for a man, especially a man of samurai stock. "Nanda, otoko no kuse ni," – "What! But you're a man!" a young man might well be told if he showed too much interest in making music.[127] Even for a woman of good family, music was never a profession. Still, women taught and studied at the Music Investigation Committee from the start. The first two Japanese sent abroad by the government to study the violin professionally were women: the sisters Kōda Nobu (1870–1946) and Andō Kō (née Kōda, 1878–1963).[128] They came from a family of former samurai and retainers of the shogun; today they are less well-known in Japan than their brother, the writer Rohan (1867–1947). Yet not only did they teach many of Japan's first violinists; their influence even extended beyond Japan, if indirectly. It was Kōda Nobu who "discovered" a young violinist named Shin'ichi Suzuki (of "Suzuki Method" fame) on a cruise to Japan's northern isles, and her sister Andō Kō who gave him his first formal violin lessons.

Like other former samurai, especially those who were on the losing side (that of the shogun), during the early Meiji years, the Kōda family had to build up a new existence after the collapse of the old regime; and like many of them they made sure their children received a good education by sending them to the new public schools. But the Kōda parents were unusual in that they sent their daughters to school as well as their sons, at a time when many regarded schooling for girls as unnecessary. Nobu attended the elementary school affiliated with the Tokyo Normal School for Women. She was in one of the classes taught by Mason during his short tenure at the Music Investigation Committee. Mason played his violin while he taught singing, and this may well have been the first time Nobu and her classmates saw and heard the instrument. The unfamiliar Western tunes were difficult for the Japanese children; even the Japanese lyrics, far removed from their everyday language, did not make learning the new songs easier. Nobu, however, learnt quickly. She later recalled that the early training in traditional Japanese music with her mother gave her an advantage, but her subsequent career suggests that she was also exceptionally talented. At any rate, Mason soon noticed her and started to give her private lessons.

Just before he left, in 1882, he recommended that she study music full-time.

Nobu duly enrolled at the Music Investigation Committee. Her teachers included two members of the imperial court's *gagaku* orchestra, Ōno Hisayori (violin) and Ue Sanemichi (voice). They had initially enrolled as students, but their slight advantage over the other students meant that they were quickly promoted to teach. The faculty already included women: Nakamura Sen, who had acted as an interpreter for Mason, and the Vassar-educated Uryū Shige (or Uriu; née Nagai, 1861–1928). In 1884, Kōda Nobu achieved 80 per cent in an exam where she performed Kreutzer's Étude No. 42. She had reached a high standard at a time when hardly any student started learning the violin as a child before entering the institute.

After graduating in 1885 – together with only two other students – Nobu began to teach while she continued her studies at the graduate department. At the graduation concert, which included traditional Japanese music, she performed on the violin with piano, on the *koto* in an ensemble, and on the piano.[129] By then she must have learnt all that the available teachers, whether Japanese or foreign, could teach her. She had to wait until the appointment of Rudolf Dittrich in 1888 for a teacher who could develop her talent. He recommended sending her abroad, and in 1889 Nobu became the first of many Japanese music students in America and Europe. In April 1889 she went to Boston to study at the New England School of Music.

Nobu later recalled that she had been told to make the piano her main instrument.[130] In fact the order from the Ministry of Education stipulated that Nobu's main instrument was to be the violin and that she would spend one year in Boston and two years in Germany.[131] Mason in a letter to his grandsons, states that she came to Boston "with a notion of studying only the violin," but that he advised her to continue with the piano,

"and this for two reasons. (1) She could not stand it to practice 5 hours a day on the violin, it would ruin her health as they always require the students on the violin to stand, while they practice. But if she practice[d] the violin three hours a day and the piano two, the piano would be a rest for her and you know she did this while she was in Buckfield. Then, when you study the piano & organ, you are obliged to know all the notes in the Bass and Treble Clefs, and all that are used in singing, both for men and women & children."[132]

Nobu's violin teacher in Boston was Emil Mahl (1851–1914), a student of Joseph Joachim's. Nobu also had her first opportunity to hear top class foreign artists in concert; one of them was Pablo de Sarasate. But she stayed only for a year, before returning home briefly and continuing to Vienna, where she studied with Dittrich's own teacher, Joseph Hellmesberger (junior). She continued to study the piano as well as the violin and (privately) harmony, counterpoint, composition and singing. She stayed with a local family while in Vienna, and perhaps it was there that she experienced music-making in the home. At any rate she joined a chorus at the home of Rosa Gerold (1830–1907), the daughter of a successful merchant and the widow of a well-regarded book dealer. Gerold even gave Nobu an Amati violin to replace the German instrument she had purchased in America. When the Amati proved too sensitive for the Japanese climate, Gerold exchanged it for a Lupot. Both Nobu and her sister Kō corresponded with Gerold for several years.[133]

Nobu returned to the Tokyo Academy of Music in 1895, and on 18 April 1896, at a concert to officially welcome her home, she demonstrated how much she had learnt. Not only did she play the first movement of Mendelssohn's Violin Concerto and the first violin part in an unspecified string quartet by Haydn, but she also sang Schubert and Brahms, accompanied an unspecified Mozart clarinet solo on the piano, and directed a violin group playing her own arrangement of a fugue by Bach. The Haydn quartet may well be the first performance by an all-Japanese string quartet, with Kōda playing first violin, Yamada Gen'ichirō second, Nassho Benjirō viola and Hiruma Genpachi cello.[134]

How well did Kōda play? In 1892 she wrote to her brother from Vienna that she had received top marks in her violin class.[135] Concert programmes listing works she performed certainly suggests that she had truly mastered her instruments; she was the first Japanese to perform challenging works like the Chaconne from Bach's unaccompanied Partita in D Minor.[136] But we cannot know how well she performed these works. Contemporary reviews by foreigners of Japanese playing are rare and Japanese reviewers as often as not had no idea what they were writing about and had not heard enough artists to make comparisons. Basil Hall Chamberlain describes her, somewhat condescendingly, as an "admirable executant" on the violin.[137] But by all accounts, Nobu was a highly talented musician.[138] She was certainly a versatile one.

Nobu's employers expected her to compose as well as play. Most of her surviving works are songs and choral works written for ceremonial occasions.[139] But she also composed two violin sonatas, the first by a Japanese, in 1895 and 1897.[140] The first sonata has three movements, two of which were completed in Vienna as an assignment for her teacher Robert Fuchs (1847–1927), known as a teacher of Gustav Mahler and other notable composers. The third movement and the single movement of the second sonata Nobu composed after her return to Japan, in 1897. The sonatas show that, by the age of 25 and after just six years of study abroad, Nobu, who had grown up to the sounds of traditional Japanese music, had completely mastered the idiom of Western classical music and was able not only to create beautifully melodic phrases, but to harmonize them skilfully.[141] Two movements of the first sonata of Kōda Nobu's sonata were performed at a concert on 5 June 1897, when Nobu accompanied her sister Kō and another violinist, Suzuki Fuku, on the piano.[142] Her achievements as a composer, however, are largely forgotten, and it is her pupil Taki Rentarō (1879–1903) who is remembered as the first Japanese composer of Western music, although he wrote little, mostly songs and two piano pieces of minor significance.

Kōda Nobu taught the violin, piano, composition and singing (her pupils included the singer Miura Tamaki, who gained international fame in the title role of *Madame Butterfly*). Besides the violin Nobu also played the viola in chamber music performances. But although Nobu had obviously mastered the violin well, she eventually made the piano her main instrument. Perhaps she felt more confident on the piano, which she had studied for longer. Possibly she was inspired by Raphael von Koeber (1848–1923), who from 1898 taught the piano at the Tokyo Academy of Music. Nobu, although a professor herself, became one of his pupils.

Nobu's own pupils at the Tokyo Academy of Music included her sister Kō, who had caught the attention of Dittrich when she accompanied Nobu to a violin lesson.[143] Like her sister, Kō, aged ten at the time, had been trained by their mother in the Japanese performing arts, including the *koto*, classical dance and reciting. Dittrich began to teach her, and three years later she was admitted into the preparatory department of the Tokyo Academy of Music. When she graduated in 1894, the *Yomiuri* Newspaper (*Yomiuri shinbun*) praised her performance on the violin. She continued into the music school proper, but that year Dittrich left, and until her sister returned the school had no violin teacher of sufficient calibre to further her considerable talent. At her graduation concert in 1894 she played the Concerto No. 7 by Giovanni Battista Viotti.[144] The *Yomiuri* Newspaper praised her performance highly; the article concluded, "(...) we have heard that although the Music Academy until now has been employing foreign teachers, now that it can produce players of such extraordinary calibre (*kisei no meishu*) as Miss Kōda Kō, it plans to dismiss the foreign employees at last and only appoint her as professor." [145] But although Dittrich did leave that year and was not replaced for several years, the Academy continued to depend on foreign teachers for a long time.

Despite not having the best possible teachers, Kōda Kō must have done well. On 24 November 1894, she performed in a charity concert at the Ueno hall. A review in the *Japan Weekly Mail* praised her performance, stating that "Miss Kōda's violin solo, 'Scene de Ballet' was not only perfect in execution, but also full of genuine artistic feeling. This young lady promises to attain a high reputation."[146] At her graduation in 1896 she played Vieuxtemps' *Fantasia Appassionata*. Like Nobu, she continued as a graduate student at the Tokyo Academy of Music until she left for Vienna in September 1899 as the first music student of a new study abroad programme established by the Ministry of Education. Before she left, on 13 April 1899, the sisters performed the Bach Double Concerto in D minor in the presence of the Empress.

In Vienna, Kōda Kō met Dittrich again, but she insisted on studying with Joseph Joachim in Berlin. She played for Joachim at his home, and Joachim was sufficiently impressed to recommend that she prepare for entrance into the conservatoire and introduce her to a private teacher. Kō was duly admitted to the conservatoire in October 1899 and received lessons from Joachim's assistant Karl Markees (1865–1926) and later (from 1900) from Joachim himself. She received official permission from the Japanese government to move to Berlin in February 1900.[147] While in Berlin, Kō also studied piano, chamber music, orchestra, harmony and counterpoint. In 1902 she played the *koto* at a lecture on Japanese music given by the musicologist Hugo Rieman (1849–1919) at the Grassi Museum in Leipzig.[148]

Returning to Japan in February 1903, Kō became professor at the Tokyo Academy of Music and concertmaster of its first full orchestra under August Junker. She and her sister regularly played in string quartets with their foreign colleagues, including Junker and the cellist Heinrich Werkmeister, Nobu taking the viola part. They performed together not only at the Tokyo Academy of Music's regular concerts, but also on tours to the Kansai area.[149] Both sisters had after all had leading representatives of the European quartet tradition as teachers.

In 1905 Kō married, unlike Nobu, who remained single all her life. Her husband Andō Shōichirō (1879–1962), a philologist, soon took up an appointment at the Third High School in Kyoto and spent the rest of his career teaching in the Kyoto and Osaka area, so the couple hardly lived together. They nevertheless had six children, who were brought up by Kō's mother and by her in-laws. The newspapers commented on the marriage, which flew in the face of the ideology of the "good wife and wise mother" propagated at the time. That Kō could get away with it – just like Uryū Shige, who also combined a busy career with a large family – shows just how much her specialized skills, polished through study abroad, were in demand.

The years around 1900 were the peak years of Kōda Nobu's teaching career at the Tokyo Academy of Music. In 1906 she was reportedly the second most highly paid woman in Japan. When a poll by the magazine *Ongaku zasshi* in 1893 asked readers to name outstanding players, Koda Nobu was among those named.[150] Soon, however, the tide turned. In 1899, when the possible candidates for a new government scholarship for music students were discussed, several journalists favoured a male candidate, because they did not expect a woman to take up a significant position after her return from abroad. When Nobu's sister was selected, a journalist attributed this to Nobu's influence.[151] In 1900, when Taki Rentarō was nominated as the third music student and the first male one to be sent abroad, a major journal praised the choice and remarked that "his responsibility must be described as huge. In particular, he must not forget that we will have the chance to compare his success with that of Kōda Kō, who has gone abroad before him."[152] From 1908, explicitly anti-female articles appeared in the press. Some writers accused Nobu of favouritism when her sister Kō was selected for study abroad, while others called her abilities as a teacher into question or criticised her for not performing in public except at Academy concerts. She had not composed anything significant, said one critic, nor did she take responsibility for training other composers.[153] Another report even insinuated that she was having an affair with August Junker, who himself was the target of attacks in the press.[154] We can only imagine Nobu's mortification. A woman from her high-class background would traditionally have been expected to lead a sheltered life in the shadow of the male family members. Yet here her character and her private life were exposed to public scrutiny.

Finally in September 1909 she left her position at the Academy. The head of the Academy claimed that she had been planning to resign for a while, but had waited until the school was able to appoint suitable replacements. According to the Academy's documents, however, she was "ordered to take leave," so it may have been a case of leaving before she was pushed.[155] Certainly the Academy did nothing to defend her against the slander or to keep her on the staff. Almost immediately afterwards, Nobu left for Europe, arriving in Berlin on 3 November. She stayed until June the following year. Her travel diary, written in Japanese and German, records that she went to concerts and the opera, took lessons in singing and piano and joined the Philharmonic Choir.[156] She also observed classes at the conservatoire, particularly those of Joachim's successor Karl Markees (Joachim had died in 1907), who had taught her sister. He did not impress her much, and she later recorded in her diary that since Joachim's death the French school of violin playing had become more significant. In April she visited Vienna. In June 1910 she left Berlin for Paris, where she continued to take lessons and observed classes at various music schools. She stayed until 10 July and then continued to London. Ten days later she sailed homewards from Southampton. Her diary records her lessons, observations of classes, impressions of competitions and concerts and summaries of conversations.[157] Most of it reads like a dry record of what might have been an officially sponsored study tour, giving the impression that Nobu expected to continue working as a music educator. But the occasional remark suggests that Nobu was still smarting from the treatment she had received back home, most eloquently in her entry for 19 July on the ship from Southampton. After writing about her exhaustion and poor health and her need for rest, she continued, "But actually, why should I become healthy? It is all pointless anyway; only as long as my parents are alive, I do have a duty to stay healthy if possible, but I do not know how my future will shape itself."[158]

Kōda Nobu arrived back in Tokyo in August 1910. A year later she and her mother moved to a new house, where she opened a piano studio. She aimed to promote music in the home, what the Germans call *Hausmusik*. In interviews she claimed that nearly all the homes in Berlin had a piano; family members also played the violin, cello and other instruments. Often a five o'clock tea would be held in the afternoon, where women gathered and would play for each other's pleasure.[159] She extolled the virtues of making music in the family; if the wife played the piano or *koto,* the husband might play with her on a flute and the mother-in-law on the *shamisen.* Moreover, if the daughters also played, they could perform for guests. Although single herself, Nobu did realize that a wife and mother needed a lot of determination to continue her musical activities after marriage and appealed for more support and appreciation from family members.[160] On the other hand, and perhaps as a defence mechanism, she seems to have cultivated a formidably serious persona. A collection of caricatures of public figures published in 1912 included one entitled "Kōda Kō dissuading [beautiful women from studying music]"; by then Kō had married and was called Andō, so the caricaturist may well have confused the two sisters, as did other reporters at the time. According to the accompanying text, when beautiful young women who wanted to study music professionally visited Kōda, she would tell them, "people like you are subject to many temptations, and it is hard to succeed, so you would do better to give up the idea."[161] Not that she necessarily was more encouraging towards men. The composer Yamada Kōsaku (1886–1965), who studied in Berlin from 1910 to 1913 and visited Nobu in her Berlin lodgings, records the conversation they had after he told her he was about to take the entrance examination for the conservatoire in Berlin. Nobu, her manner abrupt, "like a man," responded: "'What, you want to enter the Hochschule? What subject, voice? Cello? Cello is easy. With cello you might get in.' (...) 'But you're no good at the piano. (...) 'Composition? But that's impossible.' (...) I felt as if I had been slapped."[162]

Nobu taught the piano until the end of her life. Most of her pupils were daughters from upper-class families who performed regularly in student concerts at the Peers Club (in 1943 for the fiftieth time). She also gave lessons at the imperial palace and continued to compose for imperial occasions. In 1918 she had a private concert hall built and decorated with a bust of Beethoven. Mischa Elman performed there during his Japan tour in 1921, and other visiting artists, such as Jascha Heifetz, may also have done so.

Meanwhile, Andō Kō continued her career at the Tokyo Academy of Music as a full professor until 1931 and as an external lecturer until 1943. In 1932 she travelled to Europe to act as a jury member for the Vienna International Competition, fittingly won that year by a woman, Gioconda de Vito. She met Georges Enesco who told her that he remembered her sister Nobu from her student days. She also visited Carl Flesch's master classes in Baden-Baden. Possibly she felt a need to update; by the 1930s her teacher Joseph Joachim's playing style had been superseded by what is commonly described as the modern style.[163]

Back in Japan, she became a jury member for the first annual Japanese Music Competition (Ongaku Konkūru; see Part 2 Chapter 4) inaugurated in 1932. She continued to perform, mainly in concerts at the Tokyo Academy of Music. She may be the soloist on a recording made in 1931 by the Academy's orchestra (of which she was for many years the concertmaster) of Haydn's *Seven Words of Jesus on the Cross*.[164] By then world-class foreign artists had begun to tour Japan often, and Kō had to suffer being compared to them and found wanting. Her playing is discussed in a review of Japanese violinists performing publicly in a magazine article in 1927; the same issue includes brief reviews of recent performances by Mikhail Erdenko and Naum Blinder. The author described her as one of the best-known and most frequently heard players, but had little good to say about her: "When one hears that person stand on the stage and perform, it is just like being lectured to." He stated that she always included works that few other Japanese violinists attempted and that were beyond her technical abilities, as if she wanted to assert her status and authority as a veteran and observed: "Granted that she is a hard worker; but it is a big mistake to believe that this alone makes her a great performer." Letting outstanding students perform, he concluded, would be a better way of demonstrating her authority as a teacher.[165]

Whatever Kō's merits as a performer, she was one of the Tokyo Academy of Music's longest-serving violin teachers. But like her sister she received shoddy treatment from the Academy. At the beginning of the new term in 1943, she arrived to teach as usual. But she did not find her name on the new schedules. She had been fired, but no one had bothered to tell her. Her son Andō Osamu condemned the treatment of his mother in an open letter to the president entitled "A Case of Discourtesy," but to no avail.[166] Like Nobu, Kō taught privately for the rest of her life, and her pupils included members of the imperial family. She also taught three of her fourteen grandchildren.

Both sisters did, eventually, receive public honours for their service to the promotion of Western music. On 7 June 1931 the Tokyo Academy of Music officially celebrated Nobu's sixtieth birthday and her 50 years in music. In 1937, Kōda Nobu became the first representative of Western music and first woman to become a member of the Imperial Academy of Fine Arts (Teikoku Geijutsu Kaiin). Andō Kō received the same honour in 1943. In 1958 she was the first woman to be nominated a person of cultural merit (*bunka kōrō sha*) and appeared on television with her contemporary the poet Higashi Kume (née Yui 1877–1969) who graduated from the Tokyo Academy of Music in 1896.[167]

The pioneering sisters never achieved the fame of some of their male contemporaries. One reason may well be that they deliberately kept a low profile. While they performed for the public in the concerts organized by the Tokyo Academy of Music in Tokyo and in several regional cities, neither of them played for fees. Nor have they left gramophone recordings of their playing. Andō Kō did play on the radio; until 1944 the NHK's annual broadcast of her "Performance to start the New Year" was a national institution. Nobu, in one of the newspaper articles condemning her, was criticised for not performing in public more often, because she feared being regarded as no better than a geisha.[168] The author of the article might have been speculating, but he probably hit the mark. The two samurai daughters grew up in an age when performing publicly for money was regarded an occupation fit only for courtesans and outcasts.[169] Perhaps the need to set themselves apart from a tradition which associated female professional entertainers with prostitution also made them cultivate an excessively serious image of Western art music which still lingers in Japan, including a cult of Beethoven, who suffered for his art. Nobu's concert hall was decorated with a bust of Beethoven. Kō too kept one; it is said to have been the only thing she found in the ruins of her home after the bombings of Tokyo in 1945. Even at over 80, Kō practised her violin for three to five hours every morning, with an austere regime of scales, unaccompanied Bach, and Brahms, a ritual she described as her "health regimen."

But surely the fact that they were women is one of the main reasons why the pioneering sisters have been all but forgotten. Did they realize when they studied in the West, just how unusual their position was even by Western standards? Women had only just begun to make the instruments of the orchestra their own. By the late nineteenth century there were plenty of female violinists, but they were still regarded with suspicion, especially if they wished to play professionally. In Vienna, Nobu might have heard or at least learned about one of the few women who did manage a long and successful performing career: Marie Soldat (1863–1955).[170] A pupil of Joseph Joachim, whose Violin Concerto she championed, Soldat moved to Vienna in 1892 and performed there when she was not on tour. But women like Soldat were still exceptional, and Nobu may well have received and internalized the message that female violinists were not considered normal and that women should stick to the piano. Nobu's increasing devotion to the piano after her return may well have resulted from her observations in Europe, which may also have led her to concentrate on teaching girls and young women of the nobility with the aim of promoting music in the home.

Kōda Nobu and her sister, the female pioneers of the violin in Japan, both lived long enough to witness Japan's coming of age as a musical as well as a military and economic power. And as in the Western musical powers, the musical profession in Japan came to be dominated by men. Men populated the emerging professional orchestras of the 1920s and, increasingly, the faculty of the Tokyo Academy of Music. Even so, most of the violinists who attracted international attention after 1945 were women. They may not know it (any more than their international audiences do), but their success and the strong presence of women in music in general owes much to the pioneering role of the Kōda sisters and their contemporary, lesser-known female students and teachers.

## 4. The First Japanese-Made Violins and the Rise of Suzuki Violins

In order to play the violin at all the Japanese needed instruments. The first ones were imported by foreign companies, along with other goods. The British businessman Alexander Clark in Yokohama imported violins and other instruments from 1871. Initially most of them may have been for foreigners, and he only sold 20 to 30 instruments a year.[171] The demand for Western musical instruments increased when the Music Investigation Committee opened its doors in 1879. Isawa and Megata saw the procurement of instruments as a minor issue; in their memo to the education minister in 1878 they stated, "(...) we can either import them from this country [America] cheaply or make them at home with ease (...)."[172] But in fact instruments were not that easily obtained and the cost was significant. Luther Mason ordered a number of musical instruments for the Committee before he left Boston for Tokyo, including a dozen violins, two violas, two cellos and a double bass, as well as violin making tools.[173] The Committee also attempted to adapt Japanese instruments for use in teaching singing; Japan's indigenous bowed lute, the *kokyū*, was converted to a larger instrument with an all-wooden body, but it does not seem to have come into general use. Ultimately the Committee opted for Western instruments, which they initially purchased through Alexander Clark. From 1885 the Japanese company Tōkyō Kyōeki Shōsha Gakkiten took over and imported musical instruments, sheet music and other equipment through the companies of Clark and Doehring in Yokohama. Tōkyō Kyōeki Shōsha Gakkiten became the leading distributor for central and northern Japan.[174] In 1909 the company was taken over by Yamaha and renamed Nihon Gakki Seizō. Where did the imports come from? Advertisements in newspapers and magazines sometimes name the country, often Germany, for violins. Presumably they came from the centres of mass production of Bubenreuth, Mittenwald and Markneukirchen, from where several firms export to Japan to this day.

Imports, however, were expensive, and as long as musical instruments had to be imported at high prices, ordinary people could not afford them. So once they anticipated a significant market for Western instruments, Japanese craftsmen attempted to make instruments at a cheaper price. Wind instruments were in demand earlier, because of the military bands, but domestic wind instruments did not reach the quality of imported ones until well into the twentieth century.[175] Stringed instruments, on the other hand, were easier: Japanese craftsmen were highly skilled at working with wood and could apply their experience of making Japanese stringed instruments. Several started making violins soon after the Music Investigation Committee had begun teaching the violin with a view to introducing it in schools. And one man succeeded above others, so that his name became synonymous with "Japanese-made violins": Suzuki Masakichi (1859–1944). He was not the first Japanese to make a violin – indeed the first violin he saw was Japanese-made. But he was the most determined. Above all he made sure almost from the beginning that he would sell his instruments all over Japan and rapidly moved into mass production, pursuing it with more persistence than any of his rivals.

Various stories exist about who produced the first violin in Japan.[176] In the 1880s several makers of Japanese instruments tried to make violins, but not all persisted. According to one story, a certain Matsunaga Teijirō,[177] a 31- year-old maker of *koto* and *shamisen* in downtown Tokyo, looked for a new source of income because of the falling demand for traditional Japanese instruments. Hearing about violins, he went to see and hear one for himself at Tokyo's Russian Orthodox church. He asked to examine it and drew diagrams. In August 1880 he succeeded in making his own using wood from crates bought from shops selling foreign clothes and other goods. His first attempts found no customers, but after spending a fortune on research he attracted the attention of Sauvlet and Dittrich. Eventually he managed to sell his violins to *gagaku* musicians and other students of Western music.

Another story relates that a Mr. Kanda from Nagano tried making violins in 1884 or 1885, having been asked to do so by Isawa. In around 1887, Tanomogi Genshichi likewise tried to make and sell violins. Presumably he had good reason to think that violins would sell: in 1889 his daughter Tanomogi Koma enrolled at the Music Investigation Committee. But neither Kanda nor Tanomogi continued their efforts. However, a certain Yamada Hōsaburō, who had worked with Tanomogi, persisted. Like Matsunaga, he was a maker of Japanese musical instruments. From around 1907, he taught Maruyama Shin, Kamataki Kōji and a Mr Hiramatsu; Maruyama continued to make violins. This version is told by Suzuki Shin'ichi (1898–1998), Suzuki Masakichi's third and most famous son and the founder of the "Suzuki Method." He also mentions a Mr. Saitō and his younger brother Mr. Matsunaga, who may be the Matsunaga credited with having made the first Japanese violin.

While the details are uncertain, the gist is clear: several craftsmen and makers of Japanese instruments tried their hand at making Western ones, including the violin. In the Kansai area, the first mention of the violin in the newspaper in 1887 refers to Japanese-made instruments.[178] A short article in *Ongakukai* (Music World) in 1912 entitled "The first imitator of the violin" reported that a teacher from Matsumoto had brought to Tokyo a violin made in 1882 by a Matsumoto maker of Chinese-style musical instruments named Mizawa.[179] Mizawa had been asked to copy a German violin belonging to the headmaster of the newly established teacher training college. The resulting instrument had a body resembling that of a violin, but the neck looked like that of a *gekkin* (Chinese lute with a round, flattish body and frets) and the bow like a *kokyū* bow. The report does not say what it sounded like. Presumably local makers in several parts of the country attempted to make violins in imitation of instruments brought from Tokyo by newly appointed teachers, and a number may have done so successfully.

Suzuki Masakichi's first attempts were no different from those of his contemporaries. Like other early makers of violins, Suzuki Masakichi, born in Nagoya as the second son of a farmer turned samurai, originally made *shamisen* and *koto*. His father had been forced to make this sideline into his main occupation when he lost his samurai privileges and stipend in the early 1870s. Masakichi had no knowledge of Western music; certainly he had never heard the names "Stradivarius" and "Cremona," which today inspire even more awe in Japan than in the West – perhaps this was a good thing for him. He had received thorough training in the making of *shamisen*, and spent three years in Tokyo as an apprentice in his relatives' lacquerware shop before returning to learn the family trade of instrument making. He also studied *nagauta* (kabuki dance music) to deepen his understanding of Japanese music. Last, but not least, in the days before the dissolution of the old feudal domains in 1871, he had played the drum for his lord's troops and studied English at the domain's new school; the latter came in useful when he started exporting.[180]

In 1884 his father died and the business began to falter. Masakichi,

4: Suzuki Masakichi and his first violin.

reading the signs of the times and believing he could put his musical training to better use, thought of becoming a music teacher. In 1887 he sought out Tsunekawa Ryōnosuke, who taught at the Aichi Prefectural Normal College, in order to study Western music. One of Tsunekawa's pupils (Amari Tetsukichi) showed him a Japanese-made violin, told him how popular the instrument was among Westerners and suggested that he try and make one. Intrigued, Suzuki started copying it immediately. When he showed the result to Tsunekawa, he told Suzuki that it was not a bad first attempt. This violin can still be seen in the Suzuki Shin'ichi Memorial Museum in Matsumoto. It is far from flawless; the fingerboard rests directly on the body of the violin. Suzuki made a second instrument, which he sold. More orders came in and he employed assistants. A few months later he had the opportunity to see a foreign violin at the Gifu Prefectural Normal College. In fact, he did more than look at it. The humidity of the rainy season had caused its parts to come unstuck and the repair was entrusted to Suzuki. Needless to say, he made the best use of this opportunity. He realized just how poor his own efforts were, compared to the foreign violin, but although discouraged, he also knew that, crude or not, his violins were selling. He redoubled his efforts and in May 1889 showed his best violins to Rudolf Dittrich at the Tokyo Academy of Music. Dittrich judged them to be the best Japanese-made ones he had seen. In 1893 he gave Suzuki another endorsement, certifying that Suzuki violins rivalled imported ones.[181] Some years later, in 1909, Dittrich's successor August Junker likewise praised Suzuki's violins and the newspaper *Tokyo nichinichi shinbun* reported that the army and navy would be buying them.[182]

With Dittrich's endorsement, Suzuki Masakichi secured an agreement with the import company Tōkyō Kyōeki Shōsha in August 1889, and in 1890, an agreement with Miki Sasuke's book and music store in Osaka. Together, these two companies, which also handled Yamaha reed organs, distributed musical instruments nationwide. Securing their distribution network was the key to success, both for Yamaha Torakusu and his organs and for Suzuki. Early music magazines invariably carried advertisements for Yamaha organs and Suzuki violins starting with *Ongaku zasshi* (The Musical Magazine), first published in 1890. The advertisements tell us something about the reason for the violin's rising popularity: according to the early ones in *Ongaku zasshi*, in 1890 a Suzuki violin with bow could be had for from five yen upwards. Imported violins were more likely to cost 10 to 15 yen or more, although *Ongaku zasshi* carried an advertisement by the English company Besson for violins starting at five yen in 1893; bows were priced separately starting from 1 yen 50 sen.[183]

Yamaha organs started at 15 yen. A teacher's or a policeman's monthly starting salary in the 1890s was between 8 and 13 yen. Some advertisements in *Ongakukai* (World of Music) from 1907, incredibly, even list violins for as little as two yen.[184] A catalogue published in *Ongaku no tomo* (Friend of Music) in 1904 for the publisher's own instrument department listed Suzuki violins without bow from five yen and imported violins from 20 yen. Bow prices ranged from one yen for a domestic one and three yen for imported ones. Prices in general tended to rise throughout the Meiji period, while the prices for Suzuki violins remained relatively constant, so they would have become more affordable over the years.[185]

By 1897 Suzuki's firm was reportedly producing 1,200 violins a year and employing ten workers. Towards the end of the century, Suzuki heard about mechanized mass production and asked foreign trading houses for information. When they could not help him, he developed his own machines: in 1900, one to cut scrolls, followed by machines to cut the fronts and backs. Suzuki was now ready to take mass production one step further. Moreover, the quality of his violins was recognized with a prize at the Paris world exhibition that year. What flattered Suzuki even more than the prize itself was the fact that some people – including a minority of the jury members – believed that he had merely stuck his own label into European products.[186]

By 1901 Suzuki's firm was producing over 1,000 violins per year. According to figures published in 1910 production rose steadily over the following years:

1901: 1,013
1902: 1,158
1903: 1,419
1904: 2,113
1905: 3,213
1906: 5,866
1907: 6,826
1908: 9,285
1909 (November): 9,337[187]

The production of bows increased in a similar fashion, from 1,110 in

1901 to 9,954 in 1909. The author of the report estimated that if other makers like Matsunaga and Hiramatsu were included, Japan had produced about 50,000 violins to date, and that, together with imports, that amounted to over 60,000 violins in Japan, or one violin per 1,000 inhabitants. This was admittedly not a great number, but at 4 yen 57 sen for a violin plus bow and case, the violin could well contribute to the dissemination of music in private homes (p. 45).[188]

Suzuki continued to receive national and international prizes for his violins, including one at the Japan–British Exhibition in 1910. On this occasion he spent five months in Europe with a grant from the Ministry of Education to observe instrument-making and travelled to England, France, Italy, Austria, Germany and Belgium. With supreme confidence he concluded that he had little to learn from any of these countries and would start exporting his own products.[189] These included mandolins (production started in 1900) and, from 1914, guitars. In the early twentieth century, Suzuki also applied his creativity to the development of a range of instruments which (supposedly) combined the best features of Japanese and Western instruments, including the "Suzu-goto" and the "tamagoto" (which another maker developed into the *taishōgoto*, an instrument that is still popular).[190] Inventing new instruments was a fairly popular trend in those days.[191] It was not limited to Japan either. A catalogue ("Nr. 30") from Schuster in Markneukirchen, undated, but probably from the early twentieth century, includes a page of "Japanese violins" with a selection of instruments which look neither Japanese nor particularly like violins, but combined the features of several stringed instruments: variously shaped bodies with long necks, with or without frets.

The height of Suzuki's success came with the First World War, when he exported to markets formerly dominated by Germany, including Britain and North America. Suzuki expanded his premises to meet the increased demand. At the peak of the war boom (which continued into the 1920s) he employed nearly 1,000 workers producing over 150,000 violins a year. In addition, Suzuki produced and exported violas, cellos, double basses, mandolins and guitars. Suzuki had gone international, and although the boom lasted only for a few years, it showed the world that Japan could be a force to be reckoned with in the realm of classical music as well as so many other areas. It all came to an end with the conclusion of the war and the following slump. But Suzuki's importance for violin playing in Japan was far from ended, and we may as well follow the fortunes of Suzuki violins until the Second World War here. One thing that helped secure the future of Suzuki violins was that Masakichi's productivity was not limited to musical instruments: he had nine sons and four daughters. Two of the sons died young, but the remaining ones all worked for his violin factory at some time, as did one of his sons-in-law.[192] Masakichi treated the two eldest sons, Umeo (1889–1981) and Rokusaburō (1895–1945?), as his successors-to-be, training them in his firm. When Umeo was 23, his father sent him to Tokyo for additional training at his long-time business partner Nihon Gakki Seizō, established by Yamaha Torakusu in 1897. Umeo also studied the violin at the Tokyo Academy of Music with Tanomogi Koma. His progress was so good that Tanomogi invited him to play in a string quartet, but nothing came of it. In 1912 Umeo had to return to Nagoya, where he became an important support for his father during the following boom period. In 1920, as the boom was coming to an end, his father sent him abroad to learn about instrument production in America and Europe.[193] Like his father before him, he was not too impressed with what he saw. In America, he reported, violins were not mass-produced at all; most makers were German immigrants specializing in repairs. In Germany, his main destination was Markneukirchen, where Umeo, perhaps not unjustifiably, was regarded as an industrial spy and prevented from visiting the factories. With the assistance of a German guide, however, he inspected some factories from the outside and examined the discarded wood shavings. He concluded that concerning mechanized production Suzuki had nothing to learn. On the other hand he was impressed by the way whole villages were involved in the production of violins under a cottage industry system, right down to printing the catalogues.

Returning to Japan he increasingly took over the running of the family business. His father, meanwhile, had finally come to see violin making as an art and not just a business opportunity. He devoted himself to research, hoping like so many before him to discover the "mystery" of Cremona. Masakichi's third son, Shin'ichi, who studied in Berlin from 1921, managed (thanks to the inflation that ravaged Germany at the time) to purchase a Peter Guarneri.[194] When Shin'ichi returned to Japan for a few months in 1925–26, Masakichi set up his own little laboratory in his home to examine it. He wanted to make new violins that could rival the old masters. According to the German biochemist Leonor Michaelis, who met Suzuki in the 1920s, Suzuki did not have much knowledge of music, but he did have an ear for good sound in a violin.[195] He made some fine violins too. Murata Sōroku (b. 1927), a Mittenwald-trained luthier and authority on the history of violin-making in Japan, has a couple in his collection of Japanese-made instruments. One, built in 1941, resembles eighteenth-century Italian models. "It is well made, but does not sound good," Murata comments; "With better materials Suzuki Masakichi could surely have made excellent violins."[196]

Still, Masakichi took pride in his creations. In October 1926 he sent Umeo abroad once more, this time with a selection of Masakichi's hand-made violins, which he was to show to several experts. Presumably Shin'ichi helped his brother with introductions, and accompanied him. In the report Umeo wrote afterwards he cited the verdicts of Karl Klingler (1879–1971), Willy Hess (1859–1939), Josef Wolfsthal (1859–1932) and Albert Einstein (1877–1955) in Berlin and the cellist Julius Klengel (1859–1933) in Leipzig.[197] The introduction to Klengel may have been provided by another brother, Fumio (1900–45), who, after studying the cello with Heinrich Werkmeister in Tokyo, went to study with Klengel in 1923. According to Umeo, all pronounced themselves impressed and astonished that a new violin could sound as good as the old Italian masters.

Among the people Umeo visited with his violins was the deputy head of the conservatoire in Berlin, Georg Schünemann (1884–1945). Schünemann obviously found kind words for the violins, for which Masakichi thanked him in a letter dated 23 February 1927. He also offered to donate one violin a year to the school "to good student who graduate your school" (sic!). The offer was accepted with thanks; by March the following year two Suzuki violins were being played by students. By then, Masakichi had sent two more violins on their way. In a letter dated 18 January 1928 he wrote, "These are pretty good, although they are not perfect ones, and I shall be glad if you take trouble to give them to the students as prize." He did not receive confirmation that the violins had arrived until the autumn (apparently an earlier letter had got lost); in a letter dated 5 November 1928 he thanked Schünemann for a letter dated 15 October.[198] This is the last letter preserved in the conservatoire's archives and no-one knows whether Suzuki continued with the donations and for how long, who received the violins and what became of them.

Meanwhile, the Suzuki business was struggling. Umeo, on his return in January 1927 was optimistic about their chances of selling violins in Germany, but the economic slump in Japan and soon the worldwide economic depression brought the business close to bankruptcy. Shin'ichi and Fumio were recalled from Europe. In 1930 the family formed a joint stock company; Masakichi and his eldest son owned most of the shares. The other sons, sought alternatives ways of making a living. Shin'ichi and Fumio, the two returnees from Germany, formed the Suzuki Quartet, together with their brothers Akira (1899–1961) and Kikuo (1904–77). Even so, the firm had to declare insolvency and make a composition with its creditors in 1932. Masakichi followed his sons to Tokyo and continued his research into violin making, paying particular attention to tone. Umeo, meanwhile, rebuilt the business in Nagoya. For the first time in the firm's history he employed outside managers. Foreign markets having once again fallen to the European producers, he concentrated on securing distribution in Japan. By 1933 he was producing violins again; his father returned to Nagoya and continued his research into "the sound of Cremona" in a laboratory next to the factory. But the firm did not get the chance to regain the heights of the "golden" years before all-out war with China from 1937 and the National Mobilization Law in 1938 placed severe restrictions on production. The law introduced a centrally directed war economy, forcing businesses to accept rationing of vital materials and to merge. During those difficult years, Umeo proved himself a far-sighted businessman. Several of the workers trained in the Suzuki business had set up on their own, and Umeo supported them as they too struggled through the war. He also played a leading role in the local, regional and national organization of musical instrument producers; he was president of the Association of String Instrument Producers in Nagoya, and of the Chūbu Regional Association of Instrument Producers as well as founding member and vice-president of the of the Japan Federation of Musical Instrument Unions (Zenkoku Gakki Kumiai Rengōkai), founded in 1940. But as the war progressed, Suzuki Violins, like many other firms, was increasingly forced to switch its production to goods demanded by the military. By 1943 the factories in Nagoya were producing parts for aeroplanes and ships rather than violins. During this time, on 31 January 1944, Suzuki Masakichi died; he had worked on his violins to the very end. In March 1945 air raids destroyed the main factory in Nagoya and the premises in Ōfu, just outside Nagoya, where Umeo had hoped to establish a system of production similar to that he had encountered in Markneukirchen. Umeo's eldest son and prospective heir Ichirō had already died in 1941 from an illness contracted as a soldier in Manchuria. Suzuki violins seemed to have come to an end. The firm recovered after 1945, however, and today it is one of Japan's oldest companies.[199]

While Suzuki was by far the most successful maker of violins and the only one to mass-produce them on a large scale, other makers also sold violins, at least for a while. An article in *Ongakukai* in 1910 mentions several names and reports that around ten makers were active around 1900, although most of them did not stay in business for long.[200] Murata Sōroku has collected many names of makers from old catalogues and advertisements. He has also tried to find their violins, usually without success. The early makers did not always label their instruments. Most of them must have been crude things which have long disappeared.[201] Some, however, were successful enough for their names to be remembered

Miyamoto Kinpachi (1879–1970) initially worked at Yamaha Torakuzu's organ factory in Hamamatsu. In 1916 he moved to the Yamaha shop in Tokyo to repair instruments. He began teaching himself to make violins. In 1919 he presented his work to the public. He had hardly any chance to study outstanding instruments, for in those days even imported violins were usually cheap instruments from Czechoslovakia or Germany. But his first violin met the approval of the violinist Takashina Tetsuo (see following chapter) and his German professor Gustav Kron. Takashina allegedly bought it for 400 yen at a time when a Suzuki violin could be had for around 5 yen. Miyamoto was the first maker whose violins fetched high prices even in his lifetime. Several of the visiting virtuosos of the interwar period are said to have admired his instruments, and the Russian violinist Alexander Mogilevsky owned three of his violins. During his long life Miyamoto made close to 300 violins as well as several violas, cellos and guitars.[202]

Another of Japan's earliest master makers was Suganuma Gentarō (1895–1975). Like Miyamoto he started his career with Yamaha in Hamamatsu before opening his own workshop in Tokyo, where he took violin lessons with Andō Kō. After the Second World War he taught at the Musashino Academia Musicae, still one of the few colleges in Japan that teaches violin making.

In the Kansai area violin making was pioneered by members of the Minezawa family. In 1888 Tōyō Musical Instruments (Tōyō Gakki Seizō Kabushiki Kaisha) opened in Kobe Prefecture. Not much is known about it (although it existed until 1978), but in the early twentieth century Minezawa Miyazō was in charge of a workshop there which turned out between 600 and 1,500 violins a year. Here his son Minezō (1899–1978) was trained. He made some excellent violins. The violinist Tsuji Hisako (b.1926) is said to have praised them highly. Miyazō's nephew Minezawa Taizō (1901–69) likewise trained with him. In the 1920s he opened a workshop in Osaka, and after the Second World War he moved to Tokyo. Taizō's violins are said to have been praised by Heifetz, Elman and Oistrakh when they toured Japan. When Elman tested his instruments he also showed him his own 1717 Stradivarius. Minezawa discovered that the back had come unstuck. Elman implored him to repair it in time for the concert that night, which Minezawa did.[203]

Because so few violins from the early days survive, it is difficult to judge the quality of violin-making in the early twentieth century. Praise by foreign artists is hardly much of a clue. They were probably surprised that the Japanese could make their own violins at all, and anyway they would surely have felt it was churlish to say that they were not particularly good. But whatever the quality, the important thing was that Japanese makers could produce serviceable violins in sufficiently large quantities. Thanks to the skills, initiative and business sense of their craftsmen – especially Suzuki – the Japanese-made violins became available at cheap prices only a few years after the government began the systematic introduction of music education. As a result, the violin became hugely popular. The schools preferred reed organs to violins for teaching music, but although these too became cheaper, thanks to Yamaha, many schools could not afford one for years, and their teachers had to rely on violins instead, especially in the remoter parts of the country. Individuals who could never have afforded an organ could buy a violin and play it at home. For many it was just a passing fad. But more and more people studied the violin seriously, helping to create the broad base from which outstanding violinists could emerge in the twentieth century.

## 5. Early Students of Western Music and the Violin

The Kōda sisters were the first Japanese to study the violin from childhood, to continue their studies abroad and to pursue a musical career. Soon though, they were joined by other students of the violin who, while their playing did not reach the same standard, did just as much to promote Western music and violin playing among their compatriots. In the early years of the Music Investigation Committee and the Academy of Music, many students expected to use the violin to teach singing in schools after graduation. Female graduates dominated for a long time. Although many of them may have abandoned a career in music when they married, others continued to teach at schools, especially girls' schools, in Tokyo and throughout the country.

One of them, Tanomogi Koma (1874–1936), taught the violin at the Tokyo Academy of Music from 1894 to 1928. Unlike the Kōda sisters and most of the other female teachers, Tanomogi was the daughter not of a samurai but of a commoner. Her father, Tanomogi Genshichi, made instruments for Japanese music and the then popular Chinese music known as *minshingaku*, as well as for Western music; he may have been one of the first to make violins, although he did not persist. We do not know whether Koma had the chance to study the violin as a child, but probably not. In 1889 she enrolled at the Tokyo Academy of Music; she studied the violin with Dittrich and graduated in 1893. At the graduation concert, as well as singing in a choir, she played violin in three ensembles: first in a violin group with a fellow graduate and unnamed others, playing an arrangement of a *koto* piece; next in an arrangement of Haydn's "Farewell" Symphony for violins, organ and piano; and finally, again with other violinists and keyboard players, pieces by Tchaikovsky, Bizet, and Hans Sitt.[204] The programme and her part in it suggest that Tanomogi's playing was not in the same league as the Kōda sisters even before they went abroad. Nevertheless, she was hired to teach at the Academy the following year and appointed assistant professor in 1897 and professor in October 1909, a month after Nobu's dismissal. She continued to teach at the Academy and at summer schools for teachers held at the Normal School even after she married the politician Tanomogi Keikichi (1867–1940; adopted into the Tanomogi family to ensure the continuation of the family name) and had a son.[205]

Unlike the Kōda sisters, Tanomogi never had the chance to study abroad. Even so, from what we can glimpse from the programmes of the Academy's concerts, her playing appears to have improved; at least, she played increasingly demanding works. Her first recorded solo performance was an unspecified concerto by Hans Sitt in March 1897; in November that year she performed the first movement of de Bériot's Concerto in A minor (Kōda Kō played Vieuxtemps' *Fantasia Appassionata* at the same concert). In December 1903 she performed Mozart's Sinfonia Concertante, presumably the viola part, with Kōda Kō; four years earlier Kō's sister Nobu had performed the same work with August Junker playing the violin part, and a critic hinted (unsurprisingly) that there was no comparison between the two performances. While this, like all concertos at the time, would have been performed with piano accompaniment, Tanomogi played solo with the orchestra when she took the obligato violin part in Händel's Largo, conducted by August Junker, in October 1911. Her last recorded performance (for the period up to 1926) was in December 1917, when she played the first two movements of Wieniawski's Concerto Op. 22 in D minor. On that occasion a critic, although he praised her performance, added "it was merely beautiful, but without power, and skilful, but with insufficient expression."[206] Other works Tanomogi performed were Georg Hellmesberger's (1800–73) *La Mélancolie*, Mozart's Sonata No. 6, Francis Thomé's Andante Religioso, Max Bruch's *Kol Nidrei*, and Anton Rubinstein's Sonata for piano and violin.[207]

According to the musicologist Tanabe Hisao (see below), who studied with Tanomogi between 1904 and 1909, Tanomogi was beautiful, extremely refined and like a lady of the nobility, tall and imposing when she stood on the stage and performed. Because of her size she played the viola in the orchestra, the only woman to do so at the time (here Tanabe is wrong; Kōda Nobu also played the viola, at least in chamber ensembles). Kind, home-loving and maternal, she welcomed students into her home, and Tanabe, one of her favourites, often visited her. But she was a strict teacher and severely scolded lazy pupils who did not take their studies seriously. She even hit one of Tanabe's fellow students with the bow and threw him out of the room. At home she appeared as the gentle mother; her son Shinroku was ten at the time Tanabe studied with her. Tanomogi regularly invited students home at New Year for card games, an occasion Tanabe enjoyed, because she had many beautiful female pupils.[208]

Several of the earliest students at the Tokyo Academy of Music stand out as pioneers who published violin tutors and founded music colleges, or else became a driving force in establishing Western music in regional centres. One of the latter was Tsunekawa Ryōsaburō (d. 1906).[209] Most of what is known about him comes from reports in music journals praising his musical activities, first in Nagoya, and then, from 1891, in Tsu in Mie Prefecture. The son of a *gagaku* musician in Nagoya, Tsunekawa was sent by Aichi Prefecture to train as a music teacher at the Music Investigation Committee in 1884. He returned to teach at the Normal School and the Middle School in Nagoya, organized concerts, and became one of the driving forces of the city's music life. From 1887 onwards, he published general texts on music and singing as well as collections of marches and songs. Suzuki Masakichi studied the violin with him, and the two performed together at local concerts. In 1891 Tsunekawa moved to Tsu in Mie Prefecture to teach at the Mie Prefecture Normal School, and his departure from Nagoya was much lamented at a time when the presence of an enthusiastic and able music teacher made all the difference to the progress of music education in an entire region.[210] Nagoya's loss was Mie Prefecture's gain: Tsunekawa started a Music Society offering lessons in singing, organ, violin and *gagaku*. Tsunekawa maintained ties with his native Nagoya though; in 1896, for example, he performed in a concert in Nagoya playing the violin in an ensemble with several *koto* players.

Tsunekawa may have been the first Japanese to publish a violin tutor, but no one knows for sure; his tutor was advertised in the first music magazine, *Ongaku zasshi* in 1891. The advertisement reads:

The "violin" has a simple construction and is conveniently portable. Moreover its tone is elegant, and it is consequently the best-suited musical instrument for teaching music in schools. However, unfortunately there have so far been no textbooks for its study. Here Tsunekawa-sensei has written a work which is suitable, first as a textbook for normal colleges, women's high schools etc.; secondly for people who want to study the violin by themselves. It explains in detail how to use the violin and how to tune and play it. It is a rare work in which are collected over fifty lively pieces, and so we ask music lovers to buy their copy now and enjoy the exquisite tunes.[211]

The advertised tutor, however, does not appear to have been published. Tsunekawa's move to Mie Prefecture that year may have kept him too busy. His name later appears in a tutor published by Suzuki Masakichi, describing Tsunekawa as reviewer.[212]

Tsunekawa did, however, publish a textbook for teaching singing in schools in 1892, in which he recommends that teachers who play the violin well enough should use it to teach singing. Because the violin is the most beautiful instrument, he says, it will help develop children's musical sensibilities. We can glimpse further clues regarding his musical interests from the programme of a memorial concert for his father, published in 1894.[213] The programme included a mixture of traditional Japanese and Western music, the latter mostly *shōka*. Several members of the Tsunekawa family took part, and Tsunekawa himself played pieces on the violin, as well as playing a Japanese piece in an ensemble with *koto* and two violins and two marches on the organ. Tsunekawa died in 1906; according to one of his students he had ruined his health while playing the clarinet in a brass band marching through town to celebrate Japan's victory against Russia.[214]

We know a great deal more about two other earlier graduates and trailblazers of music education, whom, in the absence of evidence to the contrary we can also credit with being the first Japanese to publish violin tutors; Suzuki Yonejirō (1868–1940; no relation of Suzuki Masakichi) and Yamada Gen'ichirō (1869–1927). Suzuki enrolled in the Tokyo Academy of Music in 1885, the year Kōda Nobu and two female fellow students became the first to graduate. He himself graduated in 1888 and went on to become a pioneer in many areas of music education, including Tonic sol-fa and music education for the blind with Braille scores. In 1907 he founded the Music College of the East, now the Tokyo College of Music.

Born in 1868 as the second son of a former retainer of the shogunate, Suzuki Yonejirō, like the Kōda sisters, came from a former samurai family associated with the shogunate, although of lower rank.[215] The family left Tokyo soon after his birth in the middle of the Restoration wars of 1868–69, but returned in 1873. After graduating from primary school Suzuki attended a public middle school for a year or two before changing to a school in the Tsukiji district, apparently in order to learn English from foreign teachers. His education there did not formally include music, but he may well have first encountered Western music among the missionaries in Tsukiji; we know that other graduates of the Tokyo Academy of Music did. This would help explain why he enrolled in the Music Investigation Committee's training course. His family's reaction is not recorded; perhaps, like other families in their position, the Suzukis thought it a good idea to let their second son study a new subject. Suzuki later claimed that he had no previous knowledge of music. Certainly, his achievements on the violin when he graduated in 1888 seem modest compared to Kōda Nobu's. Asked in later years by a former student how far he had advanced, Suzuki replied that he completed the first two volumes of Christian Heinrich Hohmann's violin tutor.[216] The German music pedagogue Christian Heinrich Hohmann (1811–61) published several instrumental tutors, including his *Praktische Violinschule* (Practical Violin Method, Nürnberg, 1849). Intended as a "solid foundation for country schoolteachers," it went through several editions and was used widely in Germany and abroad. In Japan it was introduced from the 1870s, when the imperial court musicians started learning Western instruments and used it at the Music Investigation Committee.[217] Perhaps the violin tutor was also used by Mason himself, whose *Music Course* was based on Hohmann's singing course.

No sooner had Suzuki graduated than he was sent with a fellow student, Yamada Gen'ichirō to teach a summer course for school teachers in Chiba Prefecture, just north of Tokyo. The two were selected because they were among the few who played the violin, and organs were still virtually non-existent in provincial schools.[218] In August 1888 Suzuki was appointed to teach at the Normal School of Kanagawa Prefecture in Yokohama. During his time there he studied with the Australian Emily Patton (1831–1912), who arrived in 1889 and immediately established classes introducing Tonic sol-fa. Suzuki began publishing music books, including a translation of John Curwen's *How to Read Music* in 1897.[219] In 1892 Suzuki was awarded an elementary certificate and one in elementary theory from the Tonic sol-fa College in London issued by Patton, as the only Japanese candidate.[220] He had already left Yokohama in December 1889 to teach at the First Higher Middle School. From 1893 to 1904 Suzuki taught theory of music and composition at the Tokyo Academy of Music. He also taught at the Tokyo Higher Normal College, at the Tokyo School of Foreign Languages, and from 1904, at Tokyo

College for the Blind. In 1910 he published a text on Braille music notation, which is based on similar principles to Tonic sol-fa. Forty years later Wanami Takayoshi (b. 1945), the first blind violinist to win international acclaim, was one of many blind musicians who benefited from the pioneering work of Suzuki and others around the turn of the century when he studied Braille as a child. Suzuki's pioneering work even extended beyond Japan. After the Sino–Japanese War ended in 1895, Chinese students came to Japan in increasing numbers, many of them to train as teachers. Suzuki taught music to several groups of them and helped with the compilation of suitable song collections in Chinese. In 1906–07 he travelled to China himself to study the state of education there.

After his return, in 1907, Suzuki founded his own school, the Music College of the East (Tōyō Ongaku Gakkō), which produced its first graduates in 1910. Suzuki's school was in many ways more liberal than the Tokyo Academy of Music: not only was Suzuki open to a variety of musical styles; he also accepted that his students had to broaden their interests in order to make a living in music. He began to cooperate with the Oriental Steamship Company to secure jobs for his graduates on the

5: Suzuki Yonejirō (middle row, with violin) with the Meiji Music Society.

ocean liners. The first group sailed from Yokohama to San Francisco in 1914. Among the most successful graduates was Hatano Fukutarō (1890–1974), who, with his brother Kōjirō (1893–1946), led the Hatano Orchestra, also known in English as the Hatano Jazz Band, which in different permutations played not only on ocean liners, but in cinemas, hotels and dance halls. Many of the musicians who enjoyed increasing professional opportunities from around the time of the First World War were graduates of Suzuki's school. Significantly, and unlike the Tokyo Academy of Music, the Music College of the East had more male than female students.[221] Suzuki died quite suddenly in 1940, but his school survived him and recovered after the Second World War. In 1969 it was renamed Tokyo College of Music (Tokyo Ongaku Daigaku) and in 1978 it celebrated its seventieth anniversary with a concert tour to America.

Suzuki's fellow student at the Tokyo Academy of Music, Yamada Gen'ichirō (1869–1927), was another pioneer of music education. He composed songs, published instrument tutors and music textbooks as well as journal articles about the importance of music. He was especially active in promoting music education at kindergarten level, music education for women and public performances; he was a founding member of several associations that aimed to stage more concerts. Like Suzuki he founded his own music school, which still exists today as the Japan Music School (Nihon Ongaku Gakkō).

Yamada too was the son of a former samurai of Tokyo.[222] Little is known about his early years; he may have studied some traditional music and learnt the *shamisen*. He enrolled at the Tokyo Academy of Music in 1885 and studied the piano with Uryū Shige and the violin with Sauvlet and Dittrich. At a concert in July 1887 he played a piano arrangement of a movement from a Mozart symphony.[223] He graduated from the specialist department in 1889 at the top of his class. Even before graduation he was sent to teach school teachers in Chiba with Suzuki. After graduation, Yamada continued his studies while working as an assistant teacher at the Academy. He was awarded a teaching licence by the Ministry of Education in 1890, and continued to teach at the Tokyo Academy of Music in different capacities (he was appointed professor in 1899) until 1903, interrupted by a brief spell at the prefectural Normal School in Osaka in 1891–92. He also taught at other schools, public and private, as well as short courses for music teachers. Presumably he used the violin in his teaching, as he and Suzuki had done in Chiba. How much he performed on the violin is hard to know. In November 1893 he played the violin at a concert in aid of flood victims in Okayama Prefecture. In 1896 he played second violin in the string quartet led by Kōda Nobu at the concert to celebrate her return from Europe. By then, however, he appears to have virtually given up performing himself in favour of teaching and organizing musical performances. He helped found and played an active role in several associations to promote music, including the Meiji Music Society (Meiji Ongakukai).

Yamada's most lasting achievements were his contributions to the training of elementary school and kindergarten teachers in expressive play and musical games. In 1901 an earlier initiative was revived as the Association for Musical Games (Ongaku Yūgi Kai), and Yamada became a principal teacher for the Association's short training courses. Incidentally, Suzuki Yonejirō published five volumes of songs for musical games that year. Meanwhile Yamada worked to create a more permanent training course. Kindergarten education was becoming more popular and the demand for kindergarten teachers was rising, but as Yamada well knew, the Tokyo Academy of Music, with artistic as well as pedagogical ambitions, did not train anywhere near enough people to cater for the demand. In 1903 the association was renamed Ongaku Yūgi Kyōkai; Yamada organized a one-year course, which in 1904 moved to permanent premises in the Kanda district of Tokyo. That year he also started the journal *Ongaku shinpō* (Music News), which carried information about the Association's activities and those of the school and its staff; violin teachers included Ōno Umewaka and Takaori Shūichi (see below). The school had a women's division (Joshi Ongaku Gakkō) and a men's division (Nihon Ongaku Kyōkai); Yamada envisaged a co-educational school, but educating both sexes in the same school was still regarded as suspect and he did not receive official permission. Instead, in 1906, he established the Music School for Girls (Joshi Ongaku Gakkō), and continued to teach males separately. Not until 1927, shortly before his death, did he formally receive permission to re-establish his school as a co-educational school named the Japan Music School (Nihon Ongaku Gakkō).[224]

Yamada's importance for the history of violin playing rests on the publication of his *Violin Instruction* in 1892. As we do not know whether

Tsunekawa's violin tutor was ever published, Yamada's work must count as the oldest violin tutor published by a Japanese, followed closely by Suzuki Yonejirō's *Violin Tutor Volume 1*, published in 1893.[225] The two works are quite different in their approach. Yamada's tutor was based on that of Berthold Tours (1838–97), *The Violin* (Novello, London 1874, rev. 1880), to which Yamada added his own explanation for beginners. Yamada begins his preface by praising the qualities of the violin: "Although the world is not lacking in excellent musical instruments, there are few which have such an exceedingly beautiful and elegant tone and exquisite construction as the violin. Because of its excellence and beauty, Europeans name it the king of instruments." The main part (35 pages in all) begins with a brief explanation of the violin's parts using only Japanese terms. The violin and bow hold are described (with drawings) and symbols relating to bowing introduced. Then follows a detailed description of the staff notation system; unlike many later tutors, Yamada's does not include cipher notation. After a series of exercises (four of which are duets) and the introduction of all the keys, there follows a section with 20 pieces, starting with the Japanese national anthem and finishing with "Here Comes the Bride."

Suzuki Yonejirō's tutor, according to his preface, "follows the tutor by Mr. Kurē of England and explains the simplest way to study the violin." Suzuki uses cipher notation, which he describes as the easiest system for reading music. The system is based on Tonic sol-fa, which Suzuki had studied with Emily Patton. Suzuki begins his main part with a brief outline of the violin's history and concludes, "The violin, more than other musical instruments, easily appeals to and expresses the player's heart. Its playing style can be characterized by cheeriness and alacrity, but it can also be played in a solemn, gentle and affective style. Today with good reason it is called the queen among the instruments of the orchestra."[226] The reference to "the queen among the instruments" is unusual, since other tutors of the time, like Yamada's, call it "the king,", although in nineteenth-century Europe, the violin was commonly likened to a woman.

Next, like Yamada, Suzuki describes the parts of the violin; he includes English words for the parts as well as Japanese ones. After a brief discussion of instrument care and strings he explains how to hold the violin and bow (pp. 6–11). The notation system is introduced (pp. 14–18), beginning with a table that includes scales in 13 keys in ciphers; the tonic in C is "1". However, Suzuki then goes on to explain the use of ciphers independently of pitch, with "1" describing the tonic whatever the key. He includes John Curwen's "mental effects" to describe the degrees of the scale, the strong and firm tone for the tonic, the hopeful, rousing tone for the supertonic and so on.[227] A series of 75 exercises (including six Japanese songs from the school song repertoire) follow (pp. 19–59), some with hints for their execution. Because the numbers in Suzuki's system, just like Curwen's sol-fa syllables, do not describe absolute pitch, the key for each piece and the string on which to play the notes are indicated. The advantage for beginners is that if the open string is represented as the tonic, the numbers used to indicate notes on a single string are always the same and correspond to the left-hand fingers used to play them. Suzuki's tutor includes hints on how to practise the exercises and even metronome marks for each one. One could assume that his approach made learning the violin more accessible than Yamada's. However, although a tenth printing was published in 1906, no subsequent volumes appeared, despite the book being described as "volume 1."

Yamada published a second violin tutor, *How to Play the Violin*, in 1922. The preface makes no mention of his previous work, and *How to Play the Violin* is obviously no mere revision of *Violin Instruction*.[228] It has 62 pages; the violin and bow hold are explained in more detail, and many of the practice pieces and songs come with explanations. Yamada does not include an explanation of staff notation, perhaps because he could assume that most people using the work would know it. Unlike in his earlier work, however, he includes cipher notation (with "1" designating the tonic) as well as staff notation. Most of the pieces are songs from the government-issued song books for elementary and middle schools. By the time Yamada published his second violin tutor, numerous others had appeared, as we will see in the next chapter.

Yamada and Suzuki were remarkable in that they did not come from musical families. Admittedly we know little about their early years, but there is nothing to make their choice of a musical career seem an obvious one. In this they are different from the many pioneers of Western music who came from *gagaku* families. Musicians from the imperial court were among the earliest teachers at the Tokyo Academy of Music and their offspring often graduated from there.

One of them was Ōno Umewaka (1869–1920), who graduated from the Tokyo Academy of Music in 1892. His most famous achievement is the "Railway Song," published in 1900, which he composed together with Ue Sanemichi, another court musician; its opening bars still signal the closing doors of trains on the JR Tōkaidō Line from Tokyo to Kyoto. He published another early violin tutor, *Vaiorin Shohō* with the English title, *The Viorin Tutor for Beginner [sic]*, in 1899. In his preface Ōno praises the qualities of the violin in almost the same words as Yamada in 1892. He seems to have written his tutor, which he says is based on extracts from several Western publications, with school teachers in mind. There was still a dearth of tutors for beginners, Ōno pointed out, and many beginners played out of tune with irregular bowing and bad posture. His own tutor follows a common pattern, introducing the parts of the violin, explaining the violin and bow hold and the staff notation system and containing exercises and *shōka* songs.[229] At the time Ōno was teaching music in and around Osaka; a report in *Ongaku zasshi* in June 1894 noted that the violin was becoming popular and that Ōno was keeping busy with over 30 male and female pupils at the Normal College.[230] He also used the violin to teach singing, and at Osaka Middle School his pupils included the future musicologist Tanabe Hisao, who took up the violin himself.[231] Ōno Umewaka taught at the Tokyo Academy of Music from 1901 to 1903.

Another member of the Ōno family of *gagaku* musicians was Ōno Hisaharu (1884–1931).[232] His father Ōno Hisayori (1850–1924) had been among the first court musicians to study Western music and was appointed professor at the Music Investigation Committee in 1883, where he taught violin. Hisaharu was at first apprenticed into the family profession. In 1901 he enrolled in the Tokyo Academy of Music. He studied violin with Andō Kō and the *gagaku* department's foreign violin teacher Wilhelm Dubravcic. As a student his performances attracted praise from the critics. He had studied the violin before enrolling at the Academy, and so had an early start by the standards of his day and performed better than others of his generation.[233] At his graduation he played an unspecified concerto by Charles-Auguste de Bériot (A minor?) to considerable acclaim.[234] After graduating he became assistant professor in 1908 while continuing his studies at the research department and remained on the staff until 1930. In 1909 he also rejoined the *gagaku* department. That year he and three other Academy graduates formed what is believed to be the first all-Japanese regular string quartet, although it was short-lived, since it only existed until the following year, when Ōno himself and Yamada Kōsaku, the cellist, left for Berlin.[235] The magazine *Ongakukai* reported that at their concert on 30 January 1909 they played for an audience of 600. The programme included Beethoven's Allegro con Brio (from Op. 18.4?), a Haydn Allegro (unspecified), an Aria by Bach, a Molto Allegro by Mozart (fourth movement of KV 387?) and Haydn's "Emperor" Quartet, but also other items, including a violin concerto by de Bériot, played by Ōno. At its other concerts, the quartet likewise played single movements rather than an entire work and included other types of works.[236] Presumably neither players nor audience were up to an entire evening devoted exclusively to music for string quartets.

In Berlin, Ōno's teacher at the conservatoire was Willy Hess, a pupil of Joachim who had just been appointed, and whose students at the time included Georg Kulenkampff. Ōno actually performed together with Kulenkampff at the conservatoire's concert on 31 January 1914, playing fourth violin in Niels Gade's Octet, while Kulenkampff played first.[237] Returning to Japan in 1914, Ōno was appointed professor at the Tokyo Academy of Music in 1915. He concentrated on teaching rather than performing, but he played in the Academy's orchestra and performed occasionally as a soloist and chamber musician; his repertoire included the Bruch Concerto in G minor and Vieuxtemps' Concerto Op. 31 and the *Fantasia Appassionata* Op. 35. He played César Franck's Sonata on 16 November 1916 when the emperor visited the Academy, and the following May he again performed in front of the emperor at the residence of the Shimazu family (the former rulers of Satsuma domain), this time as part of a string quartet. More than once in the 1920s he performed the Bach Double Concerto with Andō Kō.[238] Ōno's private violin students included Sumi Saburō, one of Japan's leading teachers of the twentieth century (see Part 2 Chapter 4).

Ōno Hisaharu's students at the Tokyo Academy included Rudolf Dittrich's son Mori Otto (1893–1986), who also studied with his father's former pupil Andō Kō and graduated in 1917.[239] While continuing his studies as a postgraduate, Mori coached student ensembles. Conscripted for military service and sent to Korea, he was lucky enough to obtain a teaching job at a local primary school and several performing opportunities, thus becoming one of the Japanese who helped spread Western music in Korea. After returning to Japan he taught at the Yamanashi Prefecture Normal College. In 1940 he returned to Tokyo, where he continued to teach and perform. He could often be heard on the radio. Particularly interested in teaching children, he composed children's songs and published one of the first violin tutors especially for children.[240] After the war, he took over a Suzuki violin studio in Tokyo, where his pupils included the future virtuoso Wanami Takayoshi.

In the Kansai region, pioneering violinists included Ōmura Josaburō (1869–1952), a pioneer of the flute as well as the violin.[241] Although not from one of the old *gagaku* families, he apprenticed into the court music department as a player of the *hichiriki* (double-reed pipe) from the age of ten and was employed there until 1905. In 1887 he was ordered to study Western music as well, and in 1898 he became the first formally appointed teacher of the flute at the Tokyo Academy of Music, where he remained until 1905. In 1906 Ōmura moved to Osaka, where he taught at the Sōai Girls' High School (today Sōai Gakuen) which opened music school that year, as well as the Osaka Girls' School of Music and the Osaka Metropolitan School for the Blind. He frequently played the violin at concerts in the Kansai area (only two flute performances are recorded) and conducted ensembles. His fellow-promoters of Western music included Nagai Kōji (1874–1965), who had graduated from the Tokyo Academy of Music in 1896 and likewise moved to Osaka in 1906. As Nagai later recalled, there was still very little Western music in the area at the time.[242] Nagai immediately set to work, establishing the Osaka Music Association with an orchestra consisting of members of the military band and people who advertised themselves as violin teachers, with Ōmura as the leader. The level of the string players was appalling; most could not even read music, but eventually their playing improved (the hopeless ones dropped out), and their first concert was a success. In 1915 Nagai founded the private Osaka School of Music (Ōsaka Ongaku Gakkō, since 1958 Ōsaka Ongaku Daigaku), the first music college in the Kansai area, and Ōmura became one of the teachers.

As a performer Ōmura played mainly short pieces, including Johan Svendsen's *Romance*,[243] and he often performed in ensembles with *koto*, playing Japanese pieces for which he also published sheet music (see following chapter).[244] He also took an active part in various initiatives to assemble orchestras in the Kansai area, and conducted a student ensemble at Kyoto Imperial University, the nucleus of the future Kyoto University Symphony Orchestra. He was still active on the musical scene in the war years when he was in his seventies.[245]

Perhaps one of the most colourful, if short-lived violinists of this early period was Takaori Shūichi or Biō (? –1919); he was most probably the first Japanese violinist to perform publicly for money in America. Not much seems to be known about him, however. He graduated from the Tokyo Academy of Music in 1900. The programme of the graduation concert does not name any graduates who played in ensembles, while solo performances were mainly given by teachers: Koeber, Junker, and Kōda Nobu. From 1901 to 1905, Takaori and an earlier graduate of the Academy, Iwamoto Shōji, published the magazine *Ongaku no tomo* (Friend of Music). Takaori and Iwamoto also cooperated to promote the harmonization of Western and Japanese music, known at the time as *wayō chōwa gaku* (see following chapter). In addition, Takaori offered his services as a violin teacher; he is listed as one of the teachers on the programme offered by Yamada Gen'ichirō for the Association for Musical Games, and in 1904, *Ongaku no tomo* carried an advertisement for a "Takaori Music Studio" in the Kanda district of Tokyo.[246] In the same issue, however, the editors announced that Takaori, "the well-known young musician," was leaving the country to study in America and Europe for three years. He and Iwamoto left in April the following year. With virtually no money they travelled to Hawaii and North America, planning to live by performing. The timing was auspicious, Japan having just won the war against Russia. In November 1905 the pair gave a violin and piano recital as well as a performance in Japanese costume with Takaori playing the *shamisen* at a meeting of the National Society of New England Women; the programme included a lecture entitled, "Why Japan was victorious in the late war."[247] Presumably, however, they soon realized that their standard of playing was hardly in the league of world class performers, having had the chance to hear Eugène Ysaÿe and Ignacy Paderewski. In any case, Takaori later reported that, while in America, he turned away from attempting to disseminate his brand of Japanese music and concentrated his efforts on the study of Western music and conducting.[248]

Information about Takaori's life is patchy, but some can be glimpsed from his reports in the magazine *Ongakukai* (Music World), the first issue of which was published in January 1908. *Ongakukai* succeeded both *Ongaku no tomo* (which in 1905 had been re-named *Ongaku*) and *Ongaku shinpō*. The editors included Iwamoto and Takaori, and the magazine boasted an office in New York, presumably headed by Takaori. *Ongakukai* regularly carried reports of Takaori's feats abroad as well as those of his wife Sumiko, who had studied singing at the Tokyo Academy of Music. She did not graduate, but accompanied Takaori to America, where she took lessons from the famous singer Geraldine Farrar (1882–1967), then engaged at the Metropolitan Opera.[249] Soon Sumiko was performing herself, and by 1911 *Ongakukai* could report that she was more famous than her husband, who had reportedly spent the previous summer giving violin performances in over 60 hotels in New England and earning substantial sums of money.[250] In September 1911 Sumiko became the first Japanese to perform at the Met in a matinee performance of *Madame Butterfly*, although most probably in a silent role.[251] Mostly, however, she performed in vaudeville theatres, her husband acting as her musical director and as conductor. In 1910 an advertisement for an "entertainment for the benefit of the Woman's Municipal League" in the *New York Times* announced that "the Japanese Orchestra, under the leadership of Prof. Takaori, will play."[252] In an advertisement for a performance at Chase's in Washington he was described as "the Celebrated Director B.S. Takaori of the Imperial Opera House," who was to conduct "Alexander's Ragtime Band," while his wife was billed as "Madame Sumiko, the Famous Prima Donna Soprano of the Imperial Opera House, Tokio." The advertisement also promised "geisha girls, rickshaw runners etc.," suggesting that the event was to be an exotic spectacle rather than a significant musical event.[253] Like Miura Tamaki of *Madame Butterfly* fame and the geisha-turned-actress Kawakami Sadayakko, "Madame Sumiko" successfully capitalized on Western audiences' fascination with Far Eastern exoticism.

In December 1912 the couple left New York for Europe on the ocean liner *Finland*. The April issue of *Ongakukai* published Takaori's account of his voyage from New York and arrival in Berlin.[254] On Christmas Day a concert was held and Takaori was asked to conduct an orchestra consisting of the ship's ten musicians and 46 musicians among the passengers (his report included the programme). The audience included the deputy director of the famous Wintergarten Varieté theatre in Berlin, who telegraphed his director and secured Takaori an engagement for 30 December (the *Ongakukai* issue included a photograph of the Wintergarten and a copy of a newspaper cutting advertising a performance by Sumiko in a variety show). The couple remained in Berlin for about two months, then spent about a month in Hamburg, where they likewise performed; on 1 April they continued via Cologne (from where they visited Bonn, including Beethoven's birthplace) to Paris; *Ongakukai* published Takaori's reports from all these cities. In May 1913 the couple returned to Tokyo.[255] After their return, Takaori directed two operatic works at the Imperial Theatre, the only two works at the time not directed by the Italian Rossi.[256]

Soon the Takaoris were planning a second trip to America, this time accompanied by a troupe of Japanese performers with four female dancers (having advertised for chorus girls in *Ongakukai)*. They set off in autumn 1914 and after initial setbacks made a success of the venture, at least according to *Ongakukai*. American critics, although they enjoyed the exotic settings, could be scathing of the musical qualities of their performance. A reviewer for the *San Francisco Chronicle* (21 August 1916) enjoyed the four dancing girls, but was less than impressed with the Takaoris' musical accomplishments, remarking that Sumiko sounded "as though a baby voice had somehow found a tune and had whispered it into an old Edison phonograph of twenty years ago, and that then the tone waves had been turned over to the hearer through a telephone with bad connections." He was equally dismissive of Takaori's efforts as a conductor: "A very earnest Japanese gentleman, with white gloves, beat the time and seemed to feel the importance of his position, where Rosner used to be. He was – again to quote the programme – 'the musical director of the Imperial Theater of Tokio.' The Japanese are certainly a wonderful people. Already their musicians, if B.S. Takaori is a sample, have reduced the Occidental art of tone to a mathematical equation. He beat time with grave precision."[257] The troupe returned to Japan in 1917. Takaori had completely exhausted himself during the tour, and Sumiko was pregnant. Nevertheless they soon embarked on another tour to America, this time with girl singers. After their return Takaori's health broke down and he died of consumption in November 1919.[258]

In 1911–12, while still in America, Takaori published a three-part article about the violin in *Ongakukai*. He claimed to have discussed violin playing with Ysaÿe in New York.[259] The first part deals with tuning and maintenance rather than actual playing and includes references to valuable Cremona instruments. In the second part, Takaori discusses bows before presenting selected aspects of playing, based as he says on his own experience, including the merits of performing alone compared to those of playing in an orchestra. In the final part he discusses common mistakes, how to hold the violin, intonation and rhythm and recommends regular study with a teacher. Perhaps Takaori himself would have become an influential teacher (once he settled down), had his early death not cut short his career.

Tanabe Hisao (1883–1984), on the other hand, had a long and varied career, although not primarily as a violinist.[260] He played the violin enthusiastically in his youth, but later his enthusiasm for Western music faded and he gave it up. The memoirs he wrote towards the end of his long life give a wealth of detail on musical life in the late nineteenth and early twentieth centuries. Unlike many members of the musical establishment in Tokyo, Tanabe was open to all kinds of musical expression; perhaps having spent his teenage years in Osaka had something to do with it. The merchant city was known for its openness to musical innovation, including playing *shamisen* and *koto* music on Western instruments. Tanabe first encountered a violin in the hands of his music teacher at middle school in Osaka, like many of his contemporaries must have done. Ōno Umewaka used the violin to teach singing, and Tanabe was so attracted by the instrument that he wanted to learn it himself. His father agreed to buy him a violin if he did well in his other studies, and so at the age of about 15, he started to learn, practising alone in a storehouse at night until his fingers bled. After graduating from middle school he went to Tokyo in 1900 to prepare for the entrance examination to the First High School. He immediately looked for a violin teacher and found a sign advertising violin lessons given by Ōno Tadamoto (1869–1921); Ōno, another court musician and a graduate of the Tokyo Academy (where from 1898 he taught the horn and conducted research into *gagaku*), and his colleagues had just opened a studio for private pupils. Ōno was a strict teacher who hit his students' legs with his bow. He paid much attention to posture, and Tanabe practised while observing his shadow on a paper *shōji* door. In 1901 he enrolled in the First High School. It had a thriving band, in which he played as the only violinist. He took lessons from Ōmura Josaburō, who apparently was more patient than Ōno. Some of Tanabe's fellow students made fun of him: playing the violin was still regarded as a feminine occupation.[261]

While at high school, in 1903 Tanabe enrolled in the elective course (*senka*) for violin at the Tokyo Academy of Music. His first teacher was Ishino Gi (1876–1942), who taught violin there from 1900 to 1906 and in 1907 published a volume of études for the violin.[262] Tanabe studied the third volume of Hohmann's *Practical Violin Method* and Kaiser's études as well as short pieces. He gave his first performance at an Academy concert in May 1904, playing a romance by Rieding, an experience he recalled as terrifying.[263] He continued his studies at the Academy throughout his high school years and as a student at the Imperial University of Tokyo from 1904 to 1909. His teacher was Tanomogi Koma, and occasionally he had lessons from August Junker.

While studying at the Academy, Tanabe played in the orchestra; at the first desk sat the Kōda sisters, while the second violins were led by Ōno Hisaharu and Yamanoi Motokiyo (1885–1970), who taught violin at the Academy from 1908 to 1914. Tanabe also played solos at the regular concerts by the students of the elective; after the Rieding he performed a Barcarole by Friedrich Ernst Fesca, duets by Ignaz Pleyel, a concerto by Hans Sitt, and, in 1907, an Air Varié by Charles Dancla. That year Tanabe graduated from Tokyo Imperial University and became a researcher at the Institute for Research into Japanese Music (Hōgaku Kenkyūsho) established by the physicist and musicologist Tanaka Shōhei (1862–1945) in his own home. Increasingly drawn into researching Japanese music, Tanabe left the orchestra. For 30 years he taught history of music at Suzuki Yonejirō's Tōyō School of Music. He subsequently travelled all over Japan and on the Asian mainland to record folk music and published widely on Japanese and Asian Music. In 1936 he established the Society for the Research of Asiatic Music, Tōyō Ongaku Gakkai, which from 1937 published its own journal.[264] He began to practise various forms of Japanese music and dance, and today his name is mainly associated with traditional Japanese music.

The violinists of the first generation, if they did not come from *gagaku* families, tended to come from samurai families or the more well-to-do families of townspeople. These were also the groups who benefited most from new educational opportunities in general, but because music was not considered a suitable occupation for men, many of the early music students were women. Except for the Kōda sisters, most students of the violin did not reach a high standard of performance and, apart from Takaori, who died young, they soon concentrated their efforts on teaching and the dissemination of Western music in general. The violinists whose lives I have examined all made music their career in some way. But the late Meiji period also saw the proliferation of amateur enthusiasts. Unfortunately we do not know too much about individual amateurs, unless they were also writers (see following chapter). By the early twentieth century the violin had become so popular that newspapers and magazines identified a "violin boom."

## 6. The Early Twentieth-Century Violin Boom

"These days the violin is hugely popular in Osaka," remarked *Ongaku shinpō* (Music News) in September 1907. In January that year another magazine, *Ongaku sekai* (The World of Music), had already described the violin as the most widely played instrument; and several other newspapers and magazines that year also mentioned its popularity.[265] Many of them published articles about the violin; some introduced famous violinists like Paganini and Sarasate and legendary makers like Stradivari, while others provided instructions on how to play the violin.

School teachers and Suzuki's cheap instruments brought violins to ever remoter parts of the country. To be sure, schools bought reed organs as soon as they could afford them, and well-qualified teachers were still hard to find. Nevertheless, for many Japanese, like Tanabe Hisao, the violin in the hands of a school teacher must have represented their first encounter with Western music. For people who could afford one, the violin became an attractive object, at once pleasingly exotic and reassuringly familiar in its similarity to the *kokyū*, Japan's only native bowed lute, and the Chinese fiddles of the popular *minshingaku*. One of the earliest newspaper advertisements for a violin appears on a page with advertisements for factory machines, umbrellas and top hats.[266] From around 1890, individual musicians, many of them graduates from the Tokyo Academy of Music or veterans of the military bands, began to

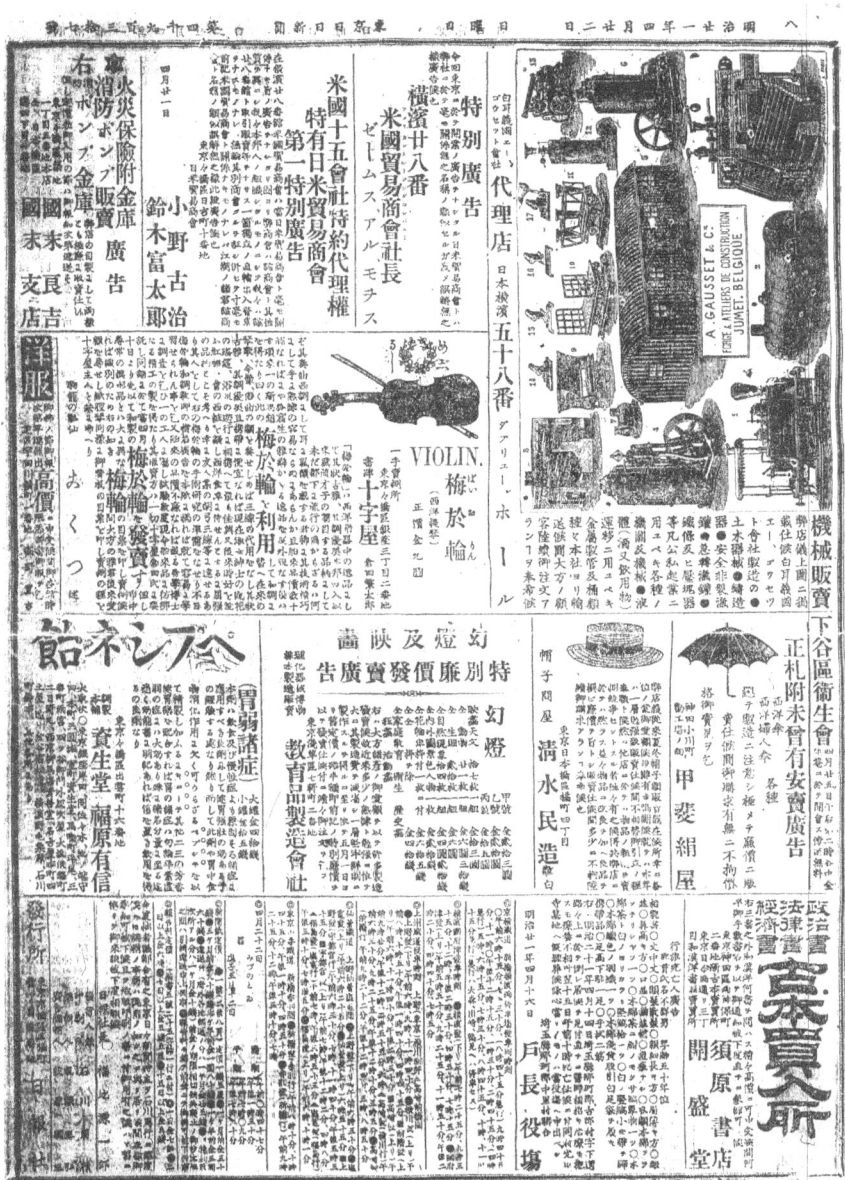

6: Page from *Tōkyō nichinichi shinbun,* 22 April 1888, one of the first mentions of the violin in a newspaper, advertising violins together with other achievements of Western civilization.

establish private music courses or give individual lessons. In Sendai in the north, graduates of the Tokyo Academy of Music established the Tōhoku Academy of Music, and one of them reportedly also taught the violin in his home. In the 1890s and early 1900s, at least nine teachers offered music courses in Osaka, four in Kobe, and five in Kyoto. From around 1907, advertisements for violin studios in Osaka, Kobe, Kyoto, and Wakayama appear in the newspapers.[267]

We can glimpse something of the progress of music education outside Tokyo from reports in the music journals, written by local teachers or correspondents connected with the journal. Music instruction spread gradually from the town and city schools to the more rural schools and from the teacher training colleges and the girls' schools to the higher and the lower elementary schools, and finally to middle schools. Much depended on the arrival of a qualified teacher, ideally a graduate of the Tokyo Academy of Music, or on the appointment of a head teacher or a local governor who appreciated the importance of music education. In Niigata Prefecture, for example, singing in schools improved after Ishihara Shigeo came as a teacher; a report in 1894 states that singing was now taught in all schools and schools were beginning to buy organs.[268] In 1898 another active teacher, Irie Kōjirō, was appointed, followed by more teachers. Irie reported in 1901 that the teacher training college in Takada had lacked a qualified teacher until the recent appointment of a music graduate from Tokyo, Chikamori Dekiji. Irie, who had travelled throughout the prefecture, observed a marked difference between districts close to towns, railway stations, and steamboat stops, and remoter parts of the prefecture. In the former, singing in schools had progressed and usually took place in a music room with a Yamaha organ (five octaves). But in the latter many elementary schools had no organ, and teachers were often ignorant of Western music.[269] The teachers at the prefectural colleges, including Irie himself, taught intensive courses, often organized by the district governors; in Mishima County in Niigata Prefecture, for example, they took place in 1902 and 1903, until which time inspectors reported that even songs like the national anthem, "Kimi ga yo," were not generally known.[270]

On the other hand, a city's or town's musical life could suffer when an enthusiastic teacher left, as we saw (in the previous chapter) from the example of Tsunekawa Ryōnosuke's departure from Nagoya. Nagoya provides a good example of how local musical associations or study groups promoted music. Music teachers and influential locals, including Suzuki Masakichi (who after all had a business interest in the promotion of Western music), organized the Nagoya Music Association in 1895, which gave its first concert in December.[271] The programme comprised a mixture of genres, and Suzuki himself took part in a performance of a *nagauta* (traditional song to *shamisen* accompaniment), playing the violin.[272] In 1902 he published his own violin tutor, *Vwaiorin dokushūsho* (A self-study manual for the violin), although most of it may have been written by his former mentor Tsunekawa, who is named as a reviewer.[273] The concert was typical in that it featured a mixture of Japanese and Western music. Nagoya was a stronghold of traditional Japanese music and is so to this day, but Western music continued to gain ground, not least due to the presence of Suzuki Violins, as a report in 1908 illustrates. In addition to Suzuki, this report also mentions the activities of a former navy band musician, Mita Masami, who had taught over 100 pupils at his studio, Mita Ongakuin.[274] According to an earlier report he encouraged his pupils to play Japanese pieces and even published suitable sheet music.[275] But despite this evidence of lively musical activity, the lack of qualified teachers in Nagoya was lamented as late as 1909.[276]

Nagoya also benefited from concerts by visiting musicians from the Tokyo Academy of Music, as it was easily accessible from Tokyo and on the way to the centres Kyoto, Osaka and Kobe. In April 1908 the violinists August Junker, Kōda (probably Nobu), Heydrich and Werkmeister performed a programme that included a Haydn string quartet.[277] In cities like Kobe and Nagasaki, the presence of foreigners increased the opportunities for Japanese to listen to and sometimes study Western music, although as the author of a report from Kobe points out, not all foreigners excelled as performers.[278]

Several reports list the available musical instruments in schools, mostly organs and violins. Clearly, most schools, even rural elementary schools, aimed to have at least one organ, and purchasing an organ, sometimes with the help of donations, was easier than obtaining qualified teachers. At least in the 1890s, though, many schools had no organ. A report from Fukui Prefecture stated that although the schools in urban areas all had organs, if all the schools in the prefecture were taken together, only about a quarter did.[279] A teacher reporting from Nara Prefecture in 1896 wrote that, when he arrived, the concertina was popular and even used for teaching music, until he explained that it was unsuitable. Now schools that could not afford an organ used the violin to teach music.[280] By the 1890s the violin may well have been the most

widely visible and audible Western instrument, because of its role in the
public education system. Students and intellectuals, including writers,
took up the violin, and it features in several literary works of the time.[281]

Famous literary writers who studied and played the violin at least for
a short time included Shimazaki Tōson and Ishikawa Takuboku.
Shimazaki Tōson began to play the violin while working in Sendai as a
teacher in 1896. He borrowed an instrument from a girl called Kiku in his
lodgings, who was studying with a graduate of the Tokyo Academy and
a pioneer of Western music in the region. Returning to Tokyo in 1897,
Shimazaki bought his own violin and enrolled in the extramural course
of the Tokyo Academy.[282] Ishikawa Takuboku borrowed a violin from a
fellow student while he was enrolled at Morioka Middle School from
1898. He later bought a violin for his wife-to-be, Setsuko, who had learnt
to play as a student at Morioka Girls' School, which she attended from
1899 to 1902. The Ishikawas loved the violin so much that they even
hung on to their instrument when poverty forced them to sell most of
their valuables.[283] Natsume Sōseki, although he did not play himself,
wrote about Western music as a symbol of modern times in several of
his works, most famously in *I am a Cat,* where he has one of the
characters, the professor Mizushima Kangetsu, tell the story of how he
bought and began to play his first violin, going to absurd lengths to avoid
detection and ridicule.[284] The model for Mizushima, Torada Terahiko
(1876–1935), was a much more interesting person and a writer in his
own right, as well as a notable physicist and an amateur musician for
whom the violin meant more than a passing fad (see Part 3 Chapter 5).

Well may a young man have feared ridicule: despite its popularity with
young intellectuals, the violin was generally perceived chiefly as an
instrument for women, and in literary works the violin as often as not
features in the hands of young women.[285] The violin was taught in schools
for girls, even before it was formally introduced into the curriculum for
girls' high schools in 1911; at the Tokyo High School for Girls it became
an elective subject for girls as early as 1887 with five weekly lessons.[286]
While in the previous era, young girls from the townspeople's class learnt
the *shamisen* to enhance their employability in samurai families, where
skilled performance could enhance their prospects to rise above their
social class, by the turn of the century playing a musical instrument had
become a desirable accomplishment for Western-style domesticity, and

carrying a violin (playing it was less important) projected a pleasing image of modern sophistication.[287]

Amateur activities, especially those that took place in the provinces, were often viewed with suspicion by commentators from the capital. The musical establishment in Tokyo, although keen to promote the practice of Western music as part of the government's campaign to civilize and enlighten the people, nevertheless displayed a condescending if not downright contemptuous attitude in their reports about musical life in Osaka, the city of merchants. An article in the *Ōsaka asahi* newspaper in 1909, for example, described a boom in violin lessons. For women, wrote the author, the violin competed with the *koto* as a desirable accomplishment for marriage. The most popular teacher was Kōga Musen (Ryōtarō), who had come to Osaka in 1888 with the band of the army's fourth division. Kōga believed that people would take pleasure in playing the violin if, rather than struggling with Western pieces, they learnt familiar Japanese tunes. He taught his students to play the violin kneeling on the floor in Japanese style, so that they could comfortably join in an ensemble with *koto* and *shamisen* in the home. Another commentator, in *Ongakukai* (Music World) in 1910, called taste in Western music of the people of Osaka superficial and childish compared to Tokyo; people treated the violin as a variant of the *kokyū* and played popular *koto* pieces on it. All *koto* teachers now had to teach the violin and taught Japanese music, taking payment for each new piece they taught. Others played Japanese pieces on the piano. The businesspeople of Osaka, the author speculated, did not want anything too demanding after a long working day. Thus, he lamented, the violin and the piano, the flowers of Western music, were abused.[288]

Abuse or no, playing Japanese traditional music, mostly *koto* and *shamisen* pieces, on the violin was so popular that for a while it looked as if the violin might truly "go native" as it were, taking up a firm place in the traditional repertoire (as it has done in Southern India and Iran and parts of the Arab world). The critics in Tokyo dubbed the practice of playing native tunes on the violin in a Japanese-style ensemble "Osaka-style," but it was not limited to Osaka at all, as concert programmes from many parts of the country show. Perhaps the sheer number of concerts in the Kyoto, Osaka and Kobe area made the Japanese pieces conspicuous in that particular part of the country; we have programmes of 405 concerts and 1,737 pieces including violins advertised between 1890 and 1912. Of these pieces, 512 were Japanese and 880 were Western; the rest are of unknown origin. At first the Japanese pieces were mainly played by violin solo or ensemble, but from about 1903, ensembles including the *koto* or the *shamisen* gained popularity.[289] The music magazines report similar performances from all over Japan; we have already seen an example from Nagoya, and a recent publication about musical life in Niigata lists numerous programmes of similarly eclectic concerts.[290] A concert in Maebashi in Gumma Prefecture, organized by the local branch of the Association for Music in the Home in May 1909, likewise featured a mixed programme. The third part consisted of popular Japanese pieces:

*First Part:*
1. Mixed ensemble (only violinists named):
"Kimi ga yo" (Japanese national anthem, arr. Peri[291]); Russian national anthem; Russian march
2. (Violin?) duet: Pleyel, Allegro Moderato
3. Violin trio: Aria from Weber's *Freischütz*
4 Violin quartet: Bortniansky, "Du Hirte Israels" (Thou Shepherd of Israel); "Glory to God in the Highest"[292]
5. Violin Solo (with accompaniment): Bach, Gavotte; Händel, Largo

*Second part*
6. Violin quartet: Schumann, "Träumerei"; Silcher, "Waldhorn: German folk song"[293]
7. Violin solo (with organ accompaniment): Martini[294], Gavotte; Chopin, Nocturne; Haydn, Serenade

*Third part*
8. Violin ensemble: *Kumoi Rokudan no shirabe* (Study in six steps, Kumoi version); *Chidori no kyoku (ikutaryū)* (Song of the plovers, Ikuta style); *Genroku hanami odori (nagauta)* (Blossom-viewing dance from the Genroku period)
9. Violin ensemble: *Haru no kyoku* (Spring piece); *Hototogisu* (Japanese cuckoo); *Chaondo (ikutaryū)* (Tea ceremony song, Ikuta style)
10. Violin and *shamisen* ensemble: *Nagauta Tsurukame* (The crane and the tortoise)

11. (Violin and *shamisen* ensemble?) *Nagauta Kanjinchō* (The subscription list)[295]

A concert in Sendai by the Tōhoku Music Academy (Tōhoku Ongakuin) in December 1912 featured a similarly mixed programme, with the following items of popular Japanese pieces:

3. One *koto*, two *shamisen*, three violins (title not specified)
7. *Shakuhachi*, violin, *shamisen*: *Nagauta Echigo jishi* (Echigo lion dance)
9. *Shamisen*, violin: *Harusame* (Spring rain)
13. *Shakuhachi*, two violins (or violin and *koto*): *Shōjō tsuru* (The crane on the pine tree)
17. *Shakuhachi*, *shamisen*, violin: *Chidori* (Plovers)
20. Violin and *shamisen*: *Kokaji* (The little swordsmith)
23. *Koto*, *shakuhachi*, violin: *Hagi no tsuyu* (Dew on the bush clover)[296]

How did the violinists learn? Some may have done so in the traditional way described in the report about Osaka; learning by ear from a teacher whom they paid for each piece of music they learnt. Teachers, however, were in short supply outside the big cities. Of course some players may well have picked up the tunes without a teacher, by listening to other musicians. But for those who could not or would not learn that way, help was at hand. As Mita in Nagoya did, other enterprising musicians published sheet music of traditional pieces transcribed into staff notation. Some were for a variety of instruments, others were explicitly for the violin and included fingering instructions. For example, Kōga Musen, the popular Osaka teacher, published a 13-volume series of transcribed *koto* pieces for the violin. Another avid promoter of Japanese music played on the violin was the *shakuhachi* player Nakao Tozan (1876–1956), the founder of the Tozan school of *shakuhachi*. From 1906 he published a series of 31 pieces for violin, starting with the *koto* piece *Song of the Plovers*. Besides his own name, this edition lists Kōga Musen and two other violinists as co-editors. Somewhat unusually for his time, Tozan also published Western pieces for the *shakuhachi*. One of Tozan's *shakuhachi* tutors includes a picture of a *shakuhachi* player standing (rather than kneeling Japanese style) and using a music stand.[297]

7: Example of sheet music with staff notation for a famous *koto* piece, *Yajio jishi,*
published in staff notation for violin: two versions edited by Machida Ōen
(Tokyo, 1918; left) and Nakao Tozan (Osaka, 1908; right).

It was not just good business sense that motivated these and similar publications. Some musicians had a mission. They saw playing Japanese music on Western instruments as a first step to playing Western instrumental music. Some even strove to develop a completely new style of music combining the best of Japanese and Western music. They hoped to "harmonize Japanese and Western music" by studying both and taking the best features of each in order to create an ideal music. Two particularly active promoters of this idea were Iwamoto Shōji and Takaori Shūichi, who expressed their views in their publication of the sheet music for a *nagauta* piece called *Aki no irokusa,* which they translated as "Autumn Leaves," in 1904. In the preface, Iwamoto extolled the beautiful elements of Japanese music and the way it suited the Japanese's sensibilities. By publishing the best examples in Western notation he hoped to promote its study. Takaori, who completed the transcription, even included an English translation of his own preface:

The musical world of our country, which is in a state of revolution and transition, is busily occupied in producing various kinds of new tunes and airs, all of which unfortunately lack refined taste and gracefulness. If left to its own course, our music will lapse into a lamentable state. My esteemed friend, Mr. Shōji Iwamoto, recognized the necessity of rescuing our music from this prevailing error by the comparative study and harmonious combination of European and Japanese tunes. Through his encouragement, I have been prompted to make a theoretical study of tunes and harmony of our native music. The result is the publication of this little song, entitled "Akinoirokusa" [sic] (Iinge [sic: Image] of Autumn Flowers). Although it is far from satisfactory both to the public as well as to the composer himself, as it is his maiden effort, yet the author's work would be more than compensated, if this little volume should become the motive of further inquiry into the proper study of our music, and should prove to be the forerunner of a more enlightened, and eventually a more highly perfected musical work in our country.

Iwamoto and Takaori put their ideas into practice at a concert in Shizuoka, on 4 and 5 November 1904, during the Russo–Japanese War, in support of soldiers' families.[298] While the mixed programme was not unusual, advertising the Japanese titles as "music harmonizing Japanese and Western styles" was. In addition to *Aki no irokusa* for violin and piano, the programme included some of the most popular Japanese pieces: *Rokudan* (Six steps) for piano ensemble with Takaori Shūichi and two other performers; *Tsurukame* (The crane and the tortoise) for violin and piano; *Yajio jishi* (Lion of eight thousand generations) for violin and piano; and *Kanjinchō* (The subscription list) for two pianists. Takaori performed again (in *Rokudan* and *Aki no irokusa*) at a similar concert in Tokyo.[299] Shortly after, he left for America to study music.[300]

Another propagator of harmonizing Japanese and Western music was Machida Ōen (?–1928). Not only did he publish popular Japanese pieces which included fingering instructions for the violin; he also wrote self-study manuals for various instruments and at least three violin tutors.[301] The first one, *Vaiorin dokushū jizai* (Learning the violin in free self-study), published in 1908, resembled other tutors published at the time. After extolling the virtues of the violin, Machida introduced its construction and parts and discussed accessories, including the pitch pipe; then he explained how to tune the violin and how to hold the violin and bow. In his treatment of notation, Machida referred to the names of the notes on the *shamisen*. Like one or two other authors of violin books, Machida used cipher notation throughout the book, which may have been familiar to some of his readers through singing lessons at school. The numbers refer to degrees of the scale, as in fixed sol-fa. The practice tunes consisted of both Western and Japanese pieces.

Machida's second tutor, *(Hōgaku sokusei) Vaiorin tebiki* (A short course of Japanese music for the violin), published in 1913, was unique in that it advertised itself as a violin tutor specifically for Japanese music. This time Machida used staff notation. In the preface he recommends playing Japanese tunes with Western instruments. His explanations of violin playing and musical notation are followed by popular Japanese pieces including *Rokudan* and *Echigo jishi*. But the book concludes with a selection of Western tunes, including "Boat Song" ("Lightly Row"), and "Rose Song" ("The Last Rose of Summer"), as well as several dances. The final page has a short glossary of Western musical terms. So even while promoting his ideal of playing Japanese music on Western instruments Machida seems to be catering to fashion by including the most popular tunes from the school song books.[302]

In 1917 Machida published his third violin tutor, entitled *Vaiorin sokusei yōgaku tebiki*. This one even included an English title page with the following inscription:

"A Short Course for Violin of Western Music
By Owen Machida
Instructor in Uyeno Musical Association of Tokyo
Author of A Short Course for Violin of Japanese Music &&&"

The introductory sections were almost identical to those of his previous book, but the practice pieces are songs from the school song books or famous pieces from the Western repertoire. Again Machida was catering to a prevailing trend, for by then, playing Japanese pieces on the violin had gone out of fashion. In his preface he explained that his earlier book suited the times and enjoyed a good reception. Now, however, times were progressing, the taste for Western music had spread widely and a national music worthy of an advanced country was not far off.

At the height of the violin boom, meanwhile, between 1902 and 1913, at least 14 violin tutors were published (including Machida's two), not counting general books on music with a section on playing the violin.[303] Some of their authors mention in their prefaces that they were responding to a trend. For example, Ōtsuka Torazō, whose violin tutor went through several editions, states in the preface to the seventh edition (1909) that the violin has recently become popular (*ryūkō*) in town and country.[304] The tutors varied in length and detail, but tended to follow the most common pattern already laid out in earlier publications: a description of the violin and its parts as well as the bow, an explanation of how to hold them, an outline of the staff notation system and how to finger the notes, and finally a series of exercises and pieces. Typically the pieces consisted of school textbook songs (*shōka*), marches, dances, and popular melodies, many from symphonies and operas. Several books included a second violin part for at least some of the pieces. Some tutors used cipher notation instead of staff notation, and some included both staff and cipher notation. Clearly, the authors of these publications were trying to make their material accessible to people with little knowledge of Western music, although it is hard to imagine that anyone learnt to play the violin well from them.

Journals carried series on how to play the violin; *Music World* alone published two longer ones, besides Takaori's three-part article mentioned in the previous chapter. Yamanoi Motokiyo (1885–1970), the author of a longer series entitled "How to play and study the violin,"[305] had studied with Wilhelm Dubravcic, August Junker and Kōda Kō. After his graduation from the Tokyo Academy of Music, he taught violin there from 1908 to 1914. He represented the orthodox view of playing the violin, as some of his remarks show. In his explanation of the violin and bow hold, he insisted that the violin should be played standing up or sitting on a chair, never kneeling Japanese style. He spoke scathingly of the way certain contemporaries played the violin. Geisha posing for postcards never held their violins and bows correctly, he maintained. Equally contemptible was the "haikara" ("high collar": faddish in a Westernized style) fashion of playing the violin, supposedly common in the Osaka area, with the bow held around the middle of the stick rather than close to the nut. Yamanoi even coined a special expression for bad players who performed vulgar songs: playing with the words "hakase" (the academic title "Doctor") and "nakaseru" (causing a wailing sound or causing someone to cry), he described such people as "violin nakase" in contrast to the expert, the "violin hakase." The violin, the king of instruments (the Chinese character has the phonetic syllables for "king" printed above it), deserved better, Yamanoi asserted.

Other authors, however, promoted precisely the style Yamanoi so abhorred. Their violin tutors not only included Japanese pieces but also hints on how to perform with ensembles of Japanese instruments. *Violin dokushū no tomo* (Violin: a companion to self-study, 1910) by Fukushima Takurō (1886–1958) has a picture on the cover of two people playing the violin: a man in a suit who is standing and a woman in Japanese dress and sitting Japanese style. Fukushima includes a section on how to tune the violin to a *koto*, *shamisen* or *shakuhachi*. Even more remarkable is the advice given in *Violin kōgiroku* (Violin lecture notes, 1913), a correspondence course. A section entitled "Posture when playing in a Japanese-style room" runs as follows:

When playing together with a *koto* or *shamisen* in a Japanese-style room, it is quite inconsiderate (*fuchōhō*) to play the violin standing straight. In other words, because the *koto* and the *shamisen* are played seated, if the violinist alone plays standing up, then the ensemble fails even before it starts playing. Those who insist on standing up, saying that is how a violin should be played, are unnecessarily inflexible. When people like that happen to play a Japanese piece, they play in a march-like style, turning a gentle and refined *koto* piece into a march and spoiling it completely. A Japanese piece does not require using the bow as harshly as for a Western piece, so it can be played well even sitting down. To play a Japanese piece, one has to play with the frame of mind (*kimochi*) appropriate to a Japanese piece. One does not hear Japanese songs sung as one sings hymns; it is the same thing. And if you fold a floor cushion twice and put it under your behind while you play, it is more comfortable to bow and your feet will not go numb.[306]

The next page carries an illustration of a woman in Japanese dress playing, kneeling on the floor with a low music stand. The caption, besides repeating the advice about the folded cushion, adds that it is alright to lower the violin slightly to look at the music. The book uses both staff and cipher notation, as well as "do re mi" in Japanese syllables.[307] The mention of people who insisted on playing the violin standing up and who treat *koto* pieces like marches is revealing. Perhaps the staff notation of Japanese pieces encouraged march-like playing because of the visual impact of the two- or four-time rhythms and dotted notes. The fact that the first kind of Western instrumental music played in Japan immediately after the enforced opening of the country was military music and that military music was relatively commonly heard might also have caused people to associate playing a Western instrument with a march-like manner. Playing a Western instrument, moreover, was never just about making music. The violin symbolized Western civilization, and, as Yamanoi's remarks show, some took up the violin to appear "high collar," fashionable in a Westernized way. Whether they were conscious of it or not, the violin may even have represented a way for them to physically act out what they saw as Western civilization. Torada Terahiko, the amateur violinist mentioned earlier, seemed to sense the importance of music as a physical activity when he wrote in his diary in 1925, "I believe that Western Music is in part something that is not just savoured with the ear, but with the whole body," and when he waved a baton to a gramophone recording of Beethoven's Symphony No. 9.[308]

So strong was the association of the violin with Western civilization, including Western music, that in the end the views of people like Yamanoi prevailed. Like the violin boom itself, the fashion of playing traditional Japanese music on the violin died down. Machida's preface to his 1917 violin tutor suggests that he saw playing Japanese music on Western instruments as a transitional phase which had now been superseded. Presumably many educators thought like Machida. Nevertheless, violin tutors with Japanese pieces did not disappear entirely. A tutor published in 1925 contains a number of Japanese tunes, reflecting a new age, its repertoire is more diverse than that of the earlier tutors, and includes popular music: an Argentinean tango (*Flor de Brazil*) by Arturo de Castro and an *Oriental Dance* by T. Lubomirsky.[309]

Gradually, however, most people came to regard playing Western rather than Japanese music on the violin as superior, although the strict separation of Japanese and Western music only became complete after 1945. Perhaps the violin was just too closely associated with Western civilization for the custom of playing traditional music on it to prevail. The violin's reputation as an instrument of Japanese music, moreover, was hardly enhanced by picture postcards of violins in the hands of geisha. Even more damaging to the violin as a status symbol was its popularity with street musicians from around the time of the Russo–Japanese War in 1904–05 until the 1920s. Wearing a bowler hat and Western shoes or else donning the garb of impecunious students, these self-taught minstrels sang political and satirical songs or sentimental love songs (*enka*). The songs used the traditional five-tone modes and vocal style, and they accompanied themselves in unison on the violin. Their performance style was raucous and their playing rough.[310] Performing these *enka* became a popular night job for students who adopted the violin for its novelty value and to enhance their chances with the ladies. Not all who posed as students were in fact students. *Enka* singers were a mixed bunch, including some less than savoury characters.[311] They contributed to the wayward image the violin acquired in the early twentieth century, as presumably, did the emergence of other musicians who played the violin for money in various types of entertainment, including the morally suspect dance halls. Popular magazines, meanwhile, began to portray the piano as the instrument of choice for music in the home, especially for women. Japanese-produced pianos became available after the turn of the century, although they were still prohibitively expensive.[312]

As a novelty item the violin was soon rivalled by other instruments. One was the *taishōgoto*. Invented in 1912 in Nagoya by Morita Gorō, it looks like a cross between an old-fashioned typewriter and a two-stringed *koto* and sounds a little like a mandolin, an instrument popular with students at this time. Much easier to play than the violin, the *taishōgoto* could be used for Japanese or Western tunes, as a solo instrument or part of an ensemble. It soon became popular and may well have contributed to the declining interest in the violin.

The violin boom, although short-lived, marked an important step on the way to assimilating Western music. And ultimately the violin remained the instrument of Western music. Like the music itself it had to be kept on a pedestal, venerated as the "king" of the "flower" of Western music, if it was to function as a way of acquiring the civilization it symbolized. That the violin's image was full of ambiguities even in the

West, the representative of both the West's perceived highest and lowest (dance) music, the instrument both of angels and of the devil and the Dance of Death, does not seem to have entered the mind of writers like Yamanoi. In Japan too though, the twentieth century brought new kinds of music played on the violin: jazz, tango and other popular dance music, played in hotels, on ocean liners and in dance halls. Those who persisted now had the possibility of earning quite a decent living from the violin – at least if they were men, for these new employment opportunities were not considered suitable for women. Even while playing in dance bands, however, many violinists and other musicians still aspired to what they perceived as the apex of Western art music; the symphony orchestra. Soon efforts were made to found the first full orchestras outside the Tokyo Academy of Music. In short, by the time the Taishō era succeeded the Meiji era and the First World War brought the "long nineteenth century" to an end, the Japanese had made the violin their own.

# Part 2: Japan's Emergence as a Musical Power: From the End of the First World War to the Bubble Economy

## I. Joining the World (1918–45)

On 1 June 1918, while the First World War still raged in Europe, the small town of Bandō on the island of Shikoku witnessed an extraordinary event. German prisoners of war in the nearby camp staged the first full performance of Beethoven's Ninth Symphony on Japanese soil. According to the programme, this was the second symphonic concert by the Tokushima Orchestra and it was assisted by a choir of 80 men and four soloists under the baton of Herman Hansen, a military band master. Unfortunately, that is about as much as we know about the performance. We can only guess how an all-male cast coped with the soprano parts, for example (a re-enactment was attempted in 1998).[1] And we should certainly not overestimate the importance of the concert for the history of music in Japan beyond the provincial towns of Bandō and nearby Tokushima. The programme was printed in German and the audience consisted largely of German fellow prisoners and a few locals.

Nevertheless, with hindsight, the performance seems to have foreshadowed much of what happened in the following years; Japan's increasing participation in international affairs, the stimulation of Japan's music life by foreigners, many of them displaced Europeans, the rise of the symphony orchestra, and the veneration for Beethoven as the "sage of music."[2] On the other hand, Japan's humane treatment of its prisoners, who in Bandō were allowed to develop a thriving cultural community, stands in stark contrast to the country's quite different behaviour during the Second World War. The First World War ushered in a period of international cooperation. Japan had declared war on Germany on 23 August 1914, invoking the terms of the Anglo–Japanese Alliance first concluded in 1902. Immediately occupying the German-leased territories in Shantung and the German-owned islands in the Pacific, Japan had also supported its European allies by assisting in sea patrols and supplying arms. Having participated in the war, Japan also participated in the peace negotiations at Versailles, the founding of the League of Nations (the forerunner of the United Nations) and conferences of the major sea powers to discuss naval arms limitations and affairs in the Pacific and East Asia.

Japan's position in 1918 was different from what it had been 50 years earlier in other ways too. The leaders of the Meiji Restoration in 1868 had largely reached their goal of "a rich country and a strong army." They had created a strong national state with a constitutional monarchy and an elected parliament, which had proved its military strength in the victories over China in 1895 and Russia in 1905. Industrialization was well underway, with a thriving textile industry and fast-growing heavy industries such as shipbuilding. Japan had also joined the Western powers in exploring the bottom of the seas in submarines and flying its own aeroplanes. Its cities were growing and the lifestyles of the people living there in many ways resembled the lives of people in Western cities.

In the 1920s and 1930s, Western culture, which had been so hastily appropriated in the Meiji years, was gradually absorbed and integrated. Practically all Japanese children went to school for at least six years, where they studied the same kind of subjects as children in Western countries. Education and, for the men, military service helped to unify and strengthen the nation, as did the railways and the postal system, which reached most parts of the country and drew the different regions together. At the same time education also gave people the means to find out things for themselves and make up their own minds. Innumerable newspapers and magazines helped create a public, whose opinion politicians ignored at their peril. As the strong group of men who had led the way in all these changes since 1868 weakened and died, new groups vied for influence, including ones that so far had little opportunity for political participation, such as factory workers and women. Political parties gained momentum and formed party governments. Inspired by the revolution in Russia, socialists united to form the Japan Socialist Party. Other international trends too were eagerly received in Japan and contributed to the more liberal and democratic atmosphere of the era.

The New Education Movement which spread through North America and Europe from the late nineteenth century inspired Japanese educational reformers, who rejected the prevailing systems and teaching methods. Instead, they emphasized ideas such as creating an environment conducive to learning, respect for the individual child, and a holistic education based on the child's stage of development and experience, which included practical subjects and the arts and which fostered emotional development as well as book learning.[3] Several educators founded their own schools. One of them was Obara Kuniyoshi (1887–1977), who in 1929 founded Tamagawa Gakuen school in Tokyo. Obara's education system laid great stress on training in the arts. In several of his many publications, Obara stressed the mother's role in a child's early education.[4] His views on the importance of the mother were shared by Suzuki Shin'ichi (see below, Chapter 4), the founder of the Suzuki Method, who experimented with teaching small children in the 1930s, and he too published his views on education.

Modern times were not just about politics and ideas. Japan was growing richer. The war had brought an unprecedented economic boom, and although this was followed by a slump and the road to economic progress continued to be bumpy after that, the overall trend was upwards. The new middle classes (officials, teachers and other professionals, and office workers), but also self-employed craftsmen, small shopkeepers and factory workers had money to spend and demanded more consumer goods and entertainment.[5] Tokyo and the bigger cities boasted department stores selling Western and Japanese goods. More importantly, perhaps, the stores presented images of a modern, Westernized lifestyle through their displays, publications and events. Western fashions became ever more widespread among those who could afford them. Women still wore their kimonos most of the time, but they adopted new hairstyles and Western accessories.

Thousands of magazines catered for different groups of readers, as did series of cheap books. New media brought new forms of mass entertainment. The first dedicated cinema, Electricity Hall, opened in Tokyo's Asakusa entertainment district in 1903, and the indigenous film industry took off soon after the Russo–Japanese War and largely contemporaneously with other countries. By 1926, Japan had over 1,000 cinemas. The phonograph came to Japan soon after its invention;

gramophone records were imported from 1903. Soon Japanese record companies were founded, many of them in the Kansai area.[6] After the First World War, prices began to fall and from the 1920s, gramophones and records became increasingly widespread. Gradually, the large international companies came to dominate the market; in 1927 Japan Polydor, Japan Victor and Japan Columbia were founded. Nationwide radio broadcasting started in 1925, at around the same time as in other countries (1921 in the USA, 1923 in Germany). The mass media promoted each other: advertisements for films with photographs would appear in magazines; the title songs of films were released on gramophone records. Newspapers and magazines sponsored concerts. Department stores not only projected images of a "cultured" lifestyle that included music in the home, complete with piano in the living room; they also held art exhibitions and recitals, published in-house magazines and even employed their own bands. Mitsukoshi in Tokyo had a refreshment room where as early as 1905 a piano and a violin were available for customers' use and where recitals with violin and piano were held.[7] Gramophone records could be heard in cafés, where waitresses served salarymen (office workers) and intellectuals. In other settings too, young women associated more freely with men, to the consternation of their elders.

Japan's greater international presence and the growing mass consumer culture had profound effects on the development of music, both Western and Japanese. In fact this distinction began to lose its meaning as the Japanese made the former thoroughly their own and their changing musical sensibilities affected the latter. While the German prisoners at Bandō celebrated German culture in Japan in 1918, the composer Yamada Kōsaku (1886–1965), gave concerts in America to considerable acclaim. He conducted two concerts at the Carnegie Hall in October 1918 and January 1919; the first concert consisted entirely, the second mostly, of his own compositions. During this time he developed his ideas on a Japanese national music in a Western idiom, and in his works from 1919 he self-consciously employed Japanese elements.[8] Yamada is generally regarded as the first Japanese composer of note; he was also one of the key figures in the organization of Japan's first professional symphony orchestras.[9] Born in Tokyo, he grew up surrounded by Western music. He sang in a church choir, listened to military bands and joined the glee club of his college, Kwansei Gakuin in Kobe, founded by Methodist Episcopalian missionaries in 1889. From 1904 to 1908 he studied vocal music, trumpet, flute and cello (with Heinrich Werkmeister) at the Tokyo Academy of Music. He continued to study as a postgraduate, and from 1910 to 1913 he studied in Berlin at what is now the University of the Arts. His many and varied activities in the years between the two world wars are impossible to chronicle here; realizing that most Japanese were still far from appreciating Western art music, he worked hard to organize concerts all over Japan given by professional musicians. He continued to extend his activities beyond Japan. Twice, in 1931 and in 1933, he toured the Soviet Union, and in 1937 he conducted the Berlin Philharmonic Orchestra.

Other Japanese musicians who performed abroad in this period were the conductor Konoe Hidemaro (1898–1973) and the violinist, composer and conductor Kishi Kōichi (1909–37). Konoe performed in Germany and the countries occupied by Germany, and did much to impress his audiences, not only with his own success, but also with his reports about Western music's triumph in Japan.[10] By the 1930s, Japanese composers were taking part in festivals of the International Society for Contemporary Music (ISCM). A number of Japanese composers won prizes at international competitions. Koseki Yūji (1909–89) won a competition sponsored by the music publisher Chester in London in 1929 for his orchestral suite *Taketori Monogatari*. Ifukube Akira (1914–2006) won first prize in 1935 for *Japanese Rhapsody* at the Tcherepnin Competition in Paris and even collaborated with Alexander Tcherepnin; their ballet *Bon Dance* was staged in Vienna in 1940. The Taiwan-born composer Kō Bunya (1910–83) won a prize in the art competition at the Berlin Olympics in 1936 for *Formosa Dances* and his work was performed in Vienna.[11] The singer Fujiwara Yoshie (1898–1976) studied in Italy and performed in several European countries as well as America between 1920 and 1934. Koga Masao (1904–78), one of the pioneers of popular song, toured North and South America in 1938 and 1939. A selection of his compositions was broadcast worldwide by NBC on 31 August 1939; Koga would have continued to Europe had not the outbreak of the Second World War prevented it.[12] While these Japanese musicians performing in the West mainly attracted interest on the strength of their "Japaneseness," they were expressing Japanese sentiment in a musical style perceived as Western by their audiences and which they had mastered completely. Composers in Western countries continued to experiment with and challenge conventional forms and absorb foreign influences; as a result they and their audiences were open to the musical ideas of non-Western composers. Indeed, one of the reasons for the Japanese composers' international success may well have been that supposedly "Japanese elements" in their works conformed to a common musical idiom perceived as "Oriental."[13]

The main impetus to Western classical music in Japan, however, came from Western musicians coming to Japan. Before the First World War, Western musicians in Japan were chiefly the professionals invited by the government to teach at the Tokyo Academy of Music or arriving in Japan on their own initiative and staying for a few years, missionaries teaching music in their churches and schools, and amateurs who had come to Japan for another reason but found their musical skills in demand. Only occasionally had touring artists from several countries found their way to Japan (see Part 1 Chapter 1): the American Jenny Claus, the Frenchman Maurel, the Hungarian Reményi, the Russian Domcheff, the Belgian Musin, the Dane Schlüter, the Germans Anna Schäfer and Dora von Möllendorff, the Pole Premislaw, and the Russian Auer-pupil Mishel Piastro who came in 1912 and again in 1918. Piastro was the first of a string of Auer's pupils who performed in Japan from the end of the First World War. The number of visiting artists increased and included names that are still legendary today. In 1918 Prokofiev came to Japan on his way to America and performed his own works at the Oriental Hotel in Kobe. While he played mainly for a foreign audience, the Japanese audience was growing. International stars included Japan on their tour circuit, thanks to the enterprising spirit of Avray Strok, a Russian-Jewish businessman and musical impresario based in Shanghai. His Japanese co-organizer was Yamamoto Kyūzaburō, the manager of the Imperial Theatre in Tokyo.[14] Artists who performed in Japan in the 1920s and 1930s included Mischa Elman, Efrem Zimbalist, Fritz Kreisler, Jascha Heifetz, Jacques Thibaud, Jan Kubelik, Arthur Rubinstein, Andrés Segovia, Gregor Piatigorsky and Emanuel Feuermann as well as dancers like Anna Pavlova, Ruth St. Denis and La Argentina. They gave Japanese music and dance enthusiasts the opportunity to experience the highest artistic standards. By this time most Japanese had a basic knowledge of

Western music through their schooling and opportunities to hear the music, so the foreign artists found an appreciative audience.

Many of the musicians who came to Japan in these years were European refugees, first from Russia, then from Nazi Germany. Persecution of Jews in the last years of the Russian empire and the Russian Revolution of 1917 caused many Russians to leave their homeland, and many, including many musicians, fled to Asia. Shanghai, already an international city, experienced an increase in its Russian population. In 1919 Mario Paci gave his first concert as the conductor of the Shanghai Municipal Council Public Band (founded in 1879), which under his leadership became a full symphony orchestra. It has been described as the first permanent professional orchestra in East Asia, and Russian refugees increased both its membership and audience. Harbin, sometimes known as the "St. Petersburg of the East," had a distinctly Russian flavour as a result of the Russian treaty with China in 1896, which secured Russia a concession to build and operate a railway in northeast China. Russians in search of work and a living had settled there and were now joined by Russian Jews and White Russians; by 1922 about a quarter of the population were Russians. Harbin had its own music academy and symphony orchestra.[15]

The Russian musicians in China played a large role in the growth of the symphony orchestra in Japan. In 1925, Yamada Kōsaku and the conductor Konoe Hidemaro succeeded in inviting over 30 Russian musicians for a well-publicized joint concert tour with Japanese musicians. Russian names dominate the list, especially in the violin and viola sections, and the two concertmasters subsequently returned to Japan and became the first two foreign conductors of the orchestra Yamada and Konoe founded later that year. The orchestra's members came from ensembles playing in cinemas and hotels or on ocean liners. The new Japan Symphony Orchestra gave its first subscription concert in 1926, but was short-lived. A split occurred in 1927, resulting in the establishment of another symphony orchestra under Konoe, the New Symphony Orchestra, predecessor of the NHK (Japan Broadcasting Association) Orchestra. These events, with typical bias towards events in Tokyo, are commonly regarded as the beginning of the orchestral movement.

Until the early twentieth century, "Western music" mainly meant military music and singing in church and in school; classical music and dissemination owed much to government efforts and official channels. Classical music continued to enjoy enormous prestige and to find new audiences, even while new kinds of music gained popularity. As the growth of mass culture in the cities offered new markets for all kinds of musical entertainment as a commercial enterprise, the variety of musical events and musical styles on offer increased. Asakusa, Tokyo's big entertainment district, gave birth to the "Asakusa opera," which mixed all kinds of musical performance, from opera proper to light music theatre and chorus line revues. Japan's first attempt to establish a permanent repertoire company for serious opera at the Imperial Theatre – which despite its name was a private venture – failed. The director employed for the purpose in 1912, G.V. Rossi, was dismissed in 1916 and left Japan in 1918 after a failed effort to establish a private theatre company. But many of the singers trained by Rossi made themselves a career in Asakusa, most famously Fujiwara Yoshie, who went on to found his own opera company.

Another operatic venture, in the Kansai area, meanwhile, was more successful, if not as the "opera" envisaged by its founder. In 1914 the Takarazuka Girls' Opera (*Shōjo Kageki*), known in English as the Takarazuka Revue gave its first performance. Established by the entrepreneur and president of the Hankyū Railway Company, Kobayashi Ichizō (1873–1957), in a popular tourist spot at the Hankyū Railway's terminus, it was intended to offer high-quality musical theatre for the masses. True to the spirit of the times, it aimed to combine the best of Japanese and Western performance art, including *kabuki* and opera (which Kobayashi regarded as too elitist in their pure forms). Kobayashi favoured Western music for its sophisticated image, and for the first performance Japanese women played the violin in kimono. A few years later a full symphony orchestra was formed (see Chapter 2). The theatre's programme included musicals based on Western and Japanese stage works. Composers included the violinist Kitamura Sueharu (1872–1931), a graduate of the Tokyo Academy of Music who created music in the *wayō* style mixing Japanese melodies and Western instrumentation. In 1938 Takarazuka toured Europe, North America and China.[16]

The Kantō earthquake of 1923 devastated most of Asakusa and hit the entertainment industry hard, but Tokyo's loss was the provinces' gain: some of the theatre companies toured the provinces until the Tokyo venues were rebuilt and several musicians moved to the Kansai area in search of new jobs. Thus the disaster actually promoted the dissemination of Western music. The disaster demonstrated, moreover, the extent to which Japan was on the world map for foreign artists, several of whom telegraphed their commiserations when they heard that the Imperial Theatre had burnt down. Mischa Elman even organized a charity concert in New York.[17] Soon Tokyo began to be rebuilt, but most of the old city had been burnt to the ground by the fires caused by the earthquake and with it, felt many, old Edo had given way to modern times – for better or for worse. As soon as recovery set in the musicians returned and a veritable golden age for musical professionals began.[18]

New settings for music included Western-style hotels, cafés, dance halls and cinemas. The large international hotels employed both Japanese and foreign ensembles to play for concerts and balls or in their cafés and restaurants. Of course the repertoire required in these settings was not the kind taught at the Tokyo Academy of Music. Internationalization (we might even call it globalization) was bringing new kinds of music to Japan, including Latin American, tango and Hawaiian, which would flourish after the Second World War, but most notably jazz, which found a strong foothold in Japan almost as soon as it came into being.[19] Jazz became popular in Asian port towns, starting with Manila, from where several Philippine jazz bands and musicians came to Japan, and to Shanghai, which became an Asian jazz Mecca, attracting many Japanese musicians. Other Japanese musicians played on the ocean liners and, while on leave in San Francisco, they had the chance to hear American jazz musicians and to buy instruments, scores and other equipment.

Jazz was also played in the dance halls, which enjoyed great popularity until government or local authorities increasingly suppressed them as morally dubious. As early as 1923 the American correspondent Grace Seton reported: "The Japanese are jazzing by day and by night. The 'foreign craze' trips merrily on its way through the sacred traditions of Nipponese etiquette and of the home... Girls and young women manage the intricate steps of the jazz in tabi and zori [traditional footwear] with surprising ease … Foreign dancing undoubtedly has come to stay."[20] The first public ballroom, the Kagetsuen in Yokohama, opened in March 1920. In Osaka, restaurants and cafés began adding dance halls to their businesses until police laws forbade the practice. From 1925 an increasing number of commercial dance halls opened, operating on a ticket system and employing female "taxi dancers." When the city of Osaka ordered them to close, many of them relocated just outside the municipal boundaries, on the main road between Osaka and Kobe. The golden era of dance halls had arrived. At its peak in 1936 there were eight major halls in Tokyo and a total of 39 halls in the rest of the country, the majority of them in the areas around Kyoto, Osaka and Kobe. Dance halls even opened in the colonies and on the Chinese mainland.[21]

Cinemas too offered musical entertainment. As in the West, the silent films were accompanied with live music, the Japanese ones with *kabuki* style music, the Western ones with Western music supplied by ensembles provided by entertainment managers. The early ones consisted mainly of wind players, but they were apt to drown the voice of the narrator (*benshi*), and mixed groups became more common. Gradually, permanent cinemas were established, and with the advent of long films from around 1914, the bigger ones employed their own orchestras, who would also play during intervals. Similar ensembles played in Kobe and Osaka. The new "talkies" (the first was shown in Tokyo in 1929) put the live ensembles out of business, but provided new opportunities through the creation of soundtracks. Film music, especially the theme songs of films, was also sold on records.

Gramophone records were even more important than film music for making foreign music known. At first the Japanese only produced gramophone records of traditional music themselves, often in "modern" styles with Western instruments. But Japan soon became the biggest market for recordings of Western music. In 1924 a set by Deutsche Grammophon, of Beethoven's Ninth Symphony (the first complete recording of a major work) sold 300 subscriptions in Japan. In 1933 the set of Beethoven's piano sonatas from Victor attracted 2,000 subscriptions from Japan, the same number as the sum of all European subscriptions. The set of Toscanini's recording of Beethoven's Fifth with the NBC Orchestra released by Victor in 1939 sold 50,000 copies in Japan.[22]

We can hardly overestimate the importance of gramophone records for making Western music known and for raising standards of performance. Before recordings became available, the only way to hear a work was either to listen to a live performance or to attempt to play it

8: Sheet music for the accompaniment of period films (Tokyo, 1927).

oneself. For a Beethoven symphony, if one was not content with playing an arrangement for piano, an entire orchestra would have to be assembled – a difficult enterprise as long as musicians of sufficient ability were still few and far between. Until the growth of symphony orchestras able to perform entire symphonies in the early twentieth century, intellectuals often discussed composers like Beethoven and Wagner without having heard their works performed in the way the composers intended. Beethoven was known from the literary work of Romain Rolland (1866–1944) rather than from his own music. Even for small-scale instrumental works the opportunities to listen to the more difficult ones were limited. The "Kreutzer Sonata," for example, was more familiar from Tolstoy's story than from Beethoven's composition. Gramophone records changed all that. Many are the stories of Japanese musicians inspired by the recordings of Elman, Kreisler and Heifetz, and numerous the violinists who attempted to imitate them to the last bowing and fingering. One was Suzuki Shin'ichi. Another, Etō Toshiya, who learnt much from recordings of Heifetz and Menuhin, later recalled that in those days slow record speeds, which could even be manipulated, enabled him to hear and imitate such details.[23] By the time the virtuosos arrived in Japan, they were eagerly awaited by aficionados who were familiar with their recordings. Several of them made recordings while in Japan.

By the 1920s the different forms of musical entertainment provided sufficient job opportunities for people trained in Western music to make a living – at least if they were prepared to branch out from their classical style and repertoire. Apart from the emerging symphony orchestras, there were employment opportunities for ensembles in review theatres, cinemas, Western-style hotels, ocean liners, dance halls and the new media. Broadcasting also offered opportunities: instrumental ensembles played for the broadcasting stations in Tokyo, Nagoya and Osaka. Many who played in the bands must have studied with private teachers or were largely self-taught. But new music colleges offering training at professional level were established in the 1920s: the Tokyo Higher Academy of Music (Tōkyō Kōtō Ongaku Gakuin), predecessor of the Kunitachi College of Music (Kunitachi Ongaku Daigaku) in 1926, the Japan Music School (Nihon Ongaku Gakkō) in 1927, the Musashino Academia Musicae (Musashino Ongaku Gakkō, today Musashino Ongaku Daigaku) in 1929. The new private colleges and schools also offered work for teachers.

Amateur music also flourished, and the first choral societies and wind bands were established throughout Japan. For young intellectuals studying at the high schools, colleges and universities, Western music represented a significant element in their Western education. As well as performing themselves in music societies, they formed the backbone of the audience for the new symphony concerts and the performances by visiting artists. For the daughters of the social elites and the middle classes the piano was becoming the instrument of choice as they aspired to the Western-inspired cultured lifestyle propagated by the department stores and in magazines.

When it came to the general public's listening preferences, however, Western music, although increasingly popular, was still far from dominant; most Japanese preferred more traditional music. *Hōgaku,* the music of Japan, dominated in the domestic production of gramophone records, and a poll of radio listening preferences in 1925 revealed that most listeners preferred the traditional genres of Japanese music (*hōgaku*) that dominated broadcasting.[24] But what does "traditional Japanese music" mean? Even performers of Japanese music could not avoid being exposed to and influenced by Western music, and many did not even want to avoid it. They experimented with new forms and with new versions of Japanese instruments, typically larger ones with a wider range of pitch. The most famous representative of "New Japanese Music," composed in the traditional idiom but influenced by Western music, is Miyagi Michio (1894–1956). A contemporary of Yamada Kōsaku, he too strove to create modern Japanese music and mixed different elements in his compositions. Miyagi Michio heard Western music from an early age; he spent his early years in Kobe with foreign neighbours. But when he lost his eyesight at the age of eight his parents made him learn the *koto,* in the tradition of blind players in the Tokugawa period. Soon family circumstances forced him to move to Korea with his father, where he had to earn a living by teaching. He began to compose himself to increase his repertoire. He also had the chance to hear concerts of Western music and imported gramophone records. Like his contemporaries in Japan he was particularly attracted by French composers like Claude Debussy and Maurice Ravel. In 1917, at the age of 23, he moved to Tokyo. He continued to study Western music from recordings and Braille scores. In 1919 he gave a public recital of his works, an event regarded as a landmark in the development of Japanese music.[25] Miyagi experimented with Western-style harmony, and although his music sounds "traditional" to today's Japanese, his contemporary audiences perceived some of his pieces as "Western." In fact, in writing and performing many types of music he overcame the strict division into genres and transformed indigenous Japanese music into a living art.[26]

However, arguably the most successful fusion of Western and Japanese music was represented in popular songs. Singing features prominently in many traditional Japanese genres, and songs played a vital role in the introduction of Western music. New popular songs reflected both traditional musical preferences and the changed musical sensibilities resulting from Western-style music education. A new type of children's song, known as *dōyō*, emerged after the First World War, in part influenced by the New Education Movement. Japanese composers made new efforts to create songs that related to children's emotional life and overcame the uncritical imitation of Western styles. The children's songs of this time successfully fuse Japanese and Western musical idioms. Popular songs for adult consumption (*ryūkōka*) were similarly eclectic. The songs of Koga Masao mixed elements from the Meiji *shōka* songs and American dance rhythms (as well as, possibly, Korean folk songs).

Like Yamada Kōsaku and Miyagi Michio, many composers were seeking to create a Japanese national music. The increasingly nationalistic climate of the 1930s encouraged this tendency, but that is no reason to dismiss the efforts of Japanese composers as nothing more than bowing to political pressure. Ever since the beginnings of Western music in Japan, its promoters had envisaged a national music combining the best of Western and Japanese elements. Indeed European composers in the nineteenth century sought to give their music a distinctly national flavour. Japanese composers were experimenting, and some experiments turned out more successful than others. Musicologists may treat the others with benign neglect or condescension, but for the cultural historian they offer fascinating evidence of the creative process, as well as of the struggle to define Japanese identity in an increasingly globalizing world, a struggle that was also evident in other art forms and in the intellectual currents of the time.

The increasing political control and ultranationalism from the 1930s onwards did not immediately have a detrimental effect on Japan's musical scene. The annexation of Manchuria in 1931 brought increased wealth to Japan. About half a million Japanese emigrated to Manchuria, taking their entertainment culture with them and adding local flavours to it.[27] Japanese musicians found new professional opportunities on the mainland and went on tours or stayed for longer. But Japan also became internationally isolated, withdrawing from the League of Nations following the League's acceptance in February 1933 of the Lytton Commission's report criticizing Japan's doings in Manchuria. Nevertheless, international artists continued to tour Japan through most of the 1930s until the war prevented it. Meanwhile, German musicians fleeing from the Nazis, and – ironically – musicians sent by the Nazis as part of the cultural exchange between the two countries allied by the Anti-Comintern Pact of 1936 contributed to Japan's musical life, continuing the German tradition.[28]

A few Jewish musicians left Germany for Japan even before the Nazis came to power, including the Russian-born pianist Leo Sirota (1885–1965) in 1929 and the musical director Klaus Pringsheim (1883–1972), the twin brother of Thomas Mann's wife Katia, in 1931. The conductor Josef Rosenstock (1895–1985) came to Japan in 1936 and the pianist Leonid Kreutzer (1884–1953) in 1938.[29] The highly successful pianist, composer and conductor Manfred Gurlitt (1890–1972), who had a Jewish grandmother, had with limited success tried to come to terms with the Nazi regime before he emigrated in 1939.[30] Eta Harich-Schneider (1894–1986), a pianist, harpsichord expert and professor at the conservatoire in Berlin, was not Jewish, but had fallen foul of her Nazi superiors. Still, she came to Japan as a part of the official cultural exchange between the two countries in 1941. The German attack on the Soviet Union made return impossible and she stayed until 1949, performing and teaching and pioneering research into *gagaku*. In her memoirs she gives a vivid picture of the tensions and rivalries between the various groups of German musicians who found themselves more or less willingly in Japan.[31] But whatever their problems with each other, each of them enriched musical life through their performances and as teachers.

After the start of the Pacific War, music from non-allied Western countries, especially American jazz and other light music, was frowned upon and the government promoted efforts to create an indigenous light music. Accounts of how classical musicians fared are mixed. Government censorship was rife, to be sure, but there were ways around it, and it affected jazz and forms of "light" music more than it did classical music, which was both too deeply entrenched to be easily uprooted and sufficiently indebted to the German tradition to escape being cast as "enemy music." Some remembered later that being seen with a violin in the streets was asking for trouble. The handsome tango violinist Sakurai Kiyoshi, who had many female fans, was rebuked by censors for his long hair.[32] But the music critic Nomura Kōichi recalled hostility mainly from the population, rather than government officials.[33]

Western classical music sometimes took the form of bombastic performances with large symphony orchestras, part of the official efforts to use music for propaganda purposes. The biggest musical spectacles during the war were the celebrations to commemorate in 1940 the 2,600th anniversary of the ascension of the first (legendary) Emperor Jimmu. The government wanted to make this an international event, and commissioned works from several foreign composers; Jacques Ibert from France, Ildebrando Pizzetti from Italy, Richard Strauss from Germany, Benjamin Britten from England and Sándor Veress from Hungary.[34] Works by several Japanese composers were also performed.

It was not so much militant nationalism and xenophobia that restricted musical activities as the increasing mobilization of people and resources for the war effort and progress of the war. In 1940, the ocean liners ceased to run and put an end to ship bands. That same year the dance halls had to close. Musicians were increasingly submitted to control and roped into the war effort, for propaganda or to entertain troops. As the war progressed, conditions for musical performances of any kind worsened. Commercial film and record production came to a standstill; the air raids on Tokyo and other cities destroyed performance and rehearsal venues, putting a stop to the activities of musicians who had not been killed, conscripted or evacuated. The last concert at the Tokyo Academy of Music was given in February 1944 under Helmut Fellmer (1908–77) with a programme that included the Bach Double Concerto.[35] The Japan Symphony Orchestra (Nihon Kōkyō Gakudan, predecessor of the NHK Symphony Orchestra) performed almost until the very end of the war, giving its last subscription concert in June 1945 with Beethoven's Ninth Symphony and its last broadcast on 5 August. Ultimately the Second World War and Japanese capitulation brought all cultural life to a standstill, but not for long, and the revival of music could build on what Japan had achieved by the late 1930s.

Foreign observers in this period often found high praise for Japan's achievements. Of course we must take into account their consideration for their hosts if they were addressing a Japanese audience. Besides, if, like the conductor Klaus Pringsheim, they had a part in Japan's success they were hardly going to belittle the fruits of their work. On the other hand, Pringsheim's assessment in the Japanese magazine *Ongaku sekai* in 1937 is nuanced enough to suggest that his praise was sincere. He praised the active concert life and the high standard of singing, remarked that there were some good string players, and gave the future of Western music in Japan a strong vote of confidence.[36] The previous year, 1936, the pianist Wilhelm Kempff performed in Japan and in his praise of August Junker's work remarked that, as he rehearsed his programme of Bach, Mozart and Beethoven with an all-Japanese orchestra and a highly gifted Japanese conductor (Kishi Kōichi; see Chapter 3): "I sometimes completely forgot, that I was in the distant Land of the Rising Sun."[37] The author of an article in *Zeitschrift für Musik* in 1935 about the reception of the German singer Maria Toll in Japan observed that Beethoven's Ninth Symphony was performed and enjoyed without difficulty in several places each winter and that mediocre artists should not be encouraged to tour Japan, because the Japanese would resent their understanding and love of Western music being underestimated.[38]

In 1929 Gustav Kron, the violinist who had taught and conducted at the Tokyo Academy of Music for 12 years, had already described the Japanese as highly discerning. While carefully avoiding judgement on performance standards, his examples illustrate the extent to which the Japanese had begun to make Western music their own. He concluded:

> The Japanese are an artistic people. Within them dwells a natural gift of receptiveness for all that is beautiful and an ability for artistic re-creation which makes it an easier task for them to accustom themselves to a completely new world. Their inborn strength of character and the continued training enables the people to face the new light without becoming blind. They just have to be offered that which is truly great. Pseudo-art the Japanese will refuse.[39]

## 1. Visiting Superstars and European Refugees

Indeed Japanese audiences had plenty of opportunity to hear world-class musicians; one of the most striking features of the years after the First World War and into the 1930s is the extent of Japan's internationalization. For music, this meant that more and more Japanese went to study music abroad and world-famous artists began to include Japan on their international tours. Moreover, the unfolding European catastrophes, the Russian Revolution in 1917 and the Nazis' seizure of power in 1933, made many outstanding musicians desperate to leave their homelands, and although Japan was rarely their first choice, several of them ended up staying there for years and helped Japan on its way to become a musical power.

The first touring violinists found their way to Japan in the nineteenth century, but they played chiefly for the foreign community. The artists who came from 1918 onwards, however, played to sizeable Japanese audiences, and several of them are still household names today. The list of visiting violinists alone is impressive:[40]

Emilio Colombo, 1918

Mishel Piastro (had already visited in 1912) 1918, 1922, 1923; he also performed with the Piastro Trio in 1937 and 1939

Alfred E. Jones (?), 1918

Mischa Elman, 1921, 1937

Efrem Zimbalist, 1922, 1924, 1927, 1930, 1932 and 1935

Kathleen Parlow, 1922

Jaroslav Kocián, 1922

Willy Burmester, 1923

Fritz Kreisler, 1923

Jascha Heifetz in 1923, 1931

Natalie Boshko, 1924

Leopold Premislaw, 1924 (Premyslav; first visit in 1909)

Boris Lass in 1925, 1926 (he settled in Japan and was still there in 1934)

Leonid (Nikolaevič) Ševčuk, 1926

Alexander Yakovlevich Mogilevsky, 1926 (see below)

Michail Erdenko, 1927

Naum Blinder, 1927

Robert Kitain, 1927

Jacques Thibaud, 1928, 1936

Cecilia Hansen, 1928

Jan Kubelik, 1929

Alfred Hoffman, 1931

Renée Chemet, 1932

Joseph Szigeti, 1932
Pierre Reitlinger, 1933
Szymon Goldberg, 1936

The predominance of Russians, many of them from the school of Leopold Auer (Elman, Zimbalist, Heifetz, Piastro, Lass and Cecilia Hansen), is no coincidence. Avray Strok, who arranged the Asian tours, knew many of them personally. Zimbalist, for example, met Strok during his student days, when Strok played timpani for the Italian Opera Company, who performed in the St. Petersburg Conservatoire's Grand Theatre and let Zimbalist sit next to him during performances.[41] In many cases the performers' fame preceded their visit. Japanese music lovers with access to a gramophone already knew them through recordings. Mischa Elman, who came in February 1921, was already famous for his "Elman tone" and had inspired Suzuki Shin'ichi.[42] Elman also won the hearts of the people by expressing a liking for Japanese music, having heard a few recordings in America, including the popular "Lion of Echigo."[43] Recordings, however, can never match the immediacy of a live performance and Elman's playing proved a revelation. The critic Nomura Kōichi later recalled that in the days before the First World War Japanese violinists sounded fairly awful; now at last many music lovers could hear the sound of the violin at its best. As a result, native players, even the eminent Andō Kō, suffered unfavourable comparisons with the world stars.[44]

Kreisler first came in May 1923 and impressed some even more than Elman. In Tokyo, he gave five recitals at the Imperial Theatre; his programmes, particularly the first, included many of his own compositions and arrangements.[45] Years later, the critic Nakajima Kenzō remembered the excitement of experiencing Kreisler's performance close up, having secured a seat in the second row.[46] Heifetz's first visit in November 1923 took place just weeks after the great Kantō earthquake on 1 September had flattened large parts of Tokyo, including the Imperial Theatre, where he was scheduled to perform. He gave his first performance on 9 November at the Imperial Hotel, which was designed by Frank Lloyd Wright and completed just before the earthquake. Some of the people who crowded in to listen to him greeted acquaintances they had not seen since the disaster. Two days later he performed outdoors in

Hibiya Park; the Hibiya concert hall had been destroyed. Ticket prices were reduced to an all-time low of one yen instead of the usual upwards of ten yen, and Heifetz donated the proceeds to a relief fund. Three thousand six hundred people braved the wind and the rain to hear him play Sarasate's *Zigeunerweisen,* Schubert's *Ave Maria* and other favourites. He concluded his recital with the Japanese national anthem and the audience thanked him with a triple "banzai" ("hurrah"). Heifetz continued to the Kansai region, where his concert in Osaka on 15 November reportedly drew record numbers and extra chairs had to be fitted into the Central Hall.[47]

Jacques Thibaud gave five recitals in Tokyo in May 1928. One of the few visiting stars who was not a student of Auer's, Thibaud represented the Franco-Belgian school, and his programmes included works by César Franck, Camille Saint-Saëns and Claude Debussy.[48] His second visit in May 1936 coincided with Charlie Chaplin's; Chaplin played the violin himself and described Thibaud as his teacher. Thibaud was also among the first to include Japan in his tours again after the Second World War and was on his way east when his plane crashed in the French Alps on 1 September 1953 and he was killed. Nomura Kōichi kept his ticket to Thibaud's scheduled recital in Tokyo.[49] Suzuki Shin'ichi, who heard about his death when a newspaper reporter rang him to hear his comments, describes the shock: "I was hardly able to coherently give the impression of the great man that he sought from me. I just stood there holding the receiver. It was like irreplaceably losing someone near and dear." Although Suzuki had not heard Thibaud live, he had, like many violinists of his generation, studied his recordings: "I could sense his personality and had been studying his impression and way of playing. (...) Thibaud had come to life in my soul and fostered in me an ineradicable love and admiration."[50]

None of the top virtuosos came as often as Efrem Zimbalist, who visited six times between 1922 and 1935. His biographer describes his six Asian tours as "by far the most significant tours of his career."[51] On his first tour he played six concerts in a week in Tokyo with as many different programmes, before continuing to Kyoto, Osaka, Kobe, Nagoya and Nagasaki, where he gave two concerts in each city. Unlike in China, where his audiences consisted almost entirely of foreigners, most of his listeners were Japanese. In his first concert, which he opened with

Corelli's *Folies d'Espagne,* followed by a Paganini concerto, the newspaper *Jiji shinpō* presented him with its honorary prize for artists, which it had previously awarded to Elman. Zimbalist continued with Bach's Chaconne and Joachim's arrangement of Brahms *Hungarian Dances* in D and E; in the third part he played Tchaikovsky's "Andante Cantabile" and Bizet's *Carmen Fantasy,* all to great acclaim and followed by several encores. The *Tokyo Asahi Newspaper* elicited comments from some of Japan's leading musicians who had attended the first concert, including Konoe Hidemaro and Kōda Nobu. Both declined to say whether they preferred Elman or Zimbalist; Konoe particularly praised the *Hungarian Dances*, and Kōda the *Carmen Fantasy* (Zimbalist recorded the Fantasy with Columbia Japan in 1932), which she could not remember having heard in Japan before. The violinist Ono Anna (see below), who knew Zimbalist personally from her St. Petersburg days, called him the best artist to have visited Japan to date.[52]

Zimbalist returned to Japan in December 1924, playing over 60 concerts in three months, many of them, at his own insistence, in small provincial towns where people had never had the chance to hear an international star before. Thus Zimbalist practised "outreach" long before his late twentieth-century colleagues. His six recitals in Tokyo were sold out. Later he recalled, "The hardest work was after performances, when the entire audience would come backstage and want autographs. I couldn't single out a single one of them by refusing."[53] Many of the fans brought his recordings for him to sign. On his third visit to Tokyo he had to give more recitals and encores than ever; as a result he had one of the few memory slips of his long career.[54] Most of his performances were recitals with piano, but in 1932 he performed with the New Symphony Orchestra under Nikolai Schifferblatt in the new Hibiya Hall, playing Mozart's Concerto No. 5 and the Glazunov Concerto.[55] In 1935 he played Mozart's Concerto No. 5 and Mendelssohn's Concerto with the same orchestra under Konoe. Like other foreign artists, Zimbalist made several recordings in Japan, including his first electrical releases with Columbia's Japanese subsidiary.[56] Like the recitals, most of the recordings were with piano, but they include one of Beethoven's Romance in G under Schifferblatt.[57] Zimbalist liked to play local tunes in his encores: Yamada Kōsaku's song "Kuruka, Kuruka" was even included in a regular programme of a Tokyo recital in 1930.[58]

We cannot measure the full extent of the influence Zimbalist and others had with their playing, but many are the anecdotes about people who were profoundly impressed by them. Many a parent who later urged their child to practise had first heard the violin played really well when Zimbalist came to play in their home town. Etō Toshiya, the first to study abroad after the war, chose America and Zimbalist, because Zimbalist had impressed him the most of all the violinists in his father's record collection.[59] Even when the stream of foreign artists ceased in the late 1930s with Japan's increasing international isolation, the memory of their playing lingered, and their recordings continued to make a lasting impression on many who heard them. Important as the touring soloists were, however, they could not exercise the same influence on musical standards in Japan as those who stayed longer. In the days when Western classical music mainly came to Japan as a result of official import, many of them were invited by the government and came for a short period, enticed by high salaries. The Tokyo Academy of Music continued to favour musicians from Germany and Austria; August Junker was succeeded by the violinist Gustav Kron (1874–?), who taught violin, strings and directed the choir and orchestra from 1913 to 1925. The other foreign violinists who taught at the Academy before 1945 were Robert Pollack (1880–1962) from September 1930 to March 1937 and Willy Frey (1907–?) from March 1936 to March 1943.[60]

But as the Russian Revolution caused numerous outstanding musicians to flee their homeland, while the increasing importance of Western music in Japan created new job opportunities, a new brand of foreign musician found employment in Japan. Many of the Russian and Eastern European musicians who settled in Japan (at least temporarily) and contributed much to musical life were experienced orchestral players and soloists who, but for the upheavals at home, would never have interrupted their careers to come to what must have seemed to them like a musical wasteland. Several of them were helped in establishing careers in Japan by the two giant pioneers of the symphony orchestra, Yamada Kōsaku and Konoe Hidemaro. They included the cellist Constantine Shapiro,[61] the pianist Leo Sirota and the pianist, composer and conductor Leonid Kreutzer. Kreutzer had also trained as a violinist, and many violinists benefited from his coaching.

Two violinists who played a vital role in raising the standards of the newly established broadcasting orchestra (now the NHK Orchestra) were Josef

König (1875–1932) and Nikolai Schifferblatt (1887–1936). Both first came to Japan as leaders of the Japanese–Russian Friendship Orchestra in 1925 and subsequently returned as conductors. Josef König was born in Prague of German parents.[62] His father Ernst König (1838–1915?), a renowned oboist, taught at the conservatoire in Prague; Antonín Dvořák composed the cor anglais part of his Symphony No. 9, "From the New World" for him. Josef König studied under Dvořák, Smetana and others at the conservatoire in Prague. In 1892, he played in the orchestra of the Vienna Theatre and Culture Exhibition. After a brief stint in Amsterdam he spent three years in the philharmonic orchestra in Helsinki, where he also played viola in a quartet with Jean Sibelius. His desk partner in the orchestra was Willy Burmester, who toured Japan from March to July 1923, during which time he gave Andō Kō violin lessons and made two recordings.[63] In 1904 König played in the Festival Orchestra in Bayreuth.[64] He later regaled Japanese musicians with anecdotes of his experiences under great conductors such as Nikolay Rimsky-Korsakov, Hans Richter, Felix Mottl and Wilhelm Mengelberg. For 20 years he was a violinist and conductor of the ballet at the Mariinsky Theatre in St. Petersburg and for a while he also played second violin in the Mecklenburg Ensemble, named after its sponsor the Duke of Mecklenburg (it toured under the name of the St. Petersburg Court Quartet and is regarded as the first truly professional Russian ensemble).

After the revolution of 1917 he left Russia and played in the orchestra in Harbin. He was hired a few months after the Japan tour, in November 1925, and in April 1927 became the first foreign conductor of the orchestra of NHK's regional JOAK radio network. Besides his work as a conductor he taught several of the orchestra's members individually, including Sumi Saburō. His pupils included Tan Shuzen, the first Chinese violinist to play with the Shanghai Municipal Orchestra, where he became a regular member after his return from Japan.[65] Katō Kaichi, another pupil, recalls that he could be very strict but also understood that Katō and his colleagues had limited time to practise, because of orchestral rehearsals and the other jobs the musicians had to keep to earn their living. He recalled practising finger gymnastics and bowing and studying études by Kreutzer, Fiorillo, Rode, Dont and Paganini's Caprices as well as famous sonatas and concertos.[66]

In April 1929 a concert was held to celebrate König's 35 years as a musician, organized by the New Philharmonic Orchestra and the

Czechoslovakian consulate. Konoe and König conducted and the soloists included Nikolai Schifferblatt, who had recently arrived in Japan to teach at what is now the Kunitachi College of Music; he played the Tchaikovsky Violin Concerto. A special issue of the orchestra's magazine *Firuhāmonī (The Philharmony)* testifies to the affection in which König was held: a caption under his photograph reads "The kindly face of our father Josef König," and several musicians paid tribute to his achievements. For his part, König praised his Japanese students in an address in the same journal. He declared, "Yes, I am convinced that within a short time the Japanese musician will be able to compete as equal colleague with us Europeans in order to bring the art we all value, which expresses what cannot be told in words or pictured, music! [emphasis by König] into full bloom."[67]

Two months later, however, he was forced to leave Japan under a cloud. The newspapers reported a domestic scandal, but as a critic observed, he had at the most made a pass at his housekeeper, a common occurrence that would not have raised many eyebrows had the offender been Japanese. König, alleged the critic, was the victim of his common-law wife's intrigues, police prejudice against foreigners and the broadcasting office's passivity.[68] König died in Harbin in 1932. In September 1942, Yamada Kōsaku led the Manchukuo Tenth Anniversary Celebratory Symphony Orchestra on a joint Manchurian tour with the newly established symphony orchestra of the puppet state's capital Hsinking (known in Japanese as Shinkyō), and the 80 musicians visited König's grave, where they had their picture taken.[69]

König was succeeded by Nikolai Schifferblatt; perhaps the broadcasting office had their sights on him even before König left.[70] Schifferblatt first studied the violin with his father and played in the local orchestra from an early age. From 1900 he studied at the Music Academy in Tiflis in Georgia and after graduation in 1906 became concertmaster in the orchestra of the Tiflis Opera. Having continued his studies in Dresden with Henri Petri and in St. Petersburg with Leopold Auer, he joined the orchestra in St. Petersburg as a soloist in 1913, before becoming a member of the Mecklenburg Ensemble. After the 1917 revolution he initially moved to Germany and performed chamber music, then joined the orchestra in Harbin. Following the Japan tour he returned to Moscow, playing as concertmaster and soloist for the Moscow orchestra. He arrived in Japan for the second time in April 1929 and gave two recitals. His piano partner was another Russian who made Japan his home, Maxim Shapiro.[71]

As conductor of the New Symphony Orchestra, Schifferblatt premiered many orchestral works. Moreover, under his baton the orchestra began to accompany visiting soloists. Members of the orchestra later particularly recalled Zimbalist's performance of the Brahms Violin Concerto at the orchestra's seventy-sixth regular concert on 22 October 1932, because Zimbalist praised the orchestra afterwards.[72] Like König, Schifferblatt gave individual lessons to members of the orchestra, including Sumi Saburō and his brother Shirō. His students found his approach to playing quite different from König's and some had difficulties adjusting. By all accounts Schifferblatt terrified his students and was a hard taskmaster at rehearsals. He told his students that he himself was terrified of Auer, but that thanks to his teacher he was able to make a living wherever he went in the world and he wanted them to be able to do the same. Thanks to Schifferblatt's dedication the violin section, indeed the whole string section, improved noticeably. Saitō Hideo, the post-war pioneer of music education, and a cellist in the orchestra, recalled playing chamber music with Schifferblatt and Andō Kō, as well as premiering the Brahms Double Concerto for violin and cello with him. He credited Schifferblatt with having introduced the Auer school of violin playing to Japan.[73]

Schifferblatt died suddenly on 14 October 1936. He had been scheduled to perform the Beethoven Violin Concerto the following month and on top of his other work was practising the violin at least two hours a day.[74] His demise profoundly shocked the members of the orchestra, as the tributes in the orchestra's magazine show. On the anniversary of his death his friends and disciples organized a ceremony at his grave in Tama Cemetery in Tokyo – another testimony to the Japanese musicians' love and respect for their foreign teachers.[75]

Two Russian violinists who lived in Japan for many years and became influential teachers were Ono Anna (née Anna Dmitrievna Bubnova, 1890–1979), and Alexander Yakovlevich Mogilevsky (or Moguilewsky as he himself preferred, 1885–1953). Ono Anna, who is credited with having been the first to introduce the teaching methods of Leopold Auer to Japan, was not exactly a refugee. Still, she would hardly have found her way to Japan had she not lived in troubled times. Born in St. Petersburg as the daughter of a government official and a lady from a noble family, she entered the conservatoire in 1904 and graduated in 1911. Among her fellow students in Auer's class were such future virtuosos as Elman, Heifetz and Zimbalist. She was working as a freelance teacher and performer when she met Ono Shun'ichi (1892–1958), the son of a Kyoto professor turned banker (Shun'ichi is also an uncle of John Lennon's wife Yoko Ono). Ono was on his way to Germany to study zoology and had reached Moscow via Siberia just as the First World War broke out. Unable to continue to Germany, he decided to study in St. Petersburg, where he knew another student and the professors spoke German. On the Trans-Siberian Railway he had met the scholar Serge Elisséeff, who engaged him to teach Japanese to his students at the University.[76] When Anna Bubnova joined his class, Ono, who had studied the violin in his youth, had already heard her play a recital with her sister. The revolution broke out, the personnel of the Japanese embassy were recalled to Japan, and Ono too had to leave. In February 1918, he and Anna married hastily and secretly and left for Moscow; from there they travelled to Japan. Anna's widowed mother and her sister Varvara, a respected painter, later joined her.

One of the first things that struck Anna about the musical scene in Japan was that most people did not start learning the violin until they were well into their teens. In Russia, she recalled, even small villages had music schools where children could start an instrument at the age of four or five; by the time they entered a conservatoire they had reached a high standard. Anna herself learnt the piano from age six – several of her pupils described her as an able accompanist – and the violin from age ten. With the support of some acquaintances who were dissatisfied with the standard of musical training, Ono Anna started to teach young children. But she also taught older pupils, provided they were willing to learn. She lived in Japan for over 40 years, mostly in Tokyo, except for a few years when she followed her husband to Kyoto, where he taught at the Imperial University. Anna taught hundreds of mainly female pupils, including many who made a name for themselves as violinists, such as Suwa Nejiko and her sister Akiko, Iwamoto Mari, Ushioda Masuko and Maehashi Teiko, Urakawa Tatsuya and the Iso brothers Tsuneo, Hideo and Yoshio, as well as the violist Imai Nobuko. Ono Anna knew many of the visiting artists from her student days. She introduced Suwa Nejiko, whom she later described as the pupil who impressed her most, to Zimbalist. After the Second World War she joined the faculty of Saitō Hideo's Music School for Children and of the Kunitachi College of Music.

Ono Anna's pupils included her own son Shuntarō, born in 1919. By the time he reached his teens she felt he needed a better teacher than Japan could offer him, and arranged for him to study with Efrem Zimbalist in America. She planned to accompany him; her relationship with Shun'ichi had deteriorated and this seemed a good way to escape from it. About a month before their scheduled departure in 1933, however, Shuntarō died of a ruptured appendix. The marriage broke down under the strain of bereavement, but also because of what Anna later described as a mutual incompatibility. The Onos had featured in an article in the magazine *Friend of the Housewife* about supportive husbands of career women in January 1926.[77] Supportive Shun'ichi may have been, but Anna did not meet his expectations of a wife. Still, the two remained on good terms, and after the Second World War Anna and her sister lived under the same roof as her husband even when he remarried, and with his widow after his death in 1958.[78]

Many of Ono's pupils remembered her for her strictness and insistence on perfection, but also for her warmth and her personal interest in the progress of each individual. Although not well-off herself, she taught several pupils for a reduced fee or no fee at all, if they could not afford the lessons.[79] So much did her students value her advice that in 1952 several of them, by now teachers themselves, formed an association of "grandchild-pupils"; they had their own pupils perform for her and received her advice. The association continued even after her departure from Japan in 1960, regularly sending tapes of student recitals to Sukhumi by the Black Sea, where she lived with her pianist sister Maria and continued to teach violin. More recently, the Ono Anna Memorial Society, as it was named after her death, has moved into cyberspace with a website detailing her achievements and the society's activities.[80]

In the 40 years she spent in Japan, Ono Anna witnessed a spectacular rise in musical standards. In 1949, when Japan had barely started to recover from the war, she expressed her belief that Japan could become a "music nation" and that music would play an important role in building

9: Ono Anna with her pupils after a performance in February 1943 at
Hongō Chūō Kaikan, Tokyo.

a future Japan.[81] In a contribution to a publication about violin playing in
1953, she observed that, while standards had risen worldwide, the
achievements in Japan were particularly remarkable, thanks to the
gramophone record, the radio, and performances by famous artists on
tour. Etō Toshiya, then studying at the Curtis Institute of Music in
Philadelphia, had risen to the highest level. Ono concluded by stating her
conviction that if such progress continued, then "in the coming age, the
Japanese will rival the Jews, who at present hold the highest rank in the
world of violin playing, and advance wonderfully."[82] Ono may have been
too modest to mention it, but she surely knew that the achievements of
Japanese violinists owed much to teachers like herself.

Equally respected as a teacher, but perhaps less loved, was Ono Anna's
compatriot Alexander Mogilevsky.[83] Born into a family of musicians in
Odessa, he had his first lessons in 1892. In 1895 he made his debut with
an orchestra, playing Lalo's *Symphonie Espagnole*. In 1898 he enrolled
at the conservatoire in Moscow, where he first studied with N. N.
Sokolovskij, then with V. Gržimali (or Jan Hřimaly). From 1905 to 1906
he studied with Leopold Auer in St. Petersburg. He graduated from the
Moscow conservatoire (Gržimali's class) in 1909 and won the

Tchaikovsky prize. In 1912 he became head professor at the Music School of the Moscow Philharmonic Society, where he had taught from 1910. He formed his own string quartet in 1909 and reportedly received a Stradivarius from Tsar Nicholas II.[84] Later (1920–21?) he succeeded David Kreyn as the leader of the Stradivarius Quartet.[85] In the First World War he was enlisted as a band conductor. After the 1917 revolution he initially fled to the Ukraine, where he performed and conducted, but returned to Moscow in 1919 to take up an appointment as head professor of violin at the National Conservatoire. In 1921 he resigned from his post and left Russia for good. He spent a year in Poland and two in Sweden and settled in Paris in 1923, where he taught at the Russian Music School. In 1926 he embarked on an Asian tour organized by Avray Strok, who is said to have engaged him to replace Jascha Heifetz when he fell sick. He briefly settled in Tokyo in 1927, but embarked on another tour at the end of the year, which took him to Manchuria, Hong Kong, Singapore, Bombay, Calcutta, Saigon, Rangoon and Java during 1928 and 1929. He returned to Japan in May 1930; according to his Japanese biographer, he was moved by the dedication of the Japanese students he had taught in master classes in 1927.[86] He married his pianist, Nadezhda Nikolaevna Duchess von Leuchtenberg de Beauharnais, a relative of the tsar, in Java in 1929, and their son Michael was born the same year.[87]

Mogilevsky taught at the Tokyo Higher Academy of Music (Tōkyō Kōtō Ongaku Gakuin, predecessor of Kunitachi College of Music) and the Imperial Academy of Music (Teikoku Ongaku Gakkō). He took private pupils, gave concerts and performed for radio broadcasts. From 1937 to 1944 he taught at the Tokyo Academy of Music; reappointed in 1948, he continued to teach at the Academy's successor, Tōkyō Geijutsu Daigaku (Geidai for short; known in English as Tokyo National University of Fine Arts and Music). Mogilevsky applied to be naturalized in 1937. He died in Tokyo in 1953, reportedly a "frustrated and bitter man."[88] His pupils included Matsumoto Zenzō, Suzuki Shin'ichi, Toyama Shigeru, Suwa Nejiko, Etō Toshiya and Unno Yoshio. Mogilevsky was by all accounts a strict teacher. As a world class violinist, he may well have found it hard to understand why his pupils had such trouble learning to play well.[89] Many of them, particularly in the early years, were late starters and had busy lives besides their lessons. Suzuki Shin'ichi was also his colleague at the Kunitachi College and the Imperial Academy besides performing with his string quartet and teaching pupils of his own. Matsumoto Zenzō was a member of the New Philharmonic Orchestra. Mogilevsky's biographer Katō Kiyoshi (1906–) was an adult by the time he studied with him. He recalled that Mogilevsky was never satisfied, and that his students often found it difficult to understand what exactly he wanted. One day Katō lost his patience, although he later apologized for his outburst. On another occasion Mogilevsky apologized to Katō, after he had lost his temper and flung a fountain pen at his feet. That time Katō remained cool, picked up the pen, adjusted the bent nib using his white handkerchief and laid it on Mogilevsky's desk.[90] In the summer, however, when Mogilevsky, like many foreigners, retired to Karuizawa (a mountain resort to the north-west of Tokyo) and his students visited for their lessons, he could become more expansive and tell his students stories from his earlier life. On one occasion someone asked him why he never played Paganini. Mogilevsky responded that he respected Bach and Beethoven most, and that rather than excite audiences and make a lot of money he wanted to end his life as a true artist.[91]

Mogilevsky inspired Japanese musicians as a performer as well as a teacher; they admired his beautiful tone and the Romantic intensity and the individuality of his interpretations. Tsuji Kichinosuke, himself a violin teacher whose pupils included his daughter Hisako, described Mogilevsky as a teacher who brought enlightenment to the world of violin playing in Japan.[92] Suzuki Shin'ichi recalled as the most important lesson he learnt that there is no one right way of playing. Mogilevsky once told him, "I am not the same person today that I was yesterday"; consequently he did not play the same way every day, and the advice he gave his students also varied from lesson to lesson. Presumably some students found this approach confusing rather than enlightening. Others found the clash of musical ideas among their foreign masters exhilarating. When Katō witnessed a rehearsal with the pianist Leonid Kreutzer, he was astonished by the vehement discussions between the two musicians.[93] Mogilevsky's clash with the conductor Rosenstock at a rehearsal for a performance of the Beethoven Violin Concerto in 1937 caused a stir among the members of the New Philharmonic Orchestra. It even made headlines in the daily newspapers, and the music magazine *Ongaku sekai* devoted the best part of an issue to the incident. Not all observers believed that the confrontation was about musical interpretation though: Matsumoto Zenzō, who witnessed the incident, believed that Rosenstock disliked Mogilevsky even before he heard him play a note and stopped him only a few notes into the first solo entry. Matsumoto did recall that Mogilevsky did not make a particularly good sound, but attributed this to his poor instrument made by Miyamoto Kinpachi. Mogilevsky used to describe it with bitter humour as "my Guarnerius" (the fate of his Stradivarius from Tsar Nicholas is not recorded). At any rate Mogilevsky never performed with the orchestra and stopped giving lessons to its members, including Matsumoto. In the end Willy Frey (1907–?) played the concerto.[94] He and Rosenstock had performed together in Berlin in the Jewish Culture Association and perhaps Rosenstock simply wanted to perform together with his friend.

By this time Russians fleeing from the revolution were joined by German Jews fleeing from the Nazis, but, as the above incident shows, the different groups of European refugees did not always mix well. Many of the Russians settled in the Kansai area and contributed much to musical life there. Their activities are not well chronicled. Presumably they often scraped a precarious living, playing in bands and ensembles and giving private lessons. Thus the decades from one world war to the next, so destructive for the European continent and its people that some people, such as the Austrian writer Stefan Zweig, saw it as the end of European culture, gave an enormous boost to European classical music in Japan. To be sure, only a minority of the outstanding artists forced by revolution and persecution to leave their homelands behind settled in Japan, and several of them left for America if they could. But thanks to their dedication, classical music in Japan achieved heights it would hardly have reached in such a short time without them, and the Japanese regarded them with respect and gratitude, sometimes with veneration and even with love.

Russian refugees played a particularly important role in the establishment of Japan's first symphony orchestras outside the Tokyo Academy of Music.

## 2. The Rise of the Symphony Orchestra
Central to Western classical music is the symphony orchestra, and the core of the orchestra is its string section, dominated by two groups of violins. Without a supply of competent violinists there can be no

orchestra. Orchestras can provide a musical and professional outlet for many an eager and ambitious violinist. Before recorded music reached Japan, there was only one way to hear the great symphonic works in the way the composer intended (rather than through a piano transcription): to form an orchestra and play them. No foreign teacher could demonstrate all by himself. Visiting performers played recitals with a pianist or a chamber ensemble. Foreign orchestras did not tour Japan until after the Second World War. Small wonder then, that the first attempts at forming an orchestra with Japanese members started early and were persisted with.

With typical bias towards Tokyo and government-sponsored, central institutions, most writers describe the present-day NHK Symphony Orchestra, founded as the New Symphony Orchestra in October 1926, as Japan's first professional symphony orchestra. But what exactly is a "professional symphony orchestra"? By 1926, several ensembles played symphonic music in the hope of earning a living, not least in the Kansai area. The New Symphony Orchestra, affiliated as it was with national broadcasting, did have a pioneering role though, and the radio represented a decisive impulse for the rise of professional orchestras – another example of how the different forms of entertainment and mass media reinforced each other.

The military bands were the first ensembles to perform arrangements of symphonic works. Franz Eckert, who trained the army band, also organized the first orchestra at the Tokyo Academy of Music, but he had few competent players to work with. His successor August Junker, who arrived on the scene nearly 15 years later, is credited with having founded the first full orchestra (see Part 1 Chapter 2). Junker's successor Gustav Kron premiered several symphonic works, including Beethoven's Ninth Symphony in 1924, which subsequently became a kind of initiation rite for new orchestras. Wind instruments other than the flute were not taught at the Academy, so the wind players came from the military bands. The military also began to train their own string players from 1907, sending students to the Academy. From 1912, the regular military band performances in Hibiya Park included string players.

Another training ground for musical professionals was the youth bands organized by major department stores as a means of advertising themselves. They were essentially wind bands, but several members later took up stringed instruments (see Part 1, introduction).[95] The Matsuzakaya department store in Nagoya even expanded its band into a full symphony orchestra in 1935. Moving to Tokyo in 1938, it merged with the Victor studio recording orchestra and was renamed the Central Symphony Orchestra (Chūō Gakudan), and in 1941 the Tokyo Symphony Orchestra (Tōkyō Kōkyō Gakudan). Renamed again in 1945, it is now the Tokyo Philharmonic Orchestra (Tōkyō Fuiruhāmonī Kōkyō Gakudan). In 1939 Manfred Gurlitt (1890–1972) was engaged as a conductor. As well as conducting symphonic works, he made efforts to establish opera in Japan.[96]

The years around 1920 saw the emergence of music societies at universities as well as the Suwa Symphony Orchestra in Nagano Prefecture, which prides itself upon being Japan's oldest amateur orchestra – founded in 1925, it celebrated its eightieth anniversary in 2005.[97] Its founder Imai Hisao came from a family of textile manufacturers. A self-taught violin and viola player, he made friends with local members of the Shirakaba (White Birches) literary movement, several of whom had become interested in Western music during their studies. The members of the Suwa Philharmonic Society continued to play throughout the war years, and after the war the orchestra expanded rapidly.

University music societies came in many forms. Some started as music appreciation societies and evolved into active ensembles and in some cases full orchestras. The Wagner Society at Keiō College (renamed Keiō University in 1918) held its first performance in 1902 with invited performers. By the early 1920s, Keiō had its own ensemble, which on 11 September 1924 accompanied Gustav Kron in Beethoven's Violin Concerto. The present Waseda University soon followed suit, establishing a music society in 1907. Gakushūin, the Peers' College, established an orchestra in 1908. Tokyo Imperial University did not establish its own symphony orchestra until 1920. Even before then, members of the university played in various groups, and some, like Tanabe Hisao, played in the orchestra of the Tokyo Academy of Music in their student days. The music department of Kyūshū Imperial University gave its first concert in 1912. By 1919 it had an orchestra with 31 members and gave a performance of Beethoven's First Symphony. A concert on 26 January 1924 included the final movement of Beethoven's

Ninth and the Bach Double Concerto with visiting soloists from Tokyo: Andō Kō and Ōno Hisayori.[98]

The best college orchestra in the 1930s was that of Kyoto Imperial University. Its beginnings resembled those of other university orchestras. At its first concert on 25 February 1917 the ensemble had only 13 players. They were conducted by Ōmura Josaburō, whom we already have encountered as a leading violinist and conductor in the Kansai area (Part 1 Chapter 5). By 1931 it had 59 members. The orchestra's success was largely due to the appointment of Emmanuel Metter (1878–1941) as a conductor in 1926.[99] Under his baton the Kyoto University Orchestra became a major orchestra of the Kansai region. Born into a Jewish merchant family in Kherson in the Ukraine, with a law degree from Kharkov and a music degree from St. Petersburg, Metter was another Russian refugee whose contribution transformed music in the years between the world wars. He was conducting the symphony orchestra in Harbin, most of whose members were Russian, when he received the invitation to conduct the new Osaka Philharmonic Orchestra, established under the auspices of the Osaka broadcasting office. His wife, the ballerina Elena Osovska, had already come to Japan the year before to teach at the school of the Takarazuka Revue.

At Metter's first performance on 1 June 1926, the Osaka orchestra was reinforced by several string players from the Kyoto University Orchestra. In fact, in both Osaka and Kyoto, various ensembles and orchestras formed, dissolved and re-formed from a limited pool of players. Attempts to stage regular symphony concerts began as early as 1906 with the establishment of the Osaka Music Society (Ōsaka Ongaku Kyōkai). Here too, Ōmura Josaburo was one of the leading lights, and the ensemble's 30 members included 15 violinists. Other ensembles included the Hagoromo Orchestra, which gave its first concert in 1915. It began as the house orchestra of Masuda Shin'ichi, a wealthy businessman; Osaka had a strong tradition of businesspeople supporting the arts. Unfortunately, the Hagoromo Orchestra had to disband when Masuda's business fell on hard times. The Osaka Philharmonic Orchestra (named after the recently established Tokyo Philharmonic Orchestra and not a direct predecessor of the broadcasting orchestra) also gave its first concert in 1915,.[100]

The most successful and long-lived of the pre-war professional symphony orchestras in the Kansai area was the Takarazuka Symphony Orchestra, which gave its first concert in 1924 under the Austrian musician Josef Laska (1886–1964).[101] Laska had studied music in Munich and had come to Japan the previous year, after a stint teaching piano at the conservatoire in Vladivostok. The hotel in Yokohama where he was supposed to be employed burnt down in the Great Kantō Earthquake just before he arrived. Instead, Laska was hired by the school of the Takarazuka Revue. Under his leadership the ensemble that had been formed to accompany stage performances became a full orchestra which also gave symphony concerts as the Takurazuka Symphony Orchestra, the most important orchestra in the Kansai region after that of Kyoto University. From September 1926 until he left Japan in 1935 and was denied re-entry, Laska conducted monthly subscription concerts under the auspices of the Takarazuka Symphony Society, 150 in all. He introduced his audiences to a wide and varied repertoire, including chamber music, symphonies and even operas. In 1927 he organized three Beethoven evenings to celebrate the hundredth anniversary of the composer's death. Nevertheless, the Takarazuka Symphony Orchestra, like the musical culture of the Kansai region in general, occupies only a minor place in the mainstream narrative, which is dominated by activities in Tokyo.

When the Osaka Philharmonic Orchestra folded in 1929 (it was re-formed on a smaller scale in 1933), Metter concentrated his activities on the Kyoto University Orchestra. During his tenure it performed all of Beethoven's symphonies. The performance of the Ninth on 17 November 1936 left several of the players sobbing like members of a football team that has just won a major tournament.[102] Apart from Beethoven, Metter's repertoire centred on the Russian composers – a marked contrast to the German-centred activities at the Tokyo Academy of Music. Metter also gave private lessons in music theory based on the harmony textbook by Nikolay Rimsky-Korsakov (1844–1908), and his students included several musicians who went on to shape musical life, such as the conductor Asahina Takashi (see following chapter).[103] Metter gave his last concert with the Kyoto orchestra in June 1937. In spring 1938 he sat in the audience as Asahina conducted his first concert with the orchestra. Metter's final broadcast conducting the re-formed Osaka Broadcasting Orchestra took place on 28 September 1939. A few days later he boarded a ship for San Francisco; whether this was in search of better musical prospects or because of the increasingly repressive political climate we cannot know for certain.

Meanwhile, in Tokyo as well, orchestras were forming and re-forming. The predecessors of the NHK Symphony Orchestra fitted the desirable image of a symphony orchestra created by representatives of the Tokyo-based musical establishment to perform serious music purely for the sake of the art. The driving forces behind them were Yamada Kōsaku and Konoe Hidemaro.[104] Soon after his return from Berlin in 1914, Yamada organized a symphony concert with financial support from the entrepreneur Iwasaki Yatarō. In 1915 he attempted to organize a professional orchestra, but it disbanded after its first concert the same year. The association of Yamada and Konoe began in 1916, when Konoe took lessons in composition with Yamada. Konoe Hidemaro, the younger brother of the later statesman and wartime prime minister, Konoe Fumimaro (1891–1945) was born into an aristocratic family in 1898. He took up the violin in 1913. In 1919 he enrolled in the Aesthetics course at Tokyo Imperial University, but he soon lost interest in the lectures and concentrated on his musical activities. In 1922 he led the orchestra of Tokyo Imperial University on a tour of the north of Japan. In 1923 he travelled to Europe, where he studied conducting and composition at the Sternsche Konservatorium in Berlin.[105] On 18 January 1924 he conducted the Berlin Philharmonic Orchestra in a programme which included four compositions of his own. After his return to Japan he founded the Konoe Symphony Orchestra.

In 1924, Konoe and Yamada joined forces and established the Japan Symphonic Association (Nihon Kōkyōgaku Kyōkai). In April 1925 they organized the Japan–Russia Joint Symphony Orchestra, which gave several performances in Tokyo before continuing to Shizuoka, Nagoya, Kyoto, Osaka and Kobe.[106] Most of the 33 Russian musicians were members of the symphony orchestra in Harbin and they dominated the list of players in the violin and viola sections. They included the first and second concertmasters Josef König and Nikolai Schifferblatt, conductors of the New Symphony Orchestra from 1927 to 1929 and from 1929 to 1935 respectively. The Japanese string players, including eight violinists, came from the various ensembles that played in cinemas, hotels or on ocean liners. The concerts of the Japan–Russia Joint Symphony

Orchestra caused a sensation; never before had orchestral music performed to such a high standard been heard in Japan.

After the Russians returned home, Konoe and Yamada merged their respective ensembles to form the Japan Symphonic Association Orchestra, which gave its first subscription concert on 24 January 1926. A few months later, however, Yamada and Konoe fell out, probably over money.[107] Most of the members, 44 of them, joined Konoe, who established the New Symphony Orchestra (Shin Kōkyō Gakudan), the forerunner of the present-day NHK Orchestra, on 5 October 1926. From the start the orchestra had a broadcasting contract, negotiated by Konoe. Its first live performance, delayed by the death of Emperor Taishō, took place on 20 February 1927, with Konoe conducting. The programme included Mendelssohn's *Fingal's Cave*, Mozart's Ballet music *Idomeneo* and Schubert's Seventh Symphony. Josef König and Konoe shared the conducting and König rehearsed the orchestra once a week. To strengthen the string section, Konoe recruited players from the orchestra of the Tokyo Academy of Music as extras.[108] Another move to improve the standard of the string section was the appointment of Saitō Hideo as first cellist and assistant conductor when he returned from his studies in Berlin and Leipzig in 1928.[109] When König was forced to leave Japan in 1929, Schifferblatt succeeded him. The orchestral profession as it formed itself in the 1920s was male-dominated, as in Europe, but the orchestra did include four female violinists: Taka Tamae and Kamahara Yoshiko in the first violins and Nakajima Tazuko and Satō Yukiko in the second violins.[110]

Konoe had high ambitions for the orchestra, including a European tour. In September 1930, he left for Europe with plans to set up an agency that would manage tours for Japanese artists abroad and for European artists in Japan.[111] Although he had not originally planned to do so, he conducted several concerts. He met Wilhelm Furtwängler and other leading conductors, whose scores he often borrowed for copying. He returned to Japan in early 1931. On the way, in Harbin, he met Yamada Kōsaku, who was on his way to Europe for what would be his last foreign tour, and the two were reconciled.

Tensions in the orchestra, however, were rising. Konoe negotiated contracts with NHK and provided the scores (purchased in Germany, where the inflation in the 1920s made his yen go a long way), while his family financed most of the running costs. Konoe took a cavalier attitude towards the players' pay and working conditions, acting as if they were his personal orchestra. It was all very well for him to prioritize his artistic aspirations over commercial considerations and expect the players to rehearse every day. But as long as they were not paid enough to make a living they had to take on other work for extra income. By 1931 many had had enough and protested. Konoe, in response, wanted to sack the oldest and weakest players. The members of the orchestra resisted, but had to give in to his demands when he resigned. Persuaded to return, Konoe fired 24 players, who established the Corona Orchestra (later Tokyo Broadcasting Orchestra), which specialized in light music. Both orchestras played regularly for radio broadcasts. The musicians' discontent with their financial situation, however, remained unresolved. The more time they were expected to devote to the orchestra, the less time they had for their other jobs on which they depended in order to make ends meet. They wanted contracts with NHK directly, but NHK felt it could not dispense with Konoe and his connections.

Konoe travelled abroad again in 1933, conducting concerts in Europe and America and returning to Japan in February 1934. In June 1935 he finally left the orchestra for good. From 1936 onwards, he travelled between Japan, the United States and Europe and ended up spending the war in Europe. In April 1946 he once more conducted "his" orchestra and in 1951 he founded the Konoe Orchestra.

The New Symphony Orchestra gave a concert without a conductor in Tokyo's Hibiya Park in August 1935 to a huge audience and to great acclaim. For a year the members played under a series of Japanese and foreign guest conductors, including König and Schifferblatt. In May 1936 the orchestra made a new contract with NHK. In future it was to give up to eight broadcasts a month under the name Japan Broadcasting Orchestra (Nihon Hōsō Kōkyō Gakudan). In August Josef Rosenstock was appointed as regular conductor. Recommended by the cellist Emanuel Feuermann, who had performed with the orchestra a few months earlier, Rosenstock was the first conductor of international renown to work regularly with a Japanese orchestra. Another Jew whose career at home was cut short by the Nazis, Rosenstock worked hard and successfully to bring the New Symphony Orchestra up to international professional standards. A strict taskmaster, he treated the members of the orchestra like recalcitrant pupils. When he was particularly angry, he reputedly scolded them, calling them "Waseda Orchestra," by which he presumably meant, "amateurs."[112]

It may have been Rosenstock who, following the example of the yearly performances at the Volksbühne in Berlin, initiated in 1938 what has become a Japanese "Rite of Winter": the performance of Beethoven's Ninth Symphony at the end of the year.[113] The New Symphony Orchestra had first performed the work in May 1927 under Konoe as part of the centenary celebrations. The performance under Rosenstock on 26 and 27 December 1938 was the first year-end performance (he had previously conducted the orchestra in a performance of the Ninth in Osaka on 30 October 1938). The choir consisted of the Tōkyō Kōtō Ongaku Gakuin (now Kunitachi College of Music), and the Tamagawa Gakuen choirs. Similar performances were given in 1940, 1942 and 1944, although the last two were not conducted by Rosenstock himself, who had been forced to retire to Karuizawa after the start of the Pacific War.[114]

From 1938, the war began to seriously affect Japan's musical life, including that of its orchestras. The National Mobilization Law subjected the country's entire economy to the demands of war. The New Symphony Orchestra began losing members to the draft, and those that remained had to play at special concerts for soldiers. Even so, in June 1939 the orchestra embarked on its first tour overseas (albeit to countries occupied by Japan) to give two concerts in Seoul, conducted by Saitō Hideo and with the violinist Wanibuchi Kenshū (1910–86) as soloist.[115] That same year, in March, the Harbin Symphony Orchestra toured Japan under its conductor Sergei Schvaikovsky. Vladimir Trachtenberg, who had led the violin section in 1925, was still concertmaster, but after the Japanese invasion of Manchuria, many of the orchestra's former members had fled to Shanghai, and although the ranks had been filled by Jewish refugees from Europe and even by Japanese (two of whom came on the tour), the orchestra's heyday had passed. The tour was advertised as "Japan–Manchukuo Defense Against Communism Friendship Artistic Mission." The orchestras made a broadcast and gave six concerts in Tokyo before continuing to Nagoya, Osaka, Hakata and Nagasaki. Returning to the mainland it also performed in Seoul and the capital of Manchukuo, Hsinking (Shinkyō). Among the soloists engaged locally was Alexander Mogilevsky, who performed the Tchaikovsky Violin Concerto with the orchestra "with gusto."[116] Japanese music lovers had high expectations of the tour and orchestra's concerts were sold out. But while the general public appeared to enjoy them, the published reviews were for the most part damning. The Harbin orchestra may have been past its best, while the New Symphony Orchestra, which gave its two hundredth subscription concert that year, had become a highly disciplined ensemble – thanks to the training received from König and Schifferblatt, and, more recently, from Rosenstock. But perhaps the stream of foreign artists in the last 20 years had simply made Japanese critics more fastidious.[117]

By 1939, however, touring artists no longer came to Japan. The New Symphony Orchestra accompanied juvenile native talent instead. In 1940 Etō Toshiya and Iwabuchi Ryūtarō, winners of that year's Music Competition (see Chapter 5), performed the Bach Double Concerto with the orchestra; Rosenstock was apparently impressed. Thirteen years later, in 1953, Iwabuchi became the orchestra's youngest ever concertmaster.

In 1944, performances by foreigners were forbidden. The last foreign soloist to perform in Japan during the war was Willy Frey, another refugee, who played the Brahms Violin Concerto in March 1943. Rosenstock himself conducted for the last time in February 1944, after which he went into virtual exile in Karuizawa, while native conductors took over. Despite worsening conditions and throughout the bombings of Tokyo from 1944, the orchestra continued to perform. Fortunately, their rehearsal venue and the Hibiya concert hall survived, and the subscription concerts continued when most other entertainment had ceased. The last wartime subscription concert, with Beethoven's Ninth, took place on 14 June 1945, nine days before American troops invaded Okinawa.

Even so, one month after the end of the war the orchestra was back for their 268th subscription concert on 14 and 15 September 1945, and for the October concert, Rosenstock returned as conductor. He remained in Japan with the orchestra for another year, giving a last concert on 16 October 1946 before leaving for his original destination, America. He would return as guest conductor in 1951 and 1956.

The new orchestras forming and re-forming in the 1920s and 1930s provided playing opportunities for violinists, whether amateurs or professionals. The best ones, such as the Kyoto University Symphony Orchestra and the forerunners of the NHK Orchestra, did much to raise the general level of playing. The earliest foreign conductors of the New

Philharmonic Orchestra, König and Schifferblatt, were outstanding violinists themselves and taught several of the rank-and-file members individually as well as rehearsing the entire orchestra. They must have found it uphill work, particularly at first. The players, late starters by today's standards, came from a variety of backgrounds. Nevertheless, the new symphony orchestras provided professional opportunities and a training ground for musicians, and contributed significantly to the foundations of Japan's post-war musical life.

## 3. New Opportunities for Violinists

Perhaps no period in the history of the violin in Japan to this day produced violinists of such diverse backgrounds with such varied careers as the years between the two world wars. The Tokyo Academy of Music, where nearly all the first-generation violinists had studied, no longer held a monopoly (not that its monopoly had ever been complete anyway) on training musicians. As school teachers and former military band members brought Western music and the violin to many parts of the country, even people far from the capital had the chance to see, hear, and sometimes play a violin. The demand for competent violinists grew faster than the still-limited learning opportunities could meet. The popularity of the violin early in the twentieth century, together with the new possibilities for earning a living with the instrument, motivated many to study it by themselves or with a minimum of formal instruction from anyone who was able to provide it. A few enterprising souls began to envisage a career as a solo performer. By the early twentieth century, several routes led to music and new career paths began to open. Although all the men introduced in this chapter – for most women, teaching remained the only career option – earned their living as musicians, not all of them stayed with the violin they had studied in their youth.

One of the earliest violinists to perform regularly all over Japan was Takashina Tetsuo.[118] Born in 1896 in the town of Namerikawa in Toyama Prefecture, he graduated from Toyama Prefecture's teacher training college in 1914 and worked for two years as a teacher before moving to Tokyo and enrolling in the preparatory department of the Tokyo Academy of Music. Whether he started to learn the violin then or earlier, perhaps during his teacher training, is not clear. Sugiyama Haseo (1889–1952), a respected performer at the time, remembered giving Takashina private lessons around the time of his entrance examination.[119] In 1917 he was accepted as a regular student and studied with Gustav Kron.[120] He graduated in 1921, playing Ferdinand David's Introduction and Variations on the Air "Je suis le petit tambour" ("I am the Little Drummer," Op. 5) at the graduation concert. By then he had already given several performances at the regular concerts staged by the Friends of the Academy, giving his first performance in November 1917 with the first two movements of Seitz's Concerto No. 32 in D minor.

After graduation, Takashina taught at the Music School for Girls and Yamada Gen'ichirō's Japan Music School, as well as continuing to give regular performances in Tokyo and the surrounding areas and in his native Toyama. In 1921 he also performed in Hiroshima, Wakayama, as well as Moji, Kumamoto and Kokura on Kyushu Island and Sapporo and Otaru on Hokkaido. His repertoire consisted mostly of short pieces; in 1921 and 1922 it included Sarasate's *Zigeunerweisen,* Schubert's Serenade, the "Garden Scene" from Wieniawski's Fantasy on themes from Gounod's *Faust*, a Polish dance by Wieniawski and a minuet by Beethoven. In 1923-24, his most performed works were Drdla's Hungarian Dance, Sarasate's Spanish Dance, Schubert's Serenade and his *Ave Maria*, and David's Introduction and Variations on the Air "Je suis le petit tambour." In 1926 his repertoire included a minuet written by himself.[121]

His most successful composition however, which won him at least local fame, is the song "The Bell on the Clock Tower" (Tokeidai no kane), composed during or after his second tour to Hokkaido in 1923. In 1922 he had married Aizawa Masuko, a native of Sapporo who graduated from the postgraduate department of the Tokyo Academy of Music as a singer in 1922. The song was supposedly inspired by a scathing review of his second performance in Sapporo and celebrates the clock tower of Sapporo Agricultural School, the forerunner of Hokkaido University. The melody was first published in January 1924 (Takashina subsequently revised it and added an accompaniment). His wife premiered it in Osaka that year.

Besides solo recitals, Takashina also performed chamber music; he was a member of a string quartet named the Haydn Quartet and established the Beethoven Trio, which among other performances played at Friends of the Academy concerts in 1923 and 1925.

Takashina played the violin "Number One" by the maker Miyamoto Kinpachi, a fact that newspapers found worth mentioning. He had considerable success as a performer – particularly in his home prefecture of Toyama, hardly spoilt for professional concerts of Western music. A review of a performance in Nagoya in 1924 described him as a genius (*tensai*).[122] In 1926, a newspaper named him as the second-most prolific performer in Tokyo after his one-time teacher Sugiyama Haseo (1889–1952). He was also one of the first to play for radio broadcasts, which began in 1925. But how good was he? In 1927 a review of contemporary performers in the magazine *Musical Star* described his playing as "teacher-style": correct but boring to listen to: "there is little or nothing in his performance that emanates [the author used the English word in *katakana* phonetic script] from himself' or in other words, 'there is no temperament' [the word in Latin script]."[123]

Indeed, he may have been more successful as a teacher. Among the several private schools he taught at was the Children's Music and Drama School, founded by the actress Kawakami Sadayakko in 1924, where his pupils included one of the school's first graduates, Aiba Minoru (1912–99). Aiba went on to a long and successful career as an orchestral violinist, concertmaster and teacher; after 1945 he played in NHK's Nagoya broadcasting orchestra for 46 years until it was abolished in 1990.[124] The Kawakami school closed after a few years, but several former students became famous actors.

In 1926 Takashina published a violin tutor based on a manuscript by his teacher Gustav Kron.[125] He spent his last years in Nagoya, where from 1941 he conducted the Central Broadcasting Orchestra. Takashina gave his last recital during his second year in Nagoya, on 25 April 1942. The week before, Nagoya, Tokyo and Kobe had experienced the first air raids. The programme was quite unlike those of his early performing career; it consisted of Händel's Sonata VI in E and three Beethoven Sonatas, op 57 in f, op 24 in E and 47 in A. In 1944 Takashina left Nagoya because of the intensifying air raids, and he died in 1945, just four months before the end of the war.

While Takashina came to the violin by the "orthodox" route of the Meiji period, through the education system and the Tokyo Academy of Music, Kiyose Yasuji (1900–81) [126] was largely self-taught. Today he is best known as a composer, and his works include violin sonatas. He contributed to the discussions about a "'Japanese" style of classical music in the 1920s and 1930s, and was one of the organizers of the Association for Innovative Composers (Shinkō Sakkyokuka Renmei) in 1930, and of the New Composers' Association in 1946.

Born in Yokkaichi in Ōita Prefecture, as the son of a prosperous local businessman, Kiyose grew up in a musical environment dominated by traditional sounds, although they mixed with the Western-style songs and pieces taught at school. His father enjoyed performing various kinds of traditional music, while the young Yasuji played in ensembles with violin, *koto, shakuhachi*, and *shamisen*. They played Japanese melodies but also Western pieces in unison, school songs, marches, waltzes and other tunes they knew from memory. "Because we played kneeling on the floor," he later remembered, "the bowing was chaotic, and we didn't worry about fingering at all."[127] After finishing school he spent some time in Beppu, where he found a teacher trained at a music school in Tokyo who gave him lessons based on Hohmann's *Practical Violin Tutor*.

Having failed several entrance examinations, he was finally admitted to Matsuyama High School, on the island of Shikoku. He still played the violin; in 1919 the local paper reported a disturbance created by a group of students including one playing the violin; this was Kiyose. At that time he preferred low-brow music and knew only a few pieces from the classical violin repertoire. One day, however, he bought his first score of a famous piece of classical music in a shop in Matsuyama. This, he later recalled, changed his life: "One day I bought a score for string quartet of a Beethoven minuet in the music shop. I could read neither the alto clef nor the bass clef, so I started playing the second violin part and continued with the first violin part. I received a huge shock. I was moved from the depths of my heart by the darkness and depth of the musical thought contained within the simple melody."[128] The minuet was a transcription from the piano sonata 49.2 (Beethoven also used this minuet in the Septet Op. 20), published in the *String Quartet Album* edited by Hans Sitt. Possibly it was left behind by a German prisoner of war when their camp was moved to Bandō; this would explain the score's presence in the shop at a time when Western music was rarely played in Matsuyama.

Determined to study music seriously, Kiyose dropped out of high school and moved to Tokyo, where he sought out Tanabe Hisao and Yamada Kōsaku with an introduction from a schoolmate. He took private lessons from Yamada, but they soon bored him. He also felt that that the kind of Western harmony Yamada taught him was too far removed from what he wanted to compose. So he continued to teach himself while enjoying the cultural and musical life of Tokyo.

In 1921 he moved back to his home village and married a local teacher he had fallen in love with while he was home for his military examination the previous year. For a year the couple lived in the hot spring resort of Ibusuki, supposedly for Kiyose's health. He began setting poetry to music, using a reed organ when he composed. His first composition was published in 1922. From Ibusuki the Kiyoses moved to Kagoshima and then back to Yokkaichi. Kiyose continued to study music by himself. But although he read magazines delivered from Tokyo, he soon realized the need to be with other musicians and composers and moved there himself. There he could associate with other composers searching for new kinds of musical expression. For a while he also played second violin in the National Orchestra (Kokumin Kōkyō Gakudan), founded in 1928 by the composer Komatsu Heigorō with the aim of performing new works, including those of the Japanese composers involved in the venture. But increasingly, he played the piano rather than the violin, often accompanying singers. His music combined elements of German Romanticism and French Impressionism with features from traditional Japanese music, especially folksongs. For a brief while he taught the celebrated composer Takemitsu Tōru.

Asahina Takashi (1908–2001) likewise started his career as a violinist.[129] He gave violin performances in and around Osaka in the 1930s. By the turn of the twenty-first century he was the most popular native conductor in Japan, having stood on the podium of the Osaka Philharmonic Orchestra for 50 years, besides conducting 70 orchestras at home and abroad. And yet he never attended a conservatoire and did not become a conductor until the age of 40; indeed he considered himself fortunate to have received a broad education, rather than one narrowly focused on music.[130]

Asahina first started playing the violin as a schoolboy, at a time when this was still unusual. He did not come from a musical family; both his father and his adopted father worked as engineers for the railways. But after the Kantō earthquake, several relatives moved into the family's Tokyo home, and one of them played the violin. He suggested that

Takashi learn too, and his grandmother, believing that exercising his arms might improve his asthma, bought him an instrument second-hand at a market selling things salvaged from the earthquake. He had lessons from his music teacher at high school, a graduate of the Tokyo Academy of Music (Tanaka Keiichi, famous for publishing works for children's music education). When he felt Asahina needed a better teacher he introduced him to Hashimoto Kunihiko (1904–49), then well known as a violinist, although he later made his name as a composer. As soon as Asahina could play a little, he and three schoolmates decided to play as a string quartet. The other violinist also had lessons from Tanaka, but the violist and cellist only learnt to hold their instruments from a clarinettist of the Toyama Officers' School's military band, who owned a viola. Somehow they got hold of a score of Haydn's "Emperor" Quartet, copied out the parts in pencil and started rehearsing; Asahina later recalled that it was more like a sport than like music-making.[131]

In 1928 Asahina enrolled in the law department of Kyoto Imperial University and played the violin in the University's orchestra. This also included alumni and townspeople and was conducted by Emmanuel Metter, whom Asahina had seen conducting the New Symphony Orchestra in Tokyo in 1927. Graduating in 1931, Asahina worked for the Hankyū railway company before returning to Kyoto University and enrolling in the Faculty of Letters in 1933. He had substituted in orchestras in the intervening two years. Now Metter told him to study the violin seriously with a view to becoming a musician; he should work hard for three years before deciding whether or not he had the ability. Metter found him an unnamed Polish teacher who taught him by the Russian method, starting from scratch. Metter himself taught him musical theory. In those days it was still rare for a young person to have studied the violin continuously for ten years, and there was a dearth of good string players, who, after all, represent the backbone of the symphony orchestra.

Asahina continued to play in ensembles and taught basic courses at the Osaka School of Music from 1934, where he was appointed professor in 1937. He played chamber music with colleagues. Soon, however, conducting became his main occupation. He made his debut with the Kyoto orchestra in 1937. His Tokyo debut with the New Symphony Orchestra followed in 1939. In 1942 he left the Osaka School of Music to become a conductor for NHK's orchestra in Osaka. But only a year later the government sent him abroad to conduct in occupied territories, first in Shanghai, where the Japanese occupation authorities had forced the celebrated Municipal Orchestra to disband and re-form. The end of the war found him in Harbin. The future concertmaster of the Berlin Philharmonic, Hellmut Stern, played under Asahina in the Harbin Symphony Orchestra and remembered him as a highly gifted young man, who soon found esteem and respect among the sceptical Europeans.[132]

After his repatriation he resumed his career as a conductor for NHK. In 1947 he made his debut with the newly formed Kansai Orchestra, whose members formed the core of the Osaka Philharmonic Orchestra in 1950. His first foreign tour took place in 1956 when he (among others) conducted the Berlin Philharmonic Orchestra. His association with the Osaka Philharmonic Orchestra lasted until his death in December 2001, by which time he was the world's oldest active conductor. In April 2001, after conducting the Osaka Philharmonic Orchestra in a Bruckner Symphony he remarked on how good the players had become.[133] No-one could know better than Asahina, for he had been part of the movement to create a permanent orchestra in Osaka almost from the beginning. Although from Tokyo, Asahina pioneered Western orchestral music in the Kansai region.

Kishi Kōichi (1909–37), another violinist turned conductor, came from the Kansai area and was very much a product of musical life there. Kishi's short life is like an unfulfilled promise: highly talented and creative in many fields, as well as playing the violin in concerts and conducting, he acted, made films, and composed solo works for violin, for voice and for orchestra.

Born near Osaka on 31 March 1909 as the eldest of eight children, Kishi enjoyed the best opportunities for his musical development. Both his parents came from wealthy merchant families. His father could afford to buy a gramophone and records, to take him to virtually all the concerts by visiting foreign artists, to pay for music lessons at home and abroad and later to support many of his son's extravagant creative projects. The Kansai region was a good place for a budding musician in the 1920s; many of the Eastern European refugees who ended up in Japan, including some outstanding musicians, settled around Kobe and taught in the area.

The Kishi family loved music. Both Kōichi's father Narajirō and his mother Kame had played the violin in their youth, and Kame sometimes played Japanese tunes on her violin for her children. Kōichi's sisters learnt the *koto* and the *shamisen* and later the piano. In 1919 the family moved from Osaka to Ashiya in Hyōgo Prefecture, where Kōichi attended the newly founded Kōnan Middle School.[134] One day their father brought home a small violin; he wanted "someone" to learn, and as Kōichi showed an interest his mother began to teach him. Eventually his father invited his mother's former teacher Ōhashi Junjirō to visit the family once a week to teach violin, piano and singing in chorus. A graduate of the Tokyo Academy of Music, Ōhashi performed regularly in the area and taught in his own studio. But his teaching was strict and unimaginative. He stuck closely to the Hohmann's *Practical Violin Tutor*, from which he had presumably learnt himself, and Kōchi soon got bored. But although he did not practise much, he listened to music on the gramophone and like Suzuki Shin'ichi was bewitched by Elman's famous tone. In February 1921 he had the chance to hear Elman live in Kobe. The "Elman shock" gripped him like so many other Japanese music enthusiasts, and he picked up his violin again. At the family's Saturday house concerts he amused them with his attempts to imitate Elman. In the following years he had the chance to listen to other world-class players, including Heifetz (1923), Kreisler, and Zimbalist (1924). But the family also attended the concerts with local musicians. When the Takarazuka Symphony Orchestra was founded in 1924, the Kishi family regularly attended its concerts, and the conductor Josef Laska became a family friend and music teacher for Kōichi and his sisters.

Laska was not the family's only connection with the community of foreigners living in and around Kobe and frequenting the beaches near Ashiya. One summer evening in 1923, Kōichi and his uncle Yoshio were playing duets, when a foreign couple knocked on the door of the Kishi's Western-style home near the beach. They turned out to be a violinist, Michael Wexler (1896–?), and his wife, who had been drawn by the sound of violin music. Wexler, a native of Lithuania, had toured northern Europe as a child prodigy, studied with Leopold Auer, and taught at St. Petersburg before moving to Vladivostok in 1917. He had intended to go to America when he stopped over in Japan, gave concerts all over the country and settled in Osaka. He did go to New York in 1930, but returned to Japan, where he continued to perform and teach.

Kōichi became Wexler's pupil. In November 1924 he gave his first recital at a concert in his school, performing one of Dancla's Airs Variés, Auguste Durand's Chaconne, an unidentified fantasy based on Bizet's *Carmen* and other study pieces, as well as a favourite of his which he would perform many times: Elman's arrangement of Giovanni Battista Sammartini's *Canto amoroso*.[135] In May the following year (1925) he gave his first public performance in Osaka, in the Miki Music Store Hall; this was organized by Wexler, who praised his tone in the programme notes. His repertoire was still basic; the most advanced piece was the Concerto in A minor by Jean-Baptiste Accolay (he regretted not being able to perform the Mendelssohn Violin Concerto). But the first generation of Japanese wunderkinder did not excite the public until a few years later, and for a high school student to give a solo recital was a small sensation. That same year Kishi also joined the newly formed orchestra of the Osaka Broadcasting Office (JOBK).

Kōichi's father's foreign acquaintances included a certain Walther F. Schulz, who ran a Swiss Rolex shop in Osaka and whose father Oskar had been the head of a conservatoire in Geneva. He urged Kishi Narajirō to send his son abroad and promised his full support. Narajirō agreed, although reluctantly; Kōichi had not even graduated from high school. In September 1926 he gave a farewell recital in Ashiya, playing both solo and as part of a string quartet. In the weeks before he left he had a few violin lessons with Eugen Klein (1893–1943), another Russian refugee, who had just arrived in Kobe.

On 9 December 1926 Kishi Kōichi left Japan, taking with him a new violin his father had bought him for 1,000 yen from the maker Miyamoto Kinpachi, Japan's finest at the time. He arrived in Geneva in January 1927, where the Schulz family welcomed him into their home and secured his enrolment at the Conservatoire de Musique de Genève in the class of Fernand Closset (1886–1962). Kishi practised hard and did well. In March 1928 he performed in a concert given by Closset's students, playing a movement from Vieuxtemps' Concerto No. 4. At the next June examination he narrowly missed graduating in first place. A few weeks later he left for Baden-Baden to attend Carl Flesch's summer school.

Here, among some of the world's top violinists, Kishi must have had a shock. He hid himself away in a monastery outside the town and practised eight to nine hours every day, until Flesch told him that four hours of really focused practising would be more effective. Flesch must nevertheless have been sufficiently impressed with him to invite him to Berlin, and Kishi arrived there in mid-September, having spent a few days in Paris on the way. Whether he immediately enrolled at the conservatoire is unclear, since the school's records only list him as a regular student for the winter semester 1930–31.[136] He did apparently have lessons with Flesch's assistant Max Rostal, and lessons in harmony with the composer Robert Kahn (1865–1951). In 1929 he again attended Flesch's summer school. This time Flesch was not enthusiastic. In a letter to Rostal in Berlin, he wrote:

> Kishi played for me again the other day, and I have to say that he did not impress me. I believe it is a mistake that he has long discontinued tone exercises. Because of this his tone has become worse again. The exercises at the bridge he must continue for the rest of his life, if he wants to produce a halfway decent tone. Also, in his bowing, a strong distortion in the form of the bow sliding to and fro at the point was noticeable which was caused by the way he pressed his fourth finger hard onto the stick when he played at the point.[137]

Among the many concerts Kishi heard in Berlin, one in particular stood out and shook his confidence profoundly. This time he was surely in good company, for the performer was the 13-year-old Yehudi Menuhin, who on 12 April 1929 made his Berlin debut with Bach, Beethoven and Brahms. Kishi and his fellow student, the Philippine violinist Ramon Tapales (1906–95) looked at each other in despair. Was there even any point in continuing their studies? Continue they did though, and that autumn Kishi returned to Japan intending to show the Japanese music world what he had learnt. He had even more to show off: just before he left Berlin he bought the "King George" Stradivarius, having persuaded his father to provide the required 60,000 yen. Even for the wealthy Kishi family this was a staggering sum, for which Kishi Narajirō had to arrange a loan. The purchase duly completed on 27 August, Kōichi boarded the train from Berlin. This time he took the Trans-Siberian railway, which proved to be fortunate, for he met the pianist Leo Sirota, who was travelling to Japan for the second time, this time with his family. Sirota became Kishi's duo partner in several recitals.

Kishi's real debut was to be in Tokyo; he planned both a recital with Leo Sirota and a concert with the New Symphony Orchestra. Perhaps driven by the memory of Menuhin's Berlin debut he told his father that he would perform the Bruch, Brahms and Mendelssohn concertos. Eventually he agreed with the orchestra, which he was hiring for hefty fees, that they would accompany him in Bruch and Mendelssohn and that his third work would be unaccompanied Bach. Meanwhile, his performance at an "audition de violiniste" at the Imperial Hotel on 10 January was not

10: Kishi Kōichi.

an unqualified success. Among the items announced on the programme was the first movement of Paganini's Concerto No. 1, a work seldom heard in Japan and therefore eagerly awaited. But the Paganini was cancelled at short notice, ostensibly because of the pianist, but most likely because Kishi lost his nerve. His recital with Sirota on 25 January 1930 with sonatas by Händel, Grieg and Beethoven met a friendly but by no means enthusiastic reception. Neither did his orchestral debut impress the critics. The Stradivarius, far from being an asset, may have worked against him. Widely reported in the newspapers, it raised expectations which Kishi – perhaps inevitably – could not meet. It is notoriously difficult to get the best out of a Stradivarius, and Kishi, who had barely had time to get to know the instrument properly, was hardly up to the task. Kishi and Sirota also played in Kyōto and Osaka. The concert in Osaka's Asahi Hall on 30 February 1930 was his biggest financial success, but the critics were again lukewarm.

Kishi's next Tokyo recital with Sirota on 28 April 1930, a Beethoven evening, was better received, especially in the English-language press – although there were hints that Sirota played a significant role in the success. Japanese reviewers were more critical. What are we to make of these differences and how well or badly did Kishi Kōichi really play? We can only draw tentative conclusions from the works he performed, but ultimately, we cannot know, since he left no recordings.[138] The foreign audience perhaps still marvelled that a Japanese could play their music at all. Presumably the old Japan hands remembered times when the efforts of Japanese musicians sounded a lot worse than they did in the 1920s. Japanese critics, on the other hand, seem to have become blasé now that they could compare their compatriots' performances with those of a stream of top-class visiting artists. Even foreign artists who were not in the same league as Heifetz or Kreisler could receive damning reviews: Jan Kubelik, for example, who performed in Tokyo a few months later. Kishi, playing on an instrument he had not yet made his own, his challenging programme almost certainly under-rehearsed, hardly did himself justice.

Kishi himself must have realized his own weaknesses as a violinist more than anyone else. He left Japan in July 1930, taking with him his Stradivarius and his father's permission to sell the instrument. He passed the entrance examination for the conservatoire in Berlin, playing Max Bruch's Concerto in G Minor; the examiners deemed his playing "brauchbar" (adequate) and his hearing "good," and he was admitted to the class of Flesch's assistant Josef Wolfsthal (1899–1931).[139] The two seem to have got on well, and it may well be that Wolfthal's sudden death the following year contributed to Kishi's diminishing enthusiasm for a career as a violinist; his enrolment at the conservatoire ceased at the end of the winter semester.

Perhaps his temperament was in any case not suited to the drudgery required from a violin virtuoso. Berlin had so much more to offer, and Kishi pursued a broad range of interests and associated with a wide circle of acquaintances. He met again with Konoe Hidemaro, whom he had first met in Geneva, and Konoe introduced him to his own acquaintances. Wilhelm Solf, the former ambassador to Japan, likewise introduced him to his circle, which included people from the highest rungs of society and famous artists. At the conservatoire he had taken classes in the new radio department, where he heard Paul Hindemith lecture, with whom he had also had personal contact. One of the most important musicians Kishi associated with was Wilhelm Furtwängler, who allowed Kishi to listen to rehearsals and to visit or telephone him and even gave him some of his scores. Not limiting himself to music, Kishi audited evening classes at Max Reinhardt's (1873–1943) theatre school. He visited the UFA film studios regularly and cultivated contacts with the staff and the actors. All kinds of ambitious plans formed in his head. He wanted to introduce

Japanese culture in Europe by exchanging films between Japan and Germany, and to inspire European musicians by introducing Japanese music.

To promote his ideas, Kishi returned to Japan in summer 1931, leaving his Stradivarius in Berlin with the dealer Emil Hermann. In the following months he gave several recitals. Again he chose ambitious works, this time with a clear leaning towards virtuoso show pieces, including the Paganini Concerto he had failed to perform previously. His self-perception as a violinist seems to have been a peculiar mixture of uncertainty and confidence: while he doubted his ability as a Japanese to truly grasp the soul of Beethoven's music, he felt that he had something of his own to communicate as an artist. Perhaps his dilemma was not as peculiarly Japanese as he apparently thought. Not all artists find fulfilment in merely performing other artists' creations; they want to create themselves. And sure enough, at around this time, Kishi began composing. He had previously written a few songs while studying music theory with Laska. Now, in keeping with his ideas about bringing Japanese and European music together, he studied traditional music, of which he had little knowledge. Fortunately he was in a good position to do so; both his parents loved Japanese popular songs (*kayō*) and some of his sisters were studying *nagauta*. He wrote his first violin pieces and experimented with mixed ensembles of Japanese and Western instruments. Pursuing his interest in dance and theatre, he associated with Takarazuka artists and wrote revues for them.[140] He frequented the dance halls around Osaka, increasing his familiarity with popular music. He even opened a violin studio and contributed to a string tutor edited by Suzuki Shin'ichi.[141]

On 20 January 1932 Kishi performed the Mendelssohn Concerto as a guest soloist at the Takarazuka Symphony Orchestra's 84th subscription concert under Laska. The review in *Ongaku sekai* was so vicious that one suspects the reviewer had an axe to grind, but looking at the many other projects Kishi was pursuing at the time it is hard to imagine that he could have practised sufficiently. At a concert on 3 May in Osaka he presented his own works, and a month later he gave another Beethoven evening with Leo Sirota, playing the same programme as two years previously. Kishi was already preparing to depart, once again, for Berlin, where he intended to introduce Japanese films and to demonstrate that the

Japanese had made Western music completely their own. He believed that works by Japanese composers should convey a "Japanese atmosphere."

Berlin in late 1932 was not the city he had left. The Nazis had won a landslide victory in the election in July, and although they lost votes at the November elections, Hitler's seizure of power was only weeks away. For Kishi the special relationship between Germany and Japan in the 1930s offered just the opportunities he needed to pursue his ideas about promoting Japanese culture. Kishi's activities in Nazi Germany will be treated later (see Chapter 6). It was in Berlin from 1932 to 1935 that Kishi metamorphosed from a violinist into a composer and conductor and celebrated some of his greatest successes.

Back in Japan, his first concert took place on 12 September 1935 (and was broadcast on 15 September), when he conducted the Takarazuka Symphony Orchestra with reinforcements from the broadcasting orchestra in Beethoven's *Coriolan* Overture, Schubert's "Unfinished" Symphony and several of his own songs, sung by Seki Taneko (1907–1990). Kishi's Tokyo debut conducting the New Phiharmonic Orchestra took place on 26 November 1935. Critics treated him more favourably than at his debut as a violinist two years earlier, but reviews of his concerts were still mixed.

On 19 February 1936, however, Kishi achieved a breakthrough when he conducted Beethoven's Ninth Symphony. He had agreed to conduct it at short notice when no other conductor wanted the job. The performance became legendary; the German conductor Klaus Pringsheim praised it even a year after the event, calling the performance unforgettable and Kishi Japan's most talented conductor. The performance was repeated on 18 March and again on 28 May, at a concert to see the Japanese football team off on its way to the Berlin Olympics. Another highlight of Kishi's career as a conductor was the pianist Wilhem Kempff's (1895–1991) Japan tour in April; on 14 April Kishi conducted the New Symphony Orchestra for Kempff's performance of Beethoven's Piano Concertos No. 3 and No. 5. Kempff later marvelled that he sometimes completely forgot he was in Japan, "while I was playing the concertos of Bach, Mozart and Beethoven with an entirely Japanese orchestra under the baton of a highly gifted Japanese conductor."[142]

Even so, Kishi, not content with conducting in both the New Philharmonic and the Takarazuka orchestras, was also pursuing his mission of promoting cultural exchange between Japan and Europe and the creation of new music in Japan. In June 1936, however, after months of overwork, his health broke down. Operated on for appendicitis, he never recovered completely and died on 17 November 1937. Kishi was widely mourned. Tributes appeared in the New Symphony Orchestra's magazine *Firuhāmonī,* which also reprinted the reviews of his performance of Beethoven's Ninth. Today, however, his achievements are largely forgotten. His memory was revived in 2009 in Tokyo, Osaka and Berlin, when the hundredth anniversary of his birth was marked with concerts and conferences. By then hardly anyone alive had known him. One of the few living witnesses was Matsumoto Zenzō (1911–2010), possibly the only violinist alive to have played under Kishi's baton.

Matsumoto himself was one of the pioneers of the orchestra movement.[143] For years he played the violin in the New Symphony Orchestra before leaving to devote himself to his string quartet. One of the first professional string quartets, the Matsumoto Quartet was the first to perform the late works of Beethoven in public. Born in Tokyo, Matsumoto became interested in the violin when he saw one in the hands of his elder brother. Until the age of 19 he largely taught himself. Like many students of the period he listened to recordings and made every effort to model his playing on those of the best in the world. He did not take lessons until he started playing in orchestras, first in an amateur group, then in the Japan Symphonic Association (Nihon Kōkyōgaku Kyōkai) under Yamada Kōsaku, who gave him his first formal lessons. From January to July 1931, he studied at the Imperial Academy of Music (Teikoku Ongaku Gakkō) with Suzuki Shin'ichi and Alexander Mogilevsky. That September he joined the New Symphony Orchestra sitting at the third desk of the second violins.

In 1934 he had the chance to study abroad, then still a privilege only a few enjoyed. He spent two weeks in Berlin, where he heard the Berlin Philharmonic Orchestra and the Karl Klingler Quartet, before he moved to Vienna to study with Ernst Moravec (1894–1980), a student of Otakar Ševčík, who taught at the Vienna Academy from 1930 to 1966. Moravec was not only an excellent teacher, but played the viola in the string quartets of Arnold Rosé and Wolfgang Schneiderhan, as well being a solo violist with the Vienna Philharmonic Orchestra. Matsumoto made the most of his one-and-a-half years there, listening to as many concerts as he could. Impressed by the Busch Quartet and by his teacher's dedication to chamber music, Matsumoto developed a love for chamber music himself.

After his return to Tokyo he rejoined the New Symphony Orchestra and tried to find congenial fellow players to form a string quartet. In 1941 the Philharmonia Quartet gave its first concert with Schubert's "Death and the Maiden," Haydn's "Lark" and Beethoven's Op. 59.3. At their second concert on 19 October 1942, the quartet, now renamed the Matsumoto Quartet, performed Beethoven's Op. 135 and 132. Until then people had not believed the notoriously difficult late Beethoven quartets could be performed in Japan.[144] In 1943 the members of the quartet left the orchestra, and the Matsumoto Quartet became the first Japanese quartet to attempt going full-time. It began making recordings with Victor, and had recorded Haydn's "Bird" (Op. 33 No. 3), when an air raid destroyed the Victor plant in Yokohama. Soon the quartet faced another problem, when two members were drafted. The quartet continued with new players, performing not only in Tokyo, but also touring Nagoya, Kyoto, Osaka and Kobe as late as February 1945.

After the war, Matsumoto pursued a busy career as a teacher and performer. He was concertmaster of the Tokyo Philharmonic Symphony Orchestra, the Gunma Symphony Orchestra and the ABC Symphony Orchestra. Between 1963 and 1968 he gave twice-yearly recitals. He also continued to play quartet in changing groups. From 1954 to 1974, he sat on the jury of the annual Music Competition (now the Japan Music Competition). He taught at Matsusaka City Women's Junior College and at the Tokyo College of Music. In 1987–88 he spent a year teaching at the Carlos Gomes Conservatoire in Belém in northern Brazil, sponsored by the Japan Foundation. In September 1987 he acted as a judge at the third Fritz Kreisler Competition. From 1979 into the 1990s, he was the president of the Japanese String Teachers Association (JASTA); he was made honorary president when he retired. Although Matsumoto's name is not very well known abroad, he did receive a citation for leadership and merit by the American String Teachers Association (ASTA) in 1982.

As late as 2003 he performed publicly in a series entitled "Great Masters" organized by Komorebi municipality in Tokyo, where he played in piano trios by Bach and Haydn. The 2010 JASTA string festival saw him playing as the oldest participant in a 176-strong orchestra. Like Asahina, he represented a link between the early days when classical music began to flourish in Japan and the post-war era when Japan attracted international attention as a musical power.

Matsumoto and the others treated in this chapter devoted most of their efforts to classical music. Tōyama Shinji (1916–2006),[145] on the other hand, is representative of a large number of gifted violinists who played a variety of musical styles in different bands in hotels, dance halls, cinemas and other venues that offered opportunities to the emerging musical profession of his time.

Nothing in Tōyama's background suggested that he was destined for a life in music. Born in 1916 as the third son of a tofu (bean curd) maker in Osaka, he was expected to take a similar job to his father's, working in a shop as soon as he graduated from higher elementary school. He was still at school when his elder brother Takeo brought a violin home, because he planned to have his friend at work teach him and make some extra money by playing in cinemas. Soon Takeo joined up with a few other musicians. They formed an ensemble with drums, a piano, a bugle and a *shamisen*. Shinji had so far shown little interest in his singing lessons at school. But he observed his brother's lessons with fascination and when Takeo lost interest and passed the violin on to Shinji, he began to study himself. His brother's friend taught him surprisingly systematically, giving him lessons twice a week and using Hohmann's *Practical Violin Tutor*. At the time Shinji only knew of one other violinist, a wandering performer (*enkashi*) named Tsuji who sang and played at the market by the local shrine and sold booklets with his songs.

At first Shinji did not like the lessons much, but fearing his brother's anger if he gave up he continued and gradually began to enjoy himself. After two years, the friend had taught him all he knew. Impressed by his progress, his brother found Shinji a new teacher, a man named Iwakuni Shigetarō. In the daytime Iwakuni played the clarinet in the Osaka City Band; in the evening he taught the violin. Around 30 years old, Iwakuni had probably trained with the Osaka Mitsukoshi Band. He commanded unusually high lesson fees for the time (50 sen), and most of his pupils were adults learning for fun. Soon Shinji left school; his mother had died, and his relatives wanted him to become a live-in apprentice at a local shop. His brother, however, protested. He wanted Shinji to continue with the violin, and found him a job at the factory where he himself worked.

Tōyama Shinji's teacher Iwakuni had good connections with local musicians, including Nagai Kōji (1874–1965), the head of the Osaka School of Music. Iwakuni joined the school's newly formed orchestra and took Tōyama and another three of his more promising pupils to play in the violin section. The orchestra was conducted by Emmanuel Metter. More importantly, Iwakuni introduced Tōyama to playing where it paid. When Tōyama was 17 and had studied with him for three years, he accompanied him to the studios in Kyoto, where they recorded music for films in the quiet of the night. They played in a 30-piece orchestra of which half were strings; Tōyama also played the trombone when the occasion demanded it. Soon he was earning 16 yen a month with his violin, a substantial income at the time.

One night he returned to the home of his sister, who ran a restaurant. Her regulars included a band man who played popular songs at a cabaret. Seeing Tōyama with his violin case, he asked him to substitute for a sick violinist in his band. Another musician asked him to join him at the "King," a dance hall just outside the boundaries of Osaka City Prefecture. Soon Tōyama was earning 50 yen a month playing in a tango band. But higher gains soon beckoned in Japan's expanding colonial empire. After the founding of the puppet state Manchukuo in 1931, many Japanese found employment on the continent. In their free time they wanted to be entertained. Dance halls sprang up, but it was hard to engage bands, so musicians had to be lured with higher wages. Tōyama joined up with some of his colleagues and in 1936 travelled to Mukden (now Shenyang), where he could earn as much as 200 yen a month, playing in dance halls and accompanying popular singers for Mukden radio.

It all came to an end in spring 1939. By then Japan had started a full-scale war with China, and Tōyama was conscripted into the army. He had to report to the office in Osaka, and only just got back before the deadline. Fortunately, he found a friend in a member of the bugle band, who had trouble reading the notation of the new sheet music the band received that year. Tōyama helped him transcribe the Western notation into the *katakana* syllables the band had used until then; in return the old soldier protected him against bullies who despised him as a performer of dance music. Soon, however, Tōyama had a more serious problem than bullying; he was sent to Southern China where he spent four years in the artillery with no opportunity for music-making. In 1943, he was temporarily discharged and went to Tokyo. The dance halls had all been closed, but for those musicians not conscripted, there was plenty of work in shows, cabaret and the cinemas which showed old films or put on concerts. Soon, however, Tōyama had to join the army again, this time to work in a ship factory in Yokohama.

In November 1945 Tōyama returned to Osaka, where he and some of his old fellow bandsmen played at American officers' clubs. He played in a tango band in a cabaret to entertain American soldiers. When the American soldiers left, Tōyama played for Japanese audiences. There were 400 to 500 bandsmen in Osaka, but Tōyama was by now a veteran and in demand. In addition to cabarets, which were highly popular at the time, he also played for radio broadcasts. In 1951 NHK's monopoly on broadcasting ended and private radio stations began to operate in Osaka. Most music broadcasts were still live; but soon the use of recordings became common. During the 1950s Tōyama even had his own programme (Maruzen Hour), where he directed the Orquesta Tipika Sud, a band of three violinists, three bandoneon players, a pianist and a bassist which played tango and popular songs in tango style. For a short while, Tōyama, who had spent most of his career in the background, became famous. The programme only lasted a year, because the band ran out of repertoire, but Tōyama continued to organize bands. He offered his services to the Rōon audience association, established in 1949 to organize and finance concerts for the working classes.[146] Organizing performances for Rōon offered opportunities for more varied and interesting music than the cabarets. He also grasped the opportunities offered by television from the mid-1950s. Tōyama continued to play himself into the 1970s. But by then opportunities for performance were decreasing. The influence of Rōon waned, cabarets had gone into decline, television music shows lost importance and their production increasingly moved to Tokyo. Eventually Tōyama gave up playing and concentrated on managing performers through his agency Shōwa Productions, which he had established in 1962. An era which had begun in the early twentieth century had come to an end.

Most of the musicians introduced in this chapter came to study the violin more or less by chance. Many started late by today's standards, in their teens, and their training, at least in the early stages, was often haphazard. This is also true of two violinists who turned from performing to teaching and who attained almost iconic status as teachers after the Second World War: Suzuki Shin'ichi and Sumi Saburō.

## 4. The Making of Two Teachers: Suzuki Shin'ichi and Sumi Saburō

Among the Japanese violinists who performed between the two world wars before devoting their lives to teaching after 1945, Suzuki Shin'ichi (1898–1998) and Sumi Saburō (1902–84) are the most famous and influential. To a Western audience this may sound surprising. Most will have heard of Suzuki and his method, which is practised worldwide. Few, on the other hand, know of Sumi Saburō, although he taught many outstanding violinists, including several who won international fame. And yet, while their lives and careers differed as much as their approaches to teaching, both tell us something about how young men could be drawn to the violin and develop as violinists and teachers at a time when, despite the rapid spread of Western music in the previous 50 years, training was haphazard and professional opportunities were uncertain. Both grew up far from Tokyo, although Suzuki's home city of Nagoya was nothing like as provincial as Sumi's native Yonago in the isolated prefecture of Tottori. Both were the third sons of samurai turned businessmen. Both were largely self-taught and did not receive formal violin lessons until they were around 20. Neither of them trained at the Tokyo Academy of Music. Suzuki received most of his formal training abroad. Sumi did not leave Japan until he was a teacher himself, but he too benefited from Japan's internationalization in the 1920s, studying with several foreign teachers in Japan.

Suzuki Shin'ichi, unlike Sumi, grew up surrounded by violins.[147] Born on 17 October 1898 in Nagoya as the third son of Suzuki Masakichi, the founder of Suzuki Violins, he graduated from Nagoya Commercial School in 1916, just as the business was benefiting hugely from the First World War, exporting to markets formerly in German hands (see Part 1 Chapter 4). Like his elder brothers Umeo and Rokusaburō, Shin'ichi was educated in the expectation that he would work in his father's violin factory. He helped out while still at school and worked there full-time after his graduation. Shin'ichi later claimed that as a young boy he did not take the violin seriously as a musical instrument, although his brother Umeo played a little. This changed when his family acquired a gramophone and Shin'ichi bought his first record: Schubert's *Ave Maria*, played by Mischa Elman. Deeply moved, he acquired another recording by Elman, of a Haydn minuet, and began to teach himself to play.

Perhaps the work in his father's booming business was too much for Suzuki. He fell ill and the doctor ordered rest in quiet surroundings. This led to a meeting that changed the course of his life. He met a businessman who introduced him to Marquis Tokugawa Yoshichika (1886–1976). The Marquis came from the branch of the Tokugawa family that had ruled the domain of Owari from Nagoya Castle under the Tokugawa shoguns. He invited Suzuki on a research expedition to the Kurile Islands in the summer of 1919. The guests on the ship included Kōda Nobu, whose brother Gunji Shigetada (1860–1924) had led the exploration and colonization of the islands during his long career in the navy. Kōda played the piano in the ship's salon in the evenings, and sometimes Suzuki would join her with his violin.

Later Suzuki would base his famous method on the premise that all children possess the same extraordinary talent. But surely he himself had a special natural aptitude for the violin; how else, with a less than promising start in his late teens, would he have impressed Nobu so much that she told him he should study music seriously and introduced him to her sister? Andō Kō agreed to teach him. She still taught at the Tokyo Academy of Music and recommended that Suzuki prepare for the entrance examination. Suzuki did not, however, follow her advice. Already he was showing his preference for doing his own thing. He continued to study with Andō privately until 1921, when Tokugawa Yoshichika invited him to join him on a world tour. Suzuki was reluctant at first. He wanted to pursue his studies on the violin. Yoshichika then suggested that he continue his studies in Germany. So Suzuki accompanied Yoshichika to Marseilles, where he and the Marquis separated, and travelled to Berlin. For three months he attended as many concerts as he could in search of a teacher. Of course, Andō Kō, who had herself studied in Berlin, could have provided him with an introduction, but Shin'ichi, strong-willed as ever, was determined to take matters into his own hands.

Berlin in the 1920s was a good place to experience the best of classical music. Some of the most outstanding musicians of their time were based in Berlin: Theodor Scheidl, Leonid Kreutzer (who would later move to Japan), Arthur Schnabel, Wilhelm Furtwängler, Paul Hindemith and Arnold Schönberg. Others performed there regularly, such as Alfred Cortot, Pablo Casals and Fritz Kreisler. Contemporary composers like Arnold Schönberg, Alban Berg, Béla Bartók, Leoš Janáček, Igor Stravinsky, Paul Hindemith, Darius Milhaud, Arthur Honegger, Kurt Weill and Ernst Křenek presented their latest works.[148] Reformers like Leo Kestenberg (1882–1962), musical advisor to the Ministry of Culture, Science and Education, and Fritz Jöde (1887–1970), professor for music education at the Academy for Church and School Music in Berlin, worked to transform music education in schools and to involve more people in active music-making.[149] But while reformers and composers experimented, the majority of music lovers in Berlin continued to cultivate their conservative tastes. "Real music," for them, still meant the classics, especially the famous composers of the nineteenth century. Yehudi Menuhin remembered Berlin as "a bastion of the traditional world … Beethoven and Brahms were gods. Furtwängler and Walter were their vicars on earth."[150]

Suzuki's highly selective personal account of his time in Berlin suggests that he mostly associated with people who represented the traditional world described by Menuhin. His choice of a violin teacher fell on Karl Klingler (1879–1971). A pupil of Joseph Joachim, Klingler is best remembered for his string quartet, formed in 1905, which in different formations continued to perform until 1936. The quartet made its name performing the Classical and Romantic repertoire, centred on Brahms and Beethoven, although it did include the occasional work by contemporaries like Hindemith and Schönberg. It drew large audiences, including a core of chamber music lovers. Besides public concerts, Klingler performed frequently at concerts in private homes, including his own, where he regularly invited guests to chamber music evenings. Suzuki tells us that he chose Klingler after hearing him perform with his quartet, and that "My ultimate desire was not to become a performer but to understand art."[151] Although he failed to gain admission to the Berlin conservatoire in spring 1923,[152] he took private lessons with Klingler and worked on acquiring a large repertoire, including concertos, sonatas and chamber music.

Klingler may well have been the ideal teacher for Suzuki. Besides performing as concertmaster of the Berlin Philharmonic Orchestra, soloist and chamber musician, he taught at the conservatoire, composed and wrote several short treatises on violin playing.[153] While his colleague the famous teacher Carl Flesch, professor in Berlin from 1908 to 1926, devoted his writings to the physiological aspects of violin playing, Klingler's approach has been described as "philosophical."[154] Although his technique was superb, his strength as a teacher lay in interpretation. In the words of his student Agnes Ritter, "he always sought the emotional content and the intellectual design in the music. He did not allow technique to be an end in itself; it had to serve the music."[155] According to his daughter Marianne Migault Klingler (1922–91), he took on Suzuki, his only Japanese student, because he was intrigued by the question of how far someone from another culture could comprehend Western music.[156] Suzuki benefited from Klingler's reflective approach as well as from his wide circle of acquaintances. Klingler invited him to his house concerts, where he met musicians but also other members of the educated bourgeoisie, for whom making and appreciating music was part of their way of life. Besides practising the violin (about five hours a day, he later reported), Suzuki went to concerts. The inflation which caused the Germans so much grief worked to the advantage of Japanese students, making their allowances go a long way. He also enjoyed the company of friends and acquaintances and attended house parties, which often included music. At one such house concert he met Waltraud Prange, an accomplished amateur pianist and singer. The two started going out together, and in 1928 they married. What with practising, concert-going and courting, Suzuki almost certainly absorbed only a small fraction of Berlin's rich artistic and intellectual mixture at the time – certainly he experienced a very different Berlin from the flamboyant Kishi Kōichi, who arrived there for the first time a few months after Suzuki left.

In his recollections Suzuki mentions only a few names of people he associated with; one of them is Albert Einstein, whom he describes as his "guardian." By the time Suzuki wrote, Einstein, already famous in the 1920s, had become an icon of the twentieth century and a popular name for any person to link their own with. Suzuki's relationship with him was surely less intimate than he suggests. Einstein travelled quite a lot in those years. He visited Japan from 17 November to 29 December

1922, and he received a hero's welcome, returning to Berlin in February 1923. Suzuki did not meet him until 1926, having received an introduction from the biochemist Leonor Michaelis (1875–1949). Formerly the head of the bacteriological department of the City Hospital in Berlin, Michaelis had become professor of biochemistry at the Aichi Prefectural Medical College (now the Faculty of Medicine at the University of Nagoya) in Nagoya in 1922. He and Suzuki met during Suzuki's temporary return to Japan in 1925–26, not long before Michaelis moved to Baltimore in 1926. Michaelis, an accomplished amateur pianist, may have known Einstein from his Berlin days and they may well have met in Nagoya during Einstein's trip to Japan. Michaelis played in a concert together with Suzuki Shin'ichi on 30 January 1926.[157] A year later, he wrote to Einstein from Baltimore and mentioned "my young friend Suzuki-san," who had visited Einstein with some of his father's violins.[158] Einstein gave Suzuki a sketch of himself with the dedication "Herrn Shinichi Suzuki zur freundlichen Erinnerung [as a friendly remembrance]/Albert Einstein November 1926."[159]

Even if Einstein and Suzuki were not as close as Suzuki later claimed, Suzuki was clearly influenced by the kind of attitudes to music Einstein shared with most members of the German educated classes. The Suzuki Method's core repertoire bears a striking resemblance to Einstein's musical preferences, revealing a distinct bias towards music from the Baroque and Classical periods, especially Vivaldi, Bach and Mozart, and a relative neglect of the Romantic and more modern periods. Einstein revered Mozart above all other composers. He also valued Johann Sebastian Bach highly. He had little interest in the Romantics or the music of his own time.[160] While Suzuki himself may not have been aware of such a connection, his years in Berlin presumably not only heightened his awareness of the spiritual dimensions of music, but also of the role of music in the lives of the people he met and of the German educated classes in general. Perhaps he also became aware of the particular affinity the Jews seemed to have with classical music and particularly the violin in the nineteenth and early twentieth centuries. Many of the virtuosos whose fame reached and inspired the Japanese were Jews, including Joseph Joachim, Mischa Elman, Fritz Kreisler, Jascha Heifetz and Yehudi Menuhin – not to mention the Russian and German Jews who lived and taught in Japan.

In spring 1928 Suzuki returned to Nagoya with his wife Waltraud. At first the couple lived in the Suzuki family home. The family business, however, was faltering, and Shin'ichi had to earn a living independently. Together with three of his brothers, Kikuo, Akira and Fumio, he formed the Suzuki String Quartet. Kikuo, who played second violin, had studied economics at Keiō University, where he had been a member of the University's Wagner Society.[161] Akira, who played the viola, had trained in his father's business before following in his brother's footsteps as a pupil of Andō Kō. In the war years he performed in Manchuria, for Mukden Radio broadcasts. Fumio studied cello with Heinrich Werkmeister in Tokyo and with Julius Klengel (1859–1933) in Leipzig. Besides playing in the quartet and teaching, he also played at the lead desk in the Tokyo Symphony Orchestra and composed. The brothers started rehearsing in Nagoya and occasionally performed on the local radio, but soon they moved to Tokyo, where they gave their first recital on 18 October 1928. A newspaper announced that the sons of the well-known violin maker Masakichi would be playing a Haydn quartet in B major, a minuet by Mozart and a scherzo and quartet in D major by Schubert.[162] By then Japanese music education was producing enough soloists for the competition to be fierce, but chamber ensembles were still rare. The quartet performed popular works from the standard repertoire and works arranged for them by Fumio. It made a few recordings, among them Fumio's Suite *The Tale of Genji* for speaker, tenor, soprano and strings. The quartet enjoyed considerable success until it disbanded during the war.

Suzuki Shin'ichi also began to teach, adults at first. He became an instructor at the Musashino Academia Musicae and joined the students and teachers who left the school to found the Imperial Academy of Music (Teikoku Ongaku Gakkō) in 1931, which he ended up running until it folded during the war years. His brothers Fumio and Akira also taught there. Their colleague, the music critic Nomura Kōichi, later described Suzuki as a man who liked to be master of his own house and could not work with others.[163] Developing his own method and starting his own school enabled Suzuki Shin'ichi to become master of his own house in the years to come. His music college students were adults, but he taught children privately. The first was Etō Toshiya, then four years old, who came to him in 1932. Next came Toyoda Kōji, only three years old.

Suzuki was not sure how to teach such a young child, but then he discovered that he preferred teaching children to young adults. He compiled collections of graded tunes. Soon he taught several other children; some later became well-known violinists. "Our house was like a kindergarten," Waltraud Suzuki wrote later.[164]

At some point during these years, Suzuki suddenly realized that something we all take for granted is in fact an astounding feat: all Japanese children learn to speak Japanese, just as all children everywhere learn their mother tongue, even those who turn out to be less than bright. If children can master something as intricate as language, then surely they can learn anything, as long as they enjoy the right kind of environment. The Suzuki Method, also known as the Mother Tongue Method, was born. Suzuki applied his ideas to teaching the violin but he believed that in principle any kind of skill could be learned in the same way. The goal of the education he postulated was not even primarily musical, but "to cultivate the qualities of sensitivity, service to others and nobility of character." He even wrote about a "Way of Music" (*ongakudō*) in analogy to Zen and training in the traditional arts.[165] Nevertheless, his inspiration came from many sources, including the international current of educational reform which swept Japan in the 1920s and early 1930s and was inspired by educators like John Dewey, Helen Parkhurst, Maria Montessori, Cecil Reddie and Bertrand Russell.

As the war made itself felt more and more, however, Suzuki had to temporarily suspend his musical activities and work for the family business. In 1943 he moved to Kiso Fukushima in Nagano Prefecture, where the factory, which was now producing supplies for the war effort, had been evacuated. He lived with his widowed sister Hinako and her two sons, while Waltraud continued to work in Tokyo. But as soon as the war ended, he went back to teaching and to developing the method that would change string education worldwide. While the success of his method outside Japan after the war made him unique, his early career in the 1930s was similar to those of his contemporaries striving to make a living in music by performing and teaching.

One of them was Sumi Saburō. He too first started teaching and performing in Tokyo between the world wars, but in other ways his early life was different from Suzuki's.[166] His father Fusatarō, in contrast to the successful Suzuki Masakichi, struggled as a businessman. His tea firm reflected what contemporaries derided as "samurai business methods," the inexperienced blundering by many forced by circumstances to adopt occupations previously regarded as beyond the pale for members of their class. As a result the family was poor. Their home town of Yonago in Tottori Prefecture was well off the beaten track compared to Nagoya. The railway station opened in 1902, together with a government railway line connecting the town with the nearby harbour town of Sakai, and in 1909 the line connecting Tottori, Yonago and Matsue became the San'in main line. Even so the region remained relatively isolated. When Saburō left for Tokyo 15 years later, his family felt like Japanese today when their children go abroad.[167] Nevertheless, the modern times of Meiji made themselves felt even here, and the sounds of the new Western music could be heard in the local church and the schools. Keijō Primary School, which Saburō and his brothers attended, boasted the first piano in town as well as a drum and fife band which played on sports days and other ceremonial occasions.

The Sumi brothers told different stories about when they first encountered the violin. Hajime (1897–?), the eldest, said he first saw one in the hands of a local railway official. Saburō claimed he first became attracted to the violin when Kawakami Otojirō (1864–1911) visited Yonago with his theatre troupe and performed a children's play entitled *The Merry Violin* or *The Merry Kokyū*. The troupe premiered *The Merry Kokyū*, written by Iwaya Sazanami (1870–1933) and based on a Swiss legend, in 1903; in the following years they performed it in many parts of Japan.[168] The play featured a boy playing the violin, possibly played by the famous geisha-turned-actress Kawakami Sadayakko (1872–1946) herself. Hajime wanted to learn the violin and attempted to build his own using a *kokyū* as his model. Saburō soon got the chance to try the real thing, when his teacher, a Mr. Anji, brought one to school and let him have a go. He handled it so well that Anji allowed him to borrow it. Meanwhile Hajime had graduated from primary school and helped his father with the business. As soon as he could afford it, he bought himself a second-hand Suzuki violin for 1 yen 50 sen. He tried to imitate the travelling street performers who came from Osaka. There was no one to teach him in Yonago, but he managed to obtain sheet music by mail order. Rumours reached him about another teacher with a violin, Terada Toshihiko (1892–1973). Hajime and Saburō went to see him, and they practised playing together. They founded the Kaede Club with a few other music lovers and performed in church at Christmas and at school functions.

Meanwhile Sumi's other elder brother Jirō bought gramophone records, including the recording of Mischa Elman which inspired Suzuki Shin'ichi. When the brothers met another classical music enthusiast who worked at the local post office, they met regularly at his lodgings to listen to items of their respective collections, including violin favourites performed by Kathleen Parlow, Efrem Zimbalist, Toscha Seidel, Pablo de Sarasate and others. Soon they got to know other record collectors, several of them primary school teachers, and helped organize gramophone concerts. They also continued to organize live concerts, and the teenage Sumi Saburō, the star, often impressed even visiting musicians. One of them was the soprano Seki Akiko (a graduate of the Tokyo Academy of Music, (1899–1973). She heard him play a Beethoven Romance and recommended that he study in Tokyo.

Like Suzuki, Sumi had two elder brothers who could take care of the family business. His parents agreed to let him go, despite dire warnings from one of the foreign missionaries about the temptations of the city lights. In 1924, at the age of 22, he left Yonago. He would return for visits, but his home would henceforth be Tokyo. At first he stayed with an acquaintance from Tottori Prefecture and then with another acquaintance, whose brother-in-law, a student at Keiō University, happened to play the violin and recommended Ōno Hisaharu as a teacher. Yet another fellow Tottori man introduced Sumi to Ōno, who agreed to teach him. Sumi's family was not able to send him much money, so he had to look for work to pay for his lessons. He auditioned for the orchestra of the big Tcikokukan cinema in Asakusa, and secured himself a well-paying job. He would arrive early for work and practise for his lessons. In 1925 Ōno secured him a place at the back of the second violins in Konoe and Yamada's orchestra, and in October 1926 he joined the New Symphony Orchestra. He had to give up his job in the cinema, although the new job did not pay nearly as well and he could only make ends meet because he had savings from the previous job. But he realized that the orchestra provided better long-term prospects if he wanted his playing to improve rather than deteriorate from scraping away in a cinema. In April 1927 Josef König was appointed as a conductor, and Sumi and his fellow-string players had the chance to learn from an outstanding and experienced violinist.

Already Sumi was teaching his own pupils. They included the future conductor Watanabe Akeo (1919–90), then still in primary school. A couple of years later Saburō began to teach his younger brother Shirō (1913–?), who joined him in Tokyo at the age of 17 in 1929. In 1932, after only three years of study, Shirō won the first prize at the first Music Competition (Ongaku Konkūru). The set piece was the Mendelssohn Violin Concerto. He won the competition again the following year.[169] Supported by leading representatives of the music world, such as the critic Nomura Kōichi, the competition was intended to promote excellent musicians and raise the level of classical music. The divisions were voice, composition, piano, violin and cello. On the jury for the violin division were Andō Kō (her sister Nobu was on the jury for the piano division), Nikolai Schifferblatt, Robert Pollack, Alexander Mogilevsky and the cellist Heinrich Werkmeister. Contestants had to pass a preliminary round before the main round, and from 1938 a separate preliminary round was held in the Kansai area. Sumi Shirō was the first of numerous Sumi pupils to win the competition for decades to come.

The father of Saburō and Shirō died around the time of the New Symphony Orchestra's first regular concert in February 1927, and their mother, sisters and younger brothers joined them in Tokyo. Saburō's income and the money his sisters earned from crafting dolls secured the family a better living than the faltering tea business in Yonago, which remained in the hands of the elder brothers. Saburō's youngest brother Gorō (1916–?) studied the piano and often acted as an accompanist for Sumi's pupils. Shirō was soon able to join his brother in the orchestra. König had been succeeded by Schifferblatt, and both the Sumis had lessons with him. Saburō never missed a chance to learn from the best teachers available to him at the time; besides Ōno, König and Schifferblatt, he also took lessons from Andō Kō, Ono Anna, and the pianist Leonid Kreutzer, who also played the violin and helped train several violinists. Soon the orchestra began to accompany visiting soloists, and the Sumi brothers had the chance to experience world-class artists close up.

Sumi Saburō's success as a teacher was already beginning to outshine his achievements as a performer. After his brother had won the Music Competition for two years running, no prizes were given to violinists until the fifth competition in 1936. This time three prizes were given and another student of Sumi's won the first, Hatoyama Hiroshi.[170] Born in 1923, he had barely reached his teens, and he began the series of child winners (there was no special category for young entrants; only after 1945 was a separate competition for students established). The boy's success caused a sensation and Sumi believed he was the reason why more children were entered and won.[171] Another of his pupils, Masukado Shōji, won the eleventh competition in 1942, although at 16 (1926–), he was past the child prodigy age.

In 1935 Sumi started teaching at Jiyū Gakuen, founded in 1921 by the educational reformer Hani Motoko. Sumi's pupils there included Hani's daughters. Like many propagators of liberal education at the time, Hani Motoko regarded music as an important part of a rounded education. She and Sumi differed, however, in their views of how lessons should be given. Sumi wanted a parent or elder sibling to be present when he taught, to make sure they could support the child's practice between lessons. Hani, on the other hand, wanted children to be as independent as possible. After the war the two would go their separate ways. Once Sumi had around 20 pupils, he started organizing recitals, which took place yearly between 1935 and 1940. Here his violin pupil Watanabe Akeo gained his first experience as a conductor. But Sumi's musical activities, like those of so many fellow musicians, were disrupted by the war. Many of his pupils left Tokyo and his own family finally evacuated to Tottori in 1944. Saburō himself travelled back and forth. The orchestra performed almost to the very end of the war, and gave concerts for the troops. As soon as the war ended, however, Sumi, resumed teaching and organized recitals by his pupils, who even played for the Occupation forces.

Both Suzuki and Sumi laid the foundations for their post-war fame as teachers in the 1930s. By then, standards of playing had risen, and more good teachers were available. Educational reformers had been extolling the benefits of early education for years, and Ono Anna had pioneered teaching the violin to young children since the 1920s. Gradually, the Japanese public came to realize that it was not only possible but highly desirable to start playing the violin from an early age. Indeed, in the 1930s, the Japanese media celebrated the first generation of home-grown violin-wunderkinder.

# 5. The First Home-Grown Child Prodigies

Ever since the Suzuki Method astonished the world with its tiny fiddlers, Japan has been seen as the country that pioneered starting children on the violin when they were barely out of their nappies. Before the 1920s, however, most Japanese who studied the violin did not start before their teens. Suzuki himself did not play until his late teens. The pioneering Kōda sisters did learn as children, but they were exceptional. When Ono Anna arrived in Japan in 1918, she found that people did not even believe children could learn.[172] She advocated an early start in magazine articles, citing music education in Russia as an example, and taught small children herself. The time was ripe for it: educational reformers were advocating more child-centred, holistic pedagogical methods with special attention to the arts, and several of them agreed with Ono. Among them was a violinist and teacher named Nakajima, then a music college professor who had taught Anna's husband for a while and whose daughter Nakajima Tazuko (1904–92), although already in her teens, became her first pupil.[173] By the 1930s, Ono Anna was joined in her efforts to teach young children by two teachers who became famous in the post-war years: Suzuki Shin'ichi and Sumi Saburō.

Soon the public could applaud the first Japanese wunderkinder. Most of them were girls, reflecting the fact that music was still not generally deemed an acceptable profession for men. Not that performing in public for fees was deemed respectable for women either. Girls, however, were acceptable. In the early twentieth century a girls' culture emerged around girl students who enjoyed a life of privilege and relative freedom between childhood and taking on the responsibilities of adult womanhood.[174] The most celebrated violin prodigies were three teenage girls, sometimes known as "the three violin maidens," [175] who performed widely in the 1930s and who led Japan's musical recovery after the war, bringing hope of a future as a "cultured nation" to audiences all over the country: Suwa Nejiko (1920–2012), Iwamoto Mari (1926–79) and Tsuji Hisako (1926–).

Suwa Nejiko first made headlines in January 1931, when the *Asahi* newspaper reported: "A violin '*tensai shōjo*' (girl prodigy) appears: the little girl from Mejiro who astonished Zimbalist."[176] The expression *tensai shōjo* has since become a cliché, but Suwa Nejiko may well have been the first violinist to be thus labelled. A photograph of her at the time of her debut in 1932 shows her in the sailor-style blouse and skirt still

common for school uniforms today, underlining her schoolgirl
innocence. Although Suzuki Shin'ichi claimed her as his pupil,[177] Nejiko
in fact had her first lessons with Nakajima Tazuko at the age of three,
continuing with Ono Anna a year later. She was the eldest of four
children, and her mother, herself highly educated for a woman of her
time, believed in early education. She played gramophone records to her
children, and Nejiko's reactions led her to conclude that her eldest was
gifted. Ono Anna also taught Nejiko's sisters Akiko and Tsugiko. Twenty
years later Ono remembered that of all her pupils (by then close to 2,000,
she claimed), Nejiko had impressed her most, not just because of her
talent, but also because of her dedication, which was only surpassed by
her mother's.[178] Soon her performances at Ono's student recitals began
to draw attention. Then, in autumn 1932, Zimbalist toured Japan for the
fourth time, and Ono introduced her most promising pupil to him. Nejiko
had already been taken to one of Zimbalist's recitals in December 1924
during his second Japan tour. Now she played the Mendelssohn Concerto
for him, and he was so impressed that he recommended sending her to
Europe and offered his support.

Around this time or soon afterwards Nejiko was introduced to a new
teacher, Alexander Mogilevsky. The music critic Nomura Kōichi later
told an interesting story about how this came about. Apparently he was
visited by a post office worker he had never met before, who told him that
on his way to work he passed a house from which he always heard the
most wonderful violin sound. One day his curiosity made him enter the
house to find out who was playing and was surprised to learn that it was
a little girl playing what looked like a fairly poor half-sized violin. The
household and its members looked poor too. They told him that Nejiko
was studying with Ono Anna. Recently, so the stranger told Nomura, he
felt concerned because the girl no longer seemed be making progress.
Persuaded by the man's eagerness, Nomura agreed to visit the house and
hear the girl. He even intended to bring along a few colleagues, but on
the appointed day it snowed and no one else turned up. Together with
his guide he listened to Suwa playing Sarasate's *Carmen Fantasy*.
Impressed, Nomura introduced her to Mogilevsky, who at the time was
his colleague at the Imperial Academy of Music and agreed to teach her
for nothing as Ono had done.[179]

Perhaps little Nejiko, by all accounts quite a tomboy who enjoyed tearing around with Ono Anna's son Shuntarō in her scarce free time, needed a firmer hand; she later recalled that Mogilevsky scolded her all the time.[180] Still, she must have progressed to his satisfaction, for on 9 April 1932 she gave her debut recital with Mogilevsky's wife Nadezhda Leuchtenberg at the piano. The programme included Vivaldi's Concerto in A minor for two violins with Mogilevsky himself playing second violin.[181] The event was preceded by a pre-debut recital for the press and a select audience which included the Belgian envoy. The debut was a resounding success. The newspapers described her as a "god child" (*shindō*), a child prodigy. It so happened that the French violinist Renée Chemet was in Tokyo on tour (see Conclusion) and heard the recital. Like Zimbalist, she recommended sending Suwa Nejiko abroad. Suwa's orchestral debut followed in December 1933 with the New Symphony Orchestra under Yamada Kōsaku. She performed the Bruch Violin Concerto in G minor. That year she also made two recordings, followed by another in 1935.[182]

Suwa's personal life, on the other hand, was troubled. Only days after the concert the *Asahi* newspaper reported that her mother had left the family home, taking her children with her. In such a situation the violin teacher might well represent stability in the life of a teenage girl. Mogilevsky, however, refused to teach her unless her parents made up. He felt strongly that a budding virtuoso needed the support of a stable family life. At this point Suzuki Shin'ichi, Mogilevsky's student and colleague at the Imperial Academy, took over and, possibly, saved Suwa Nejiko's career. Not only did he teach Nejiko, but he even tried to resolve her family problems with the help of some of his influential friends, including Tokugawa Yoshichika, who subsequently became one of Suwa's supporters. In the end, Mrs. Suwa set up home with Nejiko and her youngest sister while the other siblings returned to their father.[183] On 3 May 1934 the *Asahi* reported that the previous day Nejiko had finally returned to Mogilevsky for her first lesson after over a year. Mogilewsky even conducted her performance of the Mendelssohn Violin Concerto with the newly formed Osaka Music Society Orchestra on 26 November 1934 (the concertmaster was the Polish violinist Sigismund Lukianovich Minchinsky).[184]

Meanwhile foreign ministry officials and the Belgian diplomatic representative, who had been present at her pre-debut recital, were

11: Suwa Nejiko, report in *Asahi shinbun* (3 May 1934) about her resuming lessons with Mogilevsky.

making plans to send Nejiko to Europe. After a farewell concert sponsored by the *Asahi* newspaper, she left Tokyo on 21 January 1936 and arrived in Brussels on 1 March. Apparently she adjusted well to life abroad; having had two foreign violin teachers must have helped. Her new teacher was Émile Chaumont (1878–1942), a professor at the conservatoire in Brussels whose own teachers included Ysaÿe. Chaumont thought she had been well taught. Suwa continued to practise hard. She also enjoyed the opportunity to listen to really good performances, and in 1937 she heard all the rounds of the Ysaÿe competition, won that year by David Oistrakh. She also met winners of a different kind. In April 1937 the young pilot Iinuma Masaaki and his mechanic and wireless operator Tsukagoshi Kenji flew the *Kamikaze*, a Japanese-designed aircraft, from Tokyo to London in the record time of 94 hours. They then continued around Europe for a series of friendship visits, landing in Brussels, their first destination, on 16 April. Together with the Japanese ambassador's daughter, Suwa Nejiko presented the pilots with flowers. A month later she performed Bach and Ravel for the music-loving Queen Elisabeth of Belgium.

For a while, she did little the Japanese newspapers found worth reporting. In January 1938, her government scholarship having expired, she moved to Paris to study with Boris Kamensky (1870–1949). Kamensky had studied with Eugène Ysaÿe, Leopold Auer and Joseph Joachim before being appointed concertmaster in the orchestra of the St. Petersburg Imperial Russian Musical Society. Like so many Russian violinists, he left his country after the revolution in 1917. Suwa was introduced to him by the pianist Hara Chieko (1914–2001), who had met him when she played at the third Chopin Competition in 1937. The funding was provided by the wealthy businessman Ōkura Kishichirō (1882–1963), who also invited her to perform at several private concerts in Italy.[185] Suwa even lodged with Kamensky and his wife while she stayed in Paris. She gave a debut recital in the Salle Chopin in Paris on 19 May 1939, playing Bruch's Violin Concerto, Bach's Chaconne, Chausson's *Poème* and shorter pieces by de Falla and Wieniawski. A critic wrote, "The artist has good taste and an already sound technique and the performer has temperament and a lively intelligence."[186] Less than four months later the German attack on Poland unleashed the Second World War. Within months Germany prepared to invade France and most Japanese left Paris. Suwa, however, insisted on staying, even under German occupation. Japanese who knew her at the time reported that she was completely wrapped up in her studies, practising several hours a day. Was that what mattered most to her, her studies? Her biographer, although naming Nejiko herself among his informants, hardly ever gives us her own voice in his account; nearly all the witness accounts he cites come from third parties.[187]

Perhaps the former tomboy, who had turned into a photogenic young woman, retained an adventurous streak; perhaps her instinct told her that the war in Europe would offer more exciting opportunities than her homeland.[188] If so, subsequent events proved her right. The following five years may well have been the most exciting and gratifying ones of her life and career. Unlikely as it seems at first glance, the war gave the former prodigy the chance to prove herself as an artist when the diplomatic representatives of her homeland sought ways to promote cultural exchange. She played many concerts in France and in Germany, right to the end of 1944 (see following chapter). When the fall of Berlin was imminent she fled to Austria with the Japanese ambassador to Germany and his entourage. After the European war ended the American army shipped them to New York. The party did not return to Japan until 7 December 1945.

The *Asahi* newspaper reported their arrival the following day with a photo of Suwa Nejiko and the conductor Konoe Hidemaro.[189] Suwa told the reporters that she intended to rest and practise. She did not perform in public for ten months, but then she joined the native artists who brought music to the Japanese at a time when everything was scarce and foreign artists had not yet returned. Her first recital took place on 3 October 1946 at the Imperial Theatre with Manfred Gurlitt at the piano. In 1947 she performed the Beethoven Violin Concerto with the symphony orchestra of the Tōhō film company (which until 1951 also had an agency for classical music), conducted by Konoe in his first post-war Beethoven cycle.[190] Many more performances followed, most of them recitals with the best pianists of the time. Travelling all over Japan, Suwa enjoyed star status, as did her contemporaries, the pre-war prodigies Iwamoto Mari and Tsuji Hisako. In 1961 she performed Lalo's *Symphonie Espagnole* with the NHK Orchestra; she had already performed the work with them in 1953.

After that, however, silence began to surround the former prodigy and star. Some observers speculate that she was upset by rumours about the provenance of her Stradivarius, presented to her by Joseph Goebbels (see following chapter), and other gossip that came with being a celebrity. Her sister Tsugiko believed that she never recovered from the shock of Jacques Thibaud's sudden death. He had heard her perform in Paris and even given her a few lessons, and when in spring 1953 he wrote her a letter announcing his forthcoming Japan tour, Suwa and her mother invited him to stay.[191] Perhaps she was also tired of the tedium of performing the same popular works in provincial towns. Meanwhile, foreign artists had begun to frequent Japan again, and many Japanese music lovers displayed the kind of snobbism towards the musical achievements of their compatriots that can still be encountered in Japan today. Moreover, in 1968 she married, and it was socially acceptable, even expected, that a married woman devoted herself to her husband rather than her career. She and Ōga Koshirō (1910–91), now a professor of German literature at the University of Tokyo, had fallen in love in Berlin, where Ōga worked for the embassy. Ōga was married at the time, but his wife had been prevented from joining him when the Germans attacked the Soviet Union and the couple was only reunited after the war.

Even if Suwa no longer performed publicly, she evidently kept practising. In 1981 a recording of Suwa playing Bach's Unaccompanied Sonatas and Partitas was released (recorded between 1978 and 1980), and between 1979 and 1984, she gave a few recitals, mostly at private events. Her final public recital took place in October 1984. In 1985 she recorded Beethoven's "Spring" and "Kreutzer" sonatas, with Tanaka Sonoko at the piano Both recordings were re-issued on CD in 1994, bringing her briefly back into the news.[192]

In 1998 Hino Madoka, a violinist turned author, published a novel entitled *Sōtō no Sutoradivari* (The Führer's Stradivarius). Although Suwa Nejiko obviously provided the inspiration for the heroine, Miki Shigeko, the story is not intended to reflect Suwa's life. It ends with Miki giving up her career at 40 and travelling to Europe in order to return her Stradivarius to the son of the luthier it was stolen from, to resume lessons with her Jewish professor who fled Vienna after the annexation of Austria and to generally tie up loose ends. The story's interest lies in how Hino, writing from her own experience, explores the violinist Miki's psychology and the way her preoccupation with her art prevents her from seeing the political and cultural context of her activities as musician.[193]

Suwa Nejiko died in March 2012. Apparently the Japanese press only became aware of this after Carla Shapreau, luthier, lawyer and author of a book on violin fraud, published a major article in the *New York Times* on 21 September 2012. Only on 25 September did the *Asahi* newspaper publish a brief obituary.[194]

Suwa Nejiko's younger sister Akiko became a violinist in her own right, although with a less spectacular career. Born in 1928, she also studied with Ono Anna, and later with Wolfgang Stavonhagen (see end of next chapter). In 1944 she won first prize at the Japan Music Competition and from 1946 she performed regularly. She eventually became a professor at the Kunitachi College of Music.[195]

The second of the three girl prodigies, Iwamoto Mari, was another early pupil of Ono Anna's.[196] Her father Masahide, was the son of a pioneer of women's education in the nineteenth century, Iwamoto Yoshiharu (or Zenji, 1863–1942), and his mother Iwamatsu Shizuko had translated *Little Lord Fauntleroy*. Mari's great-uncle was Iwamoto Shōji, whom we have already encountered as a promoter of harmonizing Japanese and Western music (Part 1 Chapter 6). Among his nephews was the violinist Inoue Takeo, a graduate and later teacher at the Tokyo Academy of Music. Iwamoto Masahide spent many years in Boston and brought an American wife home with him, Marguerite Magruder. Continuing in the Iwamoto family tradition of female education, Marguerite taught English at two women's colleges in Tokyo, leaving the care of Mari to relatives or child minders.

Mari was originally called Mary Esther, but had to Japanize her name in her teens during the war years, when things foreign were frowned upon. From an early age she liked to listen to music on her parents' radio, particularly violin music. But when her father brought home a violin when she was about five, she was unimpressed. "Why, it only has four strings," she thought in disgust – or so she told a journalist, years later. Nevertheless it was decided that she would have lessons with Ono Anna. According to Ono, Mari hated practice. But she hated school even more. Mixed-race children were uncommon in Japan, and her classmates bullied her relentlessly. Unable to defend herself, she became ill. Perhaps she was an early case of "refusal to go to school," a phenomenon which, like bullying, has often featured in the Japanese media since the 1980s. Later she reported that the doctor told her parents she must either give up school or the violin for the sake of her health. Asked by her father, which activity she preferred, she chose the violin as the lesser evil. In that case, her father said, she must become Japan's number one violinist, at least as good as Suwa Nejiko, and spend several hours a day practising. This Mari did – at least nominally. Blessed with a good memory, she would learn each piece by heart quickly and spend the rest of the time repeating it mindlessly while reading the books she had placed on the stand – a trick apparently popular among budding virtuosos; Ivry Gitlis tells a similar story.[197]

Suwa Nejiko was not the only child violinist in the news: in 1936 the winners of the Music Competition in the strings and piano sections were children; Sumi Saburō's pupil Hatoyama Hiroshi won the first prize for violin. The ambitions of Mari and her parents were stimulated, and Ono Anna did not object to Mari's entering the competition the following year. She did warn Mari though: "you'll have to practise at least three hours a day," and she meant it. Mari could not fool her by reading books on her music stand. So Mari entered the sixth competition in 1937 and won the first prize; she played Tartini in the first round and the Bruch Concerto in the second. Her father now began in earnest to plan her future as a professional musician. He organized a debut recital for her on 11 November 1939 with Leo Sirota as the pianist, and a concert with the New Symphony Orchestra on 1 October 1940, where she played Beethoven's Violin Concerto. He engaged new private teachers for piano, music theory and voice. Mari also had her first taste of ensemble playing, with the cellist Saitō Hideo. She would later embrace chamber music as her favourite musical activity.

The war made life increasingly difficult for the family. Masahide worked for the American embassy and, after the outbreak of the Pacific War, for the news agency Dōmei Tsūshinsha, while Marguerite continued to teach. But times were not good for an American woman and a mixed-race teenager. Nor did carrying a violin case around enhance a person's popularity: several violinists later recalled how they were abused as "non-citizens" lacking patriotic sentiment. Nevertheless, many people were happy to forget their troubles while they listened to music, and Mari braved infrequent and overcrowded trains to give numerous concerts, many of them in factories, hospitals and military bases. On 4 March 1945 the family home was destroyed in an air raid. The family managed to flee and move to another house nearby, but on 13 April this too was hit, and

Mari fled with only her violin case, waiting for daybreak in an air shelter ditch. The next day she was scheduled to perform in Hibiya Hall. The trams were not running, and so she walked the 20 kilometres or so. When she reached the hall she found a notice on the door: "Cancelled because Iwamoto Mari missing." She played as she was, in trousers and with blistered feet.[198] A month later she was on her way to Manchuria, where she played at least 14 concerts in Harbin and Xinjing (now Changchun).[199] She liked Harbin so much that she even wanted to move there. Japan's capitulation put paid to that idea, and she was lucky to get out and back to Tokyo just in time to escape being stranded on the mainland.

Suwa and Iwamoto were sometimes treated as rivals by the press, but this may have just been media hype. They both performed at a concert in Hibiya Hall on 5 June 1949 to celebrate their teacher Ono Anna's 30 years in Japan; Iwamoto played Fauré's Sonata in A major and Bach's Chaconne, and Suwa played Chausson's *Poème* and, together with her younger sister Akiko, the Bach Double Concerto.

Although Iwamoto Mari resumed performing only weeks after Japan's capitulation, playing both as a soloist and a member of chamber music groups, she had to limit her performances when she was appointed as professor at the Tokyo Academy of Music in September 1946. She was only 20 and the Academy's youngest professor ever. The appointment was part of an effort to shake up and reform education at the Academy. But at an age where she could still be a student herself Mari did not enjoy teaching or the company of her older colleagues. Eventually her parents arranged for her to perform in her mother's homeland as an excuse to resign her professorship. She left Tokyo in March 1950. The planned concerts came to nothing, because her parents had been swindled by a supposed manager, but Mari had the opportunity to study with Louis Persinger in New York. Isaac Stern's manager (Sol Hurok) organized a recital at the New Town Hall on 14 June 1950, the first American performance by a Japanese violinist after the war. The reviewer in the *New York Times* deemed the concert a success, praising her "excellent fiddling" and continuing, "Among her talents Miss Iwamoto displayed a musical temperament that was unusually controlled by thoughtfulness and understanding, a fine ear for subtleties of pitch and phrasing, a big, colorful tone and – not unimportant in a concert artist – good looks." He particularly praised her rendition of Bach's Chaconne.[200]

After a year in New York, of which she later said it had taught her more about life than about music, Iwamoto returned to Tokyo and resumed her performing career. Many of her tours were organized by the Rōon audience association, which did much to bring classical music to a wide audience in those years. Gradually her interest turned to chamber music, and in the years from 1966 to her early death in May 1979 she devoted most of her energy to the Iwamoto Mari String Quartet (see Part 3 Chapter 4).

Tsuji Hisako, the third of the girl prodigies and the only one still active today, was born in the same year (1926) as Iwamoto Mari.[201] Unlike the other two, she came from the Kansai area and has been based there throughout her long career. Her father Tsuji Kichinosuke (1898–1985) was also a violinist. He studied with the Russian Boris Lass, performed in the Osaka area in the 1920s, and was concertmaster of the Takarazuka Symphony Orchestra, but later concentrated on teaching. Besides his daughter, his students include Kubota Ryōsaku and Wanami Takayoshi. He began teaching Hisako in 1932 when she was six, giving her daily lessons. Soon she was practising most of the day and hardly going to school, leaving Sōai School, which had a strong focus on music, without graduating. In 1938, a year after Iwamoto Mari, she won the seventh Music Competition and received a special prize from the Ministry of Education, awarded for the first time that year. The newspapers called her a *tensai shōjo*, a girl prodigy, but as her father remarked, '"I am always saying, all those people who are called virtuoso or prodigy have trained extremely hard, you know; but actually, as a parent, I don't know how often I have felt sorry [for my daughter]."[202]

The year after winning the competition, Tsuji Hisako gave a recital in Osaka with Leo Sirota at the piano, performing Tartini's "Devil's Trill" Sonata, Lalo's *Symphonie Espagnole* and other works. The *Ōsaka mainichi* newspaper expressed pride that the Kansai region had brought forth a young violinist of such talent. In the following years Tsuji Hisako regularly gave recitals in Osaka.[203] In 1940 she made her Tokyo debut, again with Sirota at the piano. In September 1942 she performed the Brahms Violin Concerto with the Tokyo Philharmonic Orchestra under Manfred Gurlitt. Like the other child prodigies she enjoyed more performance opportunities thanks to the decrease in visiting artists. In May 1943 she performed Paganini's Concerto No.1 and Lalo's *Symphonie*

*Espagnole* under Rosenstock, in November the Tchaikovsky Concerto under Asahina, and in November 1944 the Glazunov Concerto, again under Asahina. By then practically all the foreign musicians had been forced out of their jobs. Like Iwamoto, Tsuji toured Manchuria in the 1940s, where, besides giving recitals, she performed under Asahina's baton.

Once the war ended, Tsuji Hisako, like the other two young women, was in great demand as a performing artist. She played for the Occupation forces, performed concertos with the newly formed or re-formed orchestras and toured the country playing recitals. One of the highlights of her career was her performance in 1955 of Aram Khachaturian's Violin Concerto (composed in 1940), although it was not quite the Japanese premiere: the post-war prodigy Watanabe Shigeo beat her to it in 1954. Tsuji impressed David Oistrakh when he toured Japan in 1959 and he invited her to tour the Soviet Union. Tsuji premiered Kishi Kōichi's Violin Concerto in Japan; having performed the first movement under the conductor Odaka Hisatada (1911–51), she performed the entire concerto under Asahina in 1978 to celebrate the opening of a new lecture hall of Kishi's old school, Konan College. In an interview for the magazine *Bungei Shunjū,* she spoke of the special affinity she felt with Kishi, her senior (*senpai*) as a violinist, who had also played a Stradivarius. The previous year, 1977, Tsuji had famously sold her house to buy her own Stradivarius, the "Dickson-Poynder 1715."[204] The story made newspaper headlines and brought her name to the attention of people who otherwise neither knew nor cared much about her music.

In 1982 Tsuji Hisako celebrated "50 years in music" since she first started the violin. By then she was the only one of the three pre-war girl prodigies still active, Iwamoto having died in 1979 and Suwa having virtually given up performing. One observer remarked that she was in many ways the people's violinist; her yearly Christmas concert drew people who did not usually go to classical music concerts. And recently she had played five violin concertos on two consecutive evenings, and both times the hall, which seated 3,000, had been sold out.[205] Tsuji also distinguished herself as a teacher; she was appointed professor at Osaka University of Fine Arts and taught at her old school, Sōai College. In 1993 she opened a private violin studio in Osaka, which in 2010 had 37 students of all ages.[206] Besides organizing concerts for her students, Tsuji has performed herself in this millennium: she played the works of Kishi Kōichi for the hundredth anniversary of his birth in 2009. In 2012 she celebrated the eightieth anniversary of her debut at the age of six. "I am thinking of studying seriously and performing again," she told a reporter of the *Mainichi* newspaper.[207]

Boy violinists also began to attract public attention. In 1939, the year after Tsuji won the NHK/Mainichi Music Competition, the first prize went to Etō Toshiya, then 12 years old; he too received the Education Minister's Prize. The second prize went to another boy, Iwabuchi Ryūtarō. Like the three "girl prodigies," both had distinguished careers after the war.

Etō Toshiya (1927–2008) came from a musical family.[208] His father Toshiaki, a keen amateur violinist and composer of songs, named his son after the violinist Toscha Seidel. Both parents were trained teachers and actively promoted their children's education. Toshiya's musical gifts showed themselves at an early age. He started to play the piano by himself. When he was four, his father, hoping to make him into a violinist, took him to Mogilevsky, who recommended Suzuki Shin'ichi. For the next few years, Etō studied with Suzuki, who later described Etō as "my first small pupil." His mother became what could be described as Japan's first "violin mama," taking on the role of an assistant teacher, in the way that became fundamental to the system of talent education Suzuki developed after the war. According to a magazine article describing her virtues in 1949, she accompanied him to lessons and stayed to observe, so that she could practise with him. She learnt to tune the violin, and refused to buy a metronome, preferring to clap the rhythm herself. Toshiya's parents also took him and his siblings to concerts.[209]

At eight years of age, Etō gave his first public performance, and the following year he performed for the first time with his sister Reiko. In 1937, at a concert of Suzuki's pupils, he performed the Violin Concerto No.1 by Seitz with an orchestra. His first prize at the eighth Music Competition made him known to a wider public, particularly when he and Iwabuchi Ryūtarō performed the Bach Double Concerto with the New Symphony Orchestra under Rosenstock the following year. A repeat performance, this time conducted by Saitō Hideo, was broadcast in September 1941.

Etō graduated from primary school in 1940 and continued to Ikuei

School of Technical Arts, run by the Catholic Salesian Society.[210] The headmaster of the school, Vincentio Cimatti (1879–1965) allowed him to practise his violin and to study Italian while the other pupils had craft lessons. Cimatti even accompanied him to concerts all over the country and the programmes are preserved in the Cimatti Memorial Museum in Tokyo. During his time at the school Etō converted to the Catholic faith and was baptized in 1941; his family eventually followed. Several of the fathers who taught at the school were musical and sometimes came together to make music in the Etōs' home.

By then Etō no longer received lessons from Suzuki. From around 1940 to 1943 he taught himself. However, advised by a music critic that he should take formal lessons,[211] he became a pupil of Alexander Mogilevsky. In 1944 he was accepted by the Tokyo Academy of Music and studied with Inoue Takeo.[212] Already a seasoned performer, Etō circumvented the school's rules about students not performing in public outside school by assuming the name of Ezaki Toshio and formed a string quartet with Watanabe Akeo, Matsuura Kimiyo and Saitō Hideo. He graduated in 1948 and was immediately appointed to a teaching post, but left for America to study with Zimbalist the same year. He was the first of many Japanese violinists to study abroad after the war and returned in 1961 to a trailblazing career as a soloist, chamber musician and teacher of innumerable virtuosos (see Chapter 8).

Iwabuchi Ryūtarō (1928–) who came second to Etō Toshiya at the competition, was born in Dalian (named Dairen while it was under Japanese occupation) in 1928, but grew up in Tokyo.[213] He started learning the violin at the age of nine. His family was not particularly musically inclined, but his primary school teacher, impressed by his singing, recommended that he attend Ueno Music School for Children, where teachers from the Tokyo Academy of Music gave lessons on two afternoons a week. Iwabuchi also received lessons from Willy Frey. Even after winning the competition and performing with the New Symphony Orchestra, he had no ambitions to play the violin professionally and virtually gave it up while he prepared for the entrance examinations for high school and then for the prestigious law faculty of Tokyo Imperial University. Only after the war did he take up the violin again. Competent violinists were in great demand and he was soon helping out in the Tokyo Philharmonic Orchestra and the Japan Symphony Orchestra, as the New

Symphony Orchestra was now called. He left university without graduating. In 1951 he became concertmaster of the Japan Symphony Orchestra, renamed the NHK Symphony Orchestra. He was Japan's youngest concertmaster at the time. Within a few years, however, he discovered that his real passion was chamber music.[214] In 1953 he founded the Pro Musica Quartet with colleagues from the orchestra, but combining regular string quartet concerts with his responsibilities as concertmaster proved difficult. The members of Pro Musica changed, and in 1956 Iwabuchi moved to the Japan Philharmonic Orchestra, in the hope of a lighter schedule. When this hope proved vain he resigned in 1958 in order to devote himself to quartet playing. He held teaching appointments at several colleges.

The youngest violinist to perform in public in the 1930s was Toyoda Kōji, born in September 1933 in Nagoya as the son of the violinist Toyoda Yoshimichi. On 25 March 1937 the *Ōsaka nichinichi* newspaper announced that Japan's tiniest "midget violinist" (or "bean violinist," *mame teikinka*, if the Japanese expression is taken literally), only three years and seven months old, would be performing at the Grand Theatre on 27 March. The boy in the picture was indeed tiny, but posed confidently in a smart suit with knee-length trousers and a white collar, his violin under his arm, bow in his hand.[215] Toyoda had already caused a small sensation in Tokyo a month earlier. The *Asahi* newspaper reported that he began to learn the violin at the age of two, taught by his father on a specially commissioned 1/8 size violin. He performed Dvořák's *Humoresque*. His father accompanied him on guitar rather than the piano, because the piano would have drowned the sound of his tiny violin. According to the *Asahi* newspaper, his repertoire also included a gavotte by Gossec and a minuet by Beethoven. School songs he could play without being taught. The report added that this "bad-mannered violinist" sometimes interrupted his performance to scratch his nose or to look around as if the event had nothing to do with him.[216] Kōji subsequently became a pupil of Suzuki Shin'ichi. In October 1939, his performance of Bach's Concerto in A minor at a concert by Suzuki's students in Hibiya Hall elicited an encore (Dvořák's *Humoresque*). "His music shows a quality that has progressed far beyond a child's music-making," observed a critic. Etō Toshiya performed at the same concert (Adagio from Bach's Concerto No.1 and Sarasate's *Caprice Basque*).[217]

12: Toyoda Kōji, *Asahi shinbun,* 19 February 1937.

In 1941 Toyoda Kōji played the child prodigy in the film *Ai no Ikka* (Family of Love or A Loving Family) based on a bestselling story by the German writer Agnes Sapper, *Die Familie Pfäffling* (1906, Japanese translation 1930). Frieder Pfäffling, or Oda Teruo in the Japanese version, is the sixth of seven children in the family of a poor music teacher. After revealing his astonishing talent on the concertina he receives a violin for Christmas (New Year in the Japanese version). By casting Toyoda in the role of Oda Teruo, the producers hoped to draw the crowds. They put the violinist and composer Sugiyama Haseo, who had studied the violin, in charge of the film music; in the film, Toyoda played a Beethoven minuet and parts of Mendelssohn's Violin Concerto, as well as concertos by Mozart.[218]

Toyoda entered the NHK/Mainichi Music Competition in 1943 and came third (the first prize went to Hattori (née Ueno) Toyoko and the second to Hoshide Itoko, another pupil of Suzuki's). But he was already an experienced performer. He too went on to a distinguished career after the war, making his solo debut with the NHK Orchestra in 1949, winning several international competitions and enjoying a successful career abroad before returning to Japan. In this he is typical of the violinists who grew up in Japan after the war, benefiting from increased opportunities to study abroad and surprising the world with their competition successes.

The late 1930s and the 1940s were a good time for indigenous talent. With the start of all-out war in China and even more so the Pacific war, the stream of touring artists became a trickle and then ceased, and in the final years of the war most resident foreigners were forbidden to perform. Even after the war it took several years before foreign artists could once again include Japan on their tours, and the former child prodigies, maturing into adults during the years of deprivation, continued to delight their audiences. The young violinists mentioned here enjoyed successful careers after the war, as did several others. Together they represented a link between Japan's musical achievements before and after the Second World War and helped build Japan's reputation as a country where classical music flourished.

## 6. Interlude: Two Japanese Violinists in Nazi Germany

We have looked at Japan's increasing internationalization in the 1920s and 1930s mainly in terms of foreign musicians teaching and performing in Japan. But internationalization worked in more than one direction. Already early in the century we encountered the first Japanese performing Western classical music abroad, including the violinist Takaori Shūichi. After the First World War their number increased, even if it was still tiny compared to the post-1945 era. The Japanese were only just beginning to reach European standards in classical music, so their appeal as often as not lay in the fact that they appeared exotic to their Western audiences, who were impressed that they had mastered the art at all. Performing music with a Japanese flavour heightened their exotic appeal. Kishi Kōichi benefited from this trend when he abandoned the violin in favour of composing and conducting his own music. In contrast, Suwa Nejiko, who matured from a child prodigy to a fully fledged artist during her years abroad, achieved her successes performing the standard

European repertoire. Both benefited from the political situation in Europe.

Japan and Germany did not have close diplomatic relations at the time Hitler seized power, but there was a feeling of cultural affinity, particularly on the Japanese side; after all Japan had borrowed much from Germany since the 1880s. Many Japanese who later assumed leading roles at home studied in Germany. After Germany's defeat in the First World War, German scholars received financial support from Japan. As both nations isolated themselves from the international community, they drew together. Germany left the League of Nations in October 1933. Japan had already resigned in the spring, following the Lytton Commission's report after Japan's seizure of Manchuria, published in October 1932. In November 1936, Germany and Japan concluded the Anti-Comintern Pact. On the Japanese side one of the main promoters was Ōshima Hiroshi (1886–1975), then military attaché and later ambassador in Berlin. He was a great lover of German culture and actively promoted Japanese–German friendship throughout his career. The Tripartite Pact (including Italy, which had joined the Anti-Comintern Pact in 1937) followed in 1940. Politically, the alliance never really worked. The Japanese never saw eye-to-eye with the Nazis on the race issue, which was fundamental to National Socialist ideology, and both powers pursued their war goals with little consideration for their treaty partner's interests.

Cultural exchange was another matter. Many Japanese revered German science, literature and, of course, music. Germans continued to be fascinated with the exotic allure of geisha, samurai, and cherry blossom festivals. Japan still employed German teachers and Japanese students flocked to Germany. On 25 November 1938 the two countries concluded a cultural treaty with the intention of creating a framework for cultural exchanges. Even before the treaty, unofficial and semi-official exchanges flourished. In Germany, this was to a large part thanks to the German–Japanese Society. Founded in Berlin in 1890 and expanded in 1929 with the involvement of German and Japanese diplomats, scientists, artists and journalists, it was immediately brought under Nazi control in 1933. Its activities expanded as the political ties were strengthened; after 1938 the society established branches in 15 German cities. Among other activities, the society supported performances by Japanese artists.

Thus when Kishi Kōichi arrived in Berlin for the third time in autumn 1932, just months before the Nazis seized power, the timing was ideal for him to realize his ambitions to promote Japanese culture. After Hitler's victory in January 1933, the new regime lost no time in seizing control over cultural institutions, and by the end of the year, Joseph Goebbels and his Propaganda Ministry had all but succeeded. At the same time Jews were ousted from all areas of public life, including music. The loss to German musical life was devastating and Germany did not recover from it for decades. In the violin world alone, audiences were deprived of performances by virtually every big name of the time: Heifetz, Kreisler, Elman, Milstein, Thibaud, Szigeti, Huberman, Morini, Menuhin, Busch, Flesch and Goldberg. They all disappeared from German concert halls, many of them never to return.[219] Among Kishi's former violin teachers, first Rostal, then Flesch emigrated. Not that Germany had many truly world-famous violinists of its own anyway. But after 1933 only Georg Kulenkampff remained besides the Czech-born Váša Příhoda and the young Viennese Wolfgang Schneiderhan. At the same time Hitler and other Nazi leaders revered classical music and did much to promote it. They even tolerated ideological aberrations in great musicians that they would not have tolerated in others, and while Nazi musical tastes tended to be conservative, a surprising number of adventurous works found recognition.[220] After his return to Japan, Kishi would praise Hitler's regime for its promotion of the arts, although he is also on record criticizing the expulsion of Jews. He may well have benefited from the partial dismantling of Germany's music life and the potential opportunities it provided for outsiders.

Not that Kishi could impress German audiences on the violin even then. But then he had begun to concentrate his efforts on composing and conducting. He had also become a man with a mission. He wanted to bring the culture of his homeland to the Europeans – not as a culture frozen in time that had to be preserved from alien influence, but as one that could embrace that influence and become fully part of the modern times in which Japanese as well as Europeans lived. In composing his own music he absorbed the diverse musical manifestations that had surrounded him as he matured, whether Japanese or Western, classical or popular. Ironically, Kishi owed as much to Jewish musicians as to anti-Jewish measures, not only to his violin teachers, but also to the composers Robert Kahn and Edvard Moritz, both of whom subsequently left Germany.[221] Edward Moritz, a composer, conductor and violinist who had studied with Flesch, saw his career fall apart as soon as the Nazis came to power and he was forced to limit his activities to the Jewish Culture League. Kishi engaged him as a teacher at a time when he surely welcomed a well-paying pupil – Kishi still had money, although he could not afford the extravagances of his previous stays in Berlin. Moritz not only taught Kishi orchestration. He probably deserves to be called Kishi's collaborator, copying (or even editing) his scores and helping to arrange publication by Richard Birnbach. Under Moritz's guidance, Kishi completely revised many of the works he had composed in Japan, including the piano accompaniments of his short violin pieces; he also composed music to accompany the films he had made in Japan. He sold two of them to the Universum Film Company (UFA), who remade them, adding new scenes as well as Kishi's music.

In June 1933 Kishi began to work on a violin concerto, for which he had sketched out themes in Japan. He also completed two shorter violin works and worked on the music for the film *Kagami*, in which he himself appeared as an actor in the role of a student returning to Japan. *Kagami* was first shown in Berlin on 5 October 1933 and subsequently in Stettin and Detmold. On 12 December 1933 Kishi performed his violin pieces at the Japanese Sports Association Ball, while the soprano Maria Basca sang some of his songs. Basca is forgotten today, but was a popular singer in the 1920s and 1930s. She had already performed Kishi's songs at a recital in Stettin on 1 December 1933. Other performances of Kishi's works followed.

The highlight of his time in Berlin and one of the highlights of his entire career, however, was a "Japanese evening" on 29 March 1934 in the UFA's Universum Theatre on Kurfürstendamm. The event was sponsored by the German–Japanese Society and the German Winterhilfe (Winter Aid), and several diplomats were invited, although most of them did not attend. A lecture on Japanese art was also cancelled. Even so the ambitious programme lasted three hours.[222] It consisted of the films *Kagami: Traditions in the Japanese Home* and *Spring: Japanese Spring Festivals*, several songs sung by Maria Basca and accompanied by the UFA orchestra, as well as the first movement of the Violin Concerto. The soloist was Georg Kulenkampff, then Berlin's leading violinist. Kishi conducted the UFA orchestra; it was his debut as a conductor.[223]

The evening was a success. At least 35 newspapers and magazines published reviews, including the French *Courier Musicale*.[224] Most of the reviewers commended Kishi for representing Japanese culture in a language Europeans could understand. This being one of his goals, the reaction must have pleased him. Many identified influences from contemporary European music, from Romanticism as well as Russian/Slav and English or American elements; various European composers were mentioned by name: Schumann, Hindemith, Bruckner, Strauss, Beethoven, Dukas, Tchaikovsky, Wagner and Debussy. But the critics also praised him for the strong Japanese elements they believed they heard in the music. In rhetoric typical of the time, the *Berliner Lokal-Anzeiger* began its review entitled "Japanische Zukunftsmusik" with the observation, "It is the mark of a strong race and a strong national essence (Volkstum) that they overcome foreign influences, absorb them, digest them as part of their own being."[225] The article went on to praise Kishi's success in creating a new kind of music by combining Japanese and European influences, and concluded, "One should keep an eye on this eminently talented composer, for the path he demonstrates can truly lead into a future of new Japanese art music." In a similar vein the reviewer in *Germania* remarked: "The all-important thing about Kishi's music is that he has not just written works that are somehow stylized in the European way. In them, the spirit of his people lives; we hear music that is foreign to us, but results from organic growth." [226] The *National-Zeitung,* in a review likewise entitled "Japanische Zukunftsmusik," emphasized Kishi's individuality and praised his ability as a conductor.[227] The writer in *BZ am Mittag* even stated that Kishi's work, in its synthesis of Japanese and European elements, far surpassed the efforts of European composers to incorporate Japanese or Chinese elements.[228] On the other hand the *Zeitschrift für Musik* remarked that his works "showed solid ability, without being able to escape monotony in the choice of expressive means (fifths, pentatonic mode)."[229]

The Violin Concerto was the first to be composed by a Japanese and of course the first to be performed abroad. The *Völkischer Beobachter* claimed that it lay in the nature of the violin that "here the distance from the Japanese native soil is the greatest and the most obvious. Especially in this concerto, i.e. in the Allegro movement performed from it, the aim of the composer to create a connection between East and West is the strongest. Here he has also demonstrated how well he has succeeded in making the world of European thought and feeling his own."[230]

Several more performances of his works followed. The most important one took place on 18 November 1934, when he conducted the Berlin Philharmonic Orchestra. He had previously secured his status as a performer by being admitted to the Reich Music Chamber (Reichsmusikkammer), a department of Goebbels' Reich Culture Chamber, on 10 September 1934. The concert took place in the Berlin Philharmonic's series of Sunday concerts, and the orchestra had to be hired, but by then Kishi could pay for that from his earnings. The publication and performance of his compositions and the release of his films, as well as receiving critical acclaim, were an economic success; Kishi was no longer dependent on his father sending money. He had the support of the Japanese Embassy and the German–Japanese Society. Kishi was only the second Japanese after Konoe Hidemaro to conduct the Berlin Phiharmonic Orchestra; Konoe had already conducted it twice, at his debut on 18 January 1924 and in October 1933.

The final rehearsal was broadcast. The programme consisted of Gluck's Overture to *Alceste*, Kishi's own Symphony in E flat minor, entitled "The Life of Buddha," six of his songs (sung by Maria Basca), Debussy's *Prélude à L'Après-midi d'un Faune,* Kishi's Suite, *Sketches of Japan*, and Strauss's *Till Eulenspiegel.*[231] Kishi's debut with the Berlin Philharmonic Orchestra did not attract quite as much critical attention as the Japanese evening; the local papers often merely included a paragraph under "Concerts."[232] But those reviews he did receive were favourable on the whole, although his *Buddha* Symphony met with a mixed reception. Kishi was again praised for his ability to combine Japanese and European music. The reviewer in *DAZ* wrote that the symphony "glides through the stylistic phases of European Romanticism from the elevated to the impressionistic. Thematically it travels the path from Tchaikovsky via Bruckner-like horn effects to Puccini." Even so, the author remarks, these connections are more atmospheric than concrete.[233]

Already well connected, Kishi now found himself invited to even more parties and house concerts at the homes of the important and influential, including Wilhelm Frick, the Minister of the Interior, and other leading Nazis. A newspaper report of the yearly ball of the foreign press at the famous Hotel Adlon on 1 December 1934 included a photograph of him with Baron Mitsui and his wife. The ball was attended by several German political leaders, including Joseph Goebbels, and a photograph in the Kishi papers shows Kishi standing in a group around Goebbels presenting an unnamed lady with a prize.[234] By this time Kishi was perceived as representing Japanese musicians in Germany;[235] newspaper articles sometimes compared him with his compatriot Konoe Hidemaro, who was in Berlin from autumn 1933 to February 1934.

Kishi's performance could even be heard in Japan, when he conducted the Shortwave Broadcasting Orchestra on 25 January 1935 in a broadcast of his works. During his last months in Berlin, Kishi continued to compose, completing two movements of his violin sonata and a comic operetta entitled *Namiko* (the name of the heroine). Rehearsals began in autumn 1934, but a dispute with the conductor Willy Hahn (1896–1988) over his contract prevented performance. His ballet *Ama no Iwato* (based on an ancient myth) did not see performance either. Kishi decided to leave Berlin, although he planned to return and left many of his personal effects and scores behind. Just before he left, on 27 and 28 March 1935, several of his works were recorded in Berlin by Telefunken with Kishi conducting the Berlin Philharmonic. Some of these were sold in Germany the following year, a remarkable achievement at a time when very few Japanese artists were represented on recordings made abroad.[236]

Having accomplished the recordings, Kishi left Berlin and was back in Japan on 3 May. One reason for his hasty return was his wish to manage a Japan tour of the Berlin Philharmonic Orchestra, a project that had been under discussion since 1930. The Japanese press treated the visit as if it were imminent, and the German embassy in Tokyo commented on the project and on Kishi's role in it in a letter to the foreign office in Berlin dated 14 September 1935.[237] The ambassador, von Dirksen, urged that any such tour should not be a private affair, much less be used by Kishi to enhance his personal prestige, but that it should be arranged through the German embassy. Furtwängler, no less, should lead the orchestra and the Japanese veterans Yamada Kōsaku and Konoe Hidemaro should get a chance to conduct, as well as German-trained conductors of the younger generation, no doubt including Kishi, although he is not mentioned by name. According to Dirksen, Kishi was an acclaimed musician. He remarked that Kishi had been heard criticizing the effects of Aryan legislation on Jewish artists in connection with the reporting of Furtwängler's case, although he added that this should not be a reason to exclude him. The letter was passed on to the Propaganda Ministry, which contacted the office of the Berlin Philharmonic Orchestra. Ultimately the plan came to nothing and Kishi was soon involved in other enterprises. Even if he had not died prematurely, his commitments in Japan might well have prevented his planned return to Berlin.

The Japanese conductor who did return to Berlin and the Philharmonic Orchestra was Konoe Hidemaro, who arrived there late in 1938 with a passport designating him as travelling on government business. His brother Fumimaro had become prime minister the previous year.[238] Hidemaro remained in Europe until the end of the war, conducting in Germany and countries allied to or occupied by Germany, often in charity concerts for the Red Cross.[239] For a few months in 1944 he even led his own orchestra, known as the "Count Konoe Orchestra," with members from various German-occupied countries. He had first tried to assemble players through the German–Japanese Society, whose secretary wrote to the heads of 13 conservatoires in Germany, Austria and Slovakia in January 1944, asking for help in recruiting advanced students or recent graduates for a chamber orchestra to play for troops in Germany and the occupied territories.[240]

Konoe was probably the most famous Japanese musician active in wartime Germany. Suwa Nejiko initially came to Berlin late in 1942 at his instigation, to perform at an international culture festival the mayor of Berlin was planning. This came to nothing, however, and once Suwa became the protegé of Ambassador Ōshima Hiroshi and his wife, with whom Konoe was on bad terms, there was little chance of them performing together.[241] For Ambassador Ōshima, a Japanese violinist performing in the heartlands of classical music suited his aims admirably. Suwa had initially stayed in the house of the singer and actress Tanaka Michiko (1909–88) and her second husband the actor Victor de Kowa, but from January 1943 she lived with the Ōshimas whenever she was in Berlin. The ambassador made sure she received opportunities to perform and she was engaged by the German–Japanese Society.

Suwa was still studying in Paris when the Germans occupied the city in June 1940, having refused to leave at the outbreak of the war. The Kamenskys continued to look after her, although the occupation put a stop to money transfers from Japan.[242] Even as the war ravaged Europe the erstwhile prodigy developed into a mature artist. Her wartime career began when the Japanese general consulate in Marseilles mobilized Suwa and a couple of other Japanese musicians remaining in Paris to give a concert at the Opera in Marseilles. Accompanied by a French pianist, Suwa performed Chausson's *Poème* to great acclaim. Next she played with the Paris Symphony Orchestra under Jean Fournet. The start of the concert was delayed by a British air raid, but again Suwa was highly praised. Jacques Thibaud was in the audience, and praised her in person.[243]

Suwa's Berlin debut took place in December 1942. After performing two movements of Bruch's Violin Concerto in G minor for a small audience, she played at a music evening of the foreign press club. The *Deutsche Allgemeine Zeitung* reported, "For when one performs the sonata by César Franck with such noble, expansive, strong and at the same time flexible tone, with such true expressive fullness, even passion, then one has mastered the European art of the violin not merely technically, but also musically. When Miss Suwa in Manuel de Falla's Spanish Dances even achieved perfection in the spiccato bow and other virtuoso complexities, she had completely conquered the hearts of her listeners."[244]

The debut was a success and a tour through Germany followed. By the end of December Suwa Nejiko was worth a lengthy column in the section "People in the News" of the weekly Magazine *Die Woche*, entitled "Violinist from the Land of the Cherry Blossoms." According to the article, Suwa had "penetrated so deeply into the spirit of German music that she can play Bruch's famous Violin Concerto, César Franck and even Johann Sebastian Bach. (...) From her first bow stroke the listener is fascinated by the authenticity of her artistic achievement." Suwa reportedly asserted that "the great German masters to her signify the essence of music."[245]

It was playing for wounded German soldiers, however, that brought her even greater honours than rave reviews and resulted in what for Ōshima surely represented a major coup. On 24 February 1943 the *Asahi* newspaper, citing a telegram from Berlin, reported that on 22 February the German propaganda minister Joseph Goebbels had personally presented the Japanese violinist with a Stradivarius for her services in playing to German troops. The instrument, reported the *Asahi,* was made in 1722 and thus belonged to the same period as that of Elman.[246] German newspapers too reported the event, if more briefly. The *Völkischer Beobachter* wrote,

> Dr. Goebbels honours Japanese violinist. Reichsminister Dr. Goebbels presented the Japanese violinist Nejiko Suwa with a Stradivari violin in the presence of the Japanese ambassador in Berlin, Oshima. The young violinist enjoyed a spectacular success in December last year at her first performance in Berlin. She has since played in a large number of concerts for German wounded soldiers. At the presentation Ambassador Oshima expressed appreciation of the valuable present with cordial words of thanks and described it as a token of the close German–Japanese relationship also in the field of culture.[247]

The news was even worthy of mention in a news digest for the German troops, which also added that at her concert in Vienna (see below), "Reichsminister Dr Goebbels, who was unable to attend the concert, had made arrangements for the Japanese artist's room to be decorated with spring flowers in her favourite colours."[248]

After the war, it was rumoured in Japan that the Stradivarius must be one of the many instruments stolen from their Jewish owners by the Nazis. Suwa herself claimed that Goebbels had imported the instrument from a Silesian instrument shop. To this day no evidence either way is forthcoming. We know that the Nazis confiscated Jewish property, including musical instruments.[249] On the other hand, Goebbels' ministry did purchase instruments legally from dealers. The files of the Propaganda Ministry, incomplete as they are, include papers relating to the purchase of old Italian instruments with a view to loaning them to deserving artists, dating from 1941 to 1943.[250] They include drafts of documents for presenting instruments to artists, correspondence with the dealers Emil Hermann in Berlin and Hamma and Co. in Stuttgart and contracts of purchase. The violins named are a Matteo Goffriller, Venice 1698 and a Johannes B. Guadagnini, Piacenca 1748. One of the drafts also mentions a "Stradivari, Cremona 1715," and a letter from Hamma in March 1941 mentions a contract of purchase for a violin by the eighteenth-century Mantuan luthier Camillo Camilli. Because the documents are drafts, we cannot be sure that the purchases were completed, nor whether they include the violin presented to Suwa.

We cannot even be sure that the violin was truly a Stradivarius. Most of the known Stradivariuses are accounted for, but of course not all. An examination of the instrument itself might offer further clues, but Suwa Nejiko became sensitive about showing her instrument to anybody. One view has it that the violin is not by Antonio Stradivari, but by his son Omobono. Murata Sōroku, a luthier and expert on the history violins in Japan, cites a colleague who took the instrument apart for a repair and told Murata that the label said, "Francesco Stradivari." Labels are notoriously unreliable anyway.

To add to the confusion, Tanaka Michiko, who was present on the occasion and heard Goebbels' words, claimed that the violin was not even a present.[251] Presumably any ambiguity comes from the German word "verleihen," which depending on the context can mean either "to lend" or "to present someone with something as a gift." The documents in the Propaganda Ministry files speak of "Verleihung" and the draft contract with a musician suggest that a loan, albeit for an indefinite period, was envisaged.[252] However, there is no evidence that this contract was used. Goebbels himself stated in his diary, "I present the Japanese violinist Suwa with a Stradivarius violin. Oshima, who is present at the reception of this young woman, who seems most likable, is highly pleased with the gift."[253] This appears unambiguous, but the question in any case became academic once the Third Reich sank into rubble and Goebbels shot or poisoned himself (that too appears to be unclear).

The mystery surrounding the Stradivarius may never be solved, but the fact remains that the presentation represented high honours indeed for a young Japanese violinist in 1943. She was the first violinist from Japan to be honoured for her playing by a foreign government. Of course this would never have happened were it not for the political ties between Japan and Germany and the dearth of star performers during the war. But then musicians rarely receive state honours through their art alone; there is always a political context. Evidence suggests that Suwa Nejiko was an excellent violinist.

This is confirmed by the reviews of her next major performance in Berlin on 19 October 1943 with the Berlin Philharmonic Orchestra under

Hans Knappertsbusch. The programme announced that she would be playing the Brahms Concerto on the Stradivarius she had received from Goebbels. By now, wartime shortages had caused newspapers to dwindle to a few pages, with concert reviews filling only a paragraph each. The Berliner *Lokal-Anzeiger* wrote about Suwa under the heading "Japanisches Geigenwunder" (Japanese violin miracle):

> The encounter with this eminently gifted artist is a true pleasure. She coaxes from her lovely Stradivarius a tone full of noble sweetness and of substance which carries well. Moreover, she has a masterly controlled bow technique and the purest intonation. But even more admirable are the assurance of her musicality and the gift of empathy with which she was able to follow the heavy thoughts of the austere North German into the last recesses, so that her rendering of the work was a joyful experience.[254]

Of course one would expect the reviewer to be benign, but the praise mentions enough specifics to suggest that he was genuinely impressed.

Following the Berlin concert, the German–Japanese Society organized further concerts in the cities where it had branches. On 28 October Suwa played Mozart's Concerto in A major with the Vienna Symphonic Orchestra under Hans Weisbach (1885–1961). In November she was billed to play works by Beethoven, Grieg, Paganini and Sarasate in Leipzig, and in December she performed at a symphony concert in Magdeburg.[255] Throughout 1943 and 1944 the "delicate" Japanese girl played German masters in German cities while they were being bombed with increasing ferocity. She still retained her base with Kamensky in Paris, practising for several hours a day when she was not on tour. Only when the occupation of Paris by the Allied troops was imminent in August 1944 did she consent to being evacuated to Germany together with the few Japanese still remaining in France. While the men left by car, the women and children travelled by train under the constant threat of air raids. Witnesses reported that Suwa never left the train without clutching her Stradivarius.[256] Once in Berlin, Suwa stayed with the Ōshimas in the Japanese embassy, whose air shelter served them well while the battle for Berlin was reaching its climax.

And still Suwa Nejiko performed. In November 1944 Yosano Shigeru

13: Suwa Nejiko performing Brahms' Violin Concerto with the Berlin
Philharmonic Orchestra under Knappertsbusch, 1943.

at the consulate in Bern, who had heard her perform under
Knappertsbusch, organized concerts for her in Zurich, Geneva and
Lausanne – another propaganda act, to show the neutral Swiss that Japan
was not all bad.[257] Suwa travelled across Germany alone, while the Allies
at the Western borders were preparing to invade and relentless bombing

wrought havoc on the country's transportation network. The Swiss, impressed by her playing, suggested that she stay.[258] But she returned to Berlin, although not for long. Early in 1945 she accompanied the ambassador and his staff to Bad Gastein near Salzburg in Austria, where they witnessed the end of the war in Europe. The group included the cultural attaché Ōga Koshirō, whom Suwa would eventually marry. Their own country would not capitulate until several weeks later, and meanwhile the Americans shipped them to New York from Le Havre on a boat with American troops bound for the Far East. In Le Havre they were joined by Konoe Hidemaro. He had independently surrendered to U.S. troops in April and offered his services with proposals for propaganda against the military lobby in Japan.[259]

On the way to New York the Japanese passengers learnt of the atomic bomb dropped on Hiroshima and the Soviet Union's declaration of war against Japan according to the agreement of the conference in Yalta in February 1945. After landing, the Japanese, Suwa still desperately clutching her Strad, were taken to Bedford, PA, where they spent the next few months in the famous Bedford Springs Hotel. According to a local historian, the inhabitants of Bedford refused to supply food for the captives, so provisions had to be brought in from Washington.[260] In November they were finally sent on their way to Seattle to board a ship to Japan. They staged a farewell concert, in which Suwa performed with Konoe at the piano. The party arrived back in Japan in December 1945, just days before Hidemaro's brother Fumimaro took his own life after having been classified as a class "A" war criminal.

The conductor and the violinist survived and made new careers for themselves in post-war Japan, part of the all-important continuity linking Japan's pre-war musical achievements with its spectacular post-war successes. Konoe's musical connections with Germany continued. When he founded his "Konoe Orchestra" in the 1950s he invited the violinist Wolfgang Stavonhagen whom he had met during the war years. Stavonhagen (1916–), who subsequently became concertmaster of the Imperial Philharmonic Orchestra, already had a connection with Japan: in the early 1940s the Dessauer String Quartet, of which he was the leader, performed and recorded works by Japanese composers in Germany.[261]

Suwa's connection with Germany was renewed when she accompanied her husband Ōga to Cologne, where he became the founding director of the Japanese Cultural Institute in 1969. She never performed during their three-year stay and few people even knew that she was a violinist. The music at the opening ceremony on 2 September was provided by a young Japanese pianist whose father, Ambassador Uchida, had worked for the embassy at the same time as Ōga: the 21-year-old Uchida Mitsuko.[262]

## II. Recovery, Economic Growth and Cultural Ambitions (1945–1980s)

For a short while the music stopped. No band played for the arrival of the Supreme Commander of Allied Powers (SCAP), General Douglas MacArthur, at Atsugi Airbase south of Tokyo on 30 August 1945.[1] Japan had lost the war. For the first time in history foreign invaders occupied the land. The cities lay in ruins, as did most factories. The people suffered great hardship and were threatened with starvation. Elizabeth Vining, who came to Japan in October 1946 to tutor the Crown Prince, described the terrible destruction the fire bombs had wreaked in Tokyo, and the miserable lives of the people who had survived them: "In the midst of the waste people were living, some in the stone storehouses where they used to keep their treasures, some in new little wooden shacks, some in huts made of rusted iron and tin. I was puzzled to see a woman emerging from a hole in the ground, and realized with a pang that there was a low roof over it and that she was living there."[2] They ate mainly sweet potatoes supplemented with cornmeal from the U.S. Army surpluses, which in the absence of eggs, milk, fat or salt they made into steamed dumplings. "That winter when charcoal was so scarce and people had to use wood instead, they cooked in the yard beside the steps because of the smoke. I often saw them struggling in the rain to cook these meagre meals."[3]

Yet all was not lost. Even in the ruins were the seeds of Japan's spectacular post-war rise to power and prosperity. Japan's economic capacities were still stronger than they had been at the beginning of the 1930s, before the war boom brought increased growth. People might have lost nearly everything, but they still had their skills, knowledge and personal networks. Organizations and structures are not as easily destroyed as factories and houses, and could be revived more quickly.

All this was true of music too. Musical life in the major cities had already begun to resemble that of Western countries by the 1920s and early 1930s. Xenophobia and wartime austerities placed restrictions on musical activities, but music continued to play until the very last months of the war. Once Japan had recovered from the worst devastation, many of the pre-war trends resurfaced and continued, such as the internationalization of the music scene, the increasing popularity of

Western music and the rise of the musical professions. The Occupation authorities encouraged and promoted these trends.

Under the American Occupation, which lasted until 1952, Japan experienced revolutionary changes nearly as profound as those after 1868. Again the reforms were imposed by those in power, and this time ultimate power lay with the foreign conquerors. They, however, chose to work indirectly through Japanese authorities. The people, tired of war and disillusioned with the political system that had brought it about, largely accepted the changes. The infatuation with everything Western, particularly American, surpassed even the Westernization crazes of Meiji and Taishō Japan. This time the entire population embraced Western culture. Some reforms did not succeed, such as attempts to destroy the large economic *zaibatsu* conglomerates; others, such as the purge of the political right, were reversed as the Cold War began and communism seemed a greater threat than ultra-nationalism. But measures such as the land reforms and the promulgation of the new constitution in 1946 were effective and paved the way for a more egalitarian society with equal rights for women and minorities. Among the members of the SCAP committee drafting the constitution was Beate Sirota, the daughter of the pianist Leo Sirota. Her parents had sent her to study in America just before the outbreak of the Pacific War, and she returned as a college graduate in December 1945.[4]

Educational reform did much to promote equality and democracy. The School Education Law of 1947 introduced an American-style school system with nine years compulsory education for all, a comprehensive three-year high school and a four-year university. The school system expanded steadily over the next decades as children attended school for longer, and the Japanese became one of the most highly educated peoples in the world. By the 1970s, Japanese schools were drawing attention abroad, not least for the quality of education in the arts and music, but also because of the pressure on school children, driven by their "education mums," to pass through the "examination hell," enter top-ranking schools and continue into prestigious jobs in the government or big business companies. Music education had a significant place in the new school system, contributing to "the new peace-loving nation of the Cultural State of Japan." The aim of musical education was "to develop noble sentiments" and promote awareness of "the cultural aspects of life" by training children in singing, playing instruments, composition and music appreciation.[5]

Music appreciation beyond the public schools was promoted by MacArthur's Civil Information and Education Section, which made particular efforts to promote American music through live concerts, gramophone record concerts and radio broadcasting.[6] But the Occupation also contributed to the revival and enrichment of musical life in more informal ways. Soldiers craved entertainment, and Japanese musicians played for them in dance halls, hotels and officers' clubs. They picked up new styles of jazz and other American popular music which could be heard on the radio or on gramophone records. Hawaiian music, already known since the 1920s, became popular, as did Latin American music, tango, and country and western. Soon economic growth and improved technologies would bring music in many varieties to more and more Japanese through radio and television broadcasting and records.

Hungry for entertainment to brighten their drab lives, people eagerly received anything that was on offer, while the most avid music lovers of the pre-war period strove with great determination to pursue their interest once more.[7] Musicians gathered again, ensembles were formed or re-formed, instrument makers resumed production. Suzuki Umeo of Suzuki Violins started up again in 1946. As early as 28 August 1945, the NHK Orchestra could be heard on the radio again, with works by Japanese composers. On 14 and 15 September, only a month after capitulation, the orchestra gave its first regular concert after the war with a programme that included Beethoven's "Eroica." The Japan Music Competition, first held in 1932 and cancelled only in 1945, was resumed in 1946, when both the fourteenth and fifteenth competitions were held.[8] The following year, the Student Music Competition was inaugurated for children and young people up to high school. Composers' organizations re-established themselves.[9] The Tokyo Academy of Music admitted new students in September and October 1945, and teaching resumed on a reduced scale the following April. The first regular entrance examinations after the war were held in September 1946. Meanwhile, the newly appointed president, Komiya Toyotaka, strove to completely renew education at the Academy. He forced several professors to resign (some were later reinstated) and appointed a number of foreign musicians who had been forced into inactivity towards the end of the war, such as Alexander Mogilevsky, and, even more spectacularly, a roster of young Japanese performers, the youngest of whom was the former child prodigy Iwamoto Mari at barely 21.[10] In October the Academy held its first concert since the war.

Several other orchestras besides the NHK Orchestra re-formed or newly formed themselves just months after Japan's capitulation. Members included musicians from the abolished military bands, who also found work in bands formed by the police, the fire brigade and the Self Defence Forces. The centre of musical activities was still Tokyo, where most of the professional orchestras were (and are) based. The Tokyo Philharmonic Orchestra resumed its activities as the Tokyo City Philharmonic Orchestra in September 1945 under Yamada Kōsaku. It gave its first regular concert under its present name, the Tokyo Philharmonic Orchestra (Tōkyō Firuhāmonī Kōkyō Gakudan), in 1948 under Saitō Hideo.[11] Likewise, in 1945 the Tōhō Film Company founded the Tōhō Symphony Orchestra, which in 1951 became independent as the Tokyo Symphony Orchestra (Tōkyō Kōkyō Gakudan).[12] Its first permanent conductor was Konoe Hidemaro, who had returned from Europe via America in early December, just in time to conduct the NHK Orchestra in its twentieth anniversary concerts on 18 and 19 December 1946. Konoe founded his own orchestra in 1951, renamed the ABC Orchestra in 1956, but as before the war, Konoe's creations did not hold together for long, and in 1959 several of the members, including the German concertmaster Wolfgang Stavonhagen, left and founded the (Tokyo) Imperial Philharmonic.[13] The name features on several American-produced recordings of American music, including Samuel Barber's Violin Concerto, performed by Stavonhagen. The orchestra was short-lived and its members became the core of the Yomiuri Nippon Symphony Orchestra, founded in 1962.

Outside Tokyo too, orchestras formed almost immediately after the war. Within a few years NHK had radio orchestras in Osaka, Nagoya, Hiroshima, Kumamoto, Sendai and Sapporo.[14] In Hiroshima efforts to revive the local orchestra had begun in June 1945.[15] The Kansai Symphony Orchestra (Kansai Kōkyō Gakudan) gave its first concert in 1947 under Asahina Takashi, who had contributed much to its foundation. He remained its principal conductor when it was re-constituted as the Osaka Philharmonic Orchestra in 1960 and until his death in 2001. Osaka, like Tokyo, had a lively musical scene including several orchestras even before the war.

New orchestras were created. The Takasaki Citizens' Orchestra in Gunma Prefecture, formed by amateur musicians in November 1945, gave its first regular concert the following March. In May 1946 it changed its name to the Gunma Symphony Orchestra and in 1947 it formed a professional organization, whose members gave music lessons all over the prefecture. By 2010 this "Mobile Music School" had reached over six million children. The professional musicians came from Tokyo, where opportunities were still limited and the food situation poor. The orchestra's reputation increased when it became the model for a film in 1955, the year it celebrated its tenth anniversary.[16] From 1981 to 1993 the orchestra's musical director was Toyoda Kōji, Suzuki Shin'ichi's pre-war child pupil. More orchestras were formed over the following decades, including the Japan Philharmonic Orchestra (Nihon Firuhāmonī Kōkyō Gakudan) in 1956, whose chief conductor Watanabe Akeo started his musical career as a violinist. Another was the New Japan Philharmonic Orchestra (Shin Nihon Firuhāmonī Kōkyō Gakudan), formed in 1972 with members of the Japan Philharmonic Orchestra.[17]

Until foreign artists could once again visit, solo performances were given by Japanese musicians or foreigners who had lived in Japan through the war years. Among the local talent were the girl prodigies of the pre-war period, Suwa Nejiko, Tsuji Hisako and Iwamoto Mari. They performed all over the country. From the 1950s onwards, the Japanese could once again enjoy and be inspired by leading international artists. The first foreign artist to visit Japan after the war was French pianist Lazare Lévy, known in Japan as the teacher of Yasukawa Kazuko, another musician who performed widely in the immediate post-war years.[18] Next came Yehudi Menuhin in 1951 (he came again in 1954). Violinists who had toured Japan in the 1920s and 1930s returned; Szigeti came in 1953. That year, Thibaud, whose schedule included concerts in Japan, died in an air crash. Heifetz returned in 1954, Elman in 1955. New visiting violin virtuosos included Isaac Stern, who first came in 1953, David Oistrakh in 1955 and Leonid Kogan in 1958.[19] The first string quartet to tour Japan was the Budapest Quartet in 1954; the Amadeus Quartet came in 1958. American and European orchestras could be heard live in Japan for the first time, starting with the Symphony of the Air in 1955. The Berlin Philharmonic under Karajan came in 1957. Karajan had already conducted the NHK Orchestra in Tokyo in 1954. As in the

1920s and early 1930s, the visiting artists stimulated interest and inspired imitators.

The renewed appearance of leading international artists in Japan reflected the country's increasing economic power. The economy, slow to recover at first, took off spectacularly after the outbreak of the Korean War in the 1950s, and continued to boom through the setbacks of the oil crises of the 1970s and well into the 1980s when it culminated in the economic "bubble." The Japanese once again had money to spend, and besides consumer goods such as washing machines, refrigerators, television sets and cars, they spent it on cultural pursuits. Many purchased concert tickets through audience associations which provided affordable tickets for their members and made it worthwhile for artists and ensembles to tour the provinces. The first was Rōon (Zenkoku Kinrōsha Ongaku Kyōgikai Renraku Kaigi: National Allied Conference Councils for Workers' Music), established in Osaka in 1949. Rōon sponsored concerts of classical music with Japanese and foreign artists at low prices. By 1955 it had 120,000 members and in 1965 its membership peaked at 633,000; after that, competition from rival audience groups and commercial impresarios caused membership to fall. The main rival was Onkyō (Ongaku Bunka Kyōkai: Association for Musical Culture), founded in 1955 by large business enterprises. Another was Min'on (Minshu Ongaku Kyōkai: Democratic Music Association) sponsored by the Buddhist organization Sōka Gakkai and established in 1963. The audience associations did much to democratize music and other performing arts. Although their importance has declined with the increasing commercialization of entertainment since the 1970s, they still endure.[20]

Many Japanese also wanted to play music themselves as a leisure activity, or to make up for the opportunities they themselves had missed by having their children learn an instrument. In the 1950s the violin enjoyed another "boom," partly because instruments were relatively cheap.[21] Soon, however, the piano, previously reserved for the elites, became the chief object of middle-class aspirations. Thanks to the development of mass production by Yamaha and Kawai, it became affordable for middle-class families. By the end of the 1970s more Japanese were studying the piano, the most popular Western instrument, than the *koto*.[22] For those who still found the acquisition of a piano daunting, Yamaha developed the Electone, an electronic organ, in 1959. Yamaha and Kawai both established their own music school chains in order to promote the use of their products. Yamaha started experimental classes with 150 pupils in 1954. In 1959 they were renamed "Yamaha Music Schools" and had 20,000 pupils. In 1966 Yamaha established a foundation with the aim of promoting and popularizing music more widely. The Yamaha education system provided courses for everyone from pre-kindergarten age to adults. Kawai began its activities at around the same time, opening its first course in 1956; its offering included a course in general music and movement for children aged two-and-a-half to three. Soon Yamaha and Kawai each had a network of schools throughout Japan.

School education and private studios brought general music education and the chance to learn an instrument within reach of everyone. Specialist training for future professionals expanded as well. In 1949 the Tokyo Academy of Music was merged with the Tokyo Academy of Fine Arts and became the music department of Tōkyō Geijutsu Daigaku (Tokyo University of Fine Arts), commonly known as Tōkyō Geidai or just Geidai.[23] New public and private conservatoires were established. Private colleges established before the war were upgraded to conservatoires, among them the earliest private college, the Music College of the East (Tōyō Ongaku Gakkō), which became a four-year university in 1963 and was renamed the Tokyo College of Music (Tōkyō Ongaku Gakkō) in 1969. Other colleges established in the early twentieth century which attained university status included Kunitachi College of Music (1950), Musashino Academia Musicae (1949) and in the Kansai area the Osaka College of Music (Ōsaka Ongaku Daigaku: 1958). Sōai Gakuen, another pre-war institution of the Kansai area, established Sōai Womens' University with a music department in 1958.[24] Newly founded institutions included the future Tōhō Gakuen School of Music, which grew from a music school for children opened in 1948 to a high school and college to rival Geidai.

As soon as foreign travel became feasible, Japanese began to go abroad for study again, their number increasing from a trickle in the 1950s to a stream in the 1960s after the liberalization of foreign travel in the year of the Tokyo Olympics, and then to a flood in the 1980s, when the high value of the yen made studying abroad cheaper than in Japan with its hefty school fees and cost of living. While before the war most musicians had gone to Germany or France to study, America now became the country of choice for many; among the first were the violinists Etō Toshiya and Kobayashi Kenji. The former violinist Watanabe Akeo became the first conductor to study in America rather than Europe when he went to the Juilliard School in New York in 1950. As music education expanded and the possibilities for studying abroad increased, musicians who grew up after the war enjoyed opportunities only the most privileged had enjoyed earlier. From the 1960s, when Japan had once again been accepted into the international community and its "economic miracle" was well under way, more and more went abroad after receiving excellent training in Japan, often with the help of scholarships from their own or a foreign government. They began to win international competitions and to fill positions in foreign orchestras and music faculties, and international audiences began to take notice of them. An early example was the conductor Ozawa Seiji, who won the International Competition of Orchestra Conductors in Besançon in 1959 and the Koussevitsky Prize at the Tanglewood Music Center in Massachusetts in 1960. In 1961 he became assistant conductor for the New York Philharmonic, the beginning of an international career which brought him back to Japan only periodically. Toyoda Kōji, the former "midget prodigy," won prizes at several international competitions and in 1962 was appointed concertmaster of the West German Radio Symphony Orchestra in Berlin.[25]

Like Ozawa and Toyoda, many who trained abroad remained there for at least the early part of their career. Meanwhile, artists based in Japan began to embark on foreign tours. In 1960 the NHK Symphony Orchestra toured the world, with the pianist Nakamura Hiroko, then only 16, as a soloist.[26] Konoe's ABC Symphony Orchestra toured Europe the same year, before it folded. But the real sensation came in 1964, the year the Tokyo Olympics confirmed Japan's place as a wealthy and respected member of the international community. Two of Japan's larger-than-life teachers, Suzuki Shin'ichi and Saitō Hideo separately toured the United States with their ensembles of young string players. Newspapers began to carry headlines such as "Invasion from the Orient," "Young Violinists from Asia Gain Major Place on American Musical Scene" and "Suzuki's Pupils Learn Music First."[27] Observers speculated about the reasons for the Asian musicians' success. In the case of Japan, where most of the early Asian successes hailed from, the most important reason was that the country was already well on its way to becoming an international power in the field of classical music before the war. Once the country was again at peace, it could build on pre-war achievements. Composers and performers such as Takemitsu Tōru, Uchida Mitsuko and Midori became household names.

In what has been called the "reverse flow,"[28] Japan became an exporter of classical music in other ways. Yamaha and Suzuki had already exported musical instruments earlier in the century and especially during the First World War. Once the Suzuki Method became popular abroad in the 1960s, Suzuki Violins led the supply of fractional violins. Mass-produced pianos from Japan took over foreign markets in what has been described as "the most significant development in modern piano history."[29] Yamaha, like Suzuki Violins, traces its company history to the year 1887, when its founder Yamaha Torakusu built his first reed organ, and began exporting at just before the turn of the twentieth century. The other large manufacturer of pianos, Kawai, was founded in 1915. Serious expansion into markets formerly dominated by European and North American producers began in the 1950s, and by 1969 Japan had become the largest piano-manufacturing country in the world with an output of 257,000 instruments.[30] Yamaha, whose huge business empire included record players, motorcycles, archery equipment and many other products, also began to export wind instruments and electronic musical instruments. Both Yamaha and Kawai exported their music education systems in the 1960s. The dissemination of music education through commercial chains is not limited to classical music, and in fact the Yamaha Music Foundation established in 1966 focused on popular rather than classical music.[31] Besides supplying musical instruments, Japan's contribution to both classical and popular music worldwide was often indirect, through technology, from the transistor radio in the 1950s to the Sony Walkman, the karaoke machine and the compact disc in the 1980s.

Peace and economic growth, technological advances and internationalization affected all kinds of music, not just classical music.[32] The direct contact with new forms of jazz and other musical styles was just the start; soon the Japanese were eagerly consuming, and eventually playing themselves, many different musical styles from around the world.

In the 1950s contemporary American hits found an eager audience among teenagers, who were as enthusiastic for rock music as their contemporaries in other parts of the world. When the Beatles performed in Japan in 1966 they had the fans screaming as much as anywhere and inspired many imitators.[33] The 1960s also brought American urban folk music to Japan, while a modern version of the Japanese folk song developed separately. Indeed, anything that was popular in the West was bound to find a following in Japan. But the Japanese also did their own thing. In 1967 the record sales of Japanese artists overtook those of foreign artists for the first time since the Second World War.[34] By the 1990s, the term J-pop had gained currency and become an export article, often in the form of theme songs for films, a category in its own right in Japan. The 1990s also saw music reach Japan via routes other than from Europe and America, particularly ethnic music from South East Asia, reflecting Japan's efforts to strengthen its cultural and social ties with Asian countries in other areas of activity.

Older audiences, on the other hand, preferred the popular songs born out of the revival of Koga Masao's legacy and nostalgic songs expressing loneliness, yearning for home and lost love. In the 1960s and 1970s this type of song developed into the nostalgic *enka,* perceived as quintessentially Japanese. The instrumentation and musical accompaniment of *enka* varies in style, but often involves a large ensemble with a lush string sound. Immensely popular with the generations who experienced the hardships of war and its immediate aftermath, *enka* dominated the early karaoke repertoire. The audience for *enka* began to decline in the 1980s, but they are popular in other Asian countries and still have a following in Japan. Other types of popular music have roots in traditional genres, including Tsugaru *shamisen, taiko* drum ensembles and the music played at seasonal festivals (*matsuri bayashi*), as well as Okinawan popular music.

Straight traditional music (*hōgaku*) on the other hand, leads a niche existence. Although popular immediately after the war, as early as 1952 a Western observer remarked: "Thus, when one speaks about music in Japan, this means only Western music; indeed the process of assimilation has reached the extent where the younger generation virtually denies the cultivation of its country's indigenous music."[35] Still, until the 1970s, some *hōgaku* genres were widely studied, particularly by girls and young women. Before the war, the traditional arts associated with the pleasure quarters were suspect among the middle classes. Now it was respectable for middle-class daughters to study the *koto* and the *shamisen*. Businessmen studied traditional singing (such as *kouta*), an enjoyable hobby that also came in useful at company drinking parties and functions. *Hōgaku* artists composed "contemporary *hōgaku*" in continuation of pre-war "new *hōgaku*." The audience for their music (like that for contemporary and avant-garde music in the Western classical tradition) is limited.

The 1980s saw not only a bubbling economy but also a bubbling classical music scene; "internationalization" was the buzzword of the day, and Western classical music continued to represent Western civilization at its best. But it was also a commodity that could be easily bought with a strong yen. In some cases spending power exceeded discernment to the point where a foreign observer described Japan as "the world's most profitable and least critical market for classical music."[36] Foreign artists came to Japan in such numbers in the 1980s that the market appeared saturated.[37] In Tokyo two new concert halls unabashedly mixed consumerism with culture in a way that most Europeans still frowned upon, taking the "concert hall construction boom" of the 1960s and 1970s to new heights. In October 1986, the Suntory Hall was officially opened with a concert by the Berlin Philharmonic. Modelled on the Philharmonic Hall in Berlin, it was the first hall to serve alcoholic drinks (from Suntory of course) and exuded an atmosphere of luxury.[38] Bunkamura, which opened in October 1989 with a concert by the Bayreuth Festival Orchestra, displayed the marriage of classical music and luxury consumption even more flamboyantly. Situated in the Shibuya shopping and entertainment district, Bunkamura combines upmarket shopping and dining with high culture. Concertgoers pass the shops and restaurants to make their way to the third floor, (or to the second floor of the adjoining Tōkyū department store) to reach the 2,150-seat Orchard Hall, again inspired by famous European halls of Amsterdam, Leipzig and Vienna.[39] By the end of the 1990s Japan had 750 concert halls (about 100 in Tokyo), at least a third of which were built or planned during the bubble years.[40]

Excessive and extravagant concert-hall-construction might be seen as a symptom of fragile confidence and even signal a crisis of classical music.[41] Indeed, although Japan had a lively, varied and high-quality music scene with well-trained performers and receptive audiences, many observers felt that Japan still somehow lagged behind the West. The weaknesses of classical music in Japan, real or imagined, were the subject of many comments and discussions in the wake of the so-called Geidai or Kanda Affair in 1981 (see Chapter 12). Together with the privileging of Western classical music over all other forms, including Japan's traditional music, this sense of inferiority and under-achievement has led critical observers to speak of a "classical music complex."[42] Some commentators even claimed that the ambivalence towards a music imposed from outside and above and the sense of inferiority have resulted in a secret dislike of classical music.[43] But most problems commentators see with Western classical music at the end of the twentieth and the beginning of the twenty-first century are similar to those discussed elsewhere in the world and may well be a symptom of the times rather than a Japanese peculiarity. Certainly, in the early decades after the war, the growth of classical music looked like an unqualified success story.

## 7. The Post-war Violin Boom: Teaching the Masses and the Select Few

In the possession of the violinist Matsumoto Zenzō, a veteran of the pre-war professional scene, there were two identical sheets of poor-quality paper the size of a postcard, the writing produced by the kind of duplicating machine used in the days before photocopiers. "Teikin Kenkyūkai" – "Violin Research Association," says the title. "Teikin," written with Chinese characters, was the word for violin commonly used to replace the foreign word in phonetic transcription during the war years when things foreign were shunned.[44] Ten names and compositions are listed, mostly from the basic student repertoire. The final name is that of Matsumoto himself with Monti's Czardas. The date is 28 April 1946, not a year since the end of the war. Already music enthusiasts were using their new freedom to pursue the music they liked. No longer did they have to fear being accused of insufficient patriotism because they were carrying a violin case. And, as earlier in the century, the cheap price and portability of the violin made it the most attractive Western instrument to learn.

At around the same time as Matsumoto Zenzō gathered his students around him, Suzuki Shin'ichi began to turn his passion for music education into renewed action. He moved to the town of Matsumoto in Nagano Prefecture, where a group that included a former colleague from the Imperial Music School made plans for a new school. The Matsumoto Music School opened in September 1946. In December the National Association of People Interested in the Education of Small Children (Zenkoku Yōji Kyōiku Dōshikai) followed, renamed the Talent Education Research Association (Sainō Kyōiku Kenkyūkai) in 1948. The Association's aim was to publish Suzuki Shin'ichi's writings and to spread his principles through lecture tours with performances by Suzuki's pupils. In 1946 Suzuki published *Talent Education for Small Children and Its Methods.*[45]

To many Japanese, Suzuki appeared like a beacon in the bleak years following capitulation. Noda Awaji (1932–), who has been teaching children in Osaka for over 50 years, remembers how, after reading Suzuki's book, her mother insisted that her daughter commute from Nagano to Matsumoto once a week to study with Suzuki, although as a teenager who had been playing the violin for years she was well above the age group Suzuki concentrated his efforts on.[46] Interest in Talent Education spread rapidly. By 1949, 35 Suzuki Studios all over Japan were teaching 1,500 children. The following year, the Ministry of Education authorized the Talent Education Research Institute as a corporate body. Several schools and kindergartens applied Suzuki's ideas in their general education programmes. In 1951 Suzuki held his first summer school with 109 children and 11 teachers from all over Japan. It became a yearly event, as did national workshops for teachers from 1956, and "graduation ceremonies," where pupils performed set pieces to mark the completion of a grade. The first one for violin pupils took place in Tokyo in 1953, and 196 pupils performed. More spectacular were the yearly national conventions and grand concerts, inaugurated in 1955 at the Tokyo Metropolitan Hall with 2,000 children performing on the violin in the presence of members of the imperial family and diplomatic representatives of several foreign countries.

Suzuki's method appealed particularly to parents who did not themselves play a musical instrument. His insistence that nurture and the right environment were more important than natural talent chimed in well with popular beliefs. In the traditional arts, skills were passed on from father to son. Children were apprenticed from an early age and the question of talent did not come into consideration. By stressing an early start and the role of the parents, especially the mother, Suzuki gave parents the opportunity to study classical music themselves while educating their child: in the early days mothers even started learning the violin themselves first in order to capture their child's interest. In this way families could overcome their perceived disadvantage as Japanese when it came to Western classical music and make an important part of Western civilization their own. Some of the mothers, however, overshot the mark.[47] Suzuki insisted that the children should have fun while learning and progress so gradually that they did not notice the hurdles they jumped. But over-ambitious mothers pushed their children relentlessly and showered them with criticism. They brought the competitive atmosphere surrounding the school entrance exams into the violin studios. The "education mum" (kyōiku mama), the kept wife of a white-collar worker with plenty of time to devote to her children's education, whether school work or other activities, often turned Suzuki education into endless drilling. Conversely, once her children entered junior high school and the all-important high-school entrance examinations loomed, she would discourage them from continuing to study their instrument. By then many children had completed the ten Suzuki books.[48] Suzuki did not object, since he advocated musical education as a means to train good citizens rather than to produce professional musicians.

Meanwhile, parents who wanted their children to become professionals did not choose Suzuki teachers, or they sent their children to other teachers after the beginning stages. Nishizaki Takako (1944–), whose father worked with Suzuki, studied with both and became the first student to complete the Suzuki course. She subsequently studied with Broadus Erle (1918–77) and Saitō Hideo at the Tōhō Gakuen School of Music before going to Juilliard in 1962. Describing herself as a "Suzuki guinea pig," she became highly critical of Suzuki's ideas.[49] She now has her own teaching studio, where, according to her website, she "combines the best elements of the Suzuki Method with traditional teaching."[50] Other professional violinists who began with Suzuki teachers before moving on include Kuronuma Yuriko (1940–), Tanaka Toshiko (1940–), Wanami Takayoshi (1945–) and Temma Atsuko (1955–).

The Suzuki studios which sprung up all over Japan were not the only places offering music instruction to the masses from an early age. As mentioned earlier, the Yamaha and Kawai music stores began offering music classes from the mid-1950s, although they did not initially offer tuition on the violin.[51] Although Yamaha and Kawai, like Suzuki, extended their activities beyond Japan in the 1960s, neither has the same high profile abroad as Suzuki's Talent Education. In Japan, however, they attracted large numbers of pupils. Like the Suzuki Method, the Yamaha approach stressed the value of musical training for character development and the idea that everybody can learn to make music if they start early and enjoy good support from their parents. Yamaha too teaches through a repertoire of pieces, although its repertoire is more diverse in musical styles than Suzuki's. Yamaha pedagogy, like the Suzuki method, stresses learning by imitation of excellent models.[52] Other music chain stores such as Yamano Gakki and Shimamura Gakki likewise began to open music schools and of course innumerable teachers gave classes in private studios.

By the 1950s a second "violin boom" was sweeping Japan.[53] Like the first one earlier in the century, it owed much to the Japanese people's desire to make Western-style culture their own and to the fact that violins were easily and cheaply available. "After the war, you could find little grocery stores in the Japanese countryside selling cheap violins side by side with candy bars. The people needed an outlet, and music was the perfect thing," Ozawa Seiji recalled.[54] Eventually the piano would become the instrument of choice for the rising middle classes embracing Western culture through its music. Meanwhile, the violin continued to enjoy an advantage. Teaching methods, however, whether for the violin or the piano, were old-fashioned, the preferred tutors being Hohmann's *Practical Violin Method* (in Hashimoto Kunihiko's edition) for the violin and Ferdinand Beyer's (1803–63) *Preparatory School* for the piano.

Ozawa Seiji's teacher Saitō Hideo (1902–74), the cellist and conductor, was another trailblazer of the immediate post-war years.[55] Like Suzuki he had studied music in Berlin in the 1920s. Saitō's aims were quite different from Suzuki's though: he wanted to establish early training for future professionals. Before 1945 it was common for people to start in their late teens and still enter music college, whether the Tokyo Academy of Music or the increasing numbers of private colleges. But many experts realized that this was too late, and Saitō agreed. He wanted to give children a firm grounding that would enable them to become professional musicians. Saitō opened his Music School for Children (Kodomo no Tame no Ongaku Kyōshitsu) in rented classrooms in Tokyo in September 1948. He had enlisted some of the leading lights of the music world, including the pianist Iguchi Motonari, the singer Itō Takeo and the composer Shibata Minao. The administrative director was Yoshida Hidekazu, a prominent post-war music critic. "When I saw the advertisement and wanted to enrol my daughter, her violin teacher at the time said such illustrious people would never teach children, it must be a fraud," recalled the father of the violinist Furiyoshi Keiko (1946–).[56] Several of the first 30 pupils who crossed what was still a burnt desert to reach the rented classrooms were clutching small violins, mostly without cases and sometimes without bows. The youngest recruits were only four years old and included the future pianist Nakamura Hiroko and the violinist Ninomiya Yumi (1943–) who was to graduate from and join the faculty of the Curtis Institute.

Besides advocating an early start, Saitō felt keenly that music students needed a firm grounding in general musical training and that children should begin with classes in ear training and solfège. "So this is exactly the reverse of Mr. Suzuki Shin'ichi's Talent Education," Saitō later remarked.[57] Another innovation was that children (or their parents) were free to choose their teacher and studied with several teachers as a matter of course – a stark contrast to traditional ideas of teaching, where loyalty to a single teacher lasts a lifetime.[58] The children had lessons with their individual teachers and came to the school on Saturdays for general music and ensemble classes. Violin teachers included Sumi Saburō, Ono Anna and Kōno Shuntatsu (1922–), a graduate of the Tokyo Academy of Music who had studied with Andō Kō and Alexander Mogilevsky.[59]

One of the most outstanding features of Saitō's concept was that he introduced ensemble training for all children from the start: not just playing in unison like the Suzuki students, but in chamber groups with several different parts and, eventually, a full orchestra. Saitō assembled an orchestra under his baton as early as 1950. Soon its members performed Haydn's "Toy" Symphony for NHK radio. At the time people could not believe that children aged four to twelve could play together as an orchestra. When it went on its first tour to the Kansai region in 1954, the billing ran, "the girl and boy prodigies are coming."[60] The orchestra also served as a practice ground for aspiring conductors. Saitō knew the importance of competent conducting from his experience as an orchestral cellist and began training conductors systematically, most famously Ozawa Seiji (1935–), one of his earliest students.

As the first students grew older, the school expanded to accommodate them. In 1952 it moved to Tōhō Girls' High School, where a co-educational music department was opened. In 1955 Tōhō Gakuen Junior College, offering a two-year course, was established, followed in 1961 by Tōhō Gakuen School of Music, which offered a full four-year course. Branch schools in all parts of the country were added over the following decades, and in 2001 Tōhō Gakuen operated 28 music schools for children, with about 2,200 children attending.[61] Among the earliest was the department at Sōai Gakuen College for Girls in Osaka in 1955. Saitō and several of his colleagues travelled there regularly to teach. Among the violinists they taught in the 1960s was Gotō Midori's mother Setsu.

Saitō's educational achievements were presented outside Japan when the orchestra toured America for the first time in 1964. They gave their first concert in Los Angeles and continued to New York, Tanglewood, San Francisco and Honolulu. After their arrival in New York they gave

14: The orchestra of Tōhō Gakuen performing Bach's Double Concerto at its second public concert, 2 April 1956 at Nihon Seinenkan in Tokyo. The conductor is Kuyama Keiko and the soloists are Hirose Etsuko and Ushioda Masuko.

a concert in Stamford, Connecticut on 11 July with Benny Goodman as soloist. In New York City they gave eight concerts between 13 and 18 July, with four different programmes as part of a Japan Week at the Philharmonic Hall. Ozawa Seiji, who was already winning fame in America, conducted the first concert. The others were conducted by Saitō himself and four student conductors, two of them female. Soloists on the tour included Wanami Takayoshi, 19 years old at the time, and Ushioda Masuko, 22, who both performed Bach's Violin Concerto in E major, as well as Tokunaga Tsugio and Furiyoshi Keiko, who played solo parts in Vivaldi's *Four Seasons*. Reviewers were thrilled. On their first night at the Philharmonic Hall the young musicians, 35 girls and 25 boys, displayed an impressive stylistic range and "played like a million dollars." [62] Interestingly, in the light of later reactions to Asian players, a note of anxiety sounded with the praise after the second concert: "It's a little frightening, the way the youngsters of the Toho String Orchestra played last night at Philharmonic Hall. If they're this good now, what will they be when they're mature artists? So fabulous that they're unbearable, no doubt."[63] As it was, they "continued to perform miracles," not only with excellent style and technique, but with "an extraordinary buoyancy of spirit."[64] Back in Japan, Saitō's triumphs attracted considerable media attention, although not all of it was positive.[65]

In 1970 the orchestra toured Europe for several weeks. Among the orchestra's violinists was Yasunaga Tōru, the future concertmaster of the Berlin Philharmonic. For Saitō the tour was a great triumph; he even believed that classical music could become yet another Japanese export product.[66] His hope reflected Japanese confidence at the height of the "economic miracle." Already, Japanese string players, many of them trained under Saitō's baton, had begun to fill European and American orchestras. That same year, the Tokyo String Quartet won the first prize at the Coleman String Competition and four months later the first prize at the International Chamber Music Competition in Munich. The quartet was formed at Juilliard, but all its members had experienced their first ensemble training together at Tōhō Gakuen College.[67]

Saitō died in 1974 while he was preparing his orchestra for a second American tour. Although he had been ill for some time, he had hoped to go with them. Ten years later, in 1984, Ozawa Seiji and Akiyama Kazuyoshi, one of the student conductors during the first American tour, founded the Saito Kinen or Saito Memorial Orchestra to commemorate the tenth anniversary of Saitō's death. The members, nearly all of them Tōhō alumni, gave their first concert in Tokyo that year. In 1987 the orchestra embarked on a European tour. The orchestra continues to this day, and its players take time out from their regular engagements to meet for an intensive rehearsal period to perform at the Saito Kinen Festival in Matsumoto and concert tours in Japan, Europe and North America. Over the years, new Tōhō graduates joined the orchestra, which by now has many members who never knew Saitō personally.[68]

Saitō's outstanding achievements as a pioneer of professional music education in general and of orchestral training benefited many violinists, most of whom studied with his contemporary and colleague at Tōhō, Sumi Saburō.[69] For decades there was hardly a successful violinist who was not a pupil of Sumi at some stage in her or his training; his students virtually monopolized the prizes at the national music competitions and many went on to win abroad.[70] From 1945 Sumi was a regular judge at the Japan Music Competition. In 1959 his student Ishii Shizuko came third at the Long–Thibaud Competition, and Sumi was invited as a judge in 1961. For the first time he travelled abroad. The following year he was on the jury of the Paganini Competition and in 1966 the Tchaikovsky Competition. Sumi's granddaughter Eriko, who studied violin with Dorothy DeLay at Juilliard and is based in Italy, often meets people abroad who remember her grandfather.[71]

During his travels, Sumi, who never had the chance to study abroad in his youth, made a special effort to meet as many top violinists as he could. On his first trip, for example, he made contact with Max Rostal in London through the British Embassy in Tokyo. The ambassador himself wrote to Rostal, telling him that "Mr. Sumi has a very high reputation in Japan, and I am sure that if you are able to find time to see him your time will not be wasted."[72] Even in Japan he never missed a chance to learn from foreign artists. He would sit in the front row at their concerts.[73] Afterwards he would seek them out in order to learn from them and to introduce his most promising pupils. Among those who visited his home or his studio at Tōhō were Yehudi Menuhin, David Oistrakh, Joseph Szigeti, Leonid Kogan, Josef Gingold, Yuri Yankelevich, Gabriel Bouillon, Sándor Végh, Devy Erlih and Raymond Gallois-Montbrun (1918–94).[74]

While Suzuki Shin'ichi became famous abroad, Sumi Saburō, whose name is less known outside Japan, is rated higher at home, where he is sometimes called the "Auer of Japan." His student Unno Yoshio, a highly respected teacher in his own right, credits Sumi with being the first teacher to have firmly established in Japan a school of playing that gained international currency.[75] Like Suzuki, Sumi was able to build upon his pre-war teaching experience. Immediately after the war he also continued to perform, remaining with the New Symphony Orchestra until 1951. He formed an ensemble with his students, the Ensemble Fontēnu; besides playing for the occupation forces and touring Japan, Sumi's chamber orchestra also made radio broadcasts and gramophone recordings. With this group his pupil Suzuki Hidetarō (1937–) performed the Mendelssohn Violin Concerto, while Watanabe Akeo (1919–90), a violin graduate of the Tokyo Academy of Music and one of Sumi's first violin pupils, gained early experience as a conductor.

Among his pupils were two of his sons. Takeaki (1937–) followed in his father's footsteps and became a professor at Tōhō Gakuen College, having graduated from there in 1958. Yasurō (1945–2007) taught at Geidai. Sumi himself continued to teach until just before his death in 1984 at the age of 82. It is a mark of Sumi's fame and influence that his achievements continue to be commemorated. In 1986 several of his former students gathered for a grand memorial concert. Among the soloists who performed were Satō Yōko, Muroya Takahiro, Hirose Etsuko, Ishii Shizuko, Tatsumi Akiko, Tokunaga Tsugio, Sawa Kazuki, as well as Wanami Takayoshi, Sō Tomotada and Suzuki Hidetarō, who came from abroad for the occasion.[76] In 1991 an association to honour Sumi's memory was established in his home town of Yonago, no doubt with the additional purpose of boosting the cultural life of the provincial town. It organizes regular concerts featuring Sumi's students and the youth orchestra of Yonago.[77] In 2009 the Sumi Saburō Memorial Society was established to commemorate the twenty-fifth anniversary of his death. Its web pages provide detailed information about his early life in Yonago and pre-war Tokyo.[78] Like the Saito Kinen Festival and Orchestra, the activities to commemorate Sumi show how deeply Japanese revere their teachers. Here the lineage consciousness that characterizes the violin world in the West intermingles with the Confucian legacy which accords a special place to the teacher and the student–teacher relationship.[79] In Saitō's and Sumi's cases the commemorations are also a tribute to their contributions to string and violin playing in Japan in general.

Although there is no "Sumi Method," Sumi Saburō helped edit several publications, including *Atarashii vaiorin kyōhon* (*The New Violin Tutor*), published in 1964, which he co-edited with two other great teachers and contemporaries, Uzuka Tatsuo (1905–85) and Shinozaki Hirotsugu (1901–66). Shinozaki Hirotsugu, like Suzuki and Sumi, was a pioneer of music education from an early age. Enter any music shop in Japan, and beside the volumes of the Suzuki books you will find those of Shinozaki's violin tutor as well as the six volumes of the *New Violin Tutor*.[80] He taught at Musashino Academia Musicae. His students included Kishibe Momoo (1938–), who later studied with Mogilevsky, and his daughter Shinozaki Isako (1943–), who graduated from Tōhō Gakuen. In 1966 she came third at the International Paganini Competition. Besides performing, she has followed in her father's footsteps as a propagator of early music education, and recorded the accompanying cassette tapes to his violin tutor. She is a professor at Tōhō Gakuen College of Music.

Uzuka Tatsuo was less in the limelight than Sumi Saburō and Saitō Hideo, but nevertheless one of the most influential teachers of his time.[81] He graduated from the Tokyo Academy of Music in 1932, having studied with Andō Kō and Robert Pollack. Not until 1963 did he have the opportunity to study abroad, in Munich, where his teacher was Wilhelm Stross (1907–66). Before the war, Uzuka performed in recitals with pianists and in a piano trio. He taught at Geidai, his alma mater, and, after his retirement from Geidai, at Ueno Gakuen and Shōwa Junior College of Music. Uzuka was especially interested in the violin music of Bach. His pupils included Unno Yoshio, Okayama Kiyoshi, Hattori Yoshiko, Shinozaki Isako and Temma Atsuko. His son, the violist Uzuka Yoshiyuki (1939–), studied in Munich and played in orchestras in Japan and Germany before becoming professor and later president of the Tokyo College of Music.

At the Tokyo Academy of Music, reorganized as the Faculty of Music at the University of Fine Arts and Music in 1949, Uzuka's colleague Inoue Takeo (1906–86) was another teacher who represented continuity through the war.[82] Having graduated from the Tokyo Academy of Music

in 1928, he taught there through most of his career until he retired in
1974. His students immediately after the war included Etō Toshiya.
Among his later students was Temma Atsuko, who studied with him as
a teenager. She recalls that he was a "man of Meiji," "really frightening,
forceful like a *bushi* [samurai]." He wore a kimono and demanded
absolute authority. He and Uzuka were rivals, like the heads of different
schools in the traditional arts under the *iemoto* system, and when Uzuka
gave her lessons during her high school years she had to keep it secret
from Inoue. In Temma's time Inoue had several students who came from
Kagoshima and other parts of Kyushu by night train. When they arrived
he would make them have a bath and drink a glass of cold water before
their lesson.[83]

At Tōhō Gakuen College another important teacher from the pre-war
generation was Sō Tomoyasu (1904–). He graduated from the Kunitachi
Music Academy in 1929. For a time, he was a member of the New
Symphony Orchestra and received lessons from Schifferblatt. He also
led a string quartet. Beside his son Tomotada (1943–), his students
included Fujikawa Mayumi (1946–), Harada Kōichirō, who later became
a member of the Tokyo Quartet, and Isono Junko (1954–).

Although Japan now had excellent native teachers, foreign teachers
continued to play an important role. Violinists who had come to Japan in
the 1920s and 1930s continued to teach there after the war. Ono Anna
remained in Japan until 1960. Her students after the war included the
violist Imai Nobuko (1943–), Maehashi Teiko, Ushioda Masuko and
Urakawa Takaya. Alexander Mogilevsky stayed until his death in 1953,
holding professorships at Geidai and Kunitachi College of Music. His
post-war students included Kishibe Momoo, Toyama Shigeru and Hattori
Toyoko. Geidai continued to hire foreign teachers, generally on a short-
term basis, and the NHK Orchestra hired foreign conductors and
concertmasters. Other music schools invited foreign teachers to give
master classes; at Tōhō foreign teachers included Broadus Erle and
Jeanne Isnard.

As Japan became more and more prosperous and more families had
their children learn music, the demand for good teachers grew. In 1962
Masui Keiji of NHK had what proved to be a brilliant idea. The families
pursuing their cultural aspirations by making their children go to music
lessons were also buying television sets. By 1962 televisions numbered

10,222,116 nationwide. So why not use the new medium to bring the best teachers right into people's homes? Thus, the "*okeiko*" educational programmes were born; in April the first "*Piano no okeiko*" (Piano Lesson) went on air, followed three months later by the first "*Baiorin no okeiko*" (Violin Lesson).[84] *Okeiko* is the word typically used for lessons in the traditional arts; it can describe a wide range of pursuits taken up both for pleasure and because the training is regarded as beneficial in itself. The programmes proved hugely popular and ran for over 20 years until 1983. The first violin teachers on the programme in 1962 were Sumi Saburō and Etō Toshiya, and their fame as teachers was no doubt further enhanced by their participation. Sumi taught again in 1964 and 1968; that year a picture of him instructing a small boy appeared on the front of NHK's magazine with the caption, "How about you?"[85] Etō returned to the programme in 1965, 1967, 1969, 1971, 1977, 1978 and 1983. He was in charge of the programme from 1967 to 1978, and perhaps no other name came to be so closely associated with it. But the list of others who taught for one or more seasons is also impressive: Uzuka Tatsuo (1963, 1965), Iwabuchi Ryūtarō (1963, 1966), Kubota Ryōsaku (1964, 1966, 1968, 1970), Toyama Shigeru (1967, 1970, 1972, 1976), Nakajima Tazuko (1969), Shinozaki Isako (1971, 1980), Ishii Shizuko (1972, 1974, 1979), Tanaka Chikashi (1973, 1981), Tokunaga Tsugio (1973), Iso Tsuneo (1975), Sō Tomotada (1977), Muroya Takahiro (1978), Yamaoka Kōsaku (1979, 1982) and Hori Masafumi (1980).[86]

In the early years, lessons were broadcast on two days a week, later on one day, and in the 1980s every second week. Elementary lessons included "Twinkle, Twinkle, Little Star" and tunes that had been staples of violin tutors from the nineteenth century, such as "Long, Long Ago" and "Home, Sweet Home." As for all its educational programmes, NHK published accompanying textbooks, explaining the main technical points and including the practice pieces, mainly songs and other short pieces from the standard elementary repertoire. The textbook for April to September 1982 included the music for two elementary-level courses. Level one taught the basics, using folk songs as material, while level two introduced a Kayser Étude (Op. 20.), Fiocco's Allegro, part of Vivaldi's Concerto in A minor, and the second movement from Händel's Sonata No. 4 in D major. The courses continued until March 1983, and the textbook for October to March continues songs for level one and short

グラフ NHK
7 / 15
あなたもいかが —番組利用さまざま—

15: Sumi Saburō on the cover of NHK Graph, advertising the TV series
"Violin Lesson."

pieces for level two, ending with Bach-Gounod, *Ave Maria* and Henry
Farmer's Variations on "The Bluebells of Scotland."[87]

For the first programmes Sumi taught his regular pupils. Later NHK
held auditions twice a year. Many parents and teachers embraced the
opportunity for their children to have lessons from Japan's most famous

teachers, and for those children who succeeded, an appearance on the programme could change their lives. One such child was Temma Atsuko, who auditioned successfully in 1967. "I was the biggest, the oldest, but also the least advanced, and thought I would fail," she recalls. Much later she heard from the producers, that she indeed played badly, but that they had liked the way she answered their questions at the interview; they wanted children who were able to answer with a clear "yes" when told what to do by the teacher. Indeed, years later, Temma encountered people who told her they remembered the big girl who gave such clear responses. After the programme, Etō Toshiya told her mother: "Well, she plays poorly, but I have never seen a child look so happy when she plays."[88] He would have continued to teach Atsuko himself, but her parents could not afford his fees. Nevertheless, appearing on the programme marked a decisive step on her way to a professional career. She was later accepted by the high school affiliated with Geidai and had the chance to study with some of the best teachers Japan had to offer.[89] Violinists who did become Etō's pupils after appearing on the programme included Shimizu Takashi, Yabe Tatsuya, Komuro Mariko, Kai Fumiko and the violist Hasegawa Yayoi.[90] Other violinists who appeared on the programme are Tokunaga Tsugio, who himself became a teacher on the programme, Fujiwara Hamao and Satō Yōko.[91]

Presumably many more learnt to play and love the violin, even if their careers were less spectacular or they only ever played as amateurs. Indeed, many may well have watched the programme without having the slightest intention of playing the violin at all. The composer Yasuraoka Akio (1958–) observed that his composer colleagues watched the programme to learn more about the violin.[92] Others appreciated the slow motion video used to demonstrate violin technique.[93] Kurita Yoshio, one of the people responsible for the programme in the 1970s, recalled talking to a taxi driver who professed to be a great fan of the programme: "I'm not interested in classical music, but Etō Toshiya's way of teaching the children and talking to them is fascinating, and I learn from it."[94]

By the time the programme was discontinued in 1983 there were plenty of other opportunities to study the violin at any level of ability and ambition: classes run by music chain stores, private studios set up by individuals, Talent Education Institutes where Suzuki's disciples taught, and private and public music colleges. As with the general education system there was a hierarchy, and at its apex stood the national Geidai and its foremost private rival Tōhō Gakuen School of Music, both with affiliated high schools. Most of the violinists who gained national and international fame passed through one of these institutions, although, unlike in general education, a *gakureki*, that is, a CV with credentials from the right schools, is not all-important in music, as long as one has studied with the right teachers – and, in most cases, won a competition.

The Japan Music Competition, like the oldest colleges and the eminent teachers, linked pre-war achievements with post-war triumphs, having endured through the war years almost without disruption. In 1949 NHK joined the *Mainichi* newspaper for the organization of the eighteenth competition; both the preliminary and the main rounds were broadcast on the radio. Broadcasting on colour television (from 1967) further raised their profile. Winners from the early years who went on to successful, even international, careers include Kobayashi Takeshi (first prize 1949), Suzuki Hidetarō (second prize 1949, first prize 1951), Urakawa Takaya (third 1953), Kuronuma Yuriko (second 1954, first 1956), Ushioda Masuko (first 1957) and Sō Tomotada (second 1958, first 1959). The competitions reflected the improvement in music education, particularly through Tōhō, whose students virtually monopolized the prizes from around 1952. Winners became ever younger, and eventually the minimum age was set at 15. In the violin division, Sumi's pupils won most of the prizes for many years, over 100 of them, of whom 30 went on to win international prizes. From the twenty-fifth competition in 1956, winners could compete for sponsorship to take part in an international competition. The first violinist to benefit was Ishii Shizuko, a pupil of Sumi's, who in 1959, when she was only 15, went on to win a third prize at the Long–Thibaud competition. Others included Sō Tomotada, Wanami Takayoshi, Maehashi Teiko and Fujiwara Hamao in the 1960s and Horigome Yuzuko and Takezawa Kyōko in the 1980s (see Chapter 9). From 1986, sponsorship candidates were selected at the same time as the competition prizes were awarded. Various other supplementary prizes were introduced over the years, including in 1985 a Sumi Prize.

The Japan Music Competition did not remain the only competition for long. In 1946 a separate competition for younger schoolchildren was held, and in 1947 the Mainichi Shinbun Company and the San Shashin Shinbun Company organized the All Japan Student Music Competition

(Zen Nihon Gakusei Ongaku Konkūru) with the following divisions: violin, singing (solo and choral), piano and flute.[95] Prizes in the violin category were given for the first time at the second competition in 1948 and the winner in the primary school division was Suzuki Hidetarō, then in his sixth grade. He and other winners often went on to win the Japan Music Competition.

No doubt the competitions helped raise the level of performing, and preparing for and winning them helped many a young violinist on the way to a professional career both at home and abroad. As music education expanded and the number of young people seeking a career in music increased, however, the competitions' high profile and the perception of them as the only, or at least the surest, route to success led ambitious teachers and parents to over-emphasize competition success to the point that critics diagnosed "competition disease."[96] Symptoms included the kind of unremitting drilling that also characterized academic study in preparation for the "examination hell." Lesson prices soared as parents competed to send their children to the most famous teachers and secure their entry into the prestigious conservatoires, especially Geidai and Tōhō Gakuen College. Western observers were sometimes quick to explain Japanese triumphs, whether musical or otherwise, by pointing to a repressive education system characterized by mechanical drilling. But criticism of such excesses is not merely an expression of Western stereotypes. Japanese observers could be equally scathing. In 1964 the reports of the Tōhō Orchestra's American tour sparked off a discussion about early training in the leading music magazine *Ongaku geijutsu*, in which participants sharply criticized what they perceived as excessive discipline and pressure and the exaggerated ambitions of teachers and parents. The music critic Nomura Kōichi even compared the "Tōhō System" to the Nazi military. He saw it as part of the "catch-up" syndrome that Japan was still suffering from.[97] In 1969 the conductor Iwaki Hiroyuki took the discussions about music education out of the specialist journals into *Chūō kōron,* a magazine with a much broader readership. Most of his criticism was directed at conservatoire-level education, but he also touched upon wider issues, such as the over-privileging of Western classical music, the commercialization of music education, the excessive authority (and fees) of "big boss" type music teachers and over-ambitious, overbearing education mums or "*mamagon*" ("the dreaded mama-saurus"),[98] who together robbed young people of the ability to discover the joys and confront the challenges of music-making independently: "If you walk the streets you always see several young children and middle [junior high] school students carrying a violin case and not looking too happy. Come to think of it, I have never seen excessively accommodating programmes like 'Violin Lesson' and 'Piano Lesson' in other countries. It is a shock for foreign musicians who visit Japan, apparently. Many even believe that in the near future Japan is sure to grab the leadership in music worldwide."[99] The expansion of music education, Iwaki pointed out, did not in itself necessarily result in higher standards among professional musicians.[100]

Nevertheless, less than 20 years after the war, Japan's musical achievements were impressive. They owed much to the high musical standards Japan had reached even before 1945, particularly to outstanding teachers, as well as to the prevailing determination to rebuild Japan as a "culture nation." This ambition motivated the rising middle classes to devote some of their increasing wealth to cultural pursuits. The large numbers of children studying the violin may well have included many who were bored and ready to give up at the first opportunity, but they also represented a pool of well-trained violinists from which came the outstanding players whose fame reached beyond Japan.

Despite the incredible expansion and improvement of music education in post-war Japan, however, many Japanese felt and feel that in the end they could not truly make classical music their own if they remained at home. When foreign travel became possible, Japanese again studied abroad. The first went to America rather than Europe, reflecting the changed power constellations. But while study in the land of limitless opportunities could bring fulfillment, there were no guarantees.

## 8. Triumph and Tragedy Abroad: Etō Toshiya and Watanabe Shigeo

When Etō Toshiya died in January 2008, the newspapers described him as the most representative violinist of post-war Japan, active on the international stage and pioneering a soloist career at home. The first to study music abroad after the war, Etō worked with Efrem Zimbalist at Curtis, and embarked on a career in America, teaching at Curtis and performing all over the country before returning to Japan in 1961. Etō

Toshiya's career is one of Japan's post-war success stories, mirroring the rise of his country from complete defeat to economic power and international standing. In contrast, Watanabe Shigeo (1941–99), his junior by less than half a generation and billed as "a second Etō Toshiya" at his debut in December 1948, became Japan's version of Josef Hassid,[101] a tragic reminder of how badly a violinist's career can go wrong and a reflection of the fact that Japan's triumphs came at a cost. Although Watanabe survived into his fifties, as a musician and a person he effectively died as a teenager, in 1958.

Etō Toshiya, born in 1927, was one of the child violinists who won the Japan Music Competition and performed publicly before the war, demonstrating the high standard of music education Japan had already achieved. Having entered the Tokyo Academy of Music in the last year of the war he graduated in March 1948. He immediately became a teacher at the Academy and had plenty of opportunities to perform. But his dream was to study in America with Efrem Zimbalist, whose playing he knew so well from his father's collection of recordings.[102] Even before graduating he had begun to study English with Clinton Albert Feissner (1910–2010), a communications official with the Allied Occupation authority. Feissner, who had heard Etō play for Allied troops, did more than give him language lessons. He got in touch with Zimbalist and made all the necessary arrangements for the young violinist, even securing him a scholarship which later turned out to have come from his own pocket. Before leaving in October 1948, Etō described his expectations in an interview with the music critic Murai Takeo (1908–96). He named the obvious benefits: "the musical environment, which naturally I cannot have in Japan, also various technical problems I am uncertain about," and the chance to listen to world-class performers. Remarkably, he also said, "but more than that, I think I might benefit most from listening to music students perform and becoming familiar with their way of thinking. Heifetz, Menuhin and others are too distant from me to relate to, but through the performance of the various students over there now, whom I will join, I will be able to understand just how we are different from the first-class players and how far we are separated from them."[103] For a young man whose formal education had been quite limited, as his interviewer critically pointed out, Etō showed not only an impressively analytical approach to his studies, but – even more importantly – an appreciation of what he could learn by engaging with his peers. All too often Japanese students abroad isolate themselves in their lodgings with their books or their instruments, determined to learn as much as possible, but intimidated by the cultural differences and their difficulties with the spoken language. They underestimate the lessons to be learnt from association with their peers. Learn they may, but they miss out on as much as they learn.

Not so Etō. A high-profile young performer even before he left Japan, he wrote about his impressions for magazines.[104] In March 1949 he wrote a piece entitled "Friends," suggesting that he had good relations with several fellow students.[105] His writings are full of his appreciation of the opportunities Curtis offered: not just the chance to study with Zimbalist, the teacher of his choice and with William Primrose, who taught ensemble classes, but to make new friends among his fellow students and to experience the cultural life of Philadelphia and the natural beauties of the surrounding countryside. He had the chance to hear the most famous artists of the time, including the violinists Mischa Elman, Nathan Milstein, Zino Francescatti, Isaac Stern, and of course Jascha Heifetz, whom he had heard on gramophone records for 20 years. He was happy to be a student, free from the responsibilities of performing and with leisure to think and communicate with nature; Beethoven too, he reflected, had spent some of his happiest hours in the countryside.[106]

In March 1949 he received his first formal school report with top marks in all the subjects. His friends, he wrote, expected him to help them in some of the general music classes. Not long afterwards, on 26 April 1949, he gave his first performance at a student chamber recital, playing first violin in a Vivaldi concerto for four violins. "Everybody was truly happy for me," he wrote, "Here there is no unseemly envy, nor jealousy, and there is no racial prejudice or any special ethnic consciousness. I think this is why I have felt happy, full of pleasure and cheerful since coming to America."[107] In his second year, on 6 December 1949, Etō impressed his audience with a performance of Tchaikovsky's Violin Concerto to piano accompaniment, and in January 1950 he played first violin in Beethoven's String Quartet Op. 131, together with Michael Applebaum (later to become Michael Tree and the violist in the Guarneri Quartet), Richard Parnas and Leslie Parnas. Again the performance was a success. That summer he and Applebaum were invited to Zimbalist's summer residence in Maine.

On 9 November 1951 he made his debut at Carnegie Hall, sponsored by Zimbalist himself.[108] He was the first Japanese to perform there after the Second World War. Vladimir Solokoff partnered Etō at the piano, and Applebaum turned the pages for the pianist. Etō played Händel, Brahms, Glazunov, Chausson and Sarasate on a Lupot violin loaned to him by Curtis. His fellow students from Curtis came to New York on a chartered bus for the occasion. Zimbalist and his wife wrote to Etō's parents afterwards, describing the debut as "sensational."[109] The reviewer for the *New York Times* summed up, "Mr. Eto is rarely equipped for his task. The fact that he has a prodigious technique is accessory to the beauty and vitality of his tone, which is exceptionally warm, rich and vibrant, and his taste and musicianship." After giving a nuanced assessment of Etō's interpretation of Händel, Brahms and Glazunov (apparently the reviewer left without hearing the rest of the programme), he concluded, "What he needs now is experience, freedom from constraint, even when it is a constraint wisely dictated by his teachers; opportunity to profit by much playing on many platforms – in short, the maturing that only hard work and experience bring, and the consequent development of a greater measure of conviction and individuality than he can presently bring to his performances."[110]

A few months later, Etō signed a contract with Sol Hurok Attractions. His second recital at Carnegie Hall, in October 1952, was another success, and having graduated from Curtis in May, Etō now embarked on a career as a soloist, travelling all over America and to Europe to play recitals and concertos. In 1953 he began teaching at Curtis, and in September 1954 he was appointed professor. Today it is commonplace for Japanese musicians studying abroad to continue their careers outside Japan, and many hold teaching posts at American and European conservatoires, but less than ten years after the war, when Japanese were only beginning to go abroad for study, this was a remarkable achievement.

In November 1954, after having toured the Netherlands, Hawaii and Italy earlier in the year, Etō Toshiya returned to Japan for the first time. The advertisement for his first recital in Hibiya Public Hall on 19 November read, "The Greatest Hope of Japan's Music World – Back After 6 Years"; the programme was the same as at his Carnegie debut in 1951.[111] He gave recitals in Niigata, Osaka, Nagoya, Takarazuka, Fukuoka, Kumamoto and Sendai, as well as two more in Hibiya Hall.

His pianist was his sister Reiko.[112] Reiko followed him to Curtis a couple of years later, where she graduated from the piano accompaniment class in 1959. In a published discussion with Etō, Iwabuchi Ryūtarō told Etō how he had been impressed by his tone from the first note in the Händel that opened Etō's first recital. Iwabuchi, who had come second to Etō in the Japan Music Competition in 1939, was now the concertmaster of the NHK Symphony Orchestra. He had not studied abroad, unlike the other discussant, Watanabe Akeo, who had studied at Juilliard from 1950 to 1952. Watanabe had already heard Etō's Carnegie debut and recalled that Etō's tone and nuanced dynamics had impressed him most; having played chamber music with Etō before he left for Curtis, he was in a good position to assess his progress. After discussing various differences between Western music in Japan and America, the conversation turned to the question of whether or not there is a specifically Japanese way of performing Western music. A violinist named Fukui Naohiro (1912–81) had written in the *Asahi* newspaper that Etō should now work on expressing himself "as a Japanese." Iwabuchi thought that somehow Etō's performance would naturally display Japanese characteristics. Etō himself, however, categorically denied any such notion. In America and Italy people accepted that he was first and foremost himself once they got to know him: "I am a musician first and only then a Japanese," he insisted.[113]

Still, the discussion shows once again the dilemma Japanese so often found themselves in ever since the country's forced opening one hundred years earlier. They wanted to rival the West on its own terms, but they feared that by doing so they would somehow lose their Japanese identity. Etō, apparently, felt no conflict. His strong identification with the violin as an instrument that belonged to the whole world, including Japan, together with his Catholic education and faith, gave him the strength that made his time abroad hugely successful.[114] When he finally returned to his homeland in 1961 at the age of 33, he went on to a triumphant and trailblazing career as a performer and teacher of iconic status.

Watanabe Shigeo's stay in America, in contrast, started as a disappointment and ended in tragedy. While his talent was at least equal to Etō's, his early life was different from Etō's in ways that, with hindsight, boded ill. Like Etō's, Watanabe's talent blossomed early. But while Etō grew up in a stable family, Watanabe Shigeo's family broke up when he was five and he was brought up by his mother's sister Watanabe Mie and her husband Suehiko (1908–2012). While Etō's parents, both teachers, tempered their musical ambitions for their children with their efforts to give them a well-rounded education, Watanabe Shigeo's uncle was driven by the urge to give his nephew what he felt he himself had missed by starting the violin too late, and made him practise long hours at the cost of his school work. And while Etō went to America at the age of 20 as a mature young adult and a graduate of the Tokyo Academy of Music, Watanabe Shigeo was sent there as a teenager who had neither finished his general education nor learnt the social skills that might have helped him relate to the people around him in a new and unfamiliar environment.

Born on 26 June 1941 in Tokyo, Watanabe Shigeo spent his first years surrounded by the sound of the violin as his mother and uncle played together. But then the air raids worsened and the family moved to Shigeo's father's home town in Hokkaido. Already little Shigeo had expressed his desire to learn the violin, imitating playing movements with a round fan. When his parents' marriage deteriorated, his mother moved back to Tokyo with Shigeo and his little sister in 1946. She wanted her brother-in-law to teach Shigeo the violin. Meanwhile, she secured custody of her children by entering their names in her own family's civil register and found work as a violinist accompanying singers in Asakusa and playing in a band to entertain American soldiers.

Shigeo received his first lessons from his uncle Suehiko, but he did not immediately show promise. In fact he progressed so slowly that Suehiko, who had expected him to show as much talent as his mother, often lost his temper and shouted at him to forget about playing the violin, since he was hopeless. But Shigeo just stood motionless, clutching his violin in playing position, tears running down his cheeks. A determined man himself, Suehiko met his match in the stubborn five-year-old. Torn between exasperation and sympathy for the little boy who seemed to love the violin so much, he continued to teach him. And suddenly the breakthrough came. Many years later, Suehiko would explain: "There are two kinds of genius: Heifetz's kind of genius for playing immediately with perfect ease; and the kind that develops slowly with effort and hard work. Shigeo's belonged to the second kind. But then Heifetz can play all too effortlessly, so whatever he plays sounds somehow light. His

Mozart is fine, but when it comes to Beethoven and Brahms, it is ingenious, but lacking in depth. It's with people who have worked hard that one somehow feels greater depth."[115]

Suehiko's ambition burned once more. Unable to become a first-class violinist himself, he transferred all his hopes and ambitions to Shigeo. For seven or eight hours each day he would drill technique into Shigeo and make him study the most advanced repertoire, sometimes not pausing for two hours at a stretch. As Sukehiko saw it, Japanese were at a disadvantage compared to Western musicians, who had the music in their blood. Shigeo may have begun to learn fast, but for his impatient uncle progress could never be fast enough, and often he would shout, reducing Shigeo to tears that stained the varnish of his violin.

In April 1948, the year Etō Toshiya left for Curtis, Shigeo started school and could no longer practise all day, Soon, however, he was missing classes regularly. On 10 December he gave his first public recital, playing Paganini in the Yomiuri Hall, a draughty, makeshift building, filled to capacity, thanks to the *Yomiuri* newspaper's advertising. He gave his next recital in May 1949. That same month, the newspapers reported that Etō Toshiya had completed his first year at Curtis with flying colours. In the bleak years immediately after the war and in a Japan still under American occupation this was cheering news indeed.

More recitals followed. For his third one in January 1950, Shigeo was partnered by Tanaka Sonoko, an outstanding pianist who, besides accompanying other excellent violinists, also performed as a soloist. She became something like an elder sister to the friendless Shigeo, whom she later described as an ordinary, fun-loving boy when he was not playing the violin. Meanwhile, Suehiko gave up most of his other pupils to devote more time to Shigeo. He had already stopped playing for the Tōhō Symphony Orchestra in 1948 to concentrate on teaching and recommended Shigeo's mother as his replacement. Soon, however, she married an American soldier she had met while playing for the troops and the couple moved to Kure in Hiroshima Prefecture. "Are you coming with us?" she asked her son. Shigeo gave no answer and stayed behind in Tokyo. His childless aunt and uncle had for all intents and purposes become his parents. In 1953 Shigeo was formally adopted and his name entered into the Watanabe family register.

In addition to his violin lessons Shigeo began to study composition with

16: Watanabe Shigeo composing.

Ishiketa Mareo (1916–96) and then with Klaus Pringsheim, who pronounced himself deeply impressed by his talent. Shigeo's next recitals included his own works: the first movement of his Violin Concerto in G minor at his sixth recital in May 1953, and his Violin Sonata No. 1 in A minor in January 1954, at his seventh recital.[116] Shigeo also received violin lessons from Wolfgang Stavonhagen, who, having been introduced to Shigeo, was so impressed that he volunteered to teach him. Besides broadening and updating his repertoire with Bartók, Khachaturian, Glazunov and Dvořák, Stavonhagen gave Shigeo the chance to perform with the Konoe Orchestra of which he was the concertmaster. In June 1953 the 11-year-old played the Beethoven Violin Concerto in his first concert as a soloist with an orchestra. Only two weeks later he stood on the stage with the Konoe Orchestra again: Stavonhagen was scheduled to play the Beethoven Concerto himself, but had injured his hand, so he conducted while Shigeo played it for him. Ten days later Shigeo performed it again in Nagoya with an orchestra of professionals and amateurs. The concertmaster was a medical student called Wakai Ichirō. He would never forget the moving performance of the young violinist, whom he would meet again four years later under quite different circumstances.

Shigeo played the Beethoven two more times that year and the Mendelssohn Violin Concerto twice. The following year, 1954, he performed with different orchestras at least 17 times, mainly the concertos by Beethoven and Mendelssohn, but also Tchaikovsky and Glazunov. He gave the Japanese premiere of Khachaturian's Violin Concerto on 25 July 1954 with Tsukahara Tetsuo and his orchestra. The Polish violinist Sigismund Lukianovich Minchinski, who had lived and worked in Japan since before the war, told Suehiko, "I heard Heifetz play the Tchaikovsky when he was young, but Shigeo is better."[117]

That year Heifetz himself visited Japan for the fourth time. Several acquaintances, among them the Californian couple Richard and Heartie Anne Look, urged the Watanabes to let Shigeo join the crowd of hopefuls seeking an audition with Heifetz. Knowing that Heifetz might be reluctant, they arranged for Shigeo to play in his presence as if by chance while Heifetz was relaxing at a party in their home. Sufficiently impressed, Heifetz agreed to a formal audition. So on 22 May, Shigeo, with his adoptive mother and an aunt, visited Heifetz in his suite in the Imperial Hotel. "Play a C major scale," Heifetz told him. Surprised and bored, Shigeo groped around the fingerboard making two or three mistakes. Next, Heifetz told him to play Tchaikovsky. Shigeo, disconcerted and nervous in the presence of the great man, did not shine. Then Heifetz asked him to play a piece of his choice. Shigeo played Kreisler's "Tambourin Chinois." This time he did better. Animated, Heifetz began to improvise the accompaniment on the piano. But when the audition finished he did not say a word. When Shigeo asked him to sign the programme of his concert he wrote, "To Shigeo Watanabe, with best wishes, Heifetz, May 1954," still without a word. Timidly, Mrs. Watanabe told him of their plans to send Shigeo abroad. He nodded silently, made a note of Watanabe Shigeo's name on his own calling card and said laconically, "he needs to study technique more thoroughly." Disappointed, Shigeo and his aunts left the hotel. They did not know how to answer Suehiko, who eagerly asked for news.

The next day, however, the Looks received a telephone call from Heifetz. "That boy Shigeo is a wonderful violinist," he told them, "I have auditioned several people this time, but he is the only one I would take with me to America." Three weeks later he sent a telegram from California, saying he had arranged for Shigeo to study at Juilliard. A similar telegram reached the *Asahi* newspaper, which promptly published it.[118] Heifetz had told the Looks that Shigeo needed to improve his technique and the sooner he could study at Juilliard with Ivan Galamian, the better. The Looks were thrilled. But the Watanabe family and their friends did not share their enthusiasm. Could it really be right to send such a young boy to New York on his own? Suehiko, moreover, had his own misgivings. He had learnt to revere the European tradition and dreamt of sending his adopted son to Germany or Austria. America had until recently been Japan's enemy. He could not share the post-war infatuation with the power that so recently had occupied Japan; he had no time for the land of jazz and country and western and other light music. "But what with Heifetz's recommendation and the newspaper stories swaying the tide of opinion, it was a foregone conclusion," he later said.[119]

Meanwhile Shigeo continued to perform and make recordings. He played with the Tokyo Philharmonic Orchestra, the Tokyo Symphony Orchestra, the Konoe Orchestra and the NHK Orchestra. He listened to other performers, live or at record concerts, with a critical ear. "It was a performance without depth," he wrote in his diary on 17 September after listening to a recording of Yehudi Menuhin playing Bartók's Violin Concerto. He gave the Japanese premiere of the work with the Tokyo Symphony Orchestra under Manfred Gurlitt on 29 September 1954. Gurlitt and the orchestra struggled. "The orchestra lagged behind and I was worn out trying to fit in with it," recorded Shigeo, who had studied the score at the piano.[120]

The following month Shigeo played the Tchaikovsky Concerto again, this time with the Tokyo Philharmonic Orchestra under the British conductor Malcolm Sargent. Sargent, at the height of his fame, did not want a teenage soloist, but he was told that no other violinist could play it so well, and after the first rehearsal he had to agree. The concert was a huge success and when Sargent left Japan after having repeated the concert in Nagoya, Takarazuka and Tokyo, he sent Shigeo a signed photograph thanking him for an excellent performance. Ironically, one Japanese critic carped about the soloist in his review.

In November 1954 Etō Toshiya visited Japan for the first time since his departure in 1948. Etō had already heard rumours of the new wunderkind when Shigeo and his parents visited his family home on 22 November.

17: Watanabe Shigeo performing with the Tokyo Philharmonic Orchestra under Sir Malcolm Sargent, October 1954.

Naturally, the Watanabes hoped to hear about life in America and to have Shigeo's level assessed by a compatriot who knew America first-hand. Etō listened to Shigeo play a movement from the Tchaikovsky Concerto and gave him a short trial lesson before pronouncing his verdict: "He could go to Curtis right now." Years later he recalled: "His technique seemed better than mine. However I believe my ability to think about the music was superior."[121] Etō himself had read Tolstoy and looked at Russian paintings in an effort to understand the culture Tchaikovsky was part of. The atmosphere at Curtis encouraged reflection, and Zimbalist's approach to teaching gave his students the freedom to develop their own style. Curtis and Philadelphia, thought Etō, would offer Shigeo a more suitable environment than New York and Juilliard. But Heifetz, the god of the violin world, had spoken and who would gainsay him?

On February 1955, Watanabe Shigeo premiered a third concerto. This time it was a world premiere. In 1934 Manfred Gurlitt had written a violin concerto for Georg Kulenkampff, who never performed it. Ironically, in 1934, Kulenkampff premiered Kishi Kōichi's concerto. Although Shigeo had a bad cold and a fever on the day of the concert, he performed it to the composer's satisfaction. It was to be their last performance together.[122] The concerto demands both considerable agility and the ability to sing out in the extensive cantabile passages, and Watanabe Shigeo proved himself magnificently capable of both.

Not long afterwards, David Oistrakh came to Japan. Once again well-meaning acquaintances arranged an audition. This time it took place in Hibiya Hall, where Oistrakh was rehearsing Bach, Brahms and Khatchaturian, and the audience included several foreign journalists. Oistrakh was visibly impressed, although he too remarked critically on Shigeo's technique: "Your left hand technique is wonderful, but I don't like the way you use your right arm." He demonstrated his own bowing style to Shigeo and gave him his autograph.[123]

Even so, Watanabe Suehiko remained sceptical. Shigeo had been praised by two world-famous violinists. But did that really mean that Shigeo had reached the standard of Western players, or did the foreigners' praise imply that Shigeo did very well "for a Japanese"? Suehiko had no way of telling, never having had the chance to go abroad himself. Even so, he had to admit that Heifetz had done more than utter friendly words. In March 1955, Suehiko was notified that Juilliard would admit Shigeo into their preparatory course on the strong recommendation of Heifetz, who had also arranged for Shigeo to participate in the Music Academy of the West in Santa Barbara over the summer. Over the following months Shigeo became busier than ever. The news of his coming studies abroad led to even more invitations to perform and he was given intensive tuition in English. Meanwhile, his American supporters did everything to ensure his well-being in New York. They arranged for the Japan Society to act as his guardian and ensured that Shigeo had the necessary financial backup.

The only question no one but Shigeo's close family asked themselves was whether Shigeo, still only 14 and immature for his age in everything except his music, should really be sent on his own to live and study in a faraway country whose culture was alien to him and whose language he did not speak. Becoming a great violinist is not just about playing the violin well. Apart from a well-rounded education in order to deepen understanding of the music, the career of a soloist demands a high level of emotional strength. Some people, born survivors, seem to have endless emotional resources and can break free from childhood traumas. Most people, however, need the support of a stable home and dependable relationships. Shigeo's early experience of family break-up and his one-sided, excessively sheltered and controlled upbringing, dominated by a driven man, did not represent the best conditions for his emotional growth. Even if he had remained in Japan for a few years more, his teenage years might have turned out stormy. By 1955 more music students had followed Etō abroad, but like him they went after completing their general education and basic musical training in Japan. The small group already studying at Juilliard included the violinist Kobayashi Kenji, a pupil of Suzuki's, who had come to America in 1952. But America was still a long way off at a time when travel was restricted and international telephone calls an extravagance reserved for emergencies. The Watanabes in effect had to place Shigeo's fate entirely in the hands of his American sponsors.

How did Shigeo himself feel about going to America? His uncle claimed to remember Shigeo repeatedly telling him, "Japan lost the war, but I will become the best violinist in the word. I will beat America in culture." But this may well reflect more on Suehiko's sentiments than on Shigeo's. Shigeo himself told a newspaper, "First I would like to study technique, then to deepen my musical understanding. At Juilliard, there are already Kobayashi Kenji and the pianist Hirata Michi, so I'll be alright. I'm also looking forward to listening to many splendid concerts."[124] He would not be missing his friends, for he had none. Perhaps he looked forward to a freer life than he had experienced so far. If so, he would be bitterly disappointed.

On 22 June 1955 Watanabe Shigeo gave his last performance in Japan, playing the Tchaikovsky Violin Concerto with the NHK Orchestra under Niklaus Aeschbacher (regular conductor of the NHK Orchestra from August 1954 to March 1956). It was to be Shigeo's last ever performance in Japan, and by the time it was broadcast, on 6 July, he had already boarded a plane at Haneda airport the day before. He would return, but it would not be the triumphant return his extraordinary talent seemed to promise.

At the Music Academy of the West in Santa Barbara, Shigeo was by far the youngest student. Even so, his teacher the New Yorker Sascha Jacobsen (1897–), professor at the Los Angeles Conservatory and concertmaster of the Los Angeles Philharmonic, did not feel he could teach him much. In fact Shigeo caused a sensation, was voted the best student of the year and selected to play in the final concert. The critics were ecstatic, but already there were signs that all was not well. His compatriot the soprano singer Yano Shige recalls that he seemed unhappy and told her that he hated the violin. Her teacher Lotte Lehmann, watching Shigeo's impassive face as he played, whispered to Yano, "I wonder whether he really likes music."[125]

In New York, where Shigeo arrived on 12 September, he was met by Beate Sirota Gordon, who had become the Japan Society's director of student activities the previous year. After working for the American Occupation forces, the daughter of the pianist Leo Sirota had married Lt. Joseph Gordon and moved to New York. Having grown up in Japan and with musicians, Gordon was ideally suited to looking after music students from Japan, and she became Shigeo's main source of support. On the other hand, the Japan Society's decision to place Shigeo with a Japanese couple proved unfortunate. It might have offered a measure of familiarity, but it did nothing for his integration into a new culture. The couple had no interest in music and Shigeo's long hours of practice did not endear him to them. Shigeo reacted to their protest by developing violent anti-Japanese sentiments, even denying his Japanese identity. Although not an uncommon reaction among Japanese abroad, it further complicated relations, and in December Shigeo went to live with Ivan Galamian and his wife.

His relationship with his new teacher, however, was hardly less fraught. Galamian, the teacher of many outstanding violinists, reputedly could "make a violinist out of a table."[126] He gave exact prescriptions and expected his students to follow them to the letter. But Shigeo was no table; he was a fully fledged violinist and a veteran of the concert podium, whose talent had astonished the likes of Heifetz and Oistrakh. Technical weaknesses there may well have been; but were the scales and études he was given really what he needed most?[127] Etō's assessment, that he should have a teacher who would inspire him to learn and think about the music and the culture that gave birth to it, seems much more astute. Etō had no reason to shower exaggerated praise on a violinist who was being touted as a potential rival. Perhaps Shigeo would have benefited from such an approach, had he been taught by Galamian's still unknown colleague, who 20 years later would teach numerous violinists from Japan, including the child prodigy Midori: Dorothy DeLay. As it was, Shigeo received more of what was already all too familiar from his lessons back in Japan: endless technical drilling. Nevertheless he practised and practised – out of sheer loneliness and boredom, apparently. His emotional instability caused conflict with Galamian, who responded by enforcing yet more strict discipline. Shigeo, like a typical teenager, rebelled.

By the autumn of 1956 the situation became impossible, and finally Beate Gordon took him in. To her he seemed starved for love and she did what she could for him, although she had a small daughter to look after, as well as her job at the Japan Society. Galamian himself wrote to the Watanabes telling them that it was both alright and desirable for Shigeo to stay at least another year. In his letter, Galamian mentioned two recordings Shigeo had made for broadcasting in Japan. They duly went on air on New Year's Day 1957. Watanabe Suehiko recalled his deep disappointment years later: Shigeo, he thought, had learnt nothing and his playing expressed his unhappiness.[128] While Suehiko's recollections may well be influenced by subsequent events, he may have a point. Shigeo's rendition of Chopin's Nocturne tears at the heartstrings in its bittersweetness.[129]

The Watanabes, worried by what they did or did not hear from Shigeo, had written to the Japan Society a few months previously and demanded that he be sent home. Shigeo, however, refused, even threatening suicide, and the Japan Society and Galamian, no doubt reluctant to concede defeat, wanted him to continue with his studies. But though they wrote reassuring letters to Tokyo they were worried. Galamian had already consulted a psychologist friend, and now the Japan Society contacted Taketomo Yasuhiko, a young clinical researcher specializing in schizophrenia and working at Rockland Hospital in New York State. After meeting Shigeo, Taketomo suggested that he stay there as his "research assistant," so he could be kept under observation. Shigeo was to take a complete break from the violin. From March to early July 1957, Shigeo stayed at Rockland, performing simple tasks for Taketomo. In April, Taketomo wrote to Shigeo's parents, who had been informed of the situation by the Japan Society, and told them their son was "socially immature."[130]

The Watanabes were horrified. To this day in Japan views of how to handle psychological problems, not to mention any hint of mental illness, differ substantially from American attitudes, as Japanese reports about

Midori's troubles 30 years later demonstrated (see Chapter 11). The thought of Shigeo abandoning the violin even temporarily was devastating to Suehiko, who had invested so much in his adopted son. More alarmed than ever, they insisted that Shigeo return home immediately. The problem was that Shigeo still adamantly refused and Taketomo feared the worst if he were dispatched by force. Moreover, Shigeo seemed better. He even expressed a wish to attend the summer school in Santa Barbara again, where Heifetz heard him play and praised his progress.

Returning to New York and Juilliard in September 1957, Shigeo was moved into a hall of residence. Taketomo protested, but no family wanted to take in the difficult teenager. The Galamians asked the violist Natasha Gudskov, who had played quartets with Shigeo at the Meadowmount School of Music the previous summer, and the cellist Gerald Appleman, to keep an eye on him. Presumably they hoped that they would find it easier to make contact than fellow violinists and potential competitors. To draw him out of his isolation, Galamian even secured him a side job in the semi-professional National Orchestra Association Training Orchestra. Shigeo knew a couple of the members already; besides Kobayashi Kenji there was a young woman called Judy, whom he had met at Santa Barbara and who attended the same class as he did at Juilliard. In his loneliness, Shigeo developed a crush on her, but she never knew, not having received the letter Shigeo asked someone to pass on to her.

Suddenly Shigeo himself expressed a wish to return home. Twice, on 1 and 2 November, he turned up at the Japanese Society's office and asked to be sent back to Japan. Then, on 3 November, he did not leave his room all day. Appleman grew increasingly worried. Not long before, Shigeo had shown him some pills and talked of killing himself. He knocked on Shigeo's door a few times. When he knocked once more at midnight, he was told that Shigeo had been taken to nearby St. Luke's Hospital in a private car. The police had been notified at 11.45.

The Japanese Society tried to keep the affair quiet, but on 6 November Japanese newspapers reported Watanabe Shigeo's suicide attempt, supposedly brought on by unhappy love. The Watanabes had received a telegram the day before. Meanwhile, another telegram reached a young Japanese medical researcher in Albany, where he was studying anaesthesiology on a Fulbright grant: Wakai Ichirō, who, as a member of the orchestra in Nagoya in 1953 had performed the Beethoven Violin concerto with Shigeo. His mother, reading of the tragedy in the newspaper, remembered how deeply the boy's performance had moved her son and thought he would want to know the news. Wakai certainly did. He left for New York immediately, got in touch with the Japan Society and went to the hospital to see what he could do. There was very little he could do for Shigeo. The boy lay helpless and unaware of his surroundings, and his survival looked unlikely. Meanwhile the costs of his hospitalization were mounting and the Japanese Society was at its wits' end.

Finally, practical and financial arrangements were made to send Shigeo to Japan. Here at last Wakai could help. Shigeo would need expert medical care throughout the long flight if he was to survive it. On 12 January 1958, Wakai and his charge left New York, arriving in Tokyo on 16 January. No one could have foreseen such a return. Watanabe Suehiko announced to the gathering of relatives and acquaintances that his son had fallen victim to an American conspiracy. The conspiracy theory was reported in the media later that year, but apparently did not gain general currency and was soon forgotten, just like Watanabe Shigeo himself.[131] Of course the feelings that gave rise to it are easy to understand; instead of conquering America, as Suehiko and others had hoped, Shigeo had been destroyed. It did not help that, in the understandable fear of a scandal or even a diplomatic crisis, the case had been hushed up and no proper inquiry conducted, so that crucial questions remained unanswered. How, for instance, did Shigeo, who apparently could not even buy his own violin strings, manage to get hold of a large amount of prescription drugs?

Wakai never believed in a conspiracy, although 40 years later he was still struggling to comprehend what had happened to the incomparable musician he heard in Nagoya. All he knew was that Watanabe Shigeo was already an outstanding violinist when he arrived in America, who did not need the constraints of the Juilliard system or Galamian's authoritarian, rigid approach to teaching.[132] And there perhaps lies the key to the tragedy: Watanabe Shigeo was so much more than a prodigy who could play the violin well and could be taught a few more technical tricks. A sensitive and intelligent individual, he came to America hoping for greater freedom, but found himself as shackled as in Japan. He expected opportunities, but encountered tedium. He longed for love, but remained lonely. Acclaimed as a violinist, he craved attention as a human being, but failed to gain it.

Whatever the explanation of the tragedy, it did not help Shigeo. After several weeks in hospital he returned to the care of his family. Unable to talk or control his movements, he lived the rest of his life, over 40 years, as a shadow of his former self. Watanabe finally died on 13 August 1999. In 1996 his memory was revived (for a short time) by the publication of a biography and a television documentary. The documentary included footage of his former benefactress Heartie Anne Look being shown a video of the 88-year-old Suehiko, caring for the severely disabled Shigeo – hardly the last thing in good taste, and one wonders whether the showing was motivated by a lingering resentment over Watanabe's fate in America. A last photograph of Shigeo taken at around the same time, shows a pleasant-looking middle-aged man posing with a vacuous smile, a violin clutched in his right hand. The brilliant violinist Watanabe Shigeo had already died on 3 November 1958.[133]

Etō Toshiya's career, meanwhile, blazed from strength to strength. At his third Carnegie recital in October 1957 he opened with Beethoven's "Kreutzer" Sonata. Arnold Steinhardt (1937–), the future leader of the Guarneri Quartet, but at the time a not very confident student at Curtis, recalled years later:

"During that uncertain time, I went to New York to attend the Carnegie Hall debut recital of Toshiya Eto, the Japanese violinist, who had only recently graduated from Curtis. He dared to begin his program with Beethoven's notoriously difficult Kreutzer Sonata. Poised briefly in playing position as if in suspended animation next to his pianist, Billy Solokoff, Eto suddenly pounced on the first chord with great force and almost instantly melted into a sustained and delicate melody that drifted up to Carnegie's highest seats, where I sat. What control, what confidence, what artistry!"[134]

Etō did not visit his home country again until August 1959, and this time he did not return alone. He had married Angela Nudo, a student of Dorothy DeLay and Ivan Galamian at Juilliard before she came to Curtis. They he had met at the time of his second Carnegie recital. The couple had two sons: Curtis, born in 1956, and Michael, born in 1957. While

Etō gave over 20 recitals all over the country, besides playing
Tchaikovsky's Violin Concerto with the Japan Philharmonic Orchestra
under Watanabe Akeo, weekly magazines reported on the international
family. Etō was not only the first Japanese violinist to become an
international performer; international marriages too were still
exceptional. But while weeklies fastened on the romantic story of Etō
and his beautiful American wife, critics in the musical world wanted to
know why he continued to live and work in America. By then other
successful young musicians too were choosing to live abroad rather than
return to Japan – much to Japan's loss. In an interview Etō explained his
choice.[135] He saw himself first as a musician and did not want "Japanese"
to become his trademark. "Professor at Curtis" gave him a status no
position in Japan could offer. He also feared that he would soon be
forgotten abroad if he left America, because his manager would find it
harder to promote him, while restrictions on travel and currency
exchange would make it difficult for him to tour abroad while living in
Japan.

Another reason for staying away lay in the attitudes of the musical
establishment in Japan. Japanese critics, said Etō, were out to put their
juniors down. When the pianist Matsuura Toyoaki (1929–) became the
first Japanese to win first prize in the Long–Thibaud Competition earlier
in the year, Japanese critics, rather than praising his achievement, claimed
that the level must have been low. The Japanese environment was still
provincial and did not provide sufficient scope for talented musicians.
Etō did concede though, that standards were rising and that Tokyo had
become more cosmopolitan in the five years since his previous visit. At
least he was no longer accused of having become too American.

Only two years later, in 1961, he did return to Japan for good.
"Because I am Japanese," he told an interviewer.[136] He missed Japan and
wanted to live there. Meanwhile the world was changing; several
Japanese musicians had gained an international reputation (he named
Ozawa Seiji, the cellist Hirai Takeichirō, the composer Mayuzumi
Toshirō and the violinists Kobayashi Kenji and Matsuda Yōko), and
American orchestras were touring Japan. Etō had reached an agreement
with Herbert Barrett Management about giving concerts both in Japan
and America, enabling him to continue his international career as a
performer while living in an increasingly cosmopolitan Japan. His wife

was happy to live in Japan and they believed their children would receive a better education there. "I believe I have chosen the most natural course," he concluded.[137]

Although Etō's international fame would probably have been greater had he stayed in America, he had chosen a good time to return. Japan had recovered from the war and rapid economic growth enabled the arts to flourish. More students were going abroad, some of whom had even sought out Etō himself at Curtis.[138] Teaching would certainly offer him a secure income; performing as a career was more risky. Etō had, however, learnt an important lesson listening to mature performers of the first rank in America. True artistry is not exclusive to the young; on the contrary, true artistry manifests itself in performers who have reached their thirties, forties and fifties. Japan, he felt, was too fixated on young talent.[139]

Determined to change prevailing attitudes, Etō embarked on what became a trailblazing performing career, centred on Japan but with regular foreign tours. In 1964, for example, he toured North America and Canada with the Japan Philharmonic Orchestra and Ozawa Seiji. In 1975 he performed the Brahms Double Concerto with the cellist Leslie Parnas, with whom he had played chamber music in his days at Curtis; that year he also gave his fifth recital at Carnegie Hall, playing all three Brahms sonatas with William Masselos. He played at the celebrations for Zimbalist's ninetieth birthday in 1978, and in 1986, following Zimbalist's death the year before, he played at memorial concerts in both Japan and America. At home he performed with the Japan Philharmonic Orchestra, the NHK Orchestra, the Tokyo Symphony Orchestra, the Kyoto City Symphony Orchestra, the Kyushu Symphony Orchestra, the Sapporo Symphony Orchestra and others. Most of all, however, he gave recitals, including (in 1962 and again in 1985) all the Beethoven sonatas, and chamber music concerts. Many concerts were family affairs, with his sister Reiko at the piano and his wife Angela playing violin; later their son Michael played the piano. With him Etō performed all the sonatas by Bach (1996) and Schumann (1987). Etō made many recordings abroad and in Japan, of both chamber music and concertos; in the 1960s these included several violin concertos by Japanese composers: Mamiya Michio (1960), Moroi Makoto (1963), Miyashita Shūretsu (1965) and Miyoshi Akira (1966). In 1996 he recorded the second movement from Watanabe Shigeo's Violin Concerto with his son Michael at the piano.[140]

Etō's most lasting legacy, however, lies in his huge influence as a teacher. In 1963 he was appointed visiting professor at Ueno Gakuen and instructor at Toho Gakuen School of Music; he continued to teach at both schools for decades. In 1997 he became president of Tōhō Gakuen University. Hundreds of pupils passed through his hands and many of them won national and international prizes.[141] Etō himself acted as a competition judge in Japan and abroad; he was a judge at the Carl Flesch competition (1968), the Queen Elisabeth Competition (1976) and the Paganini Competition (1977). In 1996 he founded his own competition, the Etō Toshiya Violin Competition. His influence as a teacher went beyond the students he taught directly. After the television series *Violin Lesson*, he took part in the NHK series *ABC of the Violin*, which ran from 1983 to 1984. Another institution of the violin world were his "Lessons" published in the magazine *String* in the 1980s and 1990s, which would include a full score of the violin part of a work with his fingerings, bowings and suggestions for articulation. Besides several major violin concertos and famous short pieces, his lessons included the Brahms and Beethoven sonatas and the unaccompanied sonatas by Ysaÿe.

Although famously known as Suzuki Shin'ichi's first child pupil, Etō's approach to teaching was quite different. Asked about his thoughts on music education in 1979, he stated that he saw little point in starting children on the violin until they had reached the age of four to six, because he felt they lacked the necessary understanding before then. He did however emphasize the importance of early musical training even before that age, particularly in listening and possibly by playing the piano (he himself had studied the piano seriously and often impressed his students by how well he could accompany them during lessons). Etō advocated learning to read music early. While he strongly stressed technique, he also saw the dangers of overemphasizing it and criticized the tendency in Japan to focus too much on technique at the expense of a more rounded development as a musician and as a human being.[142]

Etō was by all accounts an awe-inspiring teacher. He revered his own teacher Zimbalist and was critical of Galamian, Zimbalist's colleague at Curtis, who had taught his wife, Angela Etō.[143] His own teaching style, however, sounds more reminiscent of Galamian, in that he aroused terror in his students and gave precise instructions which he expected them to follow to the letter. His earliest students in particular recalled that he

18: Etō Toshiya.

shouted at them (something Galamian reportedly never did) and that they would feel sick as they approached his house for a lesson.[144] Kawabata Narimichi (1971–), writes, "In Professor Etō's lessons I was taught a lot, from details to big things. He is a really strict teacher, and sometimes he got terribly angry. I wasn't actually hit, but I did get shouted at. I really feared him." But he asserts that he could not have learnt as much as he did from his studies at the Royal College of Music in London (he graduated top of his year in 1996), had Etō's lessons not given him a secure foundation.[145]

Kawabata's contemporary Suwanai Akiko, expresses unconditional admiration: "Professor Etō's teaching principles are truly clear-cut and perfectly logical. For example, when a student begins to learn a new piece, he gives them a copy of the music in which he has written his fingering and bowing in detail. It is written with so much care that it is completely accurate and leaves no room for doubt." She explains that he was not merely forcing his own style on his students: "Professor Etō insists on the correct tradition of European music that he himself learnt. He teaches our country's young the correct and most rational way to play the violin, and makes every effort so that they first and foremost make that their own." Suwanai, like Kawabata, praises Etō's thoroughness; she sums up his philosophy as "correct inheritance of the good traditions." [146]

His students asserted that, even while insisting on one correct way of playing, he helped each student bring out their personal strengths and his students did not all play the same way.[147] And despite his emphasis on technique, he never lost sight of the goal: becoming a musician with a message rather than just a performer. He subtitled his book *Together with the Violin* (1999) with a line from the German poet Joseph von Eichendorff (1788–1857): "I would like to know what they sing."

The music critic Hasegawa Takehisa, noting in 1988 the number of outstanding Japanese violinists and observing that Japan had become "an export country for violinists," credited Etō with having helped sweep away Japan's "Western music complex."[148] If only he were right! Even today many Japanese still believe that only study abroad can produce a good violinist and musician. Some advocate sending young teenagers abroad to prepare them for an international career. Given the high standard of training available in Japan, this seems to owe more to a lingering inferiority complex than to rational assessment. The example of Watanabe Shigeo should serve as a stark reminder of what can happen if the human being behind the musical talent is ignored.

## 9. Unprecedented Opportunities: Post-war Pathways

In 1968, the centenary of the Meiji Restoration, the Ongaku no Tomosha corporation published a special issue of its magazine *Friends of Music (Ongaku no tomo)*, entitled *Musicians of Japan*.[149] The issue even came with an English title: *Great Musicians of Japan,* a clear expression of pride in the nation's achievements. And indeed, by the 1960s Japanese musicians were gaining international fame: many of the musicians featured in the issue had won international competitions and were active abroad; several of them had made their base outside Japan.

Not so, however, the violinists depicted on two double-page spreads of photographs. The first had pictures of three teachers: Saitō Hideo, Uzuka Tatsuo and Etō Toshiya; the second depicted members of the Sumi family: the brothers Saburō, Shirō and Gorō, and Saburō's son Takeaki. Etō Toshiya's inclusion in this gallery of iconic teachers of the pre-war generation is remarkable and demonstrates the status he had already achieved at the age of just 40. Saitō, the Sumi brothers and Uzuka had been active performers from the 1920s through the 1930s, but by 1968 they had for many years devoted themselves almost exclusively to teaching. They were among Japan's greatest assets in its bid for excellence in the world of Western classical music, proof of Japan's achievements even before the war and building on these to educate the next generations. That they are chiefly remembered as teachers is hardly surprising. In their younger days between the world wars, violinists seldom had more than a brief performing career as soloists in Japan. Standards were low, teachers were in high demand, and their best pupils soon outstripped them. Gramophone recordings of international virtuosos, while providing inspiration for aspiring Japanese players, also enabled their audiences to make unflattering comparisons, as did live performances by touring foreign artists. After 1945, music education expanded rapidly, increasing the need for teachers and producing able players in ever greater numbers. So circumstances continued to favour the teachers rather than the performers. Even in the 1960s, performers tended to have a short lifespan.[150] Etō Toshiya, who moved back to Japan in 1961, was remarkable in that he continued his career as a performer even while making himself a name as a teacher.

*Great Musicians of Japan* reflected this bias towards youth. Of the 33 violinists in the string player section of the directory, only three, Suzuki Shin'ichi, Sumi Saburō and Uzuka Tatsuo, were born before the 1920s and seven in the 1920s, including Suwa Nejiko, Iwamoto Mari, Tsuji Hisako, Etō Toshiya and Iwabuchi Ryūtarō.[151] Ten were born in the 1930s and the largest number, 13, in the 1940s.[152] All of these violinists except two can also be found in another special issue published by Ongaku no Tomosha in 1976, and many can also be found in later publications, so they were more than one-day wonders in 1968. The new directory listed a total of 48 violinists, most of them (24) born in the 1940s.[153]

The generation born in the last years of the war or the early post-war years enjoyed opportunities most of their predecessors could only dream of. Knowing little or nothing of the sufferings of war, they came of age when Japan's economic boom was well under way and their country had once more been accepted into the international community. Foreign travel became easier, and after receiving excellent training at home, many young musicians studied abroad, often with scholarships from their own or a foreign government. They began to win international competitions and to fill positions in foreign orchestras and music faculties. Many did not return to their homeland for years, if indeed at all. Compared to the violinists of the period when Western classical music came of age, their careers were increasingly alike. The most successful violinists typically studied with one of the giants among the teachers and graduated from Tōhō Gakuen College or Geidai, often after attending the affiliated high schools. They then studied in Europe or North America, where for many years Juilliard dominated; some went straight after graduating from high school. Many won competitions abroad. After returning they enjoyed distinguished careers, but teaching tended to dominate over performing. If they stayed abroad after graduating and managed to capitalize on their competition successes, their chances of a performing career were better. But the violinists who pursued their fortunes outside Japan did not necessarily do much for violin playing in Japan, except boost the collective morale when they returned home for brief visits to give well-publicized performances and master classes. Still, by the 1980s several of them were moving back to Japan and taking up teaching posts at the best conservatoires.

The importance of Saitō, Uzuka and Sumi as teachers of the first generation to come of age after the war can be easily seen by looking at the biographies of the violinists from *Great Musicians from Japan* who were born in the 1930s and 1940s, nearly all of whom counted at least one of the three, or other pre-war veterans like Suzuki Shin'ichi, Matsumoto Zenzō, Ono Anna, or Alexander Mogilevsky, among their teachers. Sumi's students included Unno Yoshio (1936–), Suzuki Hidetarō (1937–), Kuronuma Yuriko (1940–), Takahashi Mihoko (1941–), Hirose Etsuko (1941–) Ishii Shizuko (1942–), Sō Tomotada (1943–), Wanami Takayoshi (1945–), Tsumura Mari (1946–), and Satō Yōko (1949–). Tsumura and Wanami, the youngest in the group, also studied with Etō Toshiya. Hirose Etsuko and Sō Tomotada also included Saitō Hideo among their teachers. He was a cellist, but naturally all the string players taking his ensemble classes learnt much from him. Hori Tadashi (1935–), Shinozaki Isako (1943–) and Maehashi Teiko (1943–) likewise named Saitō among their teachers. Maehashi, Iso Hideo (1937–) and Ushioda Masuko (1942–) were among Ono Anna's last pupils before she left Japan in 1960, while Toyama Shigeru (1935–) and Kishibe Momoo (1938–) studied with Alexander Mogilevsky. Kishibe also studied with Shinozaki Hirotsugu, who, like his contemporary Suzuki Shin'ichi, pioneered violin lessons for the very young. Toyama was 17 when Mogilvsky died; at a concert to celebrate Mogilevsky's 50 years in music he played a Paganini concerto with Tanaka Sonoko at the piano. He did not find himself a new teacher after Mogilevsky's death; nevertheless he became concertmaster of the NHK Orchestra in March 1956 at the tender age of 20. He only remained for a few months though, before resigning in order to devote himself to chamber music and solo recitals. He gave a recital in London in 1970, which marked the start of his international activities.[154] The students who continued to Geidai rather than the Tōhō Gakuen School of Music often studied with Uzuka Tatsuo, including Unno Yoshio, and Hayashi Yōko (1940–).

All the younger violinists introduced in *Great Musicians of Japan* had spent time abroad. To this day it is rare for a Japanese violinist at the top of the profession not to have done so. Among the first, in the early 1950s, were Suzuki Shin'ichi's other child pupils of the 1930s, the Kobayashi brothers and Toyoda Kōji. Both Kobayashi Takeshi (1931–) and Kenji (1933–) had also studied with Matsumoto Zenzō. Takeshi studied in Czechoslovakia in the 1950s and played as concertmaster in Brno and Linz (Austria) before returning to Japan in 1967 to lead the Yomiuri Nippon Symphony Orchestra. From 1971 he concentrated on performing as a soloist. He has taught at Tōhō and at Tokyo College of Music. His brother Kenji studied in America and the Netherlands from 1952 to 1962. He graduated from Juilliard, where he studied with Louis Persinger and Ivan Galamian, in 1959 and played with the Oklahoma City Orchestra before returning to Japan to become concertmaster of the Tokyo Metropolitan Symphony Orchestra (Tōkyō-to Kōkyō Gakudan) in 1972. Like his brother he taught at Tōhō School of Music.[155] Toyoda Kōji (1933–), the "midget violinist" of the 1930s, received a French government scholarship in 1953, and studied with Arthur Grumiaux in Paris. Toyoda became one of the many young Japanese who attracted the world's attention by winning international competitions from the late 1950s. After winning the Harriet Cohen Bach prize in London in 1956, he came second at the Geneva International Competition in 1957; in 1958 he finished sixth at the Long–Thibaud competition, and in 1959 he was a laureate (twelfth) in the Queen Elisabeth Competition.

In fact, most of the violinists featured in the 1968 publication won prizes at international competitions, which may have been one of the criteria for their inclusion.[156] Ishii Shizuko, who, after studying with Sumi Saburō and Jeanne Isnard at Tōhō, had moved to Paris to study with Gabriel Bouillon, came third at the Long–Thibaud competition in 1959 and in 1961, and at the Paganini Competition in 1963. The Paganini competition had already seen its first Japanese winner in 1962, when Hirose Etsuko came second.

1964, the year of the Olympics and of the triumphant American tours of Suzuki Shin'ichi and Saitō Hideo, also brought several Japanese competition victories. Three Japanese were among the six winners of the Paganini Competition that year: Kubo Yōko (1943–), who shared the second prize with Pierre Amoyal from France, and Tokue Hisako and Sō Tomotada, who shared the fourth prize (Kubo entered again in 1965, winning the fourth prize). Kubo had already won a third prize in the Tchaikovsky Competition in 1962. A graduate of Tōhō Girls High School, she graduated from the conservatoire in Paris in 1964 and won second prize in the Long–Thibaud Competition in 1965. In 1967 she won the first prize at the first International Violin Competition held in Naples by the Curci Foundation.

Tokue Hisako (1945–) studied with Etō Toshiya, graduated from Tōhō School of Music in 1966, and continued her studies in Moscow and Paris. She had already won a second prize at the Aspen International Competition in 1962, and won another prize at the Long–Thibaud Competition in 1969. Sō Tomotada, who had studied with Sumi and Saitō as well as his father Tomoyasu, came second in the Geneva competition in 1963; he graduated from the conservatoire in Paris in 1964, and in 1967 he won the fifth prize in the Long–Thibaud Competition.

The Tchaikovsky Competition of 1966 had two Japanese winners: Satō Yōko (1949–) came third, and Ushioda Masuko (1942–), who had been placed sixth at the Queen Elisabeth Competition in 1963, came second. Both were studying in the Soviet Union at the time, Satō in Moscow and Ushioda at her teacher Ono Anna's alma mater in Leningrad. Maehashi Teiko, her contemporary, who graduated from the

National Leningrad Conservatoire in 1964, won the third prize at the Long–Thibaud Competition in 1967, and the first prize at the Curci Foundation's international violin competition in Naples in 1969. She was studying at Juilliard at the time, having previously studied privately with Joseph Szigeti and with Nathan Milstein in Switzerland. Like Satō, Ushioda and Maehashi, many violinists were studying abroad when they entered competitions. For those still in Japan, the special prize scheme for winners of the Japan Music Competition offered the chance to compete for sponsorship to take part in an international competition. Sō Tomotada in 1962, Shinozaki Isako in 1965, Takahashi Mihoko (1941–) in 1967 and many others benefited from this scheme.

Competition prizes and the fame and concert engagements they brought provided the winners with opportunities to launch their careers abroad. Even without prizes, graduation from a conservatoire with all the networking opportunities it offered provided a powerful incentive to remain abroad. Several graduates were appointed concertmasters of orchestras in Europe and North America. While the Kobayashi brothers returned to Japan after a relatively short spell, some settled abroad permanently, such as Suzuki Hidetarō. Others, including Toyoda Kōji, Urakawa Takaya, Okayama Kiyoshi and Yasunaga Tōru, stayed longer, returning in mid- or late career.

Suzuki Hidetarō studied with Sumi and graduated from Tōhō Gakuen High School in 1956. He went to Curtis to study with Zimbalist, graduating in 1963. He then became concertmaster of the Quebec Symphony Orchestra and taught at the Conservatoire de Musique du Québec. Suzuki was a finalist at the Tchaikovsky Competition in 1962; in 1963 he finished tenth and in 1967 fifth at the Queen Elisabeth Competition; in 1966 he won second prize at the Montreal International Competition. In 1978 he was appointed concertmaster of the Indianapolis Symphony Orchestra, a position he held until his retirement in 2005. He appears to be firmly established in America, directing and performing chamber music and recitals with his wife, the pianist Zeyda Ruga Suzuki.

Toyoda Kōji became the concertmaster of the Berlin Radio Symphony Orchestra (renamed the Deutsches Symphonie-Orchester Berlin in 1993) in 1962, the first Japanese to be appointed leader of an orchestra in Europe. He held the appointment until 1979. From 1992 to 2000 he was professor of Berlin University of Fine Arts. He did, however, keep close ties to Japan, becoming the musical director of the Kusatsu International Summer Music Academy and Festival from 1980 and the musical director of the Gunma Symphony Orchestra from 1981 to 1993. In 2000 he returned to Japan to succeed Suzuki Shin'ichi as the president of the Talent Education Research Institute and principal of the International Academy of the Suzuki Method in Matsumoto. Yasunaga Tōru (1951–) too spent most of his career in Germany. Having studied with Etō Toshiya and graduated from Tōhō Gakuen College of Music in 1974, he went to study in Berlin. His teacher at the conservatoire was Michel Schwalbé, formerly concertmaster of the Berlin Philharmonic. Yasunaga joined the Berlin Philharmonic in 1977 and became its first ever Japanese concertmaster in 1983. He left in 2009 in order to return to Japan.

Urakawa Takaya (1940–) and Okayama Kiyoshi (1942–) held appointments as concertmasters in Germany for several years but chose to return to Japan in mid-career, in the 1980s.[157] Urakawa was admitted to Geidai as a student, but left the same year to study in Germany on a German government scholarship. From 1959 to 1961 he studied in Berlin with Michel Schwalbé, then in Munich with Wilhelm Stross, graduating from the conservatoire in 1964. From 1964 to 1969 he was concertmaster of the Bamberg Symphony Orchestra; from the 1970s he concentrated on solo performances. Returning to Japan he was appointed assistant professor in 1981 and professor in 1984 at Geidai.[158]

Okayama came to Hamburg with his wife Hattori Yoshiko (1943–), both of them on German government scholarships after completing the postgraduate course at Geidai. They received performance diplomas from Hamburg in 1971 and 1972 respectively, and won first prize playing in a string quartet at the annual Felix Mendelssohn Bartholdy Competition in Berlin in 1970 as well as being awarded the Ysaÿe Medal as a duo in 1971 in Brussels. They continued to perform chamber music together during Okayama Kiyoshi's tenure as concertmaster of the Beethoven Orchestra from 1971 to 1983 and after their return to Tokyo. In 1984 Okayama was appointed concertmaster of the Yomiuri Orchestra and subsequently Professor at Geidai, while Hattori became Professor at Aichi University of Fine Arts.[159]

Marriage could be another reason not to return to Japan, and could cause women in particular to end up in unexpected destinations. Kuronuma Yuriko, who in 1958 left Tōhō Gakuen High School after

having accepted a scholarship to study at the Academy of Performing
Arts (AMU) in Prague, married a fellow student. After graduating from
the conservatoire in 1962 she followed him to his homeland of Mexico,
where she remained even after their separation 20 years later. She
continued to perform, and in 1980 established the Kuronuma Yuriko
Violin Academy in Mexico City. According to her autobiography, it was
then still unusual to start children on the violin before the age of around
12.[160] Kuronuma imported fractional violins from Japan, but when the
currency exchange made them too expensive she had to collect
donations. To thank her compatriots for their generosity, she took her
pupils on a first tour to Japan in 1985. More tours followed, and on 18
January 2010, Kuronuma and her students celebrated the Academy's
thirtieth anniversary with a concert in Tokyo. On this occasion Kuronuma
was interviewed by the magazines *String* and *Sarasate*.[161] In this way,
Kuronuma and other artists abroad may periodically be brought back to
public awareness in their homeland, even if they have made their
permanent home in a foreign country.

Nishizaki Takako (1944–) initially returned to Japan after graduating
from Juilliard in 1968. She had studied there with Joseph Fuchs, Louis
Persinger and Aldo Parisot from 1961, and during this time she won a
second prize at the Leventritt Competition in 1966 and the Fritz Kreisler
Prize at the Juilliard Concerto Competition in 1969. Back in her home
city of Nagoya she opened a violin studio and performed with a chamber
orchestra. During a tour to Hong Kong she met the German businessman
Klaus Heymann, whom she subsequently married. Based in Hong Kong,
she has enjoyed an international performing career. She is one of the most
recorded violinists, no doubt helped by the fact that her husband is the
initiator of the highly successful Naxos label. She has, moreover,
championed Chinese violin music, including the popular *Butterfly Lovers*
Concerto.[162]

Nishizaki is better known abroad than in Japan, and this is also true of
other violinists who have concentrated their activities outside Japan
(although they may still feature in reference works on Japanese
musicians), such as Sō Tomotada and Fujikawa Mayumi.[163] Sō Tomotada
(or Tomotada Soh, 1943–) graduated from Tōhō Gakuen High School,
where he also studied with Sumi Saburō and Saitō Hideo, then studied
with René Benedetti at the Conservatoire de Paris for one year, and was

awarded the first prize at his graduation in 1965. Subsequently he studied with Joseph Szigeti and was his assistant in Switzerland, where he was based until he moved to London. He has performed widely in Europe and Japan, has played as a member of the Saitō Memorial Orchestra, and holds teaching posts at Tōhō Gakuen and Osaka College of Music as well as being a professor at the Royal Academy of Music in London.[164]

Fujikawa Mayumi (1946–) studied with Sō Tomoyasu, Kobayashi Kenji and Saitō Hideo at Tōhō before moving to Belgium. She studied with Franz Wigy, a pupil of Ysaÿe, at the Flemish National Music Institute and graduated in 1968. She continues to be based in London, where besides performing she teaches at the Royal Academy and at Trinity College. Nevertheless, she remains aware of her cultural background as Japanese, the magazine *Sarasate* assured its readers on the occasion of one of her regular tours to Japan in 2006, when she performed Mozart's Concerto No. 5 and the Brahms Concerto with the Yomiuri Orchestra.[165]

Maehashi Teiko, on the other hand, although she also enjoyed an international career, is still one of the most popular violinists of her generation in Japan.[166] Having won several international competitions, she made Switzerland her base and performed worldwide, often with major orchestras, including the Berlin Philharmonic, the Cleveland Orchestra and the Israel Philharmonic. She regularly performed in Japan and continues to do so. Her first recorded album was a bestseller which brought her fans outside the confines of classical music enthusiasts.[167] Maehashi has tried to reach a wider audience in her recitals too; among her more recent initiatives is a series of annual afternoon concerts in Tokyo's Suntory Hall, where the programme starts with a sonata, followed by popular short pieces. Nor were her activities limited to Tokyo. Concerts to celebrate her 50 years on the stage in 2012 included one in as small and remote a town as Yahaba, southwest of Morioka in the North-Eastern prefecture of Iwate.[168] In 2004 she was awarded the Japan Academy of Fine Arts Prize, and in 2011, on the occasion of the government's annual spring decorations, she received the Medal with Purple Ribbon awarded in recognition of contributions to arts, sports and academic fields.

Some violinists have enjoyed a successful international career while dividing their time between continents. One is Wanami Takayoshi. In many ways his biography is typical of his generation, and he himself links his own development to Japan's rise as a peaceful nation, which has given him unprecedented opportunities.[169] At the same time, Wanami is exceptional, for he was born blind, and became the first blind-born violin virtuoso to gain international recognition.[170] That Japan should produce this particular first is hardly a coincidence. Under the Tokugawa shoguns, blind *biwa* (plucked lute) and *koto* players were organized in guilds with a special system of ranks. In more recent times, the famous *koto* player and composer Miyagi Michio was blind from early childhood. Although the Meiji government put an end to the guild system, music was still regarded as a suitable occupation for the blind, and education for the blind often included musical training on Western as well as Japanese instruments. Suzuki Yonejirō, the nineteenth-century pioneer of music education, introduced Braille music notation (see Part 1 Chapter 5), and the first blind violinist was a graduate of Suzuki's Music College of the East.[171] The challenge for a blind violinist lies less with the instrument than with the almost complete reliance on the written score in the Western classical tradition.

Wanami's early life and education have been described in detail by his mother Sonoko, an "education mum" if ever there was one. Her book, *A Symphony of Mother and Child,* was published in 1977, and includes prefaces by the eminent music critic Nomura Kōichi and the playwright Tanaka Sumie. Nomura recommended the detailed record of Takayoshi's upbringing and musical education for "PTA education mums" and as a reference work for music educators.[172] By 2000 the book was in its thirteenth printing, which suggests that it has found a significant readership. Sonoko herself, although described on the jacket of the book as a "housewife," was highly educated for a woman of her generation, having graduated from Tokyo's Fifth Metropolitan High School for Girls before the war. She records Takayoshi's education (his younger brother is only mentioned in passing) with a level of detail that at times makes tedious reading, but testifies to her strong confidence and sense of purpose. When she discovered that her baby could not see, and again when he showed signs of great musicality, she did not hesitate to consult leading experts. Takayoshi first received singing lessons; then, soon after his fourth birthday, he began to learn the violin with Mori Otto (the son of Rudolf Dittrich), another pioneer of early musical education for children, who had recently taken over a nearby Talent Education violin studio from Suzuki Shin'ichi's younger brother Akira. Suzuki students do not normally learn to read music until they have mastered the basics on their instrument, but following another expert's advice, Sonoko began to study Braille, including the Braille system for reading music, which she taught Takayoshi. When he reached school age, he attended schools for the blind, but Sonoko continued to ensure that he received the best possible musical tuition. In 1950 Takayoshi's father was transferred to Osaka, and for the next few years Takayoshi's teacher was Tsuji Kichinosuke, the father and teacher of the pre-war girl prodigy Tsuji Hisako. Even after the family moved back to Tokyo, Sonoko and Takayoshi returned to Osaka regularly for lessons with Tsuji; alternatively he would commute to Tokyo. Eventually this proved too much of a burden and from January 1957 Takayoshi received lessons from Sumi Saburō. He had already won his first competitions, coming first in the sixth Japan Student Music Competition for the Blind in 1954; in 1957 he won the third prize and in 1958 the first prize in the junior high school division of the All Japan Student Music Competition, another of Sumi's many prize-winning students. He began to perform with an ensemble of blind students from his school. Takayoshi's talent, however, stood out even among his seeing peers, raising the question of his future education. An American educator strongly urged the Wanamis to let him study in America at Perkins School for the Blind in Watertown, Massachusetts,[173] but they decided against it. Takayoshi, they felt, was still too young to leave his home. His training as a violinist, moreover, needed the combined effort of parents and teacher. Later that year, 1958, Watanabe Shigeo took the dose of pills that ended his career and his life as a conscious individual. Wanami Takayoshi might well have fared better despite his youth. But at Perkins his musical education would most probably have been of the sort deemed suitable for a person labelled "blind" rather than for the highly gifted violinist he had already proved himself to be.[174]

Wanami did continue his formal education at schools for the blind, progressing to the music department of the high school for the blind attached to Tokyo University of Education (since 1973 the University of Tsukuba) in 1960. But his parents also enrolled him as an auditor at Tōhō Gakuen College, where Etō Toshiya became his violin teacher. He even attended Saitō Hideo's Saturday ensemble classes, sitting in the middle of the orchestra and following the score his mother had transcribed into Braille, until he could play his part.[175] After graduating from high school in 1963 he continued to Tōhō Gakuen University, and in 1964 took part in the Tōhō orchestra's tour of the United States, playing solos in San Francisco and New York.

*A Symphony of Mother and Child* ends with Takayoshi winning the first prize plus a special prize in the Japan Music Competition at the age of 17 in 1962 (he had come third the previous year). Winning Japan's oldest and most prestigious competition proved beyond doubt that he did not need allowances to be made for him as a blind violinist. Like his contemporaries already mentioned he went on from winning national competitions to winning international ones, coming fourth at the Long–Thibaud Competition in 1965 and second at the Carl Flesch Competition in London in 1970; that year he was also awarded the Ysaÿe medal in Brussels.

While Wanami did not enrol in a conservatoire abroad, he did study with several world-class players. In 1965 he took lessons with Joseph Szigeti and in 1967 with David Oistrakh in Moscow. He took summer classes in chamber music in Siena with Riccardo Brengola and with the pianist Sergio Lorenzi. In 1979 he studied chamber music with Sándor Végh. He made his Tokyo debut with the Japan Philharmonic Symphony Orchestra in 1963 under Saitō Hideo's baton and gave his first solo recital in Tokyo in 1966; that year he also performed with the Tokyo Philharmonic Orchestra under Watanabe Akeo.[176] In the following years he performed in several European countries as well as Japan. In 1973, besides giving concerts in 25 European cities, he travelled to America and performed with orchestras in Toledo and Albuquerque. In 1978 he and his wife, the pianist Tsuchiya Mineko, made Basel in Switzerland their European base, spending about half of each year in Europe; they moved to London in 1984. The couple continued to maintain close ties to Japan. Wanami started teaching at Tōhō Gakuen College in 1989; that year he also took part in the Saito Memorial Orchestra's European tour. In 1991 he began directing his own student orchestra, the Izumigō Festival Orchestra, whose members are students of his annual summer course in Yatsugatake, first held in 1985. He has also taught in Britain, giving master classes at the Royal Northern College of Music in

Manchester and at the Purcell School.[177] Wanami has since returned to Japan.

The many examples of Japanese violinists who launched their careers abroad may give the impression that this was a prerequisite for fame at home, but it did not have to be that way. Tanaka Chikashi (1939–2009) returned to Japan soon after completing his studies in France. Born in Tokyo, Tanaka had his first lessons with his father Tanaka Eijin (1896–1970), himself a violinist who had studied with Willy Hess at the Tokyo Academy of Music. He enrolled at Tōhō Gakuen, but left without graduating to study at the conservatoire in Paris with Gabriel Bouillon in 1955. Graduating as the top student of his year in 1962, he travelled to Austria and Italy before returning to Japan the same year and became concertmaster of the Kyoto Symphony Orchestra (Kyōto-shi Kōkyō Gakudan). From 1966 to 1979 he was concertmaster of the NHK Orchestra. He performed as a soloist with the NHK Orchestra, and other major orchestras as well as leading his own string quartet and ensemble. Until 2004 he was a professor at Geidai.

According to the "brief review" in *Great Musicians of Japan*, Tanaka's contemporary Unno Yoshio was the stronger concertmaster and concerto soloist, while Tanaka excelled at recitals and chamber music; he was at his best with French composers.[178] Not long before his death he founded his own orchestra. It made its debut on 31 January 2008, with Beethoven's Fifth and Sixth symphonies; many of the members were former pupils who had themselves become soloists and concertmasters. Sadly for the members, the first concert was also the last under Tanaka himself. He died just before the second concert on 2 February, and the concertmaster took over his baton for the orchestra's performance of Mendelssohn's Italian and Scottish symphonies. Tanaka had already been planning to do Berlioz at the third concert, so the members of the orchestra decided to meet to prepare one more concert in his name. On 10 February 2010, the Chikashi Orchestra duly gave a concert entitled "Final" with a performance of Hector Berlioz's *Symphonie fantastique* (Op. 14) at the Tōkyō Gekijō Hall. The conductor called Tanaka the Sakamoto Ryōma of music; high praise indeed, for Sakamoto Ryōma, an important political actor in the years leading up to the Meiji Restoration and one of the most popular historical characters, was the hero of the 2010 season's Sunday evening prime time "Great River" historical drama television series.[179] The concert by the Chikashi Orchestra is one of many testimonies to the way Japanese will revere their teacher, cultivating his or her memory even after their death.

One high-profile concertmaster of the first post-war generation who spent little time abroad is Tokunaga Tsugio (1946–). The son of a violinist, Tokunaga studied with his father and with Sumi Saburō as well as with Saitō Hideo at Tōhō Gakuen. Unlike many of his contemporaries, he did not go abroad after his graduation in 1965. His family's strained finances compelled him to work even while still at Tōhō, playing in studios for singers and films. He later recalled that he even worked until the small hours on the day he played in the main round of the Japan Music Competition (he won third prize in 1965) – much to Saitō Hideo's anger.[180] In 1966, when he was only 19 years old, he became the concertmaster of the Tokyo Symphony Orchestra (Tōkyō Kōkyō Gakudan), Japan's youngest concertmaster. In 1968 he had the chance to go to Berlin for a year as the second student under a new programme of the Agency for Cultural Affairs (Bunkachō), where he studied with Michel Schwalbé, then concertmaster of the Berlin Philharmonic Orchestra as well as professor at the Hochschule der Künste. From 1976 to 1994 he was concertmaster of the NHK Orchestra. He resigned to concentrate on solo performances and recordings, and in 1995 became the musical director of the JT Art Hall chamber music series. In 1998 he was appointed general producer of the Miyazaki International Music festival. In 2001 he performed the Beethoven and Tchaikovsky concertos with the NHK Orchestra – quite a remarkable feat in a country where, as he himself remarked in an interview, not many soloists are active at his age.[181] Even in 2004 he had enough popular appeal to feature in a series "We love Wine" in the music magazine *Sarasate*.[182] Tokunaga also teaches at Tōhō Gakuen, Kunitachi and Senzoku Gakuen colleges. His recent students include Miura Fumiaki, who won the Joseph Joachim International Violin Competition in Hannover in 2009 at only 16 years of age.

In short, the violinists growing up in the first decades after the war and starting their careers during the years when Japan's economy began to boom received excellent training from an early age and had opportunities for study abroad. Winning competitions, first national, then international ones, often served as a passport to a career that took them beyond their homeland. International audiences became accustomed to hearing and seeing Japanese musicians on the competition circuit, in orchestras and on the faculties of conservatoires, while back in Japan confidence in native musical achievements increased. In 1998 Ongaku no Tomosha published another survey of classical music in Japan, confidently entitled "J-Classic-shugi," which as well as articles included a directory of 443 musicians deemed to be "active performers in the front line," 74 of them violinists.[183] Thirty years after the first such publication, several of the violinists featured earlier were now accorded the status of "Pioneers of J-Classic." The special section with this title included: the first to become concertmasters in America and Europe (the Kobayashi brothers, Toyoda Kōji, Suzuki Hidetarō, Urakawa Takaya, Okayama Kiyoshi and Yasunaga Tōru); especially notable concertmasters of the NHK Symphony Orchestra (Unno Yoshio and Tanaka Chikashi); virtuosos born in the 1940s who were most famous abroad (Sō Tomotada and Fujikawa Mayumi); and Maehashi Teiko, exceptionally popular at home.[184] Meanwhile the youngest on the scene, born in the 1970s (14 of the 74 listed), were beginning to come of age.[185]

The middle generation as it were, violinists born well after the war in the 1950s (22 listings) and 1960s (13 listings) benefited as their seniors had done from Japan's increasing wealth and the rising standards in classical music. When they went abroad they were no longer met with the same astonishment that Asians could master Western classical music. At the major competitions the jury as likely as not included a compatriot or two, as did the faculties of several prestigious conservatoires. At Juilliard, for example, those such as Urushihara Asako (1966–) who came to study with Dorothy DeLay in the 1980s sometimes found that the teacher they saw most of in their first year was DeLay's long-time associate Kawasaki Masao (1951–), who, after graduation from Tōhō Gakuen, had studied with DeLay at Juilliard, graduating in 1976. He served as DeLay's assistant teacher before being appointed professor in 1987.[186] For Urushihara, and no doubt for others, he helped bridge the cultural distance they experienced and gave them the kind of detailed instructions they missed in DeLay's lessons.[187]

In other ways the violinists of this generation started out like their seniors of the early post-war years. The overwhelming majority studied at either Tōhō Gakuen School of Music or Geidai, unless they went abroad before attending a conservatoire in Japan. Among the few exceptions is Senju Mariko (1962–; see Part 3 Chapter 2), who graduated from Keiō University. She did, however, like so many others, study with Sumi Saburō and Etō Toshiya. Sumi Saburō continued to teach almost until his death in 1984. Saitō Hideo had already died in 1974. Etō and Sumi represented a link from pre-war Japan to the end of the twentieth century. No one could quite fill their place, but at Tōhō Gakuen they have been succeeded by former students. Study abroad was (and is) still regarded as essential, and for years Juilliard was the most popular destination, although many still went to Europe. Most of the top-ranking violinists had won international as well as national competitions, where Japanese winners were now so commonplace that the only way to create a stir was to be the first Japanese to win the top prize or else to win at an ever younger age. Horigome Yuzuko (1957–), who had studied at Tōhō Gakuen with Kubota Ryōsaku and Etō Toshiya, caused a sensation when she became the first Japanese to win first prize at the Queen Elisabeth Competition in 1980. An international career of performing with orchestras and in chamber music ensembles followed. Kubota Takumi (1959–), another Tōhō Gakuen graduate, was the first Japanese violinist to win the International Music Competition in Munich and has since pursued a performing career from her two bases in Tokyo and Vienna, where she studied with Wolfgang Schneiderhan from 1978. Urushihara Keiko (1963–) won the eighth Wieniawski Competition in Poznan at 18 years of age in 1981, making her not only the first Japanese but also the youngest winner of the first prize. Like her younger sister Asako (1966–), she studied with Sumi Saburō and Unno Yoshio and graduated from Geidai (in 1987). Urushihara Asako was the youngest to win the Japan International Music Competition in 1983 (although, given that the competition was only held for the second time that year this may not have been a major feat). Like her sister she performed internationally as well as in Japan. For some years she lived in Germany, but in 2005 she was appointed assistant professor at Geidai, which in recent years has begun recruiting women onto its previously male-dominated string faculty.[188]

Others whose careers were launched by winning international competitions were Takezawa Kyōko and Watanabe Reiko (both born in 1966). Takezawa, who began her studies at the age of three with the

Suzuki Method, was already a seasoned performer by the time she won the Indianapolis Violin Competition in 1986, having toured America with a group of Suzuki children as a child. She went to Juilliard straight after Tōhō Gakuen High School, after meeting Dorothy DeLay at Aspen in 1984, where she won the concerto competition. She continued to live in New York after graduating, performing with major orchestras in America and Japan as well as playing chamber music. Between 2007 and 2009 she celebrated the twentieth anniversary of her debut with a recital tour, ending with a performance of Brahms' sonatas in Tokyo's Suntory Hall in 2009. That year she moved to Paris; as she told *String,* she wanted to collaborate more with European artists and take part in festivals.[189]

Watanabe Reiko also studied at Juilliard straight after graduation from high school, in her case the high school affiliated with Geidai. In 1980 she was the youngest winner of the fiftieth Japan Music Competition, where her performance of Bartók's Violin Concerto No. 2 caused a sensation.[190] She went on to win a prize to compete abroad and came second at the Viotti Competition in 1984 and the Paganini Competition in 1986. After studying with Joseph Fuchs at Juilliard from 1985 to 1992 she retained a base in New York while pursuing an international career. But she regularly returned to Japan and in 2004 told the magazine *Sarasate* that the weight of her activities was gradually shifting towards Japan, where she had recently taken up a teaching appointment at Akita International University.[191]

Toda Yayoi (1968–), who studied with Etō Toshiya at Tōhō Gakuen and with Herman Krebbers in Amsterdam, became the second Japanese after Horigome to win first prize at the Queen Elisabeth Competition in 1993, among other competition successes. She has performed with major orchestras worldwide, but can also be heard frequently in Japan.

Back in Japan, the increased level of musical activity and rising standards offered more scope for a varied musical career than previously. Shinozaki Fuminori (1963–) did not expect to return to Japan in a hurry when he moved to Vienna as a high school student to study with Thomas Christian at the City of Vienna Conservatoire. When a Japanese conductor invited him to dinner at the time of his graduation in 1988 and asked his opinion of the classical music scene in Japan, he told him it did not interest him. Nevertheless, the conductor, who turned out to be headhunting a concertmaster for the Gunma Symphony Orchestra, persuaded him to try the job as a guest. Shinozaki stayed until he became concertmaster of the Yomiuri Nippon Symphony Orchestra in 1991; in 1997 he moved to the NHK Symphony Orchestra. He also pursued his interest in chamber music with the Hallé String Quartet and other chamber ensembles, and in education as the Musical Director of the Tokyo Junior Orchestra Society Musical Director. In 2004 Shinozaki initiated the "Maro World" music project in cooperation with Ōji Hall in Tokyo; the idea was to bring hall managers, producers, musicians and audiences closer together to create a musical experience that was different from the conventional concert, and to present classical music with a new angle by performing together with artists from other arts, such as acting, mime and even ikebana. In 2006 he published *Rufutopauze* ("Luftpause"), a book that is part autobiography, part essay, in which he presents his views and observations on topics such as his time abroad, the concertmaster's tasks, conductors, Mozart's music and music education.[192] He has also published ensemble lessons in string magazines.

Shinozaki's contemporary Morishita Kōji (1963–) is another violinist who, after studying abroad, has spent most of his career as a concertmaster and chamber musician in Japan. He studied at Tōhō Gakuen and at Cincinnati Conservatory of Music in Ohio. Returning to Japan in 1988 he played in a string quartet, as a soloist and as a guest concertmaster until he was appointed concertmaster of the Sendai Philharmonic Orchestra in 1994. He resigned in 2000 and is currently concertmaster of the Hamamatsu Philharmonic Orchestra and the Osaka Symphony Orchestra. Morishita continues to play chamber music and give solo recitals. The orchestra in Sendai was just over 20 years old when he joined, and the audience for classical music in the region was limited. Morishita saw a role for himself and his colleagues there and they gave regular chamber concerts in small towns around Sendai which were designed to be accessible to people with little experience of classical music. Meanwhile he kept his links with Tokyo by giving regular recitals there.[193]

"J-Classic-shugi" also presented violinists who had left the beaten track of mainstream classical music. Performing on period instruments was already a firmly established niche by 1998 and one of the top players was Terakado Ryō (1961–).[194] After graduating from Tōhō Gakuen and a brief spell as concertmaster of the Tokyo Philharmonic Orchestra, he moved to the Netherlands in 1985 to study with Sigiswald Kuijken at the Royal Conservatoire in The Hague. As a student at Tōhō he had already led his own Baroque ensemble. During his studies in Europe he played in a large number of Baroque and period ensembles, and expanded his repertoire to other periods. In 1987 he founded Tokyo Baroque; a string quartet, Mito dell'Arco, followed, which made its debut in 1999. In 2010 he founded Concerto Terakadino with young musicians. He teaches at The Hague Royal Conservatoire and at Tōhō Gakuen.

Other classically trained violinists have experimented with genres other than classical music. Labelled "crossover" (in Japanese as well as in English), this is perhaps less novel than exploring period performance. The latter marks a departure from the musical traditions the Japanese absorbed when they imported Western music in the nineteenth century. Playing music other than Western classical, on the other hand, was common for violinists in the early twentieth century, when the routes to becoming a professional musician were more varied and the scope for earning a living with classical music were limited. Many violinists played in ensembles accompanying films or in jazz and dance bands as well as symphony orchestras. While making a living is of obvious interest for today's violinists too, exploring the possibilities of the violin and attracting new audiences also motivate the crossover violinists. One of the first to break the mould was Furusawa Iwao (1959–), although his early career resembled others described here.[195] Graduating from Tōhō Gakuen, where he studied with Suzuki Tomoko and Etō Toshiya, in 1982, he continued his studies at Curtis and at the Mozarteum in Salzburg. His competition successes included a fifth place at the Wieniawski in 1981 and a first prize at the Michelangelo Abbado Competition in 1982. From 1988 to 1992 he was solo concertmaster of the Tokyo Metropolitan Symphony Orchestra. Furusawa began performing at his own series of "Violin Evenings," which have been described as a landmark.[196] His collaborators were the pianist Takahashi Yūji and the violinist Hakase Tarō (1968–), then still a student at Geidai, who went on to become a crossover performer in his own right. They departed from the conventional classical concert format. Furusawa also made music with foreign artists. He formed the group Typhoon with Phillip Bush, Paul Coletti and Francis Guton and has collaborated with the jazz violinist Stéphane Grappelli, the cellist Yo Yo Ma, and the pianist, conductor and composer Mikhail Pletnev. In 1999 he produced an album with the Brazilian guitar duo Sérgio and Odair Assad.

Hakase Tarō, a native of Osaka, started playing the violin at four. His early training was conventional, and he graduated from Geidai.[197] It was during his student days that he discovered rock music. He found that his fellow students in the fine arts department gave classical music a miss in favour of the Rolling Stones, Bob Marley or the Sex Pistols.[198] While still a student, he debuted in 1990 with his own band Kryzler & Kompany, a trio of violin, bass and keyboards. The trio performed pop versions of the classics wearing bright costumes and sometimes dancing to their music. When it disbanded in 1996, Hakase concentrated on solo performances. He achieved a major success together with the Canadian singer Céline Dion when they recorded "To Love You More" (music by David Foster), created as the title song for the Fuji TV drama series *Koibito yo* (My Dear Love, October to December 1995). "To Love You More" became a hit which stayed at the top of the charts for a record period of five weeks, an unusual feat for a foreign production in Japan.[199] Hakase took the stage with Dion for the song on her world tour in 1996–1997. In 2002 he established his own recording label, HATS. Besides performing music that crosses genre boundaries and producing CDs he has also been involved in television productions, as well as writing and performing his own compositions.

Hakase has since returned to performing classical music, although without giving up his engagement with other genres. In September 2007 he fulfilled his long-cherished wish and moved to London with his family, where he hoped to devote more time to practising, as he told his interviewer for *String*.[200] He needed it too, according to a review of his first recital of Händel, Beethoven and Brahms in London. The reviewer called his playing "sometimes suspect." But he did conclude that "ultimately the sheer fun of it all won the day."[201] That, presumably, was Hakase's priority.

Hakase's contemporary Takashima Chisako (1968–) is best known for performances of popular classics that appeal to wide audiences. She has also appeared in TV commercials.[202] After graduating from Tōhō Gakuen, where she studied with Etō Toshiya and Tokunaga Tsugio, she continued her studies at the Yale School of Music. From 1994 to 1997 she played in the New World Symphony in Miami. Returning to Japan in

1997, she performed as a soloist and as a duo with the pianist and composer Mino Kabasawa, giving over 100 concerts a year. Her numerous television appearances include talk shows, and she has published books introducing popular classical pieces. In 2006 she established "Takashima Chisako 12 Violinists," a group of young women who perform popular classics and arrangements of other popular tunes in showy costumes and at unconventional venues. Takashima has also published two books that aim to popularize classical music, *A Violinist's Guide to Music: 50 Selected Classical Masterpieces* and *An Introduction to Classical Music from Zero Knowledge.*[203]

Violinists crossing boundaries of genre and style are far from exclusive to Japan, and musicians like Furusawa, Hakase and Takashima are part of worldwide trends, including the globalization of music. Indeed, looking at the pathways of violinists since the end of the Second World War, the most striking, although hardly surprising, phenomenon is the extent to which they cross borders. Japanese violinists are not limited to Japan: many are equally at home in other countries, often moving between countries. While they may still be labelled "Asian" in the West, they are not that different from their counterparts from other parts of the world. We might even ask how meaningful it is to speak of a violinist as "Japanese," a question we will come back to as we look at Japan at the turn of the millennium.

Meanwhile, in the second half of the twentieth century, Japan was not just producing violinists who could compete with their counterparts anywhere in the world, but making a revolutionary contribution to string pedagogy worldwide.

## 10. From "Talent Education" to the "Suzuki Method": The Japanese Violin Goes Global

Mention "Japan" and "violin" anywhere in North America and Europe, and many people will think of the Suzuki Method. Apart from a small number of Japanese musicians that have become household names, nothing has done more to make Japan famous in the world of string playing than Suzuki Shin'ichi and his pedagogy. Some people think that any Japanese violinist they hear must have learnt their instrument by the Suzuki Method. Little do they realize that the Suzuki Method is far less dominant in Japan than its fame abroad suggests. Indeed Suzuki's success

19: Suzuki Shin'ichi with children.

in North America raised interest in Japan, and what was originally known as "Talent Education" is now commonly called "Suzuki Method" or "Suzuki mesōdo" in its Japanized version. Suzuki was neither the only one to promote music education from an early age, nor the only one to extend his activities beyond Japan. But the missionary zeal of his supporters almost from the start was unmatched. The timing, moreover, was just right. After all, Japan's economic recovery from the war, its increasing wealth and its cultural aspirations had parallels in other countries. In Europe from around 1960, countries like Germany, France and Britain saw great increases in public funding for the arts. In North America, generous corporate grants produced similar effects.[204] As education, including music education expanded, educators were looking to reform outdated pedagogical practices and to explore new ones.

The first grand Suzuki concert in Tokyo in 1955, attended as it was by diplomatic representatives of several foreign countries, attracted international attention. The spectacle of thousands of children from as young as four years old playing famous and challenging works from the classical repertoire presented compelling evidence for Suzuki's belief that any child could learn to play the violin well. Soon internationally famous musicians became interested and their endorsement contributed to the method's prestige within Japan and its international renown. One of the first was Pablo Casals, whom Suzuki especially revered and who in 1961 attended a concert held in Tokyo to honour him. Other world-famous artists who visited Suzuki and his pupils were Arthur Grumiaux, David Oistrakh, Marcel Moyse, William Primrose, Yehudi Menuhin, Alfred Cortot, and Mstislav Rostropovich; all praised Suzuki's work.[205]

At around the same time, Japanese musicians were beginning to make a name for themselves abroad, including Etō Toshiya and Toyoda Kōji.[206] Strictly speaking, Etō and Toyoda had not been taught by the "Suzuki Method," which was only fully developed after the war. Nor did Suzuki intend primarily to train professionals, but, ironically, it was the professional success of his students that helped fuel interest in the method. Still, successful pupils alone would not have done it. Saitō Hideo's students at Tōhō performed at least as well as Suzuki's – better in the long run, for unlike Suzuki, Saitō and his colleagues did aim to train professionals. But they were content to achieve success in Japan and enjoy the occasional foreign accolade when the orchestra staged a tour to North America or Europe. Saitō's first tour to the United States took place in 1964, the same year as Suzuki's, and was not only a success abroad: unlike Suzuki, Saitō also attracted media attention at home (see Chapter 7).

Suzuki's supporters, on the other hand, wanted to spread his teaching across the world. Perhaps equally importantly, they included key people with English language skills. The physician Honda Masaaki, who organized and led the foreign tours, had lived in America as a boy. Suzuki's wife Waltraud translated his works into English and handled much of the foreign correspondence that resulted from his international renown. Mochizuki Kenji, who introduced Suzuki's work to America, was studying at Oberlin Graduate School of Theology. In 1958 he showed Clifford A. Cook, professor of stringed instruments and music education at Oberlin College Conservatory of Music, a film of children playing Bach's Double Concerto. Cook was impressed:

"[...] Huge numbers of Japanese children were playing from memory violin music ranging up to the level of the Vivaldi and Bach double concertos. Aside from the sheer weight of numbers and the appeal of cute tots performing seriously, the outstanding features for the string specialist were these: (1) There was not a poor left hand position or bow arm visible in the entire group. (2) Intonation was good and pleasing tone was modulated expressively. In short, this was not just mass playing of 1200 children from 5 to 13 years of age – it was *good violin playing!*"

Cook concluded, "It is evident that Mr. Suzuki is a humanitarian as well as a highly skilled violin teacher and psychologist."[207]

Once the film became known, it caused a veritable "Suzuki Explosion."[208] In 1959 John Kendall of Southern Illinois University became the first of many American teachers to study with Suzuki in Matsumoto. In 1964 the Japanese government liberalized foreign travel and Suzuki and Honda Masaaki brought a group of children to perform in the United States. From 1966 to 1994 Honda accompanied Suzuki students on an annual tour of North America. The performances attracted wide attention, and the "Suzuki Method" was soon adopted in the United States. By 1965 a few qualified teachers were available, including Honda's own daughter Yuko (1945–2007).[209]

So great was the enthusiasm for the Suzuki Method that many teachers set themselves up as Suzuki teachers with minimal qualifications or knowledge of the method. Some of them introduced "Suzuki teaching" in public schools in the mistaken belief that Suzuki's method was about group lessons. With more enthusiasm than knowledge or skill these teachers gave the Suzuki Method a bad name. Soon teachers with a serious interest in the method were writing to Suzuki, imploring him to do something about the situation. Most of the complaints did not even reach him: his wife Waltraud, who opened the letters, did her best to protect him. In any case he could not prevent the misuse of his name, since the name "Suzuki Method" was not legally protected.[210] In 1966, however, a group of American string teachers enlisted Suzuki's support and gained substantial public funding to establish "Project Super," a major study carried out by Rochester and New York State universities. The Eastman School of Music at Rochester University became the first American music school to introduce a training programme for Suzuki teachers and Suzuki classes for children. At least twice a year Suzuki visited to give workshops. Soon other universities followed suit. In 1972 Suzuki teachers formed the Suzuki Association of the Americas to secure the quality of Suzuki teaching. Their efforts have led to well-functioning Suzuki programmes nearly everywhere in the United States. Suzuki received more invitations to teach than he could accept. When he did agree to come, he often met with a schedule that gave him no time to rest and gather his thoughts, with undisciplined children, and even with people who, under the pretence of asking for his autograph, tricked him into signing diplomas, endorsements of services or products and even contracts. After 1969 he gave up visiting the United States regularly and sent his teachers from the Matsumoto Institute instead.[211]

Why did the Suzuki Method attract so much interest among Americans? In some respects, America is not unlike Japan in its relationship with Western classical music. There is a similar consciousness of having introduced it from the outside, as is evident from a remark made by an American Suzuki teacher after visiting Europe: "The Japanese and Americans are studying European Music as foreigners!"[212] Americans could also readily identify with Suzuki's emphasis on music as a means to develop good people and citizens. They saw their belief in individualism and democracy reflected in his ideas. Even the stress he laid on the mother's role harmonized well with American values,[213] although American mothers could seldom match the heavy involvement of Japanese mothers. Other aspects of the method, such as the strict discipline, were less compatible and never gained ground. Rather than systematically conditioning their children to want to learn a musical instrument, American parents preferred to wait for a spontaneous (if casual) indication of interest from the child. Because they spent less time playing recordings to their children or supervising lessons, their children practised less. Since many believed in learning to read music as soon as possible, this was often introduced earlier than in Japan. American parents and teachers sometimes question Suzuki's belief that unceasing effort, daily practice with many repetitions and imitating recordings are the most reliable way to succeed. And Suzuki's emphasis on spiritual and character development is largely ignored.[214]

Despite its success, Suzuki's method also provoked criticism in America, most famously from Isaac Stern.[215] More benign reports talked about "fiddling legions," using the same kind of rhetoric that characterized reports of Japan's economic success. In fact, the method's elements of group lessons and massed performances received attention out of proportion to their importance within the method and many believed them to reflect the stereotypical "Japanese group mentality," although they have European antecedents, even the mass performances, which were pioneered by the Maidstone Movement in England earlier in the century.[216]

The Suzuki Method's association with armies of fiddlers mercilessly drilled to perform in unison and uniformity was particularly strong in Europe. Articles describing the Suzuki Method first appeared in journals in the 1960s, just when Japan's "economic miracle" began to attract attention – and fear. In 1966 Japan's GNP overtook Italy's, in 1967 the UK's, in 1968 France's and in 1969 Germany's. In the late 1960s numerous articles painted a sinister picture of hordes of Japanese businessmen, the successors of the samurai, conquering Europe, masterminded by "Japan Inc." and its most awesome representative, MITI. Books published at the time had titles like *The Japanese Challenge; Japan: The Planned Aggression; The Japanese Threat; The Japanese Industrial Challenge; Japan: Monster or Model; The Japanese Miracle* and *Peril: Stop the Japanese Now.* They portrayed Japan as a polluted monster, where economic animals, or robots, living in inhuman conditions single-mindedly pursued economic conquest.[217]

In such a climate, films showing hundreds of Suzuki children playing classical music with great precision and serious expressions fitted in only too well with the prevailing warlike images. A photograph in a book published in Germany in 1967 showed a mass of children, presumably at a Suzuki concert, with the caption, "Japanese children, who perform concertos by Vivaldi, Bach, or Mozart in hundreds with identical bowing and articulation." Another picture just below it shows a scene from the Yamaha piano factory in Hamamatsu, reinforcing the image of factory-like mass production projected by the children.[218] Criticism of "military-style" drilling was for many the obvious reaction.[219] Nevertheless, even Germans could not help being impressed by small children performing classical pieces previously regarded as too difficult for them. Germany's intellectual elite, however, still tends to cling to a sense of musical superiority. Music had an important place in the cultural nationalism of nineteenth-century Germany and in the self-perception of the middle classes.[220] In the education reform movement of the late nineteenth and early twentieth centuries, notions about the importance of education in the arts were linked with nationalist ideas about German dominance. Nowhere is this more vividly expressed than in Julius Langbehn's (1851–1907) *Rembrandt als Erzieher* (Rembrandt as Educator), published in 1890 and hugely popular at the time. He even uses the violin as metaphor for German political dominance: "The violin is the specifically German musical instrument; the German has invented it, cultivated it, and still leads on it as a master; he is called to play first violin also in the political world concert. *Primus inter pares.* The violin is an instrument of peace; [...]."[221] Post-war Germany, chastened by the horrors of the Third Reich, no longer made such extravagant claims. But a sense of superiority lingered when it came to music and was reinforced by the knowledge that Japan had taken Germany as a model for its modernization and that to many Japanese music students Germany remained the country of choice for study abroad.

Germans, and even more so Japanese, tend to invoke a "traditional" friendship between the two countries going back to the Meiji period, when German teachers helped the Japanese build up their own expertise in many areas, including music, and the Meiji government sent young Japanese to study in Germany. Cultural relations between Germany and Japan have usually been good. There was a particularly lively cultural exchange in the 1930s, and although neither side is too keen on recalling it, post-war relations were able to build on ties forged in those years. The 1960s and 1970s too saw a high level of cultural exchange and cooperation. The Japanese Culture Institute in Cologne was opened in 1969. This climate also explains a 1967 German publication about music in Japan, which might otherwise seem somewhat esoteric. Interestingly, the book hardly mentions Suzuki; instead readers are informed that music education for pre-school children is highly controversial in Japan and the point was driven home by translations of articles debating the American tour of Saitō Hideo's string orchestra to America in 1964.[222]

If German educators nevertheless wanted to learn about the Suzuki Method, they had virtually no opportunity to read about it in German. The German version of *Nurtured by Love* only appeared in 1975. But German music educators were discussing how to reform music teaching and wanted to learn more. Accordingly, the Association of German Music Schools (Verband deutscher Musikschulen, VdM) sent representatives to visit Suzuki in Japan in 1975. In 1976 the Association initiated a pilot project to establish whether the Suzuki Method could be successfully introduced in Germany.[223] The project ran from September 1976 to summer 1979, and the concluding report had many good things to say about the Suzuki Method; with some modifications and with further practical training for the teachers the method might well be introduced in German music schools. The report from the group working with violin teaching pointed to the similarities between Suzuki's overall educational aims and those of German music schools. In fact there was a general tendency to emphasize similarities between Suzuki's approach and that of music education in Germany.

Perhaps because German educators felt that the Suzuki Method did not offer anything radically new, the Association of German Music Schools as a whole did not take further steps to introduce it, despite the report's positive conclusions. Just as the Suzuki Method was becoming known, Egon Sassmannshaus was presenting his teaching methods at German and European conferences; his *Early Start on the Violin* was first published in German in 1976.[224] Like Suzuki, he advocated an early start and used familiar tunes, mainly folk songs. Unlike Suzuki, he introduced note-reading early, and given that one of the most widespread criticisms of the Suzuki Method was that children did not learn to read music from the start, this must have heightened Sassmanshaus's appeal.

While the public music school system treated the Suzuki Method with benign neglect, some individual schools and teachers persisted.[225] Several private teachers also applied themselves to serious study and propagation of the Suzuki method. The first German to study in Matsumoto for a substantial period of time was Kerstin Wartberg, who went there in 1980, soon after her graduation in violin performance and teaching from Cologne, and stayed until 1982.[226] Suzuki, who had spent some of his formative years in Germany, must have been thrilled to welcome a German student. He himself no longer spoke much German, but Waltraud of course did. Wartberg developed a close relationship with the couple and returned to Matsumoto for shorter periods several times between 1981 and 1987.[227] Soon she realized that Suzuki was at his best in practical lessons for a small audience. She made careful notes after lessons, often in the evenings. Her *Step By Step* series makes good use of what she learnt directly from Suzuki.[228] The series was published with Suzuki's permission. Several of the volumes are available in English, French and Spanish, but not in Japanese.

Following Wartberg's return, Marianne Migault Klingler, the daughter of Suzuki's teacher Karl Klingler and a psychologist and teacher, initiated the establishment of the German Suzuki Association and Institute in 1983. She had already established the Karl Klingler Foundation in 1979. The Association and the Institute have since been separated; the German Suzuki Association (DSG) supports Suzuki music education and the work of the German Suzuki Institute (DSI), which conducts teacher training.[229]

In 1987 Suzuki and his method came full circle. For the first time after 59 years he and his wife visited Berlin together for the eighth Suzuki Method International Conference in (West) Berlin with around 4,000 active participants from 32 countries. During the conference, Suzuki's former pupil Toyoda Kōji conducted Karl Klingler's Violin Concerto, with Rudolf Gähler (concertmaster of the Beethoven Orchestra in Bonn) and the Berlin Symphonic Orchestra.[230] Local papers praised the event, which attracted 3,000 participants from 30 countries, including 400 from Japan. But the Suzuki Method still leads a niche existence in Germany, where private initiative has to compete with a highly organized system of public music schools. German experts in music education, even those benign towards the Suzuki Method, trot out the usual stereotypes about Japan being too different for its approaches to be compatible with German ones.[231]

If the Suzuki Method has a hard time in Germany, it has fared rather better in neighbouring Denmark, one of the European countries where Suzuki's ideas were quicker to take root. Denmark has a similarly well-developed system of public music schools, but the country is smaller, and its inhabitants are, perhaps, more open to innovation. More importantly, the pioneers of the method in Denmark were respected representatives of the musical establishment. Tove Detreköy and her husband Béla had both been members of the Royal Danish Orchestra (Kongelige Kapel). Like several other European pioneers of the method, they first encountered it in America, when they moved to Bellingham in Washington State in 1967, where they soon discovered the existence of a Suzuki group taught by a Japanese teacher. Sceptical at first, Tove Detreköy became interested when she heard that the method was about more than proficiency on a musical instrument. The following year she had a chance to meet Suzuki himself and hear his pupils on their

American tour. Impressed by the musical performance and Suzuki's personality, she decided to visit him in Matsumoto. In summer 1971 she spent a few weeks at the institute, one of the first Europeans to do so.

In 1972 the couple returned to Denmark and Tove began teaching children according to Suzuki's principles, first in Aarhus, then in Copenhagen. Soon she and some of the children's parents were making plans to establish Suzuki camps and an institute, and in 1977, the Suzuki Institute was established in Copenhagen and a camp in Aarhus. Their initiatives received no kind of public support at first, and the parents agreed to pay much higher fees than it would cost them to send their children to the local authority music schools. In a country, where – unlike Japan – parents and students expect education to be free or at least cheap, this is dedication indeed. Despite practical and financial difficulties, the institute hosted national and international workshops. In 1981 Suzuki himself was present at a workshop in Helsingør (Elsinore) near Copenhagen, and in 1986 the institute's chamber orchestra, established and conducted by Béla Detreköy, even travelled to Japan at the invitation of Suzuki Shin'ichi and gave concerts in Tokyo, Nagoya, Matsumoto, Nagano, Kanazawa and Osaka.

Once more, it was the professional success of Suzuki children that helped the method gain attention and recognition. Today many, perhaps even most, of the leading string players in Denmark have had their early training at the Suzuki Institute, most famously Nikolaj Znaider (1975–). In 1998, after years of tireless work to gain financial support from private sponsors or public coffers and the respect of the musical establishment, the Danish Suzuki Institute finally secured a measure of financial support from public sources. Three years later the city of Copenhagen provided a house in Gentofte, a well-to-do suburb, just in time for the Danish Suzuki Institute to celebrate its twenty-fifth anniversary in 2002 in its own home as well as with the now traditional annual concert in Tivoli Gardens. By then it had 170 students, of whom 105 played the violin. In 1989 the Danish Suzuki Association was established to secure the training of Suzuki teachers, and cooperation with the other Nordic countries was initiated.

The Detreköys and Marianne Migault Klingler were among the driving forces behind the establishment of the European Suzuki Association (ESA) in 1980. Its aim was "to further Dr Shin'ichi Suzuki's approach to education in Europe."[232] Trained Suzuki teachers were already establishing the method in France, Britain, Belgium, the Netherlands, Sweden and Switzerland, besides Germany and Denmark. Some, like the Detreköys, had learnt about the method in America, such as Helen Brunner, a pioneer of the Method in Britain. Patricia McCarthy, having studied with John Kendall at Southern Illinois University, helped introduce the method in Cork in Ireland. Several teachers studied in Matsumoto for varying lengths of time; apart from Tove Detreköy the first Europeans in 1970–71 were Jean Middlemiss from the UK and Jeanne Janssens, sent by her music school in Belgium. Felicity Lipman became the first British teacher to graduate from the Talent Education Institute in Matsumoto in 1977.[233] Pioneers of the method in North America, such as John Kendall and Alfred Garson, who trained with the Project Super from 1966 and invited Suzuki to Canada the same year, regularly held workshops in Europe.

The European teachers learnt from the experience of their American colleagues. They realized that if they wanted to protect the integrity of Suzuki's method and stop poorly trained teachers giving the method a bad name, they had to establish a system of training and of authorizing qualified teachers. By 1980 the Suzuki Method had become fashionable enough for teachers to claim it for themselves without having received proper training. To regulate Suzuki teaching the ESA immediately devised a certification system. Today the ESA acts as an umbrella organization for 20 national associations.[234] It has been granted the sole rights to the Suzuki name in its area by the International Suzuki Association (ISA), of which it forms part, and only qualified teachers belonging to its member associations have the legal right to call themselves "Suzuki teachers." The ISA was founded in 1983 in Dallas, Texas as a coalition of Suzuki Associations throughout the world and comprising the Talent Education Research Institute (TERI) of Japan, the Asian Suzuki Association (ASA), the ESA (which also represents Africa and the Middle East), the Suzuki Association of the Americas and the Pan-Pacific Suzuki Association (PPSA).[235] Even earlier, in 1975, the first World Convention was held in Hawaii with more than 870 participants from America, Australia, Japan and other countries. The sixth world convention, held in Matsumoto in 1983, was attended by 1,500 students, parents and teachers from 22 countries.

In other parts of the world, interest in the Suzuki Method grew roughly at the same time as in Europe. In Asia, Korea in 1965 and Taiwan in 1971 were the first countries to form Suzuki Associations. The eleventh world convention was held in Seoul in 1993. In Australia the method was introduced in the early 1970s.[236] In Latin America it was first introduced to Argentina in 1967, and has since spread to other countries. Teacher training is often conducted by North American teachers. In 1986 Alfred Garson led a group of teachers and students on a tour sponsored by the ISA to Brazil, Uruguay and Argentina, where they performed and gave workshops in Rio de Janeiro, Porto Allegro, Montevideo, Buenos Aires and Cordoba.[237]

Meanwhile another South American country, Venezuela, was developing its own system of music education, which has gained worldwide fame as El Sistema. At first glance, apart from the focus on Western classical music, El Sistema seems to have little in common with the Suzuki Method. Despite efforts by individuals to apply Suzuki's ideas to teaching underprivileged children, most children who learn by the method come from middle-class families with time and money to spare for educational activities outside school. El Sistema, in contrast, explicitly addresses children from underprivileged backgrounds and aims to promote positive social change through making music at a high level.[238] Its founder, José Antonio Abreu (1939–), an economics professor and a politician as well as a musician, started teaching a small group of children and formed an orchestra in 1975. Within a few years the state began supporting the programme, which was renamed Sistema Nacional de Orquestas Juveniles e Infantiles de Venezuela (FESNOJIV) or National System of Children and Youth Orchestras of Venezuela. Students play in groups as soon as they start, and rehearse for several hours every day in 184 centres across the country.

Appearances to the contrary notwithstanding, El Sistema does owe some of its inspiration to Suzuki Shin'ichi.[239] Abreu had learnt about the Suzuki Method while a graduate student at the University of Michigan. In 1979, following a request from the Venezuelan government, Kobayashi Takeshi was invited to Venezuela as a cultural ambassador sponsored by the Japan Foundation. Kobayashi did not find the reception he received to his liking. As one of Suzuki's earliest pupils he was not himself trained by the Suzuki Method and such direct experience as he had of it was with teacher training. Now he found that, as well as training three ensembles at kindergarten, junior and semi-professional level, he was expected to teach 34 children flown into Caracas from an indigenous community 2,000 km away. There were not even enough instruments to go round. Kobayashi nevertheless persisted and had them playing the "Twinkle Variations" after two months. They performed at a concert where several Sistema orchestras played for an audience which included government members and representatives from the Japanese Embassy. Abreu hoped to open a Suzuki academy and Kobayashi was invited back the following year. But when he arrived the children he had taught previously had been flown home, and the Suzuki academy looked like a distant prospect. He taught for two weeks and left. A few months later, he learnt that Venezuelan newspapers were reporting his return in the summer for the opening of the academy and three months of teaching. "It was a bolt out of the blue and I was completely taken by surprise, and although I had got used to this way of doing things in Venezuela, I found the country too exhausting. Because I had nothing to do with these advertisements and announcements, I ultimately ignored these one-sided dealings and gave up going to Venezuela."[240] Suzuki Method or no, El Sistema went from strength to strength: in Venezuela 368,000 students and teachers are currently involved in the programme. Moreover it is finding imitators in other countries.

In December 2008 the Simon Bolivar Youth Orchestra of Venezuela visited Japan for the first time. Its performance in Tokyo was a resounding success. The same month saw the publication of a book about El Sistema by Yamada Shin'ichi, an arts manager and researcher who had travelled to Venezuela. The Suzuki community was quick to pick up the references to Suzuki, and the following year the Talent Education Research Institute's journal published a discussion between the book's author, the managing director of the Talent Research Institute Taida Hideya and the Venezuelan ambassador to Japan, Seiko Luis Ishikawa Kobayashi.[241] Taida stressed the affinities between the Suzuki Method, especially its humble beginnings, with El Sistema, and he and Ishikawa expressed the desire for collaboration: Japan could provide instruments and teachers, while Venezuela might help Japan to establish orchestras along Sistema lines.

Taida and other representatives of the Suzuki Method in Japan had good reason to consider new ventures. For while the method continued to spread internationally, in Japan it faced something of a crisis. Suzuki teacher training in Japan for a long time depended almost entirely on the personal teaching of Suzuki himself. As long as he personally had charge of the teacher training, he did not spell out a curriculum or explicitly discuss pedagogy, and students would graduate when Suzuki decided they were ready.[242] From around 1966 there was what Alfred Garson described as a "rush to Japan," and in the 1970s most of the students were from abroad and stayed between a month and a year or more.[243] Only when Suzuki reached his nineties were serious efforts made to give the training a permanent foundation, and in 1997 the institute was accredited by the government as a specialist training college called the International Academy of the Suzuki Method (upgraded to a professional training college in 2003).[244] Teacher training courses, including entry requirements, were formalized. There are now three courses; one of them can be taken in Tokyo as a supplement to conservatoire training. All include lectures about the Suzuki Method.[245] When Suzuki died in 1998, he was succeeded as the principal of his school by Toyoda Kōji, as Suzuki himself had wished. In 2010 Toyoda was succeeded by Tate Yukari, who played as a soloist during Suzuki's first American tour and later studied in Paris, where she pursued a distinguished career as a performer and teacher. It is surely significant and another sign of the Suzuki Method's globalization that both Toyoda and Tate have spent most of their careers abroad. Experience of working abroad also characterizes the careers of Taida Hideya and Nakajima Mineo, the president of the Talent Education Research Institute, both of whom were Suzuki's pupils in the 1940s before turning to international management and academia respectively. Perhaps what Matsumoto has lost by Suzuki's death it has gained through the globalization of the method he established. Certainly, the formalization of teacher training in Japan, while an obvious move to secure the future of the method, reflects international trends.

The biggest challenge to the Suzuki Method in Japan however, is not surviving without Suzuki – after all, the method's global success shows that his method can thrive without the man himself – but adapting to demographics and social change. Japan has one of the world's most rapidly ageing populations. Yamaha, Kawai, and other music chains

offering tuition have long adapted to the changing market and offer tailor-
made courses for adults. But Suzuki himself had lost interest in teaching
adults by the 1940s.[246] Other changes too have affected the Suzuki
Method adversely. As Taida, reflecting on Sistema and Suzuki, observed,
"We too, when we encountered the Suzuki Method 60 years ago, were
really poor. That the Suzuki Method could spread so spectacularly shows
that we were yearning for something. The children learning at the time
were unbelievably happy. When we become too affluent, there is too
much to choose from, in a way it is sad."[247] This is of course no different
from the situation in other affluent societies.

Indeed, the dissemination of the Suzuki Method worldwide and the
ways its development abroad has influenced practices back in Japan is a
prime example of how global currents can operate. Above all, it proves
wrong those critics who claim that a "Japanese" method cannot work in
other countries. The method has proved sufficiently open to be adapted
to a wide range of local circumstances. Suzuki himself encouraged the
teachers he trained to develop their own ideas and adapt his principles to
the situations they worked in.[248] Anyway, virtually all the individual
elements of the method have European antecedents, and many of his
ideas are similar to those of contemporary educational reformers,
particularly Maria Montessori. The revolutionary part is the way Suzuki
combined and applied the elements.[249] This does not prevent either
enthusiasts or critics, whether Japanese or Western, from insisting on the
method's "Japaneseness" and making much of the fact that Suzuki
mentions Zen among his formative influences. Some authors even argue
that Western proponents of Suzuki's ideas have not fully understood
Suzuki and cannot fully appreciate the depths of his philosophy; they
then claim to enlighten their readers, as often as not by citing popular
Western literature on Zen or their experiences in Japan.[250] Conversely
and ironically, Mochizuki Kenji, contemplating the success of the method
in America, claimed that the method was better understood there than in
Japan.[251] No doubt, the method has been enthusiastically received in
many countries because it is based on sound pedagogical principles
which recent research tends to support, including the idea that it is
continuous practice rather than inborn genius which brings people to the
top of their profession, whether in music or anything else. This was
perhaps the biggest challenge Suzuki presented his Western audiences

with. His fiddlers demonstrated the truth of his claim that their astounding achievement was not due to inborn talent, but a result of the right environment and good teaching. The prevailing belief in the early twentieth century was – and to a large extent still is – that musical talent is something inborn or bestowed by God or, in Paganini's case, by the Devil. Romantic notions of genius have persisted despite developments in teaching, and despite research proving that a supportive environment and intensive practice are the most crucial factors in the making of any expert.[252]

In Japan, Suzuki's claim harmonized with the existing belief that people can overcome any obstacle and achieve great things if they put in enough effort. Pre-war school textbooks told the story of Noguchi Hideyo (1876–1928), the peasant boy who, thanks to his determination and his mother's dedication to his upbringing, overcame physical handicap and poverty and became a world-class scientist.[253] To the Japanese, Suzuki's pupils only proved what they already believed: anybody can achieve anything if only they are taught well and work hard enough, a belief shared in other Asian countries.[254] In the best cases this belief helps children to overcome difficulties and experience the joy of achieving something they thought they could never do. In the worst cases, children suffer as misguided teachers or parents relentlessly work to drill something into them and fail, or succeed only at a high cost. Although this is not unheard of in Western countries, it seems to happen more often in Japan. It was not what Suzuki intended, but it fuelled Western stereotyping of the method as mindless drilling. Not that this type of criticism is limited to Western observers. The music critic Nomura Kōichi spoke favourably of Suzuki himself (his colleague of the 1930s), but he roundly condemned Suzuki assistants, whom he saw as wanting to train musical specialists despite Suzuki's emphasis on educating rounded human beings.[255]

Suzuki Shin'ichi, meanwhile, clearly rose above stereotypical distinctions between "the East" and "the West." To Tove Detreköy, who met him in America, Japan and Denmark, he appeared "Japanese" in Denmark, but seemed "Western" in Japan. Kerstin Wartberg describes him as open, spontaneous, lively and full of humour and in no way conforming to the stereotypical image of the Japanese.[256]

Nakajima Mineo, too, sees him as a man in a class of his own; to him he is an "uncrowned king," representing the free spirit of the people (*min*), untainted by officialdom (*kan*): "After his return from Berlin, he founded our country's first string quartet and contributed largely to the proliferation of Western music in the Shōwa era. He never joined the formalized academism that prevailed in the field of music. In the confusion of the post-war years he founded the Matsumoto Music School in Matsumoto and achieved the formation of the Talent Education Research Association, but this was essentially a private musical venture, a sort of *shijuku*." And he summarizes Suzuki's achievement succinctly: "Of course, experiments with early education had antecedents in both East and West, but by redeveloping a method of mastery in Japan's favourable climate and by his capacity to organize a worldwide educational and artistic movement, Suzuki's Talent Education movement has achieved miraculous success."[257]

## 11. The Legend from Japan: Midori

Even as Suzuki's pedagogy challenged deep-seated Western notions of inborn genius by, as it were, mass-producing wunderkinder, a Japanese child emerged as "an icon of the child prodigy"[258] whose name was mentioned in conjunction with Heifetz and Menuhin.[259] Midori did not learn with the Suzuki Method, nor did her mother who taught her and whose methods could not have been more different from Suzuki's. But Suzuki and Midori have in common that their reputation in Japan was decisively influenced by their fame in the West, starting with America. Midori's rise to fame began with her sensational Carnegie Hall debut under Zubin Mehta in December 1982 at the age of 11. Unknown in Japan at the time, Midori had emigrated to New York with her mother earlier that year and has not lived in Japan since. Even her stage name, like the name "Suzuki Method," was coined abroad; in Japan she continues to be known as Gotō Midori.

Midori was born in Moriguchi, a suburb of Osaka, on 25 October 1971. Her mother Setsu had been pressurized by her family to marry Midori's father Gotō Teruo, an engineer who worked for a public office. Like many a typical "salaryman" (a word coined in Japan which has found its way into the *Oxford Dictionary*), he spent long hours at work and came home to slump in front of the television, leaving everything to do with the home and his child's education to his wife. But Setsu was an unusual salaryman's wife (See Part 3 Chapter 2); she continued to perform and teach. Setsu originally wanted the three-year-old Midori to learn the piano, but Midori seemed much keener on her mother's violin. So Setsu made the three-year-old kneel in front of her in Japanese-style and told her that learning the violin would be tough. Then she began to teach her with a vengeance; Midori quickly realized that the violin was not just another toy. "She got angry with me all the time; yes, I was afraid; she hit me or kicked me away; those are my most unpleasant memories," Midori recalls.[260] Almost from the start Setsu made her study music that would challenge even an advanced violinist.

Setsu introduced Midori to her own former teachers, to Tōgi Yūji and his wife Sachi and to her mentor Sumi Saburō.[261] They sometimes allowed Midori to perform in their student recitals. Midori played in public for the first time in March 1976 at the age of four, performing Dancla's Air Varié No. 6 in Osaka at a student recital organized by Tōgi. The following year she performed the third movement of de Bériot's Violin Concerto No 9; she had not started primary school, and already she had the technique of an advanced teenager. By her first year in primary school she was studying Paganini, and in her fourth year she performed the first movement of his Concerto No. 1 at a recital organized by Sumi Saburō. Her mother began to feel that Midori needed a better teacher. But could such a teacher be found in Japan? Sumi, Japan's most eminent teacher at the time, did not think so.

Setsu's first thought was France; through colleagues she gained an introduction to Gabriel Bouillon, a professor at the conservatoire in Paris, whom she had heard perform in Japan and whose Japanese students in Paris had included Ishii Shizuko and Tanaka Chikashi. Setsu took the eight-year-old Midori to Paris to play for him. He agreed to teach Midori, but Setsu disliked his attitude and nothing came of it. About a year later, one of Tōgi's pupils now studying at Juilliard suggested taking a tape of a performance by Midori to New York. The recording duly made, Midori forgot all about it, and months passed; finally, in spring 1981, the response came: Dorothy DeLay wanted to meet Midori at the festival in Aspen that summer. Dorothy DeLay? The name was new to Setsu. In December 1998 DeLay would be awarded the Order of the Sacred Treasure with Gold Rays and Neck Ribbon by the Japanese government in acknowledgement of the many Japanese artists she had trained at

Juilliard and at regular master classes in Japan. In 1981, however, she was still virtually unknown there. She had, however, worked with Ivan Galamian, and Galamian's fame as a teacher *had* reached Japan and Gotō Setsu's ears. So, with a mixture of hope and trepidation, mother and daughter prepared for another trip abroad.

They spent nine weeks in Aspen, and Midori caused a sensation. Harada Kōichirō, the original first violinist of the Tokyo Quartet, witnessed the audition: "This nine-year-old bespectacled girl from Japan ambled along and played Bach's Chaconne and Paganini's Caprice No. 17 fantastically. Everybody was dumbfounded. Her technique was fantastic. Neither DeLay nor anyone else knew Midori until then. They were simply astonished. After that, Aspen was in uproar."[262] Meanwhile Setsu waited outside with rising trepidation as the scheduled 15 minutes stretched to 30 and 40. When she first came face-to-face with Dorothy DeLay, her first thought was, "she's our teacher." Her charisma, her courtesy, her warmth and the way her face expressed the English words Setsu had trouble understanding won Setsu's admiration from the start. DeLay showered Midori's playing with praise and promised to do all she could so Midori could study with her in New York.

As soon as the Gotōs returned to Japan, Setsu began to prepare for their move. That Setsu's husband and her parents violently opposed her plans did not deter her – on the contrary. Her marriage had gone from bad to worse; the couple quarrelled constantly, and Midori had to witness her mother being hit by her drunken father. The education of her daughter gave Gotō Setsu the chance to escape from her parents, her husband, and from the constraints of Japanese society in general. In New York it would be up to her to determine the shape of their new life.

On 11 February 1982, the legendary anniversary of the founding of the Japanese empire and a national holiday, mother and daughter left Japan. In future, Japan would be for Midori a country she visited regularly but no longer her home. In the 1980s an increasing number of Japanese and other East Asian music students flocked to America in the hope of superior teachers and increased performing opportunities. Many families sacrificed economic security and social status for the sake of their musical children.[263] Gotō Setsu too made sacrifices, but she had made her decision as much for her own sake as for Midori's.

A time filled with new experiences began for Midori. Once formally accepted into the Juilliard's Pre-College Division, she took Saturday classes in general musicianship and theory. From Monday to Friday, following DeLay's recommendation, she attended the private Professional Children's School. Unlike DeLay's other students, who were taught by her assistants for much of the time, Midori received at least one lesson a week from her personally. After all, Midori had an outstanding personal teacher in her mother, as her flawless technique proved. Setsu, meanwhile, must have learnt at least as much from DeLay as Midori herself. She asked the questions she thought Midori needed answering. When DeLay recommended listening to recordings of different artists and studying the lives and times of composers, Setsu was the one who went to the New York Public Library for the Performing Arts in the Lincoln Center to research and bring home books and records, which they studied together.[264] She also helped Midori with her school work. Thus, far from home, living alone in cramped quarters in a strange city whose language they yet had to master, mother and daughter developed an ever closer relationship that ultimately became unhealthy for both of them. As DeLay later described it, "It was almost as if they were one person. How much of the desire to play came from Midori and how much of it came from her mother I don't even know."[265]

So what could DeLay teach Midori, whose playing already seemed perfect to those who heard her? Critics have claimed that DeLay did not really teach at all; that her lessons were too lax and haphazard; that her star pupils already knew how to play when they came to her. They only kept coming because of her power with agents and potential employers. But for every Itzhak Perlman, Nadia Salerno-Sonnenberg, Nigel Kennedy, Shlomo Mintz or Gil Shaham, there are many less famous students who benefited equally or more from her teaching. They did not become soloists, but they played in orchestras and chamber ensembles, taught music, or organized musical events. Some even left music altogether, having realized it was not for them. Talents would not have continued to flock to her studio, had she not had more to offer than a few professional contacts. Those who praise her unanimously point out the same strengths of her teaching: her ability to size up a student – and their parent(s) – and to meet them where they were at, her encouraging, straightforward approach, her ability to make students think for themselves and her concern for the student as a person and for all aspects of performing, right down to details like dress.

These qualities made DeLay an ideal teacher for Midori. DeLay recognized Gotō Setsu's competence and let her continue the good work as her unofficial teaching assistant. She accepted Setsu's insistence that Midori cover a lot of repertoire; presumably she agreed with Setsu and enjoyed the proposition. She expanded the horizons of Midori and Setsu beyond anything either of them could have imagined. In Japan, the "catch-up" mentality encourages an approach focusing on technique and imitating excellent models. Under DeLay's guidance, Midori learnt to reflect and to explore; to hear different interpretations and make up her own mind about them, to study a composer's life and the historical background of a piece. Perhaps even more importantly, DeLay acted as a mother figure as well as a teacher. She gave Midori something that she seldom if at all got from her own mother: she made her feel comfortable and she encouraged her and praised her. She also began to build up Midori's career from the start, cautiously, but systematically. She invited a television crew to one of Midori's first lessons. A few months later, she introduced Midori to Zubin Mehta and Isaac Stern, both of whom would play a vital role in Midori's development.

Mehta was so impressed that he planned for Midori's debut with the New York Philharmonic Orchestra at the end of the year; she was to play the first movement of Paganini's Concerto No. 1 with the cadenza by Emile Sauret. On 30 December 1982 he surprised his audience with a special guest.[266] Midori caused a small sensation. The debut also made "Midori" her stage name. Her mother told her that a woman's surname could change while her first name would remain the same, but Gotō Setsu had other reasons. Midori's father came to New York for his Christmas holidays and demanded that his wife and daughter return home with him. The couple quarrelled, Teruo had another of his drunken rages, and Setsu fled with her daughter and moved into a hotel on the day of Midori's first concert. No wonder one of her unwitting critics lamented the absence of "unmarked innocence" in Midori's playing.[267]

After her New York debut Midori performed in America and abroad as a soloist with leading orchestras and conductors, occasionally at first, then with increasing frequency. In 1985 she performed Mozart's Violin Concerto in A major with the European Community Orchestra under Leonard Bernstein and Ōue Eiji as the soloist on the "Hiroshima Peace Tour," organized by the manager Sano Mitsunori. The tour took her to several European capitals and to Hiroshima. Midori had not been in Japan since 1982. Travelling with the legendary Bernstein, who was constantly surrounded by the press and various admirers, was a novelty and contributed to her own growing fame.

Midori's real moment of fame however, came at another performance under Bernstein a year later. The story of Midori's famous debut in Tanglewood has been told many times; it even made the front page of the *New York Times* on 28 July 1986 under the headline "Girl, 14, Conquered Tanglewood With Three Violins." While playing Bernstein's Serenade, Midori snapped an E-string – in itself not an uncommon occurrence on a hot and humid summer evening. Midori did what soloists usually do when this happens: she borrowed the concertmaster's violin and played on. But not for long; again the E-string broke, and again Midori borrowed an instrument from the concertmaster, who was now playing on the associate concertmaster's violin. On this third violin, which like the second was larger than her own, Midori completed her performance. The audience went wild. On her return to New York Midori was pursued by the press. She herself could not see what the fuss was about, having acted in the conventional way. Nevertheless such presence of mind and power of concentration in a teenager are impressive. Clearly the qualities that distinguish a top-class violinist from the crowd are not merely musical.

Midori's legendary performance at Tanglewood came just in time for her "official"[268] debut in Japan, when she was to play the Mendelssohn Concerto with the St. Louis Symphony Orchestra under Leonard Slatkin in Osaka and Tokyo. Triumph abroad is the best advertisement for Japanese artists returning to perform in their native land. Mochizuki Kenji (who had made Suzuki Shin'ichi's achievements known in America) wrote a most dramatic account of the Tanglewood story for the leading music magazine *Ongaku no tomo* (Friend of Music), which had previously reported her successes in America, comparing her early debut to those of Heifetz, Menuhin, Elman and Zukerman.[269] Once Midori herself arrived, she and her mother were beleaguered by journalists, and Midori reports that she eventually became very quiet, giving rise to speculations that she had forgotten her Japanese. The following year, summer 1987, she returned to Japan for what the reporter in *Ongaku no tomo* described as her "real" debut, giving recitals.[270] Having interviewed her in New York, the reporter told his readers that she was outspoken like an American, that she thought in English rather than in Japanese and felt she needed more than a couple of days in Japan to regain her confidence speaking Japanese. The Japanese, meanwhile, celebrated the "girl prodigy" and longed to know how one of their own had managed to achieve international fame at such a tender age. Her mother Setsu was asked to write a book, and in July 1987 *Ame no uta* (Rain Song) her account of her and Midori's life together was published (see Part 3 Chapter 2). Still, the Japanese did not quite know what to make of Midori. In her book, Setsu expresses disappointment that the reviews in 1987 hardly mentioned the fact that her daughter was Japanese and the hard work she put in to overcome this perceived disadvantage.[271] The *New York Times* summed it up: "In Japan, Midori Is a New Yorker."[272] That does not quite fit either, however. Midori's mother was obviously Japanese, even if her behaviour in leaving her husband flew in the face of Japanese expectations. Midori herself looked and spoke Japanese and was Japanese in the eyes of the world. Japanese journalists continued to feed their readers with details about her life in New York and her international triumphs and to comment on her Japanese language skills. In 1988 a lengthy portrait appeared in *AERA*, a general news magazine, reflecting the interest in Midori outside musical circles.[273] The overall theme was the former prodigy facing the challenges of approaching adulthood, and the author devoted more space to Midori's personal difficulties than to her musical career, which was taking her all over America and Europe as well as to Japan and East Asia.

Certainly, by this time Midori's personal life was running rather less smoothly than her music, and not just because of the usual difficulties experienced by prodigies as they face the transition to adulthood.[274] Setsu's book of 1987 reads a little like a farewell to their life together. For years their relationship seemed like several rolled into one: mother and daughter, sisters or friends, teacher and pupil, as well as manager and artist, the violin tightening the bond between them. Now, however, not only was Midori growing up and becoming more independent, her mother too was changing; she had entered a new relationship.

Among the Japanese students Midori and her mother met soon after their arrival in America was a young man named Kaneshiro Makoto. Born in 1958, he grew up in Takasaki, north-west of Tokyo. In 1979 he moved to New York to study with DeLay, and after graduating from Juilliard he became her assistant. He married a Japanese fellow student at Juilliard, and the couple sometimes met the Gotōs socially.[275] In 1986 Kaneshiro came to Tanglewood without his wife, and Midori noticed that he and her mother were spending a lot of time together. In fact everybody noticed. Back in New York, the affair soon became an open secret. Gotō Setsu had divorced her husband soon after their dramatic row on the eve of Midori's New York debut, but Kaneshiro was still married. He considered giving up teaching and asked DeLay for advice. She responded by replacing him with one of the many keen aspirants for teaching posts. Without a job Kaneshiro lost his visa status and had to leave the country. The tensions accompanied Midori on her tour to Japan in 1987. Not only did the members of the Juilliard orchestra gossip, but Setsu's family knew of the relationship and violently opposed it. As Midori struggled through her engagements at Aspen, Tanglewood and elsewhere, she decided that she would not return to Juilliard for the new term.

The stir caused by her mother's affair with DeLay's teaching assistant may well have been the last straw, but they were part of a larger issue. From the start, her mother and DeLay had formed a close relationship. Setsu, as well as being the mother of her star pupil, was in effect her assistant teacher. Together they engineered Midori's career. When Midori had an engagement, DeLay decided which work would show off her pupils most effectively – Paganini's Concerto No. 1 as often as not. Midori, meanwhile, had never got used to the competitive and oppressive atmosphere of the Juilliard School. She had few friends there, and was missing more and more Saturday classes as a result of her performance engagements.[276] To break free from the prodigy aura Midori had to free herself from the control of both her mother and her teacher, however excruciating the separation. DeLay made a last-ditch attempt to get her back by confronting her with some recent negative reviews and warning her that her career would soon come to an end.[277] But thanks to DeLay, Midori was already a household name and had artistic management and other vital contacts in the music world. Despite DeLay's gloomy prophecy, her career continued from strength to strength, including an exclusive recording contract with Sony in 1988 and her official Carnegie debut at a subscription concert in 1989.

The real question was how she could continue to develop as an artist; 15 years old is very young to do without a regular teacher. Here again, Midori's previous contacts served her well: Isaac Stern became a regular mentor as well as a father figure; her new pianist Robert McDonald, nearly 20 years her senior and an experienced accompanist, guided her through unfamiliar pieces of the violin and piano duo repertoire, until she matured into an equal partner who could give him new insights.[278] Even Kaneshiro, with whom she had an uneasy relationship, provided invaluable guidance in matters of musical interpretation. He let her use his extensive record collection and urged her to attend more and more varied concert performances.[279]

The emotional fallout was another matter. More than the scandal caused by her mother's relationship with Kaneshiro, the loss of her place as the centre of her mother's life must have affected Midori. The author of the 1988 report in *AERA* remarked on the way Midori was influenced by American individualism, which he contrasted with the Japanese "family-ism," the tendency to regard the family as an indivisible, harmonious unit. The relationship between Midori and her mother, however, exhibits typically Japanese traits that – from the outside at least – make it look like a textbook case of what a Japanese psychiatrist and psychotherapist has called the "mother–child capsule."[280] The mother, unhappy in her marriage with a man who spends most of his time at work and without a satisfying career of her own, invests all her love and ambitions in her child to the point of over-identifying with her child's achievements. Mother and daughter in particular may end up in a close relationship the Japanese have labelled "identical twin parent–child," which excludes the father completely. In such a situation the child can become over-sensitive to her mother's loneliness and dependence on her and end up suffering from "low self-esteem, self-negation and self-hate."[281] She may never learn to become independent.

The difference between Setsu and her contemporaries in the same position is that she took the highly unusual step of leaving her husband, preferring to face an uncertain future rather than tolerating the status quo for the sake of material security. The struggle to survive in an alien environment drew mother and daughter even closer together. It also made them entirely dependent on Midori's success as a violinist. Ultimately, while Setsu's and Midori's escape to America strengthened the "mother–child capsule," it simultaneously brought them into an environment where different social values and expectations enabled them to break free. It is a tribute to both women's strength that they succeeded.

For Midori, Setsu's relationship with Kaneshiro reduced the burden imposed on her by her mother's sacrifices, excessive control and over-protection. Instead of feeling guilty of "abandoning" her mother, Midori could seek independence, knowing that her mother had a new focus in life. At the same time she lost her most important source of support. In July 1988 Setsu gave birth to a son whom, Midori knew, she had long yearned for.[282] Thrilled as Midori was to have a baby brother, the birth of Ryū nevertheless must have heightened her own sense of bereavement. For a while her mother continued to accompany her on tours, but increasingly Midori was touring alone, a teenager still, but leading the life of an independent adult and the difficult life of a travelling soloist at that.

In the midst of her busy career and intense personal pressures, Midori started a new project: she wanted to bring music to underprivileged children. Of course many renowned musicians engage in charity work. But few start as early as Midori, who at 20 was barely out of childhood herself. In 1992 she established Midori and Friends with the aim of bringing music to underprivileged school children. Midori's fame worked in her favour: the story of her "conquest" of Tanglewood with three violins had made it into American school textbooks, and children knew her name. Indeed Midori started by visiting the schools from which children had written to her. Her Asian background also worked to her advantage: she provided an excellent role model to the children from multi-ethnic backgrounds. Midori know what it was like to arrive in a strange country with little money, having to learn a new language and to make new friends. The venture proved a success: by 2001 it employed 14 artist-teachers and several ensembles that worked regularly in 11 New York schools at an annual cost of $800,000 and had reached more than 100,000 students.[283] Midori continued to be its driving force; she and other top class performers gave up time they could have spent earning money to give free talks and recitals in schools.[284] The organization had a branch in Japan, and in the early years both branches relied heavily on donations from Japan.[285] In 2002, the Tokyo branch office became independent as "Music Sharing," with its own projects reflecting the different needs. As Midori observed, "There is no need in Japan for an extensive instrumental program like the one in New York because most Japanese children play instruments anyway." But she saw a need to counteract "the 'paper-and-pen' aspects of music education in Japan, which is mostly by rote and offers insufficient exposure to live music."[286]

Meanwhile, her mother had begun to teach Ryū the violin. Setsu was quite as strict with Ryū as with Midori, and no doubt her experience made her even more effective. By 1994 she was preparing the six-year-old for his debut; he was to perform Paganini's Concerto No. 1 at the Pacific Music Festival in Japan in 1995. It may well be more than a coincidence that Midori's personal difficulties came to a head just at this time. For years now, she had been coping with pressures enough to wear down a stronger and more mature person. In summer 1994 she could cope no longer. The self-control with which she had achieved so much got completely out of hand; she was not eating, she had come to depend on tranquilizers, and she suffered from bouts of depression. Already at the time of her break with DeLay and Juilliard, she had followed Zukerman's advice and sought the help of a psychotherapist. "It helped," she brightly told her Japanese interviewer in 1988.[287] It did not, however, resolve her fundamental problems. Now she agreed to see a psychiatrist, who judged her to be an emergency case. She was hospitalized at the Cornell Medical Center at White Plains (New York). Midori's mother has maintained that her daughter's hospitalization was unnecessary.[288] This reflects the approach of many Japanese (and not only Japanese) to mental illness, which is to deny it. Like Midori's interviewer in 1988, who took care to explain to his readers that consulting psychologists was common in America with its rampant individualism, they tend to believe that the closeness of family ties in Japan renders such measures unnecessary. Midori's own account suggests that her condition, characterized by anorexia, depression and dependency on tranquilizers may well have been life-threatening and nothing less than the hospital treatment she received could have saved her.[289] She remained in hospital for several months, and for the first two months she did not touch her violin. The public was informed that her engagements for the 1994–95 season were cancelled while she recovered from "digestive" disorders, and the newspapers speculated about her suffering the common plight of prodigies faced with growing up.[290] Midori resumed performing in January 1995, but for the next few years she was in and out of hospital between concert engagements.

What eventually helped her overcome her recurrent illness was the discovery of a new interest in life. In 1995 she began to study at the Gallatin School of New York University. Although this added to the pressures she faced and met opposition from family and friends, it represented another important choice about her life, and the chance to immerse herself in a variety of new subjects gave her enormous personal satisfaction. In 2000 she received her Bachelor of Arts in psychology and gender studies, and immediately enrolled on an M.A. course in psychology, from which she graduated in 2005. She even (briefly) considered giving up the violin for a career in clinical psychology, but in the end she decided to stick with what she did best, while pursuing other interests on the side. Having made this conscious choice empowered her to proceed with more discernment and less regard for the opinions of others.[291] Even the critics noticed the difference. Although some compared her performances unfavourably with those of her early career, one (Schwarz) remarked as early as 1998 that Midori's performance had begun to show "a depth many had found wanting."[292]

In recent years Midori has combined a busy concert schedule with teaching and outreach activities.[293] In 2004 she was appointed to the Jascha Heifetz Chair in Violin at the University of Southern California's Thornton School of Music. Others in her position might have continued as before, finding time for their students only when there is a lull in their schedule. Not so Midori, who reportedly devotes considerable time and energy to her new job.[294] She has since become head of strings and has initiated a number of outreach and community engagement programmes locally and further afield. In 2007 the UN designated her as a Messenger of Peace.

Midori's ties to Japan have been strengthened through her outreach initiatives, establishing her as a regular presence there since the introduction of her Music Sharing programme in 1992. In 2008 *Ongaku no tomo* devoted a special section of its March issue to her, which included an interview, a biography and a summary of her achievements since 1982, a review of her discography and a description of her latest International Community Engagement Programme, which at the end of the previous year had taken her to Cambodia, together with two Japanese musicians and the German-born violinist Korbinian Altenberger.[295]

Speculations about her Japaneseness or otherwise, which had preoccupied Japanese observers in the 1980s, were absent in the 2008 feature. Perhaps her international stature has placed her beyond them.

# 12. Costs and Corruption: The Kanda Scandal and the State of Classical Music in Japan

In 1981 Unno Yoshio had reached a high point in his career. Born in 1936 as the son of a violinist with the NHK orchestra and of a pianist, he received his first violin lessons from his father (who had studied with Schifferblatt) at the age of four. He then studied with Sumi Saburō and, after his graduation from Aoyama Gakuin High School, with Uzuka Tatsuo at Geidai. Soon he was rumoured to play better than his teachers. A group of older students asked him to play first violin in a string quartet with them. In 1958 he made his Tokyo debut, performing the Tchaikovsky Violin Concerto with the NHK Orchestra, which he joined immediately after graduating. In 1959, when he was only 23, he became the orchestra's principal concertmaster and soloist. In this role he travelled abroad with the orchestra on its first world tour in 1960. Encouraged by Isaac Stern, he resigned to embark on a solo career in 1969. The following year he started teaching at his alma mater. His own teacher Uzuka Tatsuo wanted him to become his successor. Appointed assistant professor in 1972, he became a full professor in 1975 when he was only 39.

After Etō Toshiya, Unno was the next violinist to gain fame as a performer both abroad and in Japan. Unno and Etō are the only two Japanese violinists featured in Samuel Applebaum's series of books entitled *The Way They Play.* Applebaum's co-author Henry Roth talked to Unno for five hours in Tokyo in the late 1970s. Unno told him that since resigning from the NHK Orchestra he played 50 to 60 concerts a year and had performed in more than 80 cities in 27 countries.[296] As a professor at Geidai he taught 30 students per week, as well as 10 private students. In contrast to Etō, Unno was essentially home-grown, although he did study with Michel Schwalbé, concertmaster of the Berlin Philharmonic Orchestra, for a few months in 1963 and with Szigeti in Switzerland in 1964. Asked, "As an Oriental, do you feel you have encountered any special problems in becoming attuned to the more subtle, intimate nuances of the Western musical aesthetic?" Unno answered with a clear "no": "(...) both of my parents were trained in Western musical traditions, and I was exposed to these traditions at an early age." Roth left him "in the realization that the art of violin playing in the Orient had indeed come of age!"[297]

Invited to judge in several leading international competitions, Unno sat on the jury of the Queen Elisabeth Competition in 1980. That year Horigome Yuzuko became the first Japanese to win the first prize, while two more Japanese, Shimizu Takashi and Tsukahara Ruriko, came third and fourth – a mark of Japan's high international standing in the violin world. In summer 1981, Unno travelled to Europe to judge at the eighth Wieniawski Competition in Poznan and at the first Joachim International Violin Competition in Burgenland in Austria. The *Asahi* newspaper reported the appointments as the latest evidence of Unno's international standing.[298] The Wieniawski competition that year represented another Japanese triumph with the prizes virtually monopolized by Japanese: Urushihara Keiko at 18 was not only the first Japanese but also the youngest ever winner of the competition, while the second, fourth, fifth and sixth places were also won by Japanese, three of whom, like Urushihara, counted Unno among their teachers.[299]

A few months later the *Asahi* had a different story to tell. "Unno Yoshio Arrested for Taking Bribes," screamed the headline on 8 December, while a picture taken that morning showed him sitting in a car with his eyes closed and a pained expression.[300] What the newspaper described as the "Geidai Master Violin Affair," later variously dubbed the "Geidai Affair," or the "Bribery Affair," had begun a few days earlier, when it transpired that several string instruments purchased by Geidai, including a violin certified as a Guadagnini, had come with fake certificates. On 3 December the dean of the music faculty called an extraordinary faculty meeting to discuss the way the university purchased instruments for use by students at important concerts or competitions. Instruments, reported the *Asahi*, were tested by ten faculty members, who went by the sound rather than the valuation certificate. The newspaper cited Desmond Hill of the famous firm W.E. Hill & Sons in London, who commented that this was extraordinary to European experts, who would always check the certificate first.[301] The University had cancelled the purchase of several string instruments from a dealer named Kanda Yūkō, the owner of Kanda and Company. But the professors insisted that the Guadagnini was the real thing, despite its forged certificate, a claim that lead to derisive comments in the press about the "ear of Geidai," which even made their way into the German weekly magazine *Der Spiegel*.[302] Kanda had already been arrested on 26 November for forging valuation certificates. At the same time, Nakamura Kōtaro of the music college Ongaku Gakuin had been arrested for insurance fraud with fake certificates.

Kanda's dubious business practices were subsequently exposed in the press: fraud, illegal imports of foreign violins, involving entire foreign orchestras selling their second-best instruments during Japan tours, often to Kanda.[303] The international dimension of the scandal was in fact much greater than the reporting in the *Asahi* suggests, and outside Japan it was Kanda's rather than Unno's dealings that preoccupied the media.[304] Violin fraud is a tradition that reaches back at least into the nineteenth century, when the demand for old violins, especially old Italian ones by Stradivari, Guarneri and others began to vastly exceed the supply. As with other antiques and works of art, where there is a demand it will be catered to, as the music critic Yoshida Hidekazu pointed out when he commented on the case, but not everything supplied will be the genuine article.[305] In the violin world, buyers have come to rely on certificates of authenticity produced by experts from reputable firms such as W.E. Hill & Sons of London or Wurlitzer Inc. of New York to ensure that what they are paying for is not a cheap instrument that has been tampered with to appear older than it is and given a fake label. Alarm bells should therefore have rung well before they did, when two unnamed Japanese dealers bid up to £700 for a set of wooden printing blocks imprinted with good imitations of famous makers' labels – in other words, a "forger's kit" – at Sotheby's in London in 1978. What use the kit had been put to soon became clear when the insurance company that dealt with the claim from Ongaku Gakuin discovered that the instruments said to have been stolen from the college had been insured well above their real worth and their appraisal certificates had been forged. Interpol became involved and their investigations led to another dealer, Adolph H. Primavera in Philadelphia, who had been corresponding with a Tokyo dealer. A Belgian dealer was also discovered to be using forged certificates.[306] The *Strad* published a series on violin fraud in 1982 in which reference was made to a "number of court cases" and "several leading Japanese dealers" accused of forging certificates, and of offering bribes to music professors, but no names were named. The second part concluded by stating, "The Japanese press is interested in finding out if this is a world wide practice; under most circumstances in Japan the practice of giving a commission is illegal."[307]

Indeed, although Unno was initially suspected of having helped Kanda forge certificates in English, it was the question of commissions that aroused the most controversy, because, unlike forgery, which is clearly a crime, the legal situation regarding commissions was complicated. Geidai is a national university and its professors are civil servants who by law are prohibited from accepting money or gifts in return for services rendered as part of their office.

The Guadagnini with the false certificates had been purchased from Kanda in 1979, and Unno was suspected of having persuaded his colleagues to select it after having received a bow valued at 800,000 yen from Kanda as commission and in anticipation of future deals. Unno's endorsement, it was claimed, was decisive in the university's decision to buy, and his arrest highlighted the problematic relationship between professors and instrument dealers. More than that, Unno had allegedly taken cash bribes on other occasions and persuaded several of his students to buy instruments from Kanda.[308]

The arrest of a violinist described by the *Asahi* in its report as "an international violinist who represents our country" and professor at Japan's oldest and most prestigious conservatoire sent shockwaves through the world of classical music and society at large. The press had a field day and reported daily on the disharmony that had erupted amidst the sounds of Beethoven's Ninth Symphony being rehearsed for the numerous year-end performances.[309] They drew parallels to Tanaka Kakuei, the former prime minister charged with corruption in 1976 – proceedings against him were still underway. They reported the progress of the investigation by the Tokyo District Prosecutor's Office. They detailed the allegations of excessive lesson fees and extra payments, Unno's alleged dodgy dealings with Kanda and the suspicions of substantial tax evasion.[310] Geidai came under scrutiny with reports on recent instrument purchases, the atmosphere after Unno's arrest, and student reactions.[311] A certain schadenfreude about the venerable institution's embarrassment is discernible in the reporting. One article, alluding to Natsume Sōseki's famous novel *I Am a Cat,* featured pictures of three different cats from the campus and had the subtitle "I am 'Kandanīni,' a fifth-year." Like Sōseki's cat, Kandanīni pronounces himself bemused at the goings-on among university professors and the people they associate with and especially at the difference between the fat cats who study music and the mangled specimens who struggle though the fine arts course.[312]

The president of the university, Yamamoto Masao, and the dean of the music faculty, Hamano Masao, already embarrassed by the emerging details of the university's instrument purchase policy, could do little more than express their shock and sorrow and promise to do everything to restore the university's good name and trust. Hamano called Unno the faculty's star professor.[313] They also faced pressure from students who held a gathering on the day after Unno's arrest. The students sharply criticized the lack of transparency surrounding the distinction between public and private lessons, but the meeting also revealed a difference in perception between the fine arts students, who attacked what they saw as a distorted sense of money, and the music students who defended the high fees and extra payments.[314] The students demanded an explanation from the authorities, and at another meeting a tearful Yamamoto apologized and promised a complete overhaul of university practices. The students, however, were not satisfied that anything would actually be done and called for Unno's resignation.[315]

Nor was it just the students that demanded an explanation from the university. On 16 December, the minister of education, the president and the dean had to answer some tough questions at a meeting of the Audit Committee of the Upper House of the Diet. Yamamoto was reminded that the university's high reputation was at stake and essentially told to put his house in order. The principal issues were the purchase of instruments, faculty members giving private lessons, particularly to prospective conservatoire students, and university entrance procedures.[316] The music faculty held a meeting the following day to debate the measures proposed by a committee previously set up for the purpose. After nearly seven hours of discussion, the proposals were accepted: a ban on private lessons by faculty members until at least after the upcoming exam season, and a reaffirmation of the complete ban on lessons for prospective examinees; strict enforcement of the rule that no professor must judge his own private pupils at the entrance auditions; and the prohibition of commissions on instrument sales to students. The ban on private lessons was particularly controversial, not just among the professors at the meeting, but in the wider community of music experts. Individual lessons with a top teacher are after all the foundation of a professional musical education everywhere.[317] The university's investigation into the instrument purchases was still underway.[318] Predictably, it had soon transpired that Unno was far from the only professor who personally benefited from the sale of their own discarded instruments to the university and took high lesson fees and commissions from students.[319]

After weeks of intensive investigation, Unno was charged with two offences on 28 December: first, for accepting a bow valued at 800,000 yen as a bribe in connection with the sale of the Guadagnini to his university in 1979; second for accepting bribes of around 1,000,000 yen from Kanda in connection with the sale of a violin by Pressenda to a student. The instruments were judged to be teaching material, and the gifts and money therefore judged to constitute bribes accepted in connection with specific transactions, an offence punishable with up to five years imprisonment. At the same time it was acknowledged that commissions for instrument sales were widely perceived as normal. Unno admitted the charges, although he denied that accepting the gifts constituted bribery, and was granted bail.[320] So was Kanda Yūko, who had been charged the same day with bribery, fraud and forging documents and circulating them. Allegedly the connection between Unno and Kanda began in 1972 when Kanda introduced him to the seller of his 1698 Stradivarius. Since then, Unno had reportedly received commissions for the sales of 70 to 80 instruments at a total value of 20,000,000 yen. Other charges against Unno were dropped in order to protect his students.

Collecting evidence from students created enormous difficulties for the investigation team. They were the real victims in the affair. The arrest of their teacher alone was traumatic, let alone being asked to testify against him. About 20 students were heard as part of the inquiry. Many were pursued by journalists. Music students, after years of individual lessons on their chosen instrument, tend to have a close relationship with their teachers, and perhaps nowhere more so than in Japan, where teachers in general enjoy the highest respect. The question of money, moreover, led into murky waters that blurred the distinction between lesson fees, payments for expert advice on buying a new instrument, monetary gifts in accordance with the widespread custom of gift-giving in Japan, and commissions or bribes. Even today, fees for private lessons are described as "thanks" or "monthly thanks" (*sharei, gessha*) and if paid in cash are presented to the teacher in an envelope specially designed for the purpose. Traditionally, before the education reforms of the mid-nineteenth century, teachers (who often had other sources of income) did not take lesson fees, but received more or less regular "gifts." The idea of a teacher selling his services like a merchant flogging his wares seemed unbearably vulgar in a society dominated by Confucian ideology, which held merchants in low esteem. The Meiji reforms changed this, as so many other things, and introduced regular school fees. Still, old perceptions lingered and many felt and feel uncomfortable with the idea of a teacher–pupil relationship primarily defined in financial terms. The Tokyo District Prosecution Office recognized that the gifts the students – or rather their parents, often without the students' knowledge – made to Unno were in accordance with *jōshiki*, the general sense of what is socially acceptable. They could not be linked directly to special favours received from Unno; often they would be presented during the gift-giving seasons, mid-summer and the end of the year.

That Unno was far from the only teacher whose financial transactions with students merited closer scrutiny was clear from the start, and when he was charged, the *Asahi* asserted, "One is punished as a warning to one hundred others," a sentiment reiterated by others.[321] Apart from the stories reporters collected from students, the newspaper had received over 200 letters at its Tokyo office alone – a "massive choir of accusations about pollution by money," as a headline described it, with yet another reference to the year-end performances of Beethoven's Choral Symphony.[322] Many came from parents complaining about the high cost of private music lessons. One student reported being told by his father that the family could have afforded one or two apartments were it not for his music lessons. Some teachers even took money for introducing their pupils to a teacher abroad. Meanwhile, a member of a professional orchestra pointed out that, while a few musicians in Unno's position enjoyed prestige and income, many more struggled to make ends meet. A minority did criticize the media reports, however, insisting that thank-you gifts, high lesson fees and commissions were justified and perfectly normal.

The first public hearing in court took place on 28 April 1982. Unno and Kanda admitted that money had changed hands between them but denied bribery. Kanda's shop, the *Asahi* reported, had changed its name to "Music Plaza" and was doing business as usual, while Unno had spent the time since his release from detention holed up in his home, too distressed to practise his violin and refusing to talk to the press. The *Asahi* described his behaviour with the word *hikikomori*, which has since gained currency in connection with the social withdrawal symptoms of distressed young people.[323] He had been suspended by his university on the day he was charged – with undue haste, some thought – and would eventually be dismissed. On campus, things had quietened down. A new dean of the music faculty had taken office. Decisions about instrument purchase and private lessons were not yet forthcoming, however, and the university's ability to reform itself was doubted from the start.[324]

Attention now moved away from the court case, but the debate about the Geidai Affair's wider implications had only just begun. The university's controversial ban on private lessons by faculty members came under increasing attack. Meanwhile, the question whether professors at a government-funded university who were civil servants should be allowed to give private lessons to people outside the university and particularly to prospective students was closely connected to other issues and ultimately to the state of music education in general. The *Asahi* published a three-part series of articles discussing private lessons and a separate article by Yoshida Hidekazu highlighting problems concerning private lessons in February 1982.[325] In April the magazine *Ongaku no tomo* carried a special feature entitled "Can Music Colleges Train Performers?" which included: comments by several professors, Uzuka Tatsuo and Urakawa Takaya among them, about individual lessons; a survey of 40 students and 42 graduate students about their experiences; and two panel discussions (*zadankai*).[326] Other music magazines published panel discussions. Panellists, many of them active performers and teachers themselves, discussed the place of private lessons in music education as a whole, the nature of music education, the role of conservatoires and the status of Geidai, performing careers – and, repeatedly, the high costs.[327] The prohibitive cost of musical training to professional level had already given rise to criticism back in the 1960s.[328] They were particularly high for aspiring violinists, who, like pianists, commonly began instrumental lessons at a very early age; some joked that the poor therefore learnt the cello.[329] While experts disagreed about what kind of tuition was suitable for small children or at what age they needed to change to a top-class teacher, it was obvious to all that preparation for a performing career started long before enrolment in a conservatoire. Tsunematsu Yukitoshi of the Japan Musicians Union estimated that in order to become a concert violinist the investment from age 5 to 23 amounted to at least $80,000 for lessons, instruments, equipment and miscellaneous fees to teachers.[330] No wonder the price of music lessons became a subject of widespread discussion following the revelations of the high sums students paid to Unno. Unno, an active performer of international standing as well as a professor at Japan's most prestigious conservatoire, could command top fees, but he was far from exceptional. As the economy went from strength to strength in the 1970s and 1980s, ever more people could afford private music lessons. The increasing demand, especially in the cities, drove up the fees, resulting in a "pyramid system" with particularly high increases at the top end of the market.[331] Although in other countries, too, the most respected teachers command the highest fees, the most expensive teachers in Japan were charging significantly more than their colleagues in North America, France or Germany.[332]

Besides, lesson fees were only part of the costs incurred by those who aspired to study with one of Japan's leading teachers. Students living outside Tokyo often travelled long distances by plane or bullet train, and the cost of transport could easily exceed the cost of the lessons. The manager of Kurashiki Orchestra highlighted the problems for young people in Okayama Prefecture in a letter to the magazine *Ongaku geijutsu*. The local standards of music education were significantly lower than in Tokyo, so local high school students who hoped to enter Japan's top conservatoires aimed to have at least monthly lessons with a professor from a year or two before attempting an audition. These students had to commute to Tokyo by bullet train at a cost of 30,000 yen for an eight-hour round trip; the lesson fees were in fact the least of their expenses. These students, wrote the author, were the real victims of the system. As a solution, he proposed that Geidai send its teachers out to the regions and that parents, with the support of national and local governments, share the cost of lessons for the students in their home town.[333]

The problem was only in part caused by the extreme centralization of musical culture in Tokyo. It was also a result of a general tendency to emphasize educational credentials and other labels over actual performance, even (up to a point) in music, where ultimately the performer's ability to move audiences counts. The "examination hell" adolescents have to pass through to enter Tokyo University has been well-publicized even outside Japan. Geidai is to the music world what Tokyo University is to education in general, the most prestigious and sought-after institution. As more and more people learnt musical instruments from an early age, competition for places rose. Unlike the written entrance examinations at other universities, however, prospective students have to audition, and the panel may well include their own teacher. Geidai, aware of the problem, had in 1970 issued regulations forbidding its professors to teach prospective entrants once the set pieces for the audition had been published and demanding that students give their teacher's name when they applied for auditions. The regulations were difficult to police, however, and doubts persisted as to whether they made any difference. According to *jōshiki*, the general perception of social norms (a word frequently used in the discussions), preparatory lessons with a member of the faculty were indispensable for getting into Geidai, and prospective entrants strove to study with the teacher of their choice well before their audition. At the very least they would take a few lessons to be coached on the set pieces for the audition. The problem with this state of affairs was not just that individual teachers took advantage of the demand by taking excessive fees, but that it privileged pupils from wealthy families and within easy commuting distance of Tokyo. Since Geidai was a public institution and relatively cheap, study at private colleges could cost even more.

The court case was decided on 8 April 1985.[334] Unno was judged guilty of the two charges against him and sentenced to one year and six months' imprisonment; the sentence was suspended for three years. Kanda was sentenced to two years imprisonment. Both appealed immediately. Unno later retracted his appeal, not wanting to prolong the case.[335] The press reported that he had sold his house and his Mercedes and moved to a rented apartment. He gave private lessons only to a few former students who insisted. He had refused offers by well-wishers to give a party in his support and even stayed away from his own teacher and mentor Uzuka Tatsuo's funeral earlier in the year. He had judged at a couple of international competitions but not given any performances, spending most of his time practising alone.[336] Immediately after the verdict he told the press through his lawyers that he intended to resume performing soon. A few months later he disclosed his plans to move abroad and gave details of his schedule for the next few years.[337] He moved to Paris with his family in 1986 and lived there until his suspended sentence ended in 1989. In 1987 he performed in Tokyo for the first time after nearly six years, giving a concert and a recital in Suntory Hall. On 6 June he played not one but three concertos (Mozart No. 5, Mendelssohn and Beethoven) with the Tokyo Philharmonic Orchestra under Asahina Takashi, and on 28 June he gave a recital playing sonatas by Brahms, Beethoven, Debussy and Franck. In an interview, Unno told *Ongaku no tomo* that he had been impressed by the welcoming applause he had received, but that meanwhile he was happy that his life in Europe gave him the chance to recharge his batteries. Reviewers of his recital, although critical, praised his playing overall and the critic writing for the *Asahi* noted that both concerts were sold out.[338] Clearly, being judged guilty of taking bribes had not damaged his popularity as a performer.

After moving back to Japan he resumed his performing career there; he founded the ensemble Unno Yoshio Tokyo Virtuoso, which made its debut in September 1991. Geidai had fired him on the day he was sentenced, but he was appointed professor at the private Senzoku Gakuen College of Music.[339] From 2005 to 2011 he was president of Tokyo College of Music. By this time few remembered the scandal he had been embroiled in 20 years earlier.[340] He is currently visiting professor at Tokyo College of Music and at Tōhō Gakuen School of Music.

Kanda Yūkō, meanwhile, whose arrest and sentence apparently attracted far less attention than Unno's, upheld his appeal and his sentence was suspended in recognition of his services to music education; he had loaned instruments long-term to students entering music competitions.[341] The value and prices of stringed instruments, although also a subject of media attention in the months following his arrest, did not receive quite as much attention as music education.[342] Whether Kanda's business suffered is hard to tell; perhaps, like Unno, he had his unwavering supporters. Kanda & Co. had been established by his father Kanda Heishirō in Matsumoto, where he was an ardent supporter of Suzuki Shin'ichi, and moved to Tokyo in 1956. Kanda Yūkō, who had learnt to play the violin from Suzuki as a child, had taken over in 1975. Renamed Music Plaza in 1981, the shop is now located in an unassuming building in a quiet neighbourhood in Tokyo's Shibuya ward. Regular advertisements in *String* claim without false modesty that the company has one of the world's most important violin workshops.[343] Ironically, Kanda is also the author of a two-volume work about how to examine, choose and buy violins.[344]

Unno was clearly a scapegoat in the whole affair. While his dealings with Kanda and the huge sums of money he received from students appear to have been morally questionable, most commentators believed that he was no worse than others. Many of those paying the high prices felt that outstanding teachers deserved high rewards. The widespread willingness to pay for education and cultural pursuits characterized Japan during the post-war economic boom, while rising wealth and the high prestige of Western classical music produced parents who spared no expense to give their children what they themselves had missed out on. They were also keenly aware of their own ignorance, and their lack of confidence made them seek the reassurance of famous names, whether of teachers or instrument makers, with the result that demand far outstripped supply. It is conceivable that Unno's judgement was clouded by the high prestige he enjoyed as a result of his spectacularly successful career from a young age. Perhaps the luthier Murata Sōroku had a point when he remarked that many violinists had a narrow view of the world, were ignorant and might well in some cases be out of touch with what was morally acceptable.[345]

Certainly the Geidai Affair suggested to many observers that the world of music was a closed country where people did things differently. The difference in perception between musicians and the general public was reflected in the reactions to reports about the vast sums of money changing hands in music education and even in the jury's deliberations. One of the questions the jury had to grapple with was whether a violin constituted "teaching material" in the sense that its quality decisively influenced the student's performance and whether advising on instrument purchase could therefore be considered an inseparable part of a teacher's job.[346] To a violinist the close relationship between instrument and performer is obvious, but even insiders disagree about the extent to which a performance depends on the quality of the instrument played, and the jury remained confused. Meanwhile the critic Yoshida Hidekazu pronounced himself struck by the number of people who seemed to expect higher moral standards from musicians than they themselves could live up to.[347]

A striking aspect of the discussions among musical experts was the view expressed by several of them that, where classical music was concerned, Japan was in some way in a state of transition, backward and immature (*mijuku*).[348] Several referred to traces of the *iemoto* system prevalent in the traditional arts, which, they said, created an unhealthy dependency on the teacher by students and their parents.[349] Others criticized the excessive reliance on labels, which they saw as resulting both from Confucian traditions and the fact that Western music was originally imported from the outside and imposed by the authorities.[350] Yet others cited the lack of a knowledgeable audience.[351] Few of the problems revealed in the scandal, however, were peculiar to Japan alone. Even the *iemoto* system has many features familiar to classical musicians, particularly violinists, worldwide, including the strong consciousness of lineage. As for music teachers benefiting from the sale of instruments to their students, Japanese observers had no way of telling how prevalent the practice was in the West, because it is so seldom discussed openly. This lack of openness is, ultimately, the main problem, because it violates the trust that is fundamental to the relationship between student and teacher.[352]

Thus, at the dawn of the decade when the "bubble economy" and the high yen helped Western music to prosper more than ever, the confidence of the Japanese in their own musical achievements seemed to reach a new low. Nor were the problems pointed out by the commentators resolved as the new century approached.

# Part 3: At the Turn of the Millennium

On 24 February 1989 the coffin of Emperor Shōwa was borne from his palace in the heart of Tokyo to its final resting place in the mausoleum at Hachiōji to the west of the city. The ceremonies within the confines of the palace and the mausoleum were conducted according to Shinto rites and accompanied by strains of *gagaku* music. Once the cortège left the palace, the band of the Tokyo Metropolitan Police Department took over, playing the funeral march composed by Franz Eckert in 1897. This was the music the general public could hear live as part of the state ceremony. Thus, pragmatic as so often, the controversial issues related to the emperor's position as "symbol" of the nation but not head of state, and of Shinto as the religion of the imperial house but strictly separated from the state, were resolved.

Other issues Japan faced in the years around the millennium defied a similarly neat resolution. The emperor's death and the change of era name from Shōwa to Heisei which accompanied it did not in themselves change anything. But their symbolic significance was great, for the Shōwa era was divided in two by the Second World War and the emperor was the last wartime head of state still in office, even if his constitutional role had changed. His war responsibility was hotly debated in Japan and abroad in the 1980s. His son and successor expressed regret at Japan's role in the war to the President of the Republic of Korea when he visited Japan in 1990, marking the start of a stream of apologies made by Japan in the 1990s. But they did not fundamentally change the perception of Japan as a nation unwilling to own up to its murky past.

Even more problematic than the past was the present. The economic bubble burst in the early 1990s, initiating a prolonged recession. Worse still, perhaps, was the loss of confidence it entailed. In the 1980s a series of corruption scandals had already undermined the people's trust in their government and bureaucracy, which was further diminished by the government's failure to solve Japan's problems and its perceived inadequacy in the face of the Kobe earthquake in 1995. Internationally, the end of the Cold War and the increasing power of China raised questions about Japan's role in the world. "Escape from Asia" as propagated in the nineteenth century was definitely not an option – on the contrary: some public commentators have called for a "return to Asia."[1] One of Japan's problems was that it no longer had any models to follow; in some areas (education, management) it was itself held up as an example for others. What we like to call the "late modern" or even the "post-modern" era is just as puzzling to Japan's former models in the West as it is to Japan. The loss of optimism is perhaps Japan's greatest problem, together (and possibly connected with) its rapidly ageing society.

Another death in 1989, although less widely reported abroad than that of the emperor, was equally heavy with symbolic meaning to many Japanese, especially to those who had experienced the privations of the early post-war years. On 24 June the film actress and singer Misora Hibari died. Although she was only 52, her career spanned the entire post-war period, from her first great hit "Kanashiki no Kuchibue" (Sad Whistling) in 1949 when she was only 11 years old to her last single "Kawa no nagare no yō ni" (Like the Flow of the River) just weeks before her death. Misora sang in a variety of styles, but her best-known songs are *enka* ballads expressing the sorrows of life and lost love. To many who grew up hearing her songs she seemed to both share their pain and represent the hope of hardship overcome. Her last song has become something of a signature tune, sung by artists wanting to pay tribute to her or even to Japan in general, whether Three Tenors or Twelve Girls playing traditional Chinese instruments.[2] It is also the title song of a CD by the violinist Kōda Satoko, one of Kōda's two debut recordings issued in 1999. Kōda Satoko graduated from Geidai in 1993, a member of the "orthodoxy," as the music critic Hasegawa Takehisa puts it, who had previously only played classical music.[3] The CD is intended to appeal to both fans of Misora Hibari and of classical music. The violin would seem ideally suited to such an endeavour. Its sound, besides being close to that of the human voice, features prominently in the lush string accompaniment to many *enka* songs, including many Misora Hibari hits. But the violinists who accompany *enka*, like those who play for film studios, remain unnamed and unacknowledged. They are part of the "secret" history of the violin in Japan, playing music which is perceived to express the soul of Japan, but which no self-respecting classical music enthusiast would admit to even listening to, let alone being moved by.

Instead, many commentators of the classical music scene join the general chorus of angst and pessimism by continuing to lament the state of classical music in Japan in general and of the violin scene in particular. For the music critic Watanabe Kazuhiko, who in 2002 published a book entitled *Vaiorinisuto33* (33 chapters on violinists), Japan still appears backward in comparison to the West. The book contains the usual line-up of virtuosos familiar in East and West; that is to say, nearly all of the violinists are Western, and more than half of them dead. The only Japanese who receives a chapter to herself is Midori. Other Japanese violinists get a passing mention in the final chapter with the title "Violinists of Japan."[4] In this, Watanabe's book resembles Western ones, whose authors also tend to deal with "Japanese," "Asian" or even "Oriental" violinists in a few paragraphs, usually limiting their treatment to the most recent competition winners.[5] No wonder Watanabe's chapter has the telling subheading, "beyond 'competition disease'." The Japanese tend to measure the success of their violinists (and not only violinists) by their exploits abroad. Validation by the West, especially the countries seen as the heartlands of classical music, was – and is – still the chief marker of success, and validation often comes in the form of a prize at an international competition.

Clearly, Watanabe is not impressed by the Japanese violin scene. He tells us he can think of about 60 names of "plus alpha" Japanese violinists whose performance he has heard.[6] Several of them have all but given up performing and devote themselves to teaching. Of those still performing no more than 15 to 20 are likely to be invited to play concertos with the country's professional orchestras. They include young girl prodigies, recent competition winners and competition veterans, performers who have made a name for themselves abroad, a few who have a "story" to their profile, three or four outstanding concertmasters, and two or three that can be called "great masters" (*taika*). The average concert enthusiast, says Watanabe, can probably only name about ten Japanese violinists. Watanabe names no names, so we must guess whom he had in mind. The great performers-turned-teachers would have included Etō Toshiya and Unno Yoshio, and the great concertmasters Tanaka Chikashi, Tokunaga Tsugio, and perhaps Kino Masayuki.[7] Etō and Tanaka have died since

Watanabe wrote his book. Possibly the great master turned great master-teacher is a dying breed anyway; it is more common now for older violinists to continue performing publicly as well as teach. Tokunaga has played a concerto with an orchestra on this side of the millenium. "Competition veterans" who still perform, whether or not with professional orchestras, include Maehashi Teiko and Kubota Yōko. In 2009 Maehashi was featured in *Sarasate* with a full-page portrait showing her in a glamorous golden-coloured evening dress that Anne Sophie Mutter could be proud of, and an interview about her new recording of sonatas by Johannes Brahms (No. 3) and César Franck.[8] The same issue carried an interview with Kubota Yōko, looking like someone's kindly grandmother, complete with pearls, and talking about her latest recording of Paganini's 24 Caprices. In a country where one can still hear the criticism that performing careers end too soon and where there is a seemingly plentiful and endless supply of pretty young female violinists, the determination of these artists to keep on exploring and taking risks is impressive.

The "competition winners" are a fairly obvious, if fast-changing, category. They seem to get younger all the time and thus tend to overlap with the "girl prodigies." Recent ones in 2002 included Shōji Sayaka (1983–), Kamio Mayuko (1986–) and Kishima Mayu (1986–). Shōji Sayaka began to learn the violin at the age of five; her teachers included Harada Kōichiro and Unno Yoshio, before she became one of the many budding virtuosos to study with Zakhar Bron.[9] In 1997 she won the junior division of the Wieniawski Competition, and in 1999, at the age of 16, she became the youngest candidate and the first Japanese to win the first prize at the Paganini Competition, where she also won the Premio Mario Ruminelli. Kamio Mayuko has also studied with Zakhar Bron. Previously she had studied at the Pre-College Division of Juilliard with Dorothy DeLay and Kawasaki Masao and at Tōhō Gakuen with Harada Kōichiro. In 1998 Kamio became the youngest to win the Menuhin International Violin Competition; in 2000 she won first prize at the Young Concert Artist International Auditions and in 2001 she became the youngest artist ever to be presented in the YCA Series at the Kennedy Center. She has since won a gold medal at the Tchaikovsky Competition in 2007. In 2003 she featured in the film *Playing for Real*, a documentary about young musicians developing their careers produced and directed by

Josh Aronson.[10] Kishima Mayu's teachers included Etō Toshiya, Oguri Machie, Kudo Chihiro and, again, Zakhar Bron, whose seminars in Japan she attended from 1999 to 2001; she subsequently continued to study with him at the conservatoire in Cologne. International competition prizes included the Wieniawski in 2000, where she came second (no first prize was awarded). More recently, in 2009 she came tenth in the Queen Elisabeth Competition. Shōji, Kamio and Kishima have all performed internationally. Whether they and other young competition winners will match the careers of the veterans, including Tsuji Hisako, the oldest of them all and the last of the pre-war "Three Violin Maidens," who, well into her eighties, is still active (albeit mainly as a teacher), remains to be seen.

Violinists who might be described as coming "with a story attached" could include Temma Atsuko, Senju Mariko and Kawabata Narimichi (see the following chapters). Violinists who made themselves a name abroad before enjoying success in Japan are as often as not still living outside Japan. This was true (at the time) of all the violinists Watanabe mentioned by name in his last chapter: Gotō Midori, Takezawa Kyōko, Watanabe Reiko, Suwanai Akiko, Toda Yayoi, Shōji Sayaka, Kashimoto Daishin and Yasunaga Tōru. Yasunaga, the oldest of them, has recently retired from his post as concertmaster of the Berlin Philharmonic and returned to his homeland. Meanwhile, Kashimoto Daishin, appointed to the Berlin Philharmonic in 2009, looks set for a career outside Japan.

Another book, published by Yamaha Music Media in 2007, shows the same bias as Watanabe's. *Baiorin omoshiro zatsugaku jiten (*The violin: a dictionary of interesting information) is one of several books for violin lovers, introducing all kinds of facts about the violin and violinists on 223 pages. This book too only devotes a short chapter to Japanese-born violinists, of whom 16 receive a paragraph to themselves: Takezawa Kyōko, Gotō Midori, Kashimoto Daishin, Shōji Sayaka, Horigome Yuzuko, Furusawa Iwao, Terakado Ryō, Mariko Senju, Urushihara Asako, Kawabata Narimichi, Suwanai Akiko, Kawakubo Tamaki, Okazaki Keisuke, Kishima Mayu, Kamio Mayuko, Gotō Ryū. Midori and Takezawa Kyōko also feature in a chapter in a section with "episodes" surrounding violinists (as pupils of Dorothy DeLay), as does Watanabe Shigeo. Again, most of the violinists mentioned were based abroad at the time of the book's publication.[11] In addition, a few

"crossover" violinists each get a mention: Hakase Tarō (1968–), Kawai
Ikuko (1969–), Takashima Chisako (1968–), NAOTO (1973–), and
Temma Atsuko (1955–).[12]

The number of violinists claimed by the Japanese as their own, but
living outside Japan, raises the question, who is a "Japanese violinist" in
the first place? Some of the violinists named have not lived in Japan since
childhood, if at all. Midori left Japan with her mother at the age of ten;
she has since lived in the United States, where her career was launched,
and recently acquired American citizenship. Her half-brother Ryū was
born and bred in the United States, so his ties to Japan appear even more
tenuous. Kashimoto Daishin was born in London and spent only a brief
period of his childhood in Tokyo before moving to New York in 1985.
The Japanese nevertheless tend to regard these and other violinists with
Japanese ancestors, a Japanese name and Japanese looks as "Japanese"
– albeit Japanese to varying degrees and giving rise to varying levels of
unease and confusion.[13]

Least problematic are the migrant professionals and the international
students who grew up in Japan and received their training there until they
graduated from a Japanese music school, most often Tōhō Gakuen
School of Music or Geidai. Most of the violinists who went abroad in
the 1950s and 1960s belong to one of these groups. Unless they work to
maintain professional ties with Japan, however, they might disappear
from the Japanese radar altogether. Several of the younger violinists
featured in the two books mentioned belong to this category, including
Takezawa Kyōko, Watanabe Reiko, Suwanai Akiko and Shōji Sayaka.
Suwanai Akiko (1972–) is another violinist who gained fame after
winning competitions. A student of Etō Toshiya, she had won three prizes
at national competitions and four at international ones by her first year
at Tōhō Gakuen College, including second prize at the Paganini
Competition in 1988 and second at the Queen Elisabeth in 1989. In 1990
she became the youngest violinist ever to win first prize at the
Tchaikovsky Competition. After graduating from Tōhō Gakuen she
studied at Juilliard with DeLay. Determined to pursue an international
career, she is now based in Paris.

The confusion for Japanese audiences is perhaps greatest in relation to
Japanese American or mixed-race violinists, or violinists with a Japanese
parent or grandparent, but born and raised outside Japan. Many Japanese

still have difficulty in recognizing race, nationality, ethnicity, culture and language as categories that need not go together, so strong is their belief in the homogeneity of the Japanese nation and people. Violinists such as Anne Akiko Meyers and Arabella Miho Steinbacher challenge long-held assumptions, and their Japanese audiences do not always know what to make of them.

Anne Akiko Meyers has a Japanese mother and an American father and was born and raised in the United States. She made her Japanese debut in the Suntory Hall in 1987 while still at high school and a student at the Juilliard's pre-college division. The magazine *Ongaku no tomo* described her as a "cute girl prodigy" who told the press she was thrilled to perform in her grandma's country.[14] Meyers emphasizes her Japanese roots by using her middle name and performing Japanese composers of whose music she claims a special understanding.[15] Perhaps it is not without significance that Meyers, half Japanese by birth, but in most ways thoroughly American, emphasizes her Japanese side more than many violinists whose links with Japan are more obvious but who make a point of playing down their Japanese background, such as Midori.[16]

Arabella Miho Steinbacher, like Meyers, has a Japanese mother. Her father is German, and both parents are musicians who met as students in Munich. Born in Munich in 1981, Steinbacher started learning the violin at the age of three. Her mother read in a newspaper about a teacher, Helge Thelen, who had just returned from studying the Suzuki Method in Japan. At the age of nine she caught the attention of Ana Chumachenko, whose students include Julia Fischer and Lisa Batiashvili. In 2000 she won the Joseph Joachim Competition in Hannover. Her international career took off in 2004 when she performed with the Orchestre Philharmonique de Radio France under Sir Neville Marriner. During a tour to Japan she was interviewed for *Sarasate*. According to her interviewer, she speaks fluent Japanese and is often known by her Japanese middle name as Miho-*chan* in her mother's country.[17] Perhaps she represents the best of both worlds: born and bred in one of the heartlands of classical music, yet still with noticeable Japanese roots, including the ability to speak the language. Presumably it is only her relatives and close friends who address her with the familiar and endearing "–*chan*," but perhaps the interviewer finds this worth mentioning, because it stresses Steinbacher's Japanese ancestry.

Somewhere in between these two groups are the migrant geniuses –
most famously Midori – and transnational offspring returning to perform
in Japan, such as Gotō Ryū and Kashimoto Daishin. Although clearly
Japanese by name and ancestry, they still confuse Japanese
commentators, as the example of Midori shows: "Is it right to discuss
Gotō Midori, on the strength of her Japanese nationality and name, as a
'Japanese violinist'?" Watanabe Kazuhiko asked himself.[18] At her first
appearance in a talk show on Japanese television she spoke haltingly and
as if she were translating directly from English, and he thought she
looked like an Asian American. Nevertheless, not only is Midori the only
Japanese-born violinist he devotes an entire chapter to in his book
*Violinist 33,* but he holds onto the designation "Japanese violinist" and
even calls her a "Japanese pioneer in the world." In his view, her recent
performances increasingly seemed to point to "Gotō Midori" and thus a
Japanese identity.

Surprisingly, perhaps, Gotō Ryū may in some ways seem closer to
Japan than his half-sister; his career was launched in Sapporo rather than
New York.[19] Growing up with two violinist parents (albeit not active
performers), not to mention his star sister, he impressed his family with
his musical sensitivity from an early age. When Ryū showed an interest
in the violin – or was it just a baby's curiosity? – Midori bought him a
tiny violin and his mother began to teach him when he was two-and-a-
half years old.[20] The toddler surely got more than he bargained for: if
anything, Setsu was even stricter with him than with Midori. Ryū's first
public performance in 1991 took place in Osaka, where he participated
in a student recital, accompanied by Midori on the piano. Three years
later, Sano Mitsunori, whom the Gotōs had first met when he organized
the Hiroshima Peace Tour with Midori in 1985, suggested that Ryū
perform at the Pacific Music Festival in Sapporo the following year,
1995. He even arranged for a crew from Fuji Television to make a
documentary series over a period of ten years, entitled *Gotō Ryū's
Odyssey.* After some hesitation, Gotō Setsu agreed to both. She began to
prepare Ryū for his official debut, with Paganini's Concerto No. 1, the
same work Midori had first performed in public at the age of ten. The
Japanese press went wild when they heard about it. Comparing Ryū with
his sister, they called him the "super-prodigy." The conductor Sado
Yutaka, on hearing Ryū play, felt he was more than a prodigy: "he has the

mark of a great performer."[21] Even more effective in making him known in Japan were the TV commercials by Japan Rail (JR) of which Ryū has been a fan since early childhood. Moreover, in 2005 a major publisher brought out a lavish book with photographs, an essay by Gotō Ryū himself and a DVD including a film of a day with Ryū in New York, his performance of a movement from a Mozart sonata, an interview and three JR commercials.[22]

Meanwhile, Ryū's career in America was more low-key. His mother continued to teach him the violin and to see that Ryū learnt to express himself in Japanese as well as English. He has appeared as a soloist with several leading orchestras in America, Europe and Asia, and in 2005 he released his first CD with Deutsche Grammophon. In 2010 he made his Carnegie Hall debut and launched the "Excellence in Music" initiative to support music training in New York's public schools. Only time will tell whether Gotō Ryū will strengthen his ties with Japan. In 2011 he graduated from Harvard with a BA in Physics, and although he appears to have embarked on a full-time career as a violinist it is not inconceivable that he may eventually switch to something else.[23]

Kashimoto Daishin's links with Japan appear to be more tenuous than Gotō Ryū's, although he did spend a few childhood years in the country. Accepted into the pre-college division of Juilliard in 1986, he studied under Tanaka Naoko until he moved to Lübeck in Germany in 1990, having been invited to study with Zakhar Bron. From 1999 to 2004 he studied in Freiburg at the Staatliche Hochschule für Musik with Rainer Kussmaul. Kashimoto won the first prizes at the Menuhin International Junior Competition in 1993, the International Competition for Violinists in Cologne in 1994, the Kreisler Competition in Vienna and the Long–Thibaud Competition in Paris in 1996, and has won several prizes in Japan. He has performed with leading orchestras and plays chamber music. The centre of his activities is Europe; in 2005 he returned to Japan after a three-year break to perform the Shostakovich Violin Concerto No. 1 with the Tokyo Philharmonic Orchestra in the Suntory Hall under Chung Myung-Whun.[24] "I felt I needed to do the things I can only do now," he told *Sarasate*, "Until then I only worked for the concerts. But there are other things to study, such as practicing the pieces I myself want to play, deepening my relationship with my teachers and playing chamber music."[25] More recently he has strengthened his ties with Japan, however, having accepted the musical directorship of two music festivals in the Kansai region, Akō (since 2007) and Himeji (since 2008).[26]

For the musicians themselves, their Japaneseness or otherwise is presumably of minor significance.[27] As far as they are concerned, they fully participate in what we know as Western classical music. Like Suzuki Shin'ichi, Japanese violinists today not only learn in and from the West, but also give to the West, performing and teaching and generally contributing to keep the musical tradition alive. Nevertheless, emphasizing Japanese roots in some way can be a means to making a mark in a world where foreign experience is no longer reserved for a privileged few. Kōda Satoko has followed up her recordings of Misora Hibari hits with arrangements of other Japanese popular songs. Other artists have recorded Japanese composers in the Western classical tradition on the Mittenwald label, making them available for the first time (see Conclusion).

Still, the majority of classical violinists aim to assert themselves as faithful bearers of the European classical tradition. Suwanai's respect for Etō Toshiya is grounded in Etō's determination and ability to transmit this tradition to his students. For Suwanai herself the tradition was so overwhelming that she deliberately chose to study in the USA rather than in Europe. For the same reason, she concentrated her efforts on the twentieth-century repertoire, such as Alban Berg's Violin Concerto, for which she took lessons from Louis Krasner.[28] In her autobiography, published in 2000, Suwanai repeatedly refers to the challenges Japanese face when playing Western classical music, and one wonders whether she is influenced by the stereotypes that musicians perceived as "Asian" still encounter in the West.[29] Pinchas Zukerman, no less, dragged up the usual stereotype of the Japanese who imitate without ever being able to achieve true understanding in his comment on Midori: "She doesn't come from Vilna or Odessa; she comes from Osaka," says Zukerman. "As far as character goes, it's not Austrian or Middle European playing – even though she's learned to do it, it's still a *learned* process. Her mother tongue is Japanese, so everything's always going to be a bit foreign to her."[30] Quite apart from the fact that Vilna and Odessa – not to mention Tel Aviv – hardly lie in the geographical heartland of European classical music and that no one is born with an ability to play any particular type of music, this attitude shows how little most Westerners know about

Japan. For at least a hundred years now, Western music has represented the mainstream in Japan, and yet Westerners still seem to believe that all Japanese grow up surrounded by the alien strumming and piping of the *shamisen* and the *shakuhachi*. Ironically, Jewish musicians had to contend with similar stereotypes when they first attracted public attention.

Nevertheless, Western stereotypes are probably the least of the problems Japanese violinist have to contend with. Even the prevalence of the same sort of stereotypes among the Japanese themselves are a minor issue compared to the challenges faced by violinists worldwide when they want to make a successful solo career for themselves in a highly competitive market. That Suwanai Akiko wrote her autobiography at the tender age of 28, as did her contemporary, Kawabata Narimichi, at the same time,[31] may well be motivated, at least in part, by the need to stand out from the crowd. Playing the violin, however well, is apparently not sufficient to reach and secure the admiration of audiences.

## 1. With Stories Attached: Kawabata Narimichi and Temma Atsuko

*For the second half of his Fan Club Special Concert at Ōji Hall in Tokyo's elegant Ginza shopping district, Kawabata Narimichi had changed into more informal attire of light grey, loose-fitting trousers and a dark red shirt. Had we enjoyed the* stollen *during the interval, he asked; his friend had brought the Christmas cake from Germany. Our choice of request pieces had surprised him, he continued.*

*I had wondered how he would handle this one. The programme for the concert read "First half: César Franck, Violin Sonata in A; second half: performance of audience requests." But as so often in Japan, the organizers displayed impressive efficiency. At the entrance every guest received a questionnaire with a list of compositions organized in groups A, B, and C, and the instruction to choose a favourite from each group. Two assistants at a desk in the entrance lobby processed the questionnaires as they were handed in, and by the interval they had produced two large posters with the results. In group C (containing four pieces), Bach's Chaconne in D minor was the clear winner with 100 votes. Group B (four pieces) likewise produced a clear winner: Sarasate's* Zigeunerweisen *with 81 votes. Since these two pieces must be among the most often performed violin works since the nineteenth century, this result surely cannot have surprised Kawabata. In group A, which contained 49 shorter works, the votes were more widely spread, and the poster announced that Kawabata would play four of them: Paganini's* La Campanella *(20 votes); Gounod's* Ave Maria *and Dinicu's* The Lark *(17 votes each): and Caccini's* Ave Maria *(16).[32]*

*Having played his way through this not insubstantial list, Kawabata followed the performance up with encores from the works that had also received many votes: Chopin's* Nocturne, *Monti's* Czardas, *Mancini's,* Sunflower[33] *(15 votes each), and Mendelssohn's* On the Wings of Song *(10). Even then, as the applause persisted, Kawabata seemed game for more; but his pianist appeared to be telling him that enough was enough, and led him from the stage.*

*Still the evening was not over for Kawabata. In no time at all he reappeared in the foyer, looking strangely awkward without his violin, to sign his CDs and books. The audience had looked fairly mixed, but now mainly women lined up for autographs and to have their picture taken with him. "My son is a real fan of yours," said a mother leading a little boy. Indeed there is much one can like about Kawabata Narimichi; the incredible sweetness of his tone, his mastery of virtuoso passages, or even his endearing manner as he addresses the audience. His violin seems so much part of him that it hardly leaves his shoulder during the performance, remaining held in place by the weight of his head even when he takes his hands off it. His awkwardness without it stands in striking contrast to the apparent ease and naturalness of his playing.[34]*

And yet Kawabata Narimichi is a violinist made not born. To say this implies no disrespect in a Japanese context. On the contrary, a thing made (*tsukutta mono*) is a thing that, although from the natural world, has been shaped by human hand to make it appear more precious. An ikebana flower arrangement, carefully formed by an artist with many years of training brings out the flowers at their best. A tea ceremony is an artistic performance, where the tea master manipulates a number of exquisite objects in a specially designed space. Like the actor in a Nō or *kabuki* play, the karate fighter or archer performs a meticulously choreographed and rehearsed series of movements that are beautiful to watch as well as effective. Why should a violinist be different? Playing the violin is in itself not a natural activity like running or talking. Even in the West, most people will admit that talent alone is not sufficient to play the violin well; it has to be combined with dedication. Nevertheless, Westerners will not usually invoke the effort they have put into their art with the same insistence as many Japanese artists do. For the Japanese, however, the effort to improve on nature, *doryoku*, represents a fundamental value in itself. So do its companions, hardship, *kurō*, endurance, *nintai*, and above all, persevering, *ganbaru*.[35] Only a few, maybe, are blessed with talent, and they have done nothing to earn it. But effort, endurance and perseverance are within reach of all who sincerely seek them, and will in time lead to success. Even if success never comes, the process itself is so valuable that the outcome hardly matters. The "nobility of failure" described by a foreign observer is enhanced by the effort it took to achieve it.[36] No wonder that achieving success against the odds, by overcoming hardship and suffering, feature prominently in the stories told by and about violinists.

The story of how Kawabata became a violinist fits in well with prevailing attitudes and has been told both by Narimichi himself and his father Masao.[37] This in itself is intriguing. Kawabata, at just 30, was young to be engaging in autobiography (although his contemporary Suwanai Akiko beat him to it), and rather than the fathers, it is usually the mothers who have written biographies of their successful offspring (see next chapter). The father tends to be largely absent from their story. In Kawabata Masao's book, *Narimichi's Ave Maria: as a violin teacher and a father,* the silent father finds a voice. The paper wrapper around the jacket describes it as the account of "a father's battle": "Believing in the talent of his son who had suddenly lost his eyesight, he made him blossom as a highly gifted violinist."[38] Although he is himself a violinist, Masao's place in the Kawabata family was, initially, no different from that of any salaryman; he worked long hours to support his wife and three boys, Narimichi, Yoshinari and Morimichi. Born in 1945 and graduating from Geidai in 1967, he played in the Tokyo Vivaldi Ensemble and the Tokyo Symphonic Ensemble while still at university, then joined the Iso String Quartet. A member of the Geidai Orchestra, he was its leader from 1978 to 1994. He taught violin at Senzoku Gakuen College of Music in Kawasaki. He had no wish for his children to learn the violin, however, even had he had time to teach them.

But in August 1980, when Narimichi was eight years old, disaster struck and changed everything for the Kawabata family. His grandparents took him to California, but before he could enjoy any of the holiday treats they had planned for him, he caught a cold which, probably as a result of medication, turned into a life-threatening illness. The doctors diagnosed Stevens–Johnson Syndrome, a rare disease that attacks the skin and the mucous membranes; they estimated his chance of survival at 5 percent. Narimichi's grandparents, joined by his mother, spent three anxious months before they could return to Tokyo with him.

While his in-laws and his wife gathered round his eldest son's bedside, and his mother travelled all the way from Kagoshima to look after the younger sons, Masao as the family breadwinner struggled with a sense of powerlessness as he worked harder than ever, taking on additional jobs to pay for the mounting costs. His sense of powerlessness continued after his wife and son returned. Narimichi had survived, but his eyesight had suffered, and the prognosis was bleak. His mother took him from one hospital appointment to the next. For as long as they could, the parents clung to the hope that Narimichi might see again one day, but gradually they had to face the fact that their firstborn had a disability. Deeply concerned about Narimichi's future, they began to consider what he could do for a living, and eventually his mother suggested that Masao teach him the violin.

Becoming his son's teacher enabled Masao to take a more active role as a father and to help his son prepare for future independence. But he did not immediately agree to the idea. He does not record whether the Kawabatas were influenced by the example of Wanami Takayoshi. If they were, the comparison might have done little to encourage them. Wanami was a soloist, and Masao believed a solo career to be the only option for a blind violinist. Even for a violinist who can see, however the obstacles to a solo career are formidable. More than Narimichi's eyesight, it was his age that worried Masao. Wanami started to learn the violin at the age of four. Narimichi was now ten years old. His contemporary Midori performed the first movement of Paganini's Violin Concerto No. 1 at a student concert in Tokyo when she was only nine; a few months later she caused a sensation at Aspen playing Bach's Chaconne and Paganini's Caprice No. 17 for Dorothy DeLay. Suwanai Akiko, another contemporary, won the first prize in the Eastern Japan division of the All

Japan Student Music Competition at nine; for the national competition she played a movement from Mendelssohn's Violin Concerto. In the country that pioneered teaching toddlers, even starting the violin at six or seven years of age is considered late; ten seemed beyond the pale. Moreover, as if failing eyesight were not enough of a disability, there was also the problem of Narimichi's fingers. The disease had damaged his fingernails and softened his skin. Even if he could hold a bow without trouble, would the fingers of his left hand be able to press down the strings firmly enough to produce a good, clear sound?

Nevertheless, Masao started to teach Narimichi. "From then onwards martial law ruled," he told a journalist 20 years later.[39] He took over his new role with fierce dedication, striving to help his son in a way only he could. The upper floor of the Kawabata's family home was converted and soundproofed to protect Narimichi's ears and forestall complaints from the neighbours. As soon as he came home in the evenings, Masao would go upstairs to work with his son, postponing his own practice until Narimichi had gone to bed. While Narimichi's father was out at work, his mother would supervise him. His younger brothers were largely left to fend for themselves after their father had explained the situation to them. Fortunately they coped. So did Narimichi. Perhaps he even welcomed the unprecedented attention from his father, coupled with the chance to handle the instrument with which Masao provided for the family's livelihood. At any rate, he submitted willingly enough to the spartan regime, practising practically all the hours he did not spend at school, up to eight hours a day, ten on holidays, not missing a single day. In his memoir he observes, "This was not because my father forced me. One could say I did it because it was no particular hardship for me to play the violin. But I can't say that I was particularly keen. Nor did I think that it could be pleasant to perform or such like. I just thought it was the thing to do. Children don't go to cram schools because it's fun or because they like them. It's the same thing."[40]

Equally fortunately, Narimichi almost immediately showed natural aptitude; from the first he held the violin as if he had never done anything else; he possessed perfect pitch and astonishing powers of perseverance and concentration. He needed them: by the time he reached high school age he could not see even the giant notes of the sheet music his parents had hand-copied for him and had to rely entirely on his ears to learn new repertoire. Nor could he learn to play by watching his father demonstrate; but here his father had the solution. His own lack of skill on the violin (*bukiyō*), he claimed, had forced him during his own studies to analyse technical processes, breaking them up into parts to isolate the problems and work on them separately. By naming them he trained his powers of explanation, a skill appreciated by those who studied with him and particularly useful in teaching his son.[41] Even so, he eventually decided that Narimichi needed a new teacher and introduced him to his colleague Urakawa Takaya.

Soon Narimichi enjoyed his first successes. In 1984 he won third prize at the Student Music Competition of Japan. The set piece was Wieniawski's Concerto in D minor Op. 22, which he had already played at his audition with Urakawa. In 1985 Narimichi became one of five students selected from 300 applicants to receive a master class from Isaac Stern. He played Paganini's Concerto No. 1, and Stern praised him warmly. The following year Narimichi was selected again, together with only two of the other five from the previous year. More important, perhaps, than being selected twice from a large number of applicants, more valuable even than any advice Stern could give Narimichi, was the praise he received from the famous foreign virtuoso. Three times, Stern called Narimichi's playing "wonderful," and at their second meeting he remembered Narimichi from the year before and asked whether his eyes were better.[42] No matter that "wonderful" from an American teacher in a public class for children may not mean much, or that Stern hardly heard blind Japanese boys play Paganini for him every day and could be expected to remember Narimichi. What mattered was that the kindness and concern shown to him by one of the world's outstanding violinists greatly encouraged Narimichi.

All the same, Narimichi remained doubtful about whether he wanted and was able to pursue a career as a violinist. At 14, he had gone almost totally blind. For the last four years he had spent most of his waking hours with his violin in a darkened, soundproofed room. Now he was about to graduate from junior high school and the question of his future loomed large. Should he go to a general senior high school, or should he audition for a place at the high school attached to Tōhō Gakuen School of Music, one of the best vocational high schools for music? The answer seemed obvious and in the end Narimichi agreed. He auditioned with

Etō Toshiya, who told him, "Without fail I will make you a first-class violinist."[43] This assurance from Japan's greatest teacher was again encouraging, but even so there were times when Narimichi lost heart. His father recalled that once when he came home from work and as usual went straight to the practice room, Narimichi made no motion to take up his violin. Instead he suddenly said, "I'm working so hard, but if I can't make it as a soloist, there's no point, is there." At last he had voiced the nagging doubt his father must have felt many times. What could Masao say? In vain he tried to reassure his son. Finally, he left the room. He joined his wife at the dining table, and they waited in anxious silence. After a long time, the sound of Narimichi's violin came down to them from the upper floor. They smiled at each other in relief; then Masao returned upstairs as if to resume battle. Narimichi persisted, through many moments of despair, graduating from high school and continuing to Tōhō Gakuen School of Music. In 1990 he won the third prize in the Japan Music Competition. Encouraging as this was, that same year, 1990, his fellow student at Tōhō Gakuen Suwanai Akiko won the first prize at the International Tchaikovsky Competition.

Narimichi's graduation in 1994 again raised the question of his future. After much deliberation it was decided that he should have the chance to study abroad. Etō recommended London and the Kawabatas sent an audition tape to the Royal Academy. To their delight Narimichi was accepted, but he could not travel and live abroad alone. His parents decided that his mother would accompany him. For the next three years, Narimichi and his mother lived in London, while his father and brothers had to manage by themselves. Narimichi did well at the Royal Academy. He won a competition and was chosen to play Bruch's Scottish Fantasy for the Academy's 175th anniversary celebration in 1997. A day later he graduated top of his class; Yehudi Menuhin himself presented him with his diploma. His debut recital at Wigmore Hall the following year was a success, and success abroad, as so often, attracted interest in Japan. Narimichi made his Japan debut in Tokyo's Suntory Hall with the Japan Philharmonic Orchestra under Kobayashi Ken'ichirō, playing Mendelssohn's Violin Concerto.

Since then he has given numerous performances in Japan and abroad to acclaim and is also known for his charity work.[44] His first CD, released in 1999, *On Wings of Song*, reached the top of the classical charts in

Japan, as did his second one, *Ave Maria,* which came out the following year. He released his eleventh CD, with works by Kreisler, in 2011, and his performances have reached audiences who do not normally listen to classical music. Although still based in London, he frequently performs in Japan and is kept in the public mind by a stream of media reports, no doubt helped by his life story. In September 2000, 20 years after his first fateful trip to California, Narimichi made a well-publicized return to perform a benefit concert for the Japanese American Culture and Community Center.[45] The audience included several members of the staff from UCLA's Medical Center, which Narimichi visited the following day, accompanied by a TV crew from NHK, who were making a documentary. The story of Kawabata's progress from the disastrous holiday in Los Angeles to his triumphant return has been made into a television re-enactment drama and even found its way into English-language textbooks for Japanese high schools.[46] Kawabata has become a contemporary version of Noguchi Hideyo, who overcame disability to become a world-class scientist, returning triumphant to his home village, where as a child he burnt his hand in the hearth.

Temma Atsuko, although she is half a generation older than Kawabata, achieved her big breakthrough only a few years before him, with the release of her CD *Balada* in 1993, and her story too has become part of her trademark. The work that gave the CD its title was a short piece by a Romanian composer virtually unknown outside his homeland. Until then Temma had enjoyed a respectable but unspectacular career, which she describes in her memoir *Song of My Heart: Nostalgic Ballad,* published in 2000 and in its third impression by 2004.[47] Indeed, Temma's first public appearance at the age of 12 in the popular NHK television programme *Violin Lesson* in the 1960s hardly made her seem predestined for violin stardom.[48]

Temma did not come from a musical family and her parents did not push her. During the six months she took part in the television series, her mother, who could not even read music, soon gave up pretending to take notes like the other mothers and knitted an entire suit instead.[49] She did, however, support Atsuko, and when the series ended she set out to find another teacher. An acquaintance introduced her to Inoue Takeo. A professor at Geidai, a national institution, he was a civil servant, as was Atsuko's father, and he agreed to teach her for a modest fee. Three years later she successfully auditioned for the high school affiliated with Geidai. Inoue, who told her that she needed a younger and more energetic teacher, saw to it that she received lessons from Unno Yoshio; a remarkable gesture of support, for Unno was a student of Inoue's rival Uzuka Tatsuo. Unno already had the reputation of being second only to Etō Toshiya. His busy concert schedule, however, meant that his lessons were irregular. When Uzuka, the headmaster, realized this, he secretly gave her lessons himself. Still, when Unno did teach her she found in him a mentor who encouraged her to think for herself, took her to rehearsals and concerts and even listened to her talk about personal problems. He continued to be her teacher when she enrolled at Geidai and later employed her as his assistant.

Temma had a few competition successes while at university: in 1974 she came first at the Japan Music Competition; in 1975 she was awarded a special silver medal at the Long–Thibaud competition; and in 1976 she was invited to enter a new competition in Santiago de Chile, where she received a special prize.[50] She did not, however, go abroad to study; family circumstances did not permit it and she was content with her teacher Unno Yoshio, who did not urge it. Still, she attended an international summer course in Nice during her first year at graduate school to study with Leonid Kogan (whom she had met through a relative). In 1986, when she was already pursuing a performing career, she was introduced to Herman Krebbers, who came to Tokyo to judge in the International Music Competition. For nearly 15 years she flew to Amsterdam five or six times a year for one and a half days of intensive study with Krebbers[51] – possibly a record in long-distance commuting for violin lessons.

Meanwhile, her career plodded along in an unremarkable fashion. She had given her debut recital in 1979, a year before finishing graduate school, and continued to give yearly recitals at Tōkyō Bunka Kaikan, one of Tokyo's premier classical music venues; she regularly performed with the pianist and doyen of chamber music, Tamura Hiroshi. She taught as an instructor at Geidai from 1981 to 1984 and then at the affiliated high school. She had a manager and producer; she had opportunities to perform in Japan and abroad and had made recordings. She even played a 1735 Stradivarius, bought for her use in 1987.[52] Even so, she could just about pay her bills, which included the costs of the recitals given at her own expense and the cost of her lessons in the Netherlands. She might one day secure a more permanent teaching post, but real fame seemed likely to elude her.

Temma's breakthrough came as a result of coincidence, and the story has been told many times by Temma herself and the other people involved. In summer 1992 Temma toured Romania, Bulgaria and Czechoslovakia as a cultural ambassador sponsored by the Japan Foundation. After her concert in Bucharest, she was approached by Okada Masaki of the Japanese Foreign Ministry, himself an accomplished amateur violinist. Okada told her that about ten years previously he had been given a score by a Romanian emigrant violinist in Vienna, who had asked him to pass it on to a suitable Japanese violinist who could introduce it to Japan. The music was *Balada* (*Ballad)* for violin and piano, composed in 1880 by Ciprian Porumbescu (1853–83), one of the most celebrated Romanian composers of his time.[53] One of the most famous of his over 250 compositions, *Balada* is well-loved in Romania, but little known anywhere else.

Back in Japan, Temma duly received the score, studied it and began playing *Balada* to herself. She was doing this during a tea break in a recording session, when her producer, Nakano Takashi, overheard her and asked what she was playing. Temma told him how she had come by *Balada* and Nakano decided then and there to record another CD with *Balada* as its title piece. The CD was launched at a recital in December 1993 and quickly became a hit. It is easy to understand why *Balada*, or "Nostalgic Ballad" as it was called in Japanese, would appeal to a Japanese audience: a deeply Romantic piece with a bittersweet, haunting melody, it conjures up similar sentiments to some of Japan's most popular songs, from the school song classic "Moon over the Castle Ruins" by Taki Rentarō (who, like Porumbescu, died young) to Kishi Kōichi's short violin pieces to the sentimental *enka* ballads. Moreover, if ever a composition and a violinist whom the composer never knew were made for each other, it was *Balada* and Temma Atsuko. The piece suited her playing style down to the ground and her performance had the audience in tears. The premiere in Yokohama was followed by several sold-out concerts in Tokyo; numerous television appearances followed. In short, with *Balada* as her trademark, Temma achieved the kind of star status seldom accorded to classical musicians. Her name became known beyond the confines of classical music and even inspired a novel by

Takaki Nobuko, a winner of the prestigious Akutagawa literary prize, with the title *A Hundred Year Prophecy*. Serialized in the *Asahi* newspaper in 1998, the novel features a passionate main character modelled on Temma, and, of course, the *Balada*.[54] The original CD was reissued in 2003 (after she had switched labels) to mark the tenth anniversary of the first launch. Other albums followed, most of them themed compilations of short pieces: *Japanesque* (May 2005), *Prayer* (September 2005), *Zigeunerweisen* (with a travel theme, September 2006), *Salut d'amour* (June 2007) *Monologue* (October 2009). In May 2004 *Balada* became the theme of her first DVD, entitled *Balada: Temma Atsuko in Hayama, 2004*. Other offerings for fans have included a nine-day canal cruise through Belgium and Holland for fans, featuring Temma's performances, no doubt with renderings of the *Balada*.

Tacky marketing aside, in her memoir Temma appears as a serious musician in the classical tradition, dedicated to her art and well prepared to seize the moment when it came. Her recordings include Bach's unaccompanied works and she has also given unaccompanied recitals playing Bach, Bartók and works by Japanese composers, as well as the inevitable *Balada*. Clearly, a popular image and serious playing are not mutually exclusive. Perhaps the combination adds to the attraction of Temma's story. Although quite different from Kawabata's, it too tells of perseverance bearing well-earned fruit. For both violinists, their stories help keep them in the public mind in a world where conservatoires spew out talented graduates every year, where every year produces a new crop of competition winners, and where study abroad with famous teachers has become too commonplace to make a player stand out.

## 2. Violin Mums Speak Out: Gotō Setsu and Senju Fumiko

She travels all over Japan and even across continents with her child in pursuit of famous teachers. She videotapes lessons. At public master classes, she avidly takes notes not only during her child's lessons but all the lessons. She leaves her other children to fend for themselves and accepts daily conflict, estrangement from her husband and near-bankruptcy in the pursuit of her talented violinist child's development. This is how (in 2005) the weekly magazine *AERA* described the "violin mama."[55] And, the magazine could have added, she writes a book about it. Perhaps this is the most salient difference between Japanese stage mothers and their European or North American counterparts.[56] In Japan a striking number of mothers have written books about how they brought up their successful children (not just violinists). And these books sell, thanks to the widespread belief that the environment, the parents' (particularly the mother's) involvement, and unceasing effort are more important for success and stardom than inborn genius. Small wonder then that ambitious parents want to know how other parents managed their children's success. The violin mum's career starts earlier than that of most education mums, since even toddlers can be taught to draw a bow over the string of a 1/32-sized violin.

As far back as 1949, Etō Toshiya's mother, although she did not write a book herself, was the subject of a magazine article detailing the way she had educated her successful son.[57] Wanami Takayoshi's mother Sonoko's book, *A Symphony of Mother and Child,* published in 1977, has been reprinted several times. She wrote a sequel, *Symphony of Life*, published in 1981 and likewise reprinted.[58] The book tells the story of how she accompanied her son on his travels around the world, as he gave concerts, made recordings and won international acclaim. Meanwhile his father, diagnosed with cancer, is represented as the silent martyr in the background, left alone to battle with terminal illness and finally dying in 1977.

The largely absent father is also a characteristic of the books written by Gōtō Setsu and Senju Fumiko. In Setsu's case this is understandable, since her marriage effectively ended when she took Midori to New York.[59] Because Midori's spectacular debut and her famous "conquest" of Tanglewood happened outside Japan, the Japanese did not immediately take notice. When they did, Setsu was asked to write a book about her and her daughter's life together. *Ame no Uta/Regenlied* (Rain Song) was published in 1987. Since then Setsu has achieved what may well be unique in the history of violin prodigies so far; 14 years after producing one wunderkind playing Paganini at the tender age of ten, she produced another playing the same Paganini at the even younger age of seven. Of course, ever since the days of Wolferl and Nannerl Mozart, child prodigies have come in pairs or even threes of siblings, often to be presented to the public as an ensemble. But Midori and Ryū each grew up as an only child and the only time they performed together was when Midori played the piano at Ryū's first recital.[60] Small wonder that Gotō Setsu has received media attention. In 2007 her second book, a slim volume based on lectures she gave around the country, was prominently displayed in Tokyo's music shops. By then she had herself become the subject of a detailed biography by the journalist, Okuda Akinori.[61]

Gotō Setsu was born in 1949. Her grandfather Masataka was for many years the mayor of her hometown of Moriguchi, a suburb of Osaka. Her mother Kizaki Mieko, a trained pharmacist, opened a pharmacy two years before her second daughter Setsu's birth – an unusual step for a woman of her generation. Setsu's father Tomoharu was adopted into the Kizaki family when he married Mieko, a common pattern in traditionally minded families bent on securing their continuity even in the absence of a male heir. From the Kizakis' point of view he was a disappointment: leaving his wife to run the shop, he devoted himself to karate training. Setsu received her first violin from her mother at the age of five. Not that the Kizaki family was particularly musical, but times were uncertain, the family had no major assets, and music, thought Mieko, was universal, so even a woman might be able to somehow make a living from it.[62]

Setsu studied with Tanaka Heisaburō. When he died in 1959, his wife introduced the Kizakis to Tōgi Yūji.[63] Setsu also attended classes in ensemble playing and musical theory at Sōai Gakuen School for Girls, which had a music department and a branch of Saitō Hideo's Music School for Children. In 1967 Setsu graduated from the music department of Sōai Gakuen High School with top marks for her violin performance. While still at school she had earned money accompanying popular songs in the studio of Shōwa Productions (the agency managed by the violinist Tōyama Shinji). She continued her studies at Sōai Music College. During her first year (in 1967) she took part in the Japan Music Competition and came first in the preliminary round in Osaka. Not believing that she had a chance of winning, however, she gave up before the next round. Sumi Saburō, who taught her during his regular visits to Osaka, was so angry that he refused to teach her forthwith. She also fell out with Saitō Hideo during an orchestra rehearsal. When Saitō Hideo yelled at the young women in the violin section, "you lot aren't here to prepare for marriage," she countered, "I *am* preparing for marriage," and left the rehearsal.

Without waiting for her graduation Setsu secretly auditioned for the Tokyo Symphony Orchestra. It was the second time she had tried to run away from home. This time the Kizakis, a traditionally minded family who rated the honour of their house higher than the personal fulfilment of an individual member, apparently felt that desperate measures were required to keep their recalcitrant daughter on the rails. They decided to marry her off. Setsu's mother, having snatched Setsu's violin in Tokyo, promised to return it if Setsu consented to marry a man of their choice. Reluctantly Setsu agreed, having elicited the promise from her future husband that he would allow her to play in a professional orchestra. In April 1970 she married Gotō Teruo, the son of a wealthy family from Himeji and a graduate of Osaka University.

If Teruo, who had taken a liking to Setsu, thought she would settle down and become a typical suburban housewife, he was wrong. Setsu's pursuit of a musical career may not have been wholehearted, but she still devoted far more time to her violin than Teruo liked. Nor did the birth of Midori improve their relationship. Setsu had hoped for a boy and at first had no maternal feelings for her baby. Once she did, however, and especially when she began teaching her three-year-old the violin, she developed the close bond with her child that was typical of many mothers in her situation. Unlike these other mothers, however, Setsu's talent for the violin gave her a measure of independence even after her marriage. She gave private lessons and freelanced in recording studios and college orchestras. The money she earned she spent on Midori's musical education, taking her to concerts and to private lessons with Sumi Saburō in Tokyo. When did Setsu realize that developing her daughter's talent could not only secure Midori's future, but provide Setsu herself with an escape route out of a marriage she hated and into an interesting and challenging life abroad in which she would learn as much as her daughter? Setsu's teacher Tōgi told her that Midori, with her individual style, would not do well at national music competitions; Sumi Saburō and Urakawa Takaya said Midori needed the best teacher, better than anyone Japan could offer.[64] But it is hard to see such assertions as anything but an expression of Japan's 'Western music complex," even though Midori would hardly have enjoyed the same early fame and spectacular career she did had she remained in Japan. For Setsu, Midori's teachers' advice provided the justification for giving up the security of a suburban home for an uncertain life in a foreign city, in a tiny apartment, with no steady income and no guarantee of success. Quite possibly, her first encounter with Dorothy DeLay, to whom she appears to have taken an instant liking, strengthened her resolve.

The title of Setsu's first book, *Regenlied,* was inspired by Brahms's Violin Sonata in G major, Op. 78 of 1879, which Midori was playing at the time.[65] To Setsu, Midori's liking for the sonata represented her daughter's maturing sensibilities as she left childhood behind her. Setsu wrote the book at a time of crisis; while Midori confronted the challenges of adolescence, her mother, in her late thirties, faced the confusion of a relationship with a married man ten years her junior. Setsu's book expresses her sense that the close relationship she shared with her daughter was coming to an end. She shows a keen awareness of the emotional difficulties Midori is burdened with as the result of her mother's choices: the absence of a father and an excessive sensitivity to her mother's feelings.

In contrast, Setsu's second book, published 20 years later in 2007, largely lacks the self-doubt that characterizes the first; or rather, the self-doubt is countered by a high degree of self-righteousness. Entitled *How to Bring up "Geniuses,"* it is based on transcriptions of her taped lectures and interviews. By now Setsu had brought up another "child prodigy" in Gotō Ryū and was in demand as a speaker – unlike the early years of Midori's rising fame, when the Japanese media had often criticized her for putting too much pressure on her daughter and acting like a "stage mama." Despite the book's title, Setsu emphatically denies that her children are "*tensai*" at all, or at least that they are more so than other children. She even describes Midori as "clumsy" (*bukiyō*).[66] Midori and Ryū succeeded because they grew up in an environment filled with violin playing. While Setsu's emphasis on the importance of the environment and the mother's role is reminiscent of Suzuki's *Nurtured by Love,* her approach to teaching the violin is certainly not. Suzuki aimed to encourage the children and to let them learn playfully. Setsu, in contrast, rejects the idea that learning the violin can be fun for the child. Because it is important to get everything right from the start, she advocates strictness, and even defends her use of corporal punishment; praise, she asserts, amounts to spoiling the child. Setsu categorically denies being an "education mum" who pushed her daughter to compensate for her own failed career. Even Japanese observers think otherwise.[67] For Western observers it is difficult to imagine anyone who better fits the image of the quintessential Japanese education mum.

Japanese who write about their experiences of life abroad often praise conditions there in order to highlight what they perceive as weaknesses in Japan. Setsu sometimes does the same, but she also advocates values the Japanese like to think of as their very own: learning through imitation and repetition, and the cultivation of endurance. She stresses the virtue of difficulty overcome by effort; Midori's "clumsiness" proved an asset, because she learnt to master difficulties by intensive practice; children who learn too easily often practise too little, because they can play something at the first attempt.[68] Her observation is reminiscent of Watanabe Shigeo's father Suehiko's similar view about Shigeo's early struggles, and of Kawabata Masao's remarks about his own development.

Setsu's claim that she did not intend her children to become violinists, and that she would not mind if they stopped any day, sounds like self-deception on a monumental scale. More likely, she was compensating for the career she had herself missed out on; the year the book was published she told an interviewer that she had pursued her own studies too half-heartedly.[69] By emphasizing her own role as the mother she takes most of the credit for her children's achievements. Given the role she played in their education this might seem reasonable enough, but the extent to which she downplays her children's considerable talents is puzzling, if not disturbing. Another issue she downplays is Midori's illness. She admits that she had never previously heard of anorexia or depression and that she may not have understood Midori as well as she thought. But she links the illness almost exclusively to the role of the violin in Midori's life. And while Setsu expresses a great deal of concern that Ryū would feel pressure from his elder sister's high achievements, she gives no indication of having considered how the excessively close relationship between mother and daughter, her own new relationship with Kaneshiro, the birth of Ryū and his early debut as a "super-wunderkind" might have affected her daughter and contributed to her breakdown in 1994.

It is hard to see what an ambitious Japanese mother might learn from *How to Bring up "Geniuses"* (imagining a father reading it is even harder). Like others before her, Setsu stresses the importance of the learning environment and of the mother's dedication. She defends blind imitation and repetition as an effective way of learning for children and stresses the virtues of endurance and hard work. She urges mothers to regard bringing up their children as a "mission,"[70] to have confidence and not to be afraid of being labelled "over-protective." Far from advocating anything new and innovative, Setsu reiterates well-established values. Some of these values, however, have come under criticism in recent years, having revealed themselves as ineffective in a changing world, as many of the problems Japanese society is confronting today show.[71]

In 2007 Setsu opened a non-profit private music school named "Ongaku Dōjō." Under the motto "Effort, Perseverance, Respect," the school offers morning classes for children wishing to learn the violin and training classes for teachers and parents. The term *dōjō* more commonly describes a training hall for karate than a violin studio, and, as with martial arts, the school's aims extend beyond teaching specific skills to general character training, as well as communication between educators and children and within the family.[72]

If Gotō Setsu goes out of her way to downplay the extraordinary in the story of her children, particularly her daughter, Senju Fumiko, the mother of Senju Mariko, elevates the ordinary to the extraordinary. She has produced several books in quick succession: *The Senju Family's White Paper on Education,* first published in 2001 (followed by a paperback edition in 2005); *The Day the Stradivarius Came to the Senju Family* (2005) and, together with Mariko, *Concerto for Mother and Daughter* (2005).[73]

Not that the Senju family is conventional: all three of Fumiko's children are successful artists. Senju Mariko the violinist is the youngest; Senju Hiroshi, the eldest son, is a painter and his brother Akira a composer. The brothers studied at Geidai. Fumiko believes that the seed of her children's love for art began when they all had violin lessons with Sumi Saburō. Nevertheless, it is the violinist daughter who takes centre stage in her books. Compared to those of Wanami Takayoshi and Midori, Senju Mariko's career, although busy and successful, is prosaic. Born in 1962, she studied with Sumi Saburō and Etō Toshiya and came first at national competitions in 1973 and 1977. In 1975 she made her debut with the NHK Symphony Orchestra; this marked the beginning of her career as a soloist. In 1979 she won fourth place at the Paganini competition, and she has since performed abroad often. But she did not study abroad for any significant period, and her career has centred on Japan, where she performs mainly as a soloist. She has released several CDs and published edited collections of violin pieces, books and articles.

20: Cover of Senju Fumiko's book, *Senju-ke ni Sutoradivariusu ga kita hi* (The Day the Stradivarius Came to the Senju Family, Tokyo: Shinchōsha, 2005).

Like the Wanamis, the Senjus were not a family of musicians. Senju Fumiko worked as a researcher for a pharmaceutical company before her marriage. Her husband Shizuo was a professor at Keiō University. He died in September 2000, and Fumiko began writing a few months later.

Her first book *The Senju Family's White Paper on Education,* billed as "the record of the mother who brought up three international artists" and reprinted several times, appears to have found a wide readership. Not that Fumiko's book offers direct advice on how to bring up artists. Instead she has written a story replete with the kind of values regarded as "traditional" and held dear by many Japanese, the story of a three-generation family living on the same premises, close enough together for Fumiko to carry the proverbial bowl of hot soup to her parents' house without it going cold.[74] Held together by strong emotional bonds, grandparents, parents and children draw together in difficult times, suffer together, overcome hardship through cooperation and persistent effort, and finally achieve success.

Only gradually does the violin come to play a central role in the family story. When Fumiko wanted Akira to have violin lessons (Hiroshi was learning the piano), an acquaintance introduced her to Sumi Saburō, whose name Fumiko knew from the NHK *Violin Lesson* series. Sumi, despite his reputation as a teacher of virtuosos, told Fumiko he liked teaching amateurs best and urged her to let all her children learn, so they could enjoy playing together. Mariko was too small at first, but a few months after her second birthday he began to teach her as well as her brothers. Perhaps because he began to teach her so early, Sumi took a special interest in her. When she was ten, he suggested that she take part in the Student Music Competition, just for the experience of playing for an audience in a party frock and with a smile – or so the Senju family story goes. From then on Mariko was singled out among the Senju siblings. While the boys spent their summer holidays in club activities and at summer camps, mother and daughter worked all hours on the competition repertoire. The violin forged a bond between mother and daughter, drawing them together in a relationship not unlike that between Gotō Setsu and Midori, except that it flourished within a close-knit family. Mariko, despite being one of the youngest entrants and having to play on a damaged violin, won second prize. Not content with her success, she entered again the following year. Another summer of incessant practice ensued, cementing the closeness between mother and daughter. This time, in 1973, Mariko came first and won the chance to perform with the NHK orchestra in a concert introducing budding talents in 1975. She played Bach's Double Concerto in D minor with Etō

Toshiya. Etō's fame as a teacher rivalled Sumi's, and the Senjus decided that Mariko should study with him. Changing teachers is a tricky business in Japan, more so than elsewhere perhaps, because of the lingering *iemoto* tradition, in which transferring one's loyalties to another teacher was unthinkable. Mariko's mother went to Sumi to apologize profusely. Wanami Sonoko had similar scruples when she transferred Takayoshi from Tsuji to Sumi.

The lessons with Etō are described in *Concerto for Mother and Daughter* as a succession of twice or thrice weekly dramas. At the first meeting he told mother and daughter, not without a hint of sarcasm, that he would get the blame if the "girl prodigy" did not become an outstanding virtuoso. The contrast to Sumi, whom Fumiko portrays as a benign grandfather, although he too has been described as instilling fear into his pupils and their parents, could not have been greater. Fumiko claims she was even more afraid of him than Mariko was, and when they got into her car together after the lessons the sense of relief was palpable. Mariko asserts that she could never have survived without her mother's constant support.

When Mariko turned 15, the minimum age for the Japan Music Competition for adults, Etō recommended that she enter. He would be touring America between the first of the three rounds and the final one, but promised to give Mariko extra-intensive lessons before and after his trip. In any case, he appears to have relied on students' parents as assistant teachers at least as much as Suzuki Shin'ichi, and Fumiko was by then an experienced competition coach. Mother and daughter spent yet another summer rehearsing competition repertoire (an unaccompanied fugue by Bach, a Paganini caprice and the Dvořák Violin Concerto). Despite being the youngest participant since the introduction of the age limit, Mariko went on to win the 1977 competition, having already caused a media sensation in the first round, and solidified her reputation as a prodigy.

In the following years Mariko worked hard to keep up school work while pursuing an increasingly busy performance schedule. But, like Midori in her late teens, Mariko, at the age of 20, suffered a period where the pressures of a solo career and the transition to adulthood became too much. Ever since her first public successes she had been plagued by the envy and backbiting that too often result from being in the limelight.

Years of gruelling practice and the strains of combining full-time study with a professional career had worn down her resilience, and her health suffered. For a year she abandoned the violin. If Fumiko is to be believed, the whole family suffered excruciatingly during this time; after all, the whole family had invested in Mariko's success. Suffering is one of the themes in Fumiko's story. During the years her children grew up, she was also caring for her own parents. Initially, they lived next door. Eventually their house was converted and the three generations lived there together.[75] Undoubtedly the Senjus' family life was challenging. But whether the family's suffering was unique, as Fumiko and Mariko claim (Fumiko even uses the word *junan* in connection with preparing for a competition, a word suggesting martyrdom, which is also used to describe the passion of Christ), is open to question.[76] Caring for ageing parents in the home is still perceived as the ideal in Japan and many a Japanese woman must have spent years combining the roles of mother, assistant teacher, devoted wife and housewife and dutiful daughter.

Perhaps this is the appeal of Senju Fumiko's books; under her pen the mundane becomes special. Events familiar to many of her readers become unique. Violin lessons represent a drama (or melodrama) in which Etō, simultaneously villain and hero, turns each meeting into a test of survival. Mariko may not have a disability like Kawabata Narimichi, but she is always fighting against higher odds than her rivals: at competitions she is the youngest, the only one not already billed as a prodigy or embarked on a professional career, the least prepared, with the hardest pieces to play and the most catching-up to do. Her "professional debut" (never a mere "debut") at age 12 with the NHK Orchestra gives rise to waves of hostility which finally leads to her collapse eight years later. And through all the suffering the strong family bonds provide support.

The drama reaches a new climax when in 2002 Mariko receives the chance to try out the 1716 "De Duranty" Stradivarius which is being offered for sale. In *The Day the Stradivarius Came to the Senju Family*, Fumiko exploits the Stradivarius myth to the full; Mariko's suffering and her Quest for the Perfect Violin take on epic dimensions. The Strad and Mariko appear made for each other, even foretold 20 years previously in a deathbed prophecy by Fumiko's mother. Mariko's brother Akira calls it a symbol for the paternal support she has lost. The family has one month to find the money; they all rally round and help Mariko secure a loan that will keep her playing to the end of her days, but enabled her to purchase the instrument of her dreams. Skilfully blending the mundane with the mystique, Fumiko's story conveys a powerful message that fits in well with widespread beliefs: through hard work, overcoming suffering, and family loyalty, even ordinary people can win seemingly unattainable rewards. A violinist, we are constantly told, has a hard life, which only the toughest can survive.[77]

For Mariko, the Stradivarius takes the place of a husband or even the need for one: "When I began to play the Duranty two years ago, I came to feel I'd tightened my belt and resolved, 'I might as well not be a woman.' (...) Apart from playing the violin I no longer want to do anything else now." She even claims to have discarded her womanhood entirely. To perform a concerto with an orchestra, she insists, she has to become a man. She describes her profession in words reminiscent of the samurai tradition: playing a solo is like crossing swords (*tachiuchi*), a "struggle to the death (*shinimonogurui*)." Her brother, the composer Senju Akira, even likens his sister's performances to that of a kamikaze unit (*tokkōtai*). Her mother adds to the picture when she laments her daughter's battle-scarred body: "Haven't you always got plasters stuck all over your body," and, "your body has changed (...) that is not the body of a normal woman, all your bones and sinews." Instead of the well-rounded feminine forms most mothers would like to see in their daughter, Fumiko declares, Mariko's body is angular and deformed by the violinist's mark under her chin; indeed "you have almost become a violin yourself." Mariko's rejection of the conventional female role has repercussions for her mother: "I have no daughter at home," she states categorically at the start of *Concerto for Mother and Daughter.*[78] Contrary to the traditional family values which Fumiko's books otherwise extol, her unmarried daughter does not stay at home to care for her ageing mother, but dashes around the country (and beyond) with her violin, coming home from her "battles" to be tended by Fumiko while she prepares for the next round. Even if she had children of her own, her schedule would not permit her to devote as much time and energy to their education as her mother did to hers. Nevertheless, with a harmony in keeping with the book's title, mother and daughter agree that both life choices, the devoted wife and mother and the devoted artist, are equally valid.

In 2006 Fumiko's health finally failed, and Mariko had to assume a more conventional role. Realizing that her mother was seriously ill, she had to override Fumiko's protests that it was nothing, and ensure that she received the best possible medical help.[79] In 2009 Fumiko published yet another book, *The Senju Family's Tale of Life*. The blurb reads: "The mother of the Senju family broke down with heart disease. Her three children Hiroshi, Akira and Mariko once again join forces and face up to the difficulties of an operation at an advanced age. A moving document detailing how, with heart disease overcome, the family gained new life."[80]

As with Gotō Setsu and Midori, the violin forges a close bond between mother and daughter. While Mariko's brothers seem to have pursued their chosen paths with little parental involvement beyond encouragement, to Mariko her mother's role was crucial. Fumiko is not a violinist herself like Setsu; she learnt the piano in her youth, on an Ibach piano her parents brought back from Germany, where her father studied biochemistry. Still, classical music was a well-established part of the family folklore. Fumiko's mother often told her how, on their voyage out, Albert Einstein had played the violin for them on deck in the middle of the Indian Ocean. While the circumstances of Midori's and Mariko's upbringings are different, the excessively close relationship between mother and daughter centred on the violin, and the resulting difficulties for the daughters in gaining independence, are similar, as is their mothers' invocation of widely held values in their books.

Meanwhile the father is largely absent in the story. Senju Mariko speaks about her relationship with her father as barely existent until the last years of his life.[81] In Fumiko's books he is portrayed in a similar way to Wanami Takayoshi's father: the silent corporate warrior in the background whose hard work enables his wife to devote herself completely to the family and the education of her children, and who dies a martyr's death.

The violin provides Gotō Setsu and Senju Fumiko with a purpose in life as they find a fulfilment in their daughters' careers which they did not seek in their own professional lives because they married. Meanwhile, their daughters have no children of their own and seem married to their violins. Ironically, both mothers express hopes that they will find Mr. Right (Setsu) or lament their failure to meet conventional expectations (Fumiko) although they themselves have played a large part in wedding their daughters to the violin.

## 3. In the Shadow of Cremona and Xiqiao: Violin Making Today[82]

*The annual Stringed Instrument Fair organized by the Japan String Instrument Makers Association's (JSIMA) Tokyo is a hands-on affair, where visitors are encouraged to try out the instruments. Accordingly, the hall echoed with phrases from the great concertos played with practised hands, but also rather less skilful attempts at student staples like Vivaldi's Concerto in A minor (RV 356). To boost active engagement, the fiftieth exhibition in 2007 featured a kind of competition-cum-rally. Participants could test up to twenty violins, five violas and nine cellos, all by Japanese makers, and stamp a mark next to the maker's name on a form handed out to visitors on entering the hall. They were then asked to name the makers of their favourite instruments. From the ballots submitted two quartets of stringed instruments would be selected and presented in an all-Mozart programme on the second day of the exhibition.*

The rise of the violin in Japan owed much to the ability of Japanese craftsmen to produce cheap instruments. Without Suzuki Masakichi and his factory, the violin could never have become as popular as it did. The downside was that the name Suzuki and by extension that of Japan became associated with cheap violins of dubious quality. But Suzuki himself and other luthiers were not content with a reputation for cheap products; they strove to make fine violins that could rival the best foreign ones. Japan has a long tradition of expert woodworkers, whether makers of fine buildings or of cabinets or of Japan's native musical instruments. More recently, Japan has produced some fine luthiers. But the myth of the superior "old Italians," invoked so eloquently by Senju Fumiko, will continue to weigh heavily on them as long as Japanese musicians believe that the real thing can only be found abroad. Instruments with a Cremona label sell well in Japan, better than even German and French master instruments. Even these sell better than Japanese ones. The mystique surrounding the names "Stradivarius" and "Cremona" in the West pales before the tremendous awe they inspire in Japan.

Once rising wealth and the rising yen brought "old Italians" within reach, institutions and individuals vied to acquire what was on offer on the international market. By the 1970s the purchase of a Stradivarius was no longer newsworthy, unless the buyer, like Tsuji Hisako, had sold their house for it.[83] As the economy bubbled to new heights the number of Stradivariuses in Japan increased steeply; from 18 to over 70 between 1983 and 1985.[84] Evidently the scandal of 1981–82 had not diminished the faith of the Japanese in brands, even though it had proved that obsession with big names and spending power combined with ignorance provided a fertile ground for fraud, a problem experts had pointed out in the subsequent public debates.[85] An obvious solution was offered by the music critic Hasegawa Takehisa. Reporting on his visits to several workshops of contemporary violin makers, he did his best to convince the public that old and foreign was not necessarily best and that an excellent-sounding violin could be had at a reasonable price.[86]

The Japan String Instrument Makers Association (JSIMA), whose address Hasegawa included in his report, has been doing its best to spread the same message. Every year it holds an exhibition in Tokyo in order to introduce works by its members to the public. Held for the first time in 1957 in an instrument shop in the Ginza district of Tokyo, the Stringed Instrument Fair attracts a mixed audience, among them teachers and music students and the odd mother with her child who needs their first full-size violin. Over the years, it has expanded, and in 2007 it filled seven halls (2,419 square metres) at the Museum of Science and Technology, six of them devoted to bowed, the seventh to plucked instruments. It has also internationalized. While 28 companies and 45 individual makers of bowed instruments were Japanese or based in Japan, one came from China and 16 companies and individuals had come from Europe, particularly Italy (7) and France (5). Even so, showcasing Japanese makers is still central to the event. In his address in the programme, Sonoda Nobuhiro, the president of JSIMA, stated that Japanese makers today win international competitions and need not fear comparison with their European colleagues. Several exhibitors displayed information about prizes they had won; Sonoda himself won a gold medal in Cremona in 1982.

But how much exposure do Japanese makers receive between the annual fairs? At two string instrument exhibitions held in Tokyo by Shimamura Music and Yamaha in Tokyo that same November, their instruments were conspicuously absent. The instruments came from Italy,

France and Germany and ranged from commercial brands to old and new master instruments, although Yamaha included models from its own ranges. "It's what the customers want," explained Moteki Ken, who trained with Murata and spent ten years in Germany before returning in 2003 with a German Meister diploma to take charge of Shimamura Music's string instruments section. He did, however, concede the possibility of a future boom in Japanese master instruments.

The veteran luthier Murata Sōroku seemed less optimistic about the future of violin-making. In 2007 he closed his violin-making school and retired. Several other schools still teach violin making to some extent: Kunitachi Music Academy (Kunitachi Ongakuin) has a lutherie department, as has Daikan'yama Music Academy, founded and managed by Shimamura Music. But Murata believes Japanese wanting to become truly proficient need to train abroad. Returning to Japan, they may well find that the high prices of imported materials and the prevailing infatuation with foreign brands render it impossible to make a living by selling their instruments.[87]

Meanwhile, where does Japan's oldest violin factory, Suzuki Violins stand today? Beset from both ends of the market, it would seem. At the cheap end, competition from China looms, while at the higher end, players pursue their dreams of owning a violin with a famous foreign name, ideally an "old Italian." Nevertheless, so far, the firm has managed to occupy a secure niche by concentrating on violins for the education market. Located in a quiet part of Nagoya, where small factories alternate with houses and small apartment buildings, the firm's premises look inconspicuous.[88] The office section faces the road; there is no showroom. Suzuki does not sell directly, but through designated wholesalers. In the courtyard stands a bust of Suzuki Masakichi holding his first violin. The ground floor of the factory building contains machines for cutting out the fronts, backs and scrolls. Not all the machines were running when I visited in November 2007, and I saw only two men at work. "We run the machines as necessary," explained Taniguchi Akio, the factory's managing director. In fact, although Masakichi carried mechanization further than most of his contemporaries, 85 per cent of the work today is done by hand. On the next floor several men and women worked with evident concentration, planing fronts and backs, giving the scroll its finished shape and assembling parts. The varnish is applied by hand in a separate, glass-enclosed space. In another room, workers were absorbed in finishing the varnished instruments. Suzuki Violins produces 8,200 stringed instruments a year, including 7,000 violins; bows come from a separate maker.

Compared to its heyday during the First World War, Suzuki Violins today is a tiny business employing only 30 people, including office staff. Exports have never again reached the peak they attained in those early boom years, and today only a small proportion, about a hundred instruments, is exported, mainly to America, Thailand, Taiwan and Hong Kong. The export market has been hit hardest by cheaper competition from China and elsewhere. The Japanese market, on the other hand, has remained relatively stable. In 2004 Suzuki received a "Made in Nagoya" award; according to the English webpage of the Nagoya Chamber of Commerce and Industry "the company enjoys the top market share" in "educational violins."[89] Today, Suzuki Violins wants to be known for quality rather than low prices; although beginners' outfits start at 56,000 yen, the pre-tax catalogue price of Suzuki's top-of-the range "Evidence," made from the best available imported wood costs 1,500,000 yen.[90] But Japanese parents, who take education seriously, are prepared to pay for quality.

Even in this price and quality range, however, Suzuki has competition. In the late nineteenth century, Suzuki Masakichi and Yamaha Torakusu, after a few attempts at encroaching on each other's territory, reached an agreement that they would each stick to their own patch; Yamaha would concentrate on keyboards and Suzuki on violins. More recently, however, Yamaha has expanded into stringed instruments. In 1997 they introduced the Silent Violin, an electric violin which reportedly feels and sounds like an acoustic violin when played, but with only a tenth of the volume; the upmarket models can be amplified for stage performances.[91] Yamaha, moreover, was conducting research into acoustic violins, and in 2000 the company launched its first model "Braviol" violin, followed by "Artida" in 2004. "Braviol" (the name is an amalgamation of "bravo" and "violin"), is modelled on Guarneri del Gesù's violins, while "Artida" comes in a Guarnerius ("G") and a Stradivarius ("S") version. Glossy brochures describe how Yamaha has discovered the famous makers' "secrets" and uses state-of-the-art digital technology, as well as superior craftsmanship and excellent materials, to reproduce them. The resulting product does not come cheap; the most expensive models cost 630,000 yen for the "Braviol" and 945,000 yen for the "Artida" in 2005. Makers at the JSIMA fair in 2007 were offering their violins from around 400,000 yen, although the better-known makers were asking for over 1,000,000 yen. Yamaha has also ventured into fractional violins and bows; its carbon bows are reportedly developed in cooperation with leading performers and include "signature models" endorsed by Pinchas Zukerman and Zakhar Bron; Bron also endorses the "Braviol" as an ideal instrument for young musicians in Yamaha's advertisements.

In the sales brochures, Yamaha skilfully addresses the inclinations of its Japanese customers; representing a well-known brand name itself, the company can invoke its own tradition as well as that of Cremona. Traditional "secrets" are associated with the high tech Japan is famous for and which therefore inspires confidence. Whether Yamaha violins and bows will be able to hold their own in the long run remains to be seen; given the success of its keyboard and wind instruments it is far from unlikely. Perhaps Yamaha's violins represent another step on the way to Japan's increasing confidence and self-reliance in a domain which was long regarded as belonging to the West.

## 4. Music for Love: Chamber Music

*For their thirty-second regular concert on 18 January 2010, the Morgaŭa Quartet had prepared an unusual programme. There was a "Chaikovsky," but the composer was Boris Alexandrovich Tchaikovsky (1925–96), not Pyotr Ilyich. His Quartet No. 3 (1967) was followed by Moisey Vainberg's[92] Quartet No. 6 (Op. 35, 1946) and Benjamin Britten's String Quartet No. 1 (Op. 25, 1941). All three composers, the programme explained, had a connection with Dmitry Shostakovich, Tchaikovsky and Vainberg being his students and Britten his closest friend among composers on the other side of the Iron Curtain. Unsurprisingly, the audience for this latest concert was small; the Recital Hall of the Tōkyō Bunka Kaikan (649 seats) was no more than half filled with what looked like regulars. Several violin cases were in evidence, the younger bearers perhaps students from the nearby University of Fine Arts and Music. But even in Europe such a programme would be unlikely to draw the crowds and I had myself noted the total absence of standard fare with apprehension. The Morgaŭa Quartet, however, played with such*

*conviction that my fear of boredom was soon dispelled, and when the
evening finished with Alfred Schnittke's Polka, I left the hall with regret
and an awareness of having enjoyed an unusual treat.*

The Morgaŭa Quartet is one of many active in Japan today, albeit one of
the more long-lived ones. The large number of professional string quartets
in Japan is surprising, considering the country's history of Western music.
For when the Japanese began to play Western classical music in the
nineteenth century, they did so mainly in choirs, military bands, and mixed
string and wind groups which grew into symphony orchestras once they
had enough competent players. Making Western music was about
edification, about joining the modern world, about demonstrating power.
Western music was the music of public places, the school, the concert (or
multi-functional) hall or the bandstand in a city park.

Chamber music is different, private, intimate even, like "whispering
among friends."[93] It is music played for the love of music itself and for
the enjoyment of those playing it together, perhaps with a few family
members or friends listening. By the time the Japanese encountered
Western music in the mid-nineteenth century, chamber music had moved
from the private salon into the public concert hall, and was increasingly
becoming something to listen to rather than to play. Even so, music-
making in the home was still a popular pastime, something the Japanese
could not fail to notice. The foreign teachers who came to Japan were
for the most part members of the middle classes, for whom singing and
playing a musical instrument were part of their education, and while they
lived in Japan it could serve to express and assert their cultural identity.[94]
The private nature of chamber music means that we cannot know how
many Japanese heard or even took part in informal music-making in the
homes of foreigners at home and abroad. But we have good reason to be
interested in the question. The extent to which Japanese have embraced
chamber music, whether as a private pastime in the home or as a
professional activity, provides a good indicator of their engagement with
Western classical music in general, beyond political and social
expectations.[95] For those aiming to make a living from music, forming a
chamber ensemble is more risky than joining an orchestra and less
lucrative than performing as a soloist.

Nevertheless, many professional string players (as well as amateurs), dream of playing in a string quartet.[96] The special sound created by music spread around four stringed instruments, three different sizes and pitch ranges made this particular combination of instruments popular soon after its emergence in the second half of the eighteenth century. Since then, almost all major composers have tried their hand at writing for the string quartet, providing it with a wide and varied repertoire. "String quartets are not just part of the classical tradition. They are its physical embodiment."[97] Musicians who left Europe, whether from choice or because they had to, recreated the civilization they had left by playing string quartets.[98] Several foreign violinists in Japan, amateurs and professionals played and performed string quartets with foreign or Japanese fellow musicians, among them August Junker, Leopold Premislaw, Josef König, Boris Lass and Willy Frey. After the Second World War, violinists from abroad, for example, Wolfgang Stavonhagen, likewise formed quartets with Japanese colleagues.

Meanwhile, more and more Japanese musicians performed chamber music, including string quartets from the beginning of the twentieth century. Violinists who led their own string quartets (besides Suzuki Shin'ichi and Matsumoto Zenzō, see Part 2 Chapters 3 and 4) included: Sueyoshi Yūji, the court musician; Hibino Aiji, concertmaster of the New Symphony Orchestra; Kuroyanagi Moritsuna, another member and concertmaster of the orchestra; and the violinist (later conductor) Watanabe Akeo. Hibino, Kuroyanagi and Watanabe resumed their activities soon after the war, another illustration of the continuity from the pre-war to the post-war period.

The year 1966 saw the establishment of two comparatively long-lived string quartets, the Iso Quartet and the Iwamoto Mari Quartet. The Iso Quartet holds the record, albeit with changing members; in the original line-up, the three Iso brothers, Hideo, Tsuneo and Yoshio, who had all studied with Ono Anna, played the top parts, while Nakajima Takahisa played the cello. Hideo left in 1969 to embark on a solo career and Tsuneo took his place, while Kawabata Masao (the father of Narimichi) joined the quartet as second violinist. In 1976 the cellist was replaced. Over the years more players came and went, but Iso Tsuneo continued to play first violin. The quartet cultivated a wide repertoire, with the Romantic period as its particular strength. Its recordings include works by the Japanese composers Moroi Saburō and Hattori Kōichi.

The most successful quartet of the early post-war period was the

Iwamoto Mari String Quartet, one of the first, if not the first all-Japanese string quartets that could have held its own on the stages of America and Europe and even "pass for a Central European quartet of the first rank."[99] But it made only one foreign tour, to Australia and New Zealand in 1971. Although Iwamoto Mari, the girl prodigy of pre-war days, gave her name to the quartet, she was the first to admit that its driving force and real leader was the cellist Kuronuma Toshio. Born in 1918, he graduated from the Tokyo Academy of Music in 1941, where he gained his first experience of playing chamber music. Soon after that he was drafted, sent to the northern territories and taken prisoner by the Russians. Repatriated to Japan in 1949, he joined the Tokyo Philharmonic Orchestra, and in 1956 the newly founded Japan Philharmonic Orchestra conducted by his friend Watanabe Akeo. He played in various chamber music groups, most importantly in a string quartet with Broadus Erle (1918–77), a Curtis graduate who had led a string quartet in New York before his appointment as concertmaster of the Japan Philharmonic Orchestra from 1956 to 1960. Erle and Kuronuma shared an interest in twentieth century composers.

Kuronuma had first met Iwamoto just after joining the army, at a charity performance in a Tokyo hospital, where she was playing quartet with Watanabe Akeo, Matsuura Kimiyo and Saitō Hideo. They first performed together in a concert by the Rameau chamber music group in September 1953, where Iwamoto played the solo violin in Ernest Chausson's Concerto for Violin, Piano and String Quartet, a work they performed together more than ten times over the next three years. In the following years they frequently played together in changing formations, including a piano trio with Date Jun. In 1961 Kuronuma was invited to the Malboro chamber music festival. Later that year he and Iwamoto performed Bartók's String Quartet No. 6 with Tomoda Yoshiaki and Kitazume Kisei; it was their first performance together as a string quartet and for Iwamoto the first quartet performance in 14 years. They continued to play string quartet with changing players. Kuronuma, who left the orchestra in 1962 also played with another group, the New Direction String Quartet, until its leader Kobayashi Kenji left for America.

The Iwamoto Mari String Quartet with Tomoda Yoshiaki and the violist Suganuma Junji (Suganuma was replaced by Oinuma Seiji when he became first violist of the NHK orchestra in 1976) officially started under that name in February 1966, with a broadcast of Dvořák's

"American" String Quartet on the Saturday night Fuji Seitetsu Concert programme; by then the four had been playing together since 1964. In 1965 they performed Brahms' complete chamber works. For the last concert of the series they were joined in the Sextet No. 2 by the future cellist of the Tokyo Quartet, Harada Sadao. In 1966 they became the first Japanese quartet to perform all six Bartók string quartets. Thanks to Kuronuma's enthusiasm for playing as many new works as possible, the quartet steadily built up a wide repertoire. From 1967 they gave their own series of eight yearly concerts in Tokyo, and until the fiftieth they avoided playing the same work twice. Iwamoto's fame helped them get engagements all over the country; in Nagoya they gave six yearly performances from 1973. Besides regular broadcasts, the quartet also made gramophone records and their discography includes not only Haydn, Mozart, Beethoven and Schubert, but also Sibelius, Grieg, Schönberg and works by Japanese composers.

The quartet's successful progress was cut short by Iwamoto's early death. On 12 April 1979 the Iwamoto Mari Quartet gave its ninety-fourth and last regular concert. Iwamoto Mari died on 11 May 1979, on the day the ninety-fifth concert should have taken place. The remaining members gave a final concert for the audience of their regular series on 12 June with works for string trio and strings with piano, playing under a portrait of Iwamoto and beside an empty chair on which was placed her violin. A few more memorial concerts followed before the quartet officially disbanded in November. Japan's first really outstanding quartet had come to an end. Oinuma, young and undaunted, wanted to start a new quartet. Kuronuma helped him find players, but he himself did not have the heart to continue. He still performed, but the programmes included in his biography the paradoxical statement, "with Iwamoto Mari's death the quartet ceased and he gave up his performing activities." He even, briefly, accepted an invitation from Kobayashi Kenji to join his New Arts Quartet, but trouble with his left hand forced him to stop. Increasingly, he directed his efforts towards teaching and coaching ensembles, travelling from Yamagata in the north to Hiroshima and Tokushima in the south. Many were the players and groups that benefited from his experience; even so, when he died in 1992, no quartet had achieved quite the same rapport with the audience as the Iwamoto Mari String Quartet.[100]

Even as the Iwamoto Mari quartet was performing successfully, another outstanding all-Japanese quartet, the first to gain international renown, launched its career. The Tokyo Quartet has been described as "largely an American creation," but that is only part of the story.[101] We could with equal justification call it a Japanese creation. True, its members were studying at Juilliard when they formed the quartet, but they had all had their first taste of chamber music playing as students of Saitō Hideo at Tōhō Gakuen School of Music. Without Saitō's school, and the ensemble training he provided, the world might well have had to wait much longer for the first Japanese chamber group to attain a worldwide reputation. And when in 1966 the Juilliard Quartet came to Japan for two weeks to perform and conduct open rehearsals and a workshop, their audience included Harada Kōichirō (1945–), Isomura Kazuhide (1945–) and Harada Sadao (1944–), the future first violinist, violist and cellist of the Tokyo Quartet. The three were contemporaries at Tōhō; now they decided to continue their studies at Juilliard. Together with the violinist Nakura Yoshiko (1945–), another contemporary from Tōhō, they formed a quartet and received tuition from the Juilliard Quartet. In 1970 they won first prize at the Coleman String Competition (judged by the Amadeus Quartet) and four months later won first prize at the International Chamber Music Competition in Munich. Just as they had established their reputation in Europe, Nakura left the quartet; she settled with her husband in Belgium, from where she embarked on a career as a soloist and chamber musician. The remaining members recruited Harada Kōichirō's friend Ikeda Kikuei. He was a couple of years younger, and the other two did not know him well, but he too had studied at Tōhō Gakuen, graduating in 1970; like Harada Kōichirō, his teacher was Sumi Saburō. He now enrolled at Juilliard as a student of Dorothy DeLay, but the quartet's busy schedule meant that he was thrown in at the deep end with little time for acclimatization. Between tours the quartet continued to learn the basic standard repertoire, which it had yet to master comprehensively. Asked about the secret of their rapid rise to fame, Isomura told a journalist: "We are careful. We were educated that way by Professor Saito. I always try to find the authentic style."[102] Indeed, without their early training from Saitō, it is hard to imagine how they could have become so successful in such a short time.

Forty years on, the Tokyo Quartet was still performing, although not in its original line-up; Harada Kōichiro left in 1981 to concentrate on solo performances and form a new chamber group. He has taught at Geidai and still teaches at Tōhō Gakuen. His replacement with Peter Oundjian, a Juilliard graduate, caused some to ask what a first violinist from outside the Saitō stable would do to the quartet. But the three other members felt that a heterogeneous element would represent an asset: "The essential thing is the music, not nationality. We mustn't get too settled in our own ways. The sensibilities of a member from abroad have brought a new style, and we have become freer."[103] Harada Sadao left in 1999, at the time of the quartet's thirtieth anniversary. In the early years, the Tokyo Quartet did not have much of an audience in Japan, but that has changed over the years. In February 2010 the quartet celebrated its fortieth anniversary with a series of three concerts at Ōji Hall in Tokyo.[104] For the first they recreated the programme of the quartet's Japan debut.[105] For the second, fans were asked to register their requests on the hall's home page, an unprecedented experience for the quartet. Three winners were announced at the end of 2009: Haydn's "Emperor," Ravel's only quartet and Beethoven's Op. 59.3. Ikeda expressed his astonishment: he had expected Schubert's "Death and the Maiden" to win the day and among the Beethoven quartets perhaps Op. 18.2, while Debussy seemed to him a more obvious choice than Ravel.[106] While the Amadeus and the Guarneri quartets disbanded after 40 years the Tokyo Quartet expressed their intention to keep going. In autumn 2011, however, the Japanese members of the quartet announced their decision to retire after the 2012–13 season, and in July 2013 the quartet disbanded.[107]

The rise in the popularity of chamber music since the early days of the Tokyo Quartet may well be one of the most significant developments in the world of string playing in Japan in the last 30 years. In the 1980s, Western classical music still seemed to be dominated by the genres that were privileged at the time of its introduction in the nineteenth century.[108] But already by the mid-1980s, Hasegawa Takehisa remarked on the rising numbers, quality and popularity of chamber music and particularly string quartet performances in Tokyo. For many of them, he observed, studying the genre and becoming better performers was as important as the joy of playing together.[109] By 2008, although chamber music concerts were still fewer compared to other genres, there were still enough of them for two string quartet concerts to take place on the same evening and dilute the potential audience.[110] In Japan as elsewhere, string quartets struggle to draw an audience, and many quartets are short-lived.

The Morgaŭa Quartet is among the more permanent quartets, having survived for almost 20 years. Established in December 1992, it started giving twice yearly regular concerts in 1993.[111] Its members, Arai Eiji, Tozawa Tetsuo (who replaced Aoki Takashi in 2001), Ono Hisashi and Fujimori Ryōichi are principal players in orchestras, and had played chamber music previously. Arai Eiji (1957–), is solo concertmaster of the Tokyo Philharmonic Orchestra. He studied at Tōhō Gakuen School of Music with Etō Toshiya and Suzuki Kyōko.[112] Tozawa Tetsuo is concertmaster of the Tokyo City Philharmonic Orchestra, a post to which he was appointed in 1995, while still a graduate student at Geidai. As well as giving solo recitals he played in two string quartets before joining the Morgaŭa Quartet. In 1998–99 he studied in Berlin with Rainer Kussmaul. Ono Hisashi (1955–), the violist, graduated from Geidai in 1981 and was principal violist in the Tokyo Philharmonic Orchestra for four years, before joining the NHK Orchestra as solo player.[113] Fujimori Ryōichi (1963–), leader of the cello section in the NHK Symphony Orchestra, studied at Tokyo College of Music and in Munich. He also performs solo and in 2000 founded a cello quartet.[114]

The Morgaŭa Quartet's name derives from the Esperanto "of tomorrow," and it owes its birth to the desire shared by Arai and Ono to play Shostakovich's chamber music and perform all his string quartets after hearing his operas performed by a foreign troupe touring Japan. As Arai expressed it: "There are many composers who represent the distress and confusion of the twentieth century, but among the mass of music which like that of Schnittke ends in despair and ruin, Shostakovich's music seems to associate hope with the future; this I sense quite strongly."[115] In this, Ono observes, his music, is comparable to Beethoven's late works, which the quartet has also performed, as well as all Bartók's quartets, and Haydn and other staples from the repertoire. Shostakovich continues to be their trademark though, and in the anniversary year of Shostakovich's birth, 2006, the Morgaŭa performed all 15 quartets in three days. In 2008 it performed Bohuslav Martinu's Concerto for String Quartet and Orchestra with the Tokyo Philharmonic Orchestra. Besides Shostakovich's quartets, they have recorded those of Borodin. With their CD *Destruction: Rock meets Strings*, released in

1998, they challenged the divide between classical string quartet music and other genres.

While the Morgaŭa Quartet specializes in twentieth-century music, two string quartets founded by Okayama Kiyoshi with his wife Hattori Yoshiko emphasize the classical tradition and especially Beethoven: the Eleonore Quartet and the Okayama String Quartet, founded in 1993 and 2008 respectively. In a way, however, their history goes back much further, to the founders' days in Germany. Okayama Kiyoshi and Hattori Yoshiko had played in string quartets and other chamber music groups together as students, and in the 1970s, during Okayama's tenure as concertmaster of the Beethoven Orchestra in Bonn, they established a string quartet which performed first as the Quartett der Beethovenhalle Bonn and then as the Bonner Streichquartett, with Horst Enger and Werner Solle, both section leaders and Okayama's colleagues. The couple also continued to play chamber music in other formations, including as a string duo, and, together with the violist Fukai Hirofumi, a graduate of Tōhō Gakuen and principal violist with major German orchestras, as the Japan String Trio. After returning to Japan in 1984, Okayama and Hattori gave chamber music recitals with different ensembles, but establishing a string quartet that rehearsed and performed regularly proved more difficult. In 1992 they finally teamed up with two younger musicians, Sutō Michiyo and Kitamoto Hideki, principals of the viola and the cello section respectively in the Tokyo Philharmonic Orchestra. Sutō graduated from Geidai in 1982 and received a soloist diploma from Hamburg in 1987. Kitamoto, a Tōhō graduate, studied at Juilliard and won first prize in the chamber music division of the Tokyo International Music Competition in 1980.

The Eleonore Quartet, true to its name (an allusion to Beethoven's alleged first love, Eleonore von Breuning), included Beethoven's works in all its twice yearly concerts from 1994 to 2000. The quartet's repertoire, although it included modern works, centred on the German Classic and Romantic works. In 1995 the quartet embarked on its first foreign tour, centred on Germany. The tour included two concerts in Bonn, where the house in which Schumann spent his last years and the newly opened chamber music recital hall of Beethoven's birthplace provided fitting venues for a quartet that made the continuation of the Austro–German heritage its principal aim.

The Okayama String Quartet, founded in 2008, represents an even more pronounced desire to connect with the quartet tradition and "to re-examine closely the origins," as Okayama Kiyoshi told the press.[116] The violist and cellist are again younger musicians: Sasaki Ryō, principal violist of the NHK Symphony Orchestra, and Kōno Fumiaki, professor for cello at Geidai. "There is a difference in age, but the musical direction we envisage is the same."[117] From the start, a series of regular concerts in Tokyo and Nagoya featuring the works of Haydn, Mozart and Beethoven was planned. Between June 2009 and November 2011, the quartet gave six regular concerts in both Tokyo and Nagoya featuring each of Beethoven's early quartets (Op. 18) together with a quartet by Haydn and one by Mozart to highlight the connections between the three composers. Their following series featured the quartets of Beethoven's middle period (Opp. 59.1-3, 74 and 95) together with quartets by Schubert, Mendelssohn and Schumann. In 2010 the quartet was invited to perform at the Westfalen Classics Festival in Germany.[118]

Even before embarking on its first foreign tour, the Okayama String Quartet had the opportunity to engage in an international event at home in Tokyo. In 2009, to celebrate Felix Mendelssohn's two hundredth birthday, Kurt Masur, Peter Schreier and the Gewandhaus Quartet performed in Japan, and as part of their programme the Okayama Quartet and the Gewandhaus Quartet teamed up to play Mendelssohn's Octet Op. 20. Kurt Masur had in 1991 inaugurated the Felix Mendelssohn Bartholdy Foundation (FMBF), which aimed to restore Mendelssohn's former house in Leipzig.[119] The restoration was completed in 1997 with significant financial support from the Japanese Mendelssohn Society (founded in 1996), of which Okayama was an active member.

Okayama was, moreover, involved in a pioneering international venture by the Chamber Music Department of Tokyo University of the Arts and the Joseph Haydn institute for Chamber Music of the University of Music and Performing Arts in Vienna. To celebrate the two hundredth anniversary of Haydn's death, the two institutes cooperated to produce recordings of all the 68 string quartets acknowledged as original works of Haydn.[120] The quartets are played by students of both institutions under the guidance of Okayama Kiyoshi and Johannes Meissl, professor for string chamber music in Vienna, and their colleagues, and they are recorded in Tokyo and Vienna. Students of sound engineering and producing participated in the technical process. This joint venture with custodians of the quartet tradition in its homeland is yet another indication of Japan's high standing in the world of Western classical music. At the same time it reminds us that the classical tradition which Haydn represents does not belong to the Austrians any more than it does to the Japanese; it is foreign to young Europeans and Japanese alike.[121]

To work with the classical tradition and train young generations in it is the mission of Okayama's latest venture following his retirement from Geidai, where he taught chamber music for 20 years, in 2010. In April 2011 the non-profit organization TAMA Music Forum held its first chamber music seminar in a studio built for the purpose in the grounds of the Okayama family home. Students for the masterclasses are recruited by tape audition and receive free tuition by leading Japanese and international performers, composers and musicologists. The "Studio Concertino" seats around 50 people and the seminars are open to the public. The venture comes at a good time, with young musicians showing an increasing interest in chamber music. "Young people, students with the talent to become soloists are most interested in the second violin part," Okayama told *String* magazine and Hattori added, "It's the interest in the middle parts. Perception of these has changed hugely." Cellists and violists, continued Okayama, have also embraced the idea of playing in an ensemble. "This change in consciousness seems to mean that musicians are coming closer to the heart of chamber music."[122]

The rise of chamber music and the string quartet is part of an international trend in the second half of the twentieth century, evidenced by increased attention to chamber music training, chamber music competitions, an increasing number of summer festivals and a proliferation of touring ensembles. At the same time the rising interest shows how Japanese musicians are shaking off the musical preferences that characterized the introduction of Western music in the nineteenth century and going their own ways in exploring the musical heritage that originated in Europe but belongs to the world. Exploring chamber music, moreover, is not limited to professional musicians. Like playing in an orchestra, playing in a small group, especially a string quartet, attracts many amateurs.

# 5. Serious About Music: Amateurs

*The Takadanobaba Orchestra had mobilized a substantial audience for its seventy-fifth regular concert on the last Sunday in January 2010; Tokyo's Nakano Zero Hall, built in 1993 and seating 1,292 people, looked packed. Its members had prepared an ambitious programme with French and Spanish flavours: Georges Bizet's Symphony in C major, Manuel de Falla's ballet* The Three-Cornered Hat *and Claude Debussy's* La Mer. *For the de Falla, a premiere for the orchestra, players decorated their black attire with red ribbons and flowers, while the conductor practically danced on his podium. A bit obvious, perhaps, but the performance had plenty of oomph. A few days previously my Japanese violinist friend from Cambridge Philharmonic Society days had spoken scathingly of his native country's amateur orchestras, but maybe he had never heard "Babakan." Although the bow movements of some of the fiddlers at the back desks suggested that in the fastest passages not everyone was playing every note, enough players were getting them right for the overall effect to be impressive.*

Western music was not promoted in Japan for the love of it. Yet an amateur musician is someone who plays without being obliged to for financial or other reasons: for fun and for love. With the rise of the musical profession in Europe, however, the word "amateur" came to have negative connotations in some languages, including English, despite its origin in Latin, denoting "love." Often the emphasis is not on love but on lack of skill.[123] This negative meaning of "amateur" is a major issue in a rare book about amateur musicians by Tsuji Eiji (1930–), a graduate of Waseda University who spent his working life in the employment of Tokyo Metropolitan Government and his free time playing the violin and the cello in amateur orchestras and chamber ensembles. In *Amachua no ryōbun: vaiorin no shūtokujutsu* (The domain of the amateur: the art of mastering the violin), he claims that the general level of amateur music-making is "too low" (one wonders by whose standards) as a result of poor training fixated on technique. He details the lack of skill at great length. In a section entitled "The Japanese and the violin" he alleges that Japanese regard the violin as an instrument far removed from ordinary people and extremely difficult to learn. Studying the violin is perceived as *shugyō*, self-cultivation and spiritual training with a strong ascetic element.[124]

Etō Toshiya, interviewed by *String* in 1987, expresses a different view, claiming, albeit jokingly, that some Japanese amateurs play better than professionals; he was particular impressed by the level of amateur music-making in America.[125] Urakawa Takaya, in an interview in 2009, likewise expresses his admiration for the amateur players he encountered during his time abroad, in his case Germany, from the early 1960s. He even claimed that learning from amateur musicians was one of the most stimulating aspects of studying abroad.[126]

Whatever the level (and the spectrum is likely to be as wide in Japan as anywhere), the extent and diversity of activities by musicians playing for pleasure alone is impressive and a good gauge of how much the Japanese have made Western classical music their own.[127] Etō's interviewer for *String* observed that, among string players, amateurs (many of them readers of *String*) outnumbered the professionals. To do the amateur music scene justice would require a book in its own right; the examples in this chapter are merely intended to underline the importance of amateur music-making.

Many amateurs play in orchestras; amateur orchestras began to form at around the same time as professional ones or even earlier; some professional orchestras began as amateur ensembles, such as the Gunma Symphony Orchestra and the Sendai Philharmonic Orchestra, which started life as the Miyagi Philharmonic Orchestra in 1973.[128] University orchestras are among the oldest amateur orchestras, reflecting the close connection between Western classical music and education in the nineteenth and early twentieth centuries. The Waseda University Symphony Orchestra traces its history to 1913. In 1927 it gave the Japanese premiere of Mozart's "Haffner" Symphony. Today it has around 300 student members and gives five to six concerts a year. It has appeared on television and conducted 12 foreign tours between 1978 and 2009. Its patrons have included Herbert von Karajan, who conducted the orchestra when he received an honorary doctorate from Waseda University in 1979.[129]

The real rise of the amateur orchestra, however, came after the Second World War, when the number of ensembles increased dramatically as people became more affluent and had more time to pursue their hobbies. The inhabitants of provincial cities without their own professional orchestras would hardly have the chance to hear symphonic music live

without their local amateur orchestra. The Shizuoka Philharmonic
Orchestra, for example, founded in 1977 (after failed attempts in 1960
and 1970), has over 100 members and plays an important role in local
cultural life; it even accompanies opera and ballet performances. Not
only that, but they have even travelled abroad to perform in China and in
the United States (in Shizuoka's twin town Omaha), in France (in
Cannes) and twice in Britain.[130] Similarly, the Toyohashi Symphony
Orchestra began in the early 1960s as a school band at a city junior high
school under teacher Morishita Motoyasu. Expanding into a full
symphony orchestra it gave concerts in and around Toyohashi, and in
1971 it gave its first concert in Tokyo. In 1975 it took its present name,
reflecting the fact that it had become the local amateur orchestra, rather
than a school orchestra, and an important cultural institution in the town.
Motoyasu and the Toyohashi orchestra were the driving force behind the
establishment of the Federation of Japan Amateur Orchestras (JAO) in
1972 with 23 orchestras; today JAO has 143 members spread from
Hokkaido (five members) to Okinawa (three).[131] Its president was Prince
Takamado, and honorary members include the distinguished
concertmasters Tokunaga Tsugio and Yasunaga Tōru. The federation's
stated aims are to promote "youth and common citizens' amateur
orchestras' activities" and to contribute to the development and
enhancement of musical culture.[132] The Federation is a member of the
World Federation of Amateur Orchestras, which it helped create in 1998,
and its activities include international exchange. Its biggest regular event
is the annual National Amateur Orchestras' Festival, which is attended
not only by members of affiliated orchestras, but also by members of
foreign orchestras, particular from Germany. Regional and local events
include workshops for orchestral players and the Toyota Community
Concerts.

Amateur orchestras vary considerably in size, age, membership,
ambition and general circumstances, including whether or not they
receive support from local authorities. As with professional orchestras
there is a concentration of amateur orchestras in Tokyo, significantly
more than the ten registered for the metropolitan area with the JAO. The
Takadanobaba Orchestra, for example is not a member. Takadanobaba is
the name of an area in Tokyo close to Waseda University, and its
founding members in 1973 were mostly graduates of the university. One

of them, Imai Hiroyoshi, the leader of the second violins, had not missed a single concert when he was interviewed by *Sarasate* in 2005 (he was still at it at the concert in January 2010).[133] Today the "Babakan," as members affectionately call it, has no connection with Takadanobaba. The 80 or so players formerly played in student orchestras nationwide; there are no auditions. Run by its members, players pay 30,000 to 35,000 yen per concert. The orchestra rehearses at weekends twice a month and holds training camps twice a year in preparation for its regular concerts. It employs professional coaches as well as a conductor.

While the Takadanobaba Orchestra only hired Nakano Zero hall for the concert in 2010 and has to rent the halls it can find for its rehearsals, the Nakano citizens' orchestra has the good fortune of being able to call the complex housing Nakano Zero Hall its base. Established in 1981, when a professional violinist in the area placed a notice in the Nakano newsletter, it now has 55 members, who meet every Wednesday, which leaves their weekends free for other activities. In Tokyo, even orchestras not so fortunate as to have their own hall enjoy considerable choice when it comes to hiring rehearsal spaces and concert halls. The same is true for coaches and conductors. But provincial orchestras can have difficulties. The Sendai City Orchestra, for example, cannot easily find conductors and often has to hire one from Tokyo for a short burst of rehearsals just before the concert, while regular rehearsals are taken by the principle cellist of the orchestra. It also has to compete with other groups for rehearsal space. The orchestra began as a youth orchestra in 1969; in 1990 it finally dropped "youth" from its name, because it no longer fit reality, although with an average age of 35 in 2007 its membership could be still called youthful. There is no audition, only a two-month trial period. Several of its members are married couples; often only one of them attends rehearsals at a time while the other looks after the children. Concerts frequently include a soloist, either a member of the Sendai Philharmonic Orchestra or a winner of the Sendai International Music Competition. The orchestra pays for them through grants or with earnings from playing for community events.[134]

Even further from Tokyo, in Hokkaido, the Farmers' Philharmonic Orchestra of Hokkaido considers itself "to be the only one of its kind in the world."[135] It is the brainchild of Makino Tokio, who runs an organic farm when he is not playing the violin. Born in 1962, he started to play the violin and the piano at the age of three, but like so many Japanese children gave up his music lessons when he entered junior high school. He resumed playing as an agriculture student at Hokkaido University and played in the university orchestra, which he later led. The orchestra currently has 67 members, who rehearse at weekends during the winter months (November to February), when there is little to do on the farms, and gives a concert each year. It gave its first concert in January 1995. The idea to found an orchestra for farmers owes much to the philosophy of the Danish poet and pastor N.F.S. Grundtvig (1783–1872) and the farmers' cooperative movement and folk high school movement he inspired, as well as to Japanese thinkers inspired by Denmark, such as the poet and social reformer Miyazawa Kenji (1896–1933), who tried to found a farmers' orchestra himself.[136]

Makino conducts the orchestra himself, and the concertmaster is Nomura Satoshi, a former fellow student, who now runs a private violin studio. Not all the members are farmers; they include, for example, students and lecturers from Rakunō Gakuen, a private educational institution including a university, high school and dairy science research institute.[137] The players' levels range from seasoned performers like Makino and Nomura to adult learners, but as Nomura remarks, playing in the orchestra brings out the best in them. This was evident at a joint concert the orchestra gave with the local chamber orchestra in Silkeborg near Aarhus on its first foreign tour to Denmark in February 2011. The programme included the Hokkaidō Caprice for Violin, Japanese Drums and Orchestra, composed and played by Makino himself.[138] The orchestra seems to embody the same enterprising spirit that characterized the colonization of Hokkaido under the Meiji government in the nineteenth century.

Some orchestras have been founded by enthusiasts who wanted to play the works of a single composer. One of them is the Orchestra Dasubidānya, established in 1993; named after the Russian phrase for "goodbye," *do svidánija*, it is devoted to performing the works of Shostakovich. It gives a concert each February, starting rehearsals in October. While there is a fair amount of coming and going among the violinists, some members are loyal to the point of continuing to take part even after moving away from Tokyo, with one member commuting by plane from Kōchi on the island of Shikoku and one from Fukuoka in

Kyushu. The Ainora Orchestra, named after Jean Sibelius' home of Ainola outside Helsinki was, as its name suggests, founded by lovers of the composer's symphonic work and gave its first concert in 2004 after a long gestation period. Both orchestras aspire to winning audiences for the composer's music as well as enjoying it themselves.[139]

Orchestras, while popular with many amateur violinists, are not the only place for them to pursue their passion. In Japan, as elsewhere, many amateurs prefer to play solo or in smaller groups. Their activities are varied and, for the early days, hard to track. The most famous early amateur violin enthusiast may well be Terada Torahiko (1878–1935), the physicist and amateur violinist immortalized by Natsume Sōseki in his humorous novel *I Am a Cat*.[140] Terada first saw and heard a violin in the hands of his physics professor in 1898, while he was studying at the government's Fifth High School in Kumamoto. Natsume Sōseki was his English teacher and later his colleague at Tokyo Imperial University. Fascinated by the violin, Terada bought his own at the price of eight yen eight sen, then a considerable sum for a student, and started practising on the hill near his dormitory. He had little time to play in the following years as he continued his studies, spent three years in Germany, was appointed professor at Tokyo Imperial University, married three times (he was widowed twice), fathered several children, wrestled with bouts of illness, published groundbreaking research in the field of physics as well as literary works and essays and pursued a number of other interests. In September 1922 he bought himself an expensive violin. His resolve to study seriously again was strengthened when he heard his fellow physicist Albert Einstein perform Beethoven's "Kreutzer" Sonata on 1 December, at a welcome reception at Tokyo Imperial Hotel during his lecture tour. The audience went wild and the newspapers praised his playing to the skies. They could hardly have done less for the distinguished guest, who had just been awarded the Nobel Prize and was well on his way to becoming one of the century's icons. Besides, most Japanese at the time were more likely to know the sonata through Tolstoy's *Krejcerova sonata* (published in 1889, first Japanese translation published in 1895) than a live performance of Beethoven's challenging music.[141] Terada may well have decided then and there that he too would play the "Kreutzer" Sonata, for after 20 years of attempting to teach himself, he started taking lessons. In December 1924 he heard Efrem

Zimbalist perform the sonata on the second of his six tours to Japan and realized that he still had a long way to go from his current assignment, the third volume of Christian Heinrich Hohmann's *Practical Violin Tutor.* Nevertheless, by 1934 he was working on the sonata, and on 30 January 1935 he recorded in his diary that he played it with his fellow physicist Tsuboi Tadaji. Eventually it came together well enough to be recognizable and Terada even talked half-jokingly of hiring a hall to perform it and making a gramophone recording. They might well have done so, had Terada not died at the end of that year.

Modern-day university students, too, often prefer more flexible, individual musical activities to the rigid rehearsal schedules of orchestras. Tokyo University, as in Terada's time, has many music enthusiasts, and besides an orchestra (founded in 1920 as one of the earliest orchestras), there is the Tokyo University Chamber Music Society, which started in around 1960 (not much is known about its early history). In the late 1980s it seemed to offer a space for undergraduates who, after working hard to get into the country's most prestigious university, now enjoyed a breathing space before the rigours of corporate employment. Many had given up their instrument while they prepared for entrance examinations. The society was a casual affair, where people got together to play as they wished. Tokyo University in those days had a few derelict halls and rooms on its Hongō campus (apparently relics from the student protests of 1968–69 when violent clashes between students and riot police paralyzed the university for months) which could serve as rehearsal space. Alternatively, students rented practice rooms and small studios. Several times a year the society organized weekends away, for intensive playing and partying. The society also staged regular concerts, where members would perform anything from duos to works for small orchestra. By around 2000 it was close to extinction, but it has since been revived [142]

Outside university, finding fellow players and a space to play can be a challenge, particularly in big cities. An organization can help with both. The Amateur Music Players' Association of Japan (APA), established in 1974, had 1,054 members in 2009, the majority of whom lived in the metropolitan areas of Greater Tokyo and Osaka. Ten were registered as living abroad. Most were string players, with violinists the biggest group (316). Members' ages reflected work and life patterns and how they are likely to affect the time amateurs can devote to playing: the older generations, especially men in their sixties and seventies, were overrepresented; among women the majority were in their forties and fifties.[143] In cities where many members live regular meetings are held. Other events include the Autumn Music Festival at Lake Kawaguchi at the foot of Mount Fuji.

Like the JAO, APA maintains links to the wider world; it has adopted the self-grading system of the American-based worldwide network, Amateur Chamber Music Players Inc. (ACMP) and has an English web page, which includes a testimony by Jan R. Magnus, who joined some of the association's activities during his three-month stay in Tokyo as a guest researcher and concluded: "Musicians are pretty much the same everywhere, and I can now count till (sic!) four in Japanese. I wondered before whether music making would be different in Tokyo and in Amsterdam. Not much different, I think, except perhaps that I found the discipline to be very high in the groups I played with. They like to take fast movements not too fast, and they stick to this tempo all through the movement, also in the easier passages"[144] In 2008 APA received the status of a non-profit organization, and its annual festival has the support of the Nippon Music Foundation.

Other events for amateurs include the Amateur Chamber Music Festival (ACF), held for the first time in 1988. By 2010, 556 ensembles had participated in the festivals, with over 4,000 individuals. Applicants have to submit an essay detailing their musical activities and their motivation. Instruments include the *koto* and the *shakuhachi* as well as Western instruments and the "royal way" of chamber music, the string quartet.[145]

Perhaps more than in other countries, amateur musicians like to read about their interest. This seems true of almost of any kind of amateur culture in Japan and may be a result of the high level of education, or it may be because when Japan first imported Western culture, many had to rely on books to learn about what they could not observe first hand. The absence of a continuous tradition where people can learn from more experienced players may be another reason. This propensity has been called "knowledge fetishism" or (more neutrally), "knowledge accumulation".[146] But it is not just about theoretical knowledge; particularly fascinating is the practical approach in many books and magazines on offer, as if the authors set out to answer all the questions a novice may not dare to ask for fear of looking stupid. Books include translations of such classics as *The Well-Tempered String Quartet*, which does offer a fairly down-to-earth perspective.[147] But, written by veterans of the genre, it does not address the concerns of the complete novice, who is better served by a recent special feature in *Sarasate* entitled "Mastering Chamber Music: Quartet for Beginners."[148] It follows the progress of the fictional characters Makimura Tōru, Saitō Kaori, Imamura Junko and Takahashi Seitarō as they establish themselves as a string quartet, from choosing their first piece to play together to performing in a hall. Their story is accompanied by a running commentary with practical advice from "Kuarutetto-sensei" (Professor Quartet), an experienced professional and chamber music coach. The characterization of the players at their first discussion is faintly reminiscent of that in *The Well-Tempered String Quartet,* except that the book's authors did not envisage playing with women. The first violinist, Makimura, aged 35 and a veteran of student orchestras, although not of chamber music, wants to play something not too difficult which will nevertheless sound good and, presumably, allow him to display his superior skills. Saitō, 27 years old, who assembled the group because she wanted to take up her neglected violin again, keeps quiet as one might expect from the second violin. Imamura, 44, a housewife and apparently the archetypical viola player, insists that they should choose something unusual, while Takahashi, 66 and an adult beginner, thinks only of whether the cellist has a prominent part. Eventually the group wisely decides that their first piece had better not be too difficult. We are not told what they finally settle on – perhaps Haydn, Mozart or an early Beethoven, which Saitō later learns from a more experienced musician are manageable for even inexperienced players, as long as the first violinist can play the notes. Meanwhile, Kuartetto-sensei suggests searching for possible works on the internet and then buying Urtext editions of the chosen work (never mentioning that Urtext has its own perils for inexperienced players). After a less than well-tempered first rehearsal, followed by several more, the quartet takes some lessons with a coach, and readers are strongly urged to do likewise. Finally the group decides to perform. Again readers are encouraged to follow suit in order to boost their motivation. Kuartetto-sensei recommends informal concerts in the first instance, perhaps together with other groups. She has some special advice for shy young women who tend to hide behind their long hair: "show your face!" If the players are too tense and perfectionist the audience will feel tense too. "Is this a special characteristic of the Japanese?" she asks and stresses the importance of a positive attitude.[149]

Leaving aside the question of whether hiding behind a curtain of hair is a Japanese speciality, the scenario presented by *Sarasate* seems quite typical of amateur chamber music anywhere, confirming Jan R. Magnus's impression (and my own). Perhaps the *Sarasate* feature suggests an overly structured approach, complete with coaching and performing, but some amateurs outside Japan favour a similar approach, so there seems little reason to label it "Japanese." The way the Japanese organize their musical activities may differ as a result of circumstances, but when it comes to actually playing, the music-making transcends cultural differences. The diversity of activities and the determination and dedication shown by amateurs make it difficult to believe those who claim that the Japanese do not "really" like or understand Western music.

## 6. "Never Too Late": Japan's Ageing Population and New Markets for the Violin[150]

*Shimamura Music Salon looks more like the lobby of a luxury hotel than a music school. Located on the tenth floor of the Metropolitan Plaza shopping and office complex at Tokyo's busy Ikebukuro station, it boasts a generously designed reception desk, a carpeted floor and easy chairs grouped around tables and racks with brochures. Muzak streams out of loudspeakers. Only the glass cases displaying musical instruments and the shelves with sheet music indicate the place's true purpose. On my second visit the chairs stand in rows facing a Steinway and a table displaying three violins on stands with a selection of bows lying in front of them; the second in a series of four Autumn Concerts is about to begin. At the entrance, visitors receive a clipboard with a programme leaflet, a flyer announcing Shimamura's upcoming Stringed Instrument Fair and the inevitable customer questionnaire. Two violinists and two pianists, all of them young female graduates from well-known music colleges, are going to play six pieces, arranged for two violins and piano: Elgar, Salut d'Amour; Mendelssohn, On the Wings of Song; Scott Joplin, The Entertainer; two pieces by the well-known crossover violinist, composer and producer Hakase Tarō; and* Amazing Grace. *The programme leaflet includes information on how to book trial lessons with the performers.*

*As the young women play, their music mingles with the sounds of wind instruments from one of the lesson rooms along the corridor to the left of the Steinway. After* The Entertainer, *the taped muzak comes back on, while an assistant announces Shimamura's upcoming stringed instrument exhibition at the Shinjuku store. She invites prospective buyers to make an appointment. One of the violinists, Mariko, plays a few bars on each of two of the violins on display, commenting with one-liners: "a typical old Italian"; "a new instrument which will improve with playing."*

*Once* Amazing Grace *has concluded the recital, tea is served, and the audience is invited to try the violins for themselves. Several who do are obviously beginners and pupils of one of the performers. A lady in her thirties tells me, "I started violin lessons with an instrument hired from Shimamura; now I'd like to buy my own." A young woman looks as if she is holding a violin for the first time; she plays a few hesitant strokes while an instructor guides her arm and her boyfriend watches. A great number of Shimamura staff swarm around, offering tea, inviting visitors to try the instruments and bows or to make appointments for the string fair, and generally going out of their way to make everyone feel welcome.*

*Then, suddenly, nearly all the guests have left and the chairs are being returned to their usual positions with amazing efficiency. One of the violinists, Mayuko, accompanies me to the door amidst a chorus of thanks from all the staff and urges me, once again to come to the string fair in a few weeks' time.*[151]

Shimamura Music, founded in 1962, has as its stated mission, "to offer the joys of music to the customer, and to create and expand a music-loving population." The company has shops and schools in 110 locations nationwide. Like the internationally known schools of Yamaha and Kawai, Shimamura catered to the post-war boom in cultural pursuits. With their weekly individual or group lessons they welcomed adults as well as children, but in the baby boom years the focus was on children. Today, however, the country that brought the world the Suzuki Method with its fiddling tiny tots has one of the world's most rapidly ageing societies. Obviously, it makes good business sense for music schools to extend their efforts to adult learners.

By the time the Japanese version of John Holt's book *Never Too Late,* first published in New York in 1978, graced the shelves of music stores in 2006 (the translation first appeared in 2002), managers of the same stores and their affiliated schools had already got the message and were well on their way towards developing new ideas to attract adults who wanted to start or resume playing musical instruments. Shimamura Music Salon opened in 2003 and introduced a new concept of music lessons, designed exclusively for adult learners. The generously designed lobby offers a relaxing space away from the daily grind. The members of staff act as "music advisors." Shimomura recruits them based on their individual qualifications. In practice this usually means graduation from a conservatoire or university music department. Besides the instructors, young university graduates hired on a full-time, long-term basis, Shimamura also hires teachers who work part-time as freelancers for at least one day a week. Together with the student – or should we say client? – the Music Advisors will design a "lesson plan." "Our lessons for adults are centred on repertoire they like," says Yoshida Naofumi, manager of Shimamura's Ikebukuro salon and its shop in Shinjuku, "many of them join because they want to play a certain piece."[152] The "salon" system allows for maximum flexibility in other ways too. By joining, members can freely arrange lessons with the instructor of their choice, who is on standby when not teaching. Ambitious beginners sometimes come three or four times a week, but the system is particularly popular with people whose unpredictable work schedules make it difficult to attend regular lessons at a particular time. "Many company employees come to us on the way home from work. But our students also include pensioners or people who are looking for a hobby in preparation for their retirement," Yoshida explains.

While most people enrolling at Shimamura choose to learn the piano or the saxophone, the violin comes a close third, despite its reputation for being so difficult that you hardly have a hope of mastering it if you start after the age of three, and despite requiring a prohibitively expensive instrument. The autumn concert at Shimamura was presumably designed to reassure the audience on both counts. The programme comprised pieces a beginner might realistically expect to play in the not too distant future, and the violins on display, although not cheap, looked affordable. Anyway, prospective beginners need not invest in their own instrument immediately. They may begin on an instrument provided by Shimamura without having to worry whether or not they will continue. If they do and decide to buy their own instrument, their violin teacher may quite literally hold their (bow) hand as they play a selection of violins in their chosen price range. Of course the teacher will also play the instruments for them. The instructors at the salon are employed to sell musical instruments and equipment as well as to teach and recruit students. Sceptics might question this arrangement in which the teacher is also a salesperson. But teachers all over the world advise their students on instrument purchase – sometimes at considerable benefit to themselves without the student knowing.

The Shimamura stringed instrument exhibition announced at the concert opened on a weekend in November in Shimamura's Shinjuku store, located on an upper floor of a multi-storey shopping centre at one of Tokyo's busiest stations. The display was decidedly user-friendly; the violins and bows had different coloured price tags, red for Italian, green for German and blue for French ones. Prices ranged from around 600,000 yen for mass-produced instruments to 1,500,000 yen and more for old and new master instruments. "Master workshop instruments sell particularly well, because they offer good value for money," explains Moteki Ken. "Most of our customers are amateurs who want a decent instrument that doesn't cost the earth."[153] Italian violins are particularly popular, and to provide relevant expertise and, no doubt, to impress prospective customers, Shimamura employed Shōichi Ebata, a luthier who trained in Cremona.

Shimamura Music is not the only company exploring new avenues to draw in new customers. Yamaha, with a history going back to the early days of Western music in Japan and a post-war record of offering musical training for children from pre-school age, is doing the same. In 1986 it broadened music education into the Yamaha Popular Music schools catering to teenagers and adults of all ages. While children still represent the core of Yamaha's 100,000 Popular Music Schools nationwide, "we want children to remember Yamaha as a good brand they will return to later in life," says Kitajima Tomohisa, Manager of Rifra Plus, Yamaha's version of the "music salon" approach.[154] Today Yamaha even offers special beginners' classes for the over-fifties and a course "Music and Health" intended for the mature clientele, described as *shinia* ("senior"), who is not too old to understand the meaning of yet another piece of Japanized English.

Adults may enrol at Yamaha's regular music schools such as the one near Ikebukuro Station.[155] Two separate lobbies, one for children and one for adults ensure that the latter can wait for their lesson undisturbed by Yamaha's younger clientele. A large screen shows slides of nature photographs, possibly to soothe pre-lesson nerves, and on the table lies the latest issue of the Yamaha publication *Myūjin,* a lifestyle and travel magazine for music lovers and Yamaha customers. The nearest door, leading into a fairly large lesson room, looks like the door of a ferry or aeroplane. Although a woman playing the keyboard is visible through a window, not a sound reaches the lobby, demonstrating the effectiveness of another Yamaha product line; sound-proof cabins. Students can choose between individual lessons and group lessons of up to six learners. But, while some adult learners may feel that there is safety in numbers, their busy schedules may well mean that the group is unstable. On the day I observed an intermediate violin lesson, the "group" initially consisted of a solitary young woman, although another joined her while she was playing her scales to a metronome beat from the keyboard, which the teacher also used to correct her intonation. The scales were followed by short pieces from Yamaha's own tutor and repertory books, complete with karaoke versions on CD. After one hour the lesson seemed to fizzle out. The teacher looked bored. She might well have been frustrated by the patchy attendance and irregular practising habits of her adult students. Perhaps she preferred to teach children, who can be scolded if they arrive late and poorly prepared.

A school designed exclusively for adults may well be the best solution for both teachers and students. Rifra Plus Shinjuku, opened in July 2004, has a spacious lobby, providing a place of respite just three minutes from Shinjuku station (assuming the visitor found the nearest station exit). Most of the students at Rifra are in their thirties and forties and may take lessons in cello, violin, classical and jazz piano, jazz vocal, jazz saxophone, harp, *shakuhachi,* and even *erhu,* the Chinese two-stringed fiddle that has gained considerable popularity in recent years. Here too though, the piano, saxophone and violin are the most popular choices.

The approach to teaching, however, seems different from Shimamura's. "Teaching adults is not that different from teaching children," explains Kitajima, "both like to experience success."[156] Still, Yamaha's recipe for achieving this experience at an early stage comes as a surprise, unless one regards it as a cheap ploy to sell another Yamaha product: "We encourage adults to start on the Silent Violin." The Yamaha Silent Violin celebrated its tenth birthday in 2007, and admittedly has significant advantages over an acoustic violin, especially for adults. In the cramped living conditions of many Tokyoites, there is something to be said for an instrument that sounds like a heavily muted violin while its player can adjust the volume she hears through headphones to something close to the real thing. The student can practise late at night after work without suffering complaints from the neighbours. Add a karaoke CD like those provided with Yamaha's "Violin Repertory" series of graded pieces, and even a beginner can feel confident without being disillusioned by snide remarks from family members. The pieces in the Yamaha series, sold exclusively to enrolled students, together with Yamaha's own violin tutor, mainly come from the classical repertoire, but also include jazz and pop music. While this suggests that Yamaha prefers a more standardized approach than Shimamura, Kitajima assured me that teachers do take students' wishes into account, including a preference for starting on an acoustic violin. Students at Rifra generally enrol for a course of regular individual lessons with the same teacher and often stay for four to five years. Even when they are ready to join a group, they need not stray from Yamaha, but can join the special ensemble courses offered at the studio. Yamaha's apparent preference for standardization extends to recruiting teachers; it has its own qualification system requiring prospective teachers to pass a series of graded exams.

Like Shimamura, Yamaha holds regular instrument fairs. To promote the string fair held at Rifra in November 2007, Kitajima invited the violinist Yamase Rio, who performed a short programme of mixed pieces playing her speciality, the Hardanger fiddle (see next chapter), as well as three Cremonese violins for sale at the fair. Here too, *Amazing Grace* concluded the event, leaving the audience to buy CDs and get them signed, register for the trial lessons with Rifra teachers advertised on the programme or inspect the instruments on exhibition in a separate room. Most of the violins on display cost less than 1,000,000 yen and ranged from German mass-produced ones by Höfner to Cremona violins that come with a "Hallmark," an impressive-looking certificate detailing maker and workshop. Of course Yamaha's own ranges, "Braviol" and "Artida," also featured. As at Shimamura, students may begin lessons with a hired instrument and enlist the help of their teacher when they decide to buy their own.

Both Shimamura Music Salon and Yamaha Rifra Plus school have been designed to make them approachable for adults aspiring to begin a new instrument or return to one they abandoned when university entrance exams or their career took up their time: an inviting physical environment, friendly staff trained to meet their needs and wishes, and the opportunity to buy everything they need from the same company. If a student's heart's desire is to perform on stage, Yamaha and Shimamura have an answer. Rifra, for example, holds informal mini-concerts on Sunday afternoons, where "classmates" can play to each other and staff have the opportunity to practise their skills by playing with them as compère – and, of course, to advertise Yamaha products. Shimamura arranges similar events and even hosts a major yearly event called "Your Stage." Members of Shimamura's music salons from Kyushu to Hokkaido have the chance to perform in Tokyo's Suntory Hall, hired for the purpose.[157]

Other music stores besides Shimamura and Yamaha have started to target the adult market. One of the largest is Yamano Gakki, which established its first store in 1892. Yamano's main store, like Yamaha's, is in the elegant Ginza district, but it also runs three music salons in central Tokyo. The Ikebukuro salon, a couple of minutes' walk from Ikebukuro Station, boasts a spacious lobby, a "setup room" where students can prepare themselves and their instrument for their lesson, soundproof lesson rooms, instruments for hire and a shop selling instruments and sheet music. The salon is open for lessons every day of the week from 10:00 a.m. to 9:30 p.m., giving even people working overtime the chance to fit in lessons.

Meanwhile, a special display at Yamano's main store on the Ginza in April 2006 featured not only John Holt's book (first published in Japan in 2002) but other books, magazines and sheet music of interest to adult beginners. Here the timid, reluctant to face the hard sell at a reception desk, could start by indulging in a practice the Japanese have even given its own name: *tachiyomi* or "standing and reading." Books for the amateur violin enthusiast include biographies and autobiographies of foreign and Japanese violinists, books about the famous violin makers and books about everything to do with the violin. *The Dictionary of*

*Interesting Knowledge about the Violin,* for example, published by Yamaha, includes a chapter on the history of the violin, a general knowledge chapter in question and answer form, another on the violin's function in ensembles, one on "curiosities" and two chapters on violinists, with an emphasis on the anecdotal. The question-and-answer chapter begins with "Why are there so many infant prodigies on the violin?" Because it is possible and desirable to start the violin early, is the answer, but the author hastens to assure his readers, who are likely to be adults: "It is certainly not too late to start the violin as an adult."[158]

The same reassuring statement also appears in *A Reader about the Violin* in answer to the question, "Is it terribly difficult to start the violin as an adult?"[159] This book too offers all kinds of information and curious facts about the violin, either in question and answer form or in the form of columns. Aspects of violin making and instruments feature particularly prominently, which is hardly surprising: one of the authors is the veteran violin maker Murata Sōroku. Even the merits of the Silent Violin for beginners and late-night practising are discussed. Another remarkable feature of this book is the comparatively generous amount of space given to violin making and violin playing in Japan. Of course, given the origin of the violin, it is understandable that Western names and stories dominate the books; but this dominance still suggests that the accumulation of knowledge about Western culture plays an important part in many adults' pursuit of classical music, whether by learning the violin or otherwise.

New magazines which have appeared in recent years cater for an amateur audience which clearly includes the adult beginner. For string players they include *Sarasate,* first published in spring 2003 by Sequirey (which also acts as an artists' agency), and *Gengakki Fan* (String Instrument Fan), first published in June 2005.[160] *Gengakki Fan*, published by Yamaha four times a year, included articles and series of varying length portraying famous artists and instruments past and present, luthiers, shops, teachers' studios, amateur orchestras as well as interviews, a few concert reviews and information about new books, CDs and other products. Many articles offered instruction and advice to adult learners. The Spring 2006 issue contained a special section about starting the violin (with references to the viola and the cello); "it is fine to start even at 60," assured Kino Masayuki, concertmaster with the Japan

Philharmonic Orchestra. The feature covered everything from choosing and relating to a teacher and buying and looking after an instrument and bow to various aspects of playing. For more advanced players, another issue (Autumn 2007) included an article about Shinozaki Fuminori, concertmaster of the NHK Orchestra, soloist and chamber musician, coaching an amateur string quartet in that amateur favourite, Beethoven's String Quartet Op. 18.4.[161]

Every issue of *Gengakki Fan* had a substantial sheet music section of graded pieces for different instruments and ensembles, complete with CD. These were usually famous masterpieces in easy arrangements, for example (Autumn 2007), Tchaikovsky's famous "Scène" from *Swan Lake* (Op. 20) for elementary level violin, Bach's Chaconne for intermediate level violin and piano – guaranteed to make purists writhe – or, for complete beginners, the theme from the second movement of Dvořák's Ninth Symphony "From the New World," known in Japan as "The Road Home" and, like "Auld Lang Syne," a favourite tune for chasing people out of libraries and parks at closing time.

*Sarasate* addresses a similar audience, but runs more articles covering a wider range of topics, including folk, jazz and pop music. Regulars include special viola and double bass sections, as well as pages devoted to the Japan String Teachers' Association and the Suzuki Institutes and a calendar of upcoming amateur orchestra concerts. *Sarasate* too regularly offers advice for beginners. A special section in Volume 14 (Winter 06–07) included checklists to guide readers through choosing an instrument and selecting the right teacher or school, suggestions for the first stage performance and portraits of three adult learners. For readers who took up the challenge, Volume 18 (September/October 2007) had a special section in question and answer format about how to progress. The questions included technical issues, but also more mundane problems, such as finding time to practise, playing with a practice mute and resolving feelings of dissatisfaction with the teacher.

The new interest in learning a musical instrument as an adult is part of a wider trend towards lifelong learning, a connection that was not lost on Tsuji Eiji, who in 1998 followed up his 1990 book for amateurs with another publication, entitled "Lifelong learning: the pleasure of the violin."[162] In the preface Tsuji noted the increase in the amount and scope of amateur playing since his last book; it had even become common for adults to study the violin, which he compares to the piano and the *shamisen* in its appeal for the general population. The change, he argued, had implications for teaching, which has to pay more attention to the demands of adult learners, who take up the violin solely for their own pleasure.

Nakajima Mineo (1936–2013), the president of the Talent Education Research Institute, likewise saw the implications of lifelong learning for the study of musical instruments. The Suzuki Method is known for its success in teaching small children, but if it is to survive in Japan's ageing society, it has to widen its scope. Nakajima advocated broadening the Suzuki Method's application to lifelong educational activities.[163] An obvious group to address is the large number of people who learnt an instrument in their youth and later abandoned it. Japan, Nakajima estimates, must be among the world's top countries when it comes to households with violins and pianos collecting dust. He believes that, compared to Europe and America, there is too much emphasis on acquiring technical skills and too little on the pleasure of music-making. But besides offering what he calls lifelong "aftercare" for young learners, Nakajima believes the Suzuki Method also needs rethinking in relation to adult beginners: "Starting to learn the violin, cello, flute or piano at 50 or 60, perhaps to play oneself the famous work of one's longings, is that not one of the real joys of life?"[164]

Will Japan, which pioneered teaching the violin to small children on an unprecedented scale, play a similar role in bringing the violin to adult learners? It will be intriguing to find out.

# Conclusion: Going Native, Going Global: the Violin as Part of Japanese Culture

*On its visit to Switzerland in 1980, the Toyama Youth Orchestra presented the inhabitants of Neuchâtel with a pleasant but conventional programme of classical compositions. Only one item stood out as a special advertisement of the orchestra's home country.* Sea in Springtime, *the title read, by Miyagi Michio (1884–1956), for* koto *and orchestra. The* koto *with its long, narrow body and many strings was carried onto the stage and a lady in a kimono seated herself behind it. When the conductor lifted his baton, she began plucking the strings. The resonance of the* koto *came as a surprise and contrasted with the quiet entry of the orchestral strings after the first notes. Such was my introduction to Japanese music.*

Many a Westerner must have been introduced to Miyagi's most famous piece in a similar way: by Japanese performers of Western music wishing to accommodate their Western audience's desire to hear something "Japanese." When an American classical radio channel advertised a forthcoming interview with Anne Akiko Meyers,[1] whose new CD contained two "Japanese folk songs," strains of *Sea in Springtime* sounded in the background. To the Japanese, too, *Sea in Springtime (Haru no umi),* originally composed for *koto* and *shakuhachi,* represents what they think of as traditional music. Even if they do not know the title, they will recognize the piece: "Oh of course, the one you always hear at New Year!"[2] And played in its original instrumentation it certainly sounds more Japanese than Western, at least on first hearing. But careful listening a second and third time round, especially after hearing more traditional Japanese works, will reveal, for example, a structure familiar to Western ears – not the sonata form exactly, but an A–B–A form with two contrasting sections and finishing with the return of the first section. Contemporaries who first heard the piece in 1929 would often have been more familiar with traditional Japanese music than today's Japanese; some hailed *Sea in Springtime* as proof of how well Japanese musicians had assimilated Western music, while others dismissed it as a travesty of *koto* music and a poor imitation of Western music.[3] The fluidity of the *koto*'s preludes and the *shakuhachi*'s melody lines may even sound faintly reminiscent of Debussy, whom Miyagi Michio, trained in Western classical as well as Japanese music, admired.

Indeed, it may well be its "Western" elements as much as its "Japanese" character that attracted the violinist Renée Chemet to the piece when she heard Miyagi perform it during her Asian tour in 1932. She was so impressed by *Sea in Springtime* that she asked for the score.[4] By the following day she had arranged the *shakuhachi* part for violin and wanted to perform the piece with Miyagi. They rehearsed it together and it was included in Chemet's recital on 3 May 1932, when she also performed Tartini's Sonata in G minor, Kreisler/Paganini's Allegro, and the violin concertos by Bruch and Mendelssohn. Chemet's performance with Miyagi was well received; some critics preferred it to the original version.[5] In June 1932 Miyagi and Chemet recorded the work, and the recording sold well over 10,000 copies in the first six months. British and American Victor then sold it worldwide, and it helped make Miyagi Michio known internationally. In July 1953 he attended the Second World Festival of Folk Song and Dance – Biarritz – Pamplona, where he met Chemet again. He also played for the BBC during the trip.[6] Miyagi performed *Sea in Springtime* with a visiting violinist for a second time in 1953, when Isaac Stern was introduced to him and a joint performance of the piece was included in his farewell concert. Stern later regretted that their performance was not recorded. He recorded Japanese melodies together with the *shakuhachi* player Yamamoto Hōzan in 1979.[7]

While it would be fascinating to be able to compare both recordings, we do at least have Chemet's version. Chemet took liberties with the printed score, changing some of the notes and playing others at a different octave. Although she used harmonics, she did not necessarily aim to imitate the effects produced by a *shakuhachi*. She even employed pizzicato, achieving an effective interplay with the quite different plucking sound of the *koto*. Her performance is all the more satisfying because she does not self-consciously try to sound "Oriental." Nevertheless, *Sea in Springtime* is the only well-known piece which is perceived as traditional Japanese music and yet also has a tradition of

21: Miyagi Michio performing *Sea in Springtime* with the French Violinist
Renée Chemet, 1932.

performance with a violinist, sanctioned by the composer just three years
after the work's premiere. So *Sea in Springtime* is in a sense unique. At
the same time it reflects musical trends in the 1920s and 1930s, when
composers of both indigenous and Western music were striving for
renewal. Western-style composers debated the question of "Japanese-
style music."

Kishi Kōichi took part in the debate, and his Violin Concerto and short
pieces for violin are representative of works by composers whose
education was almost exclusively in Western music. Kishi's concerto
follows an approach familiar from European (and American) classical
composers who worked melodies and other musical elements from their
countries' folk music into their symphonies and concertos. Kishi's
audience in Berlin had no trouble accepting his music. Reviewers
recognized the variety of musical influences that went into it and named
nineteenth- and early twentieth-century composers, as well as what they
described as "Japanese" or "Oriental" elements, which in fact were well-
established musical idioms of the Western Orientalist tradition (see Part

2 Chapter 6). Such Japanese elements as there are owe more to the popular music of Kishi's time than to more traditional Japanese music. The first lyrical theme after the Violin Concerto's strongly rhythmical and Orientalized opening does recall a Japanese melody: that of Koga Masao's famous popular song "Sake wa namida ka tameiki ka" (Sake: Is it tears or sighing?), first released on gramophone record in 1931.[8]

These endeavours of composers like Kishi are often attributed to the nationalistic ideology of the time, but this hardly does them justice. For one thing, they are not fundamentally different from those of European and North American composers in the nineteenth and early twentieth centuries, who likewise strove to create national music by incorporating musical elements of their homelands into their music. In other words, the efforts of Japanese composers were part of a global trend. For another, the search by Japanese composers for a way to express their identity in a language that was universally understood (in the Western world) is a reflection of trends in the other arts and in the intellectual sphere.[9] The contributions to the debate by composers like Moroi Saburō, who may have heard Kishi's works performed in Berlin in 1934, showed, moreover, that they had more in mind than the superficial incorporation of Japanese folk tunes into the kind of bombastic orchestral works favoured by the government at the time.[10] Kishi himself, once back in Japan, changed his views about "Japanese-style" composition and was critical of his own works, recognizing them as superficially orientalized pieces of Western music, or, to use his image, like a Westerner dressed up in a *happi*-coat with a Japanese-style parasol and fan.[11] He came to believe that Japanese identity would be expressed without resorting to self-conscious constructions from orientalist topoi.

After the Second World War, Japanese composers did amalgamate Japanese and Western elements successfully, but their works owed much to musical developments outside Japan in the course of the twentieth century, such as efforts to overcome the limitations of tonal music and to incorporate elements from non-European musical styles. Before the war, some Japanese composers had already interacted with their Western contemporaries. In the post-war period, as they studied the avant-garde music of their contemporaries, they truly perceived themselves as contemporaneous with their Western counterparts.[12] Whether they studied abroad or remained in Japan, their music transcended national and East–

West borders, as did that of Western composers. Identifying "Japanese" elements in the music of Takemitsu Tōru only highlights the point that the distinction between "Eastern" and "Western" has largely lost its meaning and "Western" classical music is no longer a European or even a Western art. Takemitsu, like Miyagi, counted French music among his sources of inspiration, including Debussy, who for his part was inspired by the Javanese and Vietnamese ensembles he heard at the world exposition in Paris in 1889.[13] Japanese contemporary music in the classical idiom "is now a fully functioning part of the international music scene."[14] As in the West, however, it leads a niche existence. Japanese audiences of classical music, like Western ones, prefer the works of dead European composers. Takemitsu's fame in Japan rests chiefly on his film scores, particularly those for Kurosawa Akira's films.[15]

Film music provides an excellent illustration of how music that originated in the West has become Japanese. In film music we find the most obvious synthesis of indigenous and Western, or rather global, characteristics, reflecting both local aesthetic sentiments and the spirit of the times. The growth of cities and within them a consumer-orientated mass culture since the nineteenth century was a worldwide trend, which was well underway in Japan before the country's enforced opening to the West.[16] The technological advances that transformed the place of music in society reached Japan almost immediately. In film, Japan soon went its own way, certainly not separate from other countries, but not merely following or imitating them either. Films became (among other things) a vehicle for expressing and celebrating Japaneseness, most obviously in period films.[17] Yet the music is as often as not easily recognizable to a non-Japanese audience (it would be interesting to investigate how many Japanese films owe their popularity in the West to their music as well as their visual appeal). A good example is Mizoguchi Kenji's film *Genroku Chūshingura* (The 47 Rōnin) produced in 1941–42, in the war years when nationalism was at its height, and still popular today. Mizoguchi's film deals with the famous vendetta of the 47 Rōnin, based on a historical event that took place in 1703, a story often perceived to illustrate peculiarly Japanese values and which Ruth Benedict discusses in detail in her famous study of Japanese character, *The Chrysanthemum and the Sword*. The event inspired numerous dramas, including a *kabuki* play and a *bunraku* puppet play. To summarize briefly,

Lord Asano Naganori is forced to commit suicide after a confrontation with Kira Yoshinaka, master of ceremonies in the shogun's palace. His loyal retainers kill Kira and are sentenced to death themselves. In a particularly moving scene in *Genroku Chūshingura*, Lord Asano walks to the place of execution, amidst falling cherry blossoms; on the way he meets his most loyal retainer, who has taken great pains to see his lord one last time. The scene reflects Japanese sensibilities, and yet the music with its lamenting strings is not so different from the language of Hollywood, where it was especially when someone was "dying or making love that the violin came on."[18] The composer, Fukai Shirō (1907–59), was critical of Western music that purported to be inspired by Japanese music and he himself looked to his European contemporaries.

Closely linked to film is popular song; many films have title songs that become hits in their own right. Misora Hibari, whose singing career spanned the post-war Shōwa era, is particularly famous for her performance of the sentimental popular ballad form known as *enka*. Although its roots go back at least to the interwar period, the *enka* really came into its own after the war (Koga Masao enjoyed a post-war revival). It "combines Western instruments with Japanese scales, rhythms, vocal techniques, and poetic conventions in melodramatic songs of love, loss and yearning." Like period films, the *enka* has been described as a representation of Japaneseness. Since the 1970s it has been firmly established as "the heart of the Japanese." Although declining in popularity, *enka* can be widely heard in Japan and are familiar to people beyond the diminishing group of fans.[19] The accompaniment of *enka* usually includes an orchestra with a lush string sound and soaring violins. A striking recent example because of its opening is the song *Higurashi* (Cicadas; *higurashi* literally means "clear-toned cicada"), with which Nagayama Yōko made her debut in 1993. It begins with a dramatic, if brief, violin solo. *Higurashi* is certainly typical of its kind; it is sung by a woman in a kimono, accompanied by an orchestra in which strings and especially a solo violin emphasis the pathos, and the lyrics express the transience of life and love:

Short is the season which kindles the flame of life
How much shorter then is the time when a woman is beautiful
I am like the cicada at the end of summer, crying with yearning for
love (...).

Like the music in films such as *Genroku Chūshigura*, the musical language of *enka* is easily accessible to foreign listeners, who might describe it as "Western." Like Japan's modernity in general, however, the music is not Western just because many of its elements originated in Europe. The musical expression of modern times is both local and global, part of what we might call "world music." The sentiments it expresses can be found in other modern urban song styles around the world, including the songs of, for example, Umm Kulthūm (1904–75), Egypt's version of Misora Hibari. They too are widely perceived as representing traditional music and aesthetic elements. They too often feature the sound of violins to express sentiments of nostalgic yearning and unrequited love. [20]

It is perhaps here, in film music and in *enka*, more than in any other genre, that the violin has most obviously become part of a modern Japanese tradition, by playing a leading part in art forms widely perceived as an expression of the Japanese soul. But it may well make more sense to talk about the violin as part of the story of the Japanese increasingly taking part in global musical culture. Much of the music popular in Japan today is the same as the most popular music in other parts of the world, including jazz, Latin American music, hip-hop and pop music, to which J-pop is closely related. At the same time, most violinists play Western classical music, which itself is played and enjoyed worldwide and which the Japanese have made fully their own. Japanese musicians are quick to point this out, and foreign observers with knowledge of Japan have long agreed with them: "From the outside, everybody looks at this as a Japanese orchestra," said Imai Nobuko, who led the viola section during the Saito Memorial Orchestra's European tour in 1989. "But, individually, I don't think we are Japanese musicians. We are very privileged to play the European music and to express something we have learned over the years. We want to play how we feel, and there is so much joy in it – that's something that's important." And John Wheeler, vice president of the Japan Society in New York, commented, "Music in Japan means Western music. Classical Western music is a part of Japanese cultural life and even a part of primary school education" – a level of schooling, he added, that "certainly doesn't happen in this country."[21]

The fact that the Japanese are not the only East Asians playing Western classical music and have long been joined by Koreans and Chinese on the international stage emphasizes the point that the West does not own the classical music to which it gave birth. It has already been observed that "China and Japan are becoming as important to Western classical music as the music is to them," and that "as the West casts aside music education, if not the music itself, the countries of East Asia will become the great conservators of Western classical music."[22] The veteran violinist Ivry Gitlis, who has been teaching and performing in Japan for the last 30 years, summed it up in his message to young Japanese musicians: "Believe in yourselves, express yourselves in your performance. (...) In music there is no East or West; strictly speaking there is no Western music. Come to think of it, perhaps it is easier for non-Europeans to play the music without prejudice (...)"[23]

A more light-hearted demonstration of Western classical music as a fully integrated part of contemporary Japanese culture is Ninomiya Tomoko's bestselling manga series *Nodame Cantabile,* a comedy about the lives and loves of a group of students at a fictional music college in Tokyo, which has also been filmed, both as anime and as live action drama.[24] The story's two leading characters are a female pianist and a pianist/conductor (male of course): Noda Megumi, nicknamed Nodame, whose genius and childish ways are reminiscent of Mozart (in *Amadeus,* the play by Peter Shaffer and the film by Miloš Forman), and Chiaki Shin'ichi, whose brooding obsession is implied to be reminiscent of Beethoven, his favourite composer. The other main characters include two violinists, who seem to represent two types common at the turn of the millennium. Miki Kiyora, the female concertmaster of the college's elite A-orchestra, seems all set for a career typical of so many we have already encountered; freshly returned from studies in Vienna she plans to return there after graduation, enter competitions and embark on a solo career abroad. Her playing is technically flawless. The peroxide-blonde Mine Ryūtarō, on the other hand, initially prefers to play rock music on his electric violin and with his band, until he is converted to classical music by Chiaki when they perform Beethoven's "Spring Sonata" for Mine's exam. He carries his flair for showmanship over into spectacularly choreographed performances of Beethoven's Symphony No. 7 and Gershwin's *Rhapsody in Blue* when he becomes concertmaster of the "S-Orchestra." Although he appears to have abandoned rock music for the time being, one hopes he will not confine himself to the classical mainstream altogether.

However light-hearted, *Nodame Cantabile* bears witness to the continuing reverence for Europe as the heartland of classical music. Chiaki and Miki, like many real-life musicians in Japan, long to study in Europe. Like Chiaki, many Japanese have little time for their own country's musicians and tend to prefer Western performers, or at least Japanese performers who have achieved fame in the West. Aspiring violinists learn to revere the Western gods of the violin world, as in Tanaka Chikashi's book *Gohon no hashira: violin-dō: shugyō no tabi* (The Five Pillars: The Way of the Violin. A Journey of Training, published in 2001, reprinted 2005), which is presumably addressed to serious young students with professional ambitions.[25] It chronicles the progress of the fictional violin student Sengoku Yoshiya (the name Yoshiya is deliberately reminiscent of Jascha Heifetz), and Yoshiya's training may well be taken as typical of that received by most of the post-war violinists whose careers we examined earlier. Yoshiya's parents love music, although they do not play themselves. When little Yoshiya shows an interest in the violin, the family's neighbour, a music graduate, urges them to send him to the local (Suzuki?) studio where her daughter attends group lessons. Soon the eight-year-old Yoshiya is performing in unison with his fellow students. After one such recital, Yoshiya's father recalls his own experience of boxing at his university club. A violinist on the stage needs a similar frame of mind to a boxer in the ring and therefore equally careful training in individual lessons. "He's a man," he concludes, "He has to be able to make a proper living later."[26]

With the help of their neighbour they find Isawa Yūjin, the ideal teacher: a first rate performer, whose playing they have heard and liked, who has also made himself a name teaching and – an important criterion – who has studied abroad. Isawa auditions Yoshiya and pronounces him talented. He reassures Yoshiya's mother, who is anxious because there are no musicians in the family. Thus begins Yoshiya's journey to becoming a competition-winning soloist, which at the end of the book culminates in the lone hero stepping onto the stage in front of the orchestra in the last round of the International Paganini Competition.

Tanaka's book devotes much space to discussing violin and bow technique; the "five pillars" turn out to be *son filé, detaché, martelé, spiccato* and *sautillé*. Yoshiya is urged to work on his technique before anything else, preferably starting with bow practice in the morning before school and aiming for three hours of quality practice a day. "Don't Play, Practice," runs one chapter heading; the English stands out and drives the point home. Still, Isawa/Tanaka stresses the need for everyday activities such as reading, TV, sports. He draws attention to other musical styles, namely *enka, min'yō* and jazz as being particularly expressive and advises Yoshiya to listen to different kinds of Western music. Isawa urges Yoshiya to discover his own sound and develop his own expression, letting himself be led by Japanese sensibilities.[27] But despite his constant emphasis on the importance of individual musical expression, this notion remains vague in comparison with the advice on technique. When Isawa gives examples of challenging works from the repertoire, he names composers known for the technical (rather than the musical) challenges their works present: Paganini, Wieniawski, Vieuxtemps and Heinrich Wilhelm Ernst. Paganini appears as one of the gods in Tanaka's violin heaven, the other one being Heifetz, of whom two portrait photographs grace the book's pages.

Yoshiya progresses to a high school specializing in music. He has mastered Paganini's *Caprices* and is ready for the very different challenges of playing the viola in a string quartet and rehearsing regularly with a pianist, giving his teacher the opportunity to display his expertise in these areas too. Twice a year Isawa holds one-week training camps in the mountains or by the sea, where, besides treating a selected technical issue, he talks to his students about looking after their instrument, purchasing a new one, and maintaining a good relationship with luthiers and instrument shops.

Isawa is more than a teacher. He is the prophet who has been to the sources and returned with special inside knowledge. While he studied in Europe he heard and discussed with fellow violinists the respective merits of legendary virtuosos and heard the kind of anecdotes that come from personal experiences or conversations with the famous. He can advise on the relative merits of famous foreign concert halls. The Japanese halls apparently do not merit a mention, although several impressive venues opened in the 1990s.

Tanaka, writing at the dawn of the twenty-first century, still acutely senses Japan as being at a disadvantage when it comes to Western music.

22: Book cover, Tanaka Chikashi, *Gohon no hashira: Vaiorin-dō: shugyō no tabi* (The Five Pillars: The Way of the Violin. A Journey of Training, Tokyo: Ressun no Tomosha, 2001, Reprint, 2005).

Emphasizing Japan's short history of Western music, he insists that Japan adopted music as part of Western culture, and Western music was from the start associated with toil and suffering, personified by Beethoven.[28] The subtitle of his book "*shugyō no tabi*," drives home the same message, *shugyō* being associated with strict discipline and even ascetic practices. So does the illustration on the cover: a small figure clutching a violin case, dressed in a Japanese-style short happi coat and wearing a headband, surveys mountain peaks with clouds drifting around them. A hand rises between the peaks, forming the gesture often seen on Buddha statues and signifying teaching or reasoning (Vitarka mudra). Learning the violin is particularly hard for Japanese, Tanaka claims, because they have no history of bowed instruments or of bel canto singing. The notion of individual expression is likewise alien to them and sometimes they tend to exaggerate.[29] If Japanese and Asian musicians' tendency to prioritize technique at the expense of musical expression has become a stereotype, it is one that the Japanese themselves perpetuate. When Yoshiya is asked by people he meets in Italy at the competition about teaching in Japan, he confirms that most put technique first, because expressing feelings through music does not come naturally to the Japanese. This is one of the reasons they rely heavily on recordings and faithfully imitate their favourite model, in Yoshiya's case, Heifetz.[30]

Besides Heifetz, Tanaka's book includes pictures of Elman, Paganini, Szeryng, Milstein, Menuhin, Francescatti, Flesch (2), Ricci, Kogan, Kreisler and Oistrakh. All are Westerners, all are male, and all are dead. Of course, violinists all over the world look up to Heifetz and the other violinists whose portraits grace Tanaka's book. But given that Japanese now have been playing the violin for close to 150 years and Japan has produced some outstanding violinists, one wonders why Tanaka did not offer his young readers a few Japanese role models – not to mention female ones, given that so many successful violinists are female – to boost their confidence.[31]

Tanaka is not the only violinist who continues to insist on the alleged musical backwardness of the Japanese at the turn of the millennium. The maverick violinist and composer Tamaki Hiroki has even written a book entitled "Japan: the country where sound is underdeveloped," in which he deplores noise pollution in general and the overwhelming dominance of equal temperament in particular and advocates "pure intonation" as the "natural food of sound." The issue is hardly limited to Japan, but equal temperament came to Japan with Western music, and Tamaki is not the only one to imply an exaggerated reliance on equal temperament by the Japanese.[32]

Perhaps it is partly because of continuing unease with perceived Western dominance and self-doubts about their own mastery of Western music that Japanese violinists in the past 20 years are increasingly breaking out of the mould of the Western classical canon in various ways: by playing more music by Japanese composers, or by experimenting with other musical styles. Again, such efforts can be seen as a reflection of wider cultural trends in Japan, including the advocacy of a "return to Asia," and worldwide trends. Remarkably, one violinist who has championed violin works by Japanese composers is a Chinese, Liu Wei – although perhaps this is no more remarkable than Nishizaki Takako recording Chinese works. Liu Wei, who started learning the violin as a child during the Cultural Revolution and moved to Japan in 1986, received a doctorate from Tokyo University of the Arts with a thesis about Japanese and Chinese violin music. In 1994 she premiered an unpublished violin Sonata by Yashiro Akio (1929–76), which she recorded in 2009, together with works by other composers, including Kishi Kōichi. By performing music by Chinese and Japanese composers she hopes to demonstrate how thoroughly these composers have made the Western musical idiom their own in a short time, an achievement, she believes both countries can be proud of.[33]

Kajino Ena is another violinist who combines research into music in Japan with performing. In 2009, as she prepared for a recital of Kishi Kōichi's works (and those of other Japanese composers) during a symposium to mark the anniversary of his birth, she described the charm of his short violin pieces for *String*. Kajino herself, after graduating from Kunitachi Music Academy, studied in Europe, at the Mozarteum in Salzburg, and feels she can identify with Kishi, because like him she had doubts about her ability as a Japanese to do the Western works justice. Playing Kishi's works, with their reflection of the culture of the common people of his homeland, enable her to feel "at home."[34]

Among the increasing number of violinists who have turned from classical music to other genres in recent years is Kita Naoki (1972–), a native of Morioka, Iwate Prefecture. After graduating from Kunitachi Music Academy, he studied composition and jazz improvisation at the Liverpool Institute for Performing Arts. He went on to Buenos Aires, where he studied with Fernando Suarez Paz, who formerly performed with Astor Piazzolla. When he returned to Japan he formed his own tango band, Tangophobics. But at some point, as he told *Sarasate* in 2009, he began to ask himself about his identity as a performer: "after all I'm Japanese..."[35] He realized that for him playing was about self-expression beyond the limits of genre. Besides tango he has played jazz and Arabic music, as well as improvising and performing his own compositions.

NAOTO (the spelling of his name, like his platinum-dyed hair, is apparently a trademark), who played the violin for the character Mine Ryūtarō in the live action drama version of *Nodame Cantabile*, was born in Osaka in 1973 and started learning the violin at the age of three. Although during his high school years he was a fan of Michael Jackson, he only played classical music on the violin. Not until his years at Geidai was he attracted to other genres. He joined the rock band The Yellow

Monkey and enjoyed the different approach to performing,
communicating more directly with the audience and experiencing their
reactions. Since graduating he has played with various groups, including
his own band. He describes his main area of interest as "pop," but his
playing incorporates many styles: J-POP, rock, R&B, fusion, jazz and
Latin. In 2005 he issued his first solo album, entitled *Sanctuary*. In an
interview with *Sarasate* he said he wanted to change the hard (*katai*)
image of the violin and have people realize that the violin is not limited
to classical music but can cross genres.[36]

The genres favoured by Kita and NAOTO can be described as modern,
urban styles, which, despite, in the case of jazz and tango, being
associated with a particular ethnic group or nation, became
internationally popular almost from their inception. This is not so with the
music Kunugi Takehiro and Yamase Rio have made their speciality: Irish
fiddle and Norwegian *hardingfele*. Kunugi (1966–), a native of Nara,
graduated from Kyōto City University of the Arts (Kyōto Shiritsu Kyōto
Geijutsu Daigaku). During his university years he took part in
collaborations with artists from the fine arts department and performed
minimalist music. He also developed an interest in European folk music.
After a few years of teaching he went to Europe in 1999 to study folk
music, particularly Irish fiddling. In 2002 he taught Hakase Tarō, whom
he knew from their high school days, and the two performed together.
Kunugi released his first album, *The Man The Fiddler,* under Hakase's
"Hats" label in 2004. His performance activities are centred on the
Kansai area, where he plays with three bands: Abyss of Time, Tabula
Rasa and Karira. Asked about his identity as a performer of folk music
from an alien culture, he replied, "If you delve into the world of folk
music, you invariably hit a wall of '[indigenous] soul' or 'if you aren't a
native …' But even classical music, which the Japanese have completely
mastered, originated in the West. So I believe the same is possible for
folk music." He does not, however, aim to play the music in a strictly
traditional way. Apart from his background in classical music, Kunugi
has also played gypsy music, klezmer and hard rock. "The violin allows
you to do so many different things with one and the same instrument, so
I don't want to rattle along with Irish to the point of excluding everything
else." Thanks to the Japanese ability to adopt and adapt what they import,
Kunugi asserts, they often end up playing better than people in the

country of origin, and some people in Ireland who looked down on fiddle music as outdated have even been inspired by Japanese fiddlers to form their own bands.[37]

Yamase Rio makes the same claim about the Hardanger fiddle – or "Hardanger violin," as she calls it, since neither "fiddle" nor the Norwegian "*hardingfele*" ring sympathetic strings with the average Japanese. Her own encounter with Norway came about through her sister's marriage to a Norwegian. After graduating from Tōhō Gakuen School of Music, where she studied with Etō Angela and Etō Toshiya, she performed as a solo violinist. In 1998 Yamase Rio and her sister, a pianist, started giving annual recitals at the Munch Museum in Oslo, and her interest in Norwegian culture was awakened. She learned that Edvard Grieg was influenced by the Hardanger fiddle, and wanted to know more. Oslo, however, was not the best place to pursue her interest, since the *hardingfele*'s home are the valleys off the south-western coast. When she finally located an instrument in an Oslo music shop, she was advised not to bother with the old thing. Even while she was still searching to find out more, however, the folk revival boomed. Her interest in the *hardingfele* and her lessons with Hallvard Kvåle were reported in the Norwegian media, and for Norwegian Hardanger-enthusiasts the rising profile of their instrument in Japan through Yamase's efforts provided welcome "backup."[38] Yamase herself received support from the Norwegian Embassy and Scandinavian Airlines when she began giving recitals on the *hardingfele* in Japan. She was also invited to perform in Norway, and in October 2009 she organized a festival of cultural exchange in Hardanger. In December, she launched the Japanese Hardanger Club which aims to promote cultural exchange between Norway and Japan.[39] The club supports study of the *hardingfele* by helping with the provision of instruments; not an easy task, given that the fiddles are not mass-produced. In 2011, two of Yamase's students were able to spend a few weeks in Norway with a scholarship from the club to study the folk music and culture first-hand.[40]

Although Yamase emphasizes the importance of studying the Hardanger fiddle in its cultural context, even including learning the dances (much of the repertoire consists of dance tunes), she is far from advocating strict adherence to traditional styles. At her first guest performance at the annual folk festival in Hardanger she surprised her audience with her own arrangements of non-traditional pieces. She composes and arranges music in different styles and has composed and played soundtracks for films produced by Studio Ghibli.[41]

For both Kunugi and Yamase, a firm base in a European folk style with an awareness of its cultural context has become part of their trademark. But rather than merely imitating models in a quest for the "authentic" reproduction of a tradition, they use the style as a springboard for developing their own individual style, and their music is "authentic" in the sense that it expresses their personal sensibilities and preferences. How far their performances have inspired Irish and Norwegian musicians to reconsider their own traditions is debatable.[42] Yamase's account of how she searched for and found a Hardanger fiddle provides an interesting counterpart to this author's experience of buying a Japanese *kokyū*. Kunugi and Yamase might be overstating their case, but it is possible that it is easier for them as outsiders to a tradition to use it freely and creatively, and that their example can encourage others to experiment more. Meanwhile, in a world where increased communications and sound technology have made it possible for musicians everywhere to hear music from around the world and make it their own if they so choose, the musical explorations of Japanese violinists are part of a global exchange, where inspiration flows in several directions.

As yet, the international fame of Japanese violinists tends to rest on their faithful reproduction of the European classical tradition. In this they have been joined on the international stage by musicians from Korea, Taiwan and (more recently) mainland China. In large part due to the wholesale appropriation of Western classical music by Asians, the music of Beethoven and others from the Western canon reaches larger audiences than ever before, thus proving that the canon no longer belongs to Europeans alone, but to everyone. It can even be argued that "Beethoven is a foreign 'country' to young Germans as well."[43] Classical music from the West continues to enjoy high prestige because of its association with Western civilization, but is not exclusively a European art,[44] and both Japanese and Westerners need to accept that no one owns Western classical music or can claim an inborn superior understanding of it. Moreover, it is but one musical genre among many, and its placement on a lone pedestal makes less and less sense.

For Japanese violinists, as for violinists elsewhere, the artificial divide between classical and popular becomes increasingly insignificant in their quest for individual expression and for a wider audience. Even the distinction between Japanese and foreign loses its meaning. Violinists from Japan may seek a Japanese identity, introducing perceived traditional Japanese characteristics into their music. Their Japanese identity, however, will be inseparable from an identity as participants in a global culture and their musical language will be accessible to a global audience. The violin has "gone native" in the sense that the Japanese have made it their own. Yet, almost from its introduction, it has also been and continues to be a vehicle for the Japanese as they engage in the global community.

# Notes

## Prologue and Introduction

1  Thesis published in English as Mehl, Margaret, *History and the State in Nineteenth-Century Japan* (Houndmills, Basingstoke: Macmillan, 1998); Suchy, Irene, "Deutschsprachige Musiker in Japan vor 1945. Eine Fallstudie eines Kulturtransfers am Beispiel der Rezeption abendländischer Musik" (doctoral thesis, University of Vienna, 1992).

2  http://www.bunkamura.co.jp/english/about/index.html (accessed 27 May 2010)

3  Cooke, Peter, "The violin – instrument of four continents," in *The Cambridge Companion to the Violin*, ed. Stowell, Robin (Cambridge: Cambridge University Press, 1992), 234.

4  Steinhardt, Arnold, *Violin Dreams* (Boston: Houghton Mifflin, 2006), 12.

5  Nettl, Bruno, *Encounters in Ethnomusicology: A Memoir* (Warren, Michigan: Harmonie Park Press, 2002), 64.

6  Chamberlain, Basil Hall, *Things Japanese: Being Notes on Various Subjects Connected with Japan*, Yohan Classics (Berkeley, CA: Stone Bridge Press, 2007 (1905)), 363, 366.

7  Ibid., 367. See also Eppstein, Ury, "From Torture to Fascination: Changing Western Attitudes to Japanese Music," *Japan Forum* 19.2 (2007): 191–216.

8  Zweig, Stefan, *Die Welt von Gestern: Erinnerungen eines Europäers* (Frankfurt: Fischer, 1970 (1944)), 12.

9  Osterhammel, Jürgen, *Die Verwandlung der Welt: Eine Geschichte des 19. Jahrhunderts* (Munich: C.H. Beck, 2009), 82–83.

10  For a critical assessments of the Japanese appropriation of Western classical music, see Aikawa, Yumi, *"Enka" no susume* (Tokyo: Bungei Shunju, 2002); Hanzawa, Asahiko, "Teikokushugi, gurōbaruka to ongaku," *Kokusai kenkyū* 36 (2009): 43–52; Okada, Akeo, "Europäische Klassik in Japan – eine düstere Diagnose," in *Musik in Japan*, ed. Silvain, Guignard (Munich: iudicium, 1994).

11  "Ivrī Gitorisu no namida," *String* August (2011): 1, 24–28. Yoshida, Mayu, "'Debris violins' pull at heartstrings," *The Japan Times*, 26 April 2012.

12  Tanaka, Chikashi, *Gohon no hashira: Vaiorin-dō: shugyō no tabi* (Tokyo: Ressun no Tomosha, 2001), 35.

13  Broughton, Simon, "Spike of Life," *The Strad* July (2007): 50–52.

14  Stowell, Robin ed. *The Cambridge Companion to the Violin* (Cambridge: Cambridge University Press, 1992); Kolneder, Walter, *Das Buch der Violine* (Zürich: Atlantis Musikbuch, 1989 (1972)).

15  De Ferranti, Hugh, *Japanese Musical Instruments* (Oxford: Oxford University Press, 2000), 76–77, 91.

16  Waterhouse, David, "An Early Illustration of the Four-Stringed Kokyū," *Oriental Art* 16.2 (1970): 162–168; Kambe, Yukimi, "Viols in Japan in the Sixteenth and

417

Early Seventeenth Centuries," *Journal of the VdGSA (The Viola da Gamba Society of America)* 37. (2000): 31–67; Nogawa, Mihoko, "Kokyūgaku," in *Nihon no dentō geinō kōza: ongaku*, ed. Nihon Geinō Bunka Shinkōkai and Kokuritsu Gekijō (Tokyo: Tankōsha, 2008).

17    Harich-Schneider, Eta, *A History of Japanese Music* (London: Oxford University Press, 1973).

18    Waterhouse, "An Early Illustration of the Four-Stringed Kokyū," 164.

19    Ishii, Takashi, *Hideyoshi ga kiita vaiorin* (Tokyo: Sanshin Tosho Yūgen, 1993).

20    Schoenbaum, David, *The Violin: A Social History of the World's Most Versatile Instrument* (New York: W.W. Norton & Company, 2012), xxv–xxvi.

21    Chiba, Yūko, *Doremi o eranda Nihonjin* (Ongaku no Tomosha, 2007), 9–21. For a detailed survey of Japanese knowledge and experience of Western music from the seventeenth century to the nineteenth: Nakamura, Kōsuke, *Kindai Nihon yōgaku josetsu* (Tokyo: Tōkyō Shoseki, 2003), 9–186.

22    Malm, William P., *Traditional Japanese Music and Musical Instruments* (Tokyo: Kodansha International, 2000), 199, 206; Waterhouse, "An Early Illustration of the Four-Stringed Kokyū," 167–168; Nogawa, "Kokyūgaku," 377–378.

23    Mikawa, Ise, Shinano, Etchū and Echigo.

24    Recent treatments of music in Japan include Malm, *Traditional Japanese Music*; De Ferranti, *Japanese Musical Instruments*; Provine, Robert C., Yoshihiko Tokumaru, and J. Lawrence Witzleben, eds., *The Garland Encyclopedia of World Music. Vol 7. East Asia: China, Japan, and Korea* (New York: Garland, 2002); Wade, Bonnie C., *Music in Japan* (Oxford: Oxford University Press, 2005); Hughes, David and Alison McQueen Tokita, eds., *The Ashgate Research Companion to Japanese Music* (Aldershot, Hampshire: Ashgate, 2008). See also Mehl, Margaret, "Introduction: Western Music in Japan: A Success Story?," *Nineteenth-Century Music Review* 10.2 (2013): 211–222. The same issue contains four Japan-related articles.

25    Finnegan, Ruth, *The Hidden Musicians: Music-Making in an English Town* (Cambridge: Cambridge University Press, 1989). Finnegan uses the term to describe musical activities in different genres of Western music in one location.

26    Malm, William P., "The Special Characteristics of Gagaku," in *Gagaku: Court Music and Dance*, ed. Togi, Masataro (Tokyo: Weatherhill, 1971), 5.

27    The possible exception is the *wagon*, whose origins are disputed. Malm, *Traditional Japanese Music*, 51; De Ferranti, *Japanese Musical Instruments*, 78.

28    Groemer, Gerald, "The Rise of 'Japanese Music'," *The World of Music* 46.2 (2004): 9–34, 10–18.

29    Harich-Schneider, *A History of Japanese Music*, 550–578; Tsukahara, Yasuko, *Jūkyū seiki no Nihon ni okeru Seiyō ongaku no juyō* (Tokyo: Taka Shuppan, 1993); ———, "Meiji 30 nen no kunaishō shikibushoku gagakubu," *Tōkyō Geijutsu Daigaku ongakubu Kiyō* 31 (2006): 89–112; ———, *Meiji kokka to gagaku: dentō no kindaika/kokugaku no sōsei* (Tokyo: Yūshisha, 2009).

30    For a detailed treatment of *minshingaku* in the nineteenth century in relation to Western music, see Tsukahara, *Seiyō ongaku no juyō*. On the music itself: Malm, William P., "Chinese Music in the Edo and Meiji Periods in Japan," *Asian Music* 6 1/2 (1975): 147–172.

31    Tsukahara, *Seiyō ongaku no juyō*; Yumoto, Kōichi, *Bakumatsu Meiji ryūkō jiten* (Tokyo: Kashiwa Shobō, 1998), 186–189.

32    Kurata, Yoshihiro, *Geinō no bunmei kaika: Meiji kokka to geinō kindaika* (Tokyo: Heibonsha, 1999).

33    Chiba, *Doremi o eranda Nihonjin*, 45–46, 55.

34    For *koto* music, see Wade, *Music in Japan*, 65–77; Flavin, Philip, "Meiji shinkyoku: The Beginnings of Modern Music for the Koto," *Japan Review: Journal of the International Research Center for Japanese Studies* 22 (2010): 103–123.

35    Tanimura, Reiko, "Practical Frivolities: The Study of *Shamisen* among Girls of the Late Edo Townsman Class," *Japan Review* 23 (2011): 73–96.

36    Harich-Schneider, *A History of Japanese Music*, 596.

37    Following an educational reform in 1999, learning a Japanese instrument has been introduced into compulsory education; since 2002, Japanese junior high school students have to study at least one Japanese instrument.

38    Victor, VZCF 1004; for other examples, see Wade, *Music in Japan*.

39    Chiba, *Doremi o eranda Nihonjin*.

40    Watanabe, Hiroshi, *Nihon bunka modan rapusodi* (Tokyo: Shunjūsha, 2002). The whole idea of a "Japanese music" only developed gradually from the late nineteenth century and did not fully gain currency until after 1945; Groemer, "The Rise of 'Japanese Music'."

41    Quoted in Harich-Schneider, *A History of Japanese Music*, 477.

42    Ibid., 546.

43    Hughes and Tokita, eds., *The Ashgate Research Companion to Japanese Music*, 18–27. See also the remarks on theory and aesthetics in Galliano, Luciana, *Yōgaku: Japanese Music in the Twentieth Century*, trans. Mayes, Martin (Lanham, Maryland, and London: The Scarecrow Press, 2002), 5–25.

44    Ross, Alex, *The Rest is Noise: Listening to the Twentieth Century* (New York: Picador, 2007), 558–588.

**Part 1: Confrontation with the West**

1     Nihon Fūzokushi Gakkai, ed. *Shiryō de kataru Meiji no Tōkyō hyakuwa* (Tokyo: Tsukubanesha, 1996), 118–119. *Manzairaku* is traditionally played on auspicious ceremonial occasions. Two good recent historical surveys of Modern Japan are McClain, James L. , *Japan: A Modern History* (New York: W.W. Norton & Company, 2002). Gordon, Andrew, *A Modern History of Japan: From Tokugawa Times to the Present* (Oxford: Oxford University Press, 2009 (2003)).

2     Among the best treatments in Japanese: Nakamura, Kōsuke, *Kindai Nihon yōgaku josetsu* (Tokyo: Tōkyō Shoseki, 2003); Tsukahara, Yasuko, *Jūkyū seiki no Nihon ni okeru Seiyō ongaku no juyō* (Tokyo: Taka Shuppan, 1993). No treatment in English is as comprehensive. See Galliano, Luciana, *Yōgaku: Japanese Music in the Twentieth Century*, trans. Mayes, Martin (Lanham, Maryland, and London: The Scarecrow Press, 2002); Wade, Bonnie C., *Music in Japan* (Oxford: Oxford University Press, 2005), 7–19; Herd, Judith Ann, "Western-influenced 'classical' music in Japan" in *The Ashgate Research Companion to Japanese Music*, ed. Hughes, David W. and Tokita, Alison McQueen (Aldershot, UK: Ashgate, 2008).

On singing in schools: Eppstein, Ury, *The Beginnings of Western Music in Meiji Era Japan* (New York: Edwin Mellen, 1994).

3    Mehl, Margaret, *Carl Köppen und sein Wirken als Militärinstrukteur für das Fürstentum Kii-Wakayama (1869–1872)* (Bonn: Förderverein Bonner Zeitschrift für Japanologie, 1987), 104–142, 210.

4    Details in Nakamura, *Kindai Nihon yōgaku josetsu*, 293–312.

5    Kim, Hio-Jin, *Koreanische und westliche Musikerausbildung: Historische Rekonstruktion – Vergleich – Perspektiven* (Marburg: Tectum, 2000), 118–120.

6    The following is based on Nakamura, *Kindai Nihon yōgaku josetsu*, 403–510. Togi, Masataro, *Gagaku: Court Music and Dance*, trans. Kenny, Don (New York: Weatherhill, 1971), 133–137. On the *gagaku* musicians and the Meiji state in general: Tsukahara, Yasuko, *Meiji kokka to gagaku: dentō no kindaika/kokugaku no sōsei* (Tokyo: Yūshisha, 2009).

7    Harich-Schneider, Eta, *Musikalische Impressionen aus Japan 1941–1957: Herausgegeben, kommentiert und mit einer Einführung versehen von Ingrid Fritsch* (Munich: iudicium, 2006), 89.

8    Nakamura, *Kindai Nihon yōgaku josetsu*, 430.

9    Ibid., 500.

10   The following is based largely on Ibid., 511–630; Eppstein, *Beginnings of Western Music*.

11   Both documents (the second one in Megata's own English version) are quoted in full in Eppstein, *Beginnings of Western Music*, 31–37.

12   For details of Mason's biography and work see Howe, Sondra Wieland, *Luther Whiting Mason: International Music Educator* (Warren, Michigan: Harmonie Park Press, 1997).

13   Quoted in Ibid., 58.

14   For Mason's work in Japan: Ibid; Eppstein, *Beginnings of Western Music*.

15   According to Mason; Howe, *Luther Whiting Mason*, 95.

16   Ibid., 90.

17   Matsumoto, Zenzō, *Teikin yūjō: Nihon no vaiorin ongaku shi* (Tokyo: Ressun no Tomosha, 1995), 8.

18   Nakamura, Rihei, *Yōgaku dōnyūsha no kiseki: Nihon kindai yōgakushi josetsu* (Tokyo: Tōsui Shobō, 1993), 643–688.

19   "Academy" is used here rather than "School" because this was the English translation used in the Meiji Period. Between 1893 and 1899 it lost its independence again and became a department of the Higher Normal School (Kōtō Shihan Gakkō).

20   The process is particularly well outlined in Tsukahara, *Seiyō ongaku no juyō*.

21   The following discussion is based on Nakamura, *Kindai Nihon yōgaku josetsu*, 633–748.

22   Kitahara, Kanako and Hiroshi Yasuda, "Hirosaki to I-Ai jogakkō no ongaku kyōiku," *Hirosaki daigaku kyōiku gakubu kiyō* 80 (1998): 37–47.

23   Nakamura, *Kindai Nihon yōgaku josetsu*, 725.

24   Japanese "Morobito kosorite mukaematsure"; Ibid., 732.

25   Whitney, Clara, *Clara's Diary: An American Girl in Meiji Japan* (Tokyo: Kodansha International, 1981), 173–174, 223–224.

26   Quoted in Nakamura, *Yōgaku dōnyūsha no kiseki*, 703.

27   Masumoto, Masahiko, *Yokohama Gēte-za: Meiji Taishō no Seiyō gekijō – dainihan* (Yokohama: Iwasaki Hakubutsukan/Gēte-za Kinen Shuppankyoku, 1986), 101.

28   Kondō, Jirō, *Nihon furūto monogatari* (Tokyo: Ongaku no Tomosha, 2003), 30–37.

29   Suchy, Irene, "Deutschsprachige Musiker in Japan vor 1945. Eine Fallstudie eines Kulturtransfers am Beispiel der Rezeption abendländischer Musik" (doctoral thesis, University of Vienna, 1992), 242.

30   Ibid., 149–163,229.

31   Nomura, Kōichi, "Occidental Music," in *Japanese Music and Drama in the Meiji Era*, ed. Komiya, Toyotaka (Tokyo: Ōbunsha, 1956), 489. Ōmori, Seitarō, *Nihon no yōgaku*, 2 vols., vol. 1 (Tokyo: Shinmon Shuppansha, 1986), 56–64.

32   On the balls at the Rokumeikan: Mehl, Margaret, "Dancing at the Rokumeikan – A New Role for Women?," in *Japanese Women: Emerging from Subservience, 1886–1945*, ed. Gordon Daniels and Tomida, Hiroko (Folkestone, Kent: Global Oriental, 2005).

33   Fujimoto, Hiroko, "Meiji 20 nendai no Tōkyō Ongaku Gakkō to Nihon Ongakukai," *Ochamomizu ongaku ronshū* 8 (2006): 11–23.

34   Ōmori, *Nihon no yōgaku*, 56–57. Nihon Fūzokushi Gakkai, ed. *Shiryō de kataru Meiji no Tōkyō hyakuwa*, 256–259.

35   Matsumoto, *Teikin yūjō*, 100, 120, 202.

36   They included the Shiba Shōka Kai established in 1887 and the Ongaku Shōka Kai (1886); Ōmori, *Nihon no yōgaku*, 87; Kochō, Hisako, *Taki Rentarō* (Tokyo: Yoshikawa Kōbunkan, 1968), 23–24.

37   See Chapter 5.

38   Ōmori, *Nihon no yōgaku*, 125–128.

39   For the following see Mori, Setsuko, "A Historical Survey of Music Periodicals in Japan: 1881–1920," *Fontis Artis Musicae* 36.1 (1989): 44–50.

40   Chamberlain, Basil Hall, *Things Japanese: Being Notes on Various Subjects Connected with Japan*, Yohan Classics (Berkeley, CA: Stone Bridge Press, 2007 (1905)), 368.

41   Chiba, Yūko, *Doremi o eranda Nihonjin* (Ongaku no Tomosha, 2007).

42   Malm, William P., "The Modern Music of Meiji Japan," in *Tradition and Modernization in Japanese Culture*, ed. Shively, Donald (Princeton: Princeton University Press, 1971), 282–284.

43   Galliano, *Yōgaku*, 106.

44   Yumoto, Kōichi, *Bakumatsu Meiji ryūkō jiten* (Tokyo: Kashiwa Shobō, 1998), 174–175.

45   Melvin, Sheila and Jindong Cai, *Rhapsody in Red: How Western Classical Music Became Chinese* (New York: Algora, 2004).

46   Chin, Shōgen, *Kaikyō o wataru baiorin* (Tokyo: Kawade Shobō, 2007), 56–79. Kim, *Koreanische und westliche Musikerausbildung*, 132–139.

47   Lee, Angela Hao-Chun, "The Influence of Governmental Control and early Christian Missionaries on Music Education of Aborigines in Taiwan," *British Journal of Music Education* 23.2 (2006): 205–216; Kim, *Koreanische und westliche Musikerausbildung*, 132–142.

48   Kambe, Yukimi, "Viols in Japan in the Sixteenth and Early Seventeenth Centuries,"

*Journal of the VdGSA (The Viola da Gamba Society of America)* 37. (2000): 31–67, 3.

49  Matsumoto, *Teikin yūjō*, 3.

50  Kasahara, Kiyoshi, *Kurobune raikō to ongaku* (Tokyo: Yoshikawa Kōbunkan, 2001), 102–170.

51  Nakamura, *Kindai Nihon yōgaku josetsu*, 136–137.

52  Matsumoto, *Teikin yūjō*, 4.; Anonymous, *The Musical World* (1854); "Amusements," *New York Times*, 27 October 1855, 4; Haan, J. H., "Thalia and Terpsichore on the Yangtze: A Survey of Foreign Theatre and Music in Shanghai 1850–1965," *Journal of the Hong Kong Branch of the Royal Asiatic Society* 29. (1989): 158–251, 212.

53  Matsumoto, *Teikin yūjō*, 22–23.

54  T.H.D., "Jenny Claus as a Violinist," *The Brisbane Courier*, 15 July 1873, 3.

55  Matsumoto, *Teikin yūjō*, 35.

56  Meissner, Kurt, *Deutsche in Japan* (Tokyo: OAG, 1961), 47, 57.

57  Kochō, *Taki Rentarō*, 8.

58  Ibid., 7, 16–17.

59  Tōkyō Geijutsu Daigaku Hyakunenshi Hensan Iinkai, ed. *Tōkyō Geijutsu Daigaku hyakunenshi: Tōkyō Ongaku Gakkō hen 1* (Tokyo: Ongaku no Tomosha, 1987), 218–219.

60  Kelley, Gwendolyn Dunlevy and George P. Upton, *Edouard Remenyi: Musician, Litterateur and Man* (Chicago: A. C. McClurg & Co., 1906). "Remenyi Drops Dead," *San Francisco Chronicle*, 16 May 1898, 10.

61  Meiji Nyūsu Jiten Hensan Iinkai and Mainichi Komyunikēshonzu, eds., *Meiji nyūsu jiten* (Tokyo: Mainichi Komyunikēshonzu, 1983–86). 3: 805.

62  Yōko, "Meijiki Kansai vaiorin jijō," *Ongaku kenkyū (Ōsaka Ongaku Daigaku Hakubutsukan nenpō)* 20 (2003): 11–38, 12.

63  Matsumoto, *Teikin yūjō*, 97–98; Musin, Ovide, *My Memories: A Half Century of Adventures and Experiences and Globe Travel Written by Himself* (New York: Musin Publishing Company, 1920).

64  Matsumoto, *Teikin yūjō*, 104; Poole, Herbert Armstrong, "(family history)," http://www.antonymaitland.com/hptext/hp0001.txt (2 September 2012). Einstein, Alfred, ed. *Das neue Musiklexikon: nach dem Dictionary of Modern Music and Musicians herausgegeben von A. Eaglefield-Hull* (Berlin: Max Hesses Verlag, 1926), 568; Jespersen, Gudrun, "Max Schlüter inmemoriam," *Dansk Musik Tidsskrift* 20.May (1945): 96–97. Programme of Marquardt's performance with Alexandra Beritschuck-Marquardt (harp) in the Archives of Modern Japanese Music (No. 190110002).

65  Matsumoto, *Teikin yūjō*, 112. "Miss Schaefer's Concert," *The Japan Weekly Mail*, 16 March 1907, 287.

66  Matsumoto, *Teikin yūjō*, 104, 112, 150, 303–310. For Kansai: Ōsaka Ongaku Daigaku Ongaku Bunka Kenkyūsho, ed. *Ōsaka ongaku bunkashi shiryō: Shōwa hen* (Osaka: Ōsaka Ongaku Daigaku, 1970). Not much is known about some of these artists, and the list is almost certainly incomplete. Such details as I have found will be posted on www.notbylovealone.com

67  Matsushima, Maria Junko, "St Nikolai of Japan and the Japanese Church Singing,"

http://www.orthodox-jp.com/maria/Nikolai-JAPAN.htm (13 February 2006).

68  Nomura, "Occidental Music," 461.

69  Kurata, Yoshihiro, *Geinō no bunmei kaika: Meiji kokka to geinō kindaika* (Tokyo: Heibonsha, 1999), 208.

70  Quoted in Nagano-ken Kyōikushi Kankōkai, ed. *Naganoken kyōikushi 5: Kyōikuka hen* (Nagano: Nagano-ken Kyōikushi Kankōkai, 1974), 459.

71  Ibid.

72  Matsumoto, *Teikin yūjō*, 29–30. Nakamura, *Kindai Nihon yōgaku josetsu*, 588.

73  Tōkyō Geijutsu Daigaku Hyakunenshi Hensan Iinkai, ed. *Hyakunenshi: Tōkyō Ongaku Gakkō hen 1*, 234–236.

74  Ibid., 64.

75  Morse, Edward, Sylvester, *Japan Day by Day, 1877, 1878–9, 1882–3*, 2 vols., vol. 2 (Boston, New York: Houghton Mifflin Company, 1917), 2:212–213. Matsumoto, *Teikin yūjō*, 10.

76  Nakamura, *Yōgaku dōnyūsha no kiseki*, 356–357.

77  Ibid., 288–289.

78  Tōkyō Geijutsu Daigaku Hyakunenshi Hensan Iinkai, ed. *Hyakunenshi: Tōkyō Ongaku Gakkō hen 1*, 213, 219–220. For explanations of the programmes see Nakamura, *Yōgaku dōnyūsha no kiseki*, 278–279, 286.

79  Nakamura, *Kindai Nihon yōgaku josetsu*, 439, 476.

80  ———, *Yōgaku dōnyūsha no kiseki*, 277–279, 290–293.

81  Most of the information on Sauvlet is based on Ibid., 623–739.

82  Tōkyō Geijutsu Daigaku Hyakunenshi Hensan Iinkai, ed. *Hyakunenshi: Tōkyō Ongaku Gakkō hen 1*, 248–249.

83  Ibid., 224. Nakamura, *Yōgaku dōnyūsha no kiseki*, 711.

84  Tōkyō Geijutsu Daigaku Hyakunenshi Hensan Iinkai, ed. *Hyakunenshi: Tōkyō Ongaku Gakkō hen 1*, 228. According to the programme, Sauvlet played a piece by Hubert Léonard.

85  Quoted in Nakamura, *Yōgaku dōnyūsha no kiseki*, 738.

86  "Snuffed out a Hymn," *San Francisco Chronicle*, 30 March 1895, 5; "Footlight," *San Francisco Chronicle*, 25 February 1894, 3.

87  "Snuffed out a Hymn."

88  Nakamura, *Yōgaku dōnyūsha no kiseki*, 735.

89  "Remenyi Drops Dead."

90  For example, Endō, Hiroshi, *Meiji ongaku shikō* (Tokyo: Yūhōdō, 1958), 281. The most detailed biography is Hirasawa, Hiroko, "Rudolph Dittrich: Leben und Werk" (doctoral thesis, University of Vienna, 1996). See also Suchy, "Deutschsprachige Musiker in Japan", 100–121.

91  Krejsa, Julia and Peter Pantzer, *Japanisches Wien* (Vienna: Herold, 1989), 85.

92  Reminiscences reported in Endō, *Meiji ongaku shikō*; Tōkyō Geijutsu Daigaku Hyakunenshi Hensan Iinkai, ed. *Hyakunenshi: Tōkyō Ongaku Gakkō hen 1*, 521–522; Hirasawa, "Rudolph Dittrich: Leben und Werk".

93  Hirasawa, "Rudolph Dittrich: Leben und Werk", 87.

94  Programme in Endō, *Meiji ongaku shikō*, 286–286.

95  Matsumoto, *Teikin yūjō*, 52–56.

96  Hirasawa, "Rudolph Dittrich: Leben und Werk", 206.

97   Dittrich, Rudolf, "Beiträge zur Kenntnis der japanischen Musik," *MOAG* 6.85 (1897): 376–391.
98   Hirasawa, "Rudolph Dittrich: Leben und Werk", 244–245, 280–288. Matsumoto gives Ōtsuka Jun as the editor's name: Matsumoto, *Teikin yūjō*, 319.
99   Suchy, "Deutschsprachige Musiker in Japan", 106.
100  Krejsa and Pantzer, *Japanisches Wien*, 86–88.
101  The official history of the school states that Kōda Nobu recommended him, but it seems unlikely that she knew him better than anyone else or that her influence was decisive: Tōkyō Geijutsu Daigaku Hyakunenshi Hensan Iinkai, ed. *Hyakunenshi: Tōkyō Ongaku Gakkō hen 1*, 533. According to Endō Hiroshi, Suzuki Yonejirō first brought news of Junker to Tokyo and several members of the Academy attended his second concert in Yokohama Public Hall: Endō, *Meiji ongaku shikō*, 274–277.
102  Copy of birth certificate, August Junker collection, CSO archives.
103  Schweikert, Norman, *Interview with Iwakura Tomokazu* (1995), Cassette tape, Rosenthal Archives of the Chicago Symphony Orchestra.
104  Ibid. The Staatliches Institut für Musikforschung has a photocopy from an unspecified book in its archives of the Berlin Philharmonic Orchestra, which lists the members of the Orchestra for 1891–92; Junker's name appears on the fifth desk of the second violins.
105  According to his grandson, he renounced his American nationality when he returned to Germany in 1913: Ibid.
106  "A Violin Virtuoso," *The Japan Times*, 21 February 1898.
107  Copy of the programme in the Rosenthal Archives of the Chicago Symphony Orchestra.
108  "Saturday's Concert at Ueno," *The Japan Times*, 22 March 1898.
109  Masumoto, Masahiko, *Yokohama Gēte-za: Meiji Taishō no Seiyō gekijō* (Yokohama: Yokohama-shi Kyōiku Iinkai, 1978), 119–120.
110  Masumoto, *Yokohama Gēte-za (1986)*, 119, 120. See also the memoirs of Herbert Armstrong Poole: Poole, "(family history)."
111  Urach-Württemberg, Albrecht, "Aus 40 Jahren moderner japanischer Musikentwicklung: August Junker, der Pionier deutscher Musik in Japan," *Die Musik* 29.10 (1937): 675–677, 676.
112  Tōkyō Geijutsu Daigaku Hyakunenshi Hensan Iinkai, ed. *Hyakunenshi: Tōkyō Ongaku Gakkō hen 1*, 535.
113  ———, ed. *Tōkyō Geijutsu Daigaku hyakunenshi: Ensōkai hen 1* (Tokyo: Ongaku no Tomosha, 1990), 353–359.
114  ———, ed. *Hyakunenshi: Tōkyō Ongaku Gakkō hen 1*, 533.
115  Urach-Württemberg, "Aus 40 Jahren moderner japanischer Musikentwicklung," 676.
116  Chamberlain, *Things Japanese*, 368.
117  Crusen, Georg, "Deutsche Musik in Japan," *Die Musik* 1.1 (1901): 58–59.
118  Tōkyō Geijutsu Daigaku Hyakunenshi Hensan Iinkai, ed. *Hyakunenshi: Ensōkai hen 1*, 230–231.
119  Nishihara, Minoru, *'Gakusei' Bētōven no tanjō* (Tokyo: Heibonsha, 2000), 141–142.
120  Tōkyō Geijutsu Daigaku Hyakunenshi Hensan Iinkai, ed. *Hyakunenshi: Tōkyō Ongaku Gakkō hen 1*, 568–572.

121  Ibid., 576–577.

122  Suchy, Irene, "Versunken und vergessen: zwei österreichische Musiker in Japan vor 1945," in *Mehr als Maschinen für Musik*, ed. Linhart, Sepp and Schmid, Kurt (Wien: Literas Universitätsverlag, 1990); Suchy, "Deutschsprachige Musiker in Japan", 187.

123  Ripphausen, Josef, "Stolberg vergass einen Grossen Sohn: August Junker war Japans erster 'Karajan'," *Aachener Nachrichten*, 19 September 1969, 12 (B II). Before (and even after) the treaty between Japan and Germany in 1936, many Japanese or mixed-race residents suffered discrimination from the Nazis.

124  Tōkyō Geijutsu Daigaku Hyakunenshi Hensan Iinkai, ed. *Tōkyō Geijutsu Daigaku hyakunenshi: Tōkyō Ongaku Gakkō hen 2* (Tokyo: Ongaku no Tomosha, 2003), 1222. I have not been able to confirm this; the orchestra toured under Nikisch in 1900 and 1904 and under Strauss in 1908. The history of the orchestra mentions no details about soloists, and the orchestra's archives apparently contain no programmes: Muck, Peter, *Einhundert Jahre Berliner Philharmonisches Orchester: Darstellung in Dokumenten*, vol. 4: Die Mitglieder des Orchesters; die Programme; die Konzertreisen; Erst-und Uraufführungen (Tutzing: Hans Schneider, 1982).

125  Tōkyō Geijutsu Daigaku Hyakunenshi Hensan Iinkai, ed. *Hyakunenshi: Ensōkai hen 1*, 379–380.

126  Suchy, "Deutschsprachige Musiker in Japan", 213; Nishihara, *'Gakusei' Bētōven no tanjō*, 148.

127  Nomura, Kōichi, Kenzō Nakajima, and Kiyomichi Miyoshi, *Nihon yōgaku gaishi: Nihon gakudan chōrō ni yoru taikenteki yōgaku no rekishi* (Tokyo: Rajio Gijutsusha, 1978), 29; Tanabe, Hisao, *Meiji ongaku monogatari* (Tokyo: Seiabō, 1965), 233.

128  Part of the following discussion has previously been published: Mehl, Margaret, "A Man's Job? The Kōda Sisters, Violin Playing and Gender Stereotypes in the Introduction of Western Music in Japan," *Women's History Review* 21.1 (2012): 101–120.

129  Tōkyō Geijutsu Daigaku Hyakunenshi Hensan Iinkai, ed. *Hyakunenshi: Tōkyō Ongaku Gakkō hen 1*, 219–220. Weber, *Aufforderung zum Tanz.*

130  Kōda, Nobu, "Watakushi no hansei," *Ongaku sekai* 3.6 (1931): 33–42, 35.

131  Kōda papers; microfilm: 1990–7–5.

132  Kōda, "Watakushi no hansei," 39. Howe, *Luther Whiting Mason*, 124.

133  Hagiya, Yukiko, *Kōda shimai: Yōgaku reimeiki o sasaeta Kōda Nobu to Andō Kō* (Tokyo: Chopin, 2003), 93–94. Kōda Kō to Rosa Gerold, Berlin, 1 April 1901 & Tokyo, 8 May 1906. Manuscripts in the Austrian National Library (Musikerbriefe, KODA, Ko (Kat.-Nr. 2297), 740/25–1 & 740/25–2. The Kōda papers contain seven letters from Gerold, 1904–1906; microfilm 1990–12–90/96.

134  Tōkyō Geijutsu Daigaku Hyakunenshi Hensan Iinkai, ed. *Hyakunenshi: Ensōkai hen 1*, 29. Hiruma's biographer claims that the four played as a quartet together as early as 1887, but he cites no evidence, and it seems unlikely. See Iishima, Kunio, *Meiji Seiyō ongaku yōran jidai no kakuretaru senkōsha Hiruma Kenpachi no shōgai* (Tokyo: Zen'on Gakufu Shuppansha, 1989), 48.

135  Takii, Keiko, *Sōseki ga kiita Bētōven* (Tokyo: Chūō Kōronsha, 2004), 72–73.

136  In 1898: Tōkyō Geijutsu Daigaku Hyakunenshi Hensan Iinkai, ed. *Hyakunenshi: Ensōkai hen 1*, 66.

137  Chamberlain, *Things Japanese*, 367.
138  Nomura, Nakajima, and Miyoshi, *Nihon yōgaku gaishi*, 6.
139  Manuscripts in the Kōda papers: microfilm 1990–7.
140  Until a few years ago they were forgotten. Kōda, Nobu, *Two Sonatas for Violin and Piano. Edited by Shinichirō Ikebe* (Tokyo: Zen-on Music, 2006 ). The sonatas have been recorded by Inda Chihiro with Horie Mariko in 2008: *Nihon josei sakkyokuka monogatari: Vaiorin sakuhin,* Mittenwald 2009, MTWD99038.
141  Galliano, *Yōgaku*, 40.
142  Tōkyō Geijutsu Daigaku Hyakunenshi Hensan Iinkai, ed. *Hyakunenshi: Ensōkai hen 1*, 46–47. Details according to Takii, Keiko, "Nihon no gengaku kyōiku/kusawake no jidai," in *Tōkyō Geijutsu Daigaku sōritsu 120 nen kinen ongakusai: Geidai 120 nen o furikaette (festival programme)* (Tokyo: Tōkyō Geijutsu Daigaku, 2008).
143  Kōda, "Watakushi no hansei," 38.
144  Tōkyō Geijutsu Daigaku Hyakunenshi Hensan Iinkai, ed. *Hyakunenshi: Ensōkai hen 1*, 25.
145  *Yomiuri shinbun*, 20 July 1894, quoted in Hagiya, *Kōda shimai*, 116.
146  Tōkyō Geijutsu Daigaku Hyakunenshi Hensan Iinkai, ed. *Hyakunenshi: Ensōkai hen 1*, 3, 6.
147  Matsumoto, *Teikin yūjō*, 25. Tōkyō Geijutsu Daigaku Hyakunenshi Hensan Iinkai, ed. *Hyakunenshi: Tōkyō Ongaku Gakkō hen 2*, 1320–1321. Kōda Kō's name is listed in the *Jahresberichte der Hochschule für Musik, Berlin* for the academic years 1900–01, 1901–02 and 1902–03.
148  *Musical Times*, May 1902 excerpts; http://www.musicaltimes.co.uk/archive/misc/excerpts1902.html (accessed 6 February 2009). Iwaya, Sazanami, *Sazanami Yōkō miyage* (Tokyo: Hakubunkan, 1903), 194–197. See also Hirasawa, "Rudolph Dittrich: Leben und Werk", 47. The programme included Japanese songs arranged for violin and piano by Rudolf Dittrich.
149  For example, on 12 December 1908, at the Oriental Hotel in Kobe, Junker, the Kōda sisters and Werkmeister performed Beethoven's String Quartet Op. 18.4, Tchaikovsky's Andante Cantabile from his String Quartet Op. 11, Haydn's Serenade (presumably the second movement from his Quartet Op. 3.5) and a movement from Schumann's Piano Quintet with Heydrich as the pianist. Ōsaka Ongaku Daigaku Ongaku Bunka Kenkyūsho, ed. *Ōsaka ongaku bunkashi shiryō: Meiji/Taishō hen* (Osaka: Ōsaka Ongaku Daigaku, 1968), 231.
150  *Ongaku zasshi* 28 (25 January 1893, 20–21) The clear winner was the *koto* player Yamase Shōin, an illustration that even readers of Japan's first journal dedicated to music preferred more traditional sounds.
151  *Yorozu shinpō* Hagiya, *Kōda shimai*, 164–172, 126.
152  *Teikoku bungaku*, quoted in Ibid., 133.
153  *Teikoku bungaku*, quoted in Tōkyō Geijutsu Daigaku Hyakunenshi Hensan Iinkai, ed. *Hyakunenshi: Tōkyō Ongaku Gakkō hen 1*, 573–574.
154  *Tōkyō asahi shinbun*, quoted in Ibid., 570–571.
155  *Tōkyō nichinichi shinbun*, 10 September 1909 in: Ibid., 572.; that year the German Rudolph Ernest Reuter (1888–?) was appointed to teach singing and piano: ——, ed. *Hyakunenshi: Tōkyō Ongaku Gakkō hen 1*, 538. and Kambe Aya (see below)

returned from France. Nobu's employment officially ceased on 8 September 1911:
————, ed. *Hyakunenshi: Tōkyō Ongaku Gakkō hen 2*, 1311, 1557.

156  The Philharmonic Choir was founded in 1882 by Siegfried Ochs, who directed it
until 1929.

157  Kōda papers, microfilm 1990–9–32/33: 20 July 1910. Kōda's diaries have recently
been published: Takii, Keiko and Noriko Hirata, *Kōda Nobu no 'Tai-Ōnikki'*
(Tokyo: Tōkyō Geijutsu Daigaku Shuppankai, 2012).

158  Original in German, author's translation.

159  Kōda, Nobu, "Katei to ongaku," *Ongakukai* 3.10 (1910): 57–59.

160  ————, "Ongaku to katei," *Ongakukai* 5.2 (1912): 65–66.

161  Morita, Tasaburō, *Meiryū manga* (Tokyo: Hakubunkan, 1912), 184–185. The text
appears to contain an allusion to her brother Rohan's story *Isanatori*. For Kōda
Nobu's influence on Rohan's perceptions of music: Takii, Keiko, "Kōda Rohan to
ongaku, soshite imōto no Nobu," *Tōkyō Geijutsu Daigaku Ongakubu kiyō* 26
(2001): 87–107, 103.

162  Yamada, Kōsaku, *Jiden: Wakakihi no kyōshikyoku* (Tokyo: Nihon Tosho Sentā,
1999 (1951)), 130–131.

163  Milsom, David, "Practice and Principle: Perspectives upon the German 'Classical'
School of Violin Playing in the Late Nineteenth Century," *Nineteenth-Century
Music Review* 9.1 (2012): 31–52.

164  Hagiya, *Kōda shimai*, 145.

165  Katsura, Kinko (Chikaya?), "Gen gakudan vaiorinisuto hyō," *Gakusei* 8 (1927):
43–47, 43–44.

166  Hagiya, *Kōda shimai*, 233–239.

167  Kochō, *Taki Rentarō*, 277–278. Higashi is best known for her lyrics in colloquial
Japanese, including for some of the songs of Taki Rentarō.

168  Hagiya, *Kōda shimai*, 167.

169  The association of female music-making with women's sexual role can be found
in many cultures: Koskoff, Ellen, ed. *Women and Music in Cross-Cultural
Perspective* (Urbana: University of Illinois Press, 1989), 6.

170  Kühnen, Barbara, "Marie Soldat-Roeger (1863–1955)," in *Die Geige war ihr
Leben: Drei Geigerinnen im Portrait*, ed. Dreyfus, Kay, Engelhardt-Krajaneck,
Margarethe, and Kühnen, Barbara (Strasshof, Austria: Vier-Viertel-Verlag, 2000).

171  Matsumoto, *Teikin yūjō*, 19.

172  Eppstein, *Beginnings of Western Music*, 36.

173  Howe, *Luther Whiting Mason*, 61–62, 84.

174  Matsumoto, *Teikin yūjō*, 19; Matsuyama, Iwane, "Nihon ni okeru vaiorin no seisaku
1," *Ongakukai* 3.1 (1910): 49–51.

175  Shiotsu, Yōko, "Meijiki no yōgakki seisaku," *Ongaku kenkyū (Ōsaka Ongaku
Daigaku Ongaku Kenkyūsho nenpō)* 13 (1995): 5–35; Tanaka, Kenji, *Denshi gakki
sangyō ron* (Tokyo: Kōbundō, 1998).

176  Matsumoto, *Teikin yūjō*, 30–34; Suzuki, Shin'ichi, "Nihon vaiorin shi," in *Suzuki
Shin'ichi zenshū 1* (Tokyo: Sōshisha, 1985 (1932)); Shiotsu, "Meijiki Kansai
vaiorin jijō."; ————, "Meijiki no yōgakki seisaku."; Murata, Sōroku, *Vaiorin*
(Tokyo: Iwanami Shinsho, 1975); ————, "Nihon no vaiorin seisakushi,"
(Tokyo?n.d.).

177   Probably the same as Matsunaga Sadanosuke, according to Murata.

178   Shiotsu, "Meijiki Kansai vaiorin jijō," 12–13.

179   "Vaiorin saisho no mozōsha," *Ongakukai* 5.1 (1912): 50.

180   Ōnogi, Kichibei, "Gakki sangyō ni okeru seshū keiei no ichigenkei: Suzuki Baiorin
      Seizō Kabushiki Gaisha no enkaku (I)," *Hamamatsu Tanki Daigaku kenkyū ronshū*
      24 (1981): 1–38, 4.

181   Ibid.: 10.

182   8 March, p. 4; quoted in Nihon Kindai Ongakukan, ed. *Meijiki Nihonjin to ongaku:
      Tōkyō nichinichi shinbun ongaku kankei kiji shūsei* (Tokyo: Kunitachi Ongaku
      Daigaku Fuzoku Toshokan, 1995).

183   No.28, January 1893.

184   E.g. 1908.6, after p. 50. Also, an advertisement by Miki Gakkiten (Miki Music
      Store) in Osaka lists categories "gōgai" A, B, C, at 2, 3 and 4 yen respectively:
      Ōno, Umewaka and Tateki Ōwada, *Tetsudō shōka* (Osaka: Miki Sasuke, 1911).
      Besson, founded in France in 1837, later moved to London; today it produces brass
      instruments: www.besson.com.

185   Shiotsu, "Meijiki Kansai vaiorin jijō," 18.; Suzuki's "No. 1" is consistently listed
      at five yen, although it is not always clear whether this included the bow; the two-
      yen-model was not numbered.

186   Ōnogi, "Suzuki Baiorin seizō (I)," 14–15, 17.

187   Matsuyama, Iwane, "Nihon ni okeru vaiorin 2," *Ongakukai* 3.3 (1910): 42–45, 44.

188   Indeed, another author writing at the same time even claimed that the Japanese
      market was saturated and that Japanese instruments makers should consider
      exporting to China and elsewhere: Katō, Chōkō, "Gakki seizōka ni nozomu,"
      *Ongakukai* 3.1 (1910): 48–49.

189   Ōnogi, "Suzuki Baiorin seizō (I)," 21.

190   Ibid.: 22.

191   Chiba, *Doremi o eranda Nihonjin*, 225–237.

192   Matsumoto, *Teikin yūjō*, 71–72. Ōnogi, Kichibei, "Gakki sangyō ni okeru seshū
      keiei no ichigenkei: Suzuki Baiorin Seizō Kabushiki Gaisha no enkaku (II),"
      *Hamamatsu Tanki Daigaku kenkyū ronshū* 25 (1982): 1–46.

193   Ōnogi, "Suzuki Baiorin seizō (I)," 30; ———, "Suzuki Baiorin seizō (II)," 4–5.

194   Suzuki, Shin'ichi, "Suzuki Shin'ichi zenshū 6: Aruite kita michi," (Tokyo:
      Sōshisha, 1985), 64–67.

195   Leonor Michaelis to Albert Einstein, 25 January 1927 (Einstein Archives, No. 47
      – 618.00; microfilm copy at the Institute for Advanced Study, Princeton). Einstein
      had tried a selection of Suzuki violins brought to him by two of Masakichi's sons,
      Umeo and Shin'ichi. Michaelis taught in Nagoya from 1922 to 1926, and may have
      introduced the Suzukis to Einstein. The Suzuki Violins website includes a letter
      from Einstein to Suzuki Masakichi thanking him and praising the violins.
      http://www.suzukiviolin.co.jp/about/story3.html. (14 January 2014).

196   Interview with author, 20 November 2007.

197   Matsumoto, *Teikin yūjō*, 70–71; Ōnogi, "Suzuki Baiorin seizō (II)," 6–8.

198   Staatliche akademische Hochschule für Musik in Berlin, Acten betreffend Stiftung
      der Fa Suzuki (begonnen 1. Mai 1927), I.I.57.

199   Ōnogi, "Suzuki Baiorin seizō (I)," 1.

200 Matsuyama, "Nihon ni okeru vaiorin no seisaku 1," 50.

201 Murata, "Nihon no vaiorin seisakushi."

202 Shiratori, Tamiko, ed. *Gakki no jiten: vaiorin* (Tokyo: Shopan, 1995), 363–364. The whereabouts of most of his violins are unknown.

203 Ibid., 367.

204 Tōkyō Geijutsu Daigaku Hyakunenshi Hensan Iinkai, ed. *Hyakunenshi: Ensōkai hen 1*, 19–20..

205 ——, ed. *Hyakunenshi: Tōkyō Ongaku Gakkō hen 2*, 1320.

206 ——, ed. *Hyakunenshi: Ensōkai hen 1*, 44–45, 56, 138–140, 133, 461, 467.

207 Ibid., 72, 75, 84–85, 103, 149.

208 Tanabe, *Meiji ongaku monogatari*, 242–244.

209 Matsumoto, *Teikin yūjō*, 73–77. Nagoya-shiyakusho, ed. *Nagoya-shi shi. Fūzoku-hen* (Nagoya: Nagoya Shiyakusho, 1915), 244.

210 "Nagoya tsūshin," *Ongaku zasshi* 54 (1895): 18–19.

211 "Vwaiorin kyōkasho (advertisement)," *Ongaku zasshi* 11 (1891): before p. 1.

212 Suzuki, Masakichi, *Vwaiorin dokushūsho* ed. Tsunekawa, Ryōnosuke (reviewed)(Tsu: Toyozumi Kinjirō, 1902).

213 Tsunekawa, Ryōnosuke, *Bōfu Shigetomi tsuitō ongaku taikai ensō junjo oyobi ryakusetsu* (Tsu, Mie-ken: Tsunekawa Ryōnosuke, 1894).

214 Matsumoto, *Teikin yūjō*, 73–77.

215 The main source for Suzuki's biography is Takeishi, Midori, ed. *Ongaku kyōiku no ishizue: Suzuki Yonejirō to Tōyō Ongaku Gakkō* (Tokyo: Shunjusha, 2007).

216 Matsumoto, *Teikin yūjō*, 11.

217 Kolneder, Walter, *The Amadeus Book of the Violin: Construction, History, Music*, trans. Pauly, Reinhard G. (Portland, OR: Amadeus Press, 1998), 457; Matsumoto, *Teikin yūjō*, 11–12.

218 Matsumoto, *Teikin yūjō*, 7; Takeishi, ed. *Suzuki Yonejirō*, 20.

219 Stevens, Robin S., "Emily Patton: An Australian Pioneer of Tonic Sol-fa in Japan," *Research Studies in Music Education* 14 (2000): 40–49.

220 Takeishi, ed. *Suzuki Yonejirō*, 47.

221 According to a report in 1931: Ibid., 204.

222 The following is chiefly based on Nihon Ongaku Gakkō, ed. *Ongaku kyōiku e no chōsen: Nihon saisho no shiritsu ongaku gakkō tanjō monogatari* (Tokyo: Nihon Ongaku Gakkō, 2003).

223 Tōkyō Geijutsu Daigaku Hyakunenshi Hensan Iinkai, ed. *Hyakunenshi: Tōkyō Ongaku Gakkō hen 1*, 227.

224 Nihon Ongaku Gakkō, ed. *Ongaku kyōiku e no chōsen*, 155–157.

225 Yamada, Gen'ichirō, *Vwaiorin shinan* (Osaka: Miki Sasuke, 1892). Suzuki, Yonejirō, *Baiorin kyōkasho: Kan no ichi* (Tokyo: Kyōeki Shōsha, 1893). See also Matsumoto, *Teikin yūjō*, 6–8, 83.

226 Suzuki, *Baiorin kyōkasho*, 1–2. It has not been possible to identify the tutor by "Kurē," although I have examined several possible candidates. In any case, Suzuki may well have referred to several works, most obviously to Curwen's.

227 The previous year, 1892, Suzuki had published a work on singing based on Curwen's work and presenting the system of cipher notation.

228 Yamada, Gen'ichirō, *Vaiorin no hikikata* (Tokyo: Arusu, 1922).

229 Ōno, Umewaka, *Vaiorin Shohō (The Viorin [sic]) Tutor for Beginner)* (Osaka: Miki Shoten, 1899).

230 Quoted in Ōsaka Ongaku Daigaku Ongaku Bunka Kenkyūsho, ed. *Ōsaka ongaku bunkashi shiryō: Meiji/Taishō hen*, 89.

231 Matsumoto, *Teikin yūjō*, 20, 92.

232 Kurata, Yoshihiro and Shukuk Rin, eds., *Shōwa zenki ongakuka sōran – "Gendai ongaku taikan"*, 3 vols. (Tokyo: Yumani Shobō, 2009), 145.

233 For example, review of Academy Concert on 29 and 30 October 1904 in *Ongaku no tomo*, 7:2, (1904.12).

234 Tōkyō Geijutsu Daigaku Hyakunenshi Hensan Iinkai, ed. *Hyakunenshi: Ensōkai hen 1*, 216, 217.

235 The other two members were Kawakami Jun, Ōtsuka Jun. Kōmatsu, Hajime, "Nihon no gengaku shijūsō ensō shi," in *Kuronuma Toshio to Nihon no gengaku shijū sōdan*, ed. Ongakusai, Yufuin (Ōita: Kashiwa no Mori Shobō, 1994), 127.

236 For details see Ibid., 127–129; Matsumoto, *Teikin yūjō*, 121.

237 Königliche akademische Hochschule für Musik zu Berlin; Acta betreffend die persönlichen angelegenheiten der Eleven und elevinnen 1876–1937 (II.V.14) includes the copy of a letter dated 4 February 1914 and certifying that Ōno studied at the conservatoire from April 1911 to 4 February 1914. Jahresberichte HfM, 1913–14, 22.

238 Including his last recorded concert in Tōkyō Geijutsu Daigaku Hyakunenshi Hensan Iinkai, ed. *Hyakunenshi: Ensōkai hen 1*, 618.

239 Haga, Tōru and Tsutomu Sugimoto, eds., *Nihon jinbutsu jōhō taikei*, vol. 83 (Tokyo: Kōseisha, 2001), 466; Ongaku no Tomosha, ed. *Nihon no Ongakujin meikan: gengakkihen/Japan Musicians Who's Who: Strings* (Tokyo: Ongaku no Tomosha, 1984), 134.

240 Mori, Otto, *Jidō no tame no vaiorin sōhō to sono shidō* (Shinfuonī Shuppansha, 1938).

241 Kondō, *Nihon furūto monogatari*; Kurata and Rin, eds., *Shōwa zenki ongakuka sōran – "Gendai ongaku taikan"*, 8.

242 Nagai, Kōji, *Koshikata hachijūnen* (Osaka: Ōsaka Ongaku Tanki Daigaku Gakuyūkai Shuppanbu, 1954), 167–169.

243 Presumably G Major, Op. 26 (1881).

244 Ōmura, Josaburō and Kōichi Takahama, eds., *Neiro no tomo: Vaiorin gakufu* (Osaka: Maekawa Gakkiten, 1911). Examples of programmes in Ōsaka Ongaku Daigaku Ongaku Bunka Kenkyūsho, ed. *Ōsaka ongaku bunkashi shiryō: Meiji/Taishō hen*, 163, 165, 167, 178, 208, 209, 213, 216, 259, 272.

245 Ōsaka Ongaku Daigaku Ongaku Bunka Kenkyūsho, ed. *Ōsaka ongaku bunkashi shiryō: Shōwa hen*, 260.

246 *Ongaku no tomo* 7. 4. (December 1904).

247 *New England Magazine* November 1905, 620

248 Takaori, Shūichi (Biō), "Hōgaku no kosui kara seigaku no sūhai e," *Ongakukai* 6.7 (1913): 21–24.

249 This and the following from Masui, Keiji, *Nihon opera shi – 1952* (Tokyo: Suiyōsha, 2003), 93–94, 129–130.

250 Yamamoto, Masataka, "Beikoku no gakukai to hōjin no daiseiko," *Ongakukai* 4.7 (1911): 34–35.

251 Masui, *Nihon opera shi – 1952.*

252 "Society," *New York Times,* 20 February 1910, 3.

253 "Amusements," *Washington Post,* 10 December 1911, TA3.

254 Takaori, Biō, "Ōshū man'yū ki (dai 33 shin)," *Ongakukai* 6.4 (1913): 45–47. From the account it appears that he had spent eight years in America.

255 ———, "Gakuyū shishin (26 shin)," *Ongakukai* 6.6 (1913): 53–57; ———, "Gakuyū shishin (27 shin, 28 shin)," *Ongakukai* 6.7 (1913): 56–58; ———, "Gakuyū shishin (29 shin)," *Ongakukai* 6.8 (1913): 54–56; Takaori, Shūichi, "Kikyo raiji," *Ongakukai* 6.6 (1913): 10–11.

256 Masui, *Nihon opera shi – 1952,* 93–95.

257 Quoted in Lancefield, Robert Charles, "Hearing Orientality in (white) America, 1900–1930," Doctoral thesis, Wesleyan University, 2004, 121.

258 The couple's son did not survive. Sumiko remarried and she continued to perform and teach; she died in 1963. Shūichi's nephew Takaori Miyaji became professor of piano at the Tokyo Academy of Music

259 Takaori, Biō (Shūichi), "Gengaku shugyō no hiketsu: Violin kenkyūsha no shiranebanaranu koto" *Ongakukai* 4.11 (1911): 13–15; ———, "Vaiorin shugyō ni tsuki taika no suikun," *Ongakukai* 4.12 (1911): 16–18. ———, "Baiorin taika no suikun: Dai san sho: kashitsu kyōseihō," *Ongakukai* 5.3 (1912): 24–25.

260 Nomura, Nakajima, and Miyoshi, *Nihon uōgaku gaishi,* 18.

261 Tanabe, *Meiji ongaku monogatari,* 230–233.

262 Ishino, Gi, *Vaiorin renshūkyoku* (Tokyo: Kōseikan, 1907). The reading of his name is variously given as Gi, Takashi or Iwao.

263 Tanabe, *Meiji ongaku monogatari,* 239; Tōkyō Geijutsu Daigaku Hyakunenshi Hensan Iinkai, ed. *Hyakunenshi: Ensōkai hen 1,* 145.

264 Hosokawa, Shuhei, "In Search of the Sound of Empire: Tanabe Hisao and the Foundation of Japanese Ethnomusicology," *Japanese Studies* 18.1 (1998): 5–19.

265 *Ongaku shinpō,* 1 September 1907. *Ongaku sekai,* 15 January 1907. These and other examples quoted in Shiotsu, "Meijiki Kansai vaiorin jijō," 18–19. Part of the following has previously been published in Mehl, Margaret, "Japan's Early Twentieth-Century Violin Boom," *Nineteenth-Century Music Review* 7.1 (2010): 23–43.

266 "Violin/Baiorin (advertisement by Jūjiya)," *Tōkyō nichinichi shinbun,* 22 April 1888, 8.

267 Shiotsu, "Meijiki Kansai vaiorin jijō," 21, 34–35.

268 "Niigata-ken no ongaku," *Ongaku zasshi* 48 (1894): 21.

269 Irie, Kōjirō, "Niigata-ken ni okeru ongaku," *Ongaku no tomo* 1.4 (1901.2): 8–10.

270 "Niigata Nagano (Nagaoka?) no kyōikuteki ongaku ni tsuite," *Ongaku no tomo* 6.2 (1904): 24–26. Irie taught at least two summer courses in 1901; see Seki, Tōru, *Meiji/Taishō/Shōwa Niigata ongaku bunka shiryō* (Niigata: Koshi shobō, 2010), 20–21.

271 "Nagoya tsūshin."

272 "Nagoya ongaku rengōkai," *Ongaku zasshi* 55 (1895): 17.

273 Suzuki, *Vwaiorin dokushūsho*

274 "Nagoya no ongakukai," *Ongakukai* 1.3 (1908): 50.

275 "Nagoya ongaku rengōkai."

276  "Nagoya Aigen ongakukai," *Ongakukai* 2.12 (1909.12): 43.

277  "Nagoya dai ongakukai," *Ongakukai* 1.6 (1908), 46–47.

278  Gakudō, Kyōshi, "Kōbe yori," *Ongakukai* 5.7 (1912.7): 50–52; Takatsuka, Kōji, "Nagasaki-ken ni okeru ongaku," *Ongaku no tomo* 2.1 (1902.5): 16–17.

279  Imano, Taizen, "Fukui-ken ongakujō no ichi, ni," *Dōseikai zasshi* 4 (1896.12): 59–60.

280  "Hongenshi", "Nara tsūshin," *Ongaku zasshi* 60 (1896): 35–37.

281  Takii, *Sōseki ga kiita Bētōven*. Nakamura, Kōsuke, *Seiyō no oto, Nihon no mimi: Kindai bungaku to seiyō ongaku* (Tokyo: Shunjūsha, 2002 (1987)).

282  Nakamura, *Seiyō no oto, Nihon no mimi*, 137–230.

283  Ibid., 351–435.

284  Takii, *Sōseki ga kiita Bētōven*, 149–182.

285  Takahashi, Miyuki, "Meijiki no vaiorin: sono imēji to Nihon tokuyū no juyō no shosō," *Hitotsubashi kenkyū (Hitotsubashi Journal of Social Sciences)* 25.4 (2001): 157–182, 160–161.

286  Ibid.: 170–171.

287  Tanimura, Reiko, "Practical Frivolities: The Study of *Shamisen* among Girls of the Late Edo Townsman Class," *Japan Review* 23 (2011): 73–96, 90–91.

288  "Ōsaka no yūgei violin" (1909; quoted in Watanabe, Hiroshi, *Nihon bunka modan rapusodi* (Tokyo: Shunjūsha, 2002), 170. "Gakuhōsei", "Kansai no ongaku," *Ongakukai* 3.6 (1910): 5–6.

289  Ishihara, Mutsuko, "Meijiki Kansai ni okeru vaiorin juyō no yōsu: wayō setchū genshō ni tsuite," *Ongaku kenkyū (Ōsaka Ongaku Daigaku Ongaku Kenkyūsho nenpō)* 11 (1993): 101–110.

290  Seki, *Meiji/Taishō/Shōwa Niigata ongaku bunka shiryō*.

291  Noël Péri (1865–1922), French missionary and musician, taught at Tokyo Academy of Music 1899–1904.

292  Dmitry Bortniansky (1751–1825); The first title is given in transcribed German, the second in Japanese (*I to takaki ni kōei are*); probably his work known in Japanese as *Ito takaki ni wa kōei kami ni kishi*.

293  Probably Friedrich Silcher (1789–1860).

294  Probably Padre Martini (1706–84).

295  *Ongakukai* 2.6 (1909), 44–45.

296  *Ongakukai* 5.12 (1912), 64–65.

297  Watanabe, *Nihon bunka modan rapusodi*, 173.

298  "Shizuoka juppei ongakukai," *Ongaku no tomo* 7.2 (1904): 34.

299  "Wayō chōwa juppei ongakukai," *Ongaku no tomo* 7.2 (1904): 38–39.

300  Katō, Yōzō (Chōkō), *Nihon ongaku enkakushi* (Tokyo: Matsushita Gakki, 1909), 81; Masui, *Nihon opera shi – 1952*. See previous chapter.

301  Machida, Ōen, *Zokukyoku gakufu* 3 vols.(Tokyo: Seirindō, 1909).

302  "Lightly Row," known as "Butterfly" (*Chōchō*) in Japanese, and "The Last Rose of Summer," known as "Chrysanthemum" or "Flowers in the Garden" (*Niwa no chigusa*), were among the first Western songs to be used in song collections for kindergartens and schools.

303  According to the online catalogue of the National Diet Library.

304  Ōtsuka, Torazō, *Tsūzoku vaiorin hitorimanabi, shiyōhō no bu, jisshū no bu* (Kyoto: Jūjiya Gakkibu, 1909).

305  Yamanoi, Motokiyo, "Baiorin sōhō oyobi gakushū hō," *Ongakukai* 5.1 (1912): 32–35. Continued in: 5.2: 39–40, 5.4: 42–47, 5.5: 27–30, 5.10: 41–43, 5.11: 35–36, 5.12: 38–39.

306  "Nihon zashiki ni okeru shisei ni tsuite," Nihon Ongaku Tōitsu Kai, *(Tsūshin kyōju) Vaiorin kōgiroku* (Fukuoka: Nihon Tōitsu Ongakukai, 1913), 17.

307  The digital version of this tutor does not include a separate section of practice pieces; whether they are missing, as are some pages of the text, or were not included in the first place is not clear.

308  Quoted in Takii, *Sōseki ga kiita Bētōven*, 180.

309  *Vaiorin sokusei kōgiroku*, (Tokyo: Tokyo Ongaku Tsūshin Gakusha, 1925).

310  Seidensticker, Edward, *Low City, High City: Tokyo from Edo to the Earthquake: How the Shogun's Ancient Capital Became a Great Modern City, 1867–1923* (Tokyo: Tuttle, 1983), 163–164. Lewis, Michael, ed. *A Life Adrift: Soeda Azembō, Popular Song, and Modern Mass Culture in Japan* (London: Routledge, 2009), xxi, 136–137. Mitsui, Toru, "Interaction of Imported and Indigenous Music in Japan: A Historical Overview of the Music Industry," in *Whose Master's Voice: The Development of Popular Music in Thirteen Cultures*, ed. Ewbank, Alison J. and Papageorgiu, Fouli T. (Westport, Connecticut: Greenwood Press, 1997), 154.

311  Takahashi, "Meijiki no vaiorin," 176–177. For a first-hand account see Lewis, ed. *A Life Adrift*, 136–137, 157–158.

312  Tamagawa, Yūko, "Das Mädchen am Klavier: Entstehungsgeschichte eines Klischees in Japan," in *Geschlechterpolaritäten in der Musikgeschichte des 18. bis 20. Jahrhunderts*, ed. Grotjahn, Rebecca and Hoffmann, Freia (Herbolzheim: Centaurus, 2002).

## Part 2: Japan's Emergence as a Musical Power
## I. Joining the World (1918–45)

1    Wasserman, Michel, *Le Sacre de l'hiver: La Neuvième Symphonie de Beethoven, un mythe de la modernité japonaise* (Paris: Les Indes Savantes, 2006), 43–47, illustrations 53, 54. Hayashi, Keisuke, *Bandō furyo shūyōjo (Daiku kōkyōkyoku no rūtsu)* (Tokushima-ken Itano-gun Itano-chō: Nankai Bukkusu (Inoue Shobō), 1987 (1978)).

2    Nishihara, Minoru, *'Gakusei' Bētōven no tanjō* (Tokyo: Heibonsha, 2000).

3    On the New Education Movement in Japan, see Ehmcke, Franziska, *Die Erziehungsphilosophie von Obara Kuniyoshi : dargestellt an der "Erziehung des ganzen Menschen" : ein Beitrag zur Erziehung in Japan*, vol. 72, OAG Mitteilungen (Hamburg: Gesellschaft für Natur- und Völkerkunde Ostasiens, 1979), 43–61; Obara, Kuniyoshi, ed. *Nihon shin kyōiku hyakunenshi*, 8 vols., vol. 1 (Tokyo: Tamagawa Daigaku Shuppanbu, 1970–1971); Nakano, Akira, *Taishō jiyū kyōiku no kenkyū* (Tokyo: Reimei Shobō, 1968); ———, *Taishō demokurashī to kyōiku* (Tokyo: Shin Hyōron, 2002 ). Okita, Yukuji and Masagi Tsujimoto, eds., *Kyōiku shakai shi* (Tokyo: Yamakawa, 2002).

4    Obara published several works on the subject of women and mothers in the 1920s and 1930s. He later remarked on the affinity between his own views and Suzuki Shin'ichi's talent education. Obara, ed. *Nihon shin kyōiku hyakunenshi*, 388.

5    On the consumer culture, see Silverberg, Miriam, *Erotic Grotesque Nonsense: The*

*Mass Culture of Japanese Modern Times* (Berkeley: University of California Press, 2006), 20–28.

6     Watanabe, Hiroshi, *Nihon bunka modan rapusodi* (Tokyo: Shunjūsha, 2002), 189–218.

7     By Kitamura Sueharu, who had studied at the Tokyo Academy of Music, his wife Hatsuko and her sister; see Tamagawa, Yūko, "Mitsukoshi hyakkaten to ongaku: ongaku to shōgyō wa te ni te o totte (Music and Commerce Hand in Hand: Mitsukoshi and Music)," *Tōhō gakuen daigaku kenkyū kiyō (Faculty Bulletin, Toho Gakuen School of Music)* 23 (1997): 27–59; ———, "Seiyō – Nihon – Ajia: Mitsukoshi hyakkaten no ongaku katsudō ni okeru ongaku bunka no seiyōka to kokumin ishiki no keisei," *Doitsu bungaku* 132. (2006): 78.

8     Galliano, Luciana, *Yōgaku: Japanese Music in the Twentieth Century*, trans. Mayes, Martin (Lanham, Maryland, and London: The Scarecrow Press, 2002), 36, 48.

9     It can even be said that Western music produced by Japanese on their own initiative started with him; Chiba, Yūko, *Doremi o eranda Nihonjin* (Ongaku no Tomosha, 2007), 163.

10    Beyer, Friedrich-Heinz, "Deutsche Musik in Japan: Völkisch-nationale Musikpflege im Fernen Osten," *Zeitschrift für Musik* 6 (June) (1941): 393–396.

11    Galliano, *Yōgaku*, 66, 79–80, 116, 122. Aikawa, Yumi, *"Enka" no susume* (Tokyo: Bungei Shunju, 2002), 188–192. Kō moved to China in 1938 and became known as Jiang Wenye; see Melvin, Sheila and Jindong Cai, *Rhapsody in Red: How Western Classical Music Became Chinese* (New York: Algora, 2004), 186–187.

12    Koga Masao Ongaku Bunka Shinkō Zaidan (The Masao Koga Music and Culture Promotor Foundation), *Yume jinsei o kanadete* (Tokyo: Koga Masao Ongaku Bunka Shinkō Zaidan, 2004).

13    For an outline of Orientalism in Western music which emphasizes the creative aspects, see MacKenzie, John M., *Orientalism: History, Theory and the Arts* (Manchester: Manchester University Press, 1995), 139–175.

14    Melvin and Cai, *Rhapsody in Red*, 18,97; Nomura, Kōichi, Kenzō Nakajima, and Kiyomichi Miyoshi, *Nihon yōgaku gaishi: Nihon gakudan chōrō ni yoru taikenteki yōgaku no rekishi* (Tokyo: Rajio Gijutsusha, 1978), 148.

15    Melvin and Cai, *Rhapsody in Red*; Enomoto, Yasuko, *Shanhai ōkesutora monogatari: Seiyōjin ongakukatachi no yume* (Tokyo: Shunjūsha, 2006).

16    Yamanashi, Makiko, *A History of the Takarazuka Revue Since 1914: Modernity, Girls' Culture, Japan Pop* (Leiden: Global Oriental, 2012).

17    Matsumoto, Zenzō, *Teikin yūjō: Nihon no vaiorin ongaku shi* (Tokyo: Ressun no Tomosha, 1995), 177.

18    Ōmori, Seitarō, *Nihon no yōgaku*, 2 vols., vol. 1 (Tokyo: Shinmon Shuppansha, 1986), 149.

19    Atkins, Taylor E., *Blue Nippon: Authenticating Jazz in Japan* (Durham, N.C.: Duke University Press, 2001).

20    *Metronome,* July, 1923; quote in Wade, Bonnie C., *Music in Japan* (Oxford: Oxford University Press, 2005), 18–19.

21    Nagai, Yoshikazu, *Shakō dansu to Nihonjin* (Tokyo: Shōbunsha, 1991), 39–117.

22    Chiba, *Doremi o eranda Nihonjin*, 167.

23    Etō, Toshiya, *Vaiorin to tomo ni: Nani o uttatte iru ka shiritai* (Tokyo: Ongaku no Tomosha, 1999), 224–225. Suzuki, Shin'ichi, *Nurtured by Love: The Classic Approach to Talent Education*, trans. Suzuki, Waltraud (Miami: Suzuki Method International, Summy-Birchard Inc., 1983), 51, 97. See also Harich-Schneider, Eta, "European Musician in Japan," *XXth Century (Shanghai)* 3.6 (1942): 418–421, 420.

24    Chiba, *Doremi o eranda Nihonjin*, 37–38.

25    Ibid., 199.

26    Ibid., 190–193. See also Wade, *Music in Japan*, 70–72.

27    I thank Kotaki Haruko for sending me the results of her work to preserve the evidence of the musical culture of her childhood years in Manchuria.

28    In 1937, for example, the newly founded association, Japanisch–Deutscher Werkaustausch organized a concert with works by Fortner, Hindemith and Janáček, while another concert was staged in Karlsruhe with works by Japanese composers: Galliano, *Yōgaku*, 117.

29    Sirota, Kreutzer, Rosenstock and the singer Margarethe Netke-Löwe (1889–1971) were invited to teach at the Tokyo Academy of Music. All were registered at the German embassy in 1944 as former German nationals who had been deprived of their German citizenship: Suchy, Irene, "Deutschsprachige Musiker in Japan vor 1945. Eine Fallstudie eines Kulturtransfers am Beispiel der Rezeption abendländischer Musik" (doctoral thesis, University of Vienna, 1992), 239–240. On the Sirota family: Gordon, Beate Sirota, *The Only Woman in the Room: A Memoir* (Tokyo: Kodansha International, 1997).

30    He remained in Japan to the end of his life, his efforts to re-establish his career and reputation in Germany having failed: Galliano, Luciana, "Manfred Gurlitt and the Japanese Operatic Scene, 1939–1972," *Japan Review* 18 (2006): 215–248.

31    Harich-Schneider, Eta, *Charaktere und Katastrophen: Augenzeugenberichte einer reisenden Musikerin* (Berlin: Ullstein, 1978), 238. See also Suchy, Irene, "Verfolgung vertraulich: MusikerInnen-Exil in Japan," in *Vom Weggehen: Zum Exil von Kunst und Wissenschaft*, ed. Wiesinger-Stock, Sandra, Weinzierl, Erika, and Kaiser, Konstantin (Vienna: Mandelbaum Verlag, 2006); Nomura, Nakajima, and Miyoshi, *Nihon yōgaku gaishi*, 277.

32    Ōmori, *Nihon no yōgaku*, 271.

33    Nomura, Nakajima, and Miyoshi, *Nihon yōgaku gaishi*, 264–272.

34    Furukawa, Takahisa, *Kōki, Banpaku, Orinpikku: Kōshitsu burando to keizai hatten* (Tokyo: Chūō Kōronsha, 1998), 61–127; Ishida, Kazushi, *Modanizumu hensōkyoku: Higashi Ajia no kindai ongakushi* (Tokyo: Sakuhokusha, 2005), 99–103. Britten's Requiem Symphony was deemed inappropriate and was not performed.

35    Tōkyō Geijutsu Daigaku Hyakunenshi Hensan Iinkai, ed. *Tōkyō Geijutsu Daigaku hyakunenshi: Tōkyō Ongaku Gakkō hen 2* (Tokyo: Ongaku no Tomosha, 2003), 8.

36    Pringsheim, Klaus, "Nihon no ongaku seikatsu ni okeru shinpō to kōjō," *Ongaku sekai* 9 (1937): 10–17.

37    Urach-Württemberg, Albrecht, "Aus 40 Jahren moderner japanischer Musikentwicklung: August Junker, der Pionier deutscher Musik in Japan," *Die Musik* 29.10 (1937): 675–677, 675.

38    Stege, Fritz, "Musikleben in Japan: Erfolge einer deutschen Künstlerin," *Zeitschrift für Musik* 5 (1935): 549–550.

39    Kron, Gustav, "Die Entwicklung abenländischer Musik in Japan und über japanische Musik," *Deutsche Tonkünstler-Zeitung* 47.490 (1929): 411–412, 412.

40    The list is probably incomplete, especially for foreign artists who did not perform in Tokyo. Artists not listed include Konrad Liebrecht (1898–?), who performed as a soloist with the New Symphony Orchestra and Takarazuka, according to programmes of these orchestras. Born in Vienna, he studied at the Konservatorium der Gesellschaft der Musikfreunde and was concertmaster in Graz and Berlin. See Suchy, "Deutschsprachige Musiker in Japan", 215. Elman, Zimbalist, Kreisler, Heifetz, Thibaud hardly need introducing. Biographical details of the lesser-known violinists will be posted on www.notbylovealone.com

41    Malan, Roy, *Efrem Zimbalist: A Life* (Portland: Amadeus Press, 2004), 18–19.

42    Suzuki, *Nurtured by Love*, 69.

43    Mainichi Komyunikēshonzu Hensan Iinkai, ed. *Taishō nyūzu jiten*, vol. 5 (Tokyo: Mainichi Komyunikēshonzu, 1988), 59–60.

44    Nomura, Nakajima, and Miyoshi, *Nihon yōgaku gaishi*, 227.

45    Matsumoto, *Teikin yūjō*, 187–188.

46    Nomura, Nakajima, and Miyoshi, *Nihon yōgaku gaishi*, 230–231.

47    Mainichi Komyunikēshonzu Hensan Iinkai, ed. *Taishō nyūzu jiten*, vol. 6 (Tokyo: Mainichi Komyunikēshonzu, 1988), 683.

48    Matsumoto, *Teikin yūjō*, 223–224.

49    Nomura, Nakajima, and Miyoshi, *Nihon yōgaku gaishi*, 234.

50    Suzuki, *Nurtured by Love*, 84.

51    Malan, *Efrem Zimbalist*, 183–185.

52    Mainichi Komyunikēshonzu Hensan Iinkai, ed. *Taishō nyūzu jiten*, 380.

53    Malan, *Efrem Zimbalist*, 190.

54    Matsumoto, *Teikin yūjō*, 247–248, 256; Malan, *Efrem Zimbalist*, 191, 192, 198.

55    114th Regular concert of the orchestra; Matsumoto, *Teikin yūjō*, 247–248.

56    Details about recordings by Christopher Nozawa in Ibid., 322–332. The leading record companies switched from acoustical to electrical recording in 1925.

57    Malan's comment: "One gathers from the record that the Japanese people's appreciation of Western music and their proficiency in performing it were not yet on a par." (p. 192)

58    Matsumoto, *Teikin yūjō*, 236.

59    Etō, *Vaiorin to tomo ni*, 50.

60    Tōkyō Geijutsu Daigaku Hyakunenshi Hensan Iinkai, ed. *Hyakunenshi: Tōkyō Ongaku Gakkō hen 2*, 1572–1573. Robert Pollack (1880–1962), trained in Vienna and had previously taught masterclasses in Geneva and Lausanne and held an appointment at the conservatoire in Moscow; Polish-born Willy Frey (1907–?) had studied in Warsaw, Leipzig and Berlin and played as a soloist: Suchy, "Deutschsprachige Musiker in Japan", 219, 193–194.

61    Shapiro, Isaac, *Edokko: Growing Up a Foreigner in Wartime Japan* (Bloomington, IN: iUniverse, 2009), 81.

62    Takeuchi, Hiroshi, *Rainichi Seiyō jinmei jiten* (Tokyo: Nichigai Associates, 1983), 126; Suchy, "Deutschsprachige Musiker in Japan", 207–208; Konoe, Hidemaro,

"Kēnihi-rō no kaikyū danpen," *Firuhāmonī* 4.4 (1929): 8–13; Kurata, Yoshihiro and Shukuki Rin, eds., *Shōwa zenki ongakuka sōran – "Gendai ongaku taikan"*, 3 vols. (Tokyo: Yumani Shobō, 2009), 163.

63 Burmester, Willy, *Fifty Years as a Concert Violinist: Recollections and Reflections*, trans. Wolf, Roberta Franke in collaboration with Samuel (Linthicum Heights, Maryland: Swand Publications, 1975), 126. The discography (p.162) includes two recordings made in Japan: "11922 Japanese recordings on Nitto 955: Burmester: Rococo Hummel: Waltz."

64 Listed as "St. Petersburg 1904" in Sous, Alfred, *Das Bayreuther Festspielorchester: Geschichte und Gegenwart* (Hof/Saale: Ansporn Verlag Rudolf Schmidt, 1988), 171.

65 Melvin and Cai, *Rhapsody in Red*, 145.

66 Katō, Kaichi, "Sensei to shite no Kēnihi," *Firuhāmonī* 4.4 (1929): 23, 30.

67 König, Josef, *Firuhāmonī* 4.4 (1929). Author's translation from German.

68 Shirahama, Tatsuzō, "Naniga Kēnihishi o kikoku seshimeta ka," *Firuhāmonī* 4.8 (1929): 7–10.

69 Manshūkoku Kenkoku 10 Nen Shūnen Keishuku Kōkyō Gakudan; most of the members came from the New Symphony Orchestra: Iwano, Yūichi, *Ōdō rakudo no kōkyōgaku: Manshū – shirazaru ongakushi* (Tokyo: Ongaku no Tomosha, 1999), 260. Hsinking is also known as Changchun or Xinjing.

70 According to a newspaper article he was invited to Japan by the New Philharmonic Orchestra: Matsumoto, *Teikin yūjō*, 229. Takeuchi, *Rainichi Seiyō jinmei jiten*, 170; Suchy, "Deutschsprachige Musiker in Japan," 234; Shin Kōkyō Gakudan, "Shiferuburatto-shi o itamu," *Firuhāmonī* 11 (1936): 24–25.

71 Programme in *Fuiruhāmonī*, 4.4.

72 Recollections by members of the orchestra in "Shiferuburatto shi o itamu," *Firuhāmonī* 11 (1936): 24–47. See also Sano, Yukihiko, *N-kyō 80nen zenkiroku* (Tokyo: Bungei Shunjū, 2007), 22.

73 "Shiferuburatto shi o itamu," 40–42.

74 Ibid.

75 "Shiferuburatto shi no isshūki o oete," *Firuhāmonī* 12 (1937): 28–29.

76 Serge Elisséeff (1889–1975) studied Japanese in Berlin and Tokyo. From 1916 he taught at the Imperial University in Petrograd; in 1917 he became professor at the Institute for History of Foreign Affairs in Petrograd. He subsequently taught at the Sorbonne in Paris and from 1932 at Harvard, becoming one of the pioneers of Japanese Studies in the USA.

77 Silverberg, *Erotic Grotesque Nonsense: The Mass Culture of Japanese Modern Times*, 151, 306.

78 Ono Anna Kinenkai, ed. *Kaisō no Ono Anna* (Tokyo: Ongaku no Tomosha, 1988).

79 Tributes in Ibid.

80 www.onoanna.jp (22 February 2013).

81 ongaku kokka; Ono Anna Kinenkai, ed. *Kaisō no Ono Anna*, 23.

82 Moroi, Saburō, ed. *Sōgen ongaku kōza dai san kan: ensōhen* (Tokyo: Sōgensha, 1953), 199.

83 Takeuchi, *Rainichi Seiyō jinmei jiten*, 449; Katō, Kiyoshi, *Ongaku no kokoro: Mogirefuskī kyōju o kinen shite* (Tokyo: Ongaku no Tomosha, 1966). Tōkyō

Geijutsu Daigaku Hyakunenshi Hensan Iinkai, ed. *Hyakunenshi: Tōkyō Ongaku Gakkō hen 2*, 1263–1266. Mogilevsky's earliest teachers were G. Friman in Odessa and V. I. Salin in Rostov-na-Donu: http://www.musenc.ru/html/m/mogilevskiy.html (15 June 2011).

84   Katō, *Ongaku no kokoro*, 22.

85   Stowell, Robin, ed. *The Cambridge Companion to the String Quartet* (Cambridge: Cambridge University Press, 2003), 54.

86   Katō, *Ongaku no kokoro*, 20.

87   Tōkyō Geijutsu Daigaku Hyakunenshi Hensan Iinkai, ed. *Hyakunenshi: Tōkyō Ongaku Gakkō hen 2*, 1264–1265. He formally divorced his first wife at the same time; the couple had been living apart since 1917.

88   E-mail communication from Peter Berton, who had lessons with him after the war (6 May 2010).

89   Katō, *Ongaku no kokoro*, 29–30. Matsumoto Zenzō, interview, 25 January 2010.

90   Ibid., 28, 29.

91   Ibid., 37.

92   Ibid., 44–45, 52.

93   Ibid., 31.

94   *Ongaku sekai* 9.5, pp. 10–32; Matsumoto, *Teikin yūjō*, 269–271.

95   Ibid., 120.

96   Galliano, "Manfred Gurlitt and the Japanese Operatic Scene, 1939–1972."

97   "Rōhō no amachua ōkesutora Suwa kōkyōgakudan sōritsu 80 shūnen," *Sarasate* 11 (2006): 101.

98   On student orchestras and Beethoven: Nishihara, *'Gakusei' Bētōven no tanjō*, 152–183; Tōdai Ōkesutora 45nenshi Hensan Iinkai, ed. *Tōdai Ōkesutora 45nenshi* (Tokyo: Tōkyō Daigaku Ongakubu Kangen Gakudan, 1964).

99   Okano, Ben, *Metteru Sensei: Asahina Takashi, Hattori Ryōichi no Gakufu, Bōmeisha Ukurainejin shikisha no shōgai* (Tokyo: Rittōmyūjikku, 1995).

100  Ōsaka Ongaku Daigaku Ongaku Bunka Kenkyūsho, ed. *Ōsaka ongaku bunkashi shiryō: Meiji/Taishō hen* (Osaka: Ōsaka Ongaku Daigaku, 1968), 320.

101  Details about Laska in Suchy, "Deutschsprachige Musiker in Japan", 167–184.

102  Okano, *Metteru Sensei*, 358, 383.

103  Ibid.

104  The following discussion is mostly based on Sano, *N-kyō 80nen zenkiroku*. and Ōno, Kaoru, *Konoe Hidemaro: Nihon no ōkesutora o tsukutta otoko* (Tokyo: Kodansha, 2006).

105  Ōno, *Konoe Hidemaro*, 120.

106  Details in Iwano, *Ōdō rakudo no kōkyōgaku*, 46–52.

107  Ōno, *Konoe Hidemaro*, 151..

108  Ibid., 160.

109  Ibid., 165.

110  Matsumoto, *Teikin yūjō*, 243–244. Taka, the sister of a famous cellist, studied violin with Okumura Tsuyako, Andō Kō, Josef König and Nikolai Schifferblatt. Kamahara had just graduated from the Music College of the East. Nakajima and Satō were both graduates from girls' high schools and students of Ono Anna.

111  Ōno, *Konoe Hidemaro*, 180.

112 Sano, *N-kyō 80nen zenkiroku*, 33.

113 Wasserman, *Le Sacre de l'hiver*, 70–71. Josef Rosenstock did not, however, himself conduct any of the Volksbühne performances in the 1930s. The conductor of the performance on 31 December 1932 was Ludwig Rosenstock; it was his debut with the Berlin Philharmonic Orchestra; Josef Rosenstock's debut had been made in 1922: Muck, Peter, *Einhundert Jahre Berliner Philharmonisches Orchester: Darstellung in Dokumenten*, vol. 4: Die Mitglieder des Orchesters; die Programme; die Konzertreisen; Erst-und Uraufführungen (Tutzing: Hans Schneider, 1982), 252, 460.

114 Wasserman, *Le Sacre de l'hiver*, 71–87.

115 Sano, *N-kyō 80nen zenkiroku*, 41. Wanibuchi was born in Nagaoka in Niigata Prefecture; he went to America at the age of 11 and studied with Peter Meremblum (1890–1966), a native of Tiflis (Caucasus) and a student of Leopold Auer. At the age of 19 he went to Prague where he graduated from the conservatoire. Returning to Japan after 15 years abroad, he made his Tokyo debut in 1936. He was concertmaster of the New Symphony Orchestra from 1942 to 1944.

116 E-mail communication from Peter Berton, then a violinist in the Harbin orchestra (4 May 2010).

117 Details of the Harbin orchestra's tour see Iwano, *Ōdō rakudo no kōkyōgaku*, 140–161. See also Berton, Peter, "Prewar, Occupation, and Post-Occupation Japan: Three Vignettes," *JPRI Occasional Papers (Japan Policy Research Institute at the University of San Francisco Center for the Pacific Rim)* 35. (2005).

118 Namerikawa-shi Kyōiku Iinkai, ed. *Takashina Tetsuo no shōgai* (Namerikawa: Namerikawa Kyōiku Kinkai, 1996); Maekawa, Kumio, *Hibike "Tokeidai no kane"* (Sapporo: Alicesha, 2001).

119 Takashina, Tetsu, *Vaiorin sōhō no hiketsu* (Tokyo: Kyōeki Shōsha Shoten, 1935 (1926)), 5.

120 Kron taught at the Academy 1913–1925: Suchy, "Deutschsprachige Musiker in Japan", 213.).

121 Namerikawa-shi Kyōiku Iinkai, ed. *Takashina Tetsuo no shōgai*, 9–10. It is not clear whether "Polish Dance" refers to one of the Polonaises, Op. 4 or 21, or to the composition "Kuiyavak"; the Beethoven minuet may be a transcription from the Septet.

122 Maekawa, *Hibike "Tokeidai no kane"*, 167.

123 Katsura, Kinko (Chikaya?), "Gen gakudan vaiorinisuto hyō," *Gakusei* 8 (1927): 43–47, 44–45.

124 "Vaiorin no reimeiki kara gendai made katsudō sareta Aiba Minoru shi no goseikyo o itamu," *String* June (1999): 93.

125 Takashina, *Vaiorin sōhō no hiketsu*.

126 Kuritīku 80, ed. *Nihon no sakkyokuka 3: Hirose Yasuji* (Tokyo: Ongaku no Sekaisha, 1995); Kiyose Yasuji Chosakushū Henshū Iinkai, ed. *Kiyose Yasuji chosakushū: warera no michi* (Tokyo: Dōjidaisha, 1983); Galliano, *Yōgaku*.

127 Kiyose Yasuji Chosakushū Henshū Iinkai, ed. *Kiyose Yasuji chosakushū*, 109.

128 Quoted in Kuritīku 80, ed. *Kiyose Yasuji*, 11.

129 Asahina, Takashi, *Gaku wa dō ni michite* (Tokyo: Nihon Keizai Shinbunsha, 1978); Asahina, Takashi and Tōru Yano, *Asahina Takashi: Waga kaisō* (Tokyo: Chūō Kōron, 1985).

130  Nakano, Takeshi, *Ongakuka ni naru niwa* (Tokyo: Perikansha, 2002), 171–172.

131  Asahina and Yano, *Asahina Takashi: Waga kaisō*, 19.

132  Stern, Hellmut, *Saitensprünge: Erinnerungen eines Kosmopoliten wider Willen* (Berlin: Aufbau Taschenbuch Verlag, 2000 (1990)), 74.

133  Nakano, *Ongakuka ni naru niwa*, 171–172.

134  Today part of Kōnan Gakuen, which includes Konan University; the school has a Kishi Kōichi Memorial Room where his papers are preserved.

135  Auguste Durand or August Fryderyk Duranovski, (c. 1770–1834), Polish-born and a pupil of Viotti, toured widely as a soloist before settling in Strasbourg as concertmaster of the theatre orchestra. As Kajino points out, Sarasate's work of that name would have been well beyond Kishi's abilities at the time; Kajino, Ena, Seiji Chōki, and Heruman Gochefusuki, eds., *Kishi Kōichi to ongaku no kindai: Berurin firu o shiki shita Nihonjin* (Tokyo: Seikyūsha, 2011), 55.

136  Staatliche Akademische Hochschule für Musik in Berlin. 52. Jahresbericht, 1 October 1930–30 September1931.

137  Flesch to Rostal, Baden-Baden, 18 July 1929; Schenk, D., W. Rathert, and Antje Kalcher, eds., *Carl Flesch und Max Rostal: Aspekte der Berliner Streichertradition*, Schriften aus dem UdK-Archiv, Band 4 (Berlin: Universität der Künste, 2002), 52.

138  Kajino, Chōki, and Gochefusuki, eds., *Kishi Kōichi to ongaku no kindai*, 16–55. Kajino attempts to assess his standard of performance based on his repertoire, but fails to take account of his hectic lifestyle and numerous other interests, which cannot have been conducive to the careful preparation even an outstanding violinist needs.

139  Archives of the Universität der Künste, Aufnahmeprotokoll Violine, WS 1930–31, Best.1 No. 734: under the heading, remarks about theoretical knowledge, lessons in harmony with Professor Kahn are mentioned.

140  Apparently destroyed by his mother in the 1970s and 1980s; she considered them an embarrassment, Mōri, Masato, *Kishi Kōichi: Eien no seinen ongakuka* (Tokyo: Kokusho Kankōkai, 2006), 169.

141  Suzuki, Shin'ichi, ed. *Gengaku*, vol. 9, Ongaku kōza (Tokyo: Bungei Shunjū, 1932).

142  Quoted in Urach-Württemberg, "Aus 40 Jahren moderner japanischer Musikentwicklung," 675.

143  "JASTA Interview: Matsumoto Zenzō kaichō ni kiku," *JASTA* 101.August (1991): 2–6.; interview with Matsumoto Zenzō, 21 January 2010.

144  Matsumoto, *Teikin yūjō*, 239.

145  Ueda, Ken'ichi, *En no shita no baiorinhiki: bandoman Tōyama Shinji no monogatari* (Osaka: Seishinsha, 2005).

146  Rōon (Zenkoku Kinrōsha Ongaku Kyōgikai Renraku Kaigi: National Allied Conference Councils for Workers' Music) established in Osaka in 1949 (see introduction to the next section).

147  Suzuki, *Nurtured by Love*. Suzuki, Shin'ichi, "Suzuki Shin'ichi zenshū 6: Aruite kita michi," (Tokyo: Sōshisha, 1985); Mehl, Margaret, "Cultural Translation in Two Directions: The Suzuki Method in Japan and Germany," *Research and Issues in Music Education* 7.1 (2009).

148  Grützen, Vera, "Berliner Ausbildungseinrichtungen für Berufsmusiker in den

Zwanziger Jahren des 20. Jahrhunderts: Zu einigen profilbestimmenden Faktoren der kompositorischen Ausbildung," in *Studien zur Berliner Musikgeschichte: Eine Bestandsaufnahme*, ed. Seeger, Horst and Goldhan, Wolfgang (Berlin: Henschelverlag Kunst und Gesellschaft, 1988), 117–118.

149 Gruhn, Wilfried, *Geschichte der Musikerziehung: Eine Kultur- und Sozialgeschichte vom Gesangsunterricht der Aufklärungspädagogik zu ästhetisch-kultureller Bildung*, second ed.(Hofheim: Wolke, 2003), 163–218.

150 Quoted in Levenson, Thomas, *Einstein in Berlin* (New York: Bantam Books, 2003), 323.

151 Suzuki, *Nurtured by Love*, 76.

152 Archives of the Universität der Künste, Berlin, Best.1 Nr. 644, Aufnahmeprotokoll Violine und Bratsche, Sommerhalbjahr 1923, Nr. 6, Journalnr. 950. The records include the remark, "aufzunehmen wenn Platz" (to be admitted if space).

153 Potter, Tully, "Karl Klingler," in *Musik in Geschichte und Gegenwart, Personenteil 10* (2003); Bollert, Werner, "Karl Klingler und sein Quartett," *Mitteilungen des Vereins für die Geschichte Berlins* 82.4 (1986): 447–451. Klingler, Marianne M. and Agnes Ritter, eds., *Karl Klingler: "Über die Grundlagen des Violinspiels" und nachgelassene Schriften* (Hildesheim: Georg Olms Verlag, 1990). Klingler and Ritter, eds., *Karl Klingler: "Über die Grundlagen des Violinspiels" und nachgelassene Schriften*, viii, 155.

154 Albrecht Roeseler in Klingler and Ritter, eds., *Karl Klingler: "Über die Grundlagen des Violinspiels" und nachgelassene Schriften*, VIII.

155 Ibid., 155.

156 Klingler, Marianne M., "Zum 85. Geburtstag von Shinichi Suzuki," *European Suzuki Journal* 3.1 (1983): 2–3.

157 Yagi, Kunio (Nihon Seika Gakkai), ed. *Reactivity of Flavins* (Tokyo: University of Tokyo Press, 1975), ix.

158 Leonor Michaelis to Albert Einstein, 25 January 1927 (Einstein Archives, No. 47 – 618.00; microfilm copy: Institute for Advanced Study, Princeton). See also Part 1 Chapter 4. Einstein mentions two sons of Masakichi, probably Shin'ichi and Umeo.

159 Wartberg, Kerstin, "Shinichi Suzuki. Eine Lebensbeschreibung mit Bildern," http://www.germansuzuki.de/downloadde/suzuki.pdf (20 February 2009). A new, bilingual edition has been published: ———, *Shinichi Suzuki: Pioneer of Music Education/Pionier der Musikerziehung* (n.p.: German Suzuki Institute, 2009).

160 On Einstein and music: Rentsch, Ivana and Anselm Gerhard, eds., *Musizieren, Lieben – und Maulhalten! Albert Einsteins Beziehung zur Musik* (Basel: Schwabe, 2006); Botstein, Leon, "Einstein and Music," in *Einstein for the Twenty-first Century: His Legacy in Science, Art, and Modern Culture*, ed. Galison, Peter L., Holton, Gerald, and Schweber, Silvan S. (Princeton: Princeton University Press, 2008); Bucky, Peter A., *The Private Albert Einstein* (Kansas City: Andrews & McMeel, 1992), 147–156; Wolff, Barbara, "Albert Einstein and Music," in *Albert Einstein: Chief Engineer of the Universe* ed. Renn, Jürgen (Zürich: Wiley-VCH, 2005).

161 Matsumoto, *Teikin yūjō*, 72.

162 Ibid., 227. See also booklet of CD *The Legendary Suzuki Quartet* (Quartet Haus Japan Ltd, QHJ 1003).

163 Nomura, Nakajima, and Miyoshi, *Nihon yōgaku gaishi*, 261.

164 Suzuki, Waltraud, *Suzuki Shin'ichi to tomo ni*, trans. Selden, Kyōko (Tokyo: Shufu no Tomosha, 1987), 44.

165 Peak, Lois, "The Suzuki Method of Music Instruction," in *Teaching and Learning in Japan*, ed. Rohlen, Thomas P. and LeTendre, Gerald K. (Cambridge: Cambridge University Press, 1998), 362–363.

166 Most of the biographical information is from Sumi, Saburō, *Vaiorin hitosuji ni* (Tokyo: Kōseisha, 1983).

167 Kubota, Ryōsaku et al., eds., *Sumi Saburō: Vaiorin no okeiko* (Tokyo: Ongaku no Tomosha, 1980).

168 Minami, Motoko, "'Kodomo no tame no engeki' to wa nani ka? – Otogi shibai no tanjō to sono igi," *Saichi Kyōiku Daigaku yōji kyōiku kenkyū* 13: 39–46.

169 Sponsored by the newspaper *Jiji shinpō*; from 1937 it was sponsored by the *Tōkyō nichinichi shinbun*, the predecessor of the *Mainichi shinbun*, which became the sponsor after the Second World War, together with NHK: Yōgaku Hōsō Shichijū Nenshi Purojekuto, ed. *Yōgaku hōsō 70 nenshi 1925–1995* (Tokyo: Myūjiamu Tosho, 1997), 32,153–154.

170 A native of Okinawa, Hatoyama studied at the New England Conservatory in Boston in the 1950s and played in orchestras in Tanglewood and New Orleans. He was concertmaster of the Tokyo Symphony Orchestra (Tōkyō Kōkyō Gakudan) for several years, and had his own chamber music ensemble and concert series. Ongaku no Tomosha, ed. *Nihon no ongakujin meikan: gengakkihen/Japan Musicians Who's Who: Strings* (Tokyo: Ongaku no Tomosha, 1984). In 2009 he returned to his native Okinawa.

171 Sumi, *Vaiorin hitosuji ni*, 69.

172 Ono Anna Kinenkai, ed. *Kaisō no Ono Anna*, 17, 27. See p. 32.

173 Ibid. It is not clear where he taught or whether "ongaku gakkō" refers to the Tokyo Academy of Music. According to the office of the Ono Anna Memorial Society, nothing is known about Tazuko's parents.

174 See Yamanashi, *A History of the Takarazuka Revue*, 131–133. A similar distinction was made in nineteenth-century Europe, although for different reasons; see Hoffmann, Freia, *Instrument und Körper: Die musizierende Frau in der bürgerlichen Kultur* (Frankfurt a.M: Insel Verlag, 1991), 84–86, 309–318.

175 Vaiorin sannin musume; Shiratori, Tamiko, ed. *Gakki no jiten: vaiorin* (Tokyo: Shopan, 1995), 21–22.

176 Fukada, Yūsuke, *Bibo nare Shōwa: Suwa Nejiko to Kamikaze-gō no otokotachi* (Tokyo: Bungei Shunjūsha, 1983), 15. Most of the information about Suwa's life before 1945 comes from this source, which also appears to be the main source for much of the recent biography: Hagiya, Yukiko, *Suwa Nejiko: Bibo no vaiorinisuto, sono gekiteki shōgai, 1920–2012* (Tokyo: Alphabeta, 2013).

177 Suzuki, *Nurtured by Love*, 23.

178 Ono Anna Kinenkai, ed. *Kaisō no Ono Anna*, 21.

179 Nomura, Nakajima, and Miyoshi, *Nihon yōgaku gaishi*, 258–260. It is not entirely clear when the episode took place, and in the light of other works Suwa performed at the time one might doubt that the work they heard was Sarasate's *Carmen Fantasy*.

180  Katō, *Ongaku no kokoro*, 156–158.

181  Matsumoto, *Teikin yūjō*, 247; Hagiya, *Suwa Nejiko*, 55–56.

182  Matsumoto, *Teikin yūjō*, 249; Nozaki, Masatoshi, *Rekōdo de tadoru Nihon ongakukai no paioniatachi* (Tokyo: Chopin, 2009), 144.

183  Fukada, *Bibo nare Shōwa*, 20–23.

184  Ōsaka Ongaku Daigaku Ongaku Bunka Kenkyūsho, ed. *Ōsaka ongaku bunkashi shiryō: Shōwa hen* (Osaka: Ōsaka Ongaku Daigaku, 1970), 208. Not much seems to be known about Minchinsky, whose name is mentioned in several reminiscences.

185  Hagiya, *Suwa Nejiko*, 102–106.

186  "L'artiste a du goût, un métier déjà solide et l'interprète un tempérament et une vive intelligence." E-mail communication,18 February 2012, from Denis Havard de la Montagne, chief editor of "Musica et Memoria" http://www.musimem.com (14 January 2014).

187  Fukada, *Bibo nare Shōwa*.

188  There are several photos of Suwa Nejiko in the Belgian archives of the German occupation CEGES-SOMA (Centre for Historical Research and Documentation on War and Contemporary Society, Belgium, http://pallas.cegesoma.be), Personnalités: Suwa Nejiko, violoniste japonaise, 1942–1943.

189  Ōno, *Konoe Hidemaro*, 343.

190  Nozaki, *Nihon ongakukai no paioniatachi*, 146.

191  Hagiya, *Suwa Nejiko*, 187–190.

192  Nozaki, *Nihon ongakukai no paioniatachi*, 147–148. Details about Suwa's late recordings and recitals in Hagiya, *Suwa Nejiko*, 221–255, 291–294.

193  Hino, Madoka, *Sōtō no Sutoradivari* (Tokyo: Magajinhausu, 1998). See also "Shōsetsu 'Sōtō no Sutoradivari' no chosha Hino Madoka san ni kiku: 'Kandō suru ongaku ni wa, shakai no chikara, jidaihaikei no enerugī ga kyūshū sarete imasu'," *String* March (1999): 14–18.

194  Shapreau, Carla, "A Violin Once Owned by Goebbels Keeps Its Secrets," *New York Times*, 21 September 2012. "Tensai baiorin shōjo shikō 92 sai," *Asahi shinbun* (Morning edition), 25 September 2012, 38. Published on 24 September in the digital edition: http://www.asahi.com/showbiz/music/TKY201209240582.html (25 September 2012).

195  Nichigai Associates, ed. *Ongakuka jinmei jiten* 3rd rev. ed. (Tokyo: Nichigai Associates, 2001), 217.

196  Biographical information mostly based on Yamaguchi, Reiko, *Iwamoto Mari: Ikiru imi* (Tokyo: Shinchōsha, 1984).

197  Monsaingeon, Bruno, *The Art of Violin* (Idéale Audience, IMG Artists, 2000), DVD.

198  Yamaguchi, *Iwamoto Mari*, 72–73.

199  Details in Iwano, *Ōdō rakudo no kōkyōgaku*, 326–329.

200  C.H., "Japanese Violinist Makes Debut Here: Mariko Iwamoto Plays Works by Bach and Mendelssohn in Town Hall Program," *New York Times*, 15 June 1950, 41.

201  Kakeshita, Keikichi, *Shōwa gakudan no reimei: gakudan seikatsu yonjūnen no kaisō* (Tokyo: Ongaku no Tomosha, 1973); Koishi, Tadao, "Hito: Ongaku seikatsu 50 nen no Tsuji Hisako," *Ongaku geijutsu* September (1982): 63; Nichigai Associates, ed. *Ongakuka jinmei jiten* 226–227.

202 Kakeshita, *Shōwa gakudan no reimei: gakudan seikatsu yonjūnen no kaisō*, 62. See also Tsuji, Kichinosuke, "Musume (Tsuji Hisako) o kataru," *Ongaku no tomo* 9.1 (1951): 83–85.

203 Ōsaka Ongaku Daigaku Ongaku Bunka Kenkyūsho, ed. *Ōsaka ongaku bunkashi shiryō: Shōwa hen.*

204 Tsuji, Hisako, "Kishi Kōichi no sakuhin to watashi," *Bungei Shunjū* 10 (1978): 87. According to other sources, "Dickson-Poynder 1715."; see Murata, Sōroku, "Stradivari no denrai," (manuscript, Tokyo, n.d.); Yokoyama, Shin'ichi, *Sutoradivariusu* (Tokyo: Ascii Media Works, 2008), 183.

205 Koishi, "Hito: Ongaku seikatsu 50 nen no Tsuji Hisako."

206 Chiaki, Shin'ya, "Sainō o miidasu: Tensai sodateta kiso shidō," Kōbe Shinbun, http://www.kobe-np.co.jp/info/hyogo_jin2/57.shtml (14 February 2011).

207 Demizu, Nami, "Zokuzoku: Oda-saku mo egaita baiorin shōjo, Tsuji Hisako, Genfu no oshie mune ni 80 nen," *Mainichi shinbun (Ōsaka yūhan)*, 18 January 2012.

208 Most of the information comes from Etō, *Vaiorin to tomo ni.*

209 Reprinted in Ibid., 18–22.

210 Founded by Saint Giovanni Bosco (1815–88): www.donbosco.jp (14 January 2014).

211 Ushiyama Mitsuru (1884–1963)

212 See Chapter 7. Inoue taught at the Academy from 1930 to 1952.

213 Yōgaku Hōsō Shichijū Nenshi Purojekuto, ed. *Yōgaku hōsō 70 nenshi 1925–1995*, 32, 153; "Kao: Iwabuchi Ryūtarō: Shitsunaigaku no oni," *Ongaku no tomo* September (1960): 126–129; Nichigai Associates, ed. *Ongakuka jinmei jiten* 180.

214 He had already begun playing chamber music in 1948 when he helped out in the Tokyo Quartet (not the post-war quartet of that name) whose first violinist was still a prisoner in Siberia.

215 Ōsaka Ongaku Daigaku Ongaku Bunka Kenkyūsho, ed. *Ōsaka ongaku bunkashi shiryō: Shōwa hen*, 267.

216 Quoted in Matsumoto, *Teikin yūjō*, 268.

217 Review quoted in Ibid., 279–280. It seems unlikely that both Toyoda and Etō performed movements from the same concerto; possibly Toyoda played Vivaldi's concerto in A minor.

218 Salomon, Harald, "Agnes Sappers Wirkung in Japan: Zur Rezeption eines deutschen Familienbildes in der frühen Shōwa-Zeit," *Japonica Humboldiana* 7. (2003): 179–237, 223. Unfortunately only fragments of the film are known to exist, and the soundtrack is lost

219 Roeseler, Albrecht, *Große Geiger unseres Jahrhunderts* (Munich: Piper, 1996 (1987)), 100.

220 Ross, Alex, *The Rest is Noise: Listening to the Twentieth Century* (New York: Picador, 2007), 333–370.

221 Robert Kahn (1865–1951), who taught composition at the Hochschule in Berlin from 1897 to 1930, emigrated to England in 1937. Edvard Moritz (1891–1974) studied in Paris as well as Berlin; his composition teachers may have included Claude Debussy. He emigrated to New York in 1937, where he composed some of his works for the saxophonist Cecil Leeson: Fetthauer, Sophie, Ralph Kogelheide, and Marion Reich, "Edvard Moritz," Universität Hamburg,<http://www.lexm.uni-hamburg.de/receive/lexm_lexmperson_00002075?wcmsID=0003> (3 May 2010).

222  Mōri, *Kishi Kōichi*, 220–221.

223  The Japanese premiere did not take place until nearly ten years later, when Tsuji Hisako performed the first movement; the complete concerto was not performed until 1987: Tsuji, "Kishi Kōichi no sakuhin to watashi."

224  Press cuttings in the Kishi papers cited in Mōri, *Kishi Kōichi*; Naka, Mamiko and Kaoru Mishima, "Berurin no chōshū ni todokerareta 'Nihon no Seiyō ongaku': Kishi Kōichi no kangaeru 'Nihon ongaku', amidashita 'Seiyō ongaku)," *Dōshisha Joshi Daigaku Sōgō Bunka Kenkyūsho kiyō* 22 (2005): 145–164. The following citations have been taken directly from the German newspapers and translated by the author.

225  A-th, "Japanische Zukunftsmusik," *Berliner Lokal-Anzeiger, Morgenausgabe*, 31 March 1934, 2. 'Zukunftsmusik,' a term coined by Richard Wagner literally means "music of the future."

226  Ohrmann, Fritz, "Konzerte," *Germania*, 4 April 1934, 8..

227  He, "Japanische Zukunftsmusik," *National-Zeitung*, 7 April 1934, 8.

228  Wörner, Karl, "Ein japanischer Komponist: Koichi Kishi im Universum," *BZ am Mittag*, 31 March 1934, 7–8.

229  Stege, Fritz, "Berliner Musik," *Zeitschrift für Musik* 101.5 (1934): 506–508, 507.

230  H.R., "Japanischer Konzert-Abend," *Völkischer Beobachter*, 4 April 1934, 5.

231  Mōri, *Kishi Kōichi*, 241–242. Original programme in the Staatliches Institut für Musikforschung, Berlin.

232  For example, Bst, "Ausländische Gäste," *Berliner Lokal-Anzeiger* 1934, 2; Nüll, E. v.d., "Gieseking, Telmányi, Busoni und ein Japaner," *BZ am Mittag*, 4 December 1934, 5; "Berliner Musikleben," *Germania*, 24 November 1934, 10.

233  Wohlfahrt, "Ein japanischer Dirigent: Koichi Kishi mit den Philharmonikern," *Deutsche Allgemeine Zeitung*, 21 November 1934, 8.

234  bb., "Japan auf dem Ball der Auslandspresse im Hotel Adlon," *BZ am Mittag*, 3 December 1934, Erstes Beiblatt, 3.; Mōri, *Kishi Kōichi*. front matter, picture 6; Goebbels may have been presenting the raffle prize mentioned in the newspaper article.

235  Mōri, *Kishi Kōichi*, 248.

236  Nozawa, Kurisutofa N., "Saijin Kishi Kōichi: Berurin de jisaku o rokuon," *String* August (2001): 46–50.

237  Copy in Political Archive of the German foreign office R 85965 (Abt. IV, Politik 26, Japan, Band 3). See also Schauwecker, Detlev, "Musik und Politik: Tōkyō 1934–1944," in *Formierung und Fall der Achse Berlin–Tōkyō*, ed. Krebs, Gerhard and Martin, Bernd (Munich: iudicium, 1994), 217–218.

238  He resigned in January 1939, but acted as prime minister again from July 1940 to October 1941; under his cabinet the alliance with Germany was signed in September 1940.

239  The papers of the German–Japanese Society in the Bundesarchiv in Berlin has three entire folders of correspondence connected with Konoe's activities; R 64-IV 81–83.

240  Papers in the Bundesarchiv, R 64-IV 81, pp. 25–1 (the documents are numbered in reverse order).

241  He tended to work with pianists rather than violinists, most often Müller-Chappius. On Konoe and the Ōshimas, see Hagiya, *Suwa Nejiko*, 118–125.

242 Ibid., 116.

243 Fukada, *Bibo nare Shōwa*, 225. Fukuda does not give precise information about the concerts. Possibly he is referring here to a concert that took place on 22 October 1942 in the Salle Pleyel with the l'Orchestre Lamoureux, under Fournet; the programme included works by Saint-Saëns, Tchaikovsky and Brahms: e-mail communication from Denis Havard de la Montagne, 18 February 2012.

244 Hamel, Fred, "Konzerte in Kürze: Nejiko Suwa," *Deutsche Allgemeine Zeitung*, 11 December (morning) 1942, Beiblatt, 3. Michael Raucheisen (1889–1984) was one of Germany's leading duo partners, who had also played with Kreisler.

245 nz, "Geigerin aus dem Land der Kirschblüte," *Die Woche*, 30 December 1942, 4.

246 Fukada, *Bibo nare Shōwa*, 229.

247 The same report was published in *Völkischer Beobachter*, 23 February 1934, 6; *BZ am Mittag*, 23 February 1943, 3; *Berliner Lokal-Anzeiger*, 23 February 1943, morning edition, 6; *Deutsche Allgemeine Zeitung*, 23 February 1943, 2. For a photograph of the occasion see the digital photo collection of CEGES-SOMA (http://pallas.cegesoma.be), Personnalités: Goebbels, Joseph, Reichsminister, présence à des manifestations culturelles, 1940–1943, Image no 205761.

248 Translation of T.51, Nachrichten für die Truppe, Nr. 51, 6. Juni 1944: www.psywar.org/page.php?detail=1944NFDTT051 (14 March 2013).

249 Vries, Willem de, *Sonderstab Musik: Organisierte Plünderungen in Westeuropa 1940–45* (Köln: Dittrich, 1998).

250 R 55/853 Ankauf von Meistergeigen und ihre Verleihung an Künstler.

251 Murata, "Stradivari no denrai," 2–3.

252 This is also discussed in the documents in R 55 mentioned above.

253 23 February 1943. Fröhlich, Elke, ed. *Die Tagebücher von Joseph Goebbels, Teil 2, Diktate 1941–1945* 15 vols., vol. 7 (Munich: Saur, 1993), 400. Goebbels makes one more reference to Suwa and the Stradivarius he gave her ("geschenkt") in January 1944: Schneider, Dieter Marc, ed. *Die Tagebücher von Joseph Goebbels, Teil 2, Diktate 1941–1945* 15 vols., vol. 11 (Munich: Saur, 1994), 188.

254 Abendroth, Walter, "Japanisches Geigenwunder," *Lokal-Anzeiger*, 21 October, Morgenausgabe 1943, 6.

255 German–Japanese Society, 64-IV/27 (fol 62, 64, 66).

256 Fukada, *Bibo nare Shōwa*, 288.

257 Yosano Shigeru (1904–71) was a relative of the poet Yosano Akiko.

258 Quotes from the Swiss press in Fukada, *Bibo nare Shōwa*, 294–295. Hagiya, *Suwa Nejiko*, 149–150.

259 Seventh Army Interrogation Center, APO 758, 21 July 1945: Preliminary Interrogation Report; www.footnote.com/image/232035387 (17 May 2010).

260 William Defibaugh, quoted on http://www.pabook.libraries.psu.edu/palitmap/BSH.html (7 June 2012).

261 Correspondence with the Dessau Quartet in the papers of the German–Japanese Society in Berlin, Bundesarchiv, R 64-IV-80. Not much appears to be known about Stavonhagen. Born in 1908 in Cologne, he studied at the Cologne conservatoire from 1915 to 1923. In the 1930s and 1940s he spent ten years as concertmaster in Dessau, where he also formed the Dessauer String Quartet. After 1945 he held several appointments as concertmaster. At the time of Konoe's invitation he was

concertmaster at the Frankfurt Opera Orchestra (programme notes for violin recital in Tokyo on 26 September 1952, in the Archives of Modern Japanese Music).

262  I thank Heinz-Dieter Reese, Japanese Cultural Institute, Cologne, for providing me with this information and photographs.

## II. Recovery, Economic Growth and Cultural Ambitions (1945–1980s)

1    McClain, James L., *Japan: A Modern History* (New York: W.W. Norton & Company, 2002), 523.

2    Vining, Elizabeth Gray, *Windows for the Crown Prince Akihito of Japan* (Tokyo: Tuttle, 1989), 23.

3    Ibid., 67.

4    Gordon, Beate Sirota, *The Only Woman in the Room: A Memoir* (Tokyo: Kodansha International, 1997).

5    Hirooka, Yoshio, "Music Education in Japan," *Music Educators Journal* 36.2 (1949): 34–35, 34.

6    "Western Music in Japan," *Music Education Journal* 36.3 (1950): 31, 33,37,45–46.

7    Nomura, Kōichi, Kenzō Nakajima, and Kiyomichi Miyoshi, *Nihon yōgaku gaishi: Nihon gakudan chōrō ni yoru taikenteki yōgaku no rekishi* (Tokyo: Rajio Gijutsusha, 1978), 294.

8    Yōgaku Hōsō Shichijū Nenshi Purojekuto, ed. *Yōgaku hōsō 70 nenshi 1925–1995* (Tokyo: Myūjiamu Tosho, 1997), 153.

9    Shin Sakkyokuka Kyōkai (The New Composers' Association) and Nihon Gendai Ongaku Kyōkai (Japanese Association for Contemporary Music)

10   Press reports of the changes reprinted in Tōkyō Geijutsu Daigaku Hyakunenshi Hensan Iinkai, ed. *Tōkyō Geijutsu Daigaku hyakunenshi: Tōkyō Ongaku Gakkō hen 2* (Tokyo: Ongaku no Tomosha, 2003), 1449–1460.

11   Tōkyō Firuhāmonī Kōkyō Gakudan; www.tpo.or.jp (14 January 2014).

12   Tōkyō Kōkyō Gakudan; http://www.tokyosymphony.jp/pc/top (14 January 2014).

13   Ōno, Kaoru, *Konoe Hidemaro: Nihon no ōkesutora o tsukutta otoko* (Tokyo: Kodansha, 2006), 276.

14   Ōmori, Seitarō, *Nihon no yōgaku*, 2 vols., vol. 2 (Tokyo: Shinmon Shuppansha, 1987), 48.

15   Kunikiyo, Hiroyoshi, *Vaiorin ni miserarete* (Hiroshima: Sankō Gakki, 2003), 12.

16   *Kokoni Izumi Ari* (Here is the fountain), directed by Imai Tadashi. www.gunkyo.com/history.php (18 January 2011).

17   Nihon Firuhāmonī Kōkyō Gakudan; www.japanphil.or.jp (14 January 2014) and Shin Nihon Firuhāmonī Kōkyō Gakudan; www.njp.or.jp (14 January 2014).

18   Born in 1922, she had studied with him in the 1930s and won the international piano competition for women in Paris.

19   Nomura, Nakajima, and Miyoshi, *Nihon yōgaku gaishi*, 308, 311, 321.

20   Havens, Thomas R.H., *Artist and Patron in Postwar Japan: Dance, Music, Theater and the Visual Arts, 1955–1980* (Princeton, New Jersey: Princeton University Press, 1982), 195–202.

21   Kunikiyo, *Vaiorin ni miserarete*, 23, 64.

22   Havens, *Artist and Patron*, 188, 190.

23   The official English name was Tokyo National University of Fine Arts and Music until 2008, when it was renamed Tokyo University of the Arts.

24   It became Sōai University in 1982.

25   See Part 2 Chapter 9.

26   Yoshihara, Mari, *Musicians from a Different Shore: Asians and Asian Americans in Classical Music* (Philadelphia: Temple University Press, 2007), 35–36.

27   "Invasion from the Orient," *Time* 3 November (1967). Henahan, Donal, "Young Violinists From Asia Gain Major Place on American Musical Scene," *New York Times*, 2 August 1968, 21; Strongin, Theodore, "Japanese Tutors Young Violinists (Suzuki's Pupils Learn Music First)," *New York Times*, 28 February 1964, 3.

28   Yoshihara, *Musicians from a Different Shore*.

29   Ehrlich, Cyril, *The Piano: A History. Revised edition* (Oxford: Oxford University Press, 1990 (1976)), 195.

30   Ibid.

31   Wade, Bonnie C., *Music in Japan* (Oxford: Oxford University Press, 2005), 46.

32   For the following discussion see Hosokawa, Shuhei and Christine Yano, "Popular Music in Modern Japan," in *The Ashgate Research Companion to Japanese Music*, ed. Hughes, David and Tokita, Alison McQueen (Aldershot, Hampshire: Ashgate, 2008); Mitsui, Toru, "Interaction of Imported and Indigenous Music in Japan: A Historical Overview of the Music Industry," in *Whose Master's Voice: The Development of Popular Music in Thirteen Cultures*, ed. Ewbank, Alison J. and Papageorgiu, Fouli T. (Westport, Connecticut: Greenwood Press, 1997).

33   Tetsuo Hamada, "The Beatles Concert in Japan" http://beatles.com/#/article/ The_Beatles_concerts_in_Japan (08 February 2012).

34   Hosokawa and Yano, "Popular Music in Modern Japan," 355.

35   Margareta Wöss, quoted in Suchy, Irene, "A Nation of Mozart-Lovers: Das Phänomen abendländischer Kunstmusik in Japan," *Minikomi (Informationen des akademischen Arbeitskreises Japan)* 1994.1 (1994): 1–8, 4.

36   Lebrecht, Norman, *The Maestro Myth: Great Conductors in Pursuit of Power* (New York: Citadel Press, 1993), 230.

37   Havens, *Artist and Patron*, 212. Havens quotes Walter Nichols of Azabu Artists calling the1980s "a watershed for foreign attractions in Japan."

38   Okada, Akeo, "Europäische Klassik in Japan – eine düstere Diagnose," in *Musik in Japan*, ed. Silvain, Guignard (Munich: iudicium, 1994), 193.

39   Suchy, Irene, "Westliche Musik in Japan (1): Musik in architektonischen Konzepten," *Japan Magazin* 8 (1991): 29–31.

40   Ishida, Kazushi, "Music in Japan Today: Hardware, Software, and the 'Concert-Hall Culture'," *The Japan Foundation Newsletter* 25.6 (1998): 1–5, 1.

41   Small, Christopher, *Musicking: The Meanings of Performing and Listening* (Middletown, CT: Wesleyan University Press, 1998), 190. There are, however, indications that the excesses of the 1980s had by the end of the more sober 1990s given way to promising beginnings of a "concert hall culture" emphasizing locally based cultural activity and creative content: Ishida, "Music in Japan Today."

42   Aikawa, Yumi, *"Enka" no susume* (Tokyo: Bungei Shunjū, 2002).

43   Okada, "Europäische Klassik in Japan – eine düstere Diagnose," 188–190. The article was originally written in 1989.

44   Although *teikin* was used before the 1930s, phonetic transcriptions of "violin" were more common, perhaps to distinguish the violin from the Chinese instruments

known as *teikin*; see Shiotsu, Yōko, "Meijiki Kansai vaiorin jijō," *Ongaku kenkyū (Ōsaka Ongaku Daigaku Hakubutsukan nenpō)* 20 (2003): 11–38, 14–16.

45   Suzuki, Shin'ichi, "Yōji no sainō kyōiku to sono hōhō," in *Suzuki Shin'ichi zenshū* (Tokyo: Sōshisha, 1985 (1946)).

46   Noda, Awaji, *Machi no vaiorin-sensei: honobono monogatari* (Tokyo: Shinfūsha, 2006), 12–13.

47   Starr, William, *The Suzuki Violinist*, Revised Edition ed.(Miami: Summy-Birchard, 2000), 19; Cook, Clifford A., *Suzuki Education in Action: A Story of Talent Training From Japan* (New York: Exposition Press, 1970), 18.

48   Driver, Hiroko Iritani and Susan Shields, "Japanese–American Differences," in *The Suzuki Violinist*, ed. Starr, William (Miami: Summy-Birchard, 2000 (1976)).

49   Denton, David, "Reflections of a Suzuki guinea-pig," *The Strad* September (1993): 804–805, 805.

50   "Takako Nishizaki Biography," http:/www.naxos.com/artistinfo/Takako_Nishizaki/ 55.htm (19 November 2009).

51   In 1986 Yamaha founded its system of "Popular Music Schools" for children and adults; violin tuition was added to the courses on offer in 1997, the year the Silent Violin was introduced: www.yamaha-ongaku.com/pms/20th/index.html (14 January 2014).

52   Mönig, Marc, *Die Pädagogik der Yamaha-Musikschulen: Darstellung, Hintergründe und Kritik* (Augsburg: Wißner, 2005), 186–189.

53   Kunikiyo, *Violin ni miserarete*, 20–24.

54   "Invasion from the Orient."

55   Nakamaru, Yoshie, *Kiyūkyoku, nariyamazu: Saitō Hideo no shōgai* (Tokyo: Shinchōsha, 1996).

56   Yōgaku Hōsō Shichijū Nenshi Purojekuto, ed. *Yōgaku hōsō 70 nenshi 1925–1995*, 62. Furiyoshi later studied with Etō Toshiya and Josef Gingold. She graduated from Indiana University in 1969 and joined the Cleveland Orchestra in 1970.

57   Quoted in Nakasone, Matsue, *Ongakukai sengo 50 nen no ayumi: jikenshi to ongakuka retsuden* (Tokyo: Geijutsu Gendaisha, 2001), 35.

58   Nakamaru, *Kiyūkyoku, nariyamazu*. See also www.saito-kinen.com/e/ about_skf/saito.shtml (14 January 2014).

59   Kōno became a founding member of the Japan Philharmonic Orchestra in 1956, and of the viola department at Geidai, and played in string quartets. In 1960 he went to America, where he performed at Tanglewood and graduated from Yale in 1964.

60   Nakamaru, *Kiyūkyoku, nariyamazu*, 310.

61   www.koyo-elc.co.jp/~touhou/english/stage.html (19–09–2008); www.tohomusic-child.jp (14 January 2014).

62   Parmenter, Ross, "Music: The Toho Strings," *New York Times*, 14 July 1964, 29.

63   Strongin, Theodore, "Toho Strings Give Second Program: Saita [sic] and 3 Students Share Conducting at Philharmonic," *New York Times*, 15 July 1964.

64   ———, "Toho String Concert has Buoyant Spirit," *New York Times*, 18 July 1964.

65   Nakamaru, *Kiyūkyoku, nariyamazu*, 417. Detailed schedule of the tour with programmes in Minshu Ongaku Kyōkai, ed. *Saitō Hideo: Ongaku to shōgai: kokoro de utae, kokoro de utae* (Tokyo: Minshu Ongaku Kyōkai, 1985).

66   Nakamaru, *Kiyūkyoku, nariyamazu*, 419.

67   See Part 3 Chapter 4.

68   www.saito-kinen.com (14 January 2014). See also Pincus, Andrew L., "Music: Japanese Players Take the Grand Tour," *New York Times*, 3 December 1989.

69   Kubota, Ryōsaku et al., eds., *Sumi Saburō: Vaiorin no okeiko* (Tokyo: Ongaku no Tomosha, 1980); Sumi, Saburō, *Vaiorin hitosuji ni* (Tokyo: Kōseisha, 1983).

70   See Part 2 Chapter 9.

71   "String Interview: Sumi Eriko," *String* September (1998): 22–28.

72   Oscar Marland, Ambassador British Embassy Tokyo, 21 April 1961 to Max Rostal; Berlin Universität der Künste, Rostal Papers, Korr II-253

73   Tanaka, Toshiko, *Vaiorin hitosuji ni: Nihon Firu Watanabe Akeo sensei to tomo ni* (Tōyō Shoin 1993), 120.

74   Devy Erlih is less known than the other violinists named: see Duchen, Jessica, "'Un mauvais caractère' – Devi Erlih," *The Strad* November (2008): 76–79.

75   Kubota et al., eds., *Sumi Saburō*, 4.

76   Hasegawa, Takehisa, "Sumi Saburō tsuitō ensōkai: 1000 nin o kosu ongakujin no deshi ga atsumatte," *Ongaku no tomo* 10 (1986): 12–14.

77   Details of the yearly events since 1991 in Matsumoto, Kaoru, *Yume wa vaiorin no shirabe: Sumi Saburō o sagashite* (Yonago: Tottori-ken Kyōka Tosho Hanbai Kabushiki Gaisha, 2009), 166–169. Similar local initiatives were launched in other parts of Japan at the time; for two more examples, see Mehl, Margaret, "Local Heroes," *History Today* August (2001): 36–37.

78   http://sumi-saburo-ms.jp

79   On the violin world, see the teacher–pupil "family tree" in Campbell, Margaret, *The Great Violinists* (London: Granada, 1980), xx–xxi. It is also a recurring topic on the website www.violinist.com

80   *Shinozaki baiorin kyōhon*, 4 vols.

81   Ongaku no Tomosha, ed. *'68 Nihon no Ongakuka/Great Musicians of Japan*, (*Ongaku no tomo 10 gatsu rinji zōkangō*; Tokyo: Ongaku no Tomosha, 1968), 180; ———, ed. *'76 Nihon no ongakuka*, vol. Bekkan (Tokyo: Ongaku no Tomosha, 1976), 213; Okayama, Kiyoshi, "Uzuka Tatsuo shi o shinonde," *Ongaku no tomo* May (1985): 103.

82   Tōkyō Geijutsu Daigaku Hyakunenshi Hensan Iinkai, ed. *Hyakunenshi: Tōkyō Ongaku Gakkō hen 2*, 1335, 1315.

83   Temma, Atsuko, *Waga kokoro no uta: Bōkyō no barādo* (Tokyo: Bungei Shunjū, 2000), 108, 111, 117. Not that bad relations and rivalries between teachers are peculiar to Japan; after the breakup between Galamian and DeLay students were likewise forced to choose between one and the other.

84   Later the guitar and the flute were added. Yōgaku Hōsō Shichijū Nenshi Purojekuto, ed. *Yōgaku hōsō 70 nenshi 1925–1995*, 170–171, 220.

85   *Gurafu NHK*, 15 July, 1968.

86   Yōgaku Hōsō Shichijū Nenshi Purojekuto, ed. *Yōgaku hōsō 70 nenshi 1925–1995*, 170–171. In most but not all years there were two different teachers.

87   These are the only two textbooks held in the NHK Broadcasting Museum and Library in Tokyo.

88   Temma, *Waga kokoro no uta*, 98–102.

89   See Part 3 Chapter 1.

90   Etō, Toshiya, *Vaiorin to tomo ni: Nani o uttatte iru ka shiritai* (Tokyo: Ongaku no Tomosha, 1999), ix.

91   Yōgaku Hōsō Shichijū Nenshi Purojekuto, ed. *Yōgaku hōsō 70 nenshi 1925–1995*, 220.

92   Etō, *Vaiorin to tomo ni*, 235.

93   Nihon Minkan Hōsō Renmei, ed. *Nihon hōsō nenkan* (Iwasaki Hōsō Shuppansha, 1969), 419.

94   Yōgaku Hōsō Shichijū Nenshi Purojekuto, ed. *Yōgaku hōsō 70 nenshi 1925–1995*, 220.

95   Zen Nihon Gakusei Ongaku Konkūru, http://gaccon.mainichi-classic.jp (22 March 2010).

96   Watanabe, Kazuhiko, *Violinists 33: Mei-ensōka o kiku* (Tokyo: Kawade Shobō, 2002).

97   Partial translation in Borris, Siegfried and Verband Deutscher Musikerzieher und konzertierender Künstler, eds., *Musikleben in Japan: in Geschichte und Gegenwart, Berichte, Statistiken, Anschriften* (Kassel: Bärenreiter, 1967), 181–186, 181.

98   Translation and explanation of this colloquial expression in Kittredge, Cherry, *Womansword: What Japanese Words Say about Women* (Tokyo and New York: Kodansha International, 1987).

99   Iwaki, Hiroyuki, "Ongaku kyōiku wa kore de yoi no ka," *Chūō kōron* 84.10 (1969): 134–149, 136.

100  Ibid.: 114.

101  Josef Hassid (1923–50) born to a family of Polish Jews, showed an extraordinary talent from an early age. In 1937 he began to have lessons with Carl Flesch and soon his career took off in London. But soon he displayed abnormal behaviour, was diagnosed schizophrenic and admitted to a mental hospital, where he died from the results of a brain operation.

102  Etō, *Vaiorin to tomo ni*, 51. A shorter summary of Etō's career was previously published: Mehl, Margaret, "Toshiya Eto 1927–2008," *The Strad* June (2008): 25.

103  Etō, *Vaiorin to tomo ni*, 169–170.

104  Reprinted, together with unpublished manuscripts, in Ibid., 58–132.

105  Ibid., 74–79.

106  Ibid., 61–66.

107  Ibid., 86–87. The programme does not specify which Vivaldi Concerto.

108  Malan, Roy, *Efrem Zimbalist: A Life* (Portland: Amadeus Press, 2004), 270; Etō, *Vaiorin to tomo ni*, 53.

109  Etō, *Vaiorin to tomo ni*, 141.

110  Downes, Olin, "Japanese Violinist at Carnegie Hall: Toshiya Eto Presents Sonatas by Brahms and Handel and Glazunoff Concerto," *New York Times*, 10 November 1951, 9.

111  Etō, *Vaiorin to tomo ni*, 180.

112  Ibid., 131.

113  Ibid., 182.

114  Ibid., 200, 251.

115  Yamamoto, Shigeru, *Shindō* (Tokyo: Bungei Shunjū, 1996), 52.

116  His two sonatas were recorded by Mittenwald in November 2005 with Kino Masayuki (vl) and Yoshiyama Hikaru (pf); MTWD 99026.

117  Yamamoto, *Shindō*, 85–86.

118  Ibid., 93–94.

119  Ibid., 96.

120  Ibid., 99–101.

121  Ibid., 107–108.

122  It was recorded for broadcasting and issued on CD in 2006: Mittenwald MTWD 99025.

123  Yamamoto, *Shindō*, 112.

124  Ibid., 127,131. The pianist Hirata Michi (Michi Hirata North) later served on the faculties of Western Washington University and the University of Maine and developed a special piano programme for young students in Taiwan.

125  Ibid., 14–15.

126  Quoted in Sand, Barbara Lourie, *Teaching Genius: Dorothy DeLay and the Making of a Musician* (Newark Pompton Turnpike, New Jersey: Amadeus Press, 2000), 58.

127  In his bowing he followed what his biographer describes as the "Auer tradition," although Auer himself advocated a flexible approach to bow hold and his students did not necessarily bow that way. Photos of Watanabe Shigeo show him bowing with a high wrist and a low elbow, a style which by the early twentieth century was going out of fashion; Auer, Leopold, *Violin Playing As I Teach It* (New York: Dover Publications, 1980 (1921)), 12–13, 20–22. Kolneder, Walter, *Das Buch der Violine* (Zürich: Atlantis Musikbuch, 1989 (1972)), 454–455. Watanabe Shigeo himself described the technical changes Galamian demanded as minor: Yamamoto, *Shindō*, 168.

128  Yamamoto, *Shindō*, 205.

129  http://www.youtube.com/watch?v=0w_47rQFlCE (11 June 2011, but since removed).

130  Yamamoto, *Shindō*, 211.

131  "Tensai shōnen no saiki: Watanabe Shigeo kun no ryūgaku kara shitsuren jisatsu made," *Shūkan shincho* 9 February (1959): 74–81.

132  ———, *Shindō*, 263–264.

133  Ibid. The TV documentary was "Yomigaeru shirabe: tensai baiorinisuteo Watanabe Shigeo" (Yomiuri Telecasting Company). Previously (in 1988), Watanabe Suehiko and others interested in preserving Shigeo's memory had his recordings published on CDs. The photograph can be seen at http://www.m-pine-m.com/shop/catalog/CD/harmony/watanabe.htm (14 January 2014).

134  Steinhardt, Arnold, *Violin Dreams* (Boston: Houghton Mifflin, 2006), 97. Steinhardt heard the third recital, not the debut recital: see list of Etō's performances in Etō, *Vaiorin to tomo ni*, xxvii–xxviii.

135  *Geijutsu Shinchō* (September 1959), see Etō, *Vaiorin to tomo ni*, 193–201.

136  Ibid., 202.

137  Ibid., 206.

138  Ibid., 54.

139  Ibid., 85.

140  Watanabe, Op. 4; EMI TOCE9304, 1996.

141  Etō, *Vaiorin to tomo ni*, xiii–xv. The list includes 71 names and 173 prizes.

142  Ibid., 211–215.

143  Ibid., 229.

144  Ibid., 231. Compare Arnold Steinhardt: "To this day my stomach shifts slightly when I pass his apartment building at 170 West Seventy-third. Street." Steinhardt, *Violin Dreams*, 100.

145  Kawabata, Narimichi, *Boku wa, namida o denai me de naita* (Tokyo: Fusōsha, 2003), 103.

146  Suwanai, Akiko, *Vaiorin to kakeru* (Tokyo: NHK, 2000).

147  Etō, *Vaiorin to tomo ni*, 232, 238.

148  Ibid., 156.

149  Ongaku no Tomosha, ed. *'68 Nihon no Ongakuka*.

150  Borris and Verband Deutscher Musikerzieher und konzertierender Künstler, eds., *Musikleben*.

151  Ongaku no Tomosha, ed. *'68 Nihon no Ongakuka*, 178–193. The other two were Hattori Toyoko (1926) and Kubota Ryōsaku (1928).

152  1930s: Iso Hideo, Unno Yoshio, Kishibe Momoo, Kobayashi Kenji, Kobayashi Takeshi, Suzuki Hidetarō, Tanaka Chikashi, Toyoda Kōji, Toyama Shigeru, Hori Tadashi; 1940s: Ishii Shizuko, Ushioda Masuko, Kubo Yōko, Kuronuma Yuriko, Satō Yōko, Shinozaki Isako, Sō Tomotada, Takahashi Mihoko, Tsumura Mari, Hayashi Yōko, Hirose Etsuko, Maehashi Teiko, Wanami Takayoshi.

153  Ongaku no Tomosha, ed. *'76 Nihon no ongakuka*, 210–233. The two exceptions were Suwa Nejiko, who by then was no longer performing publicly, and Hayashi Yōko (1940). The new names are Iso Tsuneo, Urakawa Takaya, Okayama Kiyoshi, Oguri Machie, Kameda Misako, Shiokawa Yūko, Tokunaga Tsugio, Nagano Akiko, Nishizaki Takako, Fujikawa Mayumi, Fujiwara Hamao, Matsuda Yōko, all born in the 1940s, and Shimizu Takashi and Yasunaga Tōru, born in 1953 and 1951 respectively.

154  Nichigai Associates, ed. *Ongakuka jinmei jiten* 3rd rev. ed. (Tokyo: Nichigai Associates, 2001), 230.

155  Listed as professor by special appointment: brochure for Tōhō Gakuen School of Music, string instrument course, 2010.

156  The following discussion is far from exhaustive. All the names mentioned here are listed in Ongaku no Tomosha, ed. *'68 Nihon no Ongakuka*. The only exception is Tokue Hisako, who is only listed in ———, ed. *'76 Nihon no ongakuka*.

157  Fukuzawa, Mitsuomi, ed. *J(apanese) Classic-shugi! Shinsedai Nihon ātisuto gaido* (Tokyo: Ongaku no Tomosha, 1998), 184, 212, 214.

158  Nichigai Associates, ed. *Ongakuka jinmei jiten* 183.

159  Ibid., 188, 240.

160  Kuronuma, Yuriko, *Vaiorin/Ai wa hirumanai: Puraha kara Mekishiko e* (Tokyo: Kairyūsha, 2001), 10.

161  "Mekishiko Ongakusai 2010 – Minotta kajitsu to tomo ni Vaiorinisuto Kuronuma Yuriko," *String* January (2010): 41–43. "Kuronuma Yuriko: Artist Interview," *Sarasate* 32 (2010): 24–25.

162  www.naxos.com/artistinfo/Takako_Nishizaki/552.htm (14 January 2014). The *Butterfly Lovers* Concerto, composed in 1959 by two students of the Shanghai Conservatoire, the violinist He Zhanhao and the composition major Chen Gang, is inspired by a popular love story, and the composers were influenced both by their study of Western music and their familiarity with Chinese folk music and local opera. The violin part features the portamento and special vibrato of Chinese *yueju* singing and Chinese instruments like the *erhu* (two-stringed fiddle). The concerto became an instant hit, although it was unofficially blacklisted during the Cultural Revolution: Melvin, Sheila and Jindong Cai, *Rhapsody in Red: How Western Classical Music Became Chinese* (New York: Algora, 2004), 210–211, 256–257.

163  Fukuzawa, ed. *J(apanese) Classic-shugi!* , 184. Nishizaki is not listed in this publication, although she is one of the violinists listed in *'76 Nihon no ongakuka*.

164  Nichigai Associates, ed. *Ongakuka jinmei jiten* 219.

165  "Fujikawa Mayumi: Artist Interview," *Sarasate* 14 (2007): 32.

166  Ongaku no Tomosha, ed. *Ongaku nenkan* (Tokyo: Ongaku no Tomosha, 2004), 7. She is described as the most popular among the "veterans."

167  Fukuzawa, ed. *J(apanese) Classic-shugi!* , 194.

168  Flier, Maehashi Teikō afutanūn konsāto, 29 July, Yahaba-chō Bunka Kaikan.

169  Wanami, Takayoshi, *Vaiorin wa mita* (Tokyo: Kairyūsha, 1999).

170  Campbell, *The Great Violinists*, 311.

171  Sugie Taiichirō (1891–1935) graduated in 1912. He taught at Osaka Metropolitan School for the Blind. Matsumoto, Zenzō, *Teikin yūjō: Nihon no vaiorin ongaku shi* (Tokyo: Ressun no Tomosha, 1995), 121. http://www5c.biglobe.ne.jp/~obara/tenji/nenpyo10.html (19 June 2011).

172  Wanami, Sonoko, *Haha to ko no shinfonī: Mōmoku no vaiorinisuto, Wanami Takayoshi o sodateta haha no shuki* (Tokyo: Ongaku no Tomosha, 1977), 3. See also Part 3 Chapter 2.

173  Founded in 1832, this was the school Helen Keller attended; Wanami met Keller when she visited Japan and he performed at a reception in her honour in 1955.

174  Wanami, *Haha to ko no shinfonī*, 230, 254–256.

175  ———, *Vaiorin wa mita*, 102.

176  Wanami, Takayoshi, *Ongaku kara no okurimono* (Tokyo: Shinchōsha, 1994), 364.

177  Ibid., 363–369. www.music-wanami.com/english (14 January 2014).

178  Ongaku no Tomosha, ed. *'68 Nihon no Ongakuka*, 189.

179  "Ryōma den." In January 2002, in a special edition of NHK's popular history programme "Sono toki rekishiga ugoita," he was voted by viewers the greatest historical figure of all times.

180  "String Interview: Tokunaga Tsugio," *String* June (2001): 31–36, 33.

181  Ibid.: 36.

182  "We Love Wine (4): Furansusan akawain o katate ni – vaiorinisuto Tokunaga Tsugio," *Sarasate* 6 (2005): 66–67.

183  Fukuzawa, ed. *J(apanese) Classic-shugi!* , 218–189. (The directory starts on the back page.) In addition, several violinists are among the musicians not listed in the directory but featured individually in articles: Furusawa Iwao (1959–, pp. 26–29), Senju Mariko (1962–, 34–37), Takezawa Kyōko (1966–, 44–45), Watanabe Reiko (1968–, 134–135), Morishita Kōji (1968–,152–153), Yabe Tatsuya (1968–, 60–61),

Midori (1971–, 38–39), Suwanai Akiko (1972–, 14–17); as well as two violinists featured in articles entitled "Crossover Talk"; Hakase Tarō (1968–, 78–80) and Takashima Chisako (1968–, 81–83; also in a commercial feature, 104–105).

184  Ibid., 184. Suzuki Hidetarō is not listed in the directory section.

185  The youngest was Kashimoto Daishin, born in 1979 and described as "the hope of the violin world" Ibid., 211. See introduction to Part 3.

186  "Kawasaki Masao: Meimon Juriādo no seikyōju ni shukunin," *Ongaku no tomo* August (1987): 90.

187  "Doroshī Direi Shirīzu (6): Urushihara Asako," *String* March (1994): 20–23, 21.

188  http://www.geidai.ac.jp/staff/fm032e.html (7 June 2012)

189  "Takezawa Kyōko-san: Debyū nijū shūnen o kinen shite Burāmusu no sonata zenkyoku ensō," *String* November (2009): 36–40.

190  Takayanagi, Morio, "50 kai o mukaeta ongaku konkūru," *Ongaku geijutsu* 1 (1982): 68–69.

191  "Watanabe Reiko: Artist Interview," *Sarasate* 6 (2005): 26–27.

192  Shinozaki, Fuminori, *Rufutopauze (Luftpause): Uīn no kaze ni fukarete* (Tokyo: Shuppankan Bukku Kurabu, 2006). Luftpause refers to a "breathing space" ("Atempause" is the more common German expression) or the right timing while playing a piece of music, even to the Japanese concept of "*ma*" (p. 36).

193  Morishita, Kōji, "Keimō mo watakushi no shigoto: Sendai shūhen no shitsunai konsāto no kikaku," *String* March (1998). Fukuzawa, ed. *J(apanese) Classic-shugi!*, 152–153.

194  Yoshimura, Kō, "Kogakki no meishutachi," in *J-Classic-shugi*, ed. Fukuzawa, Mitsuomi (Tokyo: Ongaku no Tomosha, 1998).

195  Fukuzawa, ed. *J(apanese) Classic-shugi!*, 26–29; Nichigai Associates, ed. *Ongakuka jinmei jiten* 249. See also http://www.jp-musicet.com/en/artists/F/iwao-furusawa/ (2 September 2011).

196  Hashida Naoki, lincr notc to *Violin Summit* 2006, HUCD-10018–9

197  Fukuzawa, ed. *J(apanese) Classic-shugi!*, 78–79.

198  Interview quoted on http://tarohakase.com/about-taro/#page (14 January 2014).

199  Schermann, Susanne, "Anmerkungen zur japanischen Pop-Musik," *Minikom: Information des Akademischen Arbeitskreises Japan* 78 (2010): 20–25, 20. The charts by the company Oricon, produced since 1967, are based on sales of recordings.

200  Shigematsu, "Vaiorinisuto Hakase Tarō-san kurashikku no sekai e..." *String* May (2008): 28–30.

201  Homfray, Tim, "Concert Review: Taro Hakase (violin) Maciej Janas (piano), Cadogan Hall, London, 6 March 2008," *The Strad* June (2008): 81.

202  Fukuzawa, ed. *J(apanese) Classic-shugi!* , 81–83, 104–105; Nichigai Associates, ed. *Ongakuka jinmei jiten* 220.

203  Takashima, Chisako, *Vaiorinisuto no ongaku annai: kurashikku meikyoku 50 sen* (Tokyo: PHP Kenkyūjo, 2005).

204  Lebrecht, Norman, *Who Killed Classical Music? Maestros, Managers and Corporate Politics* (Secaucus, NJ: Birch Lane Press, 1997), 162–164.

205  Wartberg, Kerstin, "Shinichi Suzuki. Eine Lebensbeschreibung mit Bildern," http://www.germansuzuki.de/downloadde/suzuki.pdf (20 February 2009).

206 Ibid. See also previous chapters.
207 Cook, Clifford A., "Japanese String Festival," *Music Educators Journal* 46.2 (1959): 41–42, 41.
208 Mills, Elizabeth and Sr. Therese Cecile Murphy, eds., *The Suzuki Concept: An Introduction to a Successful Method for Early Music Education* (Berkeley and San Francisco: Diablo Press, 1973), i.
209 Peak, Lois, "The Suzuki Method of Music Instruction," in *Teaching and Learning in Japan*, ed. Rohlen, Thomas P. and LeTendre, Gerald K. (Cambridge: Cambridge University Press, 1998), 349. Bargreen, Melinda, "Violin teacher Yuko Honda, 61, shared Suzuki legacy," *The Seattle Times*, 14 April 2007.
210 Wartberg, "Shinichi Suzuki."
211 Ibid.
212 Timmerman, Craig, "Letter from the USA to Europe: Impressions and Ideas," *European Suzuki Journal* 5.1 (1985): 8.
213 Mari Yoshihara calls the method "quite culturally hybrid, if not even American." Yoshihara, *Musicians from a Different Shore*, 40.
214 Peak, "The Suzuki Method of Music Instruction," 349, 365.
215 Wartberg, "Shinichi Suzuki."
216 Yoshihara, *Musicians from a Different Shore*, 42–45, 244 n.287. Mehl, Margaret, "Cultural Translation in Two Directions: The Suzuki Method in Japan and Germany," *Research and Issues in Music Education* 7.1 (2009). Deverich, Robin K., "The Maidstone Movement: Influential British Precursor of American Public School Instrumental Classes," *Journal of Research in Music Education* 35.1 (1987): 39–55, 45.
217 Wilkinson, Endymion, *Japan Versus Europe: A History of Misunderstanding* (Harmondsworth: Penguin, 1983), 68–77.
218 Borris and Verband Deutscher Musikerzieher und konzertierender Künstler, eds., *Musikleben*, 145.
219 Wieck, Michael, "Begegnung mit Shinichi Suzuki," *Das Orchester* 26.April (1978): 291–293.
220 Riethmüller, Albrecht, "'Is That Not Something for *Simplicissimus*?!' The Belief in Musical Superiority," in *Music and German National Identity*, ed. Applegate, Celia and Potter, Pamela (Chicago: University of Chicago Press, 2002). Gienow-Hecht, Jessica C. E., *Sound Diplomacy: Music and Emotions in Transatlantic Relations, 1850–1920* (Chicago: University of Chicago Press, 2009), 28–39.
221 [Langbehn, Julius], *Rembrandt als Erzieher. Von einem Deutschen*, 31 ed.(Leipzig: Hirschfeld, 1891), 231; Gruhn, Wilfried, *Geschichte der Musikerziehung: Eine Kultur-und Sozialgeschichte vom Gesangsunterricht der Aufklärungspädagogik zu ästhetisch-kultureller Bildung*, second ed.(Hofheim: Wolke, 2003), 182–185.
222 Borris and Verband Deutscher Musikerzieher und konzertierender Künstler, eds., *Musikleben*, 153, 181–186.
223 Verband deutscher Musikschulen, "Modellversuch: 'Übertragung der Suzuki-Methode' – Abschlussbericht," (Bonn: Bundesgeschäftsstelle des Verbandes deutscher Musikschulen e.V., n.d.; 1981?).
224 Sassmanshaus, Kurt, "Songs of My Father," *The Strad* September (2008): 63–64, 63–64.

225 The VdM collected no data on the number of music schools that continued to work with the Suzuki Method: e-mail communication from Gisbert Möller, VdM, 28 August 2008.

226 E-mail communication from Kerstin Wartberg, 13 February 2009.

227 Telephone interviews with Kerstin Wartberg, 1 and 7 July 2008; Suzuki Shin'ichi, foreword (dated June 1994) in Wartberg, Kerstin, *Erziehung durch Musik. Die Suzuki-Methode: Unterrichtspraxis und pädagogisches Konzept*, 6 ed.(Sankt Augustin: Deutsches Suzuki Institut, 2004).

228 Interview 1 July 2008. Published by Alfred Publishing, Los Angeles.

229 E-mail communication from Kerstin Wartberg, 13 February 2009.

230 Wartberg, *Erziehung durch Musik*, 47–48. Reports about the conference in *European Suzuki Journal*, vol. 7.2.

231 Heitkämper, Peter, *Die Kunst erfolgreichen Lernens: Handbuch kreativer Lehr- und Lernformen* (Paderborn: Junfermann, 2000), 468–473, 471. Here too, Langbehn could be cited as a precedent: [Langbehn], *Rembrandt als Erzieher*, 228–229.

232 http://www.klingler-stiftung.de/ (14 January 2014); http://europeansuzuki.org/ (14 January 2014); Beyer, Anders, ed. *1977–2002: 25 år i ord og billeder. Det Danske Suzuki Institute, Jubilæumsskrift* (Copenhagen: Det Danske Suzuki Institut, 2002), 18–19.

233 Details about European pioneers of the method in Homfray, Tim, "Method Man," *The Strad* September (2008): 48–52, 48. "Global Twinkling," *The Strad* Dec (1998): 1350–1351; "Who is Who," *European Suzuki Journal* 1.1 (1981): 5–8.

234 Belgium, Great Britain, Croatia, Denmark, Estonia, Faroe Islands, Finland, Germany, Hungary, Iceland, Ireland, Italy, Lithuania, Netherlands, Norway, Poland, South Africa, Spain, Sweden and Switzerland.

235 http://www.internationalsuzuki.org/regional_associations.htm (14 January 2014).

236 "Global Twinkling."

237 Garson, Alfred, *Suzuki Twinkles: An Intimate Portrait* (Miami: Summy-Birchard, 2001), 118–131.

238 Information on El Sistema from Govias, Jonathan, "Inside El Sistema," *The Strad* September (2010): 50–60.

239 For the following discussion, see Yamada, Shin'ichi, *Eru Shisutema: Ongaku de binbō o sukuu Nanbei Benezuera no shakai seisaku* (Tokyo: Shakai Kyōiku Hyōronsha, 2008), 135–155.

240 Kobayashi, Takeshi, *Vaiorin ittei, sekai hitoriaruki* (Tokyo: Geijutsu Gendaisha, 1980), 246. See also Yamada, *Eru Shisutema: Ongaku de binbō o sukuu Nanbei Benezuera no shakai seisaku*, 153.

241 Kobayashi, Seiko Luis Ishikawa, Taida Hideya, and Shin'ichi Yamada, "'Eru Shisutema' o kataru," *Suzuki Method: Sainō kyōiku* 168 (2009): 24–32.

242 Hersh, Sarah and Lois Peak, "Developing character in music teachers: a Suzuki approach," in *Learning in Likely Places: Varieties of Apprenticeship in Japan*, ed. Singleton, John (Cambridge: Cambridge University Press, 1998).

243 Garson, *Suzuki Twinkles*, 35, 100. Garson is one of the pioneers of the method in North America.

244 In Japanese, Kokusai Suzuki Mesōdo Ongakuin; the Japanese terms are *senshū gakkō* and *senmon gakkō*.

245  http://www.suzukimethod.or.jp/english/E_mthd41.html (14 January 2014); "Tokushū: Suzuki Mesōdo no shidōsha yōsei," *Suzuki Method: Sainō kyōiku* 169 (2009): 26–40.

246  Nakajima Mineo, however, believes that applying Suzuki's principles to lifelong education may be a way forward: Nakajima, Mineo, *Ongaku wa ikiru chikara* (Tokyo: Nishimura Shoten, 2009), 160–166. On the challenges faced by the Suzuki Method in Japan today, see also Mari Yoshihara, "The Man Who Became a Method: Globalization of the Suzuki Method." (2006) I thank Mari Yoshihara for sending me the unpublished manuscript.

247  Kobayashi, Hideya, and Yamada, "'Eru Shisutema' o kataru."

248  For example, he told Helen Brunner to teach English children to sing and play scales, something he did not regard as necessary in Japan: Homfray, "Method Man," 52; Starr, *The Suzuki Violinist*, v.

249  Mehl, "Cultural Translation."; Starr, *The Suzuki Violinist*, v., Wartberg, *Erziehung durch Musik*; Kendall, John, *The Suzuki Violin Method in American Music Education* (Reston, Virginia: Music Educators National Conference, 1978), 13; Wickes, Linda, *The Genius of Simplicity* (Princeton, NJ: Summy-Birchard Music, 1982). Grilli, Susan, *Preschool in the Suzuki Spirit* (Tokyo: Harcourt Brace Jovanovich Japan, 1987), 24–38.

250  Madsen, Eric, "The Genesis of Suzuki: An Investigation of the Roots of Talent Education" (M.A., McGill University, 1990), 135; Cook, *Suzuki Education in Action: A Story of Talent Training From Japan*, preface; Bauman, Suzan C., *In Search of the Japanese Spirit in Talent Education: A Research Essay* (Secaucus, NJ: Summy-Birchard Inc., 1994).

251  Mochizuki, Kenji, "Amerika o yuriugokashita Suzuki mesōdo: Nihon no wakai shidōsha e uttaeru," in *Suzuki Shin'ichi zenshū*, ed. Suzuki, Shin'ichi (Tokyo: Sōshisha, 1985 (1968)), 339.

252  Heitkämper, Peter, "Die musikalische Erziehungsmethode Shinichi Suzukis und die moderne Gehirnforschung," in *10 Jahre Suzuki-Violinschule Münster*, ed. Schwindt, Martin (Münster: 1998); Ericsson, K. Anders, Michael J. Prietula, and Edward T. Cokely, "The Making of an Expert," *Harvard Business Review* July-August (2007): 115–121; Chaffin, Roger and Anthony F. Lemieux, "General Perspectives on Achieving Musical Excellence," in *Musical Excellence*, ed. Williamon, Aaron (Oxford: Oxford University Press, 2004).

253  Ampiah, Kweku, "Noguchi Shika: the eternal mother of modern Japan," *Japan Forum* 12.1 (2000): 77–85. The Suzuki literature includes several stories of disabled children learning to play the violin.

254  See, for example Stevenson, Harold W. and James W. Stigler, *The Learning Gap: Why Our Schools Are Failing and What We Can Learn from Japanese and Chinese Education* (New York: Simon & Schuster, 1992).

255  Borris and Verband Deutscher Musikerzieher und konzertierender Künstler, eds., *Musikleben*, 181, 186.

256  Interview, 7 July 2008.

257  Nakajima, *Ongaku wa ikiru chikara*, 46, 48. *Shijuku* (private academy) was the official designation by the Meiji government for a type of school in the tradition of early modern Japan; the word *juku* has romantic and nostalgic associations and implies independence of spirit and close relationships between teachers and pupils.

258  Yoshihara, *Musicians from a Different Shore*, 73.

259  For example Schwarz, Robert, "Glissando: The violinist Midori had sailed through Juilliard and Carnegie Hall by the time she was 18. Now she's practicing the passage to adulthood," *New York Times*, 24 March 1991, SM 30, 61.

260  Quoted in Okuda, Akinori, *Haha to shindō: Gotō Setsu monogatari* (Tokyo: Shōgakukan, 1998), 90–91.

261  Tōgi Yūji (1928–85), a native of Kyoto, was trained in the music department of the Imperial Court and at Geidai. From 1954 to 1956 he played in the Tokyo Philharmonic Orchestra. Besides performing as a soloist and chamber musician, he taught at Sōai Gakuen, where he also conducted the orchestra.

262  Okuda, *Haha to shindō*, 114.

263  Sand, *Teaching Genius*, 74–78; Yoshihara, *Musicians from a Different Shore*.

264  Okuda, *Haha to shindō*, 161–162.

265  Schwarz, "Glissando: The violinist Midori had sailed through Juilliard and Carnegie Hall by the time she was 18. Now she's practicing the passage to adulthood."

266  The concert was repeated on 31 December, 1 January and 4 January.

267  Quoted in Wright, David, "What Has Midori Done For an Encore? Plenty," *New York Times*, 19 January 2003, AR31. On Midori's personal life and conflicts see Midori, *Einfach Midori*, trans. Van Volxem, Susanne (Berlin: Henschel, 2004).

268  Midori, *Einfach Midori*, 101.

269  "Gotō Midori: 'Odoroku beki 14 sai no tensai shōjo' to Amerika de daihyōban," *Ongaku no tomo* August (1986): 90. Mochizuki, Kenji, "Amerika: Ichiya ni shite, Amerika sendo o sekken shita Gotō Midori chan no kaikyō," *Ongaku no tomo* October (1986): 234–235.

270  Takayanagi, Morio, "Gotō Midori: Juriādo no tensai shōjo ima, kokyō Nihon demo honkakuteki debyū," *Ongaku no tomo* August (1987): 88–89.

271  Gotō, Sctsu, *Ame no uta* (Tokyo: Wanibukkusu, 1987), 205.

272  Sanger, David E., "In Japan, Midori Is a New Yorker," *New York Times*, 16 September 1989, 13.

273  Muro, Ken'ichi, "Gendai no shōzō: Tensai shōjo Nyū Yōku no seishun," *AERA* 13 September (1988): 53–57.

274  Details in Midori, *Einfach Midori*. Much of the following discussion is based on Midori's own account.

275  Okuda, *Haha to shindō*, 233–235.

276  Midori, *Einfach Midori*, 94–95, 117–118.

277  Ibid., 124–126.

278  Wright, "What Has Midori Done For an Encore? Plenty."

279  Midori, *Einfach Midori*, 128–129.

280  Muro, "Gendai no shōzō: Tensai shōjo Nyū Yōku no seishun," 55. Saitō Satoru describes the 'mother–child capsule' as "one of the biggest factors in the psychopathology of Japanese children"; quoted in Kawanishi, Yuko, *Mental Health Challenges facing contemporary Japanese Society: the "Lonely People"* (Folkestone, Kent: Global Oriental, 2009), 78.

281  Kawanishi, *Mental Health Challenges facing contemporary Japanese Society: the "Lonely People"*, 109.

282  Midori, *Einfach Midori*, 116.

283  Pincus, Andrew L., *Musicians with a Mission: Keeping the Classical Tradition Alive* (Boston: Northeastern University Press, 2002), 233.

284  Tommasini, Anthony, "A Gifted Young Violinist Gives Something Back," *New York Times*, 8 May 1997, C15.

285  Midori, *Einfach Midori*, 163–162.

286  Quoted in Pincus, *Musicians with a Mission*, 262.

287  Muro, "Gendai no shōzō: Tensai shōjo Nyū Yōku no seishun," 56.

288  Okuda, *Haha to shindō*, 260.

289  Midori, *Einfach Midori*, 188–202.

290  Jepson, Barbara, "A Prodigy Still, but Uneasily Older," *New York Times*, 22 January 1995.

291  Bargreen, Melinda, "Violin legend Midori lets music, achievements speak for themselves," *The Seattle Times*, 8 April 2003; Templeton, David, "Music, Motion, and the Evolution of Midori," *Strings* 104 August/September (2002).

292  Schwarz, Robert, "Midori Surmounts the Perils of Prodigyhood," *New York Times*, 4 January 1998, AR33; Watanabe, *Vaiorinisuto 33*, 260; Eggebrecht, Harald, *Große Geiger* (Munich: Piper, 2000), 48.

293  Details on her official website, www.gotomidori.com (14 January 2014).

294  Reel, James, "Midori is reshaping collegiate string education," *Strings* August/Sepbember (2008).

295  "Tokushū II: Gotō Midori no 'ima' o ou," *Ongaku no tomo* March (2008): 93–102.

296  Applebaum, Samuel, *The Way They Play*, 13 vols., vol. 8 (Neptune City, N.J.: Paganiniana Publications, 1980), 179.

297  Ibid., 203, 205. For biographical details see also Nichigai Associates, ed. *Ongakuka jinmei jiten* and his profile at http://yoshio-unno.com (14 January 2014).

298  "Unno Yoshio shinsain ni," *Asahi shinbun*, 25 August 1981, 13.

299  Elisa Kawaguti (Kawaguchi Erisa, 1959–), Kageyama Seiji (1959–), Furusawa Iwao (1959–) and Shimane Megumi (1961–) .

300  "Unno Yoshio shūwai de taiho," *Asahi shinbun*, 8 December 1981, 1.

301  "Taisaku-i o setchi e," *Asahi shinbun*, 2 December 1981, 14; "Geidai 'waga mimi' ni fushin," *Asahi shinbun*, 4 December 1981, 23; "Yahari mimi yori kanteisho," *Asahi shinbun*, 4 December 1981, 19.

302  "'Gadanīni' wa fukuseihin," *Asahi shinbun*, 10 December 1981, 23. "Gakka ni korori Geidai no mimi," *Asahi shinbun*, 13 December 1981, 22; "Gut und Teuer," *Der Spiegel* 6 (1982): 138–142.

303  "Kanda, gakki fusei mochikomi," *Asahi shinbun*, 12 December 1981, 23. "'Gadanīni' wa fukuseihin."

304  Ongaku no Tomosha, "Tokubetsu zadankai: Vaiorin mondai ni hata o hasshita Nihon kurashikku ongakukai no genjō o tou," *Ongaku no tomo* February (1982): 123–130, 124. Reuter, Fritz Jr, "Reuter's Focus Report: Has the Violin Business Become a Criminal Racket and a Snare?" ((c) 1985, 1996, 1997, 1998), http://www.fritz-reuter.com/reports/rin024.htm 1997, 1998 #886.

     They even found their way into a German detective novel: Zorn, Günter, *Mörderische Saiten* (n.p.: Edition Chimaira, 2005).

305  Yoshida, Hidekazu, "Kaie dō kurichikku 92: mō hitotsu no 'shingan'," *Ongaku geijutsu* January (1982): 20—25.

306 Norman, Geraldine, "Many a New Fiddle," *The Times*, 27 May 1982. Reuter, "Reuter's Focus Report: Has the Violin Business Become a Criminal Racket and a Snare?" 1997, 1998 #886.

307 Harvey, Brian, "Violin Frauds, Fakes and Misdescriptions: The Law Part 1–3," *The Strad* June; July; August (1982): 93–94; 173–178; 261–262, 178.

308 "Unno Yoshio shūwai de taiho."

309 "Kamen hagareta 'purinsu'," *Asahi shinbun*, 8 December (Evening) 1981, 11.

310 "Shūhen ni kuroi uwasa," *Asahi shinbun*, 8 December (Evening) 1981, 10; "Unno ni kyogaku ribēto," *Asahi shinbun*, 9 December 1981, 1; "'Ueno no mori' kane de meidō," *Asahi shinbun*, 9 December 1981, 21. "Gyōsha to kanadeta waon," *Asahi shinbun*, 9 December 1981, 23; "Unno, Geidai ni aiki kawaseru," *Asahi shinbun*, 10 December (Evening) 1981, 15; "Unno o datsuzei yōgi de chōsa e," *Asahi shinbun*, 12 December (Evening) 1981, 11. "Unno ressun ni giwaku," *Asahi shinbun*, 16 December 1981, 19; "Unno ga shūsei shinkoku," *Asahi shinbun*, 24 December 1981, 14.

311 "Geidaisei wa okori to akirame," *Asahi shinbun*, 11 December (Evening) 1981, 19.

312 "Geidai 'hitsuwa' nyan demo shitteru: Wagahai wa 'Kandanīni' ongaku gakubu gonensei," *Asahi shinbun*, 16 December 1981, 17.

313 "Shūhen ni kuroi uwasa."

314 "'Gadanīni' wa fukuseihin."

315 "Geidaisei wa okori to akirame."; "Kanda, gakki fusei mochikomi."

316 *Sangiin kaigiroku jōhō dai 95 kai kokkai kessan iinkai dai 1 gō*, 16 August 1981.

317 "'Kinken tsuihō' kunō no 7 jikan," *Asahi shinbun*, 18 December 1981, 21; "Geidai no 'kojin ressun kinshi': Ongakukai ni ōki na hamon," *Asahi shinbun*, 18 December (Evening) 1981, 12.

318 The infamous Guadagnini was subsequently pronounced genuine; one of the certificates, issued by "Aaringu string company" proved to be authentic and the German company Fritz Steiner conducted a new appraisal and certified the instrument's authenticity: *102nd Parliamentary Session: Culture and Education Committee no. 6*, 16 April 1985.

319 "Ribēto, sara ni futari," *Asahi shinbun*, 9 December (Evening) 1981, 1; "Geidai 'giwaku no ansanburu'," *Asahi shinbun*, 9 December (Evening) 1981, 15.

320 "Unno, jutaku shūwai de kiso," *Asahi shinbun*, 28 December (Evening) 1981, 1; "Wairo to omowanu," *Asahi shinbun*, 29 December 1981, 19. The Japanese legal term for the offence is *jutaku shūwai*.

321 "Ongakukai ni ichibatsu hyakkai," *Asahi shinbun*, 28 December (Evening) 1981, 8. Sakisaka, Masahisa, "Hitobito no nasu ni makaseyo – kojin ressun tōketsu kaijo ni yosete," *Ongaku geijutsu* August (1982): 20–23, 22.

322 "Kane osen kokuhatsu no daigasshō," *Asahi shinbun*, 28 December (Evening) 1981, 9.

323 "Geidai jiken shōkōhan hiraku," *Asahi shinbun*, 28 April (Evening) 1982, 19.

324 "Wairo to omowanu."

325 "Ongaku kyōiku to kojin ressun: 'Geidai jiken' no naka de kangaeru," *Asahi shinbun*, 8 February; 9 February; 12 February (Evening) 1982, 5; Yoshida, Hidekazu, "Mitsutabi 'Geidai jiken' kō," *Asahi shinbun*, 18 February (Evening)

1982, 5.Summarized in Ongaku no Tomosha, ed. *Ongaku nenkan* (Tokyo: Ongaku no Tomosha, 1983), 15.

326 "Tokushū: Ongaku daigaku wa ensōka o sodaterareru ka," *Ongaku no tomo* April (1982): 84–119.

327 Examples: Hiyama, Rikurō et al., "Tokubetsu zadankai: Gakki no kachi wa nan de kimaru ka," *Ongaku geijutsu* February (1982): 30–43; "Tokushū: Ressunryō – shakaiteki giwaku o manekanai teido to wa," *Ongaku geijutsu* August (1982): 20–37; "Tokushū: Ongaku daigaku wa ensōka o sodaterareru ka." Chiba, Kaoru, Akihō Kurita, and Masaaki Niwa, "Tokubetsu kendankai: Ressunryō – shakaiteki giwaku o manukanai teido to wa," *Ongaku geijutsu* August (1982): 24–33.

328 Nakane, Shin'ya, "Ondai sotsugyō made ikura kakaru?" *Ongaku no tomo* March (1961): 88–89; Iwaki, "Ongaku kyōiku wa kore de yoi no ka."

329 Iwaki, "Ongaku kyōiku wa kore de yoi no ka," 136.

330 Tsunematsu Yukitoshi, Japan Musicians Union, quoted in Havens, *Artist and Patron*, 193.

331 Sakisaka, "Hitobito no nasu ni makaseyo – kojin ressun tōketsu kaijo ni yosete."

332 Sukegawa, Toshiya, "Ressunryō no jittai," *Ongaku geijutsu* August (1982): 34–37.

333 Tanabe, Mikio, "Chihō ni okeru ressun no mondai – Tōkyō geidai no kojin ressun kaikin ni omou," *Ongaku geijutsu* August (1982): 32–33. The Kurashiki Orchestra, an amateur orchestra, was founded in 1974: http://kurakan.org/kurakan-blog/profile.php (11 July 2011).

334 "Geidai oshoku: Unno ni yūzai hanketsu," *Asahi shinbun*, 9 April 1985, 1. I thank Heinrich Menkhaus for explaining the legal technicalities of the verdict.

335 "Unno no yūzai ga kakutei," *Asahi shinbun*, 30 October 1985, 22.

336 "Geidai oshoku: jutaku shūwai mitomeru," *Mainichi shinbun*, 9 April 1985, 19. "'Sekai no Unno' kibishii dan," *Asahi shinbun*, 9 April 1985, 23.

337 "Geinō/goraku: Jiken de kyōshoku o hanare Ōshū ga butai no Unno," *Asahi shinbun*, 14 August 1985, 6.

338 Takayanagi, Morio, "Unno Yoshio – 5 nen han no jūden jikan o hete, migoto ni 'fukkatsu'," *Ongaku no tomo* September (1987): 94–95; Nakagawa, Genri, "Tsuyayaka na neiro wa kenzai," *Asahi shinbun*, 1 July 1987, 7; Hasegawa, Takehisa, "Unno Yoshio vaiorin risaitaru," *Ongaku no tomo* August (1987): 158.

339 Nichigai Associates, ed. *Ongakuka jinmei jiten* 184.

340 Wikipedia articles about Unno and the Geidai scandal have only appeared quite recently; until then it was difficult to find any references on the internet; http://ja.wikipedia.org/wiki/%E8%8A%B8%E5%A4%A7%E4%BA%8B%E4%BB%B6 (08 July 2011).

341 "Gakkishō ni yūyo hanketsu," *Asahi shinbun*, 11 October 1986, 22.

342 Hiyama et al., "Tokubetsu zadankai: Gakki no kachi wa nan de kimaru ka."

343 See also http://musicplaza.co.jp (14 January 2014).

344 Kanda, Yūkō, *Vaiorin no mikata, erabikata kisohen: Machigatta kaikata o shinai tame ni*, 2 vols., vol. 1 (Tokyo: Ressun no Tomosha, 1998).

345 "Gyōsha to kanadeta waon."

346 The question was decisive, because the answer determined whether Unno had advised students on instruments qua his office and his accepting commissions

constituted bribery in connection with his office. For details about the court case see Date, Akio, "Geidai Unno kyōju jiken daiisshin hanketsuno igi to mondaiten," *Jurisuto (Jurist)* 840 (1 July 1985): 45–50. Matsumoto, Ichirō, "'Shokumu ni kanshi' no igi (4): Geidai Baiorin Jiken," *Bekkan Jurisuto (Jurist),* 117 (April 1992): 192–193.

347  Yoshida, Hidekazu, "Kaie dō kurichikku 93: Geidai jiken," *Ongaku geijutsu* February (1982): 20–25, 22.

348  Ongaku no Tomosha, "Tokubetsu zadankai: Vaiorin mondai ni hata o hasshita Nihon kurashikku ongakukai no genjō o tou," 125.

349  Kimura Eiji in "Tokubetsu zadankai: Ongakuka no tanjō kara katsudō made," *Ongaku geijutsu* May (1982): 26–37, 35; ———, "Tokubetsu zadankai: Vaiorin mondai ni hata o hasshita Nihon kurashikku ongakukai no genjō o tou," 125. "Shasetsu: Ongaku kyōiku no minaoshi o motomeru," *Mainichi shinbun,* 15 April 1985, 5.

350  This was even the subject of a panel discussion of its own: "Tokubetsu zadankai: Retteru jūshi no shakai fūchō o kangaeru," *Ongaku geijutsu* April (1982): 21; Hideo, Itokawa, "Koramu: Retteru dakai e no michi," *Ongaku geijutsu* April (1982): 31–33.

351  "Tokubetsu zadankai: Ongakuka no tanjō kara katsudō made," 36. Ongaku no Tomosha, "Tokubetsu zadankai: Vaiorin mondai ni hata o hasshita Nihon kurashikku ongakukai no genjō o tou," 125.

352  Todes, Ariane, "Opinion: Failure to declare," *The Strad* April (2011): 25. See also the December 2011 issue of *The Strad* with a special focus on money.

**Part 3: At the Turn of the Millennium**

1  Goto-Jones, Christopher, *Modern Japan: A Very Short Introduction* (Oxford: Oxford University Press, 2009), 142.

2  http://www.youtube.com/watch?v=Pi63bfUc94s&feature=related (14 January 2014); http://www.youtube.com/watch?v=tzTvJQRIWLU&feature=related (14 January 2014); "Like the Flow of the River" has also been a popular song at concerts and sing-alongs in the wake of the 2011 disaster.

3  Hasegawa Takehisa, liner note to Kōda Satoko. *Kawa no nagare no yō ni: Misora Hibari on vaiorin.* CD Denon. COCQ 83724.

4  Gotō Midori, Takezawa Kyōko, Watanabe Reiko, Suwanai Akiko, Toda Yayoi, Shōji Sayaka, Kashimoto Daishin and Yasunaga Tōru: Watanabe, Kazuhiko, *Violinists 33: Mei-ensōka o kiku* (Tokyo: Kawade Shobō, 2002), 272–278.

5  For example, Campbell, Margaret, *The Great Violinists* (London: Granada, 1980). Schwarz, Boris, *Great Masters of the Violin: from Corelli and Vivaldi to Stern, Zukerman and Perlman* (London: Robert Hale 1984).

6  Watanabe, *Vaiorinisuto 33,* 276–277.

7  Born in 1963, Kino Masayuki studied at Tōhō and at the Guildhall in London, won several international competitions and performed as a soloist and chamber musician. In 1993 he became concertmaster of the Japan Philharmonic Orchestra.

8  "Maehashi Teiko: Artist Interview," *Sarasate* 29 (2009): 8, 22–23, 8. See also "Vaiorinisuto Maehashi Teiko-san 8 nenburi no shinrokuon o furikaette," *String* July (2009): 16–20.

9    Born 1947 in Uralsk and trained in Odessa and Moscow, Bron made a name for himself as a teacher first at the conservatory in Novosibirsk and since then in Lübeck, Rotterdam, London, Cologne and Madrid. His non-Japanese students include such famous names as Vadim Repin, Maxim Vegnerov, Daniel Hope and David Garret; www.zakharbron.com (14 March 2012).

10   www.mayukokamio.com (14 January 2014).

11   Only Furusawa Iwao (1959–), Senju Mariko (1962–), Urushihara Asako (1966–) and the "crossover" violinists had been based in Japan for most of their careers in 2007; Hakase Tarō has since moved to London.

12   Okuda, Yoshimichi and Haruo Yamada, *Baiorin omoshiro zatsugaku jiten* (Tokyo: Yamaha Music Media, 2007), 210–215, 164–169, 185–188, 215–216. Whether Temma Atsuko's performance can really be described as "crossover" seems doubtful.

13   The following classification is in part based on Yoshihara's book about Asian musicians in the United States; it has been modified to reflect the Japanese perspective: Yoshihara, Mari, *Musicians from a Different Shore: Asians and Asian Americans in Classical Music* (Philadelphia: Temple University Press, 2007).

14   "Kyūto na tensai shōjo ga 'obāchan no kuni' de hajimete no koncheruto – Anne Akiko Meyers," *Ongaku no tomo* 11 (1987): 25.

15   Yoshihara, *Musicians from a Different Shore*, 208.

16   E-mail correspondence from Midori, 3 August 2009.

17   "Arabella Miho Steinbacher: Artist Interview," *Sarasate* 32 (2010): 22–23. See also Interview with Richard Eckstein on www.arabella-steinbacher.com (27 November 2010).

18   Watanabe, *Vaiorinisuto 33*, 254–255. Midori now has U.S. citizenship.

19   Although according to Yoshihara's classification Gotō Ryū and Kashimoto Daishin might figure as "hybrid" Asians, from a Japanese point of view, it appears more appropriate to describe them as transnational.

20   Midori, *Einfach Midori*, trans. Van Volxem, Susanne (Berlin: Henschel, 2004), 152.

21   Okuda, Akinori, *Haha to shindō: Gotō Setsu monogatari* (Tokyo: Shōgakukan, 1998), 317, 324.

22   Gotō, Ryū and Hirotsugu (photos) Okamura, *Gotō Ryū: foto & essei* (Tokyo: Bungei Shunjū, 2005).

23   www.ryugoto.com (12 March 2012)

24   "Kashimoto Daishin: Artist Interview," *Sarasate* 8 (2005): 20–21.

25   Ibid.: 20.

26   "Kashimoto Daishin: Artist Interview," *Sarasate* 42 (2011): 18–19. The two festivals are connected.

27   Compare Yoshihara, *Musicians from a Different Shore*.

28   Suwanai, Akiko, *Vaiorin to kakeru* (Tokyo: NHK, 2000), 171–172. Louis Krasner (1903–96), a Russian-born American, was the first to champion the violin concertos by Alban Berg and Arnold Schönberg. He commissioned the Berg concerto and was in contact with the composer during its inception: Schwarz, *Great Masters of the Violin*, 517–519.

29   Yoshihara cites several examples related by her informants: Yoshihara, *Musicians from a Different Shore*.

30 Schwarz, Robert, "Glissando: The violinist Midori had sailed through Juilliard and Carnegie Hall by the time she was 18. Now she's practicing the passage to adulthood," *New York Times*, 24 March 1991, SM 30, 61.

31 Kawabata, Narimichi, *Boku wa, namida o denai me de naita* (Tokyo: Fusōsha, 2003). The author's postscript is dated December 2000.

32 Actually composed by Vladimir Vavilov and first published and recorded by him in 1972.

33 Henry Mancini (1924–94)

34 "Narimichi Kawabata Fan Club Special Concert 2007," 29 November 2007.

35 Yano, Christine R., *Tears of Longing: Nostalgia and Nation in Japanese Popular Song*, Harvard East Asian monographs 206 (Cambridge (Massachusetts): Harvard University Asia Center, 2002), 16, 46, 53, 70.

36 Morris, Ivan, *The Nobility of Failure: Tragic Heroes in the History of Japan* (Tokyo: Tuttle, 1982 (1975)).

37 Kawabata, *Boku wa, namida o denai me de naita*. Kawabata, Masao, *Narimichi no Ave Maria: Violin no shi toshite, chichi toshite* (Tokyo: Kōdansha, 2003).

38 The paper wrapper (*obi*: kimono sash) with the publisher's sales pitch is a common feature of new books in Japan. The following is based on Kawabata, *Narimichi no Ave Maria*; ———, *Boku wa, namida o denai me de naita*.

39 Murao, Kunio/Kikuchi, Takeshi, "Tensai baiorinisuto no chichi Kawabata Masao," *AERA* 2001.8.13–20. (2001): 62–67.

40 Kawabata, *Boku wa, namida o denai me de naita*, 57.

41 Murao, "Tensai baiorinisuto no chichi Kawabata Masao."

42 Kawabata, *Boku wa, namida o denai me de naita*.

43 ———, *Narimichi no Ave Maria*, 142.

44 Details about his recent and current activities from his official website www.kawabatanarimichi.jp (7 June 2012).

45 Moster, Roxanne Yamaguchi, "Blind Violinist Grateful for Diagnosis 20 Years Ago," *UCLA Today* (2000).

46 "Handi norikoeru sugata kandō yobu: Kō 2 no Eigo kyōkasho ni hanseiki," *Mainichi shinbun*, 16 June (Evening) 2004.

47 Temma, Atsuko, *Waga kokoro no uta: Bōkyō no barādo* (Tokyo: Bungei Shunjū, 2000).

48 See Part 2 Chapter 7.

49 Temma, *Waga kokoro no uta*.

50 Ibid., 138–139.

51 Ibid., 179–183.

52 The details are not recorded in her biography nor in a recent interview in *String* where she describes her relationship with the instrument: "Temma Atsuko debyū 30 shūnen: kono 30 nen no dai no kazukazu," *String* November (2009): 46–49.

53 An orchestral version was later composed by Theodor Rogalski (1901–51).

54 Details about Temma's activities: http://www.officetemma.co.jp/main/profile.html (13 July 2011).

55 Saitō, Juri, "Baiorin mama jōnetsu rapusodī," *AERA* 25 April (2005).

56 On the indispensable role of the mother (parent) in violinists' careers outside Japan, see Steinhardt, Arnold, *Violin Dreams* (Boston: Houghton Mifflin, 2006), 32.

57   Etō, Toshiya, *Vaiorin to tomo ni: Nani o uttatte iru ka shiritai* (Tokyo: Ongaku no Tomosha, 1999), 18–22.

58   Wanami, Sonoko, *Haha to ko no shinfonī: Mōmoku no vaiorinisuto, Wanami Takayoshi o sodateta haha no shuki* (Tokyo: Ongaku no Tomosha, 1977). ———, *Inochi no shinfonī: Mōmoku no vaiorinisuto, Wanami Takayoshi o sasaeta haha no kiroku* (Tokyo: Ongaku no Tomosha, 1981).

59   "Gotō Midori: 'Odoroku beki 14 sai no tensai shōjo' to Amerika de daihyōban," *Ongaku no tomo* August (1986): 90.

60   Midori, *Einfach Midori*, 152.

61   Okuda, *Haha to shindō*. The following biographical details are largely based on Okuda.

62   Ibid., 29.

63   Tanaka was the concertmaster of the orchestra of Kyoto University and the uncle of the violinist Tanaka Chikashi; he died in 1959. On Tōgi Yūji (1928–85) see Part 2 Chapter 11.

64   Gotō, Setsu, *Ame no uta* (Tokyo: Wanibukkusu, 1987), 18.

65   Based on two songs composed in 1872.

66   Gotō, Setsu, *"Tensai" no sodatekata* (Tokyo: Kōdansha, 2007), 149.

67   Ibid., 46–48; Okuda, *Haha to shindō*, 104, 225.

68   Gotō, *"Tensai" no sodatekata*, 150.

69   Yamaguchi, Saneko, "Special Interview: Gotō Setsu," *Sarasate* 15 (2007): 16–20. She even claimed she disliked music; in her book she adds that she prefers cleaning: Gotō, *"Tensai" no sodatekata*, 150.

70   Gotō, *"Tensai" no sodatekata*, 122.

71   Kawanishi, Yuko, *Mental Health Challenges facing contemporary Japanese Society: the "Lonely People"* (Folkestone, Kent: Global Oriental, 2009).

72   http://www.gotosetsu.jp/ (14 January 2014).

73   Senju, Fumiko, *Senju-ke no kyōiku hakusho* (Tokyo: Shinchō bunko, 2005 (2001)). ———, *Senju-ke ni Sutoradivariusu ga kita hi* (Tokyo: Shinchōsha, 2005). Senju, Fumiko and Mariko Senju, *Haha to musume no kyōsōkyoku* (Tokyo: Jiji Tsūshin Shuppankyoku, 2005).

74   Hendry, Joy, *Understanding Japanese Society* (London: Routledge, 1987), 30.

75   Senju, *Senju-ke no kyoiku hakusho*, 147.

76   Senju and Senju, *Haha to musume*, 188; Senju, *Senju-ke no kyōiku hakusho*, 212–213.

77   Senju and Senju, *Haha to musume*, 6.

78   Ibid., 252,339,231–232, 232, 228, 231, 256.

79   Senju, Mariko, *Utatte, vaiorin no uta* (Tokyo: Jiji Tsūshin Shuppankyoku, 2009).

80   Description in MARC database. Quoted on www.amazon.co.jp (8 September 2010).

81   Senju, *Utatte, vaiorin no uta*, 166–169.

82   Parts of this chapter were published previously: Mehl, Margaret, "Made in Japan," *The Strad* May (2008): 58–64. On Xiqiao, "a contender for the title of violin capital of the world" and "home to an estimated 40 violin factories," see Hume, David, "Quality and Quantity," *The Strad* October (2008): 38–42. Pellegrini, Nancy, "The rise and rise of Chinese Lutherie," *The Strad* March (2010): 50–54.

83 Murata, Sōroku, "Sutoradivari no denrai," (Tokyo, n.d.), 3.

84 Yokoyama, Shin'ichi, *Sutoradivariusu* (Tokyo: Ascii Media Works, 2008), 156.

85 See for example Hiyama, Rikurō et al., "Tokubetsu zadankai: Gakki no kachi wa nande kimaru ka," *Ongaku geijutsu* February (1982): 30–43.

86 Hasegawa, Takehisa, "Nihon no vaiorin seisakusha o tazunete: koko made kita Nihonsei no shinsaku vaiorin," *Ongaku no tomo* March (1982): 140–153. The makers he visited were Yamamoto Kōshi, Kinoshita Tarō and Ueki Shigeru.

87 Interview, 20 November 2007.

88 Factory visit and interviews, 5 November 2007, with Taniguchi Akio, factory managing director, and Shigeri Masahiko, factory manager.

89 http://www.nagoya-cci.or.jp/mono/list_e.html (16 March 2012).

90 Sales brochure, undated, picked up in 2007.

91 Yamaha Strings: Silent Series, sales brochure, Tokyo 2005.

92 Or Mieczyslaw Weinberg (1919–96).

93 Pellegrini, Nancy, "Chamber Music in China," *The Strad* October (2010): 62–68, 63.

94 This is particularly evident in the diary of the legal expert Georg Michaelis, a keen amateur singer: see Becker, Bert, *Georg Michaelis. Ein preußischer Jurist im Japan der Meiji-Zeit. Briefe, Tagebuchnotizen, Dokumente 1885–1889* (Munich: iudicium, 2001).

95 This is only partly true of the kind of music-making in the home praised by writers in magazines from the turn of the twentieth century, especially for women and preferably on the piano, which can be seen in the context of the family ideology promoted by the state and leading intellectuals.

96 See Bashford, Christina, "The String Quartet and Society," in *The Cambridge Companion to the String Quartet*, ed. Stowell, Robin (Cambridge: Cambridge University Press, 2003). Lebrecht, Norman, "Comment (string quartets)," *The Strad* November (2010): 25.

97 Lebrecht, "Comment (string quartets)."

98 Bohlman, Philip V., "Of Yekkes and Chamber Music in Israel: Ethnomusicological Meaning in Western Music History," in *Ethnomusicology and Modern Music History*, ed. Blum, Stephen, Bohlman, Philip V., and Neuman, Daniel M. (Champaign, IL University of Illinois Press, 1991). Levin, Walter, "Immigrant Musicians and the American Chamber Music Scene, 1930–1950," in *Driven into Paradise: The Musical Migration from Nazi Germany to the United States*, ed. Brinkmann, Reinhold and Wolff, Christoph (Berkeley: University of California Press, 1999).

99 Potter, Tully, "The Concert Explosion and the Age of Recording," in *The Cambridge Companion to the String Quartet*, ed. Stowell, Robin (Cambridge: Cambridge University Press, 2003), 92.

100 Yufuin Ongakusai, ed. *Kuronuma Toshio to Nihon no gengaku shijū sōdan* (Ōita: Kashiwa no Mori Shobō, 1994), 110–111.

101 Potter, "The Concert Explosion and the Age of Recording," 92.

102 Epstein, Helen, "A String Quartet from Tokyo – It Had to Happen," *New York Times*, 9 March 1975, XI.

103 Quoted in Yoshida, Junko, "40 shūnen mukae mikka renzoku kōen Tōkyō Kuarutetto," *Asahi.com*, 24 January 2010.

104 "Tokyo Kuarutetto," *Ongaku no tomo* February (2010): 152. Yoshida, "40 shūnen mukae mikka renzoku kōen Tokyo Kuarutetto."

105 Alban Berg, No. 3; Bartók No. 1; Beethoven, Op. 74, "Harp."

106 "Tokyo Kuarutetto."

107 "Tokyo Quartet to Lose Japanese Members," *The Strad* December (2011): 10. www.tokyoquartet.com (11 January 2014).

108 Suchy, Irene, "A Nation of Mozart-Lovers: Das Phänomen abendländischer Kunstmusik in Japan," *Minikomi (Informationen des akademischen Arbeitskreises Japan)* 1994.1 (1994): 1–8.

109 Ongaku no Tomosha, ed. *Ongaku nenkan* (Tokyo: Ongaku no Tomosha, 1985), 6.

110 *Ensō nenkan*. (Tokyo: Bunkachō (Agency for Cultural Affairs)/Nihon ensōsha renmei (Japan Federation of Musicians), 2009), 8.

111 Fukuzawa, Mitsuomi, ed. *J(apanese) Classic-shugi! Shinsedai Nihon ātisuto gaido* (Tokyo: Ongaku no Tomosha, 1998). Programme of the thirty-second subscription concert, 18 January 2011, Tokyo Bunkakaikan Recital Hall.

112 Nichigai Associates, ed. *Ongakuka jinmei jiten* 3rd rev. ed. (Tokyo: Nichigai Associates, 2001), 173.

113 Ibid., 191.

114 Fukuzawa, ed. *J(apanese) Classic-shugi!* , 195.

115 Ibid., 160.

116 Yomiuri Online, "Okayama Kiyoshi gengaku shijūsōdan kessei "genten mitsumenaosu"," *Yomiuri online Chūbuhatsu* 2009.

117 Ibid.

118 Another foreign tour took place in 2012.

119 Leipzig has a particular significance in the history of Western music in Japan as the city where Taki Rentarō, the third government-sponsored music student after the Kōda sisters, studied.

120 Liner notes to *Haydn total: Streichquartette*, promotional CD, HAY 00001-2 (2009). The project is supported by the Japanese charitable foundation Kikin Midori no Kaze.

121 Compare Steinberg, Michael P., "Afterword: Whose Culture? Whose History? Whose Music?," in *The Oxford Handbook of the New Cultural History of Music*, ed. Fulcher, Jane F. (Oxford: Oxford University Press, 2011).

122 "Ansanburu o shūchū shite manabu 'shitsunaigaku no dōjō' no yō na ba o: Okayama Kiyoshi shi shuzai TAMA Ongaku Fōramu," *String* June (2011): 18–22, 21–22.

123 Booth, Wayne, *For the Love of It: Amateuring and Its Rivals* (Chicago: University of Chicago Press, 1999), 8–9. An exact definition of "amateur" is elusive, and it is more appropriate to speak of an amateur–professional continuum: Finnegan, Ruth, *The Hidden Musicians: Music-Making in an English Town* (Cambridge: Cambridge University Press, 1989).

124 Tsuji, Eiji, *Amachua no ryōbun: Vaiorin no shūtokujutsu* (Tokyo: Shunjūsha, 1990), 9–23, 27–28.The point about *shugyō* is made by other writers Havens, Thomas R.H., *Artist and Patron in Postwar Japan: Dance, Music, Theater and the Visual Arts, 1955–1980* (Princeton, New Jersey: Princeton University Press, 1982), 187. *Shugyō* is particularly associated with the traditional arts, but similar notions apply to Western music.

125  Etō, *Vaiorin to tomo ni*, 217.

126  "String Interview: Urakawa Takaya," *String* July (2009): 50–56.

127  Needless to say, not all amateur musicians play Western classical music; in Japan as elsewhere this is a minority pursuit.

128  Murchie, Maureen, "A History of the Sendai Philharmonic Orchestra, 1973–2005" (University of Illinois at Urbana-Champaign, 2010).

129  Programme for Waseda University 125th Anniversary Concert (21 October 2007), www.wso-tokyo.jp (14 January 2014).

130  "Amachua ōkesutora kita kara minami kara 2: Shizuoka Firuhāmonī kangen gakudan," *Sarasate* 15 (2007): 98–99.

131  www.jao.or.jp/members.html (12 November 2010).

132  Ōmori, Seitarō, *Nihon no yōgaku*, 2 vols., vol. 2 (Tokyo: Shinmon Shuppansha, 1987), 317–322. www.jao.or.jp/ (12 November 2010).

133  "Sukiru appu shirīzu: Sekando vaiorin o kiwameru," *Sarasate* 8 (2005): 41– 47, 47.

134  "Amachua ōkesutora kita kara minami kara 5: Sendai Shimin Kōkyō Gakudan," *Sarasate* 18 (2007): 82–83.

135  Hokkaidō Nōmin Kangen Gakudan: http://www.jdnet.dk/jdnet/front/osusume/ 2011-01_Farmers-EN.pdf   Profile:   http://www.phoenix-c.or.jp/~m-ecofar/ profile2.html (14 January 2014).

136  http://www.kenji-world.net/english/who/who.html (14 January 2014).

137  Founded in 1933 by Kurosawa Torizō, another thinker and activist inspired by the example of Denmark.

138  Makino: Capriccio Hokkaidia for solo violin, Japanese *wadaiko* drum and orchestra (1998) (FPOH, conducted by Satoshi Nomura); violin solo: Tokio Makino.

139  "Amachua ōkesutora de tanoshimō! Mokutekibetsu ōkesutora 1: Sakkyokuka ni miserarete," *Sarasate* 8 (2005): 54–55.

140  *Wagahai wa neko de aru*; first serialized 1905, English 1972. For Terada's biography see Suenobu, Yoshiharu, *Terada Torahiko: Baiorin o hiku butsurigakusha* (Tokyo: Heibonsha, 2009).

141  This is confirmed by a contemporary foreign observer: Werkmeister, Heinrich and Frederick H. Martens, "Impressions of Japanese Music," *Musical Quarterly* 13.1 (1927): 100–107, 106.

142  http://cmc.sakura.ne.jp (12 November 2010); Author's impressions 1988–89.

143  www.apa-music.org/what/constituent/index.html (12 November 2010).

144  www.apa-music.org/english/index.html (12 November 2010).

145  www.tvumd.com/festival.htm (12 November 2010).

146  Crooks, Sam, "Exoticisation and Identity in Amateur Jazz in Japan: A Case Study" (BA thesis, Oxford, 1999), 5.

147  Heimeran, Ernst and Bruno Aulich, *Das stillvergnügte Streichquartett*, Second ed. (Munich: Heimeran, 1969). Japanese, *Kuwartetto no tanoshimi*, translated by Nakano, Yoshirō. Tokyo: Akademia Myūjikku, 1975.

148  "Tokushū Shitsunaigaku o kiwameyō: Hajimete no kuarutetto," *Sarasate* 31 (2009): 52–59. The musical advisor behind "Professor Quartet" is Ōshima Michiko, a graduate of Tōhō School of Music with a performance diploma from Eastman, a former member of the Manhattan-based Cassatt String Quartet and current member of the Cantus String Quartet.

149 Ibid.
150 Parts of this chapter were published as Mehl, Margaret, "Japanese Salon Schools: Adults Only," *The Strad* December 2008 (2008): 48–52.
151 Concert on 27 October 2007.
152 Interview, 9 November 2007.
153 Interview, 16 November 2007.
154 Interview, 28 October 2007.
155 Yamaha Music Center Ikebukuro, Visit on 13 November 2007.
156 Interview at Rifra Plus Shinjuku, 28 October 2007.
157 Description in "Shimamura gakki YOUR STAGE 2 Santorī Hōru de 5 nichikan 500 mei ga sanka," *Sarasate* 19 (2007): 98.
158 Okuda and Yamada, *Baiorin omoshiro zatsugaku jiten*, 33.
159 'Ongaku o yomu hon' henshū iinkai, ed., *Vaiorin o yomu hon: motto shiritai vaiorin no hanashi* (Tokyo: TO-ON Music Publishing, 1998), 136–137.
160 *Gengakki Fan* has since ceased publication with volume 12, published in spring 2008. *String*, published since 1985, is more likely to appeal to music students, young professionals and possibly advanced amateurs; it ceased publication in 2013.
161 Shinozaki, Fuminori, "Maro no ansanburu ressun," *Gengaku fan* 10 (2007): 52–55.
162 Tsuji, *Amachua no ryōbun*. Tsuji, Eiji, *Shōgai gakushū vaiorin no tanoshimi* (Tokyo: Shunjūsha, 1998; reprint, 2001).
163 Nakajima, Mineo, *Ongaku wa ikiru chikara* (Tokyo: Nishimura Shoten, 2009), 160–166.
164 Ibid., 165.

## Conclusion
1 WWFM The Classical Network, New Jersey (20 February 2009).
2 Chiba, Yūko, *Doremi o eranda Nihonjin* (Ongaku no Tomosha, 2007), 6.
3 For a description of the reception of the piece at the time, see Ibid; Watanabe, Hiroshi, *Nihon bunka modan rapusodi* (Tokyo: Shunjūsha, 2002). The harmonic features of the piece are described in Galliano, Luciana, *Yōgaku: Japanese Music in the Twentieth Century*, trans. Mayes, Martin (Lanham, Maryland, and London: The Scarecrow Press, 2002), 53–55.
4 The score was published in September 1931 in Fukuoka by Dai Nihon Katei Ongakukai, a company which began publishing Japanese melodies in staff notation in the late Meiji period.
5 Watanabe, *Nihon bunka modan rapusodi*, 41–43.
6 Recording: *Miyagi Michio,* Japan Traditional Cultures Foundation 2005, VZCP–1101;. Ishida, Kazushi, *Modanizumu hensōkyoku: Higashi Ajia no kindai ongakushi* (Tokyo: Sakuhokusha, 2005), 75.
7 Surprised to hear a Beethoven string quartet and one of Bach's Brandenburg concertos even in a Sapporo coffee shop, Stern wished to meet representatives of indigenous music. Until then Stern had never heard a *koto* played: interview with Isaac Stern in Miyagi Michio Kinenkan (Miyagi Michio Memorial Hall Foundation), ed. *Miyagi Michio no sekai: Miyagi Michio seitan 100 nen kinen* (Tokyo: Miyagi Michio Kinenkan, 1993), 28–33.
8 Columbia: lyrics Takahashi Kikutarō, singer Endō Ichirō.

9 See, for example, the writings of Nishida Kitarō, Watsuji Tetsurō, Yanagida Kunio or Tanizaki Jun'ichirō.

10 Galliano, *Yōgaku*, 99, 115–116.

11 Nakamura, Jin, "Berurin no Nihonjin: Kishi Kōichi to 'Nihon' no hyōshō," in *Kishi Kōichi to ongaku no kindai: Berurin firu o shiki shita Nihonjin*, ed. Kajino, Ena, Chōki, Seiji, and Gochefusuki, Heruman (Tokyo: Seikyūsha, 2011), 81.

12 Ishida refers to *dōjidaiteki ishiki:* Ishida, *Modanizumu hensōkyoku*, 191.

13 Fauser, Annegret, *Musical Encounters at the 1889 Paris World's Fair* (Rochester, NY: University of Rochester Press, 2005), 139–206.

14 Galliano, *Yōgaku*, 312.

15 Wade, Bonnie C., *Music in Japan* (Oxford: Oxford University Press, 2005), 49, 148.

16 Ishida, *Modanizumu hensōkyoku*, 28.

17 On Japanese period films as search for the essence of Japaneseness: Mellon, Joan, *The Waves at Genji's Door: Japan Through Its Cinema* (New York: Pantheon Books, 1976).

18 Studio concertmaster Israel Baker, quoted in Heiles, Anne Mischakoff, "The Golden Fiddlers of the Silver Screen," *The Strad* November (2009): 24–30.

19 Yano, Christine R., *Tears of Longing: Nostalgia and Nation in Japanese Popular Song*, Harvard East Asian monographs 206 (Cambridge (Massachusetts): Harvard University Asia Center, 2002), 3,4,7, 28–29.

20 On the music of Umm Kulthūm, who has sometimes been compared to Edith Piaf, see Gsell, Stefanie, *Umm Kulthum: Persönlichkeit und Faszination der ägyptischen Sängerin* (Berlin: Das Arabische Buch, 1998), 1143–1154. Her music is described as "world music" in: Bohlman, Philip V., *World Music: A Very Short Introduction* (Oxford: Oxford University Press, 2002), 54–55.

21 Both quoted in Pincus, Andrew L., "Music: Japanese Players Take the Grand Tour," *New York Times*, 3 December 1989.

22 Oestreich, James R., "Japanese Musicians Still Turn to the West," *New York Times*, 12 September 2010.

23 "Ivrīū Gitorisu no namida," *String* August (2011): 1, 24–28, 27.

24 *Nodame Cantabile* first appeared in a women's comic magazine from 2001 before being published in book form; by 2008, 21 volumes had appeared. The first nine volumes had been dramatized for television and aired between October and December 2007. My observations are based on the live action drama.

25 Tanaka, Chikashi, *Gohon no hashira: Vaiorin-dō: shugyō no tabi* (Tokyo: Ressun no Tomosha, 2001).

26 Ibid., 10–11.

27 Ibid., 132–133.

28 Ibid., 15, 107.

29 Ibid., 35, 107, 111.

30 Ibid., 183, 194.

31 In fairness it should be added that Tanaka edited another book accompanied by a CD with works performed by Urushihara Keiko; other Japanese violinists introduced in the volume are Midori, Kashimoto Daishin, Shōji Sayaka and Kamio Mayuko: ———, ed. *Vaiorin no meiki to meikyoku* (Tokyo: Natsumesha, 2008).

32	Tamaki, Hiroki, *Oto no kōshinkoku Nihon: Junseiritsu no susume* (Tokyo: Bunka Sōsaku Shuppan, 1998). Tamaki Hiroki (1943–2012), a native of Kobe, graduated from Tokyo University of the Arts, where he studied violin, conducting and composition. He has composed for television programmes. See also Hanzawa, Asahiko, "Teikokushugi, gurōbaruka to ongaku," *Kokusai kenkyū* 36 (2009): 43–52, 46–47. For a Western critique of equal temperament see Duffin, Ross W., *How Equal Temperament Ruined Harmony (and Why You Should Care)* (New York: W.W. Norton & Company, 2007).

33	*The Famous Japanese Violin Works Played by Liu Wei.* 2009. VZCC-1025 According to the liner notes, Liu Wei has also released three CDs of the violinist and composer Ma Sicong's (Sitson; 1912–87) violin works. "Chūgoku to Nihon no kakehashi kara sekai e hasshin: vaiorinisuto Ryū Wei (Liu Wei) san," *String* November (2009): 50, 52.

34	Kajino, Ena, "Kishi Kōichi no ongaku no miryoku," *String* November (2009): 32–33, 33.

35	"Kita Naoki: Artist Interview," *Sarasate* 29 (2009 ): 15, 24–25, 24.

36	"NAOTO: Artist Interview," *Sarasate* 8 (2005): 18–19.

37	"Kunugi Takehiro: Artist Interview," *Sarasate* 43 (2011): 7, 22–23, 22.

38	"String Interview: Yamase Rio," *String* June (2010): 38–43, 39–40.

39	www.rioyamase.com/english and http://hardanger-club.or.jp/english.html (14 January 2014).

40	"Harudangeru vaiorin no Nihonjin sōsa Senkusha Yamase Rio San 'Nihon Harudangeru Kurabu' o hossoku," *String* March (2010): 26–29; "Bunka wa genchi ni iku koto ni yotte rikai shi, jikkan suru koto ga dekiru dai ikkai Harudangeru vaiorin sukarāshippu shōhō," *String* August (2011): 52–55.

41	*Mizugumo monmon* and *Gedo senki*; "String Interview: Yamase Rio," 39.

42	The folk revivals in Norway and Ireland (as well as Scotland and other countries) have been going on for some time: Cooke, Peter, "The violin – instrument of four continents," in *The Cambridge Companion to the Violin*, ed. Stowell, Robin (Cambridge: Cambridge University Press, 1992), 240–241.

43	Steinberg, Michael P., "Afterword: Whose Culture? Whose History? Whose Music?" in *The Oxford Handbook of the New Cultural History of Music*, ed. Fulcher, Jane F. (Oxford: Oxford University Press, 2011), 552.

44	Parakilas, James, "Classical Music as Popular Music," *The Journal of Musicology* 3.1 (1984): 1–18, 1, 18–19; Ross, Alex, *The Rest is Noise: Listening to the Twentieth Century* (New York: Picador, 2007), 562–567.

# Select Bibliography

This bibliography contains works on music in Japan (and a few on Korea, Taiwan and China) in European languages referred to in the book, as well as a small number of the most recent publications in English and German that might be of interest to readers. For a full bibliography of works cited in the book see www.notbylovealone.com

ATKINS, TAYLOR E. *Blue Nippon: Authenticating Jazz in Japan*. Durham, N.C.: Duke University Press, 2001.

BORRIS, SIEGFRIED, and VERBAND DEUTSCHER MUSIKERZIEHER UND KONZERTIERENDER KÜNSTLER, eds. *Musikleben in Japan: in Geschichte und Gegenwart, Berichte, Statistiken, Anschriften*. Kassel: Bärenreiter, 1967.

CHAMBERLAIN, BASIL HALL. *Things Japanese: Being Notes on Various Subjects Connected with Japan*, Yohan Classics. Berkeley, CA: Stone Bridge Press, 2007 (1905).

CROOKS, SAM. "Exoticisation and Identity in Amateur Jazz in Japan: A Case Study." BA thesis, Oxford, 1999.

DAY, KIKU. "The Effect of the Meiji Government's Policy on Traditional Japanese Music During the Nineteenth Century: The Case of the *Shakuhachi*." *Nineteenth-Century Music Review* 10.2 (2013): 265–292.

DE FERRANTI, HUGH. *Japanese Musical Instruments*. Oxford: Oxford University Press, 2000.

DE FERRANTI, HUGH, and ALISON TOKITA, eds. *Music, Modernity and Locality in Prewar Japan: Osaka and Beyond*. Farnham, Surrey: Ashgate, 2013.

DITTRICH, RUDOLF. "Beiträge zur Kenntnis der japanischen Musik." *MOAG* 6.85 (1897): 376–391.

DRIVER, HIROKO IRITANI, and SUSAN SHIELDS. "Japanese-American Differences." In *The Suzuki Violinist*, edited by Starr, William. Miami: Summy-Birchard, 2000 (1976).

EPPSTEIN, URY. *The Beginnings of Western Music in Meiji Era Japan.* New York: Edwin Mellen, 1994.

———. "From Torture to Fascination: Changing Western Attitudes to Japanese Music." *Japan Forum* 19.2 (2007): 191–216.

FLAVIN, PHILIP. "Meiji shinkyoku: The Beginnings of Modern Music for the Koto." *Japan Review: Journal of the International Research Center for Japanese Studies* 22 (2010): 103–123.

GALLIANO, LUCIANA. *Yōgaku: Japanese Music in the Twentieth Century.* Trans. Mayes, Martin. Lanham, Maryland, and London: The Scarecrow Press, 2002.

———. "Manfred Gurlitt and the Japanese Operatic Scene, 1939–1972." *Japan Review* 18 (2006): 215–248.

GORDON, BEATE SIROTA. *The Only Woman in the Room: A Memoir.* Tokyo: Kodansha International, 1997.

GOTTSCHEWSKI, HERMANN. "Nineteenth-Century *Gagaku* Songs as a Subject of Musical Analysis: An Early Example of Musical Creativity in Modern Japan." *Nineteenth-Century Music Review* 10.2 (2013): 239–264.

———."Traditionelle und westliche Musik als Identitätssymbole der Moderne: Die Nationalhymnen Japans und Koreas um 1900." *OAG Notizen* 12 (2013): 39–48.

GOTTSCHEWSKI, HERMANN, and KYUNGBOON LEE. "Franz Eckert und ,seine' Nationalhymnen. Eine Einführung." *OAG Notizen* 12 (2013): 27–30.

GROEMER, GERALD. "The Rise of 'Japanese Music'." *The World of Music* 46.2 (2004): 9–34.

HARICH-SCHNEIDER, ETA. "European Musician in Japan." *XXth Century (Shanghai)* 3.6 (1942): 418–421.

———. *A History of Japanese Music.* London: Oxford University Press, 1973.

———. *Charaktere und Katastrophen: Augenzeugenberichte einer reisenden Musikerin.* Berlin: Ullstein, 1978.

———. *Musikalische Impressionen aus Japan 1941–1957: Herausgegeben, kommentiert und mit einer Einführung versehen von Ingrid Fritsch.* Munich: iudicium, 2006.

HAVENS, THOMAS R.H. *Artist and Patron in Postwar Japan: Dance, Music, Theater and the Visual Arts, 1955–1980.* Princeton, New Jersey: Princeton University Press, 1982.

HERD, JUDITH ANN. "Western-influenced 'Classical' Music in Japan" In *The Ashgate Research Companion to Japanese Music*, edited by Hughes, David W. and Tokita, Alison McQueen. Aldershot, UK: Ashgate, 2008.

HERSH, SARAH, and LOIS PEAK. "Developing Character in Music Teachers: A Suzuki Approach." In *Learning in Likely Places: Varieties of Apprenticeship in Japan*, edited by Singleton, John, 153–171. Cambridge: Cambridge University Press, 1998.

HIGUCHI, RYŪICHI, SHUKUKI LIN, SHINICHIRŌ OKABE, TAIJIRŌ AMAZAWA, YOSHIHIRO KUROTA, YASUKO TSUKAHARA, MIEKO MORIMOTO, and RIEKO SUENAGA, eds. *Gosenfu ni egaita yume: Nihon kindai ongaku no 150 nen/150 Years of Modern Japanese Music* (exhibition catalogue). Trans. Art ka (Shimpei Shirafuji, Nina Horisaki-Christens), Tokyo: Meiji Gakuin University, 2013.

HIRASAWA, HIROKO. "Rudolph Dittrich: Leben und Werk." Doctoral thesis, University of Vienna, 1996.

HIROOKA, YOSHIO. "Music Education in Japan." *Music Educators Journal* 36.2 (1949): 34–35.

HOSOKAWA, SHUHEI. "In Search of the Sound of Empire: Tanabe Hisao and the Foundation of Japanese Ethnomusicology." *Japanese Studies* 18.1 (1998): 5–19.

———. "'Salsa no tiene frontera': Orquesta de la Luz or the Globalization and Japanization of Afro-Caribbean Music." *Revista transcultura de Música/Transcultural Music Review* 3 (1999?).

HOSOKAWA, SHUHEI, and CHRISTINE YANO. "Popular Music in Modern Japan." In *The Ashgate Research Companion to Japanese Music*, edited by Hughes, David and Tokita, Alison McQueen, 345–362. Aldershot, Hampshire: Ashgate, 2008.

HOWE, SONDRA WIELAND. "The Role of Women in the Introduction of Western Music in Japan." *The bulletin of historical research in music education* 16.2 (1995): 81–97.

———. *Luther Whiting Mason: International Music Educator*. Warren, Michigan: Harmonie Park Press, 1997.

HUGHES, DAVID W. *Traditional Folk Song in Modern Japan: Sources, Sentiment and Society*. Folkestone, Kent: Global Oriental, 2008.

HUGHES, DAVID, and ALISON MCQUEEN TOKITA, eds. *The Ashgate Research Companion to Japanese Music*. Aldershot, Hampshire: Ashgate, 2008.

ISHIDA, KAZUSHI. "Music in Japan Today: Hardware, Software, and the 'Concert-Hall Culture'." *The Japan Foundation Newsletter* 25.6 (1998): 1–5.

JOHNSON, HENRY. *The Shamisen: Tradition and Diversity*. Leiden: Brill, 2010.

KAJINO, ENA. "A Lost Opportunity for Tradition: The Violin in Early Twentieth-Century Japanese Traditional Music." *Nineteenth-Century Music Review* 10.2 (2013): 293–321.

KAMBE, YUKIMI. "Viols in Japan in the Sixteenth and Early Seventeenth Centuries." *Journal of the VdGSA (The Viola da Gamba Society of America)* 37. (2000): 31–67.

KIM, HIO-JIN. *Koreanische und westliche Musikerausbildung: Historische Rekonstruktion – Vergleich – Perspektiven –*. Marburg: Tectum, 2000.

LANCASHIRE, TERENCE A. "When is Japanese, Japanese? A Tale of Two Musicians." In *Performing Japan: Contemporary Expressions of Cultural Identity*, edited by Jaffe, Jerry C. and Johnson, Henry, 239–272. Folkestone, Kent: Gobal Oriental, 2008.

———. *An Introduction to Japanese Folk Performing Arts*. Farnham: Ashgate, 2011.

LEE, ANGELA HAO-CHUN. "The Influence of Governmental Control and early Christian Missionaries on Music Education of Aborigines in Taiwan." *British Journal of Music Education* 23.2 (2006): 205–216.

LEE, RILEY KELLY. "Fu Ho U vs. Do Re Mi: The Technology of Notation Systems and Implications of Change in the Shakuhachi Tradition of Japan." *Asian Music* 19.2 (1988): 71–81.

LEWIS, MICHAEL, ed. *A Life Adrift: Soeda Azembō, Popular Song, and Modern Mass Culture in Japan*. London: Routledge, 2009.

MADSEN, ERIC. "The Genesis of Suzuki: An Investigation of the Roots of Talent Education." M.A., McGill University, 1990.

MALM, WILLIAM P. "The Modern Music of Meiji Japan." In *Tradition and Modernization in Japanese Culture*, edited by Shively, Donald, 257–300. Princeton: Princeton University Press, 1971.

———. "The Special Characteristics of Gagaku." In *Gagaku: Court Music and Dance*, edited by Togi, Masataro, 3–25. Tokyo: Weatherhill, 1971.

———. "Chinese Music in the Edo and Meiji Periods in Japan." *Asian Music* 6 1/2 (1975): 147–172.

————. *Six Hidden Views of Japanese Music.* Berkeley: University of California Press, 1986.

————. *Traditional Japanese Music and Musical Instruments* Tokyo: Kodansha International, 2000.

MEHL, MARGARET. "Land of the Rising Sisters." *The Strad* May (2007): 60–64.

————. "Made in Japan." *The Strad* May (2008): 58–64.

————. "Toshiya Eto 1927–2008." *The Strad* June (2008): 25.

————. "Japanese Salon Schools: Adults Only." *The Strad* December (2008): 48–52.

————. "Cultural Translation in Two Directions: The Suzuki Method in Japan and Germany." *Research and Issues in Music Education* 7.1 (2009).

————. "Japan's Early Twentieth-Century Violin Boom." *Nineteenth-Century Music Review* 7.1 (2010): 23–43.

————. "A Man's Job? The Kōda Sisters, Violin Playing and Gender Stereotypes in the Introduction of Western Music in Japan." *Women's History Review* 21.1 (2012): 101–120.

————. "Introduction: Western Music in Japan: A Success Story?" *Nineteenth-Century Music Review* 10.2 (2013): 211–222.

MELVIN, SHEILA, and JINDONG CAI. *Rhapsody in Red: How Western Classical Music Became Chinese.* New York: Algora, 2004.

MIDORI. *Einfach Midori.* Trans. Van Volxem, Susanne. Berlin: Henschel, 2004. Second, expanded edition: Henschel, 2012.

MITSUI, TORU. "Interaction of Imported and Indigenous Music in Japan: A Historical Overview of the Music Industry." In *Whose Master's Voice: The Development of Popular Music in Thirteen Cultures*, edited by Ewbank, Alison J. and Papageorgiu, Fouli T., 152–174. Westport, Connecticut: Greenwood Press, 1997.

MÖNIG, MARC. *Die Pädagogik der Yamaha-Musikschulen: Darstellung, Hintergründe und Kritik.* Augsburg: Wißner, 2005.

MORI, SETSUKO. "A Historical Survey of Music Periodicals in Japan: 1881–1920." *Fontis Artis Musicae* 36.1 (1989): 44–50.

MORSE, EDWARD SYLVESTER. *Japan Day by Day, 1877, 1878–9, 1882–3.* 2 vols. Vol. 2. Boston, New York: Houghton Mifflin Company, 1917.

MURCHIE, MAUREEN. "A History of the Sendai Philharmonic Orchestra, 1973–2005." University of Illinois at Urbana-Champaign, 2010.

NOMURA, KŌICHI. "Occidental Music." In *Japanese Music and Drama in the Meiji Era*, edited by Komiya, Toyotaka, 451–507. Tokyo: Ōbunsha, 1956.

OKADA, AKEO. "Europäische Klassik in Japan – eine düstere Diagnose." In *Musik in Japan*, edited by Silvain, Guignard, 179–197. Munich: iudicium, 1994.

PEAK, LOIS. "The Suzuki Method of Music Instruction." In *Teaching and Learning in Japan*, edited by Rohlen, Thomas P. and LeTendre, Gerald K., 345–368. Cambridge: Cambridge University Press, 1998.

PELLEGRINI, NANCY. "Chamber Music in China." *The Strad* October (2010): 62–68.

———. "The rise and rise of Chinese Lutherie." *The Strad* March (2010): 50–54.

PROVINE, ROBERT C., YOSHIHIKO TOKUMARU, and J. LAWRENCE WITZLEBEN, eds. *The Garland Encyclopedia of World Music. Vol 7. East Asia: China, Japan, and Korea*. New York: Garland, 2002.

RICHARDS, E. MICHAEL, and KAZUKO TANOSAKI, eds. *Music of Japan Today*. Cambridge: Cambridge Scholars Publishing, 2008.

SCHAUWECKER, DETLEV. "Musik und Politik: Tōkyō 1934–1944." In *Formierung und Fall der Achse Berlin-Tōkyō*, edited by Krebs, Gerhard and Martin, Bernd, 211–253. Munich: iudicium, 1994.

SHAPIRO, ISAAC. *Edokko: Growing Up a Foreigner in Wartime Japan*. Bloomington, IN: iUniverse, 2009.

STEVENS, ROBIN S. "Emily Patton: An Australian Pioneer of Tonic Sol-fa in Japan." *Research Studies in Music Education* 14 (2000): 40–49.

SUCHY, IRENE. "Versunken und vergessen: zwei österreichische Musiker in Japan vor 1945." In *Mehr als Maschinen für Musik*, edited by Linhart, Sepp and Schmid, Kurt, 89–121. Vienna: Literas Universitätsverlag, 1990.

———. "Westliche Musik in Japan (1): Musik in architektonischen Konzepten." *Japan Magazin* 8 (1991): 29–31.

———. "Deutschsprachige Musiker in Japan vor 1945. Eine Fallstudie eines Kulturtransfers am Beispiel der Rezeption abendländischer Musik." Doctoral thesis, University of Vienna, 1992.

———. "A Nation of Mozart-Lovers: Das Phänomen abendländischer Kunstmusik in Japan." *Minikomi (Informationen des akademischen Arbeitskreises Japan)* 1994.1 (1994): 1–8.

―――. "Verfolgung vertraulich: MusikerInnen-Exil in Japan." In *Vom Weggehen: Zum Exil von Kunst und Wissenschaft*, edited by Wiesinger-Stock, Sandra, Weinzierl, Erika and Kaiser, Konstantin. Vienna: Mandelbaum Verlag, 2006.

―――. "Österreich – Japan: die Musikbeziehungen der österreichischen Zwischenkriegszeit (bis 1945): Ein skeptischer Beitrag." In *Die Republik Österreich und Japan während der Zwischenkriegszeit 1918 – 1938 (1945)*, edited by Getreuer-Kargl, Ingrid and Linhart, Sepp:, 105 – 114. Vienna, 2013.

SUZUKI, SHIN'ICHI. *Nurtured by Love: The Classic Approach to Talent Education*. Trans. Suzuki, Waltraud, Miami: Suzuki Method International, Summy-Birchard Inc., 1983.

TAMAGAWA, YŪKO. "Das Mädchen am Klavier: Entstehungsgeschichte eines Klischees in Japan." In *Geschlechterpolaritäten in der Musikgeschichte des 18. bis 20. Jahrhunderts*, edited by Grotjahn, Rebecca and Hoffmann, Freia, 209–219. Herbolzheim: Centaurus, 2002.

TANIMURA, REIKO. "Practical Frivolities: The Study of *Shamisen* among Girls of the Late Edo Townsman Class." *Japan Review* 23 (2011): 73–96.

TOGI, MASATARO. *Gagaku: Court Music and Dance*. Trans. Kenny, Don. New York: Weatherhill, 1971.

TOKITA, ALISON. "Takarazuka and the Musical *Modan* in the Hanshin Region 1914–1942." In *Rethinking Japanese Modernism*, edited by Starrs, Roy, 408–427. Leiden: Brill, 2012.

―――. "Bi-musicality in modern Japanese culture." *International Journal of Bilingualism* online (2012): 0(0) 1–16.

TSUKAHARA, YASUKO. "State Ceremony and Music in Meiji-era Japan." *Nineteenth-Century Music Review* 10.2 (2013): 223–238.

WADE, BONNIE C. *Music in Japan*. Oxford: Oxford University Press, 2005.

WARTBERG, KERSTIN. *Shinichi Suzuki: Pioneer of Music Education/Pionier der Musikerziehung*. n.p.: German Suzuki Institute, 2009.

WASSERMAN, MICHEL. *Le Sacre de l'hiver: La Neuvième Symphonie de Beethoven, un mythe de la modernité japonaise*. Paris: Les Indes Savantes, 2006.

WATERHOUSE, DAVID. "An Early Illustration of the Four-Stringed Kokyū." *Oriental Art* 16.2 (1970): 162–168.

WERKMEISTER, HEINRICH, and FREDERICK H. MARTENS. "Impressions of Japanese Music." *Musical Quarterly* 13.1 (1927): 100–107.

"Western Music in Japan." *Music Education Journal* 36.3 (1950): 31, 33, 37, 45–46.

WHITNEY, CLARA. *Clara's Diary: An American Girl in Meiji Japan.* Tokyo: Kodansha International, 1981.

YAMANASHI, MAKIKO. *A History of the Takarazuka Revue Since 1914: Modernity, Girls' Culture, Japan Pop.* Leiden: Global Oriental, 2012.

YANO, CHRISTINE. "Defining the Modern Nation in Japanese Popular Song." In *Japan's Competing Modernities: Issues in Culture and Democracy, 1900–1930,* edited by Minichiello, Sharon A., 247–264. Honolulu: University of Hawaii Press, 1998.

————.*Tears of Longing: Nostalgia and Nation in Japanese Popular Song.* Harvard East Asian monographs 206. Cambridge (Massachusetts): Harvard University Asia Center, 2002.

YOSHIHARA, MARI. "The Flight of the Japanese Butterfly: Orientalism, Nationalism, and Performances of Japanese Womanhood." *American Quarterly* 56.4 (2004): 975–1001.

————. *Musicians from a Different Shore: Asians and Asian Americans in Classical Music.* Philadelphia: Temple University Press, 2007.

# Index

Page numbers followed by the letter 'i' refer to pages that contain illustrations. References to notes consist of the page number followed by the letter 'n' followed by the number of the note, e.g. 424n101 refers to note no. 101 on page 424.